Towards an International Criminal Procedure

CHRISTOPH J. M. SAFFERLING

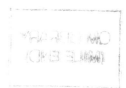

OXFORD
UNIVERSITY PRESS

OXFORD

UNIVERSITY PRESS

Great Clarendon Street, Oxford OX2 6DP

Oxford University Press is a department of the University of Oxford.
It furthers the University's objective of excellence in research, scholarship,
and education by publishing worldwide in

Oxford New York

Auckland Bangkok Buenos Aires Cape Town Chennai
Dar es Salaam Delhi Hong Kong Karachi Kolkata
Kuala Lumpur Madrid Melbourne Mexico City Mumbai Nairobi
São Paulo Shanghai Taipei Tokyo Toronto

Oxford is a registered trade mark of Oxford University Press
in the UK and in certain other countries

Published in the United States
by Oxford University Press Inc., New York

© Christoph J. M. Safferling 2001

The moral rights of the author have been asserted
Database right Oxford University Press (maker)

First published 2001
First published new in paperback 2003

British Library Cataloguing in Publication Data

Data available

Library of Congress Cataloging in Publication Data
Safferling, Christoph Johannes Maria, 1971–
Towards an international criminal procedure / Christoph J.M. Safferling.
p. cm.
Includes bibliographical references.
1. International Criminal Court. 2. Criminal procedure (International law) 3. Human
rights. I. Title.
KZ6310.S24 2001
341.7'7—dc21   00–067833
ISBN 0–19–924350–6
ISBN 0–19–926450–3 (pbk.)

Typeset in Palatino by
Cambrian Typesetters, Frimley, Surrey
Printed in Great Britain
on acid-free paper by
T.J. International Ltd, Padstow, Cornwall

OXFORD MONOGRAPHS IN
INTERNATIONAL LAW

General Editors: Professor Ian Brownlie CBE, QC, FBA
*Former Chichele Professor of Public International Law in the
University of Oxford and Member of the International Law Commission,* and
Professor Vaughan Lowe, *Chichele Professor of Public International Law in
the University of Oxford and Fellow of All Souls College, Oxford*

TOWARDS A.   'ONAL CRIMINAL PROCEDURE

OXFORD MONOGRAPHS IN
INTERNATIONAL LAW

The aim of this series is to publish important and original pieces of research on all aspects of international law. Topics that are given particular prominence are those which, while of interest to the academic lawyer, also have important bearing on issues which touch upon the actual conduct of international relations. None the less, the series is wide in scope and includes monographs on the history and philosphical foundations of international law.

RECENT TITLES IN THE SERIES

**Just War or Just Peace?
Humanitarian Intervention and International Law**
Simon Chesterman

**State Responsibility for Transboundary Air
Pollution in International Law**
Phoebe Okowa

The Responsibility of States for International Crimes
Nina H. B. Jørgensen

**The Law of International Watercourses:
Non-navigational Uses**
Stephen C. McCaffrey

**International Justice and the International Criminal
Court: Between Sovereignty and the Rule of Law**
Bruce Broomhall

Human Rights in International Criminal Proceedings
Salvatore Zappalà

FORTHCOMING TITLE:

**Universal Jurisdiction: International and
Municipal Legal Perspectives**
Luc Reydams

to my parents

Preface

Towards an International Criminal Procedure was first published in April 2001. International criminal law has continued to change in the intervening time. The Rome Statute for the International Criminal Court (ICC), signed in July 1998, has provoked an immense amount of academic work. The Statute came into force on 1 July 2002, Rules of Procedure and Evidence have been drafted, and a list of persons to be elected as judges and prosecutor has been assembled. The ICC has set sail.

International criminal law has also developed through the work of the UN Tribunals for the Former Yugoslavia and for Rwanda: several decisions of their chambers have influenced procedural law. The multitude of amendments to the Rules of Procedure and Evidence at the UN Tribunals illustrate the insecurity of the judges, coming from a great variety of legal cultures to The Hague and Arusha, with regard to procedural issues.

The goal of an international criminal procedure has not yet been reached. The maxim 'towards an international criminal procedure' understood as a working programme of a law in progress is therefore still valid. The Statute and Rules of the ICC provide a framework within which the rights of the accused and of victims must be balanced. The ICC has been given a procedural order that combines Continental and Anglo-American criminal procedure, and that procedural order is still incomplete, and sometimes inconsistent.

Towards an International Criminal Procedure aims to put international criminal procedure into the context of comparative law and human rights law. It attempts to promote understanding of differing traditions on the one hand and adherence to universal principles on the other. Using these two pillars, this volume seeks to establish a solid and commonly acceptable foundation from which answers to special procedural questions may be derived.

Furthermore, in addressing the entire process of criminal prosecution from beginning to the end, it indicates the necessity to view criminal procedure in its entirety, in order to develop the 'whole system'. This volume is not, however, a commentary to the Rome Statute or other documents. The reader will not find a discussion of every article of the ICC Statute or of the Rules of Procedure and Evidence (which were, at the time of writing, only available as a first and incomplete draft). There are other publications which fulfil that purpose. Instead, this volume guides the reader through the individual steps of criminal prosecution. It explains their underlying rationale, how they are carried out in general in national jurisdictions (using Germany, the UK, and the USA to represent the differing legal systems), and illustrates how they can be dealt with before international institutions.

I am very grateful to Oxford University Press for producing this paperback edition, which makes the book affordable to a wider readership. Hopefully it will serve its purpose for practitioners as well as students and academics as a worthwhile compendium of comparative and international criminal procedural law.

C.J.M.S.

Erlangen, December 2002

Acknowledgements

The idea of the thesis on which this book is based was born in 1996 during a seminar at the Ludwig-Maximilians-Universität in Munich on the development of international criminal law ('Von Nürnberg bis Den Haag') held by Professor Dr Bruno Simma. I had the pleasure of looking at the procedural order at the International Criminal Tribunal for the Former Yugoslavia. This task was handed over to me mainly because I had at that stage no history in public international law but was believed to be familiar with German national criminal law. In the course of the work for a paper presented at this seminar, which was drafted with the kind help of Markus Zöckler, I realized that not much literature on the Anglo-American criminal process was available in Munich and that a thorough analysis and comparison between what I knew of German criminal procedure and 'the other' system was not available. This seemed to me to be the main snag in the discussion of an international criminal procedural order, that there is a major misconception of 'the other' system on both sides of the water. We just do not know enough about one another. With the aim of forming a criminal order for an International Criminal Court I thought it would be worth looking at both systems and comparing them in greater detail. The *tertium comparationis* in international law could only be human rights law, which serves as a basis for all executive actions.

I am greatly indebted to Professor Dr Bruno Simma who encouraged me to make this the topic of a doctoral thesis under his supervision and gave me all the support that I needed. Many thanks to Professor Dr Klaus Volk, who functioned as a second supervisor. I am grateful to the Law Faculty of the University of Munich that not only gave me permission to submit this thesis in English, the first doctoral thesis there ever to be written in English, but also awarded the faculty prize of 2000 to this book. I would like to thank Oxford University Press and Mr John Louth for accepting the manuscript despite many procedural difficulties at the beginning.

Most of my knowledge of public international law and human rights law in particular I gained from my stay at the London School of Economics and Political Science, where I took part in the postgraduate master of law course in the academic year 1996/7. To do further research I stayed at the University of London for another six months, during which time most of this thesis was written. I am grateful for everything I learnt there and for having had the opportunity to use the wonderful British Library of Political and Economic Science. Many thanks also to the British

Institute of Advanced Legal Studies and its library. The Registry at the International Criminal Tribunal for the Former Yugoslavia made it very easy for me to access the important cases and material, not only via the internet but also by sending out copies. I got invaluable support from Professor Christopher Greenwood (LSE) for whom I had the pleasure to work as an occasional research assistant and who supplied me with much material and ideas. I am also thankful in particular for help in understanding human rights from Professor Christine Chinkin and Dr Chaloka Beyani (both LSE), who also both discussed problems with me to clear my mind. As English is not my mother tongue, I was dependent on native speakers to help with grammar and orthography. Without the help of Mrs Mary-Louise Eisenberger, MA, Sarah Green, M.Sc. (LSE), Farrhat Arshad, BA (Oxon.), LL.M. (LSE), Caroline Neenan, BA (Oxon.), Annecoos Wiersema, LL.B. (LSE), and Daniel Taegtmeyer, this thesis would probably be linguistically unintelligible. I am very thankful for their advice, support, and friendship. Most important as concerns moral support, apart from Newman House and Father Jim Overton and Father Jeremy Fairhead, were Fiona Muklow, Dr Ludger Helms, Paul Rosario, Günther Treppner, Tamara Repolust, and Billy Swan. Many thanks also to Professor Dr Christian Wolf (Munich) for his time and precious advice. I would also like to thank my fiancée Natascha Etminan for her endurance and love. Last but not least I am deeply indebted to my parents who made all my education possible and never let me doubt their support, not only financially, in a way that no one could expect. As my mother died only a few weeks ago, I would like to dedicate this publication to her in particular.

C.J.M.S

Munich
October 2000

Contents

Table of Cases

Human Rights Committee

European Court of Human Rights

European Commission on Human Rights

The Inter-American System

International Criminal Tribunal for the Former Yugoslavia (selection)

Appeals Chamber

Prosecutor v. Dusko Tadic, Judgment on Jurisdiction 2 October 1995, Case No. IT-94-1-AR72, published in 35 ILM 32 (1996).

Prosecutor v. Tihomir Blaskic, Judgment 29 October 1997 Case No. IT-95-14-AR108 bis.

Prosecutor v Drazen Erdemovic, Decision 7 October 1997, Case No. IT-96-22-A.

Trial Chambers

Trial Chamber I

Prosecutor v. Drazen Erdemovic, Sentencing Judgment I, 29 November 1996, Case No. IT-96-22-T.

Djukic case, Decision rejecting the application to withdraw the indictment and order provisional release, 24 April 1996, Case No. IT-96-20-T.

Karadzic and Mladic Decision rejecting the Application presented by Mr. E.M. Medvene and Mr. T.F. Hanley III, seeking leave to file briefs challenging the fairness of the Statute and the Rules of Procedure, 24 July 1996, Case No. IT-95-5-R61 and IT-95-18-R61.

Review of the indictment pursuant to Rule 61 of the Rules of Procedure and Evidence:

Karadzic and Mladic, Rule 61 Decision 11 July 1996, Case No. IT-95-5-R61 and IT-95-18-R61.

Milan Martic, Rule 61 Decision 8 March 1996, Case No. IT-95-11-R61.

Mrskic, Radic and Sljivancanin (Vukovar Hospital), Rule 61 Decision 3 April 1996, Case No. IT-95-13-R61.

Nikolic, Rule 61 Decision 20 October 1995, Case No. IT-94-2-R61.

Trial Chamber II

Tadic Decision 10 August 1995 Case No. IT-94-I-T.

- Decision 10 August 1995 on the Prosecutor's Motion Requesting Protective Measures for Victims and Witnesses, Case No. IT-94-1-T.

- Decision 27 November 1996 on Prosecution Motion for Production of Defence Witness Statements.

Erdemovic Sentencing Judgment II, 7 March 1998, Case No. IT-96-22-T.

Review of the indictment pursuant to Rule 61 of the Rules of Procedure and Evidence:

Ivica Rajic, Rule 61 Decision 13 September 1996, Case No. IT-95-12-R61.

German Courts

BVerfG Restructuring Federal States Judgment 23 October 1951, in BVerfGE 1, 14.

English Courts

American Courts

Other Courts

Abbreviations

AfCHPR	African Charta on Human and Peoples' Rights
AJIL	American Journal of International Law
BayObLG	Bayerisches Oberstes Landgericht (Bavarian Supreme Court)
BGH	Bundesgerichtshof (German Supreme Court)
BGHSt	Reports of the Bundesgerichtshof Criminal Division
BGHZ	Reports of the Bundesgerichtshof Civil Division
BVerfG	Bundesverfassungsgericht (German Constitutional Court)
BVerfGE	Reports of the Bundesverfassungsgericht
BYIL	British Yearbook of International Law
CPS	Crown Prosecution Service
Crim.App.R.	Reports of Criminal Appeals Cases
CrimLR	Criminal Law Review
Draft Statute ILC	Draft Statute for an International Criminal Court by the International Law Commission
ECJ	European Court of Justice
ECHR	European Convention on Human Rights
ECommHR	European Commission of Human Rights
ECourtHR	European Court of Human Rights
EJIL	European Journal of International Law
Eur. J. Crime Cr.L.Cr.J.	European Journal of Crime, Criminal Law and Criminal Justice
UN GA	General Assembly of the United Nations
GA	Goldmanns Archiv
HRC	Human Rights Committee
HRComm	Commission on Human Rights
IAmCHR	American Convention on Human Rights
IAmCourtHR	Inter-American Court of Human Rights
ICC	Permanent International Criminal Court
ICCPR	International Covenant on Civil and Political Rights
ICESCR	International Covenant on Economic, Social and Cultural Rights
ICJ	International Court of Justice
ICLQ	International and Comparative Law Quarterly
ICTY	International Criminal Tribunal for the Former Yugoslavia

ICTR	International Criminal Tribunal for Rwanda
ILC	International Law Commission
ILM	International Legal Materials
ILR	International Law Reports
IMT	International Military Tribunal
JA	Juristische Ausbildung
JuS	Juristische Schulung
LG	Landgericht (Regional Court)
LJIL	Leiden Journal of International Law
MLR	The Modern Law Review
NILR	Netherlands International Law Reports
NJW	Neue Juristische Wochenschrift
NStZ	Neue Zeitschrift für Strafrecht
NZWehrr	Neue Zeitschrift für Wehrrecht
PACE	Police and Criminal Evidence Act
PCIJ	Permanent Court of International Justice
PrepComm	Preparatory Committee for the Establishment of an International Criminal Court
Rome Statute	Rome Statute of the International Criminal Court
Rule	Rule of the Rules of Procedure and Evidence of the International Criminal Tribunal for the Former Yugoslavia
SC	Security Council of the United Nations
Statute ICTY	Statute of the International Criminal Tribunal for the Former Yugoslavia
StGB	Strafgesetzbuch (German Penal Code)
StPO	Strafprozeßordnung (German Code of Criminal Procedure)
St.Tr.	State Trials
StV	Strafverteidiger
UDHR	Universal Declaration of Human Rights
UN	United Nations
YB	Yearbook of the European Commission on Human Rights
WLR	Weekly Law Reports

Introduction

At the end of the twentieth century the international community is pursuing the institution of an International Criminal Court. Recent experiences of two world wars and innumerable 'minor' armed conflicts in particular have brought about the idea of prosecuting war criminals as a means to prevent future atrocities. As purely political methods have often proved to be ineffective in this regard, the international community has now decided to add legal sanctions to these political efforts. An International Criminal Court should hold individuals responsible for human rights violations. In the course of the twentieth century, several attempts were made to enforce international criminal law directly. With the establishment of Criminal Tribunals for the Former Yugoslavia and Rwanda through the UN Security Council this became reality for the first time in history. In consequence of these Security Council activities the world community is pressing for establishing a permanent International Criminal Court, which would have jurisdiction over crimes such as genocide, crimes against humanity, war crimes, and grave breaches of the Geneva Conventions. One of the main difficulties with this institution will be the procedural order that this international court should apply. On 17 July 1998 the UN Diplomatic Conference of Plenipotentiaries on the Establishment of an International Criminal Court adopted a Statute for an International Criminal Court (so-called Rome Statute). This statute represents many years of political and legal struggle and contains a certainly impressive compromise. However, the discussion about a correct procedural order for this court, which is now being established, is far from over. The Rome Statute provides a workable framework and basis to be filled in and built on by legislative acts, for example the Rule of Procedure and Evidence, or judicial acts, that is, case-law, as soon as the statute enters into force.

When talking about criminal procedure in an international context the first thing one must do is respond, in some way, to the wide gap between the Anglo-American and the Continental traditions of criminal procedure. The former, which is usually referred to as being adversarial or accusatorial, developed by way of an historical evolution compared to the latter, often called inquisitorial, which emerged, to a great extent, but not exclusively, by imposition of a systematic structure.[1]

The International Criminal Tribunal for the Former Yugoslavia (ICTY) has embarked on the great challenge of overcoming the gulf that exists

---

[1] J. Hatchard, B. Huber, and R. Vogler (eds.), *Comparative Criminal Procedure* (London, 1996), 224.

between the different legal traditions. Thus far the work of the ICTY 'demonstrates the difficulties inherent in melding civil law and common law rules and international human rights standards into a truly "international" body of procedural and substantive criminal law'.[2] The two main systems, adversarial and inquisitorial, surely play a major role in finding an appropriate procedure for an International Criminal Court (ICC), indeed, these traditions form the basic structure of the Rome Statute. However, the aim must be a truly international criminal procedure[3] which should not be used as a test for the credibility of domestic penal systems,[4] but stands solidly on the various traditions of criminal procedure.

This work intends to confront this problem of how to reconcile the two main systems of criminal procedure in a conclusive international process order. The view taken here stands on two approaches. First is the approach of a comparative lawyer, looking at the individual steps of criminal procedure and how they present themselves in the different systems. Secondly, human rights prerequisites have to be taken into account. This second requirement is by no means subordinate to the first; every procedural step must be measured against human rights imperatives and rooted in them. Despite the fact that the underlying philosophical foundations of civil and common law, as well as their distinct procedural steps, differ in many respects, both systems must be committed to ensuring fundamental human rights in a democratic society. In this the two traditions have an overlapping goal: to actualize fundamental human rights within a fair procedure. Alongside this common objective, the differences could even be understood as being in a sort of competition: which system is capable of better protecting the rights of the offender; which system provides for a greater possibility of balancing the different rights and interests that are at stake? Starting from an international human rights perspective one has to compare carefully both approaches and contemplate how they try to safeguard the individual rights in each stage of the procedure. There, we face the problem of having to determine these rights when the major human rights treaties enlist a rather incomplete and vaguely phrased set of provisions. The Human Rights Committee (HRC) rightly points out in its General Comment on Art. 14 ICCPR: '[T]he requirements of paragraph 3 are minimum guarantees, the observance of which is not always sufficient to ensure the fairness of a

---

[2] King and La Rosa, 8 EJIL (1997), 123 at 125.

[3] Melding elements of one model into another does not seem to be the appropriate way but is frequently adhered to, e.g. Cassese, 10 EJIL (1999), 144 at 168.

[4] *Report of the Preparatory Committee on the Establishment of an International Criminal Court,* i (Proceedings of the Preparatory Committee during March–April and August 1996) GAOR 55th Session, Suppl. No. 22, UN Doc. A/51/22, para. 215. (= Report of the PrepCom I).

hearing as required by paragraph 1'.[5] But even more than that, as we scrutinize a procedure for an International Criminal Court we have to look for a well-rounded system of criminal procedure. In other words, it is not enough to spell out the distinct rights and name the forms of protection in the different systems; rather it must be suggested which system provides better safeguards. It is also crucial to keep the whole system in mind so as not to destroy a carefully balanced system with a simplistic, eclectic approach.

This work looks at criminal procedure in chronological order. But before the particular stages of the procedure are examined the historical and philosophical background and underpinnings will be briefly outlined. Through this the main problem with this issue, that is, the differences between the adversarial and the inquisitorial system, will be clarified. In addition the question of why human rights can and should serve as a common denominator in the search for a conclusive procedural structure will be discussed (Chapter 1). The following chapters follow the course of the prosecution. The pre-trial inquiry (Chapter 2), the confirmation of the indictment (Chapter 3), the trial (Chapter 4), the stage after the conviction (Chapter 5), and finally the post-trial stage (Chapter 6) will be discussed according to human rights provisions and national law and practice in England and Wales, and the United States on the one hand, and Germany on the other, taking the suggestions for an International Criminal Court, in particular also the Rome Statute, and the law and practice at the International Criminal Tribunal in the Hague into due account. It might not be obvious to take the German system as representing the civil law system, since the French legal system is traditionally conceived of as being the 'classical' civil law system.[6] Today, however, the pure civil law system of criminal procedure is history, and despite existing differences, the structural equalities are such that, for the purpose here, it does not matter which national legal order is exemplified.[7] Furthermore, the differences between France and Germany are mostly limited to the pre-trial stage.

---

[5] Human Rights Committee, General Comment 13, Article 14 (21st session, 1984), Compilation of General Comments and General Recommendations Adopted by Human Rights, Treaty Bodies, UN Doc. HRI/GEN/1/Rev.1 at 14 (1994) at para. 5 (= HRC General Comment 13).

[6] Kai Ambos differentiates the civil law system into two subgroups, one being the French system, the other being the prosecutorial system. Germany belongs to the latter subgroup; compare Ambos in L. Arbour *et al.* (eds.), *The Prosecutor of a Permanent International Criminal Court* (Freiburg im Breisgau, 2000), 495–6.

[7] The difference lies mainly with the prominent role of the *juge d'instruction* in French procedural system. The examining judge appears elsewhere in Europe only in Spain, Holland, and Belgium. In France he is only responsible in certain instances; compare Volger, in Hatchard *et al.* (eds.), *Comparative Criminal Procedure*, 42 and 229.

The selection of problems that are discussed is certainly somewhat arbitrary. However, they are, in my view, the most severe problems found in criminal prosecution and most likely to endanger the fairness of the procedure and human rights of the persons involved in this process. The results will be summarized in Chapter 7. I will suggest that the flaws of both systems, Anglo-American and Continental, could best be avoided in a structural combination of these two approaches. Such a combination would serve best the aim of criminal prosecution, that is, to find the true offender and sentence him to the punishment he deserves in a system that can truly be called 'fair'.

1

About the Necessity of Respect for the Alleged Offender

The search for an international criminal procedure has to be based on the two main systems of national criminal procedure, namely the Anglo-American and the Continental European traditions. In order to decide how different these systems really are and whether or not they can be reconciled at all, I look first at the historical development of the two systems (I) and at their underlying ideas (II). This will help us to understand the actual differences, and will bring to light the similarities in both theory and practice.

(I) Criminal Procedure from Ancient to Modern Times

A historical sketch will clarify the roots and legal bases on which the different criminal justice systems are built. At this stage I will give a brief descriptive narrative of how the criminal justice systems developed and how they were justified in Germany, England, and the United States. A purely descriptive and neutral presentation is certainly difficult, perhaps impossible. One difficulty that stems from the differing legal systems lies in the different sources of law. While the common law development is principally a collection of cases, the history of the criminal justice system in Germany is mainly an explanation of different statutes and acts. This contrast is explored below.

1. Germany

Due to the fragmentation into many states, kingdoms, dukedoms, independent towns, and other similar divisions, several procedural systems existed in parallel with each other. It was not until the foundation of the German Empire after the war against France in 1870–1 that legislation was unified. The character of criminal procedure was originally similar to that of civil litigation. It was mainly privately brought. The victim or his family would accuse the offender. The constitution of the court was democratic; the assembly of the people was called upon to act as judge over the allegations.[1] The trial was public and oral. The rules of evidence were primitive and mainly based on ordeal or on some form of God's judgment like a fight.[2]

Charlemagne undertook a reform of the criminal system, in particular, introducing lay judges, so-called 'scabini', which were meant to represent the people and convict on behalf of the people. However, these reforms did not prevail in the rural communities and the 'old thing' was reinstated in the post-Carolingian era. Further reformative steps gradually appeared in the towns during the second half of the medieval age (about 900–1450). The previously private accusatorial system was superseded by an ex officio procedure, inquisitorial in character. The responsible judges inquired, accused, and judged all in one person. The aim was primarily to find the material truth. Although witness testimony was introduced, at the centre of the proceedings was the confession. This was produced by penal questioning, that is, torture.[3] The trial became secret and written.

At the turn of the sixteenth century German procedure came under the decisive influence of the much further developed Italian law.[4] Under this influence German procedural law developed systematically and academically. Carl V codified German criminal law both materially and procedurally for the first time in the so-called Constitutio Criminalis Carolina (1532).[5] Amongst the major changes was the complete abolition of the accusatorial principle.[6] The prosecution of criminals was perceived as an exclusively executive duty. A judge would institute proceedings ex officio and place the suspect in detention for purposes of the inquiry. There were strict rules of evidence and exact prescriptions on how to weigh evidence; a conviction was conditional on either a confession (CCC, Art. 60) or the testimony of two impeccable witnesses (CCC, Art. 67, 69). To gain a confession torture was permissible (CCC, Art. 6, 8, 9, 20–61) yet there were two novelties that were meant to protect the accused: first, torture was only allowed if there was a certain degree of suspicion; second, a confession made under torture was only admissible as evidence if it was corrob-

---

[1] C. Roxin, *Strafverfahrensrecht* (24th edn. Munich, 1995), § 67 No. 1.
[2] Cf. e.g. the legend of Lohengrin who stood as knight on behalf of Elsa to defend her against the criminal accusations of Telramund in a fight which was considered as proving the truthfulness of the allegations.
[3] Torture was permissible from 1270, documented in the so-called *Schwabenspiegel*.
[4] Italian law was received in Germany mainly through two channels: (1) by German students who studied law at the universities of Upper Italy and (2) via private collections of law, so-called *Rechtsspiegel*.
[5] Hereinafter referred to as CCC. Compare the short description of this impressive code by K. Peters, *Strafprozeßrecht* (4th edn. Heidelberg, 1985), 61–4.
[6] Although a complaint from a third person was possible (CCC, Art. 11–17) nevertheless the procedure was held *ex officio*. Such a complaint procedure was particularly dangerous as the complainant was held responsible in case of an acquittal, had to give security beforehand, and was taken into custody if he could not do so.

orated after the questioning under torture. Certainly the prospect of being tortured even further in the case of a denial of the previous confession made this an unpromising possibility. The trial was secret and written and only the pronouncement of the judgment was public. As the judges were not necessarily jurists, they would in unusual cases consult law faculties of universities and eventually simply publish the opinion of the professor, who had not even seen the accused, as the verdict.

The common German criminal procedure can be summarized as purely inquisitorial; it saw the accused as a mere object of the inquiry, almost defenceless in the hands of the inquisitor. The only defence possible was a written legal comment on the material produced by the prosecution.[7]

At the times of absolute monarchy the people were expelled from the judges' benches and replaced by professional judges who were highly dependent upon public authority both personally and institutionally. Serious cases needed the *placet* of the political leader. He had the power to acquit, to reduce or increase sentence, and to pass verdict. Until the nineteenth century the monarch would exercise the highest judicial authority in criminal matters. This was the situation in most parts of Europe during the time of absolutism.

A fundamental modification came about during the Enlightenment. The seeds of reform were sown by pre-Enlightenment thinkers, namely Christian Thomasius (1655–1728) and the Jesuit Friedrich von Spee (1591–1635), both writing against witch-trials in particular.[8] Most heavily criticized was the inquisitorial process with its inherent legitimization of torture. In Prussia torture was eventually abolished in 1740, soon after Friedrich the Great came to the throne, for ordinary offences, and for serious cases in 1754 and 1756. Other states followed this example slowly. In Bavaria it was ruled out by the then Minister of Justice and famous lawyer Anselm von Feuerbach on 7 July 1806; in Gotha it was set aside as late as 1828.[9]

Prominent amongst the Enlightened Thinkers in criminal matters were Voltaire (1694–1778) in France and Beccaria (1739–94) in Italy. Montesquieu (1689–1755) also pleaded for a reform of criminal procedure to make it similar to the English system. The French Revolution and its postulates of civil liberties and republicanism led to the adoption of, amongst other things, the accusatorial principle, the principle of an oral and public trial, and the principle that the burden of proof lies on the party of the prosecution. The jury system was introduced. In 1808 the

---

[7] Roxin, *Strafverfahrensrecht*, § 69 No. 10.

[8] Von Spee is famous for his work *Cautio criminalis* (1631), Thomasius is known for *De Crimine Magiae* (1701).

[9] See Peters, *Strafprozeßrecht*, 67.

Napoleonic *Code d'instruction criminelle* compiled these principles.[10] The inquiry was presided over by the prosecutor (*procureur d'état*) who would accuse the suspect before an examining magistrate (*juge d'instruction*). Upon the confirmation of this indictment the case was transferred to a trial by jury. Rules of evidence were totally abandoned in favour of the principle of free consideration of the evidence. The jurors had simply to ask themselves whether they had *intime conviction* of the guilt of the defendant.

These principles were postulated in Germany amongst the civil liberties proclaimed at the conference in the Paulskirche on 27 December 1848 and were part of the Frankfurt Constitution of the German Empire (Frankfurter Reichsverfassung, FRV) of 28 March 1849. An independent prosecuting authority was introduced (§ 179 FRV) and in addition special tribunals were prohibited (§ 174 (II) 2 FRV). Furthermore the need for an arrest warrant issued by a court was formulated in order to protect against arbitrariness by the police (§ 138 (II) FRV).

In the aftermath of this most of the German fragmented states codified new procedural systems that were in accordance with these principles.[11] This is called the Reformed German Criminal Process. Both the Austrian Penal Procedure (1973) and the German Code (StPO 1877) are rooted in this reformed system. The German StPO was codified after the foundation of the German Empire in 1871, was ratified by Parliament on 1 February 1877, and came into force together with the other *Reichsjustizgesetze* (Judiciary Acts) on 1 October 1879. It has remained in force until today although it has undergone several changes. The first reform of this system came in 1924, the so-called *Emminger'sche Reform*.[12] This brought the abolition of the jury. Instead lay judges (*Schöffen*) were introduced to sit alongside the professional judges.

During the Third Reich several perversions of criminal procedure and procedural fairness were introduced, partly to bypass the guarantees of the StPO. Most commonly known amongst these is the so-called Volksgerichtshof (court of the people), responsible for political crimes, acting as an appeals chamber for the Reichsgericht. Several other tribunals existed for political delicts at a lower instance,[13] best described as 'Scheinverfahren ohne alle Garantien und mit vorher feststehendem Ergebnis'.[14] The StPO itself was submitted to several modifications.

---

[10] This code was then applicable also in the German territory west of the River Rhine (*Linksrheinische Gebiete*).

[11] e.g. Bavaria 1848 and 1861 and Prussia 1849.

[12] Named after the then Minister of Justice Emminger.

[13] Cf. the description of special tribunals during the Nazi regime by H. Rüping, *Staatsanwaltschaft und Provinzialjustizverwaltung im Dritten Reich* (Baden-Baden, 1990).

[14] 'procedures without any guarantee and a result that was obvious in advance' (trans. by the author), compare H. Rüping, *Grundriß der Strafrechtsgeschichte* (2nd edn. Munich, 1991), 103–4.

Amongst them was the strengthening of the powers of the prosecutc increase in the number of possible reasons for detention as well a abolition of the prohibition of *reformatio in peius* on appeal. At the beginning of the war lay judges were dismissed from the courtroom.[15] On 26 April 1942 the separation of powers was finally eliminated and Hitler as the *Führer* simultaneously proclaimed himself highest judge.

After the war this Nazi legislation was overturned[16] and several reforms were instituted to enhance the foundations of a procedure which is in accordance with the rule of law. The fathers of the German Constitution of 1949 (*Das Bonner Grundgesetz*) embodied in the text several explicit references to judicial independence and the rights of the accused. Interestingly these were not included in the beginning Articles 1 to 19 of the Bill of Basic Rights but rather further on in the document, in Articles 101 to 103, the so-called Judicial Basic Rights (*Justizgrundrechte*).

§ 136a StPO was introduced to guarantee respect for the human dignity of the suspect and the accused. In 1964 the position of the defence was buttressed by further rights to disclosure and enhanced visiting rights. Other reforms and modernizations will be referred to in the course of this work. The structure of German procedure has, however, not changed since then.

2. The development in England

From the time of William the Conqueror the basic reason for having a criminal justice system has been to keep the peace. Criminal prosecution, as part of this broader system, was necessary in order to keep the 'King's Peace'.[17] The criminal trial was understood as contributing to this aim by channelling the private revenge of a person wronged into an official process. Victims were called upon to entrust their cases to the public authorities.[18] This perception has several consequences: first, the criminal trial resembled, and still does today, civil litigation, and secondly, the onus was and is on the private person to denounce the alleged offender and institute proceedings.[19] As the Crown was responsible for maintaining order in society, that is, the 'King's Peace', it had to provide effective institutions for doing this. This was done by several officers, mainly the Justices of the King's Bench as the chief servants appointed by the Crown,

---

[15] Compare Peters, *Strafprozeßrecht*, 72.

[16] Mainly in West Germany through the *Vereinheitlichungsgesetz* 1950 which also aimed at instituting a uniform procedure after the fragmentation of the several occupation zones.

[17] Stephen, Criminal Procedure from the Thirteenth to the Eighteenth Century, in Association of American Law Schools (ed.), *Selected Essays in Anglo-American Legal History*, ii. 443 at 444.

[18] Ibid. 480.

[19] For a compilation of the several possibilities of private accusation, see ibid. 479–85.

and the coroner, appointed to investigate death. Both institutions used the same instruments to investigate criminal offences, usually the accusing jury, or Grand Jury.[20] This body consisted of people from the neighbourhood of the scene of the crime who were expected to know the true circumstances of the offence. They were put under oath to disclose their knowledge. Clearly they were not expected to be impartial towards and ignorant of the facts of the crime. The opposite was true; they were expected to represent the *fama publica*.[21] The charges against the accused, as conceived by this jury, were compiled in a document, indictment,[22] or inquisition.[23] It was not until the seventeenth century that the Grand Jury changed. Then the body was no longer expected to present its own knowledge, but became an institution that determined from material presented to it whether or not there was a case that ought to be tried.[24]

The collection of evidence, that is, a thorough inquiry into the case, was the task of the parish constable or of justices of the peace, responsible for the investigation of local crime. The effectiveness of a system such as this is questionable, especially since these persons received no salary or a minimal one and had to earn their living by other means. Furthermore the system was entirely informal: no formal description of the duties and rights of such a position existed until two statutes of 1554 and 1555.[25] These statutes require that the collection of evidence be documented in the form of depositions. Witnesses were required to appear at trial. Justices were empowered to grant the accused bail,[26] conditional or unconditional. Although practically it was the justices who decided whom to prosecute, formally the accusation was still made by the Grand Jury, and was therefore private in nature.[27] The procedure was entirely informal, with rights of the suspect non-existent.

For the trial that followed the investigation there were several possibilities. In ex officio proceedings there was first of all 'trial by ordeal'. On public accusation the accused might for example be submitted to 'ordeal by water' in order to verify or invalidate the charges. If the accused failed the ordeal he was punished by, for example, losing a foot or a hand in cases of theft.[28] If he was successful at the ordeal he was nevertheless

---

[20] P. Devlin, *The Criminal Prosecution in England* (New Haven, 1958), 4.

[21] Forsynth, *History of the Trial by Jury* (London, 1852), 201.

[22] So-called in the case of a Grand Jury used by the Justices.

[23] The term in the case of a coroner's inquiry.

[24] Devlin, *Criminal Prosecution*, 4–5.

[25] See Stephen, Criminal Procedure, 459–60.

[26] Bailing is, indeed, as old as English law itself. Compare E. De Haas, Antiquities of Bail (New York, 1940), ch. 1.

[27] Devlin, *Criminal Prosecution*, 7.

[28] It was not unusual for a thief to be hanged, beheaded, or pushed over a cliff, and for the owner of the stolen goods to act as executioner, see F. Pollock and F. W. Maitland, *History of English Law before the Time of Edward I* (2nd edn. Cambridge, 1923), ii. 579.

banished.[29] The charged was, one might say, presumed guilty, as he was punished either way. The practice of ordeal was probably discontinued in the course of the thirteenth century.[30]

The second possibility was trial by jury. In such a case a dispute between the Crown and the defendant would be presented to a jury. When the Crown presented the allegation orally the defendant had immediately the chance to deny his guilt and ask for proof of the accusations. The prosecution would in that case present the dispositions and if the truthfulness of these testimonies was still contested it then had to call the witness into court.[31] The main hindrances to a proper defence., however, were that the prisoner was held in confinement more or less secretly until the trial and therefore had little time for the preparation of his defence.[32] Furthermore, no notice was given of the evidence against the prisoner prior to the actual trial, and he had to defend himself in person as he was allowed no counsel. Above all, it appears that the defendant was not allowed to call witnesses on his behalf. If witnesses were allowed, however, they were not examined under oath as the prosecution witnesses were. Major importance was attributed to confessions and in particular to those of accomplices.[33] The independence of the jury, on the constitution of which the defendant had no influence whatsoever, was also dealt with in a curious manner. It appears that jurors could be held accountable and even be tried themselves if the verdict they returned was not according to the wishes of the authorities.[34] To sum up we can say that criminal trial in England as early as the seventeenth century was organized according to certain intelligible principles that are partly still in force today. However, the defendant was heavily underprivileged in the conduct of the preliminary proceedings and at trial, where he was threatened with the possibility of extremely severe punishment.

[29] Stephen, Criminal Procedure, 487.

[30] Pollock and Maitland, *History of English Law*, ii. 599, who suppose that this was a consequence of the decrees of the Lateran Council (1215).

[31] Stephen, Criminal Procedure, 491.

[32] This problem was made an issue in the trial of the Duke of Norfolk in 1571 (1 *St.Tr.* 957–1042), tried for high treason, accused of imagining the death and deposition of Queen Elizabeth. The Duke complained that he had no access to books and was not even allowed paper to make notes.

[33] Interesting in this regard is the trial of Raleigh (2 *St.Tr.* 1–60). He was tried for treason, accused of conspiring with Lord Cobham to make Arabella Stuart Queen of England with the help of the Archduke of Austria. The whole evidence amounted to the 'confession' of Cobham before the Privy Council and a letter he wrote afterwards. Cobham was not called to be examined, although Raleigh insisted that the testimony given by him was false. He was convicted and executed on 29 Oct. 1618.

[34] e.g. in the trial against Sir Nicholas Throckmorton (1 *St.Tr.* 395) who was accused of high treason in 1554, jurors who acquitted him were sent to prison for their verdict and eight of them were brought before the Star Chamber, eventually discharged on the payment of a certain sum. See Stephen, Criminal Procedure, 494.

A new institution for the investigation of crimes was founded by the 1829 Metropolitan Police Act, namely the police. Justices were therefore able to become independent and truly judicial. From then on it was the duty of the police to take statements from witnesses and collect other evidence on which the justices were then asked to decide for trial or discharge. This development made the Grand Jury institutionally redundant, and it was eventually abolished in 1933.[35]

The right to silence became a recognized right of the defendant in the Victorian era. But even before then pre-trial inquiry was not based on confession, which could ultimately be extorted by torture. Torture was, indeed, never permitted in English law.[36] However it was used during the reigns of Henry VIII and his three children, Edward VI, Mary I, and Elizabeth I, as well as during the reigns of James I and Charles I.[37] The reasons why torture was never as 'popular' a means of questioning the defendant in England as it was on the Continent are hard to guess. Stephen supposes that it had little to do with 'any special humanity of feeling' or the basic rights of the Magna Carta. Rather he finds the summary character of the early methods of the trial and the severity of the punishments inflicted as reasons for this.[38] That sentences were extremely severe can hardly be contested. Whether or not the comparatively liberal criminal process is to be seen as a counterbalance to the toughness of the substantive law, as Stephen seems to presume, or whether it was a consequence of the urge to base state authority on the rule of law, that is, a tool for controlling the executive, as Radzinowicz argues,[39] is unclear.

In the course of the seventeenth century the trial itself was given more or less the shape which, with minor modifications, it has kept until today. This was achieved because the

evils of judicial corruption and subserviency, and the horrors of a party warfare carried on by reciprocal prosecutions for treason alternately instituted against each other, with fatal effect, by the chiefs of contending parties, had made so deep an impression on the public imagination, that a change of sentiment took place which from that time effectually prevented the scandals of the seventeenth century from being repeated.[40]

After the Revolution one of the most important changes was the increased independence of the judges. They were now in office not *gratia regis* but

---

[35] Administration of Justice Act 1933, compare Devlin, *Criminal Prosecution*, 10.

[36] L. Radzinowicz, *A History of English Criminal Law and its Administration from 1750* (London, 1948), i. 26, nevertheless found an exception in the form of *peine forte et dure* up until 1772.

[37] Stephen, Criminal Procedure, 462 with further references.

[38] Ibid. 462–3.

[39] Radzinowicz, *A History of English Criminal Law*, i. 25.

[40] Stephen, Criminal Procedure, 525.

according to their skills and behaviour. A copy of the indictment was given to defendants several days before the trial, and they were allowed counsel and witness upon oath. In 1708 it was further allowed for the prisoner to be given a list of witnesses for the prosecution and of the jurors ten days before the trial. Also, representation by counsel of the defendant during trial, that is, mainly the examination and cross-examination of the witnesses, was gradually granted.[41] Further reform was also certainly to the credit of Bentham, who added to the respect for the individual rights of the subject the principle that criminal procedure should protect against the arbitrary tendencies of the state and should reduce the uncertainty of punishment.[42] Thereby he found a link between criminal law and criminal procedure.[43]

The statutes of Philip and Mary concerning preliminary inquiry continued to be in force until the Victorian age. In 1826 and again in 1848 the procedure was generally reformed. In 1848, the so-called Sir John Jervis' Act brought major improvements to the situation of the defendant.[44] Witnesses had now to be examined in the presence of the accused and he was given a chance to cross-examine them. The testimony had to be written down and signed by both magistrate and witness. The accused was then asked to comment on the allegations, but was cautioned that he did not have to say anything. If however he wished to do so, his statements could be used against him at trial. The defendant could then call witnesses on his behalf. Finally, the justices would decide whether the case 'raises a strong or probable presumption of guilt' and commit for trial, grant bail, or discharge. The accused was entitled to copies of the dispositions and had the right to be represented by counsel.[45] Yet the procedure did not take place in open court; new proceedings were not excluded even if the justices decided to discharge. Since the reign of George III the course of the trial has not much altered. Changes since that

---

[41] In the trial against William Barnard (19 *St.Tr.* 815) in 1758 it seemed that his counsel cross-examined all witnesses fully, whereas at the trial against Lord Ferrers (19 *St.Tr.* 886) in 1760 the defendant himself was left to examine the witnesses, which was particularly delicate as he had to prove the defence of insanity which he had set up. The Act of 1836 finally laid down the right to be represented by counsel; see Holdsworth, *A History of English Law* (London, 1965), xv. 157.

[42] Radzinowicz, *A History of English Criminal Law*, i. 370.

[43] This seems to be a logical consequence of Bentham's utilitarian point of view. The aim of peace and happiness in society can only be achieved by an effectively working criminal justice system as a whole. Arbitrariness in the enforcement system produces unreliability and as such is one of the main hindrances of deterrence.

[44] See Stephen, Criminal Procedure, 460–1; the substance of this Act still governs the conduct of preliminary inquiry, although the language was changed by the Magistrates' Courts Act 1952, see Devlin, *Criminal Prosecution*, 7.

[45] Although this is not explicitly stated in the above statute, Stephen holds that this right was never disputed in practice, Stephen, Criminal Procedure, 461.

time have concerned mainly modification or even partly destruction of the jury system. The structure, however, has remained the same. I will discuss changes in the course of this work.

3. The development in the United States

The development of the criminal trial in the United States of America is of particular interest. Immigrants came from both civil and common law backgrounds, the greater part certainly from Britain. Furthermore, immigration was motivated partly by dissatisfaction with the oppressive legal system in the homeland. However, it is difficult to find statements of general validity about the criminal system in the emerging new states because of the fragmentation of the colonies, in particular the dissimilarities between North and South.

Immigrants certainly did not arrive in the 'new world' with libraries of statutes and law books. On the other hand, they did have a strong sense of what they wanted, and in particular of what was wrong in their former home. If a cautious attempt to generalize may be allowed, the criminal process in the emerging American states was a mixture of a simplified structure of the English law and religious principles. There was a profound awareness of the injustices and exigencies of the criminal justice system in England.[46] The protection of the accused soon became an important part of the colonial codes. The Massachusetts Body of Liberties of 1641, for example, blended common law and Puritan theology. The list of rights contained numerous safeguards for the defendant, like a speedy and equal justice, bail, right of counsel, trial by jury, challenge of jurors, double jeopardy, cruel and unusual punishment, and prohibition of torture. Other colonial documents expressed similar rights, like the Pennsylvania Frame of Government of 1682. Although this reads almost like a modern human rights treaty, in practice procedure was not 'fair' by modern terms, as we shall see.

In the Puritan colonies of New England the inquisitorial structure of summary justice was adopted. It relied greatly on magistrates who would, as experienced and God-fearing people, execute justice according to the righteous rules of God's word. The examination of the alleged offender was in the hands of the magistrate with the aim of gaining a confession. He could then either punish summarily or commit for trial (in some states a Grand Jury would be responsible) and had discretion over bail. The trial that followed was a model of simplicity, the accused in principle standing alone before the court. The judge would be an active participant although nevertheless generally neutral towards the accused. Since the community was mainly religious the system of summary trial was

---

[46] D. J. Bodenhamer, *Fair Trial* (Oxford, 1992), 14.

sufficient and was generally unimpeded, as crime was conceived of as sin that would destroy the unity of the community before God. The aim of the procedure therefore was to secure a confession and guide the offender to true repentance. As these communities were quite strongly bound together it was difficult to conceal crime in the first place and it was a relatively rare phenomenon in the early colonial years. This situation changed as more and more settlers came, for reasons other than religious ones, and lived outside the Puritan orbit. They demanded justice by jury trials. In Virginia a similar two-track system existed, the summary trial being the favoured procedure here as well. However, in contrast to the North, the indictment carried a presumption of guilt. Consequently most accused persons pleaded guilty in order to avoid the costs of a full-scale trial.

The Revolution, it seems, brought a shift in focus. The central idea was the right to liberty. The protection of this right became the focal point of the crusade against the mother country.[47] Rights in this sense were conceived of as limiting governmental power, restraining unwarranted interference in private affairs. At that time also privacy was understood very much as community-based and not so much as an individual right. The desire to uphold these rights fuelled the urge to independence from England. Numerous documents during the 1760s and 1770s contained liberty rights, with fair trial articles usually amongst them. The peak was certainly reached in the Declaration of Independence and the Virginia Declaration of Rights on 12 June 1776. Certainly here also the writings of Montesquieu and Beccaria were influential enough to underpin the belief that governmental power needs to be bound by general principles by means of a written constitution. Finally, on 25 September 1788, a Bill of Rights came into existence. Four of its ten articles were concerned with a fair trial. From that time on, every federal state would establish an accusatorial jury system similar to the English criminal process. Despite a pronounced anglophobia in American politics after the Revolution state courts relied heavily on British precedents to guide their definitions of due process of law.[48] As a reaction to the sentencing habits of England, which were thought of as too bloody, long discussions arose about the abolition of the death penalty.[49] Likewise the institution of the Grand Jury was contested during the first half of the nineteenth century in particular. However, the system was kept because the Grand Jury was seen as a

---

[47] Ibid. 31. [48] Ibid. 53.

[49] From this background it seems anachronistic that nowadays the USA is one of the few Western countries not only not to rule out the possibility of capital punishment but with an ever-increasing execution rate. Nor are the USA amongst the signatory states of the 2nd Optional Protocol to the ICCPR, GA Resolution adopted 15 December 1989, entered into force 11 July 1991, UN Doc. A/Res/44/128, and Protocol 6 of the ECHR (ETS 114 adopted 28 April 1983, in force since 1 March 1985).

bulwark of liberty, a controlling instrument of prosecutorial activities. The Petit Jury also underwent criticism and experienced a major shift in the course of the nineteenth century. It was formerly responsible for both the determination of fact and law. The relationship between judge and jury entered into a new phase from around 1845 onwards. From then, the judge decided on matters of law whilst the jury determined questions of fact.[50] As a corollary, stringent rules for the admission of evidence evolved, as well as the right to state appeal and the possibility for the judge to set aside verdicts contrary to the evidence.[51]

Law enforcement in the emerging cities was entrusted to a police force which was poorly paid and ill-trained as well as interfered with by political hacks. Little respect for the rights of a suspect could be expected from this side. The protection of the suspect's rights began in court, not on the street. It was the trial judge who had to ensure that the dignity of the suspect was respected and, if necessary, the police would be disciplined by evidence being declared inadmissible that was gathered in breach of proper conduct. Still, equality before courts was not given. Slaves and blacks in general were treated more harshly than whites and had to fear greater penalties that were inflicted upon them for no other reason than their colour.[52]

How the singular instruments and rights developed from the mid-nineteenth to the end of the twentieth century will be discussed in the course of this work. The criminal justice system of the United States has experienced further unification through the application of the Fourteenth Amendment to most of the 'fair trial' rights. Serious crime is mostly prosecuted by the police in collaboration with prosecutors and tried before a jury. The further unification of the federal systems and the elaboration of the rights of the accused are mostly due to the cases decided by the Supreme Court. This highest court of the United States has developed as the main protector of the constitutional rights of the individual and has produced a respectable case-law which has been highly influential on the rights of suspect and accused and on the conduct of law enforcement agencies.

(II) About the Nature of Penal Prosecution

We have seen from this brief historical sketch that over the centuries two systems of criminal prosecution developed, the adversarial and the

---

[50] This was heavily contested as it was considered by some to be against the constitutional right to trial by jury. It developed however through the ever explicit instructions by judges concerning the law, compare DeWolfe Howe, Juries and Judges of Criminal Law, 52 *Harvard Law Review* (1939), 582.

[51] Bodenhamer, *Fair Trial*, 61.   [52] Ibid. 64–5.

inquisitorial trial, roughly attributed to the Anglo-American world and the Continental European world respectively. Both systems evolved over a long period of time and have certainly influenced one another. The mutual influence can be traced to such a degree that the boundaries of the classical systems are blurred.[53] Certainly within the Member States of the Council of Europe, the European Court of Human Rights (ECourtHR) and also the European Commission on Human Rights (ECommHR), have played their part in assimilating the systems. Yet opinions about the comparability of the two main concepts are diverse. Some are convinced that the differences between the systems are such that any comparison is impossible.[54] At the other extreme, some go as far as to deny any importance to the structural uniqueness of the different traditions.[55] How much truth is there to either of these opinions? How similar or how far apart are the different types of criminal system really?

1. The aim of criminal prosecution

To answer this question we first have to ask ourselves what actually happens during a criminal trial. From the historical development we have seen that there are two main roots of criminal justice, the first being related to the individual, the second being related to society as a whole. The first is personal revenge. The victim or the victim's relatives need to be compensated for the evil the offender has done to them. A public trial will ensure that this is done justly and that private wars are prevented. The second is the keeping of the peace. By trying and sentencing offenders society is protected from further crime. Both of these aims can only be fulfilled effectively and work properly if the truly guilty are punished. This is the goal of the trial.[56]

The development in all systems was more and more towards state-controlled prosecution. Keeping the peace, ensuring security and order within society, was transferred to the public authorities, away from private prosecution. This is so despite the formality that in some jurisdictions the Grand Jury indicts, which means that, strictly speaking, the accusation is private. The initiative nowadays is taken by a public institution, that is, prosecutor or police. With the inquiry into the criminal events

---

[53] Compare the analysis of Tulkens in Delmas-Marty, *The Criminal Process and Human Rights* (Dordrecht and Boston, 1995), 8.

[54] This view is held for example by J. Niblett, *Disclosure in Criminal Proceedings* (London, 1997), 212.

[55] P. Bal, 'Discourse Ethics and Human Rights' in H. Deflem (ed.), *Habermas, Modernity and Law* (London, 1996), 22 n. 5 in particular, argues that a systematic comparison between the two systems reveals more similarities than differences.

[56] Similarly K. Volk, *Prozeßvoraussetzungen im Strafrecht* (Ebelsbach, 1978), 183–203, sees as the main aim of the trial the ensurance of the peace under the law (*Rechtsfrieden*) which is mainly achieved through truth (*Wahrheit*) and justice (*Gerechtigkeit*).

the facts need to be established. Interviewing witnesses and collecting evidence should lead to full knowledge of the crime and point to the guilty person.

At the stage of the trial it is officially established whether the offence that occurred is a punishable criminal offence and whether or not the accused person is guilty of committing this crime. The criminal law of the state is applied to the offence in a formal and institutional procedure, the convicted person is thereby publicly censured for his deviation from the law.[57] By this process the punishment of the offender is legitimized.[58]

Consequently, states have tried to establish a procedure they consider best at establishing the truth. On the Continent they inclined towards having an inquisitor who would question the suspect, whereas the English form developed as a more discursive process. In countries where torture was applied, there was a strong belief that this method would reveal the true conduct of the crime.[59] From our viewpoint today we know that the opposite is true: truth is distorted by questioning under torture.[60] On the Continent the belief was and is still held that the material truth is there and just needs to be detected.[61] Common law systems were rather established according to the view that the truth would come out in a discussion between adversarial parties. The underlying aim of criminal prosecution however is the same in any system: to discover the truth. Criminal process is understood as '[t]he complex set of rules and practices which have as their aim the application of the rules of the substantive criminal law and of criminal responsibility, mainly by means of making the appropriate determinations of fact, so as to bring into play the rules of criminal punishment'.[62] The system of criminal courts could be called diagnostic, as it serves '[t]o identify and determine the disposal of those who should, because they have broken the law, be liable to special coercive measures'.[63]

This aim of the criminal system has major influences on the procedure that can be applied. Already the goal of finding the truth obviously lays certain restrictions upon state authorities. The end is not just to punish somebody for a crime that occurred, but to find the person who has actu-

---

[57] See e.g. R. A. Duff, *Trials and Punishment* (Cambridge, 1986), 135.

[58] N. Luhmann, *Legitimation durch Verfahren* (2nd edn. Frankfurt, 1989), sees in this gaining of legitimacy the main sociological reason for criminal trials.

[59] See Peters, *Strafprozeßrecht*, 64.

[60] K. Volk, *Wahrheit und materielles Recht im Strafprozeß* (Konstanz, 1980), 13–14, argues that torture was not abolished because of a loss of belief in the defendant's duty to truthfulness, rather because of humanitarian grounds and perhaps mainly because it was understood to be ineffective in finding the truth.

[61] In general to the concept of material truth, Volk, *Wahrheit*.

[62] Maher in T. Campbell *et al.* (eds.), *Human Rights* (Oxford, 1986), 197 at 198.

[63] Duff, *Trials and Punishment*, 104.

ally offended. To punish by any means is therefore ruled out. The means have to be selected with the aim of stigmatizing and sentencing the truly guilty.[64] The aim of a criminal procedure is therefore the same both on the Continent and the Anglo-American context. Epistemologically different, however, is the concept of how to achieve this aim.

2. The 'new', democratic approach to criminal prosecution

With increasing democratization another factor came into play: the notion that government or executive powers cannot arbitrarily interfere with human beings. As the state was no longer conceived of as an absolutist monarchy in which citizens were subjects of the ruler, but shifted to being perceived as a democratic republic,[65] where free and equal individuals decided over their common fate themselves, criminal trials had to be restructured according to this. On the one hand, criminal law from this time onwards could only serve as a tool for protecting the common and individual legal goods (*Rechtsgüter*), that is, the very basis of the secular society. On the other hand, all through investigation and trial state authorities had to pay respect to the inviolability of the individual suspect. This notion prevailed in states which emerged from the Enlightenment and were based on written constitutions encompassing a Bill of Rights. Therefore the emphasis on the respect of the individual's inviolability is more commonly observed in the United States and on the Continent than in the legal system in England. As the United Kingdom never had a written constitution or a Bill of Rights, and indeed has only recently made efforts to make the ECHR applicable in English courts,[66] civil liberties do not seem to play a major role there in the rhetoric of discussions on criminal justice reforms.[67] This might also still be related to the influence of utilitarian thought, Bentham in particular, on English law. As utilitarian theory tends to subordinate means to ends, and aims at maximizing utility at the lowest cost, criminal procedure and the rights of the accused are perceived as means to the goal of achieving a reliable verdict. With this

---

[64] Ibid. ch. 4, derives more or less the whole collection of rights attributed to the defendant only from this aim: to find the true offender.

[65] Republic is to be understood in the sense of *Kant* as mainly describing separation of power. In modern terminology the term mostly used as equivalent is democratic *rechtsstaatlich*. See Kant, *Perpetual Peace* on the one hand, and J. Habermas, *Faktizität und Geltung* (Frankfurt/Main, 1993), on the other.

[66] This was one of the first achievements of the Blair government after their election victory on 1 May 1997.

[67] Maher in Campbell *et al.* (eds.), *Human Rights*, 197 at 199, stresses this point and is convinced that the 'right to silence' would not have been abolished if the criminal process in England was understood and justified according to human rights. This thesis is corroborated by the writing of Duff, *Trial and Punishment*, ch. 4, in which the right to silence is discussed as not stemming from procedural fairness but is scrutinized with a view to the contribution it makes in finding the true offender.

there is the risk of ignoring the liberal understanding of how individuals ought to be treated at all stages of criminal prosecution.

Although above we found a major difference in how the path to the aim of finding the truth is pursued, we are here confronted with an important similarity. The respect for the human being must be at the centre of any criminal procedure.

In recent discussions of criminal justice this civil liberties approach has come more and more under attack from efforts to increase security and protection for society against the threats of organized crime and terrorism.[68] This dilemma could be described as *Crime Control v Due Process*.[69] In this context one could go as far on the first side as the exclamation after the end of the Second World War: '[i]f ever there was a gang of malefactors who deserve extermination without the privilege of legal defence, it is the Nazi ringleaders'.[70] Understandable though this sentiment might be, it is entirely unjustifiable from a human rights point of view. As every human being is of the same value, in theory there can actually be no conflict between crime control and due process. The state authorities owe the same respect to every individual whether suspected or accused of a crime or not.

Furthermore, the conception of procedure changed fundamentally in the modern democratic state. The modern secular state must accept the plurality of incompatible and irreconcilable doctrines, be they religious, philosophical, or moral, which coexist within the framework of democratic institutions.[71] The vital consensus and thus stability can only be achieved through open and fair procedural systems. Justice is often not perceived as some material concept but rather as procedural fairness.[72] This is true as well for the criminal trial. Fairness is absolutely essential in order to arrive at a just verdict. Stemming from the principle of the separation of powers, the trial is not the place where the question of whether or not the offence constitutes morally wrong behaviour is discussed.[73]

---

[68] An illuminating example is the discussion in Germany around what is called *Großer Lauschangriff* (large-scale bugging operation). To legalize all the newly proposed police powers, Art. 13 *Grundgesetz* (Basic Law) protecting against arbitrary interference in the private home had to be changed. This shows that even states with written constitutions and a Bill of Rights are not entirely protected against repressive policy. Differences are that changes might take more time and need a broader compromise.

[69] See Tulkens in Delmas-Marty, *Criminal Process and Human Rights*, 9, referring to the situation in America as described by H. Packer.

[70] Glueck, 59 Harvard Law Review (1946), 396 at 397–8.

[71] See A. Giddens, *The Consequences of Modernity* (London, 1990).

[72] Cf. J. Rawls, *Political Liberalism* (New York, 1993); B. Barry, *Justice as Impartiality* (Oxford, 1995); Habermas, *Faktizität und Geltung*.

[73] Nevertheless Bal, *Discourse Ethics and Human Rights*, 83–4, argues in favour of such a concept. The problem with this approach is that the legal system is then bereaved of the effect it usually has of producing security under the law. Furthermore, the separation

During a trial there is no 'practical discourse' in the sense of a 'normative validity claim' (*Geltungsdiskurs*), but a 'legal discourse' about the application of the norm (*Anwendungsdiskurs*). This discourse is not limited to the determination of the facts and the assurance of proof but is concerned also with the personality of the perpetrator, how far he can be held responsible, and how much punishment should be imposed.[74] Procedural fairness is crucial for the realization of justice in a democratic society.

B. DEVELOPMENT OF 'FAIR TRIAL' AS A HUMAN RIGHT

(I) From France 1789 to Yugoslavia 1993 and Rome 1998

As a human right 'fair trial' was born alongside the other rights of the 'first generation'. Absolutist monarchs used criminal justice as a tool to suppress non-conformist individuals. Ultimately, accused persons were dependent on the grace and favour of the monarch or the colonial power. For subjects there was no protection whatsoever against the arbitrariness of their sovereign. During the Enlightenment the ontological understanding of 'citizen' changed fundamentally. From formerly being mere objects of state authority, human beings changed to being the actual reason for statehood and needed to be treated accordingly, that is, as subjects of governmental powers. Consequentially, no power of the executive over the liberty and security of the person was to be without limits. Only in cases that had previously been established by law, like a strong suspicion of having committed a criminal offence or a conviction by a competent criminal tribunal, could a person be legally detained.[75] Similarly, a number of inalienable rights stemming from the duty to respect the dignity of the human person were formulated, like the right to silence,[76] the right to be informed of the accusations and have time to prepare one's defence,[77] and to be presumed innocent until state authorities can convincingly establish guilt.[78] Furthermore, liberty against arbitrary criminal conviction by state authorities was to be guaranteed by participation

---

between legislature and judiciary becomes blurred, and the principle *nullum crimen sine lege* is distorted or abolished altogether. The results that Bal wants to achieve are sufficiently pursued by the system of justifications and excuses for behaviour that under 'ordinary' circumstances would constitute a crime.

[74] M. Walzer, *Spheres of Justice* (Oxford, 1983), 269–70, refers to the criminal trial as a 'distributive institution' in which punishment, as stigmatization or 'loss of honour' is distributed according to where it is deserved.

[75] Compare Art. 7 Déclaration des Droits de L'Homme et du Citoyen, 26 Aug. 1789.

[76] As to be found in Art. 5 Virginia Bill of Rights, 25 Sept. 1788.

[77] Art. 6 Virginia Bill of Rights, 25 Sept. 1788.

[78] Compare Art. 9 Déclaration des Droits de L'Homme et du Citoyen, 26 Aug. 1789.

of the public, through jury and publicity of the proceedings.[79] Punishment was only feasible where and as much as strictly necessary, and where previously established by law.[80] As we have already seen, both instruments, the American as well as the French Bill of Rights, were of great influence on other European criminal justice systems.[81] Most of them sooner or later adopted the 'fair trial' principles that were laid down there.

As these rights permeated to the different systems they were soon understood as essential in a democratic society. However, it took two world wars to establish a document that would enshrine human rights at the international level. After the Second World War the time was right for the birth of both international human rights documents and international enforcement of international criminal law. On 8 August 1945 the victorious Allied states established an International Military Tribunal (IMT) for the most prominent German war criminals[82] and on 29 April 1946 a similar tribunal was established for the Far East. On 8 December 1948 the General Assembly of the young United Nations agreed on a Resolution that is known as the Universal Declaration of Human Rights (UDHR).

Art. 16 Statute IMT Nuremberg paid respect to the rights of the accused and, despite some flaws in the procedural order, one could say, especially considering the atrocities that had taken place and the suffering that was involved, that the procedure was 'fair'. Although praised as a triumph of law[83] and justified as morally legitimate,[84] and despite the further 'blessing' by the UN General Assembly,[85] the Nuremberg and Tokyo trials cannot be seen as legally binding institutions and indeed cannot even serve as proper precedents as both were not truly international tribunals.

The UDHR enshrines in Art. 10 and 11 the principle of a 'fair trial'. This document has never gained binding effect on the Member States of the UN. Although Cassese likes to attribute to the provisions encapsulated in this document moral and political weight that would bind all states in the world, he admits that legal norms they are not.[86]

It was therefore with the establishment of the United Nations that human rights endeavoured to obtain international character. From this

---

[79] Art. 6 Virginia Bill of Rights, 25 Sept. 1788.

[80] The *nullum crimen, nulla poena sine lege* sentence is embodied alongside the necessity principle in Art. 8 Déclaration des Droits de L'Homme et du Citoyen, 26 Aug. 1789.

[81] About the influence of the Virginia Bill of Rights on the French Déclaration, see L. Richer, *Les Droits des l'homme et du citoyen* (Paris, 1982), 15–18.

[82] London Agreement 8 August 1945, and the Charter of the IMT annexed thereto.

[83] B. B. Ferencz, *An International Criminal Court* (London, 1980), i. 71.

[84] Radin, International Crimes, 32 Iowa Law Review (1946), 33.

[85] Adoption of the Nuremberg principles: *Principles of Inernational Law Recognized in the Charter of the Nuremberg Tribunal and in the Judgment of the Tribunal* UN Doc. A/1316 (1950).

[86] A. Cassese, *Human Rights in a Changing World* (Cambridge, 1990), 48.

moment on, the verification of basic rights attributed to all human beings was no longer conceived of as a purely national matter important only for domestic legal and constitutional orders. The UN as an international body was made responsible for the promotion of and respect for fundamental human rights.[87] It was under the auspices of this UN that the international community, soon after the UDHR, started to draft two covenants on human rights that would serve as truly legally binding instruments for their signatories. Two documents, one on economic, social, and cultural rights and another on civil and political rights, were open for signature in 1966 and entered into force in 1976. The right to 'fair trial' was enshrined in the second of these treaties, the International Covenant on Civil and Political Rights (ICCPR), mainly in Articles 14 and 15. Alongside these global developments, four main regional instruments evolved. Most prominent amongst these is probably that of the Council of Europe with its European Convention on Human Rights (ECHR), which entered into force in 1950. This, because of its functioning supervisory machinery comprising the European Court of Human Rights (ECourtHR), has the power to issue legally binding decisions. It is mainly in Art. 6 and 7 ECHR that the 'fair trial' principle is addressed. In the American context we find Art. 26 of the American Declaration of Rights and Duties of Man (1948) and the American Convention on human rights (1969), which enshrines 'fair trial' in Art. 8. The most recent embodiment of human rights on a regional basis is the African Charter on Human and Peoples' Rights (1981) containing the right to a 'fair trial' in Art. 7 AfCHPR. On the states party to these agreements the provision certainly has binding impact to the extent that a 'fair' procedure could even be enforced through the equivalent supervising body.

The right to a 'fair trial' was in the limelight again as the UN Security Council decided to establish a truly international tribunal *ad hoc* for the former Yugoslavia[88] and shortly after for Rwanda.[89] The Secretary General called the compliance with the principle of a 'fair trial' axiomatic for the tribunal.[90] Although he was referring to Art. 14 ICCPR in particular, this can hardly be seen as anything more than a political statement, having no legally binding force.[91] Similarly the Rome Statute of the ICC

---

[87] See Preamble of UN Charter and Art. 1 Charter UN.

[88] UN Security Council Resolution 827, 25 May 1993.

[89] UN Security Council Resolution 955, 8 November 1994.

[90] Report of the UN Secretary General pursuant to para. 2 of Security Council Resolution 808 (1993), UN Doc. S/25704, of 3 May 1993, para. 101, 106 (= Report of the Secretary General).

[91] See Reinisch, 47 Austrian JPIL (1995), 173 at 183 and 184–5. It must be considered very unfortunate that the report does not mention other rights that are concerned with fair and humane treatment during prosecution, like Art. 9, 10, or 15 ICCPR.

contains several references to the right to a 'fair trial', partly taken literally from Art. 14 ICCPR, for example, Art. 55, 66, and 67 Rome Statute.[92]

(II) The 'Fair Trial' Amongst Other Human Rights

In order to explain the role 'fair trial' plays among other norms that are understood to be entailed in the concept of human rights we have to address several questions which are contested and as yet unsolved. The first is a dogmatic or methodological problem. Among which of the sources of public international law should human rights, and the 'fair trial' principle in particular, be counted? Of course there are several human rights treaties. But is there beyond this a customary rule and, if so, what content should this custom have? Or should we conceive of human rights as 'general principles of international law' altogether? A second, separate question, but a related one, is the issue of friction between civil and political rights on the one hand and economic and social ones on the other. Although the former attribution of these rights to specific separate political systems, that is, civil and political rights to capitalism and social and economic ones to communism, might have been expected to have ended, there is still no overall concept of human rights.[93] The question of where 'fair trial' stands in the 'war of the generations of human rights' needs to be solved. Lastly we seek to explain what 'fair trial' consists of. The most known and influential 'fair trial' codifications, namely Art. 14 ICCPR and Art. 6 ECHR, consist of long lists of 'rights'. But in what regard are these norms really 'rights'? This is again a methodological question, different from the one above which was concerned with the sources of international law. It is related more to the concept of application and the consequences for the individual.

---

[92] Rome Statute of the International Criminal Court UN Doc. A/Conf.183/9, 17 July 1998; see Ambos, Der neue Internationale Strafgerichtshof—ein Überblick, NJW (1998), 3743, Hermsdörfer, Zum Statut des Internationalen Strafgerichtshofs – ein Meilenstein im Völkerstrafrecht, 40 NZWehr (1998), 193, and Kinkel, NJW (1998), 2650; Cassese, The Statute of the International Criminal Court, 10 EJIL (1999), 144; Arsanjani, The Rome Statute of the International Criminal Court, 93 AJIL (1999), 22; M. C. Bassiouni (ed.), ICC Compilation of UN-Documents and Draft ICC Statute before the Diplomatic Conference, Rome 1998, *The Statute of the International Criminal Court: A Documentary History* (Ardsky, 1998).

[93] This is so although in particular in state theory many writers have emphasized the importance of respect for both liberty and equality, see e.g. Isaiah Berlin, 'Two Concepts of Liberty', in Berlin, *Four Essays in Liberty* (Oxford, 1969), 126, or J. Rawls, *A Theory of Justice* (Oxford, 1972). In jurisdiction one can also observe trends in this direction. One example is the understanding of the 'principle of a social state' (*Sozialstaatsprinzip*) by the German BVerfG as a right to 'equally participate', see BVerfG *numerus clausus* judgment 18 July 1972, in BVerfGE 33, 303 at 331: '[D]as Freiheitsrecht wäre ohne die tatsächliche Voraussetzung, es in Anspruch nehmen zu können, wertlos.'

1. The status of 'fair trial' today

The problem that is of interest here is the teaching of the sources of human rights law. Where do human rights come from as international norms? As part of public international law human rights stem from the same sources as international law in general. This question may be answered by referring to the list to be found in Art. 38 Statute ICJ. Three main sources are given there. Although this list may be seen as non-exhaustive[94] the concentration here will nevertheless be on treaty, custom, and general principles.

As we have seen, the principle of a 'fair trial' has gone through several codifications since the end of the Second World War. It is therefore well established in treaty law. Nevertheless, human rights in treaties have the great disadvantage of not binding states or other authorities, like the UN, that are not party to the particular treaty. The right to a 'fair trial' would be binding beyond signature and ratification, if one could establish a customary obligation on states to organize their criminal justice system in a 'fair' manner. In American literature one observes a strong inclination to include 'fair trial' among customary norms. Lillich, for example, treats the whole UDHR as customary, a statement which appears rather axiomatic in the absence of further material corroboration.[95] However, he excluded 'fair trial' from his list of *jus cogens* as this would go 'too far'.[96] Likewise, Meron states that he

[b]elieve[s] that at least the core of a number of the due process guarantees stated in Art. 14 of the Covenant [ICCPR] have a strong claim to customary law status. Such rights include the right to be tried by a competent, independent and impartial tribunal established by law, the right to presumption of innocence, the right of everyone not to be compelled to testify against himself or to confess guilt, the right of everyone to be tried in his or her presence and to defend himself or herself in person or through legal assistance of his or her own choosing, the right of everyone to examine witnesses against him or her and the right to have one's convictions and sentence reviewed by a higher tribunal according to law.[97]

The enumeration chosen by Meron seems somewhat arbitrary and is left with no further explanation.[98] It is astonishing that none of these writers actually scrutinizes 'fair trial' according to the elements that are commonly thought to establish custom, that is, state practice and *opinio*

---

[94] Meron, *Human Rights and Humanitarian Norms as Customary Law* (Oxford, 1989), 88.

[95] See Lillich in Meron, *Human Rights in International Law* (Oxford, 1984), 116–17, with further references to legal writing, international conferences, state practice, and court decisions, mainly from US background.

[96] Ibid. 117, a statement which is also left without further elaboration.

[97] Meron, *Human Rights and Humanitarian Norms as Customary Law*, 96–7.

[98] e.g. why is the right to a 'public trial' not included? What about 'equality before the courts'?

juris,[99] but are satisfied with some general expression of belief. A thorough examination of the customary status of the 'fair trial' principle would take much more than that. The task is made greater by the problem that it is by no means obvious what 'fair trial' really encompasses, and what the singular rights within the 'fair trial' concept actually stand for.

Alston and Simma have criticized this approach and plead for a different concept of the perception of human rights.[100] In their view human rights belong to a different category of sources of international law altogether. They conceive of human rights as 'Principles of International Law' mentioned as a third source of international law in Art. 38 Statute ICJ alongside treaties and custom. The urge to do this, which is shared by many European writers,[101] is mainly rooted in the desire not to blur the concept of customary law. I would like to follow the Alston and Simma approach for three main reasons.

(a) 'Fair trial' is a whole concept that influences the criminal justice system from the start of the investigation to the release of the offender. It can therefore hardly be called a 'right' in the traditional way as a legal claim (*Rechtsanspruch*). It is not even restricted to one article of, say, the ICCPR. If understood as a principle, the nature of this overall concept is more visible.

(b) Different systems may look differently at issues within the 'fair trial' concept. A customary norm warrants a globally applicable 'right'. Meron wants to derive *opinio juris* mainly by looking at the domestic practice of states.[102] The question of whether or not this is at all a sensible way to establish custom left aside, it would prove particularly difficult in our context. The answers that would be given by states in criminal matters would be far too ambiguous and equivocal, as the national systems adhere to varying ideals of criminal prosecution. If 'fair trial' is conceived of as a 'general principle', the domestic system is given far more room to fulfil this international duty in the way it believes is most appropriate.

---

[99] Meron, *Human Rights and Humanitarian Norms as Customary Law*, 79–114, gives a general analysis of the development of human rights custom. Nevertheless when it comes to individual rights, he paints with a rather broad brush. Compare ICJ *North Sea Continental Shelf* case (*Germany v Denmark, Germany v The Netherlands*) Reports 1969, 44; and the prevailing view amongst scholars, e.g. A. Verdross and B. Simma, *Universelles Völkerrecht* (3rd edn. Berlin, 1984), § 560–6, or I. Brownlie, *Principles of Public International Law* (Oxford, 1979, 5th edn. 1998), 10.

[100] See Alston and Simma, Sources of Human Rights, 12 *Australian Yearbook of International Law* (1992), 82. That the concept of 'general principles' should be further developed regarding human rights is also submitted by Meron, *Human Rights and Humanitarian Norms as Customary Law*, 88–9.

[101] See also the analysis and further references by Reinisch, 47 Austrian JPIL (1995), 173 at 196–8.

[102] Meron, *Human Rights and Humanitarian Norms as Customary Law*, 132.

(c) If understood as a principle it is clear that all executive or judicial power, regardless of its origins, has to be organized in accordance with this principle. Consequently every authority that exercises penal powers over individuals, whether national, multinational, or international, could only operate within the limits of fairness.

The human right to a 'fair trial' is therefore to be seen as a 'general principle of international law'. It has to be emphasized that the finding that 'fair trial' is to be understood as stemming from 'general principles' as regards the question of the sources of law does not make the whole concept of 'fair trial' a 'principle' in the way Dworkin understands 'principles' in contrast to 'rights'.[103] The category of 'general principles' as a source of law does not prejudice the methodological question of application of the concept of 'fair trial'. This will be discussed below. A question left open is the actual content of these 'general principles'. Should the entire Art. 14 ICCPR, for example, be seen as a 'general principle', or could one only make the case for a minimum, core right which would have this status?[104] If one does not rely on deducing 'general principles' from national practice but also accepts international fora, like the UN General Assembly, or international conferences, as media to establish 'general principles', it seems that one could claim this status for the entire UDHR and ICCPR.[105] The question we are addressing is somewhat limited in this regard. We only seek to establish an international criminal procedural order for an ICC. The question of which standard of human rights is to be applied there will be addressed below, separately.

2. The dichotomy between civil and political and economic and social rights

'Fairness' in criminal procedure is in human rights treaties systematically included among what are traditionally called civil and political rights. The reason for this can be derived from the historical development. The criminal process was one of the main means for the monarch to suppress his citizens, political enemies in particular. 'Fair trial' therefore stood for freedom from absolutist arbitrariness and oppression, as did the other basic rights. In the post-absolutist era it stands as a bulwark against the sometimes more subtle oppression by the 'police' state. Chronologically speaking, 'fair trial' is among the 'first generation' of human rights.

---

[103] R. Dworkin, *Taking Rights Seriously* (London, 1977).

[104] Alston and Simma, 12 Australian Yearbook of International Law (1992) 103 are not quite clear about this. Presumably they plead for a common minimum standard. Likewise Kaufmann-Hevener and Mosher, 27 ICLQ (1978), 596 at 612–13 derive from their comparative legal analysis that not the whole list of Art. 14 (III) ICCPR could be seen as 'general principles'.

[105] Reinisch, 47 Austrian JPIL (1995), 173 at 199–201.

Civil and political rights are in their classical sense understood as legal titles to renounce any interference by state authorities into the private life of an individual. The 'right to life' gives the individual a claim not to be killed by the government, the 'right to free speech' gives him the privilege to speak and publish his own views without state censorship. Certainly a more progressive understanding of these rights could add an economic and social side to these rights, like the 'right to life' encompassing a claim to be given food,[106] the 'right to free speech' entailing the positive obligation to provide space for the speaker and to protect him from undue interruption by third persons.[107]

However, while all these rights could be connected solely to the dignity of the human person as such and the respect that humans mutually owe one another, the right to a 'fair trial' necessarily presupposes some sort of authority to conduct criminal prosecution. The state must actively do something. It must provide institutions that prosecute, it must establish independent tribunals with impartial judges, and must equip prisons in such a way that human dignity is not violated, to name but a few actions.

If we look at the traditional criticism that economic and social rights usually have to endure we will find a great number of these censured points also fulfilled in the 'fair trial' principle.[108] Civil and political rights are considered to be negative and cost-free. As just said, a 'fair trial' requires positive action and is resource intensive. Civil and political rights are conceived as being precisely definable and readily justiciable. 'Fair trial' is inherently intractable and difficult to adjudicate, in particular from a human rights perspective, considering the different procedural systems. To confirm this it suffices to point to the jurisdiction of the Strasbourg authorities which mostly abstain from giving precise definitions of a 'fair trial' and leave a great deal of margin of appreciation to the Member States.[109] To what extent the 'fair trial' principle springs from widely shared values to which governments are committed, beyond ideological differences, is likewise not always easy to tell. Some states seem to

---

[106] Human rights bodies are very cautious in this regard, although the 'right to life' has been stretched to such a degree that the state must take necessary measures to prevent people from 'disappearing', whether government forces or private organizations are responsible, see IAmCourtHR *Velásquez Rodríguez case* Judgment 29 July 1988, Series C No. 4. Although this speaks of a more integrated approach, it nevertheless does not view economic circumstances as vital preconditions for civil and political rights. See for a description of this case, S. Davidson, *The Inter-American Court of Human Rights* (Aldershot, 1992), 155–8.

[107] e.g. the protection of demonstrations against counter-demonstrations, as done in ECourtHR *Plattform 'Ärzte für das Leben' v Austria* Series A No. 139, para. 32.

[108] The following critical points are taken from the list given by Alston and Quinn, 9 HRC (1987), 156.

[109] A. Rupp-Swienty, *Die Doktrin von der Margin of Appreciation* (Munich, 1999), 52–61, observes that the margin of appreciation is relatively narrow with Art. 6 ECHR compared to other articles. This might be due to its relatively strict wording.

be just as neglectful towards a 'fair' treatment of defendants as they are towards people living in urban slums. Even in the Western world which claims to lead the way in human rights protection, maltreatment of prisoners[110] and 'efficient' questioning of suspects, tantamount to torture and inhumane treatment,[111] are on the daily agenda. Similarly, the argument about whether inquisitorial or adversarial systems are 'better' is sometimes reminiscent of disputes of ideological colouring where different views are condemned as heretical tenets.[112] These characteristics seem to put 'fair trial' amongst the 'second generation' of human rights.

No matter what the precise attribution of 'generations' should be, it is certain that the principle of a 'fair trial' is still to be counted among human rights. The fact that the right presupposes state powers and penal prosecution in particular does not alter this.[113] The criticism has been made that a right to a 'fair trial' is not available for every person at any time. This however is nothing unusual for human rights. The right to travel freely abroad for example is also a human right for the one who does not want to leave his own country. It becomes applicable the moment he waves his passport at the border guard to be granted leave. Likewise, everyone can theoretically have the right to a 'fair trial', including those who are never in conflict with the law. These aspects cannot therefore preclude the human rights status of the 'fair trial' concept. Another aspect of human rights is their indispensability. In this regard it is of utmost importance that a 'fair trial' guarantees the respect for the dignity of the suspect in a situation where he is jeopardized most. Criminal proceedings must never treat the defendant like an object. The subjectivity of the person must be guaranteed, that means he must be put into a situation where he can effectively participate in the proceedings.

Despite the special character a 'fair trial' seems to have, it is still a human right. With regard to the above, it might be questioned whether it would not be better to count 'fair trial' among economic and social rights. There is also evidence to the contrary, however, which suggests that 'fair trial' has civil and political roots.[114] A 'fair trial' can be deployed immediately and fully realized. It must not be seen as a long-term aspirational goal. Either a trial is 'fair' or it is 'unfair'. There cannot be a compromise

---

[110] Compare A. Cassese, *Inhumane States* (Cambridge, 1996).

[111] Compare e.g. police questioning in Northern Ireland, reported and condemned in ECourtHR *Ireland v United Kingdom* Judgment 18 January 1976, Series A No. 25.

[112] It is often surprising how vehemently pressure groups like the Lawyers' Committee on Human Rights defend what is in their eyes the indispensable right to cross-examination, while research, which comes mainly from England, shows that this technique cannot be regarded as the incarnation of truth-finding (more later).

[113] Maher in Campbell *et al.* (eds.), *Human Rights*, 197 at 203, discusses the universality of the 'fair trial' in great detail.

[114] Reference here once again to the list given by Alston and Quinn, 9 HRC (1987), 156.

of a little bit unfair, or not quite as fair as it could be. It is also easily enforced. This might be done by all sorts of means; one effective but for the prosecuting agencies certainly painful means, is an exclusionary rule concerning illegally obtained evidence and an instance of cassation (*Revisionsinstanz*) in cases of 'fair trial' violations. These are serious reasons for not viewing 'fair trial' as an economic and social right. It would be particularly dangerous if one applied the ways of implementation that are proposed for the economic and social rights to the implementation of the 'fair trial': the realization of 'fair trial' can neither be viewed as succumbing to sustainable development nor as an optimal balance between the state as the respector and the state as the provider.[115]

In view of all this it would be better not to include the right to a 'fair trial' in either of the 'classical' groupings. 'Fair trial' is a concept that bears first of all an objective institutional function. More than any other right it obliges the state to create certain institutions and to give these institutions a certain structure. On a second level it equips the individual with certain legal positions that must be legally enforceable in order to be effective. If these include budgetary claims, like the right to free legal assistance, one could rely on the concepts developed for economic and social rights by relating the granting of aid to the financial situation of the claimant. But this has to be considered according to the importance of individual rights within the overall concept of a 'fair trial'. Amongst human rights the right to a 'fair trial' therefore has a unique status and can neither be classified as a civil and political nor as an economic and social right.

3. 'Fair trial' as a 'kaleidoscope of rights'

It is soon clear from reading the texts of the human rights treaties, Art. 14 ICCPR in particular, that 'fair trial' does not just comprise one peculiar right. It consists of a whole range of different rights and obligations. Nevertheless it is one concept: how to make a trial 'fair'. Several positions are meant to be indispensable to achieve this aim as they are outlined in the human rights treaties. We can differentiate between three different components that are inherent in what we call 'fair trial'.

Amongst these are, first, institutional guarantees, such as the independence and impartiality of the tribunal or court. These address, first of all, the legislator. He is called upon to establish the institutions needed in a way compatible with human rights.

Secondly, there are moral principles that should preside over each step of the procedure, like the presumption of innocence or the principle of equality of arms. These principles are certainly to be closely complied

---

[115] Cf. the proposition by Eide, 10 HRLJ (1989), 35, who argues that this balance is as such not a political one and results in an ideal, distributive justice.

with by the legislator when forming procedural systems; perhaps their main impact lies however within the interpretation and application of the law to the individual case. In particular, in difficult cases with conflicting interests, the solution has to be found according to these legal principles. It is this second component that Dworkin would conceive of as 'principles of law'.[116] According to the terminology of the German BVerfG one could call this 'objektive Menschenrechtsordnung' which stems from the individual 'rights' and penetrates all areas of criminal procedure.[117]

Finally, there are rights, conceived of in a classically narrow manner, as legal claims to be free of something or to be given something,[118] like the right not to be arbitrarily detained or the right to counsel. Some of these rights are of overall validity and are precise enough to be called 'self-executing'. They are not a merely accidental reflex, but grant the individual a realizable legal claim.[119] All three concepts, institutional guarantees, moral principles, and individual rights, are compiled in one 'right': the right to procedural 'fairness'. The individual is entitled to have all three components verified in his confrontation with the penal system. In that sense the individual has a 'right' to a 'fair trial'.[120] What this means in the different stages and situations the individual finds himself in during the course of prosecution and trial is the subject of this work.

C. THE INTERNATIONAL CRIMINAL PROCEDURE

(I) A Short History of International Criminal Procedure

As is well-known, the prosecution of offences against the international legal order is a rather recent phenomenon. The reasons for this fact are mainly twofold: first, an international system of penal norms only emerged in the course of the twentieth century. Secondly, the idea of criminal prosecution on an international level, that is, over and above the

---

[116] Dworkin, *Taking Rights Seriously*. It is again pointed out that the question here has little to do with the previous question as to the sources of human rights law.

[117] BVerfG decision 2 May 1967, in BVerfGE 21, 362 at 372.

[118] Compare the different possibilities of how to interpret human rights given by C. S. Nino, *The Ethics of Human Rights* (Oxford, 1991), 25–9: (*a*) the absence of a prohibition, (*b*) a direct permission, (*c*) the correlation of active and passive duties of others, (*d*) right as a claim, or (*e*) right as immunity. What is defined here as the 'classic', narrow approach is alternative (*d*).

[119] Verdross and Simma, *Völkerrecht*, § 423.

[120] According to J. Raz, *The Morality of Freedom* (Oxford, 1986), 166, one speaks of someone having a right if some aspect of one's well-being is sufficient reason for holding some other instance to be under a duty. Applying this to the criminal process, one can easily develop a right to a 'fair trial' by saying that otherwise the liberty and security of the accused would be in danger.

sovereignty of a nation-state, was not agreeable to political leaders. These two causes are obviously related, in that the chances of developing a code of international crimes were curtailed by the reluctance of states to allow any transference to an international level of what was perceived of as their national heritage: criminal law.

The two major historical events that brought international prosecution of individuals onto the agenda were the two world wars. After the First World War attempts had been made by the victorious Allies to prosecute the former German Emperor William II of Hohenzollern before an *ad hoc* tribunal which was to be established for this purpose only.[121] All other 'war criminals' were to be tried by 'ordinary' national military tribunals.[122] The 'Kaiser' sought refuge in the Netherlands and was there granted asylum on the grounds that he was immune from prosecution as head of state; thus Art. 227 of the Versailles Treaty remained a 'dead letter'.[123] The Turkish massacre of the Armenians did not attract enough international attention to make the prospect of international prosecution of persons responsible possible.[124] The dawn of international criminal prosecution broke with the end of the Second World War. On 8 August 1945, barely three months after the unconditional surrender of Germany, the Allied powers signed the London agreement by which they adopted the Charter of the International Military Tribunal.[125] Twenty-four of the most prominent German Nazi leaders were indicted, twenty-two eventually tried, of whom three acquitted, twelve sentenced to death, and seven

[121] See Treaty of Peace between the Allied and Associated Powers and Germany, Versailles, 28 June 1919, reprinted in M. C. Bassiouni, *International Criminal Law* (New York, 1987), iii. 109. Art. 227 (II) of this treaty. It contains a reference to the right to a 'fair trial' of the defendant which shall be assured by this tribunal.

[122] See Art. 228 of the Treaty of Versailles.

[123] Bassiouni in Bassiouni (ed.), *International Criminal Law*, iii. 26. Arguably the Allies, the USA and the UK in particular, were not unhappy about these hindrances as they allegedly never had the intention of establishing the tribunal that the peace treaty envisaged; compare J. F. Willis, *Prologue to Nuremberg* (Westport, Conn., 1982), chs. 4 to 6. The surrender of German 'war criminals' to the victorious powers according to Art. 228 Versailles Treaty was not a great success either. Instead of extraditing, the German Reichsgericht in Leipzig was supposed to carry out prosecution and punish its own war criminals, which was done very reluctantly and against the national feeling of many Germans; see Willis, *Prologue to Nuremberg*, ch. 8.

[124] The British government was perhaps the only one that pressed for the prosecution of war criminals in Turkey. The enterprise had little success. From an international criminal law perspective it was difficult to envisage genocide organized by a state against its own people as an offence against the international criminal order. The Genocide Convention was only agreed upon in 1948. See Dadrian, 14 Yale Journal of International Law (1989), 221, and Willis, *Prologue to Nuremberg*, ch. 9. The reluctance to prosecute the persons responsible for the massacre of the Armenian people arguably encouraged Hitler to continue with his plan of the 'Endlösung', compare Cassese, 16 MLR (1998), 1 (2).

[125] Agreement for the prosecution and punishment of major war criminals of the European Axis, 8 August 1945, 82 UNTS 279. Nineteen other states subsequently acceded to this agreement.

imprisoned for life or at least fifteen years.[126] The procedural order in Nuremberg was based exclusively on the Anglo-American adversarial system, with the exception that trials *in absentia* were permitted by Art. 12 Statute IMT.[127] Despite its name, the Nuremberg Tribunal was not a genuine international judicial body. It was created by the victorious allies who, instead of prosecuting individually, combined their efforts in one multinational tribunal. The equivalent in the Far East, the Tokyo Tribunal, was established by unilateral proclamation and therefore had even less of an international character.[128] Both tribunals are certainly to be considered as the major steps forward in elaboration and enforcement of international criminal law. Nevertheless many doubts remain as to whether the procedure was actually 'fair', in particular with regard to the principle *nullum crimen sine lege*.[129] Both in Germany and the Far East national prosecution of less important war criminals followed.[130] These trials, although of major importance for the development of material international criminal law,[131] can barely constitute authority for an international criminal procedure as they were held solely under the auspices of national procedural systems.[132] The emerging United Nations Organization made some effort to establish a permanent international criminal court but did not succeed. In an unprecedented step the UN Security Council created an *ad*

[126] Compare the list: Disposition and Outcome of the Nuremberg Trial, in Bassiouni, *International Criminal Law*, iii. 127.

[127] Martin Bormann who was Hitler's Deputy for Nazi Party affairs and later Secretary to the Führer was sentenced to death without being present. His whereabouts were uncertain and it was considered likely that he was already dead. The case of this and of the other defendants are to be found in T. Taylor, *The Anatomy of the Nuremberg Trials* (New York, 1992).

[128] It was established by General Douglas MacArthur, Supreme Allied Commander, who also appointed all the judges on the bench, S. R. Ratner and J. S. Abrams, *Accountability for Human Rights Atrocities in International Law* (Oxford, 1997), 163–5.

[129] It is not surprising that critical voices mostly come from German authors, compare e.g. H.-H. Jescheck and T. Weigend, *Lehrbuch der Straftrecht Allgemeiner Teil* (Berlin, 1996, 5th edn.), § 14 II 2, or D. Oehler, *Internationales Strafrecht* (2nd edn. Munich, 1983), no. 1060, and n. 24 for further references; also K. Ipsen, *Völkerrecht* (4th edn. Munich, 1999), § 38 No. 32. It is surprising, however, if a comparison between the IMT Nuremberg and the ICTY is allowed, that whereas the former terminated its proceedings against twenty-two defendants, sentencing twelve to death after barely a year in court, the latter needed more than two years to sentence one (Tadic) to twenty years imprisonment, with the appeals decision on the verdict not included.

[130] In Germany this was done so mainly by virtue of the Allied Control Council Law No. 10, 20 December 1945.

[131] The UN General Assembly shortly after these trials voted for the so-called Nuremberg Principles: Principles of International Law Recognised in the Charter of the Nuremberg Tribunal and in the Judgment of the Tribunal, UN Doc. A/1316 (1950) and thereby accelerated the process of developing substantive criminal norms in international law.

[132] The importance of these war-crime trials after the IMT in Nuremberg became obvious in the case against *Erdemovic* at the ICTY. In its Appeals Judgment of 7 October 1997 the Appeals Chamber was seriously split over the authority of these trials, in discussing his sentence with regard to duress as a defence.

hoc tribunal for atrocities committed on the territory of the former
Yugoslavia pursuant to Chapter VII of the UN Charter.[133] Soon afterwards it took the same measures to establish peace and security for
Rwanda.[134] These two *ad hoc* tribunals are the first real international
enterprises to prosecute international criminal law 'directly', on an international level. From a procedural point of view this is the birth of international criminal procedure, illustrated by the fact that the statutes and
rules of both tribunals do not adhere to one specific national procedural
order, but endeavour to combine several systems. Since the creation of
these two tribunals the attempt to create an international criminal court
on a permanent basis has been given a kick start. Discussions have been
conducted in a special committee which is to propose a possible statute
for an effective, just, and fair procedure at an international court.

In June and July 1998 a conference was held in Rome with the aim of
establishing a permanent International Criminal Court.[135] On 17 July 1998
the conference agreed upon a statute (henceforth Rome Statute[136]) with an
impressive majority of 120 states voting in favour, seven states voting
against, and twenty-one states abstaining.[137] Although this statute is
certainly a milestone in the development of international criminal law, it
will not end the discussion about suitable procedural rules. Rather the
dispute will be fuelled as the statute needs to be ratified and the court-to-
be needs rules of procedure and evidence to fill in the framework given
by the statute.[138]

The discussion, not surprisingly, is marked by two main difficulties:
first, the need to reconcile different criminal procedural ideas and systems
and, secondly, the necessity of realizing human rights in the procedural
order. We will now take a look at the question of why the international
procedural system needs to be organized in accordance with international
human rights standards.

---

[133] Security Council Resolution 827, 25 May 1993.

[134] Security Council Resolution 955, 8 November 1994.

[135] A short introduction to the organization and the work of the conference is given by
Kirsch and Holmes, 93 AJIL (1999), 2.

[136] Rome Statute of the International Criminal Court, UN Doc. A/Conf.183/9, 17 July
1998, reprinted in ILM 37 (1998), 999.

[137] The most prominent states voting against the treaty were the USA, China, and Israel.
For a report on the conference: NZZ (20 July 1998), 3. The Rome Statute has prompted much
writing, most of which was published after this work was drafted. Nevertheless, I have tried
to incorporate texts that were published up until Easter 2000. A shorter overview of the
Rome Statute is given by Ambos, JA (1998) 988, most recently also Ambos in Arbour *et al.*
(eds.), *The Prosecutor of a Permanent International Criminal Court*, 3, and Hermsdörfer, 40
NZWehrr (1998), 193; compare also the Special Issue on the ICC in 6 European Journal of
Crime, Criminal Law and Criminal Justice (1998), 319–460.

[138] According to Art. 26 (I) Rome Statute the Statute will enter into force as soon as 60
states have ratified the treaty. According to Art. 51 (I) Rome Statute the Rules of Procedure
and Evidence shall be adopted by a two-thirds majority of the members of the Assembly of
States Parties.

(II) The Human Rights-Centred ICC

Measuring the conduct of international institutions according to human rights law is a relatively recent phenomenon. Since the emergence of human rights, they have been perceived as basic rights each nation-state had to consider and guarantee in the relationship with its citizens, or any human being within its territory, or more precisely within its jurisdiction.[139] Their importance was and is still seen to be in national constitutional law. When addressing the human rights compatibility of a criminal procedure at an ICC the focus shifts. No longer is the main problem the question of how much interference from outside the nation-state will permit, that is, how far 'interior sovereignty' may be limited.[140] The question now is, can the 'exterior sovereignty', if exercised through an international organization, be limited by human rights?[141]

I will first take a look at modern answers to the original problem of human rights and interior sovereignty and then try to find a solution to the new question of human rights and international activity.

1. The usual way: human rights as a basis for national constitutional law

Human rights are claimed to be inalienable principles that are to be respected by all state authorities. They are meant to be meta-positive rights, unchangeable by government. Human rights are described as a blueprint for constitutions, a model of relations between government and

---

[139] The principle of responsibility according to jurisdiction has recently been substantiated by the ECourtHR *Loisidou v Turkey* Judgment 18 December 1996, 23 EHRR (1997), 513, paras. 52–7 in particular. The ECourtHR ruled that the concept of jurisdiction is not restricted to the national territory of the state. If a state exercises effective control on territory outside its national borders it is responsible for human rights violations occurring on such territory. Turkey was therefore held responsible for the violations in the Turkish Republic of Northern Cyprus. Similar is the concept of state responsibility applied by the ICJ in the *Case Concerning Military and Paramilitary Activities in and against Nicaragua* (*Nicaragua v US*), Judgment (*merits*) ICJ Reports 1986, 14 (= *Nicaragua* case), for actions of US agents on Nicaraguan territory.

[140] I refer to the common distinction between *exterior* (i.e. intra-state relations) and *interior* sovereignty (i.e. internal legal order); see e.g. J. Habermas, *Die Einbeziehung des Anderen* (Frankfurt/Main, 1996), 175.

[141] The ICJ has to address this question in two pending cases, *Lockerbie* (*Libyan Arab Jamahiriya v UK*, ICJ Order 14 April 1992, ICJ Reports 1992, 3) and *Genocide* (*Bosnia and Herzegovina v Yugoslavia (Serbia and Montenegro)*, ICJ Order 8 April 1993 and 13 September 1993, ICJ Reports 1993, 3). In the latter case in particular the question arises of whether or not Security Council Resolutions under Chapter VII of the UN Charter can be invalid (*ultra vires*) if they run counter to international human rights law (in this case the friction may exist between UN Security Council Resolution 713 (1991) imposing a weapons embargo upon the former Yugoslavia and the Genocide Convention). This point is especially elaborated by Judge *ad hoc* E. Lauterpacht is his Separate Opinion attached to the Order of 13 September 1993, in ICJ Reports 1993, 439, paras. 98–104.

citizen, covering all important aspects of social, political, economic, and legal life.[142] Philosophically, however, there are difficulties in justifying the origin of these rights. Most commonly they are derived from some conception or other of natural law, nowadays mostly referred to as 'human dignity'.[143] This concept is certainly based on the enlightened liberal-individualist perception of human nature. Thereby 'natural' is by no means self-explanatory, as it tends to claim to be, but merely reflects what the writer believes to be 'natural'.

Against the enlightened liberal conception of the relationship between state power and citizens arose the philosophical school of communitarianism, in particular in North America during the 1980s, referring to the writings of Aristotle as an alleged alternative to Kant.[144] The focus was shifted away from a universal ethic towards inherited ways of life and grown communities.[145] This has an obvious impact on human rights. A communitarian approach to human rights must be characterized by cultural relativism. Furthermore the emphasis lies on state sovereignty rather than on the individual citizen. It is the community (nation) of men and women, who live as members of a historic community, and express their inherited culture through political and social forms worked out among themselves, that gives the state its necessary legitimacy.[146] This tends to the consequence that the precedence of nation, people, community, or family over the individual is incompatible with the idea of human rights.[147] These could only be derived from the shared values of each society, and therefore could not be universal in character.[148]

The very opposite track is followed by a cosmopolitan conception of human rights.[149] Here human rights are understood as basic rights in a world-state. The cosmopolitan idea is directed towards a global society.

---

[142] Fox in S. Hashmi, *State Sovereignty* (University Park, Pa., 1997), 105 at 126.

[143] Compare e.g. M. McDougal, H. Lasswell and L. Chen, *Human Rights and World Public Order* (New Haven, 1980). See also Schachter, 77 AJIL (1983), 848. This is also the approach of the German Constitution; Art. 1 GG reads: 'Human dignity is inviolable. It is the duty of all governmental power to respect and protect it.' This is the only basic right which is eternally unchangeable, see Art. 79 (III) GG. The following enumeration of basic rights Art. 2 to Art. 19 GG as well as the Judicial Rights in Art. 101 to Art. 104 GG are understood as rooting in Art. 1 GG.

[144] One of the first and most influential writings in this regard was MacIntyre, *After Virtue* (London, 1st publ. 1981). That communitarians are reluctant to take European writing into account and that their perception of Aristotle is wrong is claimed by O. Höffe, *Vernunft und Recht* (Frankfurt/Main, 1996), 164–85.

[145] Compare for a critical analysis Gutmann, 83 ARSP (1997), 37 at 51–66.

[146] Walzer, 9 Philosophy and Public Affairs (1980), 209 at 211.

[147] MacIntyre, *After Virtue*.

[148] Compare the critical description of communitarianism and human rights by Nino, 7 Ratio Juris (1994), 14, in particular 20–4.

[149] See e.g. Held, Kosmopolitische Demokratie und Weltordnung, in: M. Lutz-Bachmann and J. Bohman (eds.), *Frieden durch Recht* (Frankfurt/Main, 1996), 220.

International law in the sense of inter-state relations will cease to exist; it will be transformed into a global interior order. Statehood as such will be transferred from the national state to the global state. Human rights will be the basis of this world-statehood. The case for this view is certainly difficult to argue. For the time being it is entirely unrealistic. Although the European Union might be seen as an attempt at a process of national states dissolving and a single European state emerging,[150] other parts of the world are experiencing the complete opposite. In places like the former Soviet Union[151] or the former Yugoslavia,[152] the world has seen new nation-states evolving and separating from one another.

There are other theoretical systems which could be described as situated in between the communitarian extreme on the one hand and the cosmopolitan on the other. I will pick out two approaches, political liberalism and discourse theory. As representative for the former I will discuss Rawls, the latter I will describe with reference to Habermas.

Rawls derives his concept of basic rights from a social contract.[153] In a hypothetical situation people that have no knowledge of their situation in society (a 'veil of ignorance') agree upon a concept of justice. According to Rawls they would then agree that everybody has the most extensive civil rights compatible with the rights of other persons (liberty), and also arrange social and economic inequalities to an extent that would benefit the least advantaged the most, and further equal opportunity for all (equality). All state acts have to be measured against this basis as regards legitimacy. Rawls's reading of human rights can therefore be called an institutional approach.[154] Human rights manifesting the 'overlapping consensus' of all liberal and well-ordered hierarchical societies express the minimum standard for well-ordered political institutions for all peoples who belong, as members in good standing, to a just political society of people. They serve as the basis for both liberal and hierarchical societies. Human rights understood in this way do not depend on any particular comprehensive moral doctrine or philosophical conception of human nature. Cultural relativism has no place in Rawls's conception of human rights, in particular he finds it irrelevant whether these rights are attributed to persons as individuals or as members of a specific group.

---

[150] This is certainly heavily disputed and many people sharply oppose the emergence of a European state. The German BVerfG vehemently denied statehood of the European Union after Maastricht, see BVerfG *Maastricht*-Judgment 12 October 1993, BVerfGE 89, 155. Compare also Grimm, 1 European Law Journal (1995), 303 on the one hand and Habermas, *Die Einbeziehung des Anderen*, 185, on the other.

[151] Compare Schweisfurth, 52 ZaöRV(1992), 541.

[152] See Weller, 86 *AJIL* (1992), 569.

[153] See Rawls, *A Theory of Justice*.

[154] In particular the elaboration of the problem in J. Rawls, 'The Law of Peoples', in S. Shute and S. Hurely, *On Human Rights* (New York, 1993), 42, especially 68–74.

Human rights exist to lay boundaries to states' interior sovereignty. Therefore they are distinct from constitutional rights or the rights of democratic citizenship.[155]

Although Habermas's concept of a discourse ethic tackles the problem of the origin of rights differently and is outspokenly against the idea of a 'veil of ignorance',[156] the conclusions are comparable. Human rights in the discursive theory serve as preconditions for communication.[157] In contrast to the concept of political liberalism where human rights are understood as 'classic' liberties which protect the individual against state interference, liberties are here seen as resulting from a self-legislation where all free and equal parties conceive of one another as common creators of laws to which each of them are bound.[158] As such human rights are no moral heritage but specific engravings of a modern understanding of subjective rights. Human rights are genuinely judicial rights.[159] As every state action is based on communication,[160] human rights necessarily need to be granted as otherwise a discourse is not possible and the state action therefore illegitimate. Again, with this approach human rights constitute a major restraint on the interior sovereignty of states.

Both Rawls and Habermas ground their theories on a modern interpretation of Kant, who was the only enlightened philosopher to think about how to achieve worldwide peace.[161] Kant's conception of a world order is based on a community of republican states which are founded on liberty and equality of people.[162] He denies, however, the positive idea of a world republic and adapts a negative surrogate of a confederation of states. In the absence of public coercive laws (*öffentliche Zwangsgesetze*) between states, these states must be made to comply with the *jus gentium* voluntarily. A republican interior order would guarantee this.[163] A human

---

[155] So far the ideal theory of Rawls. The problem lies in the relation between liberalism and tolerance. How much ground may liberalism lose to tolerance in trying to find the 'overlapping consensus' with non-liberal societies? A critical discussion of Rawls' concept is given by McCarthy in Lutz-Bachmann and Bohman, *Frieden durch Recht*, 200.

[156] Habermas, *Die Einbeziehung des Anderen*, 67–77 in particular.

[157] See also J.-P. Müller, *Demokratische Gerechtigkeit* (Munich, 1993), 174–80, with regard both to political and judicial decision-making.

[158] In discussing Rawls this is Habermas's idea of reconciling public and private autonomy, see Habermas, *Die Einbeziehung des Anderen*, 126–7.

[159] Ibid. 222.

[160] Habermas, *Faktizität und Geltung*, 135–6.

[161] His treatise *Perpetual Peace* attracted much attention on the bicentenary of the complete version 1996. See e.g. Lutz-Bachmann and Bohman, *Frieden durch Recht*.

[162] Kant understood by 'republican' what modern writing calls 'democratic'. Most important for Kant is the realization of a separation of power and a constitution based on freedom and equality. The antithesis of 'republicanism' would be 'despotism': arbitrary execution of laws according not to the public will but to the private will of those in power.

[163] This premise is certainly very optimistic. Empirical research shows that republican states do not become involved in less wars than authoritarian states, but that nevertheless

rights-oriented state is therefore a precondition for 'eternal peace'; Kant gave human rights great international importance. Nevertheless, his perception of global order is heavily based on state sovereignty—to such an extent that any rights attributed to the individual outside the canopy of the national, republican state are reduced to a minimal concept. What Kant called *jus cosmopoliticum* as a concept of rights, next to *jus civitatis* of people within a state, and *jus gentium* of states in relation to each other, that are attributed to human beings wherever they are, that is, even outside the domestic legal order, he wants to be limited to a right to common hospitality (*allgemeine Hospitalität*).[164] Even this limited concept of universal rights breaks with total state sovereignty. It can be seen as the beginning of modern human rights.[165] For Kant this was no philanthropically utopian concept, but 'law'.[166]

If we try to give a summary of what human rights are generally conceived of as, we could say that they constitute the epistemic basis of every state because they express the universal value that every human being wants to be a being capable of acting (*handlungsfähiges Wesen*).[167] This we can call a universal, reciprocally respected claim of every human individual (*jus cosmopoliticum*).

2. The changing focus: human rights as basic rights of an international legal order

The situation of an international body is slightly different. An ICC is an authority exercising judicial powers that stretch beyond national boundaries. In the classical conception of public international law the individual was not a subject. He could only feel enforcement through the mediation of the nation-state.[168] The nation-state, however, is restrained by human rights for the protection of the individual. Human rights norms were

their belligerent undertakings are of a different character. It seems that internal pacifistic behaviour does influence the motives of foreign policy, compare Habermas in Lutz-Bachmann and Bohman, *Frieden durch Recht*, 12.

[164] See Kant, *Perpetual Peace*, Third Definitive Article. This right has a duty, as a corollary, to respect the people living in a certain territory. In this context Kant criticizes deportation and oppression by colonial powers.

[165] See J. P. Müller in P. Zen-Ruffinen and A. Auer (eds.), *De la constitution: Études en l'honneur de Jean-François Aubert* (Basel, 1996), 133 No. IV 3 b.

[166] Kant, *Perpetual Peace*, Third Definitive Article.

[167] Compare Höffe, *Vernunft und Recht*, 77, who derives this from an existentialist-based social anthropology which says that every human being is a positive social being and at the same time a negative endangered victim. This form of anthropology is essentially different from the usual ideal of aiming for the 'good life' as in the classical conception of anthropology, which is e.g. found in Howard in A. A. An-Na'im, *Human Rights in Cross-Cultural Perspectives* (Philadelphia, 1991), 81. This classical conception certainly makes it difficult to build human rights on anthropology.

[168] See e.g. I. Seidl-Hohenveldern, *Völkerrecht* (8th edn. Munich, 1994), nos. 540, 617, 621, and Verdross and Simma, *Völkerrecht*, no. 47.

among the first actually to address the individual as a subject.[169] Yet the enforcement of this body of rules lies within national boundaries, if we may leave supervising bodies like the Council of Europe and the HRC aside, as they are special enterprises. Why then would an ICC be obliged to respect the human rights of every person it comes into contact with?[170] What is the legal reason why an ICC must necessarily be compatible with human rights? In the following I will argue that respect for human rights is obligatory for an ICC. Four main reasons will be put forward to support this position.

(a) *The argument of analogy to national jurisdiction*   An international court would exercise power over individuals directly in analogy to national courts. This is by no means altered by the cautious approach adopted by the drafters of the statute of an ICC which contemplates the court as a superseding instrument exercising additional jurisdiction if national law enforcement is for some reason or other not available or unwilling to prosecute properly (complementary jurisdiction).[171] Quite the opposite is true. If the international court were to serve as a substitute to national courts it would have to operate at the same level of restraint as the national court would, that is, the ICC must be bound by human rights. Any other concept would be discriminatory. This is so because the decision on whether the international criminal is prosecuted by national authorities or an international court would, first, have no compelling support in substantive law, secondly, would be different from case to case, and thirdly, be arbitrary and accidental. This could be a first reason for arguing that the ICC must fulfil human rights standards.

(b) *The argument of restricted national power*   A second reason could be found in a more technical argument. The international body will be established by several states. For the moment it is irrelevant in what way the court will actually be established. It will always need states to participate, either by signing a special treaty or by giving a vote in the UN bodies.[172] The court will always be a creature of a multi-state agreement.[173] These states—or at least several among the creators—are bound by human rights even in the strongest form possible, treaty law. If these states were

---

[169] Compare Dinstein, 20 Israel Law Review (1985), 206 at 208.

[170] The aim of this treatise is merely to scrutinize the 'fair trial' principle, which comprises mainly the rights of suspects and defendants. Nevertheless, the human rights implications would stretch to other areas as well, like the treatment of victims and witnesses, or labour policy towards the employees of the court.

[171] ILC Draft Statute Preamble, Commentary para.1.

[172] The proposed ways of establishing the court will be discussed later.

[173] The possibility of founding the ICC on a UN Security Council Resolution is slight, although it undoubtedly has advantages; see the discussion of this issue in the ILC Draft Statute Commentary, Art. 2, paras. 1–6.

now to collaborate with an ICC they must ensure that this international judicial authority would be at least under the same level of restraints as their national courts are. Everything else would constitute a circumvention of their human rights obligations. In this regard one could say that human rights operate as restrictions to the exterior sovereignty of states. Just as states are impeded in their interior sovereignty from treating human beings as mere objects, their power to do so via exterior, that is, international bodies is likewise curtailed.

One might explain this in other terms through jurisdiction. Jurisdiction is usually understood as the carrier of human rights responsibility.[174] National criminal courts have to comply with the state's human rights obligations as they are part of the national jurisdiction. An ICC exercises international jurisdiction which is not attributed to any state. However, it derives its competence from all the states that cooperate with it. These states that would be in a position to exercise jurisdiction over international crimes (principle of universality) transfer their jurisdiction over these offences (partly) to the international court. This is so although the ICC exercises international jurisdiction which is primarily allocated to the international community. This community, however, consists formally of several states that create this international institution to perform this jurisdiction. Technically the national state that agrees to cooperate with the ICC gives up its power to adjudicate in the matters dealt with by this body. This originally national power was always limited by human rights. By transferring it to the international level it cannot suddenly lose these commitments. The international institution must therefore necessarily be under the same restraints as the national.

(c) The argument of restricted international power A third reason comes from the above outline of justification of human rights. If human rights are, as was argued above, restraints on executive powers of states, there are no grounds whatsoever why this should be different in an international context. Indeed, human rights are to be seen as limits on any infringing power, disregarding the question of whether the power is legally stemming from a national or an international authority. In this regard it is also unimportant that the ICC is not connected to overall governmental powers but is an independent, solely judicial authority.[175] As the human being is the reason for the protection of human rights, and not the state as such, any infringing power is enough to trigger the applicability of these rights. In other words: the respect human beings owe one another when founding the state with its institutions, must be the same

---

[174] See once more ECourtHR *Loisidou v Turkey* Judgment 18 December 1996, 23 EHRR (1997), 513.
[175] Compare Art. 1 Rome Statute.

when human beings, already organized in states, create international institutions.

(*d*) *The argument of the nature of human rights*   Finally, if we understand human rights as a legal position that human beings occupy, no matter where and when, the claim for a 'fair trial' is also valid if the person is confronted with an international body. A *jus cosmopoliticum* would be applicable in any situation, independent of nationality or even state-hood.[176]

3. The standard to be applied

The second question, then, is which standard the international body is to apply. Above I looked briefly at the discussion about the extent to which human rights have gained customary law status. It was pointed out that, even if one derives human rights from 'general principles', the content of these principles is still not clear by itself. An international human rights standard has not been developed and agreed upon yet. I now have to address this question in the context of the ICC and ask which standard of 'fairness' the international court would have to apply. The very way I formulated this question indicates the direction where the answer may be found. One can hardly imagine different standards of 'fairness'; a trial is either 'fair' or it is 'unfair'. The question concerns what the international community considers as 'unfair' treatment. Each step of the procedure will be scrutinized in the course of this work in order to examine what should be thought of as 'fair' behaviour.

If one follows the idea of Rawls the answer would probably have to be found in an 'overlapping consensus' between the creator-states. That would mean that an imagined 'social contract' would be drawn up between representatives of states, both liberal and hierarchical.[177] The main reason why Rawls adopts this complicated procedure is state sovereignty, which he sees as equivalent to individuals' autonomy in the national context. This reason, however, is invalid in our context. Human

---

[176] Kant, from whom I have borrowed the term, certainly did not foresee international institutions being created as the ICC. His writing was rather concerned with a right and just internal legal order. All executive power would be exercised by national institutions. The *jus cosmopoliticum* was merely understood as a right to respect for those who are, as foreigners, under the power of a state of which they are not nationals. This is comparable to international institutions. Under the power of this international body, everybody is a foreigner. Furthermore, the respect for human beings, necessitated by the *jus cosmopoliticum*, states have to exercise with regard to everybody, nationals and non-nationals alike. Consequently states cannot infringe this concept when creating an international institution to prosecute individuals.

[177] See Rawls, 'The Law of People', in Shute and Hurely, *On Human Rights*, 42, especially 68–74.

rights operating at an ICC do not infringe upon state sovereignty.[178] They are binding upon the international body and not upon the national state. Accepting this understanding, Rawls's original theory of a social contract between individuals may indeed be applied at the international level. It is individuals who are actually concerned and who agree upon a structure of rights at the ICC. This means that we would construct an 'international social contract' for the foundation of human rights,[179] yet in a limited way. It would be an international institution with jurisdiction over international crime. It is widely accepted that the international criminal law that the court adjudicates on would address the individual directly, unmediated by the nation-state.[180] If this is so, we can also expect this international institution to respect human rights, which are also widely believed to address the individual directly, without further mediation by national states.

Another more state-based approach could be derived again from the fact that states create an ICC. If states that now have a high standard of procedural fairness want to be able to collaborate with the international body, must they not ensure that the protection given to the defendant there does not fall short of their domestic safeguards? If a state with very high standards were to cooperate with a court that did not fulfil its idea of the rights of the defendant, the state would not only be behaving hypocritically but would actually be in violation of the rule of law. This is expressed in the principle *nemo plus iuris transferre potest quam ipse habet*.[181] Consequently the international body would have to adopt the highest standard of human rights of the defendant. Only then could the court be called truly international because only then could all states be potential members of it.

A different avenue has been taken by the European Union/European Community, as expressed in the case-law of the European Court of Justice (ECJ). Although all the Member States of the European Union are at the same time within the Council of Europe and party to the European Convention on human rights, the ECJ does not accept the ECHR as the

---

[178] The conflict with state sovereignty lies in another field: prosecution of nationals. I will look at this topic shortly.

[179] Such an international social contract is avoided by Kant and Rawls as they both attribute crucial importance to state sovereignty. In the context here this reproach is not valid as the institution of an international body is a different issue where there is no intrusion into the state's sovereignty on the question of the realization of human rights.

[180] See e.g. Dinstein, 20 Israel Law Review (1985), 206 at 206–7.

[181] This is pointed out by J. P. Müller, in R. Rhinow, S. Breitenmoser, and B. Ehrenzeller, *Fragen des internationalen und nationalen Menschenrechtsschutzes FS Luzius Wildhaber* (Basel, 1997), 45 at 65. Müller says that, just like any legal subject, the constitutional state is not justified in transferring a lower standard of rights than it has according to its domestic order. It is therefore not possible for a state to empower a supra-national institution to infringe upon international human rights.

constitutional human rights basis for the European Union. The judges in Luxembourg prefer to speak of 'fundamental rights' that are 'inspired by the constitutional traditions common to the Member States, [and] must be ensured within the framework of the structure and objectives of the Community'.[182] Unfortunate as this is, it is technically speaking certainly true that the European Union has itself not ratified the ECHR and is therefore not legally bound by it. However, the ECJ went further and made reference to the ECHR as a possible source of law: '[i]nternational treaties for the protection of human rights on which the Member States have collaborated or of which they are signatory, can supply guidelines which should be followed within the framework of Community law'.[183] Thereby the ECJ declared the rights within the ECHR as general principles of law which are binding on the organs of the European Union.[184] The ECJ does not however take case-law of the Strasbourg court into account, which is rather anachronistic but it is within the tradition of international courts to neglect one another respectfully.[185] This approach was vindicated by the German Bundesverfassungsgericht when it found that the protection of human rights through the Court in Luxembourg was sufficient and declared itself in a status of cooperation with the ECJ as regards the protection of basic rights.[186]

(III) The Aim and Nature of International Criminal Procedure

1. International criminal law as protection against human rights violations

Not much has been said about the aim and purposes of an international criminal order. Although this work is not concerned with the justification of international criminal law, a brief theoretical outline seems indispensable.[187] This is so because an international court needs to be certain about its intentions in order to understand its functions, powers and limits. The question needs to be divided into three separate parts: (*a*) the justification

---

[182] See ECJ *Internationale Handelsgesellschaft mbH v Einfuhr- und Vorratsstelle für Getreide und Futtermittel* Judgment 17 December 1970, Case No. 11/70, ECJ Reports 1970, 1125 at 1134.

[183] ECJ *Nold, Kohlen- und Baustoffgroßhandlung v Commission of the European Communities* Judgment 14 May 1974, Case No.4/73, ECJ Reports 1974, 491 at 507.

[184] Compare Reinisch, 47 Austrian J Publ.Int.Law (1995), 173 at 185 with further references.

[185] See in this context B. Dickson, *Human Rights and the European Convention* (London, 1997), 35–45, with a discussion which rights the ECJ has actually applied in Community law.

[186] The foundation stone of this was laid by the BVerfG *Solange II* Decision 22 October 1986, BVerfGE 73, 339 at 387 and was *expressis verbis* phrased in BVerfG *Maastricht* Judgment 12 October 1993, BVerfGE 89, 155 at 175. This relationship of cooperation was however declared unilaterally by the BVerfG and still awaits confirmation by the ECJ.

[187] I have discussed this problem in greater detail elsewhere, see Safferling, ARIEL (2000).

of an international criminal legal order, (*b*) the trial, and (*c*) the enforcement of the sentence.[188]

As regards international criminal law, one can see from looking at the term that it consists of two elements, an international one and a criminal one. As concerns the 'criminal' aspect, international criminal law should be under the same restraints as any national criminal law system. Commonly, the objective of criminal law, the most infringing and harshest form of law, is seen as lying in the protection of legal goods (*Rechtsgüterschutz*).[189] Legal goods mean individuals as well as institutions of society.[190] With regard to the international context, and an international norm needs a specific international connection,[191] these goods are to be seen in peaceful coexistence (collective good) and the protection of individual human beings as part of humankind (individual good). These goods find their expression in particular in human rights law. Criminal law therefore serves mainly to enforce the order that derives from human rights. A further limiting principle is to be derived from the international setting of the problem: the principle of sovereignty needs to be respected. Criminal law is generally considered as a matter of local public policy only.[192] Therefore we should leave criminal law to the domestic systems as long and as far as it is effective and appropriate enough on the national level. The crimes to be tried at the ICC, namely genocide, crimes against humanity, war crimes, and grave breaches of the Geneva Conventions,[193] are widely accepted as international crimes in

[188] This seems to be a fragmentation common to all criminal justice systems. Already v. Liszt placed it at the very beginning of his famous treatise on the purpose of criminal justice, the so-called 'Marburger Programm', reprinted in 3 ZStW (1883), 1. As state authorities infringe on the private lives of individuals differently in all three fields, the state needs a justification for all three of them, see Roxin, JuS (1966), 377 at 381; compare also A. v. Hirsch, *Doing Justice* (New York, 1976), 46–7, who supports this differentiation, although he is mostly concerned with the second stage only. Likewise Hart, *Punishment and Responsibility* (Oxford, 1968), 5–6, differentiates in this way.

[189] Bal, *Discourse Ethics and HR*, 83, following *Günther*, wants to see this changed from 'legal goods' to the protection of the conditions of a normative discourse. This is, in my understanding, more of a new dressing according to a discursive theory, rather than an actual material change.

[190] See e.g. Roxin, *Strafrecht AT I/1*, para. 3 no. 1.

[191] See e.g. Bassiouni, *International Criminal Law*, i. 2–9, who gives a list of characteristics an international criminal norm has to fulfil. He differentiates between international and transnational elements and a buttress of 'necessity'. His approach is empirical and statistical, trying to shed light on existing norms whether they are international in character or not. The interest here lies rather on the epistemological reasons for an international criminal norm and the philosophical justification for its execution.

[192] Crawford, 89 AJIL (1995), 404 at 406.

[193] Compare Art. 5 Rome Statute, Art. 6 Genocide, Art. 7 Crimes against Humanity, Art. 8 War Crimes, which is a combination of the concept of grave breaches and war crimes. Art. 5 (I) d Rome Statute also contains the crime of aggression. Before the ICC can exercise jurisdiction over the crime of aggression, however, the Member States must agree on a definition according to Art. 5 (II) Rome Statute.

this sense. Whether or not this list can be extended, as is suggested by many,[194] is not a subject of this work which is only concerned with procedural law.

In order to give this system efficiency international criminal law needs to be enforced. The first rationale for so doing is the need to communicate with the offender and censure him for his defiance of the internationally protected order.[195] Secondly, the international legal system is corroborated and vindicated by the execution of international criminal law. It prevents acts of revenge by victims[196] and thereby returns peace and reliability.[197] It has pedagogical influence[198] on the world community and deters others from offending against the established order.

Finally, the imposed sentence must be enforced in order to give effect to the criminal law system. It furthermore serves to rehabilitate and resocialize the offender and so prevent him from committing further crimes.

The main rationale for international criminal law is therefore the protection and promotion of human rights in the global society.[199] By enforcing this system through prosecutorial means it is given the seriousness and persuasiveness it needs.

2. The limits of the prosecution: human rights of the defendant

The aim of protecting human rights is itself limited. Human rights can only be protected through human rights. If human rights are to be protected via criminal prosecution, the applied system must itself be strictly compatible with human rights.

As we have seen in the national context, the criminal process is based on two pillars: the finding of who is guilty and the protection of the dignity of the persons involved. International prosecution must be based on the same foundations. The guilty must be found because if the innocent are sentenced none of the positive effects of the criminal justice system can be achieved. The communication with and censure of the innocent is useless because they are not capable of repentance, and do not

---

[194] Compare e.g. Bassiouni, *International Criminal Law*, i. 1 ff., 135, or Dinstein, Israel Law Review 1985, 207–21, who give a list of twenty-two international crimes.

[195] This element of censure is emphasized by A. v. Hirsch, *Censure and Sanctions* (Oxford, 1993), 9. In his view it has to prevail over utilitarian aspects and over general preventive theories in particular, see Hörnle and v. Hirsch, GA (1995), 261.

[196] Compare the ICTY First Annual Report (1994), para.15.

[197] This is stressed by the UN Security Council Resolution 955 (8 November 1994) in particular.

[198] Compare the Trial Chamber II *Tadic* case (IT-94-1-T) Decision 10 August 1995 on the Prosecutor's Motion Requesting Protective Measures for Victims and Witnesses, para. 32.

[199] In Allott's understanding of human rights as a manifestation of a 'spontaneous and tentative self-ordering' of international society this would probably mean a further step towards self-recognition of international society as a society, see P. Allott, *Eunomia* (Oxford, 1990), 279.

need rehabilitation. Also, the utilitarian effects will fail to bear fruit. How can global society grow in knowledge and reliability towards human rights if the system falls short of punishing the actual offender? In particular, the feelings of revenge on the side of the victim will certainly prevail if the system does not succeed in taking the place of vengeful acts. One will never arrive at the point where revenge can be replaced if the system does not produce punishment for the real offender. In this regard the procedural system of an international criminal law must be comparable to the national systems. Most importantly, it must pursue the goal of finding the real offender.

The second pillar we have found in the protection of human rights for the offender. Apart from the epistemic reason for protecting the dignity of the human being discussed above, which says that even if the accused is suspected of a heinous crime such protection is essential for every authoritative act of every system, there are also utilitarian grounds why the human rights of the offender must be safeguarded through the whole criminal process. If we look again at the aim of the criminal system, to prevent revenge from taking place, only respect for human rights towards all sides can stop a vicious spiral of violence from further expanding. The prosecuting court in this regard takes the place of a revenging victim. The court publicly stigmatizes the offender, censures and punishes him. The victim's desire for revenge should thus vanish as the victim has the feeling that justice has been done. In order to achieve this goal one has also to take into account the personal dignity of the victim and his family. If the victims' rights are disrespected they will not feel vindicated by the trial process.

On the other hand, if this quasi-revenge comes about in a biased and unfair manner the party of the offender will be outraged. This side will consequently call for satisfaction and ignore court and victim. In order to re-establish peace and calm the conflict between the accused and the victim, both parties involved need to have the feeling that justice is being done impartially and independently. In the national context this aim of pacification plays its role mainly between the parties.[200] In international crimes the stakes are much higher. By the very nature of international crimes they do not concern a single person only. The number of victims is much higher and the amount of suffering is immense as protracted violence is deployed. Usually there are groups of people involved, peoples or minorities, fighting for their physical and cultural survival. Therefore pacification is not only needed between the offender and the actual victim, but between the groups that were engaged in hostilities. It

---

[200] This is the way 'pacification' is introduced and understood by Roxin, *Strafrecht AT I/1*, para. 3, no. 27.

is not only needed to heal the wounds of severe injuries or the loss of a person, it is also needed to help to develop healthy and constructive relations among ethnic groups.[201] Hence the rights of the offender must be guaranteed and the trial must be fair and must be seen to be fair. Without this, pacification of the conflict between victim and offender, which can be so severe in international crimes, is an unachievable goal.[202]

Finally, a human rights enforcement system that is itself not compatible with human rights loses a great deal of impact and persuasiveness. How should one generally rely on and trust in a system that is meant to protect human rights but is intrinsically at odds with them? An inconclusive system can in the short run only be upheld by a further suppressive policy which the international community can neither afford nor execute, and which is in the long run doomed to failure anyway. This shows that human rights must be an integral part of the procedural scheme of an ICC. The protection of human rights by using criminal law at an international level can only be effective if it is done with respect for human rights. The enforcement of human rights is therefore limited by human rights themselves.

(IV) How to Solve the Conflict with State Sovereignty

State sovereignty and international criminal prosecution confront one another in a slightly different way than the sovereignty problem posed by human rights, which was discussed above.[203] The question here is to what extent has the state to tolerate the prosecution of its own nationals by an international court. Technically, the question could be answered in accordance with the ratification documents or similar signs of willingness to cooperate: if a state has agreed upon the ICC, it has simply already given as much of its interior sovereignty to the international institution as is necessary.

Philosophically the question may cause greater problems, in particular as the prosecution of individuals by an ICC seriously challenges state sovereignty. Certainly nobody would want to claim nowadays that nation-states are completely free to act in whatever way they want. There clearly exist international obligations that limit states' actions.[204] But the

---

[201] This reminds us of what the former UN Secretary General *Boutros-Ghali* called 'peacebuilding' in his pamphlet *An Agenda for Peace* (2nd edn. New York, 1995), 39.

[202] This seems to be the approach of the ICTY as is found in the First Annual Report (1994), para. 15.   [203] See above, C II.

[204] See the PCIJ in the *Lotus* case, Series A No. 10, 18–19, and repeated by the ICJ in the *Nicaragua* case ICJ Reports 1986, 14 at 135, and most recently in the advisory opinion *The Legality of the Use and Threat of Nuclear Weapons*, ICJ Reports 1996, 66 (= the *Nuclear Weapons* advisory opinion), for a summary of the reactions to this advisory opinion, see Safferling, 40 NZWehrr (1998), 177.

other extreme seems to be equally far-fetched, that state sovereignty only exists ex gratia of the international community.[205] This would mean that states are not actually born sovereign (*geborene Souveränität*) but are given sovereignty (*gekorene Souveränität*). Such a view is borne out of the cosmopolitan idea of a world-state that delegates the exercising of power to inferior entities, as for example to federal states. States have (still) to be conceived of as the main actors in international law. Nevertheless the concept of state sovereignty needs to be 'de-absolutized' and de-monopolized to create a modern global order of integration.[206]

The answer that I will try to develop is related to the concept of human rights that was outlined above. The starting-point is an appropriate concept of sovereignty as regards international criminal law. After this I can address the question of prosecution of nationals by an international body.

1. State sovereignty revisited

It is first of all in state societies that peoples establish community and government. This is what sovereignty means: the exercise of self-determination.[207] For a people that decide to organize their life together in a community of free and equal parties, the exercise of (interior) sovereignty lies exactly therein.

The connection between self-determination and sovereignty might not be blatantly obvious as the development of self-determination has often been troublesome and difficulties in defining the real meaning remain.[208] As a major tool of international law the term self-determination of peoples was essential in the age of decolonization. As such it was included in Art. 1(2) Charter UN to accelerate the process of solving colonial dependencies that still existed after the Second World War.[209] Although not enshrined in the UDHR, the principle of self-determination of peoples was given an eminent position in Art. 1 of both of the two 1966 Covenants.[210] It was further elaborated as a main governance of interna-

---

[205] See Fox in Hashmi, *State Sovereignty*, 105 at 112–13.

[206] See e.g. the discussion with regards to the European Union by Oeter, 55 ZaöRV (1995), 659, with many references.

[207] Compare J. P. Müller, 'Föderalismus, Subsidiarität, Demokratie' in H. Vollkommer (ed.), *Föderalismus-Prinzip und Wirklichkeit* (Erlangen, 1997), pleading for a material understanding of governmental structures and statehood in contrast to the formalistic terminology usually applied. Compare also Habermas, *Die Einbeziehung des Anderen*.

[208] Compare the summary of the development by Koskenniemi, 43 ICLR (1994), 241.

[209] See Doehring in Simma *et al.* (eds.), The Charter of the United Nations (Oxford, 1995), Art. 1 (II) Self-determination, No. 17–18.

[210] The HRC refused to rule on the principle of self-determination of peoples, saying it was not within its jurisdiction *ratione materiae*, and thereby cleverly avoided the difficult question of what constitutes a people. It discusses the problems that were derived from the principle of self-determination under the heading of minority rights in Art. 26 ICCPR, compare HRC

tional relations in the UN General Assembly Resolution on Friendly Relations.[211] The 'orthodox' understanding of this principle could be described as 'state independence'. By gaining independence from the imperial power, the peoples exercise their right to self-determination, which is consequently then used and 'dead'. The concept of self-determination was therefore only accepted in the context of independence from colonial influence. It was soon understood as being monolithically focused on one specific historic problem. Self-determination was not to outlive the process of decolonization. It was therefore suggested that self-determination should be understood as a more flexible 'right', disconnected from its historic emergence[212] as a principle of self-governance of peoples.[213] This means that all peoples exercise this right through choosing their form of constitution and government. Later this was developed further into a right to participate, a right to democracy. Self-determination is more about inclusion of 'peoples' and minorities,[214] than exclusion and dismemberment,[215] and can be interpreted as the right for citizens to choose freely their government, their social, economic, and cultural development, as long as human rights are respected.[216] Modern understand-

---

Mikmaq v Canada Opinion 29 July 1984, Communication No.78/1980, 2 Selected Decisions 23, and *Lubicon Lake Band v Canada* Opinion 26 March 1990, Communication No.167/1984, CCPR/C/38/D/167/1984 at 29.

[211] Declaration on Principles of International Law concerning Friendly Relations and Co-operation among States in Accordance with the Charter of the United Nations, GA Res. 2625 (XXV), 24 October 1970.

[212] That all human rights need to be disconnected from their historic, cultural, and geographical origins is argued by Höffe, *Vernunft und Recht*, 55–61.

[213] Whether or not and to what extent the right to self-determination of peoples entails a right to secession from the original state will not be discussed here, compare e.g. R. Mullerson, *Human Rights Diplomacy* (London, 1997), 50–61, who supports secession for a minority that is unable to exist and develop its identity in the framework of an existing state, and Koskenniemi, 43 ICLQ (1994), 241 at 264–9, who argues that in an 'abnormal situation' the primacy international law gives to statehood has to be put aside. However, there is no 'applicable' concept of self-determination, so that locally and regionally idiosyncratic arrangements have to be found, something not done in the case of the former Yugoslavia.

[214] Heavily disputed is the question of what constitutes a 'people'. More traditional views understand 'people' as in 'nation', pre-existent to any state order, determined by elements like ethnicity, religion, culture, and history. This could be described as an a priori understanding of people (Walzer). A more modern approach would define a 'people' as that which has the will of organizing social life together by means of establishing a state structure. This determination of a people coincides with the establishment of the state, and it could therefore be called a posteriori concept of 'people' (Habermas). See also Oeter, 55 ZaöRV (1995), 659 at 683.

[215] Communitarians would probably go as far as this and derive from it the inviolability of this self-determined state from outside interference, see e.g. M. Walzer, *Just and Unjust Wars* (New York, 1977). As to a 'right to democracy' see also Frank, 86 AJIL (1992), 46, who does not further elaborate on the concept of democracy.

[216] See e.g. in ECourtHR *Loisidou v Turkey* Judgment 18 December 1996, 23 EHRR (1997), 513, Concurring Opinion of Judge Wildhaber (joined by Judge Ryssdal), denying the right to exercise self-determination to the Turkish Republic of Northern Cyprus because it did not

ings make self-determination synonymous with material principles of democracy. Not only do the constitutional foundations of a state make visible the exercise of self-determination of a people, but every governmental act expresses self-determination. If not, self-determination of peoples is infringed upon. Therefore self-determination equals state sovereignty.

The 'international level' has historically evolved from the idea of regulating the relations between these sovereign entities, that is, it purely pertains to exterior sovereignty. That a people wants to exercise its life together in a peaceful coexistence with neighbouring or other states and find ways to deal with disputes in a peaceful way is very much an expression of this interior sovereignty.[217]

The international legal order is now developing into more than just that. Originally provoked by the horrific experiences of war and tyranny in the first half of the twentieth century in particular, the international community has shifted its focus and now aims at becoming a protector for peoples and nations against exactly this, war and tyranny. It thereby develops with the premise of actually guaranteeing sovereignty, as understood here, to all peoples, that is, providing for the conditions of interior sovereignty. In so doing it cannot possibly be in conflict with sovereignty. Sovereignty, in its interior aspect in particular, can only be exercised in circumstances of peace and security, in an environment that is obliged to human rights in a non-oppressive manner.

2. The prosecution of nationals by an international court

International criminal prosecution deals with individuals who are endangering the international order and holds them responsible for disturbing the conditions of peaceful coexistence of states and enjoyment of human rights. These individuals are of course nationals of some state. As they offended against the international criminal system they violated the very fundament of their own nation-state and most likely that of other states as well. Indeed, they have infringed upon the sovereignty of these states. First of all these individuals are under the executive and judicial power of their nation-state. Nevertheless, the international character of the crime makes it something that is beyond national jurisdiction as it concerns matters that are of pre-sovereign importance.

In some cases one could leave the prosecution of international criminals to the enforcement systems of national states. As the international

---

itself respect minority rights and the right to self-determination for the Greek Cypriots in the Constitution of 1985.

[217] This can be derived from the idea of Kant, *Perpetual Peace*, that republican states will abstain from warfare in international relations.

criminal has also violated the sovereignty of his own state his prosecution does lie in the interest of the national state. This might be a way of coming to terms with its own history and be an irreplaceable condition for the exercise of self-determination again.[218]

The situation is different if the international crime involved other states or peoples and they were prevented from exercising their sovereignty. In these cases it is more obvious that a state prosecuting the criminal would only exercise jurisdiction on behalf of the international community.[219] If states are strong enough to do so, one should perhaps leave it to the national level. Nevertheless, the international community bears generic responsibility for providing a safe environment for the exercise of sovereignty. If it seems necessary to that end to hold individuals responsible, it is the right of the international community to do so without intruding into national sovereignty, because these things lie logically before national sovereignty.[220]

If sovereignty is understood as being rooted in and actually meaning self-determination of the group of people that decides to organize its life in a local community, and if the international community is understood as being called upon to provide the circumstances for them to be able to do so unimpeded, then criminal prosecution to the end of guaranteeing these conditions enforced by the international community cannot infringe upon the national sovereignty of the state, a national of which is being indicted at the international court. International prosecution, then, only serves as providing the circumstances in which sovereignty can be exercised, the International Criminal Court being the institution through which this aim is executed.[221]

---

[218] In this context is the urge of the German people to prosecute former Nazi leaders after the Second World War and to bring to trial SED and STASI chiefs after the collapse of the Berlin Wall, as well as the enterprise of the South African people to overcome the former apartheid regime by taking a combined stand of a truth commission and criminal prosecution.

[219] See e.g. the Judgment of the Supreme Court of Bavaria against *Djajic* Judgment 23 May 1997, reported in 1998 Neue Juristische Wochenschrift (NJW), 392, see also Safferling, 92 AJIL (1998), 528.

[220] S. R. Ratner and J. S. Abrams, *Accountability for Human Rights Atrocities in International Law* (Oxford, 1997), 295–302, argue in favour of an approach uniting prosecutorial and non-prosecutorial measures. They would want to see only the most serious culprits tried at an international criminal court, only those with policy-making responsibility or those who played important roles in the most heinous massacres. If we apply these conditions, both Tadic and Erdemovic, the first persons sentenced by an international tribunal, have been dealt with by the wrong institution, as they were of low rank in the chain of command.

[221] As such the ICC would be one of the international institutions that Simma and Paulus refer to when they talk about the shift of international law away from the consent base 'Lotus principle' towards an institutionalized body of law, 'in which states channel the pursuit of most or their individual interests through multilateral institutions', see 9 EJIL (1998), 266 at 276.

Having found human rights as the necessary legal basis for any procedural order, I will now look at the individual steps of prosecution and trial as they derive from the Anglo-American tradition on the one hand and the Continental tradition on the other, in order to find the structure that would suit the International Criminal Court.

2

The Pre-Trial Inquiry

The 'pre-trial inquiry' is the period between the discovery of the crime and final formulation of an indictment which is handed over to a court. It is not an easy task to define the end of the pre-trial inquiry precisely, especially because different systems give different answers thereto. According to the German stop, the pre-trial inquiry ends as soon as the public prosecutor transfers public legal action to the court by filing an indictment and a request to the court to open trial (§ 170 (I) StPO).[1] The prosecutor must approach the competent court (*zuständiges Gericht*); the question of competence depends mainly on the seriousness of the offence.[2] The court then decides whether or not to set a date for the trial.

In English law, the situation is far more complex. This is so because of the court organization in England and Wales, which may seem confusing from a Continental point of view. Without looking at it in detail, English law distinguishes between trial on indictment and summary trial. The former takes place before judge and jury at the Crown Court, the latter at a Magistrates' Court. Which court will hear the case depends on the seriousness of the offence. Offences are classified in three categories: either exclusively triable only on indictment (generally speaking, the most serious crimes[3]), triable only summarily (the least grave offences[4]), or triable either way (offences of medium gravity[5]). Trial on indictment is generally preceded by a committal proceeding, when the evidence is reviewed by a Magistrates' Court on a prima facie basis. In minor cases, information is laid before a magistrate, who decides whether or not to summon the person charged. This is when the prosecutor's inquiry ends.

---

[1] Compare Kleinknecht and Meyer-Goßner, *StPO* Einl. No. 60.

[2] Compare the German Organization of the Courts Act (Gerichtsverfassungsgesetz, GVG) §§ 24, 74 and 120 GVG. In principle the Court of first instance (Amtsgericht) is competent unless the penalty is more than four years' imprisonment or within the list of offences triggering the competence of the Regional Court (Landgericht), § 74 GVG, or of the Upper Regional Court (Oberlandesgericht), § 120 GVG.

[3] Crimes like murder, manslaughter, robbery, rape, incest, causing grievous bodily harm with intent, and so forth. See the list by Sprack in *Emmins on Criminal Procedure* (6th edn. London, 1995, hereinafter referred to as Emmins), 1.3.

[4] Apart from trivial criminal offences, not even punishable with imprisonment, Magistrates' Courts deal with assaulting a police officer, interfering with a motor vehicle, drink-driving offences, and many juvenile cases.

[5] Such as theft, handling stolen goods, obtaining property by deception, most forms of burglary, non-aggravated criminal damage, assault occasioning actual bodily harm, unlawful wounding, and indecent assault.

Generally speaking, the inquiry ends when the institution that is responsible for the investigation seeks the action of a judicial body. On the other hand, the importance of the differences between the systems when it comes to determining the precise beginning and end declines, if we focus on the investigating methods, which are basically the same all over the world. This is where the main human rights concerns lie.

The repeatedly invoked differences between the inquisitorial and the adversarial systems vanish at the investigating stage. Both 'systems' necessarily rely on a pre-trial inquiry, which is essentially inquisitorial in nature.[6] Despite these similarities in structure, there are major dissimilarities in operation. Because of the divergent approaches to procedural law, different principles have evolved and different solutions are presented to similar questions. The effect that this has on the suspect may very well vary from system to system. This must be scrutinized from a human rights point of view.

I will start with a look at the individual institutions involved in the pre-trial process. The division between the participating institutions will be highlighted in the discussion in the first section below, which will deal with the reasons for this distinction and the underlying human rights concerned, as well as the differences in the participants' roles. I will then proceed to individual investigation measures. One of the most important means of finding out about a crime is to question both suspect and witnesses. I will discuss the rights that play a role at this stage. Serious mischief is done to the suspect if he is subjected to pre-trial detention; a very basic human right, that is, the right to liberty and security of person, is thereby breached. Finally, other measures for collecting evidence, like search and seizure, will be discussed. I will look at the consequences of a potential violation of the rights we have found to play a role in the investigation later on, when the rules of evidence are under scrutiny in the trial stage.

A. THE VARIOUS INSTITUTIONS

In the pre-trial inquiry, we find all three previously named parties involved. Let us start by looking at the state authorities, who they are, and why they have to be kept apart. I will then take a look at the prosecution and the court and discuss the role, or rather the roles, that they play in the different procedural systems, before I turn to the offender and his professional jurist.

---

[6] J. Hatchard, B. Huber, and R. Vogler (eds.), *Comparative Criminal Procedure* (London, 1996), 224.

(I) The Investigating Bodies

Unless there is a proper inquiry, and unless prosecution and accusation exist as independent institutions there can be no trial, no judge. Is this merely a truism? Have we simply accepted the system so uncritically that we do not even realize how important a division between investigation and court is? This simple idea is of major human rights importance, a first step towards guaranteeing a fair trial. The human rights treaties we are looking at do not explicitly refer to the need for a division between these institutions. They do, however, allude to the right for everyone who is 'charged with a criminal offence' to a 'fair hearing' by an 'independent and impartial tribunal established by law'.

1. The applicable human rights norms

Before we can start to analyse the consequences of this human rights provision for the process of investigation, we must first ascertain whether we can apply this rule to the first stage of criminal procedure at all. Following the four basic steps of interpretation of legal instruments in general,[7] and treaties in particular,[8] I must first take issue with the letter of the provision (literal interpretation). In Art. 14 (I) (2) ICCPR, it says: 'In the *determination* of any criminal *charge* against him . . . everyone shall be entitled to a fair and public *hearing* by a . . . *tribunal* established by law' (italics added). The same words can be found in Art. 6 (I) ECHR. Taken literally, the provision seems to presuppose an inquiry. The charge has already been laid, the trial is merely about determination of charges. On the other hand, before a charge can be brought, there must be some sort of investigation, that is, the deploying of time and measures to obtain evidentiary material. Furthermore, Art. 14 (I) ICCPR only refers to hearings before tribunals. The commencement of investigations can hardly be understood as a hearing before a tribunal. Spanish wording, *'en la substanciación de cualquier acusación de carácter penal formulada contra ella'*, and French wording, *'un tribunal . . . qui décidera soit du bien-fondé de tout accusation en matière pénal dirigée contre elle'*, allude to an even greater extent to an 'accusation' already made before a tribunal and therefore also exclude the application of this provision to the stage of inquiry.

What can easily be seen from the aforesaid is that the interpretation of 'criminal charge' is crucial to answering the question of the scope of application. Is 'charge' to be read as a technical term, as in national law, and identical, for example, with the 'charge' as in English criminal procedure, which would make Art. 14 (I) ICCPR applicable during the pre-trial stage

---

[7] See the ICTY Appeals Chamber in *Tadic* para. 71
[8] See Art. 31 Vienna Convention on the Law of Treaties (1969).

as soon as the suspect is formally charged by the police?[9] Or does it refer to the Continental system of 'accusation' which would probably mean the review of the indictment by a judge in order to decide whether or not the suspect should be tried?[10] Likewise, there might be several charges in the course of criminal proceedings.[11] Because we cannot decide which interpretation to choose, and indeed the drafters of the different conventions did not have a common approach in mind, we must find an 'autonomous interpretation'[12] of the Covenant.[13] The ECourtHR disapproves of any formal interpretation of the word 'charge' in favour of a substantive meaning, because '[t]he prominent place held in a democratic society by the right to a fair trial favours a "substantive", rather than a "formal" conception of the "charge" referred to by Article 6; it impels the Court to look behind the appearances and examine the realities of the procedure in question'.[14] The Court then defines 'charge' as: 'the official notification given to an individual by the competent authority of an allegation that he has committed a criminal offence' or some other act which carries 'the implication of such an allegation and which likewise substantially affects the situation of the suspect'.[15] There is no reason why such an approach should be inappropriate for interpretation of Art. 14 (I) ICCPR. The test of application would therefore be: is the suspect substantially affected by the allegations made by state authorities?[16]

Another difficulty that needs to be taken into account for interpretation of Art. 14 (I) ICCPR or Art. 6 (I) ECHR is the fact that they both refer to the 'determination' of a criminal charge.[17] For this reason, some authors argue that the norm is inapplicable to the pre-trial stage; it expressly refers only to court hearings.[18] This argument is certainly not available for paras. (II) and (III) of Art. 14 ICCPR or Art. 6 ECHR, but could be transferred to

---

[9] Emmins, 21.3.6.   [10] Compare §§ 199ff StPO.

[11] F. G. Jacobs and R. C. A. White, *The European Convention on Human Rights* (2nd edn. Oxford, 1996).

[12] This is the prevailing view in the literature; compare M. Nowak, *International Covenant on Civil and Political Rights* (Kehl and Strasbourg, 1993), Art. 14 No. 13.

[13] The doctrine of 'autonomous interpretation' is applied by the ECourtHR when interpreting legal terms within the Convention and has been applied above all with regard to Art. 6 ECHR. With regard to 'charge', compare e.g. *Deweer v Belgium* Judgment 27 February 1980, Series A No. 35, paras. 43 ff. Cf. also D. J. Harris *et al.*, *Law of the European Convention on Human Rights* (London, 1995 = Harris), 16.

[14] ECourtHR in *Adolf v Austria* Judgment from 26 March 1982, Series A No. 49, para. 30.

[15] ECourtHR in *Corigliano v Italy* Judgment 10 December 1982, Series A No. 57, para. 34; likewise *Eckle v FRG* Judgment 15 July 1982, Series A No. 51, *Foti v Italy* Judgment 10 December 1982, Series A No. 56; cf. also Harris, 171, and Peukert, EuGRZ 1979, 261 at 269–71, with further references to case-law.

[16] See Nowak, Art. 14, No. 14.

[17] The wording of Art. 10 UDHR is similar.

[18] D. Poncet, *La Protection de l'Accusé par la Convention Européenne des Droits de l'Homme* (Geneva, 1977).

Art. 8 (I) AmCHR, as the latter speaks of the 'substantiation of any accusation of a criminal nature'. Only the most recent of these universal human rights documents, the African Charter, is wider and less precise in its wording, in Art. 7 (I) AfCHPR. On the other hand, both Art. 14 ICCPR and Art. 6 ECHR refer to a temporal limit, namely 'reasonable time'. This requirement also pertains to the pre-trial stage, as it sets a time limit ('reasonable time') within which the trial must start. Furthermore, determination of the charge is necessarily linked to and conditioned by the formulation of a criminal charge; the charge triggers the court proceedings. This influences, even governs, the pre-trial procedure. It is therefore not a convincing interpretation, even from a literal point of view, if the applicability is limited to the trial stage.

Definition of the term 'criminal' has inspired numerous judgments and much literature. As states might evade such applicability and circumvent the conditions of Art. 14 ICCPR simply by slipping purely criminal matters in amongst administrative offences, an autonomous definition has to be found here as well.[19] Interpretation of this provision by the European institutions is equally extensive and controversial. From its early years onwards, the ECourtHR provided a three-criteria test: (*a*) the classification of the offence in domestic law, (*b*) the nature of the offence, and (*c*) the degree and severity of the possible punishment.[20] We do not face excessive difficulties in this field with regard to our topic. The International Criminal Court can only apply international criminal law which meets all three criteria easily when they are rooted in the international environment; (*a*) certainly, the offence must be considered criminal by the international community, (*b*) the nature of the offence must be purely criminal, as only the gravest acts against the international community can be criminalized at the international level,[21] and (*c*), these offences are sanctioned with the longest and severest punishments the international community can apply.[22]

Having discussed the meaning of the crucial decisions in this field, we unfortunately cannot find a straight answer to the question of whether or

[19] Nowak, Art. 14, No. 13.

[20] ECourtHR in *Engel v Netherlands* Judgment 8 June 1976, Series A No. 22, paras. 80–5; see details of these criteria: van Dijk in R. St J. Macdonald, F. Matscher, and H. Petzold (eds.), *The European System for the Protection of Human Rights* (Dordrecht, 1993), 363–8.

[21] Compare e.g. the ILC Draft Code of Crimes against the Peace and Security of Mankind (1996) ILC 48th Session, UN Doc. A/CN.4/L.522; the ICTY Trial Chamber, in the *Erdemovic* case, para. 32, finds, when discussing the penalty, that crimes against humanity in international criminal law cannot be equated with the underlying ordinary crime in national criminal law, e.g. murder or rape. The international norm is unique in character, as it implies an attack on the international community as a whole.

[22] Again the ICTY Trial Chamber in the *Erdemovic* case, para. 31, referring to crimes against humanity, calls it a general principle of law, common to all nations, that the severest penalties apply to international crimes.

not investigation should be institutionally separated from the judicial body. We understand that Art. 14 (I) ICCPR is applicable as soon as the suspect is 'charged' with a criminal offence. But this says nothing about the institutions involved in this stage.

Admittedly, Art. 14 (I) ICCPR also speaks of an 'independent and impartial tribunal'. This wording demonstrates that the provision is based on the liberal principles of separation of powers and independence of the judiciary *vis-à-vis* the executive.[23] But if we combine the two elements, we might find a different picture; if there must be an independent and impartial tribunal to which the suspect has a right, if a 'criminal charge' (*accusation, acusación*) has been laid against him, does this not imply that the 'charge' must come from a different institution? Leaving aside the interpretation of 'criminal charge', the mere fact that such a thing must exist encompasses the idea of a division between prosecution and tribunal. And, can a tribunal *de facto* be 'independent and impartial', if the 'charging' instance is not institutionally separated? The fact that this question must be answered in the negative becomes clear if we take a glance at the meaning of 'independent' that the Strasbourg authorities have attributed to this term in their extensive case-law. 'Independence' is merely an institutional term, in contrast to 'impartiality', the importance of which lies more in the composition of the judicial body's personnel.[24] The tribunal must be independent of the executive and also of the parties.[25] Consequently, the tribunal cannot bring a charge itself, as in so doing it would automatically be committed to one side.[26] Neither would the principle of impartiality, being closely interlinked with the previously

---

[23] Nowak, Art. 14 No. 2. How important separation of powers and democratic principles were for the drafters beyond any cold-war policy is impressively proved by the different proposals that were put forward in the preparing sessions of the Commission on Human Rights to embody a literal reference to democratic principles in Art. 14 (I) ICCPR, for example, the proposals by the Soviet Union [E/CN.4/253] and Yugoslavia [E/CN.4/284] on the one hand, the United States and the Philippines [E/CN.4/279] on the other in the 6th Session (1950).

[24] ECommHR in *Demicoli v Malta* Report 15 March 1990, Series A No. 210, para. 42.

[25] ECourtHR in *Beaumartin v France* Judgment 24 November 1994, Series A No. 296-B, para. 38; *Benthem v Netherlands* Judgment 23 October 1985, Series A No.97, paras. 42–3; *Campbell and Fell v UK* Judgment 28 June 1984, Series A No. 80, para. 78.

[26] Very doubtful in this regard is the Rule 61 decision of the ICTY Trial Chamber I in *Karadzic* and *Mladic* case No. IT-95-5-R61 and IT-95-18-R61 from 11 July 1996. In paras. 83–4, the Trial Chamber encourages the prosecutor to supplement the indictment to emphasize the individual criminal responsibility of the two accused pursuant to Art. 7 (I) of the Statute concerning the takeover of Screbrenica in July 1995. Similarly, the same Chamber invited the prosecutor reviewing the *Nikolic* indictment according to Rule 61 to amend the indictment with regard to rape, sexual assault, and genocide (paras. 32–4). This blatant intervention of court judges into the accusing prosecutor's authority is mitigated by the fact that the reviewing judges according to Rule 61 cannot sit as a member of the Trial Chamber for the trial of that accused, by virtue of Rule 15 C.

discussed independence principle,[27] be satisfied, if there was not a genuine prosecuting body. As 'impartiality' requires lack of prejudice and bias, the tribunal must comply with both a subjective and an objective test: first, on the basis of the personal convictions of a particular judge; secondly, to ascertain whether the particular judge offers guarantees sufficient to exclude any legitimate doubt in this respect.[28] Leaving aside the subjective element, the objective one, according to Harris is comparable to the English law doctrine that 'justice must not only be done: it must be also be seen to be done'.[29] The ECourtHR stated in *Fey v Austria*:[30] '[w]hat is at stake is the confidence which the courts in a democratic society must inspire in the public and, above all, as far as criminal proceedings are concerned, in the accused'. Applied to our context, this would clearly prohibit a judge from sitting on the bench that is ruling on a case that he himself investigated. Furthermore, it prohibits a system in which judges are in charge of the investigations to collect evidence, as it is this very evidence that must convince them of the guilt of the suspect. A literal interpretation leads us to the application of Art. 14 (I) ICCPR to the penal inquiry and presupposes institutional separation between prosecution and judicial body.

We cannot draw much enlightenment from a systematic perspective (systematic interpretation). Art. 14 ICCPR stands in a rather isolated position amongst other human rights provisions. The systematic order seems to be accidental rather than indicative of some kind of logical development, apart from the fact that Art. 15 ICCPR comes straight after Art. 14 ICCPR as the most closely related human rights provision (although logically, the *nullum crimen* principle should be placed before the fair-trial provision). Nor does a glance at the internal structure of Art. 14 ICCPR as a whole shed more light on the issue. No intrinsic meaning can be found in the enumeration of specific rights in Art. 14 (II) to (VII) ICCPR. These paragraphs merely clarify what a fair trial demands with regard to criminal procedure. The same is true of Art. 6 (II) and (III) ECHR. These specifications, however, from a literal point of view, seen to deal only with the trial stage. A systematic approach therefore tells us nothing about pre-trial proceedings.

A historical interpretation does not provide much help, either, as this

---

[27] ECommHR in *Demicoli v Malta* Report 15 March 1990, Series A No. 210, para. 42.

[28] ECourtHR in *Piersack v Belgium* Judgment 1 October 1982, Series A No. 53, para. 30; cf. also Harris, 234.

[29] Harris, 235: this reminds us as well of the general rationale of sentencing in criminal law. One of the main ideas of punishment is that the conviction of the offender by the court communicates to third persons the moral disapproval of the act and in so doing strengthens trust in and the reliability of the legal order. See v. Hirsch, *Censure and Sanctions*, 9.

[30] *Fey v Austria* Judgment 24 February 1993, Series A No. 255-A, para. 30.

institutional problem was not discussed during the drafting of the ICCPR or any of the other human rights treaties. The fact that the 'impartiality' and 'independence' requirement was not intended to bear any allusion to prosecuting authorities has already been discussed.

Our last resort, therefore, lies in a teleological interpretation. Going back to the finding that the wording of Art. 14 (I) ICCPR and parallel norms in other human rights treaties presupposes an institutional separation between investigating and sentencing authorities, we must now prove this by teleological arguments. What, therefore, is the general aim of Art. 14 (I) ICCPR and related articles? The HRC defines the aim of Art. 14 ICCPR in these words: 'All of these provisions are aimed at ensuring the proper administration of justice'.[31] For the ECourtHR, Art. 6 ECHR holds a prominent place in a democratic society and therefore cannot be interpreted restrictively.[32] A combination of these two statements leads to the main objective: to ensure the proper administration of justice in a democratic society. In a modern, pluralistic, and democratic society, procedure is an important, perhaps the only, safeguard of justice.[33] The institutions must therefore be established in a way that will produce the best balance of the applicable rights and duties, both theoretically and practically. It is possible to imagine criminal procedure as a purely scientific, computerized calculation of evidence. A simple hypothetical example would be one in which a murder has occurred, and the weapon has been found with which the lethal shot was fired, as can be proved with certainty through ballistic studies. Genetic studies lead to identification of the only person who could possibly have fired this weapon.[34] In a case like this, could judgment be handed down by computer arithmetic carried out by the person who collected the evidence?[35] Forensic evidence is,

---

[31] HRC General Comment 13, para. 1.

[32] *De Cubber v Belgium* Judgment 26 October 1984, Series A No. 86, para. 30, *Moreira de Azevedo v Portugal* Judgment 23 October 1990, Series A No.189, para. 66; cf. also Harris, 164.

[33] I understand justice here as a purely secular and immanent phenomenon. The transcendental equivalent of 'just' would be 'good'. Certainly, in a secular state, beliefs of what is good are legion. Justice must be achieved beyond personal religion and belief. To that end, i.e. to find a just decision, democratic societies agree on certain procedures to balance individual against common rights and duties. Justice changes from instinct to a rule of conduct, as Rousseau puts it in his *Social Contract* (bk. I, ch. 8). Criminal procedure is one such rule. Compare in general, Rawls, *Political Liberalism*, and Habermas, *Faktizität und Geltung*.

[34] According to scientists, it will be possible within the next few years to identify the offender by a single human cell only, which could be found virtually anywhere on the scene of the crime, e.g. a smudged fingerprint, saliva on the back of a stamp or a cigarette butt, a speck of dandruff, or a single sperm. See the *Guardian* (9 October 1997), 12.

[35] It is interesting to note that Germany's *Bundesgerichtshof* (BGH, Federal Court of Justice) is reluctant to accept the persuasiveness of scientific evidence, as it ruled that, even in a case where genetic studies narrow the identification of the offender down to a probability of 99.986%, the maximum limit that can be achieved by scientific proof, conviction is not automatic; it may very well be that the judges are not persuaded beyond reasonable doubt of the accused's guilt, and in any case, the trial judges cannot base a conviction solely on DNA

however, usually far from being as clear as that. Consequently, a procedure must be found allowing evidence to be weighed and rights to be
balanced, taking into account the fact that only human beings, not
computers, are involved. If evidence is collected by one person, this
person will be emotionally and psychologically fixated on his hypothesis
about how the crime took place.[36] This hypothetical presumption of how
the crime occurred, put forward by the investigators, cannot be made the
sole basis of conviction. It must be challenged. Therefore, the investigators
must persuade another institution of the correctness of their hypothesis.

2. How to apply the human rights norm

The question of whether or not to apply Art. 14 ICCPR to the pre-trial
stage has been answered in the affirmative, albeit cautiously.
Furthermore, I have found that court and prosecution must be institutionally separated. How can these two findings now be combined in a
conclusive human rights methodology? From a dogmatic point of view,
the result is still unsatisfactory. Discussion of the applicability of Art. 14
ICCPR, however, necessitates dealing with the matter of how this norm
should be applied.

The typical human rights application would be to formulate a right to
something for an individual, which would at best be enforceable through
human rights bodies. Consequently, I would have to formulate a right to
'a separate and independent prosecutor'. If I argue in this way, I
encounter several difficulties. The most obvious one is the lack of a written norm; this means we would have to find such a right implied in other
provisions. Its applicability would also be doubtful; could a right to a
separate and independent prosecutor be judicable in an isolated manner?

The correct dogmatic avenue in my view is that human rights provisions can have structural and institutional consequences lying beyond
their precise scope of application. Certain rights might be useless, if they
are not embedded in a specific procedure by certain institutions. This is
exactly the case here; a right to have the criminal charge reviewed by an
independent and impartial tribunal, as discussed above, can only be
ensured by having two separate institutions: a prosecuting one and a judging one. If what is spelt out literally in human rights treaties, for example,
the right to an independent and impartial tribunal, is called the institutional guarantee of a human rights norm,[37] we can call the phenomena of

---

evidence, BGHSt 38, 320 *2nd DNA-Analysis-judgment* 12 August 1992. At the most it can be
brought into play additionally, BGHSt 37, 157 *1st DNA-Analysis-judgment*.

[36] See, with the specific context of the presumption of innocence during the
Zwischenverfahren (interim or review proceeding) in § 203 StPO: Schünemann, GA (1978), 161
at 172.

[37] Nowak, Art. 14, No. 15.

direct consequences from institutional guarantees 'institutional reflexes' (*Rechtsreflex*) of human rights norms.

These reflexes we derive from the institutional guarantee of an independent and impartial tribunal are also backed by the general 'fair trial' provision. A 'fair trial' basically means 'equality of arms' between the parties.[38] If investigation and judgment were governed by one and the same institution, the independent and impartial tribunal, the principle of equality of arms would be null and void, as there would be no parties to which the principle could apply.[39] Furthermore, leaving aside the problem of applicability, the result is endorsed by the 'presumption of innocence' pursuant to Art. 14 (II) ICCPR; judges who have been in charge of the inquiry themselves can never presume the accused innocent.

Lastly, the separation can also be seen as deriving from the ancient principle of law that no one ought to be a judge in his own affairs, *nemo judex in causa sua*.[40] This is recognized as a general principle of law. Translated to criminal procedure, it means that the judge cannot conduct his own inquiry and convict the alleged offender on the basis of the evidence that he himself has collected and investigated.

3. Consequences

I have thus concluded that there must be two separate institutions: a court and a prosecuting body. Any international criminal court would therefore have to be coupled with a separate investigating team. In Art. 11 (b) and 16 (II) Statute ICTY, the prosecutor at this tribunal is recognized as a separate organizational entity. The prosecutor and his staff must be completely independent of the court. In the national context, the prosecutor is the public substitute for a private accusation. As such, he represents public interest.[41] Likewise, his counterpart at an international criminal court represents the international community as a whole. This duty must be fulfilled without any influence or instructions from any source and certainly without influence from judges.[42] I will now take a detailed look at this institution.

---

[38] I will discuss this provision in detail later, for now, the reference to Nowak, Art. 14, Nos. 19–21, and Harris, 207–11, should be sufficient substantiation of the meaning given to 'fair trial'.

[39] This is to be understood without prejudice to the frequently made statement that in the strict sense the German criminal process does not recognize the concepts of parties.

[40] *Dr. Bonhman's* case [1610] 8 Co, Re114a.

[41] See UN Guidelines on the Role of Prosecutors, No. 11.

[42] Compare Amnesty International, IOR 40/05/94 29.

(II) The Prosecution

The meaning of the term 'prosecution' has not yet been clearly established. So far, it has been used to refer to the investigating authorities who are independent of the judiciary. But who exactly are the authorities that are responsible for the investigation and what rules must they observe? In the following, I will take a brief look at pre-trial institutions and who they are according to the major national systems, discuss the human rights issues relating to this institutional problem, and thence attempt to demonstrate that an independent legal authority that is in charge of the investigating process and committed to the principle of objectivity has the best prospects of protecting the human rights of the suspect.

1. Relationship between prosecution and police

All legal systems operate some kind of prosecution service or authority that exists alongside the police forces. However, their respective roles differ immensely depending on the system. In England and Wales, the investigation is solely dealt with by the police, unsupervised by any superior authority.[43] It is mainly the duty of the police force itself to ensure the obeisance of the law through its own disciplinary system.[44] The system in the United States is similar, whereby the Supreme Court is the main supervisor of the investigating methods of the police.[45]

(*a*) *The system in England and Wales*   It was not until 1986 that a prosecution authority was introduced alongside the police in England and Wales.[46] Before then, it was solely the duty of the police force to investigate, obtain evidence, and commence prosecution, either by employing solicitors or instructing counsel for Crown Court procedure. In 1986, the independent Crown Prosecution Service (CPS) was finally established by

---

[43] L. H. Leigh, in J. A. Andrews (ed.), *Human Rights in Criminal Procedure* (London, 1982), 31 at 32 (= Leigh in Andrews (1982)).

[44] See the opinion of the Royal Commission on Criminal Procedure (Philips Commission) on this point. Leigh in Andrews (1982), 42, sees therein a lack of enforcement, as the Judges' Rules can only be implemented indirectly via the exclusionary rule of evidence; he complains that not even this is substantiated anymore, citing *Conway v Hotten* (1976), 63 Crim.App.R. 11 as a striking example. Given the fact that the introduction of the Police and Criminal Evidence Act (1984) (generally referred to as PACE) in the mean time has brought a major change and replaced the former Judges' Rules, the crucial criticism remains unchanged that the indirect safeguard of rules of evidence in court might not be enough. The legislative process of this fundamental reform of police powers is analysed by L. Helms, *Wettbewerb und Kooperation* (Opladen, 1997), 163–71; it is interesting to see how much influence opposition groups in and outside parliament had on the actual bill, although Labour eventually voted against the whole bill.

[45] Herrmann, JZ (1985), 602 at 608.

[46] Compare Emmins, 2.2, which contains a detailed explanation of how the Crown Prosecution Service is structured.

s. 1 of the Prosecution of Offences Act 1985. It consists of the Director of Public Prosecutions (DPP) and the Chief Crown Prosecutors. The CPS is now the link between police and court. Although not involved in the conduct of the actual investigation, the CPS reviews police reports of the inquiry and evidence gathered to decide whether or not to take legal action. The previous system offered potential for miscarriages of justice. An independent authority, it was believed, could better decide whether or not there was enough evidence to lay charges.[47] However, this 1986 reform does not seem to have had a revolutionary effect on actual practice. The CPS takes over the work of former police lawyers and solicitors in magistrates' cases and undertakes the briefing of counsel in other cases, as the CPS does not have a stand in court itself. As the CPS has only a limited function and the training and status of these prosecutors varies, direct comparison of the CPS with the office of the public prosecutor on the Continent would be inappropriate.[48] However, we should not underestimate the fact that the police now have to persuade an independent lawyer that they have a case before court proceedings can commence. Thus the investigation has become more professional.

(b) The role of the prosecutor and the role of the police in the USA The systems in the United States of America are similar to the English system. The police forces, which have developed on a local basis,[49] investigate crimes from beginning to end.[50] Only when the case has been thoroughly investigated and suspicion is strong enough to stand trial, will the police approach a prosecutor. The prosecutor does not initiate his own investigations. He relies on the results and the evidence collected through police work.[51] In the states, the prosecution is represented by district attorneys, city or county attorneys. On the federal level, a US prosecuting attorney is appointed for each US district. The prosecutor's job is to represent the case before court.[52]

(c) The German system In general, the German police have two functions: a preventive and a retributive one. These must be strictly separated according to Germany's public safety and order law (*Sicherheits- und Ordnungsrecht*), and are governed by two completely separate sets of rules: the Police Law (*Polizeirecht*) on the preventive side, the Code of Criminal Procedure (*Strafprozeßordnung StPO*) on the retributive side. The

---

[47] Smith in C. van den Wyngaert, *Criminal Procedure Systems in the European Community* (London, 1993), 77.

[48] Hatchard *et al.*, *Comparative Criminal Procedure*, 233.

[49] J. D. Brewer (ed.), *The Police, Public Order and the State* (2nd edn. London, 1996), 110.

[50] K. Kangaspunta (ed.), *Profiles of Criminal Justice Systems in Europe and North America* (Helsinki, 1995), 206.

[51] G. P. Alpert, *The American System of Criminal Justice* (Beverly Hills, Calif., 1985), 56–7.

[52] D. J. Champion, *Measuring Offender Risk* (Westport, Conn., 1994), 38–9.

strict distinction is highlighted by the fact that the Basic Law (*Grundgesetz, GG*) places the latter within the legislative competence of the Federal Parliament (*Bundestag*), whilst the former is left up to the individual federal states (*Bundesländer*), Art. 74 No. 1 GG and Art. 70 (I) GG. For now, of course, our sole interest lies in the retributive branch, i.e. criminal investigation. There, the police play the role that is defined for them by the Code of Criminal Procedure. This says that they are to be 'auxiliary officials to the prosecution service' (*Hilfsbeamte der Staatsanwaltschaft*) only (see §§ 160, 163 StPO). To put it the other way round, the prosecutor conducts the inquiry and is merely aided by the police force.[53] This means that the investigation is supervised by an institution of professional lawyers. The prosecution service (Staatsanwaltschaft) is often referred to as the 'Wächterin des Gesetzes' (custodian of the law)[54] and a 'champion of public interest'; it is an organ of the administration of justice (*Organ der Rechtspflege*), like the court.[55] However, unlike the court, the prosecutor is not independent: he is subject to the administrative supervision (*Dienstaufsicht*) of the Ministries of Justice (see §§ 146, 147 GVG).

(*d*) *The relevant human rights provisions*   Having looked at various systems, their institutions, and their procedures, I will now turn to human rights provisions applicable at this stage. My thesis is that the 'presumption of innocence' should be a governing principle of the whole of criminal procedure, from police inquiry onwards. The fact that it is applicable is certainly without prejudice to the meaning of this presumption at the different stages of the proceedings. For the actual indictment of the suspect at court by the prosecutor, it is true that the alleged offender is not, and by the very nature of the accusation cannot be, presumed innocent. Answering the question of applicability of the presumption of innocence to the pre-trial stage in the affirmative must be followed by careful scrutiny of its meaning during the different phases of criminal procedure. In the pre-trial stage, the innocence provision dictates that the authority responsible for the conduct of the investigation can only be one made up of members of the legal profession, must be institutionally independent from both the court and governmental influence, and must conduct its inquiry in a purely objective manner until it is persuaded of the guilt of the suspect itself.

---

[53] There certainly is a dichotomy between theory and practice; in practice, the police investigate independently when crimes have been committed. Nevertheless, accountability rests with the public prosecutor, which has a strong supervisory effect. Compare Hatchard et al., *Comparative Criminal Procedure*, 227–32 and 241.

[54] See BGH judgement from 8 March 1956 in BGHZ 20, 178 at 180.

[55] Roxin, *Strafverfahrensrecht*, para. 10, no. 8ff.

(*e*) *The presumption of innocence*   One very controversial issue is the question of whether the principle of the presumption of innocence is applicable during the pre-trial stage at all. Below, I will show that there can be no doubt that the suspect must be presumed innocent from the very beginning of the inquiry. If this principle were to be applied at the trial stage only, it might already be too late for the rights of the suspect to be safeguarded. Art. 14 (II) ICCPR, identical with Art. 6 (II) ECHR, reads as follows: 'Everyone charged with a criminal offence shall have the right to be presumed innocent until proved guilty according to law.'

If we adopt a literal approach in interpreting this norm, similar questions arise to those that came up in the discussion of the applicability of Art. 14 (I) ICCPR to the pre-trial enquiry. Again, when determining commencement of the applicability of the presumption of innocence, we find the word 'charge' as the apparent threshold. Earlier, I sought an autonomous interpretation and found that applicability commences with the date on which state activities substantially affect the situation of the person concerned.[56] Furthermore, in Art. 14 (II) ICCPR the exact date on which applicability ends can be found: 'until proved guilty according to the law'. Obviously, as soon as the defendant is convicted, there is no place for the presumption of innocence; on the contrary, the defendant has been proved guilty.[57]

In order to achieve a conclusive interpretation of the Covenant, it seems reasonable to apply the same meaning to the individual terms wherever they appear.[58] But what seems reasonable and easy is often not the right approach. Different provisions may have to be read differently.

It has already been mentioned that Art. 6 (II) ECHR has exactly the same wording as Art. 14 (II) ICCPR. In the American Convention, we find the presumption not as a separate paragraph but as the introduction to the list of minimum standard guarantees similar to those in Art. 14 (III) ICCPR and Art. 6 (III) ECHR. Art. 8 AmCHR speaks of 'every person accused of a criminal offence', who has the right to be presumed innocent. This wording surely alludes to the proceedings before the court. Similarly, the Statute of the ICTY refers to the presumption of innocence in Art. 21 (II) Statute ICTY as a right of the accused. As the statute differentiates strictly between the suspect (Art. 18 Statute) and the accused (Art. 20, 21 Statute), it becomes clear that the 'accused' can only claim to be presumed

---

[56] Nowak, Art. 14 No. 14.

[57] Nowak, Art. 14 No. 34. Certainly, doubts remain as to when exactly the defendant is proved guilty. Does conviction in the first instance carry enough weight or can only the final decision make the presumption vanish? I will discuss this problem later on, when dealing with the issue of appeal and review proceedings.

[58] Harris, 241, automatically applies the same autonomous meaning of 'criminal charge' in Art. 6 (I) ECHR to Art. 6 (II) ECHR.

innocent in accordance with Art. 21 (II) Statute ICTY *vis-à-vis* the judges. The African Charter seems to be more generous towards this problem. In Art. 7 (b) AfCHPR, only termination of the presumption is mentioned, whilst nothing is said about its commencement. Art 7 AfCHPR reads as: '(I) Every individual shall have the right to have his cause heard. This comprises: (b) the right to be presumed innocent until proven guilty by a competent court or tribunal'. This seems to be the best approach to an understanding of the presumption of innocence. The presumption ends with conviction by a competent court. Before such conviction, everybody is to be presumed innocent by all state authorities. The emphasis in all the norms we have looked at is not so much on the person 'charged' or the 'accused', but rather on legal conviction by a competent court as the agreed conclusion of applicability.

Looking at the historical background, the Human Rights Commission did not foresee a separate provision governing the presumption of innocence.[59] It was on the basis of a British motion in the 3rd Committee of the GA in 1959 that the presumption of innocence was attributed its significance by being put in a separate paragraph.[60] The presumption of innocence was thus given a paramount position in the Covenant. It was considered as being the most important provision foreshadowing the individual minimum guarantees enshrined in the following paragraph, which were consequently formally annexed to the presumption of innocence paragraph.[61] It seems as if the drafters saw the presumption as fundamental and necessitating all the procedural guarantees. The presumption itself is therefore the cardinal principle of criminal proceedings.[62]

Looking at pre-trial inquiry one is tempted to conclude that the whole procedure is *per se* hypothetical and presumptive, allowing no room at all for the presumption of innocence. In actual fact, this is how investigation functions; hypothetical conduct of the criminal act is presumed and the prosecution tries to prove this before the court. Prohibiting the investigator from working this way would mean rendering the whole system ineffective. The prosecutor would be condemned to persistent doubts and could not take effective action to fulfil his duty as the representative of the public interest. With regard to the European Convention organs, it has also been argued that a wider interpretation of Art. 6 (II) ECHR would endanger the effectiveness of the Convention machinery and provoke an

---

[59] See Art. 14 (II) of the Human Rights Commission draft of 1954, in E/2573, 67.

[60] A/C.3/L.792; A/C.3/SR.961, § 29; A/4299, § 56.

[61] This is the structure of Art. 8 AmCHR, where Paragraph (II) contains the minimum guarantees.

[62] So Jacobs and White, 150, concerning Art. 6 (II) ECHR.

increasing number of complaints.[63] Furthermore, it could be argued that the structure of criminal procedure would be destroyed, as the genuine separation of the parties, prosecutor and defendant, would be forfeited. Lastly, it is at the trial stage that the judges should weigh evidence independently and objectively. Arguably, there is therefore no room for the presumption of innocence in the first stage of criminal procedure.

Granted that strict application of the presumption of innocence to the investigation would destroy its efficiency, and granted as well that the inquiring authorities must, to a certain extent, proceed presumptively and hypothetically, the better arguments are still in favour of applying the presumption of innocence. First, it must be admitted that the suspect only has a defence counsel at his side and the whole administrative machinery of the state against him. Indeed, in the international context, he stands alone against all Member States of an International Criminal Court, as they are under obligation to cooperate with the court. In the case of the former Yugoslavia, suspects are up against all states, as the latter have the duty to duly cooperate with the ICTY by virtue of Art. 25 UN Charter and Art. 29 (I) Statute ICTY.[64] Allowing the investigating authority to consider the case solely on the basis of its presumptions would ridicule any chance of a proper defence and would indeed hamper any ideal of a 'fair trial' and 'equality of arms' for the parties. Secondly, the fact that criminal investigation must be hypothetical and presumptive by its very nature nevertheless encompasses the public mandate given to the prosecutor, that is, to establish whether or not a crime was committed and to administer justice. The investigator should not act as though engaged in a personal battle against a particular suspect but should, instead, attempt to discover the whole truth of the crime and establish where guilt lies. He will only achieve this goal if he is prepared to abandon his former hypothesis at every stage of the proceeding. However, this necessitates more than paying attention to evidence emerging by chance and working in favour of the suspect. It places a responsibility on the investigator to collect evidence until every other alternative explanation of how the criminal offence might have occurred is convincingly excluded. This includes the duty to look for and collect evidence that favours the suspect. Thirdly, control by the courts is not enough from a human rights perspective. A trial as such is a major evil inflicted on the suspect. If he is innocent, he surely cannot be expected to undergo a trial that might last several years only because it is his duty as a citizen not to jeopardize the proper admin-

---

[63] S. Stavros, *The Guarantees for Accused Persons under Article 6 of the European Convention on Human Rights* (Dordrecht, 1993), 51.

[64] Switzerland, as the only non-member of the United Nations, implements Chapter VII Resolutions voluntarily pursuant to Art. 2 (VI) UN Charter.

istration of justice.[65] Being tried means serious mental stress, as well as loss of social respect. The innocent must be protected as far as humanly possible from having to suffer a trial before a court. The investigating body must also provide very strong corroboration of the suspicion so that the danger of trying an innocent person is kept as small as possible. Finally, the objective of Art. 14 ICCPR and of its related provisions in regional instruments is to protect a person throughout criminal process.[66] We can thus see that it makes perfect sense to apply the provision of Art. 14 (II) ICCPR to the pre-trial inquiry.

The European human rights authorities in Strasbourg are very reluctant to expressly apply the presumption of innocence to an earlier stage than the trial. Much case-law, however, exists concerning the prolongation of applicability beyond the judgment of the first instance. In the *Minelli* case, for example, the Court held that if a conviction is impossible because of time limitation, national courts may not decide questions of cost-partition by reflecting on the likelihood of a conviction,[67] and therefore found a violation of Art. 6 (II) ECHR. The main reason for this ruling was that in this case the defendant did not have a fair opportunity to defend herself in an ordinary trial.[68] In the same case, the Court clearly rejected the argument of Switzerland that the presumption of innocence was merely a rule of evidence.[69] Art. 6 (II) governs criminal procedure in its entirety, irrespective of the outcome of the prosecution; it does not refer solely to an examination of the merits of the charge.[70] What is very important to the Court is the connection between the presumption of innocence and the opportunity for a fair defence. Before a verdict of guilt is passed, the defendant must have had a chance to reply to and rebut the accusation. This seems to be a cardinal principle of the Court and was also found in *Adolf v Austria*;[71] there the judgment of the Austrian District Court implied, in its reasoning, that the Court believed in the guilt of the applicant but that the

---

[65] See e.g. the view of the BGH in *Aufopferungsanspruch* Judgment 22 February 1973 in BGHZ 60, 302 (304 in particular). The BGH sees every citizen as obliged to tolerate investigative measures instituted against him. The proper functioning of the criminal justice system (*Strafrechtspflege*) is a superior concern and outweighs the interests of the individual in an unfettered life.

[66] Jacobs and White, 146, writing about Art. 6 ECHR.

[67] Minelli was even compelled to pay compensation to the prosecutor, who was in this case a private one, on the grounds that he would very likely have been found guilty had it not been for the statutory limitation that he went free. See ECourtHR *Minelli v. Switzerland* Judgment 25 March 1983 Series A No. 62.

[68] Ibid., para. 37.

[69] A careful distinction must be made between the principle of presumption of innocence and the principle of *in dubio pro reo*, the latter being a rule of evidence. See below, Ch. 5.

[70] ECourtHR *Minelli v. Switzerland* Judgment 25 March 1983 Series A No. 62, para. 30.

[71] ECourtHR *Adolf v Austria* Judgment 26 March 1982, Series A No. 49. According to J. Frowein and W. Peukert *ECHR* Art. 6 No. 167, this case should have been abandoned earlier on as trivial.

offence did not merit punishment. However, the Court did not find a violation of the presumption of innocence, because the decision of the Austrian Supreme Court cleared the applicant of any suspicion of guilt.[72]

These judgments unquestionably concern questions at the stage of the court proceedings only. However, the ECourtHR held that, unless there is a conviction, the presumption of innocence prevails, that is, it is allotted to individuals as long as they are not convicted by a competent tribunal.[73]

Cases where the alleged violation occurred during pre-trial proceedings were censured by the Commission and seldom reached the Court.[74] Unfortunately, the Commission never found a violation. In a very early case, *X v FRG*,[75] a scientific test was ordered against the applicant charged with homosexual relations to provide evidence of whether his homosexual tendencies were comparable with a mental defect. Despite the fact that the outcome of this medical examination would prejudice judgment of the applicant's innocence or guilt, the Commission held that a medical examination is not in itself a violation of Art. 6 (II) ECHR, as it constitutes a normal and often desirable part of a thorough and conscientious investigation of a case.[76] Similarly, the Commission permitted a blood-test on the grounds that if detention had been legitimate, then a minor interference in the form of a blood-test was admissible a fortiori.[77] Lastly, in *X v FRG*, the Commission could not find a violation in the fact that the German police did not inform the suspect of his right to silence until he had already confessed to the allegation.[78] Without actually determining the scope of application, the Commission held that the first hearing by the police clearly lies outside the limits of Art. 6 (II) ECHR. At that time, the suspect is clearly not yet charged with a criminal offence.

Calling to mind the definition of 'criminal charge' as established by the ECourtHR, as 'the official notification given to an individual by the competent authority of an allegation that he has committed a criminal

---

[72] Ibid., paras. 38–41. Judges Cremona, Liesch, and Pettiti nevertheless dissented and argued that the Supreme Court could not be held as a remedy for the obvious violation resulting from the unambiguous language of the District Court, ibid. 21.

[73] See, as concerns *Adolf* and *Minelli*, Kühl, NJW (1984), 1264 at 1266–7.

[74] To the best of the author's knowledge, not a single case concerning pre-trial inquiry has made its way to the Court.

[75] ECommHR *X v FRG* Decision 7 May 1962, Appl. No. 986/61, 5 YB (1962), 192.

[76] Ibid. 198.

[77] ECommHR *X v Netherlands* Decision 4 December 1978, Appl. No. 8239/78, 16 DR, 184 at 185.

[78] ECommHR *X v FRG* Decision 12 July 1971, Appl. No. 4483/70, 30 Coll. of Dec. (1972), 77. Previously, the German courts held that the conduct of the interrogation was contrary to German law (§§ 136, 136a, 163, 163a StPO), but X's confession to the police could nevertheless be taken into account. Besides, the Commission held that it could only rule on violations of the ECHR.

offence' or some other act which carries 'the implication of such an allegation and which likewise substantially affects the situation of the
suspect',[79] the findings of the Commission are surprising. If a suspect is
summoned or taken to the police station to be questioned about a crime,
he is certainly confronted with an allegation that he has committed a
criminal offence and his situation is certainly substantially affected, as
he finds himself in a defending position where a careless word could
immediately lead to his detention. If one also takes into account the
above discussed statements of the Court concerning the opportunity for
a fair defence as the underlying objective of the presumption of innocence, it must be admitted that this chance must be given to him as soon
as he encounters an official allegation. If the suspect is not given this
opportunity, he is an easy target for psychological tricks played by the
police.[80] Furthermore, the Court held on several occasions that the
presumption of innocence is violated by so-called pre-trial publicity,
that is, if state officials or the mass media declare that they are
convinced of the guilt of the suspect in public. This could make a fair
trial virtually impossible.[81] In the opinion of the Court, the presumption
of innocence is therefore not only applicable to courts but also to other
state authorities and not only during the formal trial but as soon as the
suspect is substantially affected. If the Strasbourg organs were to apply
their own jurisprudence, the presumption of innocence would consequently be pertinent to pre-trial inquiry. Stavros gives further evidence
of the inconsistency of the interpretation favoured by the European
bodies. For him, the main objective of the presumption of innocence lies
in the requirement of 'respect for human dignity throughout every
aspect of the criminal proceedings'.[82] This implies the need for a special
case-by-case justification, if certain pre-trial measures are imposed upon
the suspect, to ensure that public interest in the effective administration
of justice is safeguarded and the suspect's right to be treated as an innocent person upheld. Stavros draws a parallel to Art. 5 (III) ECHR, which
concerns pre-trial detention; with regard to this provision, however, the
Strasbourg authorities have repeatedly found that the national organs
must carefully weigh the state's interests against those of the individ-

---

[79] See above nn. 14–15, and cf. also Harris, 171.

[80] Concerning games and tricks played by police officers during interrogation, an interesting and shocking study on police practice in England has been published by M.
McConville *et al.*, *Standing Accused* (Oxford, 1994). This field study was made possible only
after PACE introduced the right to counsel in Britain in 1985. Before that date, interrogation
was mainly considered to be purely a person-to-person event between interrogator and
suspect, without involvement of third persons. As a logical consequence, researchers were
not allowed to attend such interrogation either.

[81] ECourt *Allenet de Ribemont v France* Judgment 10 February 1995, Series A No. 308.

[82] Stavros, *Guarantees*, 50.

ual.[83] By analogy, the presumption of innocence should be interpreted in a similar balancing process.[84]

In the view of the HRC, the presumption of innocence governs the whole of criminal proceedings. In its General Comments, the HRC points out that the provision of Art. 14 (II) ICCPR is crucial for the protection of human rights and that all state authorities must refrain from prejudicing the outcome of the trial.[85] In the same way, the 8th UN Congress on the Prevention of Crime and the Treatment of Offenders[86] stressed the important responsibility of the prosecutors to promote respect for and compliance with the principle of the presumption of innocence.[87] Similarly, in its document about pre-trial detention, this congress also emphasized the fact that the presumption of innocence governs pre-trial detention in the preamble.[88]

I therefore draw the conclusion that the presumption of innocence, as enshrined in Art. 14 (II) ICCPR, is applicable throughout all stages of criminal prosecution until the verdict of guilt is handed down by a competent tribunal.[89] This maxim is applicable especially in the stage of pre-trial inquiry, in the sense that the investigating authorities must also investigate in favour of the suspect in order to exclude any reasonable doubt from their suspicion.

(f) Consequences for the investigating institutions   If what I found above is true, the police should arguably not be solely accountable for the investigation. During the process of investigation, many valuable rights of the suspect are at risk, several of which will be discussed below. If the police were solely answerable, the risk of one-sided and biased conduct would be too high. On the other hand, correction of possible inaccuracies through rules of evidence at the trial stage is unreliable for two reasons: first, because the burden of the trial is too heavy to carry for an innocent suspect and, second, as the true offender might profit from the misconduct of the investigation, the proper administration of justice is jeopardized.[90] For the sake of both the individual and society as a whole, police

---

[83] Compare *Wemhoff v FRG* para. 5, *Neumeister v Austria* para. 4, *Fox, Campbell and Hartley v UK* paras. 28–36.   [84] Stavros, *Guarantees*, 49–52.

[85] HRC General Comment 13, Article 14, para. 7.

[86] Havana Conference, 27 Aug.–7 Sept. 1990.

[87] See the Preamble of the Guidelines on the role of prosecutors, UN Doc. A/CONF.144/28/Rev. 1 (1990), 189.

[88] UN Doc. A/CONF.144/28/Rev. 1 (1990), pre-trial detention, 157.

[89] In the PrepComm, it was proposed that the presumption of innocence be granted to 'Anyone suspected of committing a crime'; compare the Report of the PrepComm II, 194.

[90] See Hatchard *et al.*, *Comparative Criminal Procedure*, 231, who admit that the lack of judicial scrutiny of the prosecution case in the pre-trial phase in England and Wales results in the subsequent discontinuation of trials or in acquittals after evidence is not submitted or excluded because of failure to comply with PACE. This wastes precious resources and undermines the confidence of police and public in the efficacy of the administration of criminal justice.

authorities must be controlled through professional lawyers. This was admitted by the European Commission of Human Rights in the above-mentioned case, *X v Netherlands*, concerning the ordering of blood-tests. An adequate guarantee against arbitrary or improper use of blood-testing was seen in the fact that, according to Dutch law, blood-tests had to be ordered by either the public prosecutor, his deputy, or a specially authorized senior police officer in the light of the particular circumstances of the case.[91] Rather than providing remedies after a violation of human rights has occurred, which is, of course, the special duty of the state according to Art. 2 (III) ICCPR, the states must ensure that violations are effectively prevented, as is the state's obligation by virtue of Art. 2 (I) ICCPR. The UN Guidelines on the role of prosecutors state that prosecutors perform an active role in criminal proceedings and shall in particular supervise the legality of investigating measures.[92] A similar conclusion was reached with regard to false confessions by the Joint Committee of the British Institute of International and Comparative Law when reviewing French, German, and English criminal law.[93] It therefore seems more than appropriate that responsibility for the entire investigation should be transferred to the prosecutor.

In the international context, steps must be taken to ensure that the prosecutor is made accountable for conduct of the investigation beyond national borders. Even if national authorities were to assist the international prosecutor, they would still have to be guided by the latter. It is his duty to guarantee the protection of fundamental human rights during that stage.

2. Principle of objectivity

There is another huge difference between the Continental and the Anglo-American systems of criminal procedure due to the differences in the philosophical reasoning of criminal procedure. In most of the Continental legal orders, the prosecutor must be objective in that he must even investigate in favour of the suspect, that is, he has to seek evidence that might prove that the suspect is actually innocent (§ 160 (II) StPO). The reason for this approach is the belief that state organs must seek the entire truth and behave in accordance with the rule of law, and that they are sworn to justice and a fair trial for the suspect, who must be presumed innocent.[94]

---

[91] ECommHR *X v Netherlands* Decision 4 December 1978, Appl. No. 8239/78, 16 DR, 184 at 186.

[92] Guidelines on the Role of Prosecutors, UN Doc. A/CONF.144/28/Rev. 1 (1990), 192, para. 11.

[93] The committee certainly pointed out that this review procedure is time- and cost-intensive, see Hatchard *et al.*, *Comparative Criminal Law*, 245.

[94] Kleinknecht and Meyer-Goßner, § 160, No. 14.

As the system is not adversarial, state organs bear responsibility during the process for the well-being of the defendant (*prozessuale Fürsorgepflicht*),[95] as there is no other organ to do so.

The principle of objectivity has also been dealt with by English courts and legal experts. They came to the conclusion that the investigating police force must be objective.[96] Objectivity is this sense means that the police must consider not only whether there is enough evidence to charge a particular suspect; but also whether all reasonable alternatives have been rebutted.[97]

The literature on the US systems illuminates the fact that there, too, the prosecutor is not merely interested in convicting as many offenders as possible.[98] If rebutting the allegations was solely up to the defence, that is, if the prosecutor did not have to take circumstances working in favour of the suspect into consideration, the prosecutor would not be fulfilling his public mandate, which is to seek justice. The duties of the prosecutor have been described as fourfold:[99] (1) legal sufficiency, meaning that the prosecutor has to ensure himself that the case is lawful with regard to criminal law and constitutional, that is, civil liberties, issues; (2) system efficiency, which means that the prosecutor has the possibility of giving priority to cases which he considers more serious with regard to both suspect and victim; (3) defendant rehabilitation, which entails reflections about what punishment is in the best interests of the suspect and society; (4) trial sufficiency, by which the persuasiveness of the evidence in court has to be assessed.[100] Certainly, this does not indicate a high degree of objectivity. The high rate of plea bargaining,[101] especially if it takes place behind the back of the persons concerned, also demonstrates little respect for offender and victim.

The close link between this principle of objectivity and the human rights principle of the presumption of innocence has already been shown. If we take this link seriously, the responsible investigating authority must be objective and, going beyond what the Anglo-American systems fore-

[95] Cf. Roxin, *Strafverfahrensrecht*, § 42 D V.

[96] Leigh, in Andrews (1982), 33–4.

[97] See *Report of an Inquiry by the Hon. Sir Henry Fisher into the Circumstances Leading to the Trial of three persons on Charges arising out of the Death of Maxwell Confrait and the Fire at 27 Doggett Road, London S.E.5. Sess. 1977/78* H.C. 90 (Fisher Report), quoted by Leigh, in Andrews (1982), 33.

[98] Alpert, *American System*, 64–5.

[99] Jacoby, 'The Changing Policies of Prosecutors', in W. F. McDonald (ed.), *The Prosecutor* (Beverly Hills, Calif., 1979), 75–97.

[100] Cf. also Alpert, *American System*, 64–5.

[101] About 90% of all serious cases end with a guilty plea after bargaining, compare ibid. 80, which presumes that, if all crimes are included, the figure rises to 98%. Even the objective and purely descriptive survey by Kangaspunta, *Profiles of Criminal Justice Systems*, speaks of a plea-bargaining rate of somewhere between 80 and 90%.

see, must also investigate in favour of the suspect. In the UN Guidelines on the role of prosecutors, this is expressed in para. 13 (b), as follows:[102] 'Prosecutors shall: (b) . . . act with objectivity . . . and pay attention to all relevant circumstances, irrespective of whether they are to the advantage or disadvantage of the suspect'.

3. Independence from the executive

There is another side to this; for the prosecution to be truly objective it must be independent of any political influence. This is rightly pointed out in the Statute of the ICTY, Art. 16: '(II) The Prosecutor shall act independently as a separate organ of the International Tribunal. He or she shall not seek or receive instructions from any Government or from any other source.' The reason for this is the need for just and fair administration of justice. The prosecutor is not the representative of a certain state or a specific government; instead, he represents public opinion, as his duty is to safeguard the functioning of the criminal system in society. The international prosecutor therefore represents the international community and neither a state nor the UN.

This has several consequences; the prosecutor is, although independent from both the judiciary and the executive, certainly bound by the law. It is not in his discretion to decide when or whom to prosecute. Nor is it legitimate for any other organ or body to order investigations. The prosecutor has to investigate as soon as a criminal offence that lies within his jurisdiction is made known to him through whatever mediator. This is known in German criminal procedure as the *Legalitätsprinzip* (principle of legality), found in § 160 StPO.[103] The administration of criminal justice allows little space for political influence.

There is another reason why the prosecutor must be independent; one main objective of the criminal justice system is surveillance of government and police force activities. In other words, his task is also to control the executive organ. This aim can only be achieved if the accusing authority, that is the prosecutor, is not under influence of those institutions he has to restrain.[104] In the international context, this objective is even more

---

[102] Guidelines on the Role of Prosecutors, UN Doc. A/CONF.144/28/Rev. 1 (1990), 192, para. 13.

[103] As to the contrasting *Opportunitätsprinzip* (principle of expediency) see below. Independence from political or governmental influence is guaranteed in Germany by the structure of the German *Berufsbeamtentum* (civil service). Civil servants are independent from governments, as they cannot be removed for political reasons. Against this background, the recent decision to change the status of the *Generalbundesanwalt* (Federal Prosecutor) into a political servant, which implies the possibility of removing the incumbent from this post for purely political reasons, seems dangerous [§ 36 (I) No.5 *Bundesbeamtengesetz* (Federal Civil Servant Act 1985)].

[104] Compare the IACommHR in its annual report on Paraguay, OEA/Ser.L/V/II.77 rev.1,

obvious; international criminal law primarily aims at preventing governments and armed forces from committing humanitarian atrocities. This
ideal, and it is still a utopian ideal, that one day international criminal law
might operate in analogy to national criminal law, can only be achieved,
if criminal law is applied in a not arbitrary manner and without discrimination to every offender in a uniform fashion. As long as political reasons
hamper universal application, the desire for vengeance and distrust will
always be present.

4. The international criminal law context

(a) The law at the ICTY   Within the context of the ICTY, the statute recognizes the prosecutor as a separate organizational entity in Art. 11 (b)
Statute ICTY. The prosecutor's work and responsibility are defined in Art.
16 (I) Statute ICTY as consisting of the investigation and prosecution of
persons responsible for serious violations of international humanitarian
law committed in the territory of the former Yugoslavia since 1 January
1991. Art. 16 (II) Statute ICTY contains a general independence clause.
This independence is related first to the other organs of the ICTY,[105] and
secondly to any other source. The Statute ICTY bars the prosecutor not
only from receiving instructions but also from seeking instructions from
any government or from any other source.[106] This is probably meant as a
rule of conduct for the prosecutor in the sense that he must be aware of
his genuine responsibility. He cannot transfer his responsibility to any
other body. The reasons for naming governments explicitly seem to be
obvious. Governments or states form the legislative and may be part of
the executive in international law. The fact that 'any other source' is also
referred to bears witness, first of all, to the aim of general independence
from all sides and, second, to the drafters' concern that other unnamed
institutions might influence the work of the prosecutor. Institutions
included in this provision are certainly governmental institutions, the UN
in particular, quasi-government agencies, like *de facto* regimes, and
NGOs.[107] It should also include the tribunal and in particular the UN

---

doc. 7, 17 May 1990, 168–70. Quoted in T. Buergenthal and D. Shelton, *Protecting Human
Rights in the Americas* (4th edn. Kohl and Strasbourg, 1995), 382–4.

[105] See First Annual Report of the ICTY, UN Doc. A/49/342; S/1994/1007, 29 August 1994
(= ICTY First Annual Report (1994)), para. 143.

[106] See also the Report of the Secretary General pursuant to paragraph 2 of Security
Council Resolution 808 (1993), UN Doc. S/25704, 3 May 1993 (= Report of the Secretary
General), para. 85.

[107] Reference to the term 'any source' is also to be found in Art 18 (I) Statute ICTY. There,
United Nations organs, intergovernmental and NGOs are explicitly included in 'any source'.
The fact that the ICTY prosecutor is aided by staff provided for by governments, which the
ICTY greatly encourages (see ICTY First Annual Report (1994), para. 156), is not problem-
atic, as long as they operate exclusively under the orders of the ICTY prosecutor.

Security Council.[108] Nsereko concludes: '[t]he judges cannot, for example, purport to instruct the prosecutor on matters that fall squarely within his discretion. They cannot order him to prosecute a particular individual or prevent him from discontinuing proceedings at any stage before the judgment, for he is *dominus litis*.'[109] In the light of this, the practice of the Trial Chambers of encouraging the prosecutor to add other counts to the indictment when reviewing the indictment pursuant to Rule 61 seems risky.[110]

Institutional independence from the tribunal is only guaranteed if the prosecutor is not elected by the judges of the tribunal he is serving at. Art. 16 (IV) Statute ICTY gives the UN Security Council the power to appoint the prosecutor. That this is so is certainly due to the special circumstances under which the ICTY was established: it was done by the Security Council, acting under Chapter VII of the UN Charter.[111] It is, however, not without difficulties. As we have seen, the prosecutor also needs to be organizationally independent from the executive. To guarantee the independence it would therefore appear necessary to rely on other safeguards. In particular, the term of service needs to be of considerable length in order to reduce the possibility of undue pressure on the holder of the post.[112] The prosecutor at the ICTY serves a four-year term and is eligible for reappointment. This period seems sufficient to reduce the political influence exerted on the institution of the prosecutor through election.

According to Art. 18 (I) Statute ICTY, the prosecutor at the ICTY shall initiate investigations ex officio or on the basis of information obtained from any source; he must assess this information and decide whether it provides sufficient grounds for a prosecution. There is nothing new in this. What is emphasized, however, is that information given by governments does not enjoy any special privilege. It must be assessed in the same way as other information is scrutinized. Where the information comes from is not important; the prosecutor reading about crimes in the newspaper over his breakfast must assess whether there is sufficient basis to proceed.

The ICTY prosecutor's office consists of four sections, one responsible for investigation, one for prosecution, a Special Advisory Section, and the Office of the Prosecutor.[113] Lacking their own police force, the 'investigators' are under the protection of IFOR.[114] The fact that the prosecutor's staff is

---

[108] Nsereko, 5 Criminal Law Forum (1994), 507, at 517.   [109] Ibid. 517–18.

[110] See ICTY, *Nikolic* case, where the prosecutor was invited to amend the indictment and charge Nikolic with genocide and the *Karadzic* and *Mladic* cases, where the reviewing chamber according to Rule 61 suggested that a charge be laid also for the crime of rape.

[111] Established by Security Council Resolution 808 (22 February 1993) and 827 (25 May 1993).

[112] The requirements of 'independence' concerning judges are similar; see below.

[113] Compare the ICTY First Annual Report (1994), paras. 150–5.

[114] See Third Annual Report of the ICTY, UN Doc. A/51/292; S/1996/665, 16 August 1996 (= ICTY Third Annual Report (1996)), para. 75.

appointed by the UN Secretary General (Art. 16 (V) Statute ICTY) has been criticized by Bassiouni as undermining the independence of the staff and submitting the prosecutor to UN bureaucracy and the politics of that bureaucracy.[115] But given the situation with respect to domestic law, this practice is not surprising. Prosecutors are usually civil servants who are appointed, of course, by the executive of a state. Furthermore, the connection with the UN Secretary General seems to be purely formal and contractual. The prosecutor selects his staff independently from the UN.[116]

As concerns 'objectivity', the ICTY follows US practice. Nowhere in the statute is the prosecutor bound to collect evidence in favour of the suspect.[117] Rule 66 governs only the obligation to disclose evidentiary material to the defence, in particular exculpatory evidence (Rule 68) found accidentally. The tribunal itself went beyond the letter of the text, when it stated in *Kupresikic*:

[T]he Prosecutor of the Tribunal is not, or not only, a Party to adversarial proceedings but is an organ of the Tribunal and an organ of international criminal justice whose object is not simply to secure a conviction but to present the case for the Prosecution, which includes not only inculpatory, but also exculpatory evidence, in order to assist the Chamber to discover the truth in a judicial setting.[118]

The wording brings the differences in the understanding of the role of the prosecutor to light. Although the passage as a whole clearly points to objectivity in a Continental manner, the inserted 'or not only' stresses that devotion to the adversarial system, be it in a restricted sense, is present at the tribunal.

(b) Proposals for an ICC: The Rome Statute For a permanent international criminal court, it would be appropriate to have the prosecutor elected by the state parties or the UN General Assembly. Also, removing the prosecutor must be a generic power of the Member States and cannot be dealt with by the judges of the court. This procedure is now foreseen in Art. 42 (IV) Rome Statute. Fears that the prosecutor will turn out to be a 'Master of the Universe', especially if he should be equipped with the power to

---

[115] M. C. Bassiouni and P. Manikas, *The Law of the International Criminal Tribunal for the Former Yugoslavia* (New York, 1996; hereinafter referred to as Bassiouni, *The Law of the ICTY*), 833–4.

[116] Nevertheless, the prosecutor encountered difficulties, especially of a budgetary nature, from the UN office and the General Assembly. See ICTY First Annual Report (1994), para. 148.

[117] Bassiouni, *The Law of the ICTY*, 833: '[t]he Prosecutor is to enforce international law in an objective manner and not act as the agent of any nation or group of nations'. Their understanding of 'objectivity' as 'independence' is not like that proposed here.

[118] ICTY *Kupreskic* 21 September 1998, cited by J. R. W. D. Jones, *The Practice of the ICTY and ICTR* (Ardsley, NY, 1997), 165.

initiate proceedings ex officio, are sufficiently met by provisions regarding the moral character of the prosecutor (Art. 42 (III) Rome Statute).[119] Altogether, the norms concerning the prosecutor are set out most clearly.[120] Independence is achieved by the term in office of nine years (Art. 42 (IV) Rome Statute). Impartiality is obtained by excluding the prosecutor and his deputies from cases relating to a complaint involving a person of their own nationality (Art. 42 (VII) and (VIII) Rome Statute).

In light of the principles of objectivity and independence, the pre-Rome proposal for a 'permanent *ad hoc* criminal court'—as the latest ILC proposal for an ICC could be described—that is impotent unless pursuant to Art. 23 and 25 Statute ILC or unless the UN Security Council orders its unchaining or a state complaint brings the court into effect seems highly counterproductive. Amnesty International criticized this approach strongly, as the court seems to be 'a tool for state parties, rather than a tool for the general public'.[121] Likewise, the Lawyers' Committee for Human Rights wanted this proposal to be amended.[122] However, the proposition by Amnesty International to allow investigation on the prosecutor's own initiative or on the complaint of an individual is unfortunately quite unrealistic, as states are not prepared to permit intervention in what they claim to be internal affairs. It is disappointing and anachronistic that states should intervene in individuals' affairs through national criminal law but consistently resist allowing independent criminal control over the behaviour of their nationals through international criminal law.

The ICTY uses even harsher words:

It would be a travesty of law and a betrayal of the universal need for justice, should the concept of State sovereignty be allowed to be raised successfully against human rights. Borders should not be considered as a shield against the reach of the law and as a protection for those who trample underfoot the most elementary rights of humanity.[123]

From a human rights perspective, it is totally unjustifiable to sometimes prosecute and sometimes not do so.[124] The individual is completely unprotected against the often arbitrary political decisions of states in the form of a state complaint to the ICC or under the auspices of the UN Security Council. Given the fact that the state complaint procedure, as the

---

[119] The United Kingdom submitted that a reference to impartiality and integrity should be inserted and 'high competence and experience' be replaced by 'highest level of competence and experience'; see Report of the PrepComm II, 36.

[120] Jarasch, 6 Eur.J.Crime Cr.L.Cr.J. (1998), 328.

[121] Amnesty International IOR 40/05/94, 27.

[122] Lawyers' Committee for Human Rights, International Criminal Court Briefing Series, Vol. I, No. 1, 9–10.

[123] ICTY Appeals Chamber in *Tadic* para. 58.

[124] See also B. B. Ferencz, 'Von Nürnberg nach Rom' in *Humanitäres Völkerrecht* (Bochum, 1998), 4.

'little sister' of Article 36 of the Statute of the ICJ, is consent-based and restricted to genocide, the real power to start prosecution would be left to the UN Security Council. This organ is, to say the least, heavily political and easily deadlocked.[125] Establishing a prosecutor who is highly dependent on this organ might possibly make a mockery of the whole undertaking. The prosecutor would never be able to initiate investigations against heads of governments that occupy permanent seats at the UN Security Council, because these states would simply protect themselves or their 'allies' through the veto.[126] This possibility alone, apart from constituting a major inequality among states, threatens one main aim of international criminal law, namely, to prosecute systemic crimes ordered or backed by governments. Luckily the Rome Statute follows the better avenue: the prosecutor may initiate investigations *proprio motu* (Art. 15 (I) Rome Statute, based on a German–Argentinian proposal, which was heavily opposed by the United States).[127] The Prosecutor may conduct preliminary examinations and collect evidence. Before the actual investigation may be commenced the prosecutor needs authorization by the Pre-Trial Chamber.[128] The Pre-Trial Chamber must examine the supporting material presented by the prosecutor and make a preliminary determination that the case appears to fall within the jurisdiction of the ICC.[129]

The UN Security Council was given yet another power in Art. 23 (III) Statute ILC; this foresees the primacy of the Security Council over the ICC's jurisdiction.[130] 'No prosecution may be commenced under this Statute arising from a situation which is being dealt with by the Security Council as a threat to or breach of the peace or an act of aggression under Chapter VII of the Charter, unless the Security Council otherwise decides.' This provision is surprising.[131] In effect, the Security Council could again bar the prosecutor at the ICC from investigating, although the sentence is phrased in a 'positive' way.[132] The reason for this is somewhat

---

[125] The Netherlands Advisory Committee, Recommendations, 6.3 in 17 NILR (1995), 225 at 239, are strongly in favour of deleting this provision.

[126] Lawyers' Committee on Human Rights, International Criminal Court Briefing Series, Vol. I, No. 1, 10–11.

[127] Bergsmo, 6 Eur.J.Crime Cr.L.Cr.J. (1998), 355–7; the view of the USA is presented by Scheffer, 93 AJIL (1999), 12 at 15.

[128] Bergsmo, Cissé and Staker, in Arbour *et al.*, *The Prosecutor of a Permanent ICC*, 121 at 142.

[129] Sarooshi, 48 ICLQ (1999), 387 at 403.

[130] The Commentary of the ILC shows that this provision was heavily criticized by some members, ICC Draft Statute, ILC Report Doc. A/49/10 (1994) (= Report ILC), Art. 23 paras. 10–15.

[131] The Report of the PrepCom II, 75–7 reveals, however, that this norm has encountered few challenges, and indeed, seems to be widely accepted within the PrepComm.

[132] The Commentary of the ILC stresses the fact that the Security Council is not given a mere 'negative veto' over commencement of prosecution; the Security Council must be acting under Chapter VII. ICC Draft Statute, ILC Report Doc. A/49/10 (1994), 87.

vague. The Security Council appears to fear losing some of its political power to the prosecuting authority, an unheard-of consequence in the national context. Admittedly, under Art. 12 UN Charter, the Security Council is the main organ responsible for the maintenance of international peace and security.[133] But why should it forfeit this primary responsibility as the result of an international court with jurisdiction over some of the worst atrocities? In truth there is no reason to think so. The international prosecutor is responsible for bringing to justice those who commit very serious violations of international criminal law. The fact that he thereby contributes to the maintenance of international peace and security is a long-term expectation rather than an immediately visible effect.[134] By its very nature, his task is different from that of the Security Council, under Chapter VII UN Charter. Furthermore, for practical reasons, the prosecutor could hardly intervene in an ongoing armed conflict. As is the nature of criminal law, it only starts operating after the milk is spilt, meaning that international criminals are only accessible to prosecutors after the conflict is over. This means that, for both theoretical and practical reasons, there is no conflict between the tasks of the Security Council and the jurisdiction of the ICC.[135] There are therefore no reasons why the executive should have primacy over the judiciary.[136] The proposal for the ICC seems to stem from the two *ad hoc* tribunals established by the Security Council under Chapter VII UN Charter, and the reasons given therefor. The institution of both tribunals was certainly by virtue of the power of the Security Council to maintain international peace and security. An ICC, however, is not subject to the same restraints of justification and is established by a treaty.[137] This criminal court is an independent judicial organ, sharing the same underlying rationale as the Security Council only to a limited extent. The situation can be compared with the relationship between the Security Council and the ICJ.[138] It can certainly be said that the UN's main judicial organ contributes to the

---

[133] ICC Draft Statute, ILC Report Doc. A/49/10 (1994) Art. 23 para. 12.

[134] Meron opines that the establishment of the ICTY and the prospects of an ICC did have some deterrent effect on violations during the Yugoslav conflict, 92 AJIL (1998), 463. Empirical proof is not available.

[135] Bergsmo, 6 Eur.J.Crime Cr.L.Cr.J (1998), 358, sees a dichotomy between peace and justice which will continue after the establishment of the ICC. He does at least observe positive experiences in the extensive cooperation between the ICTY and the international peacekeeping forces in Bosnia and Herzegovina. This will have a positive influence on these tensions.

[136] The argument that the UN Charter assigned primacy to the Security Council, compare Wedgwood, 10 EJIL (1999), 93 at 97–8, is not convincing, as the Charter does not foresee a criminal court at all. The principal difference between criminal justice and executive powers is also overlooked by Hafner *et al.*, 10 EJIL (1999), 108 at 113–15.

[137] See below, Ch. 2 A III 1 b.

[138] Compare also Zimmermann, 2 Max Planck YB UN Law (1998), 169 at 218.

maintenance of international peace and security by means of peaceful settlement. The Security Council is even called upon to use this organ under its Chapter VI UN Charter powers. But nowhere has the Security Council primacy or the power to bar a case from being referred to the ICJ.[139] The Netherlands Advisory Committee sees an even greater threat to the independence of the ICC in this provision and recommends its deletion.[140] The Rome Statute found a compromise: Art. 16 Rome Statute gives the UN Security Council the power to delay investigation or prosecution by the ICC prosecutor for twelve months through a Chapter VII Resolution requesting the prosecutor to abstain from investigating. This request may be renewed. The norm contains no limit as to the number of possible renewals. In effect, the Security Council could therefore bar the international prosecutor permanently from conducting the investigation. India argued in Rome that, through this provision, the conference had accepted that justice could undermine international peace and security.[141] One way to read Art. 16 Rome Statute would be that continuation of the investigation (or prosecution)[142] through the prosecutor at the ICC must be determined by the Security Council as a 'threat to the peace' within the meaning of Art. 39 UN Charter.[143] It can also be interpreted otherwise. As long as there is a situation threatening international peace and security, the Security Council may bar any investigation. Arguably, the first interpretation would leave the Security Council less room to stop the prosecutor. Nevertheless, it would be an almost cynical reading, as it implies that ICC proceedings are detrimental to the maintenance of international peace and security.[144] The twelve-month limit does not create accountability, as Cassese opines. Furthermore, as the prosecutor's hands are bound, all the evidence will have disappeared after a year.[145]

For practical reasons it would appear logical for the UN Security Council to use the ICC instead of creating a new *ad hoc* tribunal under its power of 'judicial intervention' as per Chapter VII UN Charter.[146] The ICC would thereby gain jurisdiction over states that are not Member

---

[139] Lawyers' Committee for Human Rights, International Criminal Court Briefing Series, Vol. I, No. 1, 11.

[140] Netherlands Advisory Committee, Recommendations 6.4 in 17 NILR (1995), 225 at 240.

[141] See Bergsmo, 6 Eur.J.Crime Cr.L.Cr.J (1998), 358.

[142] This wording does not embrace the totality of activities of the prosecutor, as the statute differentiates between investigation and preliminary examination. The latter cannot be barred by the Security Council; see Bergsmo and Pejic, in O. Trifterer (ed.), *Commentary on the Rome Statute of the International Criminal Court* (Baden-Baden, 1999), Art. 16, No. 15.

[143] Compare Cassese, 10 EJIL (1999), 144 at 163.

[144] Bergsmo and Pejic, in Trifterer (ed.), *Commentary on the Rome Statute*, Art. 16, No. 23.

[145] Cassese seems to have lost his previous concern for the preservation of evidence when discussing Art. 16 Rome Statute, 10 EJIL (1999), 144 at 159 and 163 respectively.

[146] This term is used by H. Roggemann, *Der Internationale Strafgerichtshof der Vereinter Nationen von 1993 und der Krieg auf dem Balkan* (Berlin, 1994), 8.

States to the statute.[147] This possibility has been provided for in Art. 13 b Rome Statute.[148] Apart from that, state complaint procedures in human rights treaties have proved inefficient. Twelve states have made use of the state complaint possibility of the ECHR, whereas no such procedure has been invoked to date in the case of the ICCPR, the ACHR, or the AfCHPR. One further reason why jurisdiction is purely consent-based at the ICJ is the tenet of state sovereignty; this is justified by the fact that states claim their rights against other states before this court. In criminal law, an individual is prosecuted, not a state. Strictly speaking, state sovereignty is not involved.[149] Any criminal system, be it national or international, that does not leave the decision of whether or not to prosecute solely up to the prosecutor, but makes it dependent on previous political decisions, is contrary to Art. 14 ICCPR.

This standpoint of human rights lawyers does not seem to be reconcilable with the strict sovereignty concept of a number of states. Whether agreement can be reached must be doubted.[150] One could envisage concepts that states could agree more easily to and thus become party to the ICC. In the following, I will outline several conditions that may permit a reconciliation between the human rights position and that which fears for state sovereignty.

First, an ICC should have a reduced subject-matter jurisdiction.[151] Only crimes that are generally accepted as part of the international criminal order should be within the Court's jurisdiction; they comprise genocide, crimes against humanity, war crimes.[152]

---

[147] This possibility is welcomed by the Netherlands Advisory Committee, Recommendations 6.2 in 17 NILR (1995), 225 at 239.

[148] Cassese calls this mechanism the 'sledgehammer' of the ICC, as acceptance of the court's jurisdiction by the states involved is not required, 10 EJIL (1999), 144 at 161.

[149] Dugard, 56 Cambridge Law Journal (1997), 329 at 337.

[150] The state complaint provision, Art. 25 Statute ILC, is where the threshold for setting the ICC in motion could be lowered comparatively easily. In the PrepComm, voices called for the opening of the complaint possibility to any other source, so that it is not limited to complaints by states; see Report of the PrepComm I, para. 221. See also Dugard, 56 Cambridge Law Journal (1997), 329 at 338. The Rome Statute did not take up this proposal. The state complaint procedure has remained more or less the same; see Art. 13 a, 12 Rome Statute. How the jurisdiction problem was solved in Rome is described by Kaul, 6 Eur.J. Crime Cr.L.Cr.J. (1998), 364 ff.

[151] This book only deals with procedural law. Subject-matter jurisdiction is therefore not discussed here and nor are any aspects of substantive international criminal law. These issues are discussed, *inter alia*, by Safferling, JA (2000), 164; the articles of Kaul, Sunga, and Schabas, in 6 Eur.J.Crime Cr.L.Cr.J. (1998), 364, 377, and 400. Arsanjani, 93 AJIL (1999), 22; Robinson, 93 AJIL (1999), 43 and, before the Rome Conference, Zimmermann, 2 Max Planck YB UN Law (1998), 169.

[152] Aggression should not be within the ICC's jurisdiction, because it is too difficult to define and apply as a criminal norm and is therefore not generally accepted. This can also be seen from the discussion of the PrepComm about aggression; see Report of the PrepComm I, paras. 65–73. The Rome Statute follows a compromise influenced decisively by

Secondly, the ICC's jurisdiction should be restricted by the principle of complementarity,[153] that is, the ICC should operate at a subsidiary level to national jurisdictions. In this way the Court's interference in what could be regarded as national sovereignty[154] would be reduced to a minimum. Indeed, the national state would then have the opportunity to deal with human rights violations that have occurred within its jurisdiction without international jurisdiction altogether (compare Art. 17 Rome Statute).[155] Cassese's doubts about whether the safeguards against abuse by individual states are sound enough seem exaggerated. Any attempt to shield the culprit can be stopped early enough by virtue of Art. 17 (II) Rome Statute.[156]

Thirdly, with such a limited scope of application, the prosecutor should be able to commence prosecution of his own accord, without a formal complaint. It would then be irrelevant who has been given the power to lay a complaint. As a complaint would not be comparable with a case filed at the ICJ or a human rights body, which would have to decide on its admissibility and then on its merits, it would still be the prosecutor's responsibility to initiate investigations and eventually decide whether or not to prosecute. It would be more conclusive to give *ex officio* powers to the prosecutor. Complaints by individuals, states, NGOs, or the Security Council would then be no more than information handed on to the prosecutor, who would deal with this in an independent manner.[157] Art. 15 (I) Rome Statute adheres to this proposal and gives the prosecutor the power to initiate investigations *proprio motu*.

Fourthly, the Security Council could be given the power to refer matters to the ICC as foreseen in Art. 13 b Rome Statute. However, it must be clear that the executive may not order the prosecution of individuals.[158]

the German delegation: in principle, aggression comes within the jurisdiction of the ICC (Art. 5 (I) d Rome Statute), but only after a definition is adopted by the Assembly of Member States to the ICC (Art. 5 (II) Rome Statute). See also Hermsdörfer 40 NZWehr (1998), 192, 197–8, Wedgwood, 10 EJIL (1999), 93 at 104–5, and Sunga, 6 Eur.J.Crime Cr.L.Cr.J. (1998), 37.

[153] See Lawyers' Committee for Human Rights, International Criminal Court Briefing Series, Vol. I, No. 1, 8–9.

[154] Although, in the author's view, there is no interference, as shown in Ch. 1 above.

[155] Compare Art. 35 Statute ILC, which will be discussed in further detail in Ch. 4. The ICC adheres to the complementarity principle, as shown by Art. 17 Rome Statute and paragraph 10 of the Preamble to the Rome Statute; see Hermsdörfer 40 NZWehr (1998), 192, at 194, Ambos, NJW (1998), 3743, at 3744. The development of the principle of complementarity at the Rome Conference is described by Kaul, 6 Eur.J. Crime Cr.L.Cr.J. (1998), 364.

[156] Cassese, 10 EJIL (1999), 159. His fears that the ICC might not be in a position to preserve evidence at an early stage is, after all, not a problem of complementarity. In all cases where a state is unwilling to cooperate with the ICC, it can distort evidence fairly easily.

[157] The Lawyers' Committee for Human Rights, Legal Experts Project, working paper on 'The Accountability of an *Ex Officio* Prosecutor', proposes several ways in which the further independence of an ex-officio prosecutor could be consolidated by more political supervision of the prosecutor's cases through, e.g., an independent political organ.

[158] This is guaranteed by Art. 53 (II) Rome Statute, as the prosecutor is not bound by the referral of the case by the Security Council. He may use his own discretion.

As concerns the conduct of the inquiry, the prosecutor should comply with the principle of objectivity. In the PrepComm discussion it was submitted that '[t]he Prosecutor should conduct an independent and impartial investigation on behalf of the international community and should collect incriminating and exonerating information to determine the truth of the charges and to protect the interests of justice'.[159] With regard to the public mandate incumbent on the international prosecutor, this is the preferable view of the powers and duties of this institution. This proposal was taken up by the Rome Conference. Art. 54 (I) Rome Statute reads as follows:

Art. 54

1. The Prosecutor shall:

(a) in order to establish the truth, extend the investigation to cover all facts and evidence relevant to an assessment of whether there is criminal responsibility under this Statute, and, in doing so, investigate incriminating and exonerating circumstances equally;

(b) . . .

The prosecutor at the ICC therefore has the duty to investigate both incriminating and exonerating circumstances. The prosecutor's role extends beyond that of a mere 'party': he must aim at establishment of the truth.[160]

(III) The Court

All human rights treaties call for a competent, independent, and impartial tribunal or court established by law. However, the wording varies: the ECHR, for instance, leaves out 'competent' and the AfCHPR does not mention 'independent'. These differences vanish once the meaning of each term is examined separately.

1. The need for a 'competent tribunal'

(a) The human rights law The word 'competent' was inserted before 'independent and impartial' in Art. 14 (I) ICCPR by its drafters in order to ensure that all persons are tried in courts whose jurisdiction has been previously established by law, thus avoiding arbitrary action. Paragraph 1 was therefore amended by the Commission of Human Rights in its 8th Session (1952) in accordance with a Yugoslavian motion.[161] This concept

---

[159] Report of the PrepComm I, para. 226. Several proposals in the Report of the PrepComm II, 112–14, incline in the same direction.

[160] Behrens, 6 Eur.J.Crime Cr.L.Cr.J. (1998), 431; Cassese, 10 EJIL (1999), 144 at 168.

[161] E/CN.4/573; compare also M. J. Bossuyt, *Guide to the 'Travaux Préparatoires' of the International Covenant on Civil and Political Rights* (Dordrecht, 1987), 283.

seems to coincide with the meaning of 'tribunal' as interpreted by the European authorities. A 'tribunal' is characterized in the substantive sense of the term by its judicial function, that is to say, determining matters *within its competence* on the basis of rules of law and after proceedings conducted in a prescribed manner.[162] This means that the tribunal must be vested with the ability to produce legally binding decisions. Mere recommendations or advice would be contrary to the idea of a 'tribunal'.[163] As far as controlling and limiting the executive are concerned, the tribunal must be 'established by law'.[164] 'The judicial organisation in a democratic society must not depend on the decision of the Executive, but should be regulated by law emanating from Parliament'.[165]

The controversial issue arising here is whether the tribunal has to be *pre*-established by law, that is, whether the judicial authority must have existed before the criminal offence occurred. Art. 8 AmCHR says so explicitly. Within the American system, the Inter-American Commission did not hesitate to criticize special tribunals being established after the crime. From the *travaux* of Art. 14 (I) ICCPR, the conclusion seems apparent that the tribunal need not be *pre*-established, as the drafters rejected a corresponding Chilean motion.[166] Harris accordingly argues that the proposed amendment was rejected, *inter alia*, with the Nuremberg and Tokyo trials in mind, which were *ad hoc* tribunals established in the aftermath of the Second World War. '[T]he important consideration is whether a court observes certain other requirements once it begins to function, however it might be created.'[167] An approach like this entails a dangerous quantification of human rights, and, if generalized, would mean that one or several human rights norms could be neglected, if others, allegedly more important ones, were better safeguarded instead. Stavros, on the other hand, stresses that the drafters' primary aim was to avoid arbitrary

---

[162] See ECourtHR *H v Belgium* Judgment 30 November 1987, Series A No. 127-B, para. 50, where the Court ruled against the opinion of the Commission that the Council of the Ordre des avocats of Antwerp fulfilled these requirements and also found that the judicial function and competence of this Council was only one of several requirements. Cf. also ECourtHR *Belilos v Switzerland* Judgment 29 April 1988, Series A No. 132, para. 64.

[163] This is so even if the recommendations are normally followed by the executive, as in *van de Hurk v Netherlands*, Judgment 19 April 1994 Series A No. 288, paras. 45, 50, where the government claimed that there was not a single case where the decision of the court had not been complied with. The ECourtHR was of the opinion that a court that 'recommends' rather then 'determines' is incompatible with Art. 6 (I) ECHR.

[164] Stavros, *Guarantees*, 135.

[165] EComHR *Crociani v Italy* Decision 18 December 1980, Appl. No. 8603/79, 22 DR, 147 at 219.

[166] E/CN.4/SR.110, 4.

[167] Harris, The Right to a Fair Trial in Criminal Proceedings as a Human Right, 16 ICLQ (1967), 352, at 356. Harris does not refer to this in his commentary on the ECHR.

action by states and that a tribunal must therefore be *pre*-existent.[168] In *Crociani v Italy*, the ECourtHR relied upon the fact that the optional competence of the Italian Constitutional Court in criminal matters involving Members of Parliament, triggered by the Parliamentary Committee of Inquiry after criminal behaviour was detected by this committee, was foreseen by law before the alleged acts took place. In that sense the competence of the tribunal was *pre*-established.[169] Still, there are few European cases which stress the need for *pre*-established law as in the Inter-American system. The reasons cannot be found in different persuasions on either side of the Atlantic Ocean with regard to the content of human rights norms. As Stavros rightly suggests,[170] the reasons are, first of all, a very different political environment in Latin America to that of Europe, and second, the wide scope of application that Art. 6 ECHR has experienced through the case-law of the Strasbourg authorities, reaching far beyond the mainstream system of justice.[171] The need for a *pre*-existing tribunal can also be drawn from the provision *nullum crimen, nulla poena sine lege*.[172] In summary, it can be said that international human rights law considers it necessary for a criminal tribunal and its competence to have been established by a legislative act before a criminal offence occurs.

(b) The solutions for an international court   There would be four possibilities for establishing an ICC. The first would be an amendment of the UN Charter, making an ICC an integral part of the Charter, binding on all Member States. This would be the institutionally most desirable and 'clean' solution. This would certainly fulfil the criterion of a legal basis for a criminal court.[173] However, as previous attempts to change the Charter have shown, this is also a completely unrealistic idea; a two-thirds majority would be needed and the *placet* of all five permanent members of the Security Council.

A second conceivable scenario would be establishment via a resolution of the Security Council. Other than on a case-by-case basis, this would be hard to imagine, because binding resolutions can only emerge under the conditions of Chapter VII UN Charter. Whether this solution could fulfil human right duties is doubtful.

---

[168] Compare E/CN.4/573; cf also Bossuyt, *Guide*, 283; Stavros, *Guarantees*, 135.

[169] *Crociani v Italy* 22 DR, 147 at 219.

[170] See Stavros, *Guarantees*, 139-42.

[171] Compare e.g. one of the first cases to expand the interpretation of 'civil rights' into what, according to German national law, clearly comes within the ambit of 'public law' *König v Germany* Judgment 28 June 1978, Series A No. 27. Compare also the reasoning of Judge Matscher in his dissenting opinion explaining why he voted against this extension of Art. 6 ECHR.

[172] Found in Art. 15 ICCPR, Art. 7 ECHR, Art. 9 AmCHR, and Art. 7 (II) AfCHPR.

[173] This would also be the approach favoured by the Netherlands Advisory Committee, Recommendations 2.3 in 17 NILR (1995), 225 at 226.

Creation of the ICC by a resolution of the General Assembly has been discussed but must be discarded as unpromising. General Assembly resolutions cannot produce a binding effect on states, but must be seen as mere recommendations. The resultant institution would lack a sound legal basis for the prosecution of individuals.[174]

The final option would be a multilateral treaty. Such a treaty would surely provide the necessary legal basis for criminal prosecutions as required by human rights standards. It would certainly be the 'normal way', as Crawford puts it, for such an institution to be internationally born.[175] The Achilles' heel of the proposition lies again in its practical implementation. How effective and credible would the undertaking be if the most 'wanted' states remained outside the system?

Because of the possible scenario of an insufficiently ratified treaty or a treaty only ratified by 'good' states, it has been argued in academic writing that the international community should consider seriously adopting the statute via a Security Council resolution.[176] Admittedly, the ICTY Appeals Chamber in *Tadic* did not analyse the possibility of the Security Council creating an ICC on a permanent basis, but it did find that the power to create an *ad hoc* tribunal was implicit in Chapter VII. One would have to go one step further and justify the institution of a permanent court as a measure contributing to the maintenance of international peace. Alternatively, one could argue in favour of binding Security Council resolutions not rooted in a Chapter VII power but stemming from the general powers of the Security Council under Art. 24 (I) UN Charter.

Dugard argues that if the attempts to create a permanent criminal court should fail, the Security Council should take up the issue. For him, the risks of a major set-back to the development of international law, should the project of a multinational treaty fail, are too high.[177] This certainly gives the impression that an international criminal court should be urged for at all costs and that the end justifies the means.

As reported above, the conference in Rome in June and July 1998 established the ICC via a multilateral treaty. The majority of votes in favour was impressive, whether the process of ratification can repeat these numbers has yet to be seen. Sixty ratification instruments are required for the ICC to enter into force (Art. 126 Rome Statute)—only half of the states that voted in favour of the statute.

---

[174] Dugard, 56 Cambridge Law Journal (1997), 329 at 340.

[175] Crawford, 89 AJIL (1995), 404 at 416. The Netherlands Advisory Committee, Recommendations 2.5 in 17 NILR (1995), 225 at 227, opts for an international treaty as it believes this to be the most feasible option. For the same reason, Amnesty International also favours this approach, IOR 40/05/94, 23.

[176] Dugard, 56 Cambridge Law Journal (1997), 329 at 341; Warbrick, 5 Transnational Law and Contemporary Problems (1995), 237 at 261.

[177] Dugard, 56 Cambridge Law Journal (1997), 329 at 342.

2. The 'independence' of the tribunal

It would be incorrect to read impartiality and independence as synonyms, although, prima facie, they seem to imply the same thing.[178] By looking at the terms separately, as the European authorities do,[179] we may see what consequences there are from the fact that the AfCHPR refers to the 'independence' of tribunals only as a state obligation (Art. 26 AfCHPR), which differs from the right to an 'impartial court or tribunal' in Art. 7 (I) d AfCHPR.[180] According to European case-law, the implication of independence is threefold. The tribunal must be institutionally and functionally separate from the executive, the legislative, and the parties.[181] This is very much a purely objective test that looks at the institution and its function. In *Belilos v Switzerland*, for example, the 'judge' was a senior civil servant. The Court scrutinized the functions of courts and their internal organization. However, a purely structural point of view is not sufficient. The way in which the court appears to an outsider must be taken into account. Referring to its judgment in the *DeCubber* case, the ECourtHR stressed the crucial importance of '[t]he confidence which the court in a democratic society must inspire in the public and, above all, as far as criminal proceedings are concerned, in the accused'.[182] The ECourtHR further refers to the common law maxim that 'justice must not only be done: it must be seen to be done'.[183] The situation in *Belilos* was likely to undermine public confidence.[184]

To determine whether or not institutional and functional separation is properly in place, the ECourtHR has developed some guidelines;[185] the manner of appointment of the members of the tribunal, duration of their term of office, and existence of guarantees against outside pressures must be scrutinized. The usual manner of appointment is appointment by the

---

[178] Rädler, 'Independence and Impartiality of Judges', in D. Weissbrodt and R. Wolfrum (eds.), *The Right to a Fair Trial* (Berlin, 1997), 727 et subs.

[179] For a description of the European approach, see Leigh, 'The Right to a Fair Trial and European Convention on Human Rights', in Weissbrodt and Wolfrum, *Right to Fair Trial*, 653 et subs.

[180] Despite this textual differentiation, Ankumah fails to discriminate in this regard; E. A. Ankumah, *The African Commission on Human and Peoples' Rights* (The Hague, 1996), 125.

[181] See ECourtHR *Ringeisen v Austria* para. 95 on the one hand and EComHR *Crociani v Italy* 22 DR, 147 at 220 on the other.

[182] ECourtHR *DeCubber v Belgium* Judgment 26 October 1984, Series A No. 86, para. 26. The Court seems to treat the requirement of outward appearance as a separate generic condition of 'independence'. The better approach would be to take it as a principle of how to look at the tribunal when scrutinizing the institutional and functional separation.

[183] ECourtHR *Campbell and Fell v UK* Judgment 28 June 1984 Series A No. 80, para. 81.

[184] ECourtHR *Belilos v Switzerland* para. 67.

[185] The ECourtHR summarized these guidelines in *Campbell and Fell v UK* Judgment 28 June 1984 Series A No. 80, paras. 77–82.

executive. The ECourtHR considers this permissible.[186] Independence is endangered if the judges are subject to instructions in their role as adjudicators.

The ordinary and proper duration of term would be appointment for a fixed term or for life; in other words, judges should be irremovable by the executive and not subject to dismissal at will. If the term is too short, the pressure of the executive on the judges could be tantamount to improper influence.[187] As to the other safeguards against outside pressure on judges, the European authorities seem to be rather generous. They are satisfied with factual evidence of non-intervention and do not require formal, that is, legal, recognition.[188]

This concept of the human right of 'independence' seems to be implied in the term 'court or tribunal' in the wording of the AfCHPR. If the judicial institution were not independent from the executive and the legislative, it would not merit the name of 'court or tribunal'. Although only an institutional guarantee of 'independence' was inserted in Art. 26 AfCHPR, an individual right exists by virtue of Art. 7 AfCHPR.[189] The drafters of the AfCHPR took it for granted that a court is independent *per definitionem* and saw the only danger in partiality on the part of the judges.

3. The 'impartiality' of the tribunal

(a) Human rights law 'Impartiality', in contrast to the institutional and functional approach of 'independence', concerns the person of the judge. Bassiouni observes that this is now considered to be a general principle of law recognized by all legal systems in the world.[190] In this context it means freedom from prejudice and bias, being open-minded towards both parties. In *Piersack v Belgium*, for example, the ECourtHR found a violation of the 'impartiality' requirement, as the President of the Belgium Assize Court had previously played some part in the applicant's case, in his capacity as senior public prosecutor. Therefore he did not seem to be impartial.[191] According to European case-law, the test is twofold; personal on the one hand and organizational on the other. The personal impartiality of a judge

---

[186] *Campbell and Fell v UK* para. 79. Appointment by Parliament is also permissible, as found by the EComHR in *Crociani v Italy*.

[187] In *Campbell and Fell v UK* para. 80, the Court declared a three-year term admissible, but, as it seems, only because of the fact that the members were unpaid and might otherwise be hard to find. Cf. Harris, 232.

[188] See again *Campbell and Fell v UK* para. 80.

[189] Similarly, Rädler, in Weissbrodt and Wolfrum (eds.), *Right to Fair Trial*, 729.

[190] Bassiouni, *The Law of the ICTY*, 804; similarly Rädler, in Weissbrodt and Wolfrum (eds.), *Right to Fair Trial*, 727.

[191] ECourtHR *Piersack v Belgium* Judgment 1 October 1982, Series A No. 53.

must be presumed until the contrary can be proven.[192] This presumption makes it virtually impossible to successfully claim a judge personally biased, which is why this approach is often criticized.[193] Moreover, no violation has ever been found in case-law.[194] Organizational impartiality must be considered with respect to function and internal organization and not merely from an objective point of view. The goal of inspiring confidence in a democratic society requires that the courts' outward appearance be taken into consideration. Here we encounter similarities with the 'independence' test, which makes the law non-transparent, as it distorts the initial separation of the issues. It is therefore submitted here that there should be a strict separation of the two issues, with 'independence' understood as addressing organizational structure, as outlined above, and 'impartiality' as referring purely to the person of the judge in two respects: First, his state of mind (personal), and second, the circumstances of the case (organizational).[195]

Two questions must thus be asked. First, whether or not the tribunal is independent from the executive, legislative, and parties involved. Secondly, whether the judges are impartial both personally and organizationally. Only if it can be said that from an outside point of view there are no reasonable grounds to doubt court's independence or impartiality can both questions be answered in the affirmative.[196]

(b) The Law of the ICTY   To assess the legal position at the ICTY, we must first examine the 'independence' of this tribunal. From an objective point of view, the ICTY appears institutionally and functionally independent. It is not part of a hierarchical structure but exists as a unique body. However, the ICTY's relation to its creator, the UN Security Council, has been criticized as subverting the tribunal's independence; the ICTY addressed the legality of its creation in its reply to *Tadic*'s

---

[192] ECourtHR *Le Compte, van Leuven and De Meyere v Belgium* Judgment 23 June 1981, Series A No. 43, para. 58.

[193] See e.g. Stavros, *Guarantees*, 159, who rightly questions the sudden, purely objective approach applied here, when independence and organizational impartiality are both to be measured by outside appearances. This cautious approach towards the personal integrity of judges probably stems from a collegial attitude on the part of the ECourtHR towards national judges.

[194] The often quoted *Boeckmann* case, as an example of blatant partiality of a judge (cf. Harris, 235, and R. van Dijk and G. J. H. van Hoof, *Theory and Practice of the ECHR*, Deventer, 1984 = van Dijk ad van Hoof), 260) did not result in a decision on the merits as an amicable settlement was reached after the case was declared admissible. See ECommHR *Boeckmann v Belgium* Decision 29 October 1963 Appl. No. 1727/62, IV Y.B. (1963), 370.

[195] Similarly, Rädler in Weissbrodt and Wolfrum, *Right to Fair Trial*, 730 et subs., who discriminates between the subjective conception of impartiality and the objective or structural conception.

[196] I follow *Stavros* in his criticism and diverge from the ECourtHR as I wish to see the subjective approach applied through the 'impartiality' test.

motion challenging jurisdiction. The Appeals Chamber[197] suggested it had 'inherent' jurisdiction to determine its validity, referring in a somewhat expansive way to the principle of *compétence de la compétence* (or, phrased in German, the verbal equivalent of a car crash: *Kompetenz-Kompetenz*),[198] but it then refrained from properly addressing controversial issues like the relationship between the Security Council and the tribunal. Alvarez therefore sees the independence of the tribunal jeopardized, as the existence of the tribunal seems to be at the mercy of the political will of the Security Council.[199] The ICTY also operates formally as a subsidiary organ of the Security Council. Although this sounds strange when considering the principle of 'independence',[200] the fact that the ICTY was established in the form of a subsidiary organ says nothing about the nature of this organ, and in particular does not mean it cannot be independent.

The judges at the ICTY are elected under Art. 13 Statute ICTY. They are elected by the UN General Assembly from a list submitted by the UN Security Council. The term of office is four years (Art. 13 (IV) Statute ICTY); re-election is permitted.[201] Further conditions are those applied to the judges at the ICJ. In comparison to the ICJ, there seems to be one flaw: Art. 13 (III) of the Statute ICJ stipulates that judges shall finish any case they may have begun, although their place may already have been filled by their successor. The same provision was enacted at the ICTR in Rule

[197] The Trial Chamber previously rejected jurisdiction on the issue, presuming the legality of UN Security Council actions, ICTY Trial Chamber *Tadic* Decision 10 August 1995 Case No. IT-94-I-T, para. 7. The fact that the Trial and Appeals Chamber disagree on this issue comes as no surprise as the topic is subject to much discussion among international lawyers, especially in the context of the ICJ advisory opinion *Certain Expenses of the United Nations*, 20 July 1962 ICJ Reports 1962, 151, and in the *Lockerbie* case.

[198] The principle plays a major role in the determination of *Staatlichkeit* (statehood); according to the Bundesverfassungsgericht in the *Maastricht* judgment, it is the main threshold of state sovereignty. It held that the treaty of Maastricht does not give the European Union the *Kompetenz-Kompetenz*. Because of this it did find the treaty compatible with the Basic Law *(Grundgesetz)*, as state sovereignty stays with the national states, who are the 'Lords of the Treaties' *(Herren der Verträge)*. BVerfG *Maastricht* Judgment 12 October 1993, BVerfGE 89, 155 at 190, 192–99. Another field where one can find the concept of *Kompetenz-Kompetenz*, arguably the original meaning and the one the Appeals Chamber is referring to, is in arbitration. Arbitration tribunals, characteristically established *ad hoc* by contracting parties, are empowered to determine their own jurisdiction and interpret the underlying treaty. This power, i.e. the *Kompetenz-Kompetenz*, is therefore rooted in the free will of private contractors. Compare C. Wolf, *Die institutionelle Handelsschiedsgerichtsbarkeit* (Munich, 1992). The jurisdiction of the ICJ in this regard rests on the same pillar, i.e. dispute resolution by arbitration, compare I. F. I. Shihata, *The Power of the International Court to Determine its own Jurisdiction* (The Hague, 1965), 27 et subs. Whether or not this idea is transferable to the context of criminal law at the ICTY is doubtful.   [199] Alvarez, 7 EJIL (1996), 245 at 253–4.

[200] Sjöcrona, 8 LJIL (1995), 463 at 465 arguably alleges that this makes the ICTY dependent on the UN Security Council.

[201] The shortness of the term of office is due to the *ad hoc* character of the ICTY, although it is unclear how long the Security Council envisaged the tribunal to last. The possibility of re-election is seen by Bassiouni, *The Law of the ICTY*, 806, as a problem for independence. But second-term appointment of judges is not unusual in national jurisdictions, either.

14*bis*.[202] At the ICTY, Judges Karibi-Whyte, Odio-Benito, and Jan continued to sit in *Delalic et al.*, although not re-elected, until the trial was
finished. Security Council Resolution 1126[203] extended their terms of
service. With view to Art. 13 (III) Statute ICJ and the reference to the ICJ
in Art. 13 (IV) Statute ICTY, this practice is certainly justified. However, it
would be preferable to have a precise rule in the ICTY's own law itself, as
a Security Council Resolution creates the impression of undue interference on the part of an executive body. In this case, a resolution was not
even necessary by virtue of Art. 13 (IV) Statute ICTY and Art. 13 (III)
Statute ICJ.[204]

Furthermore, the judges must be 'impartial', both personally and institutionally. Impartiality is one of the conditions for those eligible to judge at
the ICTY (Art. 13 (I) Statute ICTY).[205] It is furthermore, by virtue of Rule
14, part of the solemn declaration the judges must make before taking up
their duties. But the personal impartiality of the judges at the ICTY is not
restricted to having no opinion as concerns the conflict on the Balkans, as
Morris and Scharf might imply.[206] It reflects a particular state of mind, as
we have seen above.[207] The most important part is the requirement of
'impartiality' in individual cases. Rule 15 gives several situations[208] where
judges must be excluded from adjudicating. This includes situations where
the judge has a personal interest (Rule 15A and B) or has ruled on the case
before, be it as confirming the indictment (Rule 15C) or as member of the
Trial Chamber, if hearing an appeal (Rule 15D). The question of whether or
not Rule 61 proceedings were included in Rule 15C was solved, as Rule 61
was included in the letter of Rule 15C.[209] Generally speaking, the words
'might affect' imply that these provisions should be interpreted broadly to
avoid even the appearance of impropriety.[210]

Statements made by the former President of the ICTY, Antonio Cassese,
have recently given rise to concern as to the 'impartiality' of the judges.

---

[202] Enacted at the 4th Plenary Session in Arusha, 1–5 June 1997.

[203] SC Resolution 1126 of 27 August 1997, noting that the trial should be finished before
Nov. 1998. The SC therefore extended the term of service for more than one year.

[204] Compare Jones, *The Practice at the ICTY and ICTR*, 160.

[205] The Report of the Secretary General, para. 74, connects 'impartiality' in particular to the
acts that fall within the ICTY's jurisdiction.

[206] V. Morris and M. P. Scharf, *An Insider's Guide to the ICTY* (Irvington-on-Hudson, NY,
1995), 143.

[207] See once more Rädler in Weissbrodt and Wolfrum, *Right to Fair Trial*, 730–4.

[208] It is therefore considerably more specific than the law concerning the ICJ; see Bassiouni,
The Law of the ICTY, 805.

[209] This amendment should certainly be welcomed, though it might lead the ICTY into an
insoluble dilemma. If a Rule 61 procedure is actually followed by an ordinary trial, six
judges will already have been involved in the case at the time of judgment. If one party then
appeals, exactly five judges will remain for the appeal (Rule 15D). The ICTY would not have
a substitute judge in case of another exclusion.

[210] Bassiouni, *The Law of the ICTY*, 805.

His 'very outspoken' criticism of world policy and his call for further action, in particular regarding the referral of war criminals to the ICTY, has been criticized by several commentators as not being the business of a judge.[211] The President cannot, however, influence the work of the prosecutor; he can only insist on the obligations under Art. 29 Statute ICTY of all states to cooperate with the ICTY.[212] Indeed, it is not the ICTY that should be criticized, but those who, for political reasons, support the work of the ICTY only half-heartedly or oppose it altogether. The whole idea of criminal prosecution is jeopardized if it is left up to a tribunal that resembles 'a giant who has no arms and legs'[213] but the problem is not one of 'fair trial'.

(c) The ICC   Arts 35 and 36 Rome Statute deal with the qualifications of the judges at the ICC.[214] When performing their functions, they must be independent and not engage in activities that might interfere with their judicial functions or affect confidence in their independence. The latter is explained itself by the fact that the ICC is not a full-time body.[215] Only the judges composing the Presidency serve on a full-time basis (Art. 35 (II) Rome Statute). The other judges are also elected on a full-time basis but must only serve full-time if the Presidency so requires (Art. 35 (I) and (III) Rome Statute). Hence, judges must be permitted to perform other salaried functions. Functions that are incompatible with work as an ICC judge include, for example, membership of the legislative or executive branch of a national state; judges should not be engaged in prosecution at a national level, either.[216]

According to Art. 36 (VI) Rome Statute, the judges at the ICC shall be elected by a two-thirds majority of the Assembly of States Parties to the ICC.[217] They serve a nine-year term and are not eligible for re-election (Art. 36 (IX) Rome Statute).[218]

---

[211] See e.g. Thornberry, 104 Foreign Policy (1996), 72 at 84.

[212] Swaak-Goldman, 10 LJIL (1997), 215 at 216.

[213] Compare President Cassese, quoted in ICTY bulletin No. 3, 22 February 1996, 4.

[214] At the Rome Conference, this was an important issue; see Jarasch, 6 Eur.J.Crime Cr.L.Cr.J. (1998), 336–8.

[215] Non-full-time judicial organs are not as unusual as it might seem. Most of the constitutional courts of the Federal States in Germany, for example, only sit when required. The members of these bodies are usually full-time judges in other functions. Likewise, the ECourtHR formerly consisted of part-time judges, until the reform of the Eleventh Protocol to the ECHR entered into force in November 1998.

[216] Report ILC Art. 10 para. 1 and 2, and now Art. 40 Rome Statute.

[217] Other bodies have been put forward as suitable to elect the judges; compare Lawyers' Committee for Human Rights, Legal Expert Project, 'The Accountability of an *Ex Officio* Prosecutor', 20. However, it seems appropriate to leave the election to the member states, at least as long as there is no closer link to the UN as regards membership.

[218] The twelve-year term first envisaged in Art. 7 (VI) Statute Working Group was criticized as too long and therefore reduced to nine, like the term of the judges at the ICJ; see Report ILC Art. 6, para. 4.

Several provisions in the Rome Statute address the issue of 'impartiality'. Personal impartiality is *conditio sine qua non* for being considered eligible (Art. 36 (III) a Rome Statute). Art. 9 (VII) Statute ILC excludes judges from hearing a case which is connected with their nation of origin.[219] In contrast to the enumerative ICTY Rule 15, Art. 11 (II) Statute ILC and now Art. 41 (II) Rome Statute contain an overall regulation excluding any judge from participating in any case in which he has previously been involved in any capacity that might lead their impartiality to be reasonably doubted. This should not be limited to involvement external to the ICC, as the Report ILC seems to say.[220] Previous involvement as a judge at the ICC should also be prohibited. For example, a member of the Trial Chamber is disqualified from membership in the Appeals Chamber in the same case. As to the review *in absentia* procedure, it is laid down in special rule Art. 37 (V) b Statute ILC that no judge who has previously been a member of the Indictment Chamber shall sit in the Trial Chamber. The general exclusion clause contained in Art. 11 (II) Statute ILC was criticized by several representatives in the discussions of the PrepComm.[221] It was submitted that further elaboration of the grounds for disqualification was needed.[222] The conflict of interest clause has proved a workable solution in many national and international settings. It would, however, be desirable, in order to prevent any criticism as to the partiality of judges, to insist that no judge may deal with the same case more than once. The Rome Statute leaves the details to the Rules of Procedure; it nevertheless contains a clarification that no judge may be involved twice in the same case before the ICC (Art. 41 (II) a Rome Statute).[223] The Rule 4.1.6 (I) of the Draft Rules of Procedure and Evidence foresee a number of grounds for disqualification. The list is not exhaustive but includes: (*a*) Personal interest in the case, (*b*) private involvement, (*c*) the performance of functions included forming an opinion on the case in question, prior to taking office at the ICC, and (*d*) the public expression of opinions that could impair the required impartiality. Interestingly, Draft Rule 4.1.7 requires that the judge in question should apply to be excused as soon as he has reason to believe that grounds for disqualification exist and not wait for a request for disqualification.

---

[219] See also Report ILC Art. 9 para.4. A similar provision is found missing in the Rome Statute. Regulation of the constitution of the Trial Chambers has been left to the Rules of Procedure.

[220] Report ILC Art. 11, para. 2, citing the example of involvement as a prosecutor or defence counsel.

[221] The Report of the PrepComm II, 30–3 contains proposals by France, Japan, Argentina, Australia, and Netherlands, all of which elaborate in great detail on the reasons for exclusion of the judge.

[222] Report of the PrepComm I, para. 45.

[223] Deschênes in Trifterer (ed.), *Commentary on the Rome Statute*, Art. 41, No. 3.

Both prosecutor and defendant may challenge the 'impartiality' of the judges. The disqualification will be decided by the majority of the chamber in question without the participation of the challenged judge (Art. 41 (II) b Rome Statute).

4. Protection of the authority of judges

When a state's executive and legislative bodies establish a judiciary that fulfils the above requirements, their responsibility is not yet over. First of all, they must recognize and implement the decisions. But mere passive recognition is not enough. Courts and judges must be actively promoted and protected. The IAmCommHR finds this crucial for the performance of the role of the judge:

Lack of support from political and police authorities in implementing the judiciary's decisions, or the lack of protection for judges against acts of vengeance or professional reprisals . . . for the exercise of their authority, which inhibits them in their role as judges attacks the credibility and confidence of the people in the democratic society.[224]

This means that understanding, acceptance of, and compliance with judgments and decisions must be actively fostered. In Germany, this has recently been an issue in the aftermath of the so-called '*Kruzifixbeschluß*' (crucifix decision) of the *Bundesverfassungsgericht* (Federal Constitu-tional Court).[225] Some (at least one) of the Federal States publicly denounced the finding of Germany's highest court.

Furthermore, judges must be effectively protected against criminal assault. This is especially necessary in highly political trials. Judges must be protected from attempts at intimidation by influential groups taking an interest in the outcome of the trial. They must certainly be safeguarded against attacks on their lives, which is a particular high risk in trials against so-called organized crime or terrorism. Special protection needs to be afforded for the 'investigating judge' (*Ermittlungsrichter*), who will shortly be discussed in detail. Being involved in the prosecutor's inquiry, he will be a possible target of attack. Lack of protection will render the judiciary ineffective and leave it at the mercy of groups who are willing to use violence. This will sooner or later destroy confidence and trust in a democratic society, which the IAmCommHR[226] and the European authorities[227] rightly point out to be the main objective of an independent and impartial judiciary.

---

[224] Annual Report of the IAmCommHR *Nicaragua* 1993, OEA/Ser.L/V/II.85, doc. 9, rev., 11 February 1994, 455; reprinted in Buergenthal and Shelton, *Protecting Human Rights*, 379.

[225] BVerfG *Kruzifix* decision 16 May 1995, BVerfGE 93, 1.

[226] Buergenthal and Shelton, *Protecting Human Rights*, 379.

[227] Compare e.g. ECourtHR *Belilos v Switzerland* Judgment 19 April 1988, Series A No. 132, para. 67.

5. Investigating judge

What role will the independent and impartial judge play during the pre-trial stage? As I previously argued that the investigation is the responsibility of the prosecutor, who is institutionally independent from the court, it might be considered strange that I now ask what role the judge should play during the inquiry. I will argue in the following that whenever the human rights of persons who are the subject of an investigation process are involved, a judge must be consulted and must approve any infringement of human rights before action is taken.[228]

(a) The system according to the German StPO   In the German system, as in several other Continental systems, this is provided for by the figure of the 'investigating judge' (*Ermittlungsrichter*). The role of the *Ermittlungsrichter* has certainly changed, in particular by virtue of the Criminal Procedure Reform Act 1974. The existing institution, a figure resembling the French *juge d'instruction*, a judge who is responsible for the investigation,[229] was abolished. According to German criminal procedure, any potential infringement of the right to liberty and security of person, and his right to privacy, cannot be permitted without a court order (§ 162 StPO). The institutionally competent authority at court is the *Ermittlungsrichter* (§ 21e GVG). The system generally operates on two levels: (1) in principle a judge must authorize the interfering action; (2) in urgent cases (*Gefahr im Verzuge*), an order issued by a prosecutor or a senior police officer is sufficient.[230] The legality of the action is subject to scrutiny by the judge; he is not called to address necessity or expediency.[231] The test he applies is twofold: first, he examines whether the legal requirements exist and, secondly, he asks whether or not the demanded action is excessive.[232] That means that, when appreciating all personal and factual circumstances of the individual case, the action has, first, to be relevant (*geeignet*) and necessary (*erforderlich*) to achieve its objective. This would not be the case if less stringent measures (*milderes Mittel*) were sufficient to meet that end. Secondly, the planned interference must be found to be in proportion

---

[228] This is also requested by the Freiburg Declaration on the Position of the Prosecutor of a Permanent ICC, No. 8, repr. in Arbour *et al.*, *The Prosecutor of a Permanent ICC*, 667.

[229] A description of the examining magistrate's role in France can be found in Hatchard *et al.*, *Comparative Criminal Procedure*, 41–2.

[230] As *pars pro toto* may serve the searching of the suspect's house (*Hausdurchsuchung beim Verdächtigen*) §§ 103, 105 StPO.

[231] Compare BVerfG Decision 27 April 1971, in BVerfGE 31, 43.

[232] The Prohibition of Excessive Action (*Übermaßverbot*), also known as the Principle of Proportionality (*Verhältnismäßigkeitsgrundsatz*), is, according to the jurisdiction of the BVerfG (see BVerfG Decision 8 March 1972, in BVerfGE 32, 373, at 379 or BVerfG Decision 31 January 1973, in BVerfGE 34, 238, at 246), a German constitutional principle stemming from the *Rechtstaatsprinzip* applicable to all state action.

to the importance of the case and the degree of suspicion.[233] The interference is judicially reviewable, in all cases. Thus, if special human rights provisions are supposed to be infringed, there must be an independent third person, namely, an 'investigating judge', to review the legality of the interfering action. Only if this person is convinced that the legal conditions are met will he sign the order. This does not create an institutional link between the judge and the prosecuting bodies. He acts purely in a review capacity and has no authority to initiate inquiries himself. He can only act at the request of the prosecutor.[234]

(b) Similar institutions in the USA   The systems of criminal procedure in the USA do not have any equivalent to the Continental investigating judge. However, the inquiring police officer is often dependent on a judge's warrant. This is the case, for example, when the police want to arrest a suspect. A warrant will only be issued by a magistrate, or another duly authorized official, if probable cause that the suspect has committed a felony is found.[235] But there are exceptions to this rule, exceptions that seem to be the rule in terms of quantity. A warrantless arrest is possible whenever a police officer has reasonable grounds to suspect that a felony has occurred and that the prospective arrestee has committed it, or that there are reasons to believe that a felony has occurred and that the perpetrator might escape if not immediately arrested. This is apparently police practice in the majority of cases and was explicitly upheld by the US Supreme Court in *US v Watson*.[236]

A warrant is also theoretically necessary for police search and seizure, as set out in the Fourth Amendment of the US Constitution. Over the last thirty years or so, the scope of the Fourth Amendment has been considerably reduced.[237] Although the court does not play a substantial role in the investigation, I have found that some kind of *ex ante* control over human rights and civil liberties is also recognized in the United States.

(c) Judge's ex ante *control in England and Wales*   The same seems to be true of the English system. Instead of the suspect being arrested and charged, he can be warned for summons and then summoned for trial by the magistrate. Empirical studies show that arrest is the widespread

---

[233] Kleinknecht and Meyer-Goßner, StPO, Einl. 20.

[234] Only in a state of emergency could the investigating judge take action himself, if no prosecutor is available (§ 165 StPO).

[235] Osakwe in Andrews (1982), 267.

[236] US Supreme Court *US v Watson*, 423 US 411 (1976).

[237] e.g. property that had not been described in the warrant was still allowed to be seized (Osakwe in Andrews (1982), 277 with references), although the exclusionary rule, which is often criticized as too strict, declares evidence obtained illegally as inadmissible in trial; see Supreme Court *Silverthrone Lumber Co. v US*, 251 US 385 (1920); see also Ch. 4 below.

practice.[238] Leigh suggests that this is so because arrest is a simpler alternative for the police compared to the complicated system of applying to a magistrate with all the paperwork involved.[239] Furthermore, arrest triggers several other rights like search and seizure, powers for which the police would otherwise need a warrant.[240] The 'proper' avenue according to common law is still the warrant for search and seizure, issued by a magistrate and based on positive law,[241] although both alternatives are foreseen in PACE (1984) ss. 17, 18, and 32. In the English legal system, too, we can find the attitude that important human rights are reliably safeguarded if their observance is reviewed by an independent, judicial authority.

(d) What human rights say about the investigating judge The concept of this third person as an impartial guarantor of human rights during inquiry is rooted in the principle of the separation of powers. The judge's duty is to control the application of democratically established legal rules on behalf of the people.

In human rights treaties we find hints that such procedure is the most appropriate for democratic societies. Art. 9 ICCPR establishes the right to liberty and security of person. In order to ensure that no one is subject to arbitrary arrest or detention, that is, detention that is not justified or not in accordance with procedures established by law, the detainee should be brought before a judge promptly (Art. 9 (III) ICCPR) and be entitled to have his case reviewed by a judicial authority (Art. 9 (IV) ICCPR). The right to liberty and security of person is certainly of paramount importance, as detention virtually prevents enjoyment of liberty. The judge is clearly foreseen by the human rights norm as the controlling authority. What is correct as a remedy after the infringing act has occurred cannot be wrong prior to its occurrence. Indeed, prior review is even safer, as clearly unfounded warrants will not be executed and the person in question will be left unharmed.

In *Funke v France*, this problem came before the ECourtHR[242] in a slightly different context, namely, with respect to the right to privacy in

---

[238] Ashworth, The English criminal process: a Review of Empirical Research, 2.

[239] Leigh in Andrews (1982), 37.

[240] Leigh (ibid. 44) calls this extra power vague and dubious and suspects (ibid. 38) it is another reason for the excessive use of powers of arrest.

[241] This is based on the 18th-century cases: *Leach v Money* (1765) 19 St.Tr. 1001 and *Entice v Carrington* (1765) 19 St.Tr. 1029; cf. L. H. Leigh, *Protection of Human Rights in Criminal Procedure* (Kerala, 1993; hereinafter referred to as Leigh (1993)), 33.

[242] ECourtHR *Funke v France* Judgment 25 February 1993, Series A No. 256-A. It is perhaps surprising that France had to defend warrantless search and seizure before the Court, as it is known to have an *Ermittlungsrichter*, having a Continental system of criminal procedure. However, the case concerned taxation and customs. Traditionally, different laws and rules apply here than in 'ordinary' criminal procedure.

Art. 8 ECHR. The French government argued that the pertinent law, concerning the powers of customs officers to search premises, was strictly supervised by the courts *ex post facto* in a very efficient manner. Furthermore, it argued that Art 8 ECHR does not require judicial authorization in advance of search and seizure.[243] Unfortunately, the ECourtHR did not take issue with the applicant's allegation of breach of the French Constitution. However, if, as the French pleading suggests, *ex post* and *ex ante* control are interchangeable and rest in the discretion of the government, as they are equally efficient and both eliminate arbitrariness, it is remarkable that the French parliament changed the law to *ex ante* authorization after the case was filed.[244] The reasons given for this legislation were that it was intended to provide better protection for individuals.[245] We can thus draw the conclusion that, although the defending government did not consider *ex ante* authorization by a judge obligatory from a human rights point of view, it nevertheless believed it to be a more effective and better guarantee of human rights.

This principle must be applied to all human rights provisions the compliance of which are potentially endangered by the investigation. The court must ensure that the planned act of inquiry is lawful and not arbitrary. Of course, such *ex ante* control must be modified if it would invalidate the effectiveness of the investigation. Here again, a balance must be found between the human rights of individuals and public interest in an effective criminal prosecution system. The only reason why a court warrant might be unnecessary in order to implement what is a justified human rights infringement is that of time; if time is pressing, if, for example, the suspect is likely to destroy evidentiary material or abscond entirely while the judge's signature is being sought, police and prosecutor must have powers to react accordingly without delay. In such cases, court supervision of the lawfulness of the action will consist in *ex post* control.

The allegation that judges merely rubber-stamp the police request[246] is a serious and, certainly, valid criticism. However, it addresses the practice and not the theoretical structure. First, judges do not blindly sign any application by the police. Secondly, the effect on the police should not be underestimated. Police officers will probably be more cautious, and commit fewer human rights infringements, if they have to justify their actions in writing.

---

[243] Ibid. para. 50.

[244] Budget Acts from 30 December 1986 and 29 December 1989.

[245] See ECourtHR *Funke v France*, paras. 29 and 50. The ECourtHR did not comment on this issue, as it had already found a violation; it held that the law authorizing the interference did not provide for sufficient restrictions and limitations, ibid., para. 57.

[246] See e.g. the Royal Commission 1981 para. 3.37; K. Lidstone and C. Palmer, *Bevan and Lidstone's The Investigation of Crime* (2nd edn. London, 1996), para. 4.08.

In sum, the role of the court during the stage of investigation of a crime would be to supervise actions by the investigating authority that might infringe human rights and to ensure that human rights are carefully observed.

(e) The ICTY system   The Statute of the ICTY does not assign any function to the judge during the investigation. Art. 18 (IV) Statute ICTY brings the judge into play only to review the indictment, that is, after the investigation has come to an end. Rules 39 and 40 of the Rules of Procedure address the conduct of investigation. In very broad terms, Rule 39 (ii) gives the prosecutor the power to 'undertake such . . . matters as may appear necessary for completing the investigation'. This is connected with Rule 39 (iv), which empowers the prosecutor to 'request such orders as may be necessary from a Trial Chamber or a Judge'. It is submitted here that these two paragraphs should be read in conjunction with each other. Any measure that endangers human rights needs authorization from a judge.[247] Rule 40 addresses provisional measures; in case of emergency, the prosecutor may request that a state take certain measures against a suspect, for example, arrest, seizure, and so forth. The requested state must comply with this order in accordance with its own law in respect of human rights.

Rule 54 is also of interest here. A judge or a Trial Chamber may issue any orders, summonses, subpoenas, warrants, and transfer orders necessary for the purposes of an investigation or for preparation of the trial. The difference in the scope of application of this provision as compared with that of Rule 39 is hard to discern. While the latter is included in the section about the inquiry, the former is included in provisions governing the regulation of pre-trial proceedings. The difference lies in the fact that the former addresses preparation of the indictment, whilst the latter is directed at the preparation of the trial after the indictment has been issued. Nevertheless, the prosecutor has occasionally sought orders pursuant to both rules simultaneously.[248] President Cassese elaborated on this issue when ruling on a prosecutor's motion in the *Celebici* case.[249] He treated Rules 39 (iv) and 54 as a joint concept, to be subject to the following twofold test: (1) an order must be issued by the ICTY for the prosecutor to obtain such material; and (2) the material sought must be relevant to an investigation or prosecution being conducted by the prosecutor. The

---

[247] Arguably, this is not the view of Bassiouni, *The Law of the ICTY*, 872–5, who does not mention Rule 39 (iv), but is of the opinion that the Statute ICTY clearly follows the adversarial system, where supervision by a judge is not *usus*.

[248] Compare Jones, *The Practice of the ICTY and ICTR*, Rule 39, 253.

[249] Decision 11 November 1996 of the President on the Prosecutor's Motion for the Production of Notes Exchanged Between Zejnil Delalic and Zdravko Mucic, Case No. IT-96-21-T.

prosecutor's request will only be granted if he provides material that establishes a sufficient degree of probability that these criteria are met.[250]

We can thus see that the prosecutor is subject to considerable *ex ante* supervision on the part of the judges when requesting orders and warrants. The judges will not merely rubber-stamp any motion made by the prosecutor.

Since the Eighteenth Plenary Session on 9–10 July 1998, the Rules of Procedure and Evidence have embodied a provision relating to the pre-trial judge in Rule 65*ter*. Although it refers to the civil law 'juge d'instruction' (*Ermittlungsrichter*),[251] the norm is systematically only applicable to the stage after the indictment (Chapter 3 below). The pre-trial judge, whose appointment is dependent on the decision of the Trial Chamber in each individual case, seems to serve mainly as an instructor or director of communications in complicated and lengthy trials. He therefore does not merely control the prosecutor judicially. His main advantage lies in the acceleration of the second stage of the proceedings, from confirmation of the indictment to commencement of trial.

(f) The ICC Art. 58 (I) Rome Statute, like its predecessor Art. 28 (I) Statute ILC, envisages *ex ante* supervision of provisional arrest of the suspect. The Pre-Trial Chamber (before the Presidency) may, at the request of the prosecutor, issue an arrest warrant.[252] Furthermore, Art. 58 (VII) Rome Statute, like Art. 26 (III) Statute ILC, gives the power of issuing warrants and subpoenas to the Pre-Trial Chamber upon request by the prosecutor. Art. 91 and 92 Rome Statute, like Art. 51 to 53 Statute ILC, deal with cooperation of the states with the ICC. Measures taken by the states in order to meet the request are to be implemented in accordance with national law.

(IV) The Defence

Faced with the entire machinery of the state authorities and police powers, the suspect might appear a little defenceless, but at least he apparently has the right to counsel or a legal assistant (Art. 14 III b ICCPR, Art. 6 III c ECHR, Art. 8 II d AmCHR, Art 7 I c AfCHPR). According to human rights treaties, however, this right is once again only applicable to someone 'charged with a criminal offence'. When exactly does this right come into existence?

---

[250] Morris and Scharf, *An Insider's Guide*, 195, who refer to the Fourth Amendment of the US Constitution. As we have seen above (5a), a similar test is applied by the German authorities.

[251] Jones, *The Practice at the ICTY*, Rule 65*ter*, 332.

[252] Behrens, 6 Eur.J.Crime Cr.L.Cr.J. (1998), 432–33.

I have already looked at the problem of determination of the scope of application. According to the EcourtHR, the provision is applicable as soon as the suspect is substantially affected by the allegations.[253] Consequently, the right to legal assistance would arise the first time the suspect is confronted with the allegation. During interrogation by the police, the suspect would then already have the right to counsel.

1. The right to counsel

Generally speaking, this is the practice in most Western legal systems.

(a) The German system   In Germany, this right is guaranteed in the StPO. According to §§ 163 (IV), 136 (I) StPO, the suspect has the right to consult an attorney before being interrogated by the police. However, at this stage, the attorney does not have a right to be present during interrogation, although he may be admitted and, if so, he has a right to intervene for the purpose of counselling and questioning and is not restricted to the role of mere observer.[254] When his client is questioned by the prosecutor, the counsel has a right to be present according to §§ 163a (III), 168c (I) StPO. The system operates on two levels; first, the police have the power to interrogate, then they transfer the files to the prosecutor, who reviews and weighs the evidence and prepares the indictment. The interrogation by the police more or less seems to play the role of a preliminary measure. It is called the 'first interrogation' by the police (*erste Vernehmung*) and the suspect cannot be compelled to appear. His presence can only be compelled for the interrogation conducted by the prosecutor.[255] This explains why treatment of the counselling lawyer is different in the two situations. As the suspect is, at least in theory, voluntarily participating in the police interrogation, there is no obligation to admit counsel to the interrogation room. However, as he may be forced to attend the interrogation by the prosecutor, counsel's presence must be allowed.[256]

(b) The Anglo-American tradition   In England and Wales a compulsory right to counsel at the pre-trial stage was introduced for the first time by s. 58 of PACE (1984); this provision replaced the former one of the Judges' Rules which awarded the right to a solicitor only if it was not likely to cause unreasonable delay or hindrance of the process of investigation or

---

[253] See above Ch. 2 A I 1.

[254] See Kleinknecht and Meyer-Goßner, StPO, § 163 No. 16.

[255] BGH Judgment 26 November 1992, BGHSt 39, 96.

[256] This difference is not clearly carved out in Hatchard *et al.*, *Comparative Criminal Procedure*, 228, which creates the impression that the presence of counsel during investigation is entirely at the discretion of the interrogating police. It clearly is not, for the reasons given. In practice, the police will usually permit defence counsel to be present.

the administration of justice.[257] This weak formulation had certainly given the police investigators carte blanche.[258] The situation is now radically different. Only in exceptional circumstances, as spelt out in s. 58 PACE, can the right to consult a solicitor be denied. Denial would be possible if the suspicion concerns a serious arrestable offence and the delay is authorized by an officer of at least the rank of superintendent. Circumstances permitting, denial of the rights to a solicitor might be justified by the fact that either evidence or other persons might be harmed, or other persons connected with the crime unduly alerted.[259] Mere fear that the solicitor might advise the suspect to remain silent[260] cannot be sufficient reason to refuse the right to a solicitor.[261] To facilitate access to a solicitor, a duty solicitor scheme was introduced in Britain in 1986.[262]

In the United States, the right to counsel is embodied in the Sixth Amendment to the Constitution. This right is understood to apply to every critical step of the proceedings, not only the trial stage but also pre-trial proceedings. According to the case-law of the US Supreme Court, the right to counsel applies in particular to all in-custody pre-trial examinations,[263] and increases in importance as soon as a person is in custody or otherwise deprived of freedom of action in any significant way, unless that person 'voluntarily, knowingly and intelligently' waives the right.[264] The lower limit for applicability is the initiation of any kind of adversary judicial proceedings.[265] It might be said that the right to counsel comes into play when the suspect is 'substantially affected' by the activity of the prosecuting bodies, which makes the similarity with the jurisprudence of the ECourtHR obvious.

---

[257] For a short summary of the historical development of the right to a solicitor in England and Wales, see McConville *et al.*, *Standing Accused*, 72–6. The former Judges' Rules were not really supervised *ex post* by courts; e.g. a confession was only excluded if it was considered unreliable, despite having been obtained in breach of the rules, see *Reg. v Elliott* [1977] CrimLR, 551.

[258] Emmins, 21.5.3. In the first scientific study on police interrogation, McConville *et al.*, *Standing Accused*, give empirical evidence that this event is even now generally seen by both police and solicitor as an inter-subjective matter solely involving the police officer and suspect.

[259] Compare Emmins, 21.5.3, and s. 58 PACE. The reasons for the refusal must be given and added to the custody record.

[260] This advice is by no means the most common advice given to persons interrogated by solicitors at police stations. See McConville *et al.*, *Standing Accused*, 104–8.

[261] *Alladice* [1988] 87 Crim.App.R. 380.

[262] The efficiency of this duty solicitor scheme has been widely criticized. Because it is notoriously underfunded, good solicitors refuse to cooperate with the scheme and participating solicitors are often negligent and content to give advice over the telephone. Compare Leigh (1993), 53–4.

[263] US Supreme Court *Escobedo v Illinois*, 378 US 478 (1964) and already mentioned in *Powell v Alabama (The Scottsboro Boys case)* 287 US 45 (1932).

[264] US Supreme Court *Miranda v Arizona*, 384 US 436 (1966); cf. also Osakwe, in Andrews (1982), 259 at 280–1.

[265] US Supreme Court *Kirby v. Illinois*, 406 US 682 (1972).

(c) Human rights law   The above look at the national systems leads us to the underlying rationale for granting a right to a solicitor at this early stage, long before the court hearing begins. The defendant before the court is helpless in the face of the professional court lawyers, who apply a strict codex of procedural rules when discussing his guilt and future fate. It is therefore a matter of 'equality of arms' that he, too, should be assisted by an experienced lawyer.[266] In addition, counsel may also serve as guarantor of procedural regularity.[267] A similar problem arises in the pre-trial stage of police interrogation. Notwithstanding the fact that the police caution the suspect, he is still in the position of an *extraneus* facing the police, who know the rules and govern the questioning. Furthermore, the interrogee is always in a situation of mental stress. A third person present during interrogation can challenge and perhaps prevent coercive measures.[268] Lastly, the safeguarding of human rights during the pre-trial stage is important because the whole inquiry is intended to determine the legal and factual basis for trial by obtaining evidence and preparing court procedure. The foundations for potential conviction are being laid here. It is a crucial stage for the suspect.[269] Rightly Nsereko holds that '[u]nless this right [i.e. the right to counsel] is recognised to operate at this stage [i.e. the pre-trial stage], it would have little significance to the accused later on, because the fate of a criminal case is usually determined by what goes on at the pretrial interrogation sessions'.[270] Therefore, already at this stage, the suspect must be assisted by legal counsel.[271]

It is an interesting point that the ECHR does not mention the 'right to counsel' in its text. The ECourtHR and ECommHR do concede, however, that the right to legal assistance is implicitly embodied in the Convention's text.[272] Art. 6 (III) c ECHR creates a sufficient basis for a

---

[266] Compare ECommHR *X v FRG* Appl. No. 10098/82, 8 EHRR (1984), 225.

[267] Compare ECommHR *Ensslin, Baader and Rape v FRG* Decision 8 July 1978, Appl. Nos. 7572/76, 7586/76, 7587/76, 14 DR, 64 at 114.

[268] See Stavros, *Guarantees*, 56.

[269] Compare ECourtHR *Quaranta v Switzerland* Judgment 24 May 1991, Series A No. 25, para. 67, and, ECommHR *Can v Austria* Report 12 July 1984, Series A No. 96, p. 17, para. 52, and ECommHR *Murray v UK* Report 27 June 1994, 22 EHRR (1996), 29 at para. 69.

[270] Nsereko, 5 Criminal Law Forum (1994), 507 at 524.

[271] Philips Commission, para. 4.89. Compare also Emmins, 21.5.3; McConville *et al.*, *Standing Accused*, 274–82, who concede that the English system, which even separates the pre-trial from the trial stage institutionally by the use of barristers and solicitors, traditionally focuses on rights at the trial stage and therefore tends to underestimate the importance of pre-trial protection for the defendant.

[272] However, they seem to disagree on the actual location of this provision. Whilst the Commission favours Art. 6 (III) b and c ECHR (*Can v Austria* Decision 12 July 1984, Series A No. 96), the Court considers that it is laid down in Art. 6 (III) c ECHR only (*S v Switzerland* Judgment 28 November 1991 unpublished, cited in Stavros, *Guarantees*, 57).

right to counsel that is applicable throughout the proceedings.[273] It is widely accepted that the ECHR guarantees the right to a lawyer.[274]

The IAmCourtHR had to judge several cases concerning deprivation of liberty, mostly in connection with forced disappearances. The Court found, that '[p]rolonged and coercive isolation is by nature, cruel and inhumane treatment, harmful to the mental and moral integrity of the person and the right to dignity inherent to the human being. Thus it also violates article 5 of the Convention.'[275] The HRC has stated on several occasions that the right to counsel must be safeguarded during pre-trial interrogations. The HRC condemns incommunicado detention on two grounds: first, because it is in breach of Art. 10 (I) ICCPR and, second, because it hinders the preparation of defence at a critical stage of the prosecution.[276] The fact that the HRC is also concerned about the accessibility of legal counsel during preliminary proceedings becomes clear from the discussions on State Reports summarized by McGoldrick.[277] In its General Comment the HRC even connected incommunicado detention to torture and inhumane treatment[278] and has repeated this opinion several times.[279]

Art. 14 (III) b ICCPR must therefore be understood in a broad manner; the right to counsel begins with the pre-trial inquiry at the police station and is particularly relevant when the individual is being held in pre-trial detention.[280] This is the only way through which the dignity of the individual can be protected against the enormous potential threat and pressure he encounters when facing the huge machinery of the investigating authorities.

(d) The Law of the ICTY The Statute of the ICTY reiterates the text of Art. 14 ICCPR almost verbatim when it comes to speaking about the rights of the accused. As concerns the right to counsel, Art. 21 Statute ICTY is therefore

---

[273] See also ECourtHR *Campbell and Fell v UK* Judgement from 28 June 1984, Series A No. 80, para. 99.

[274] Compare *Quaranta v Switzerland, S v Switzerland*, Harris, 256, Frowein and Peukert, Art. 6 No. 187. Stavros states very cautiously at *Guarantees*, 56: 'The Commission appears to be gradually accepting' the applicability of the right to counsel in all legal orders.

[275] IAmCourtHR, *Fairén Garbi and Solís Corrales* cases Judgment 15 March 1989, Series C No. 6 (1989), para. 149.

[276] HRC *Caldas v Uruguay*, Doc. A/38/40, 192, similarly in *Machado v Uruguay*, Doc. A/38/40, 148.

[277] D. McGoldrick, *The Human Rights Committee* (2nd edn. Oxford, 1994), 406.

[278] HRC General Comment 7 (Article 7), para. 1.

[279] Recently the HRC criticized incommunicado detention in Spain (HRC Comments on Spain, UN Doc. CCPR/C/79/Add.61 (1996), para. 18, concerning terrorist cases) and in Peru (HRC Comments on Peru, UN Doc. CCPR/C/79/Add.67 (1996), para. 17).

[280] See Nowak, Art. 14 No. 42. The explicit reference to a right to communicate with counsel was adapted by the Third Committee 14th Session on a motion by Israel (A/C.3/L.795/Rev.3); see A/4299, §§ 56, 63.

not any clearer than the human rights provisions just discussed. Art. 18 (III) Statute ICTY grants a right to counsel to the suspect. The Rules of Procedure are even more telling in this regard. Rule 42 names a number of rights of suspects during investigation. Rule 42A (i) gives to the suspect 'the right to be assisted by counsel of his choice or to have legal assistance assigned to him without payment if he does not have sufficient means to pay for it'. Interrogation of the suspect may not proceed unless counsel is present or the suspect has voluntarily waived his right to counsel. This waiver can be revoked at any time. In such cases, interrogation must cease and may only be continued when counsel is present (Rule 42B). Because of these clear provisions, Bassiouni sees the law at the ICTY as providing greater protection than both US law and the ICCPR.[281] One former shortcoming of the practice at the ICTY was the fact that only one counsel was assigned to accused persons who did not have the means to pay for legal assistance.[282] The ICTY recognized this flaw and changed its practice, for example in the *Tadic* and *Djukic* cases.[283] What has also been criticized, and is certainly problematic in all domestic legal systems, too, is the professional fee the UN are willing to pay.[284]

According to the interpretation of human rights proposed here, the right to counsel is applicable before a formal 'charge' is issued, so that Art. 14 (III) d ICCPR actually provides for a 'right to counsel' at the prosecutor's office. This has been rigorously transferred to the law of the ICTY.

(e) The Statute of the ICC   The right to prompt access to a lawyer has not been clearly incorporated in the Draft Statute ICC, which has provoked criticism.[285] However, Art. 41 (I) b Statute ILC repeats the words of Art. 14 (III) b ICCPR. As stated above, this right must be applied from the beginning of the prosecution and not only at the stage of the trial. In order to comply with human rights, Art. 26 (VI) a ii Statute ILC puts the onus on the prosecutor to inform the suspect prior to interrogation that he has the right to assistance from counsel of his own choosing or, if he cannot afford this, to have legal assistance assigned to him by the ICC.[286] The ILC incorporated this right because it was of the opinion that it was too late to

---

[281] Bassiouni, *The Law of the ICTY*, 876.

[282] Sjöcrona, 8 LJIL (1995), 463 at 467, criticizes this as totally inadequate, because it forces the assigned counsel to withdraw from his 'normal' cases and his regular clients and income, in order to handle the difficult cases of international criminal law.

[283] Compare ICTY Third Annual Report (1996), para. 106.

[284] Sjöcrona, 8 LJIL (1995), 463 at 467–8, alleges that the fees paid per day amount to about half of what a specialized Dutch advocate earns per hour. Perhaps it would be a good idea, for a change, to give some thought to the question of whether advocates' fees might not be excessive.

[285] Lawyers' Committee for Human Rights, International Criminal Court Briefing Series, Vol. I, No. 2, 2.

[286] Compare Report ILC Art. 26, para. 5.

provide for counsel only at the trial stage.[287] The Statute ILC thus appears to be compatible with human rights in this regard, although the right to counsel could be addressed more clearly.[288] The PrepComm has discussed proposals in this regard and has found it necessary to elaborate further on the suspect's rights. In its report, it proposes a concrete right to legal assistance.[289] The Rome Statute contains a provision on the 'Rights of persons during an investigation' (Art. 55 Rome Statute). It thus pays more attention to the situation of the suspect. Art. 55 (II) c Rome Statute stresses that the suspect shall have the right to legal assistance when being questioned.[290] The Pre-Trial Chamber supervises the suspect's rights (Art. 57 (III) c Rome Statute).[291] Hence the shortcomings of the Statute ILC are remedied in this regard.

2. Qualifications of counsels

Perusal of human rights provisions concerning counsel reveals different terms that refer to the 'assistant'. Art. 14 (III) d ICCPR speaks of legal assistance, as does Art. 6 (III) c ECHR, while Art. 14 (III) b ICCPR speaks of a 'counsel of his own choosing', as does Art. 7 (I) c AfCHPR; Art. 8 (II) e AmCHR, however, specifies him as 'legal counsel'. These differences must be reconciled. What qualifications are demanded by human rights provisions for 'assistants' of suspects? Is the practice of compulsory representation by a lawyer, common to most Western criminal systems, compatible with human rights?

(a) Interpretation of the applicable human rights provisions   As it stands, the term 'legal assistance' does not necessarily mean assistance in the form of a lawyer. It refers, instead, to assistance in the legal conduct of the case.[292] So these norms appear to say that the suspect may call any person he trusts to his assistance.

It seems clear, however, that every suspect has the right to counsel of his own choosing, if he has the necessary means. He must be given this possibility at all costs.[293] But may certain qualifications be required by the state? May the state even require that the assistant be from the legal profession? Harris argues that the drafting history of Art. 14 ICCPR shows that representation was not intended to be limited to that provided

---

[287] Ibid. para. 6.   [288] See also Amnesty International IOR 40/05/94, 34.
[289] Report of the PrepComm II, 116.
[290] Hall, in Triffterer (ed.), *Commentary on the Rome Statute*, Art. 55, No. 13.
[291] Behrens, 6 Eur.J.Crime Cr.L.Cr.J. (1998), 431. Guariglia and Harris in Triffterer (ed.), *Commentary on the Rome Statute*, Art. 57, No. 14, do not mention Art. 55 Rome Statute in this respect.
[292] Compare Harris, 16 ICLQ (1967) 352 at 364, n. 62, with reference to the drafting history of the ICCPR.
[293] Frowein and Peukert, Art. 6 No. 192.

by lawyers.[294] The HRC, on the other hand, ruled against a government that appointed a defence counsel who was not a lawyer. In the Committee's view, the defendant was deprived of his right to adequate legal assistance in preparing his defence.[295]

Strictly speaking, the state already interferes by regulating the way in which the legal profession is organized. This may be justified by the necessity to guarantee a certain ethical code and professionalism for jurists. States also have a tendency not to admit lawyers as representatives of political criminals or members of minorities if they are known to be sympathetic to such political dissidents[296] or minorities. Lawyers might even be threatened with criminal prosecution themselves if they are suspected of bias and thus fail to fulfil their duty as a lawyer to remain independent and objective. Although these practices are widely tolerated by the European human rights bodies, Stavros heavily criticizes this approach and argues in favour of a change in policy: 'wide and imprecisely formulated grounds, such as "disrespect for the trial court", should be automatically excluded' and 'special domestic criminal laws regulating counsel's conduct in the proceedings should be viewed with caution, if not suspicion'.[297]

Once more, the test must be based on what is necessary in a democratic society. In this context, 'democratic society' refers, more precisely, to the functioning of the judicial system and the interests of justice. Non-admittance of lawyers on the basis of their personal, political inclination may seem contrary to basic principles of a democratic society. As long as there is no clear proof that the lawyer chosen by the suspect is actually violating his professional obligations, he must be admitted as counsel.[298] Similar concerns are expressed by members of the HRC when discussing state reports. With regard to Guinea, Tomuschat pointed out that legal counsel for the defendant must consist of an independent lawyer. If defence counsel is a public official, proper administration of the rights of the defendant is jeopardized.[299]

---

[294] Harris, 16 ICLQ (1967) 352 at 364, especially n. 62, pointing to Muslim law and cases judged according to native tribal law and custom which might cause difficulty if legal representation is insisted on.   [295] HRC *Vasilskis v Uruguay* Doc. A/38/40, 173.

[296] Compare e.g. ECommHR Appl. No. 509/59 3 YB, 174, concerning a case in Germany where a solicitor sympathizing with the illegal organization Freie Deutsche Jugend (FDJ) was not allowed to represent a member of this organization in court. See in this connection, Harris, 16 ICLQ (1967), 352 at 366. Other cases quoted in Stavros, *Guarantees*, 205–6, revealing the wide margin of appreciation left to the states by the European authorities.

[297] Stavros, *Guarantees*, 206, see also 221.

[298] If applied restrictively, the German regulation in § 138 a StPO would be compatible with this test, although it contains a special provision for political crimes. Generally speaking, the lawyer can be excluded only if there is strong suspicion that he has participated in the crime.

[299] SR 475 para. 50. The Guinea report is to be found as Doc. CCPR/C/6/Add.5 (1980). Cf. also McGoldrick, *Human Rights Committee*, 408.

Another restriction becomes apparent in complex and protracted cases in particular: the restriction in the number of those providing assistance.[300] Stavros finds this beyond criticism, as long as the restriction is generally applied. In some cases, however, this restriction in number nevertheless seems doubtful. Above all in complicated cases, for example, in the field of economic crimes, three lawyers might not be enough, as various specialists are necessary. The same might be true of international crimes; international criminal law is a relatively new field of uncodified law, also poor in case-law, especially as regards general principles. Several specialists might well be needed. It seems odd, with regard to the principle of 'equality of arms', that the prosecutor's office does not face similar restrictions.

A second statement of Art. 14 ICCPR is clear in principle: if the suspect does not have sufficient means, he will receive free legal assistance, if the interests of justice so require. This principle comes into force in cases involving difficult legal or factual issues. In most countries, this means that legal representation becomes compulsory before higher courts, as such cases are automatically referred to them.[301] This inherent generalization of dissimilar cases seems unproblematic from a human rights perspective for the following reason: as the lower court can only impose a minor sentence,[302] the risk of abuse, in the sense that the case is deliberately discussed at a lower court in order to deprive the indigent defendant of legal counsel, becomes negligible. The ECourtHR emphasized that such representation must be an effective one, in *Artico v Italy*. In this case the assigned lawyer could not represent the applicant and no substitute was ever formally appointed despite numerous requests; the ECourtHR therefore found a violation of Art. 6 (III) C ECHR.[303]

But if human rights treaties speak of a 'right to counsel', do they not also imply the flip-side, that is, the freedom not to be represented by a lawyer? Should this not be even more the case, given that human rights norms under scrutiny here speak of a right to defend oneself in person?

---

[300] ECommHR *Ensslin, Baader and Rape v FRG* Decision 8 July 1978, Appl. Nos. 7572/76, 7586/76, 7587/76, 14 DR, 64 at 114. In Germany the defendant is only allowed at most three counsels, see § 137 (I) StPO.

[301] The German criminal system requires legal representation from the Landgericht (Regional Court) upwards, § 140 StPO. Yet in the English system the persuasion that the defendant has to be allowed to defend himself in person, if he so wishes, is prevalent. This becomes particularly difficult in cases concerning rape or involving children witnesses. I will discuss this at the trial stage.

[302] In Germany, the Amtsgericht can inflict a maximum penalty of four years' imprisonment; see §§ 24, 74 GVG, but a single judge only has the power to imprison for a maximum term of two years, § 25 GVG. The English Magistrates' Court can only impose a sentence of up to twelve months, see Emmins, 13.3, ss. 31, 32, and 123 Magistrates' Courts Act (1980).

[303] ECourtHR *Artico v Italy* Judgment 13 May 1980, Series A No. 37.

In *Croissant v FRG*, the ECourtHR[304] found '[t]he requirement that a defendant be assisted by counsel . . .—which finds parallels in the legislation of other Contracting States—cannot, in the Court's opinion, be deemed incompatible with the Convention'. In this case, Mr Croissant was himself a lawyer, facing criminal prosecution because of his connections with and representation of members of the Rote Armee Fraktion, RAF ('Red Army Faction'). The Landgericht (Regional Court) Stuttgart appointed two lawyers of his own choosing to represent him in court and a third lawyer whom he opposed as redundant and personally unsuitable. The ECourtHR held that the appointment of several defence counsels is not in itself incompatible with the Convention, and 'may indeed be called for in specific cases in the interest of justice'.[305] Nevertheless, the interests of the defendant must be taken into account, especially as he will have to bear the costs in case of a conviction. The Court may, however, appoint lawyers against the wishes of the defendant, if this is necessary to provide for adequate representation throughout the trial, as was the case here according to the ECourtHR.[306] Two consequences must be drawn therefrom; first, according to the ECourtHR, the 'right to counsel' does not entail the right to repudiate legal representation and, second, the right to free choice of counsel is not absolute but dependent on approval by the court. Both restrictions find their justification in the requirement of the interests of justice.

It could be argued that the different systems of criminal procedure require their own specific standards of legal representation.[307] The Continental court system, with the inquiring judge, carries an obligation to be procedurally responsible for the defendant (*richterliche Fürsorgepflicht*). The English judge, completely separate and somewhat 'retreated' from the parties, naturally does not advise and question the defendant. In England, the defendant would be a helplessly lost figure, unable to defend himself against the prosecution, if he did not have the defence counsel at his side, whereas the defendant on the Continent faces the judge who arguably only wants his best. Clearly, this is not the real situation and, as practice shows, the Continental judge often sides with the prosecutor, with the two of them appearing, in crass cases, almost as one party.[308] A distinction should therefore not be made between the two systems with regard to the necessity of legal counsel for the defendant.

Let us now sum up the principles that we have found: legal assistance must be granted, if so desired, and paid for by the defendant. The free

---

[304] ECourtHR *Croissant v FRG* Judgment 25 September 1992, Series A No. 237-B, para. 27.
[305] Ibid.   [306] Ibid. para. 28.
[307] Nowak Art. 14, Nos. 48–9, apparently seems to make this point.
[308] Compare Schünemann, *Verfahrensgerechtigkeit* (1995), 215.

choice of the defendant may be limited, if the interests of justice so require. In a democratic society, this must be interpreted restrictively. If the defendant cannot afford counsel, legal assistance must be granted free of cost, if the interests of justice so require.

(b) Law and practice at the ICTY   The law at the ICTY addresses the question of the qualification and appointment of counsel in Rules 44 to 46. Obviously, several additional requirements must be met, due to the international character of the tribunal. Rule 45A therefore lays down as a necessary precondition the ability to speak at least one of the tribunal's working languages.[309] Rule 45A was amended during the Eleventh Plenary Meeting of the ICTY, 25 June 1996: under special circumstances, a counsel may be assigned who speaks neither of the ICTY working languages but the language of the client. Prior to the amendment, Erdemovic had made a request to be assigned counsel who did not speak either of the ICTY languages. This request was supported by the prosecutor and granted by Judge Jorda on 28 May 1996. In the proceedings against Erdemovic, this led to major and fatal difficulties, as the assigned counsel misunderstood the effect of a guilty plea, which had to be rectified on appeal by granting a replea.[310] Repetition of such an unfortunate development could easily be prevented by abolishing the plea procedure altogether.[311]

In contrast to many national jurisdictions (like Germany), the counsel is not, however, assigned by the judge but by the Registry. This has a number of major advantages from a human rights' point of view. If assignment is effected by an administrative organ not present in the court room, there is less danger of the judge choosing advocates who will cause the least trouble rather than advocates that benefit the suspect most. The Registry is called upon in Rule 45A to keep a list of qualified advocates who have indicated their willingness to represent war criminals. It has done so in close consultation with the judges and lawyers from the various bar associations and has also proposed regulations concerning the status and conduct of assigned counsel, calculation and payment of fees and disbursements. It has furthermore established an advisory panel.[312]

There are no other grounds on which counsel may be excluded apart from misconduct during the proceedings. The Chamber may, in such cases, and after warnings, 'refuse audience' to counsel (Rule 46A), or even complain to the disciplinary authority of the person who has misbehaved (Rule 46B).

---

[309] See Jones, *The Practice of the ICTY*, Rule 45, 262.
[310] ICTY Appeals Chamber *Prosecutor v Erdemovic* 7 October 1997, Case No. IT-96-22-A, and the Trial Chamber II *Prosecutor v Erdemovic* 5 March 1998, Case No. IT 96-22-T.
[311] The guilty plea will be discussed in Ch. 4 p. 272 et subs. below.
[312] ICTY, Second Annual Report (1995), paras. 96–7.

(c) Proposal for an ICC   If the above principles are transferred to the international context, it is obvious that legal counsel must be granted under all circumstances (Art. 55 (II) c Rome Statute).[313] As the defendant faces the most serious allegations and the severest punishments, the interests of justice always require that legal counsel be assigned. The right to defend oneself in person may be restricted likewise in the interests of justice because of the complexity and the length of the procedure.

The Draft Rules contain several requirements with regard to the qualifications of counsel (Draft Rule 5.3): counsel shall have competence and experience in international or criminal law and procedure and be fluent in one of the working languages of the ICC. The Registrar will maintain a list of potential counsel who meet the criteria (Draft Rule 5.2 II). The ICC will establish a code of professional conduct for counsel (Draft Rule YY).

B. QUESTIONING BY THE INVESTIGATION

The very first contact with the police that suspects, whether innocent or not, and witnesses have is when they are interrogated after a crime has occurred.[314] This can take place in many ways: it may be carried out in the street, a frequent practice, for example, after road accidents; at the home of the person being questioned, for example after a robbery in the victim's house; or lastly, at the police station, which is mostly the case if a longer statement is required and the case is possibly on the point of being solved. The police will probably prefer the latter because of the relatively coercive atmosphere.[315] Several human rights may be at stake here. First, the freedom of movement (Art. 2 Prot. 4 ECHR) seems to be involved. When the police stop citizens on the street or the latter are requested to accompany a police officer to the station, without arrest, this would seem to interfere with a person's freedom to walk around in peace. This right, as laid down in Art. 2 Prot. 4 ECHR must be distinguished from the right to liberty and security of person as found in Art. 5 ECHR.[316] The difference lies in the 'deprivation of liberty'. Only if the person is actually detained can one speak of Art. 5 ECHR being triggered.[317] The ECourtHR distinguishes

---

[313] See Hall in Trifterer (ed.), *Commentary on the Rome Statute*, Art. 55, No. 14.

[314] C. Osakwe, in Andrews (1982), 259 at 267, sees arrest as a citizen's first contact with the criminal justice system. In my view, it is usually preceded by some form of questioning. No matter which of these two views is empirically correct, the questioning is the broader and less serious measure, because it not only involves the suspect but also witnesses, lasts for a relatively short time only, and does not necessarily involve detention. For these reasons, the questioning comes before detention.

[315] Leigh in Andrews (1982), 37.

[316] Harris, 560.

[317] Compare hereto the case at the ECourtHR *Guzzardi v Italy*, Series A No. 39.

between the two articles on the basis of the degree or intensity and not the nature or substance of the case.[318] This must be considered with regard to the type, duration, effects, and manner of implementation of the measures in question.[319] For the present, I wish to focus on the interrogation. I will differentiate between the questioning of suspects and witnesses, whose protection seems to be of major importance in international criminal law.

(I) Questioning of the Suspect

The guilty party is surely the most sought-after person during the whole inquiry—to find the offender is the whole aim of the investigation. A statement from the suspect, at best a confession, could change, accelerate, or perhaps even end the prosecutor's efforts. To make the suspect confess, after having found him, is the first wish of every investigator. There is one obstacle in the investigator's path that may have devastating consequences for the prosecutor's case: the suspect cannot be forced to talk, indeed he has a right to remain silent. This principle, also known as *nemo tenetur se ipsum prodere*, is expressed in different ways in human rights treaties:

Art. 14 ICCPR
(III) (g) not to be compelled to testify against himself or to confess guilt

Art. 8 AmCHR
(II) (g) the right not to be compelled to be a witness against himself or to plead guilty;
(III) A confession of guilt by the accused shall be valid only if it is made without coercion of any kind.

The ECHR does not include an explicit reference to this right. However, the case-law of the ECourtHR shows that the right to remain silent and not incriminate oneself is part of the overall maxim of a 'fair trial'. The ECourtHR confirmed this recently in *Funke v France*,[320] *Saunders v UK*,[321] and *Murray v UK*.[322]

I am of the opinion that, before a suspect can be questioned by the police or any other investigating authority, he must be duly informed of the allegation, the reasons therefor, and his right to silence. Below, I will discuss how these provisions follow on from human rights treaties and from international and domestic practice.

---

[318] ECourtHR *Guzzardi v Italy*, para. 93.
[319] Ibid., para. 91. Guzzardi was actually held in a hamlet under curfew and not, as one would expect, behind bars in a prison cell. The ECourtHR held nevertheless that he was 'detained' and that Art. 5 ECHR was applicable and in this case even violated—rightly so.
[320] ECourtHR *Funke v France*, Series A No. 256-A.
[321] ECourtHR *Saunders v UK* Judgment 17 December 1996, 23 EHRR (1997), 313.
[322] ECourtHR *Murray v UK* 22 EHRR (1996), 29.

1. Notification of the charge

The suspect can only profit from the freedom from self-incrimination if he is made aware of the fact that he is under suspicion and in a situation where this right is likely to be jeopardized. In other words, the suspect must be duly informed that he is actually under suspicion, and specifically that he is being questioned for this reason, and the allegations against him must also be disclosed to him.

In Art. 14 (III) a ICCPR, Art. 6 (III) a and Art. 8 (II) b AmCHR, we find similar wording to describe the right to be informed promptly and in detail 'of the nature and cause of the charge against him'. A similar provision is found in the articles governing the liberty and security of persons, for example, Art. 9 (II) ICCPR and Art. 5 (II) ECHR, which also states that the detained must be informed promptly of the reasons for his detention. However, the differences between the norms are clear: liberty and security of person are only concerned with the act of detention. The detainee must be put in a position where he can challenge the lawfulness of his detention. The person suspected of a criminal offence needs to prepare his defence against the criminal allegations.[323] Art. 9 (II) ICCPR therefore targets Art. 9 (IV) ICCPR, which guarantees a possibility for the detained of challenging the lawfulness of his detention. Art. 14 (III) a ICCPR serves to ensure the right to prepare the defence as laid down in Art. 14 (III) b ICCPR. As criminal law is involved here and the issue is of crucial importance for the suspect, this right must be expressed in a more precise and detailed manner.[324] This can be seen from the wording: while, in Art. 9 (II), detained persons must be informed of the reason for their arrest, persons suspected of a criminal offence must be informed 'in detail' of the 'nature and cause' of the charges brought against them.[325]

The burden to inform the suspect lies on the shoulders of the state authorities. This implies steps to contact the suspect. In *Mbenge v Zaire*, the HRC found it untenable that the accused learnt about his convictions through the press, although the Zairean tribunals knew of the correct address of the accused.[326] It held that the state party must show that it has made 'sufficient effort' to inform the defendant.[327]

(a) The domestic systems   The right to information found its expression in the Sixth Amendment of the US Constitution. Case-law has interpreted this as meaning that the suspect needs to know whether the accusation is

---

[323] Harris, 250.
[324] Frowein and Peukert, Art. 6, No. 175; Nowak, Art. 14, No. 38.
[325] This gradual difference was also emphasized by the ECommHR in *Nielson v Denmark* Appl. No. 343/57, 2 YB, 412 at 462.
[326] HRC *Mbenge v Zaire* Doc. A/38/40, 134.
[327] Ibid., cf. also McGoldrick, *Human Rights Committee*, 420.

in the form of a presentment, indictment,[328] or information;[329] that the charges must be spelt out with clarity and particularity; that a vague and indefinite charge will not suffice.[330] It has therefore been found as in breach of the Constitution if the accused is sentenced on the basis of a different norm from that with which he was charged.[331]

In the UK, the suspect must likewise be cautioned before he is interviewed.[332] He must thus be informed of the accusations against him. Unfortunately, the law is not precise in this regard. However, it would seem to be inherent in the definition of interview, which reads as: '[a]n interview is the questioning of a person regarding his involvement or suspected involvement in a criminal offence or offences which, by virtue of paragraph 10.1 of Code C, is required to be carried out under caution'.[333] The questioning must therefore comprise the legal aspects ('criminal offence') and the factual material ('his involvement').

As we have already seen, there are two levels of inquiry in Germany: the police and the prosecutor. With respect to the former, § 163 a (IV) StPO rules that the interrogating officer is obliged to disclose the factual allegations to the suspect. However, the police officer does not have to name the precise norms of the Criminal Code (StGB), which might be sometimes difficult to determine. Such disclosure should not be considered a mere formality. The suspect must be genuinely informed, if necessary in the form of a conversation.[334] At the prosecutor's, where the first compulsory interrogation takes place, the caution must include the criminal norms that are under consideration (§§ 163 a (III) and 136 (I) 1 StPO). The information must be precise and detailed with regard to both the legal underpinnings and the alleged facts.[335]

(b) Human rights case-law   The European authorities differentiate likewise between the 'nature' and 'cause' of the allegation. The former refers to the legal grounds, the latter to the material facts upon which the allegation is

---

[328] 'Presentment' means that the initiative came from a Grand Jury, 'indictment' that the accusation was reviewed by a Grand Jury. The Fifth Amendment guarantees that one of these two procedures is compulsory for a capital or other infamous crime. Offences punishable with the death penalty must be presented by indictment.

[329] In this case, the prosecutor has filed the case on his own initiative.

[330] Osakwe in Andrews (1982), 273.

[331] US Supreme Court *Cole v Arkansas* 333 US 196 (1948).

[332] According to English legal terminology, an interview is the questioning of a person regarding his involvement or suspected involvement in a criminal offence. An interview must be carried out under caution, see paras. 10.1 and 11.1A Code C (Code of Practice (according to ss. 66, 67 PACE (1984)) C—The detention, treatment and questioning of persons by police officers).

[333] Code C 11.1A

[334] Kleinknecht and Meyer-Goßner, StPO, § 163 a No. 4.

[335] Ibid., § 136, No. 6.

based.[336] The same interpretation underlies the wording of Art. 14 (III) a ICCPR according to its drafting history.[337]

In practice, the European bodies have required relatively few details in the information that is supplied.[338] The term should be interpreted on the basis of the aim, which is to enable proper preparation of a defence. From this point of view, the ECommHR has not considered it necessary for the interrogator to mention all the evidence on which the charge is based.[339] The ECourtHR likewise held, in *Brozicek v Italy*, that the obligation to inform the suspect is satisfied when the offences are listed with references to the relevant rules, and the date, place, and name of the victim are mentioned.[340] Rightly, Harris asks where the difference to Art. 5 (II) ECHR then lies.[341] The difference is reduced to the word 'prompt' (*dans le plus court délai*). For Harris, any lack of precision with respect to the information at this stage of the procedure is offset by the fact that Art. 6 (III) b ECHR requires not only sufficient time but also facilities, that is, more information, to be made available to the suspect later on.

This requirement of 'prompt' information has not caused major problems for the European authorities. However, it is not so very easy to define the requirement precisely. Again, according to the wording, the information is related to the 'charge', that is, as soon as the person is charged, he must be informed of the details. If the formal 'charge' was the relevant time of application, the investigating authorities could question the suspect as long as they wished without informing him of the suspicion. We have seen before that European case-law provides an autonomous definition of the term 'charge', a substantive one.[342] This induces us to apply the same question, that is, whether the suspect is substantially affected here too. This must be measured against the background of the aim of the right to information: the preparation of a proper defence. Is it necessary to this aim to inform the suspect of the suspicion at the first interrogation by the police? It could be claimed that, at this early stage of the trial, the police are only collecting evidence in order to formulate a charge. As long as there is no actual charge, it is not possible

---

[336] ECommHR *Ofner v Austria* Decision 19 December 1960, Appl. No. 524/59, 3 YB, 322 at 344.

[337] See E/CN.4/SR, 156 the comments of the USA and Yugoslavia (p. 11), France and the UK (p. 12).

[338] Harris, 251.

[339] ECommHR *X v Belgium* Appl. No. 7628/76, 9 DR, 169 and also *Ofner v Austria* Appl. No. 524/59, 3 YB, 322.

[340] ECourtHR *Brozicek v Italy* Judgment 19 December 1989, Series A No. 167, para. 42.

[341] Harris, 252.

[342] The European system has not yet had to answer the question of the applicability of Art. 6 (III) ECHR. Nevertheless, the authorities seemed not to be generally disinclined to accept the applicability during pre-trial investigation. See Frowein and Peukert, Art. 6, No. 174.

to talk about preparing a defence of any kind. This is certainly true of the period when the investigating officers are still working without full knowledge. Does this situation not change as soon as there is reasonable suspicion? We have seen that, in all the national systems under scrutiny, the prosecuting authority must caution and inform the suspect before questioning him. The question is, therefore, what makes the suspect a suspect? May the interrogator interview someone against whom he has a suspicion not as a suspect but, for example, as a witness? Considering the object and purpose of Art. 6 ECHR or any other corresponding human rights provision, the answer must be in the negative for the following reasons. First, if the investigator has a certain suspicion, the position of the suspect is substantially affected, because certain coercive measures are allowed against such a person, for example, surveillance, tapping, and so forth. These measures are mostly dependent upon the probability of factual grounds for suspecting the person of having committed the offence.[343] According to the autonomous meaning of 'charge' assigned to it by the ECourtHR, Art. 6 (III) a ECHR would be applicable from that time on. Secondly, if the interrogee is not informed of the allegation against him, not only is preparation of a defence impossible, but defence is made entirely unrealizable. This is so because everything the suspect says can be used as evidence against him during trial.[344] Thirdly, it is a matter of 'fairness' to disclose allegations and suspicions to the one person who is being interviewed in order to equalize the imbalance of information between suspect and prosecution. Police forces certainly like situations in which the suspect is not aware of the allegations or of the police listening to conversations without the knowledge of the suspect.[345] Situations like these seem to be highly risky, especially for the innocent; the interrogator wants to prove his hypothesis, which is unknown to the person questioned; the danger of drawing incorrect conclusions from innocent answers is great. Being informed of the suspicion gives the suspect a fair opportunity to defend himself effectively against the allegations from

---

[343] Compare e.g. § 100a StPO: 'Surveillance and recording of telephone correspondence may be ordered, if there are certain facts justifying the suspicion that someone has committed or assisted in one of the following offences . . .' [translation by the author].

[344] From this perspective, the judgment of the US Supreme Court in *Rhode Island v Innis* [1980] 446 US 291 is very dubious; the court admitted evidence stemming from a 'conversation' in the police car on the way to the police station. English law tries to avoid entirely interviews outside the police station; 'conversations' in police cars (Lidstone and Palmer 8.12) and the famous 'chat' with the suspect are to be avoided in particular (Lidstone and Palmer 8.05).

[345] Compare e.g. the ECourtHR in *Saunders v UK* Judgment 17 December 1996, 23 EHHR (1997), 313, where the suspect was interviewed not by police officers but by investigators from a commercial board to which he was accountable. Also *A v France* Judgment 23 November 1993, Series A No. 272-B, where an 'acquaintance' called the suspect and allowed the police to tape the conversation in which the suspect clearly admitted the offence.

the very beginning. The right to information must therefore be applied as soon as there is reasonable suspicion that could trigger other measures against the suspect.[346]

What would seem to be a truism is not always unproblematic: the information supplied must be in a language that the suspect understands. This stems from the obligation to respect the suspect as an individual subject and not see him as a mere object of the proceedings against him. The suspect's right to be informed of the allegations in a language he understands is explicitly stated in every human rights treaty, for example, Art. 14 (III) a ICCPR, Art. 6 (III) a ECHR, Art. 8 (II) b AmCHR.[347] The problem was addressed before the ECourtHR in *Brozicek v Italy*. Despite the fact that *Brozicek* complained to the Italian authorities that he did not fully understand the accusation and asked for a translation into either his mother tongue or one of the official United Nations languages, there was no reaction on the Italian side.[348] The ECourtHR held that, as the Italian authorities could not support their assumption that the applicant was capable of understanding Italian with conclusive evidence, they had to presume that he did not understand the language, not only because of his complaint but also because of the fact that he was neither a national nor a resident of Italy.[349]

We can conclude therefrom that, if the suspect is either a national or resident of the prosecuting state, the authorities may presume him capable of understanding the official language of the national state. However, if this is not the case, the organs must ascertain whether the suspect understands the allegations.

(c) Law at the ICTY   Art. 21 (IV) (a) Statute ICTY contains the same right to prompt information about the nature and cause of the allegations as the above discussed human rights treaties. It is unfortunate, however, that this right is not also explicitly entrenched in Art. 18 (III) Statute ICTY and in the Rules about the interrogation of suspects. It nevertheless seems logical to presume the applicability of Art. 21 (IV) (a) Statute ICTY to this stage from the picture drawn by Rules 42 and 43: a suspect must be

---

[346] English law speaks of 'grounds to suspect' that provoke the obligation to caution the interrogee before the interview; see Code C 10.1.

[347] Art. 8 (II) b AmCHR speaks of 'notification' instead of 'information'. This difference in the letter should not lead to the presumption of any difference in substance.

[348] ECourtHR *Brozicek v Italy* Judgment 19 December 1989, Series A No. 167, paras. 16, 39. This approach chosen by Brozicek seems very brave or speaks of his phenomenal language skills, as the Italian authorities could have complied with his request by translating the accusations into Chinese or Arabic.

[349] Ibid., para. 41. An interesting case concerning language in criminal proceedings was decided by the ECJ recently (*Bickel and Franz v Italy* 24 November 1998, C-274/96). However, the decision was based on European Community law and not on human rights law; compare Safferling, 94 AJIL (2000), 155.

cautioned about the fact that he has a right to counsel and that a recording is being made in a language he understands. The aim of these rules is scrupulous honesty towards the suspect. Against this background, it seems unlikely that the drafters of the Statute and Rules wished to exclude the right of the suspect to be informed of the allegations against him as soon as possible.

(d) The ICC Statute Art. 26 (VI) a Statute ILC required that the suspect be informed of his situation as a suspect. The fact that this includes information about the nature and cause of the allegations against him must be expressed more clearly. Furthermore, he must be informed of his right to silence and that he cannot be compelled to incriminate himself (see also Art. 41 (I) g Statute ILC). Finally, steps must be taken to ensure that the suspect understands the allegations against him (Art. 26 (VI) c Statute ILC). The PrepComm proposes an extensive list of rights of the suspect, amongst them the right to be informed fully of the charges against him and of all the rights to which he is entitled under Art. 26 Statute ILC.[350] Art. 55 (II) Rome Statute addresses these proposals.[351] It contains the suspect's right to be informed that there are grounds to believe that he has committed an international crime.[352] Although this goes one step further than the ILC draft, it should be clear that the information must pertain to the cause and grounds for the suspicions.[353]

2. The right to remain silent

The next caution, after the suspect has been informed of the allegations against him, is to tell him that he does not have to comment on the allegations and questions put to him by the investigator. This is a 'landmark' in the development of procedural guarantees,[354] rejecting the former practice of questioning the accused under oath to obtain both evidence and confessions. This right to silence stems from the privilege against self-incrimination, *nemo tenetur se ipsum prodere*. To properly safeguard this privilege against self-incrimination, the suspect must be informed of his right to remain silent. If this right is not disclosed, it is of no value at all to the person who should benefit from it.

The right to freedom from self-incrimination is embedded in Art. 14 (III) g ICCPR and Art. 8 (II) g AmCHR. The ICCPR draft was amended in

---

[350] See Report of the PrepComm II, 116–18.

[351] Hall in Trifterer (ed.), *Commentary on the Rome Statute*, Art. 55, No. 10.

[352] Behrens, 6 Eur.J.Crime Cr.L.Cr.J. (1998), 431.

[353] Art. 67 (I) a Rome Statute, which is applicable to the stage of the trial, is more illustrative in this regard: the person charged must be informed promptly and in detail of the nature, cause, and content of the charge.

[354] H. G. Abernathy and B. A. Perry, *Civil Liberties under the Constitution* (6th edn. Columbia, SC, 1993), 84.

1950 correspondingly, on a proposal by the Philippines.[355] The ECHR is not equipped with such a provision, but it is understood to be part of Art. 6 ECHR as a whole, being generally recognized as a principle of international law.[356] This right is rooted in respect for the human dignity and free will of every individual.[357]

The US Constitution acknowledges the privilege against compulsory self-incrimination. The Fifth Amendment provides that 'no person shall be compelled in a criminal case to be a witness against himself'. According to case-law, this not only applies to evidence that incriminates directly but has also been applied to evidence that incriminates indirectly, that is, only tends to incriminate.[358] Cross-examination by the prosecutor and any comments by the prosecutor or judge to the jury that tend to draw inferences from the defendant's silence are prohibited. However, a jury can scarcely be hindered from drawing inferences from the behaviour of the accused.[359] Nevertheless, the defendant may voluntarily waive this privilege and give incriminating evidence. Once he has waived this right, he can no longer claim it for further testimony on the subject; in other words, the choice is all or nothing. To safeguard this important constitutional principle, the suspect must be cautioned, that is, warned of his right to remain silent.[360] This principle stems from the famous US Supreme Court decision in *Miranda*.[361] Since this decision, the police must read what are commonly called *Miranda* warnings to any individual taken into custody.[362] This case is primarily concerned with custodial interrogation. Yet, as it refers not only to express questioning but also to its functional equivalent, that is, '[t]o any words or actions on the part of the police . . . that the police *should know* are reasonably likely to elicit an incriminating response from the suspect',[363] interrogation is therefore

---

[355] See Bossuyt, *Guide*, 305; E/CN.4/365; E/CN.4/SR.159, §§ 41–2; A/2929, 43 (§ 88).

[356] ECourtHR *Saunders v UK* Judgment 17 December 1996, 23 EHHR (1997), 313, at para. 68.

[357] ECourtHR *Murray v UK* and *Funke v France* emphasizing the close link with the presumption of innocence provision.

[358] *Patricia Blau v US*, 340 US 159 (1950); see also *Hoffmann v US*, 341 US 479 (1951).

[359] Abernathy and Perry, *Civil Liberties under the Constitution*, 84–5.

[360] Kangaspunta, *Profiles of Criminal Justice Systems*, 206.

[361] US Supreme Court *Miranda v Arizona* 384 US 436 (1966).

[362] The *Miranda* warnings read as follows: 'You are under arrest. Before we ask you any questions, you must understand what your rights are. You have the right to remain silent. You are not required to say anything to us at any time or to answer any questions. Anything you say can be used against you in court. You have the right to talk to a lawyer for advice before we question you and to have him with you during questioning. If you cannot afford a lawyer and want one, a lawyer will be provided for you. If you want to answer questions now without a lawyer present you will still have the right to stop answering at any time. You also have the right to stop answering at any time until you talk to a lawyer.' Reprinted in L. Epstein and T. G. Walker, *Constitutional Law for a Changing America* (Washington, DC, 1992), 385.

[363] US Supreme Court *Rhode Island v Innis* 446 US 291 (1980) (italics added). The case-law

defined not so much by the perspective and intent of the police but rather by the impression made by the behaviour of the police on the suspect.

English law likewise recognizes a right to silence. Generally speaking, nobody can be compelled to answer a police officer's question.[364] The police officer must caution the suspect that he need not say anything. According to Code C 10.4, this caution reads as follows: 'You do not have to say anything. But it may harm your defence if you do not mention when questioned something which you later rely on in court. Anything you do say may be given in evidence.'

In Germany, all three potential interrogating authorities are obliged to remind the suspect that he is free to comment on the allegations (§§ 136 (I) 2 and §§ 163 a (III) and (IV) StPO). He is considered to have refused to testify if he does not comment on the allegation. If, however, he comments on part of the allegations only and declines to testify on them in full, inferences *in malam partem* can be drawn from this behaviour.[365]

The right to silence not only serves to protect the suspect against torture or undue pressure. It also contains the general sentiment that a 'fair trial' demands that the state authorities should build their case without the suspect convicting himself.[366] The consequences of the right to remain silent on the evidence will be discussed later at the trial stage.[367]

The ICTY refers to the 'right to silence' in Art. 21 (IV) (g) Statute ICTY using the same words as the above human rights treaties. This right was originally not mentioned alongside the right to have legal counsel in Rule 42; the amendment found in Rule 42 (iii), and dating from 30 January 1995, contains an explicit reference to the right to silence. The new subclause, (iii), was added on the basis that the right was of such fundamental importance that it should be set forth expressly in the Rules.[368] The suspect must now be cautioned that any statement he makes may be used in evidence. This 'right to silence' is also referred to in Rule 63 (Questioning of the Accused), which was amended in this way at the twelfth plenary session (2–3 December 1996) in order to achieve consistency with Rule 42.[369] This provision governs the questioning of the

of the US Supreme Court after *Miranda* is summarized in Epstein and Walker, *Constitutional Law for a Changing America*, 393–5.

[364] Leigh in Andrews (1982), 39.

[365] Kleinknecht and Meyer-Goßner § 261 No. 17.

[366] Abernathy and Perry, *Civil Liberties under the Constitution*, 84.

[367] See Ch. 5.

[368] Jones, *The Practice at the ICTY*, Rule 42, 257.

[369] The Argument of Morris and Scharf, *An Insider's Guide*, 199–200, that the suspect need not be informed of this right and that the law at the ICTY deviates from the *Miranda* jurisprudence, is most probably outdated, because of the above cited amendments of the Rules of Procedure. It is furthermore inconsistent to rely on the assistance provided by counsel as Morris and Scharf do, because the suspect must be informed of his rights, regardless of whether he wishes to avail himself of his right to counsel.

accused, that is, after the charge and after his initial appearance before the tribunal. We have held above that it is necessary from a human rights point of view to inform the suspect of his 'right to silence'. The procedure envisaged in the Rules of Procedure as amended incorporates this right from the earliest stage possible and is thus compatible with human rights. Art. 21 (IV) (g) Statute ICTY is therefore to be seen as being applicable to the initial interrogation of the suspect, too.[370]

Art. 26 (VI) a i Statute ILC includes explicitly the obligation to inform the suspect of his right to silence, without such silence being taken into consideration in the determination of guilt or innocence. The latter annex is a welcomed clarification that inferences from silence are prohibited.[371] This provision has been included in the Rome Statute in Art. 55 (II) b. What is missing is the warning that any statement may be used in evidence.[372] This should be remedied in the Rules of Procedure.

3. The right to counsel

(a) General   The main aim of the presence of a legal assistant is to safeguard the proper conduct of the interrogation. I have already discussed the right to counsel as part of the institution of 'defence' at an earlier stage.[373] What needs to be added is the importance of the caution. The suspect must be made aware of the fact that he has the right to legal assistance.

The US criminal system has inherited this compulsory warning from the Supreme Court's *Miranda* decision.[374] The UK system has embodied the caution in PACE 58 and Code C 3.1 and in Germany it is found in §§ 136 (I), 163a (IV) StPO. From a human rights perspective it cannot be denied that the right to legal assistance is worthless if the suspect is not informed of this right. Furthermore, the right must be respected by the investigator; it is his duty to abstain from questioning until the request for counsel is fulfilled or the suspect willingly and deliberately waives his right to counsel. This means, of course, that not only direct questioning but also its 'functional equivalent'[375] must be prohibited. In *Brewer v Williams*, the US Supreme Court put this into practice and excluded evidence disclosed by the suspect to police officers who were transporting him by car and whilst so doing, discussed their compassion for the

---

[370] The ICTY First Annual Report (1994), para. 60, speaks of the right to be protected against self-incrimination as being already entailed in the Rules of Procedure. Due to the amendments outlined above, the Rules now also explicitly state this.

[371] This issue will be discussed later at the stage of the trial in Ch. 5.

[372] Hall in Trifferer (ed.), *Commentary on the Rome Statute*, Art. 55, No. 12.

[373] See above A IV, p. 103 *et subs.*

[374] US Supreme Court *Miranda v Arizona* 384 US 436 (1966).

[375] Ibid.

parents of the murdered child, for whom a 'Christian burial' was not possible as long as the body of the girl was not found.[376] Shortly afterwards, however, in *Rhode Island v Innis*, the Court upheld the suspect's evidence as to the location of the weapon, when, in a similar situation, police officers spoke of their concern for the safety of children who find dangerous weapons.[377] In both cases, it seems quite obvious that the police officers were putting undue pressure on the suspect, without even addressing him directly, by appealing to his compassion. In the setting of a police car, such behaviour is especially deceptive and is a blatant denial of the suspect's right to consult legal advice before deciding whether to testify or not. Such tricks must be considered as conflicting with the human right to freedom from compulsory self-incrimination and the right to counsel.

(b) International A different question might arise in an international context. If a person is accused and even detained by a state that is not his national state, the question of whether this person has a right to communicate with a representative of his home state might be asked. Such a right is enshrined in Art. 17 Convention on Safety of UN and Associated Personnel (1994)[378] pertaining to a context that is comparable to the present one. As the name suggests, the Safety Convention addresses crimes committed against UN or associated personnel. This hastily drafted convention aims at preventing similar scenarios to those suffered by UN peacekeepers in Somalia and the former Yugoslavia.[379] The former UN Secretary General Boutros Boutros-Ghali drew particular attention to these incidents in his publication entitled *An Agenda for Peace*.[380] The convention approaches the protection scheme from two sides, (*a*) finding equilibrium between the rights and duties of state parties on the one hand and of the UN and associated personnel on the other, and (*b*) establishing individual criminal responsibility on the part of alleged perpetrators of attacks against such personnel.[381] Although comments on the Safety Convention have not always been approving,[382] it enshrines in Art. 17 (I)

---

[376] US Supreme Court *Brewer v Williams* 430 US 387 (1977).

[377] US Supreme Court *Rhode Island v Innis* 446 US 291 (1980).

[378] UN Doc. A/Res/49/59 (1994) 9 December 1994, adopted without a vote; reprinted in 34 ILM (1995), 482 (= Safety Convention).

[379] A general analysis of UN military operations and the applicability of international humanitarian law is given by Greenwood, International Humanitarian Law and United Nations Military Operations, 1 YBIHL (1998), 3.

[380] Boutros Boutros-Ghali, *An Agenda for Peace*, 2nd edn. (New York, 1995).

[381] Compare to this Convention in general Bourloyannis-Vrailas, 44 ICLQ (1995), 560.

[382] Bloom, 89 AJIL (1995) 621, draws a positive picture; Sharp, 7 Duke J. Com&Int'l L (1996), 93, argues in favour of a general status of UN personnel similar to that of police forces, whereas Greenwood, 7 Duke J. Com&Int'l L (1996), 185, favours the principle of uniform application of humanitarian law and finds difficulties in the scope of application of

Safety Convention a general reference to 'fair trial', unfortunately without any further specification or reference to other human rights treaties. Art. 17 (II) Safety Convention reads as follows:

(II) Any alleged offender shall be entitled:
  (a) To communicate without delay with the nearest appropriate representative of the State or the States of which such person is a national or which is otherwise entitled to protect that person's rights or, if such person is a stateless person, of the State which, at that person's request, is willing to protect that person's rights; and
  (b) To be visited by a representative of that State or those States.

Although this right is not enshrined in any of the major human rights treaties, it seems a sensible additional right within the context of international criminal procedure. The state of which the prisoner is a national should, and probably will, take an interest in and responsibility for the future fate of this person. In cases in which both the state and the defendant wish to be in contact, the visit of a state representative should at least not be denied. The circumstances covered by the Safety Convention and of international criminal procedure in general are similar. In both cases a national from one state has been detained by a 'foreign' power. This foreign power, in our case the international court, should recognize the interest and responsibility the state has in and for the protection and well-being of its nationals.

The legal regime at the ICTY includes the obligation to inform the suspect of his right to have counsel assigned to him prior to interrogation (Art. 18 (III) Statute ICTY) and to be informed of this right (Rule 42A). However it does not speak of any right to have contact with a representative of one's national state. According to Art. 55 (II) c and d Rome Statute, the suspect must be informed of his right to legal assistance and of the right to be questioned in the presence of counsel.

4. Conduct of questioning

What we have said before about the right to silence, or—to give it a better name—freedom from compulsory self-incrimination,[383] has particular

---

the Convention. Bourloyannis-Vrailas, 44 ICLQ (1995) 560 at 589–90, is critical about the immediate effect the Convention will have, especially in its intention to enforce criminal law; despite the recent efforts towards establishing a Permanent International Criminal Court, the Convention does not mention such an institution (reasons given at p. 580) and relies solely on the indirect enforcement avenue. Zwanenburg has recently scrutinized the effects of the ICC Rome Statute on peacekeeping operation, 10 EJIL (1999), 124, and argues that peacekeepers are bound by the Rome Statute, but does not discuss their protection under the Rome Statute.

[383] Roxin, *Nemo tenetur... die Rechtsprechung am Scheideweg*, NStZ 1995, 466.

importance for the conduct and method of interrogation. The suspect should be spared all undue pressure out of respect for his free will.

(a) The prohibition of torture in human rights law   It should be absolutely clear from international conventions (Conventions against Torture[384]) and major human rights treaties[385] that torture is prohibited in any circumstances. Torture has in fact been outlawed for centuries.[386] Yet the world is far from being free of inhumane and degrading treatment, especially when suspects are interrogated by the police.[387] Although thumbscrews and the like are fortunately 'out of fashion' in most Western democracies, at least, blatantly inhumane and degrading treatment still persists even there.[388] Above all, more subtle techniques of suspect interrogation must be scrutinized. For example, pre-trial detention can be used to break the suspect's will-power, or even the mere threat of being detained could constitute undue pressure.

It is not an easy task to define torture or inhumane and degrading treatment accurately. To compose a conclusive list is probably impossible and ultimately counterproductive, as it can easily be subverted.[389] The jurisprudence of the ECourtHR, above all as elaborated in *Ireland v United Kingdom*,[390] makes it clear that torture is to be distinguished from degrading and inhumane treatment, although both are unconditionally[391] prohibited by Art. 3 ECHR.[392] Both torture and inhumane and degrading

---

[384] Convention against Torture and Other Cruel, Inhumane or Degrading Treatment or Punishment (1984), in ILM 1984, 1027 and 1985, 535. European Convention for the Prevention of Torture and Inhuman or Degrading Treatment or Punishment (1987), European Treaty Series, No. 126.

[385] Art. 7 ICCPR, Art. 3 ECHR, Art. 5 AmCHR, Art. 5 AfCHPR.

[386] Leigh in Andrews (1982), 39.

[387] The UK was called to book in Strasbourg, when it was asked to justify the interrogation techniques employed in Northern Ireland; see ECourtHR *Ireland v United Kingdom* Series A (1978).

[388] A distressing report on the European situation is given by A. Cassese, *Inhumane States* (Cambridge, 1996), 109–12, recounting his experiences as President of the European Committee for the Prevention of Torture and Inhumane and Degrading Treatment or Punishment from 1989 to 1993.

[389] Ibid. 45–6, reporting the reasons why the Torture Committee could not and did not agree on a definition of torture.

[390] ECourtHR *Ireland v United Kingdom* Judgment 18 January 1976, Series A No. 25.

[391] There is neither a limiting clause in a 2nd paragraph that would 'justify torture to the degree necessary in a democratic society', which would certainly make a mockery of both the individual's protection against torture and democratic society; nor is Art. 3 derogable in a state of emergency by virtue of Art. 15 ECHR. The same is emphasized by the HRC with regard to Art. 7 ICCPR in HRC General Comment 7 (Article 7) para. 1.

[392] Of course, there is a third position mentioned in Art. 3 ECHR, i.e. the prohibition of degrading and inhumane punishment. For the part of the procedure discussed here, the problems concerning punishment can be left out. N. Rodley, *The Treatment of Prisoners under International Law* (Paris and Oxford, 1987), 71, argues that the formula stemming from Art. 5 ECHR was not meant to be distinguished. The distinction was first made by the ECommHR in *The Greek case* 12 YB, 186. This case was brought by Denmark, Norway, Sweden, and the

treatment are prohibited in absolute terms, irrespective of the conduct of the victim.[393] In the opinion of the Court, there is a gradual difference between the two prohibitions, torture being the graver assault on human integrity. Treatment that causes bodily harm or intense physical and mental suffering is 'inhumane'. 'Degrading' treatment is treatment capable of provoking feelings of fear, anguish, and inferiority, possibly with humiliating and debasing effects and breaking down the physical or moral resistance of the victim.[394] The ECourtHR attaches a special stigma of particular seriousness and cruelty to torture by referring to UN GA Res 3452 (XXX) Art. 1.[395] In the crucial para. 67 the ECourtHR cites a number of reasons why it does not consider the level of torture to have been reached: neither the 'object of extraction of confessions' nor the 'systematic application of the measures' can be seen as substantive conditions of torture.[396]

The HRC has not yet expressed a definite view on what constitutes 'torture'. The General Comments merely state that both physical and mental suffering can amount to torture, but do not provide any further definition or distinction between torture and inhumane or degrading treatment.[397] However, it does rely on the interpretation of Art. 1 (I) of the 1984 UN Convention against Torture, although this document is certainly not binding for Art. 7 ICCPR. It therefore understands torture as acts of public officials that intentionally inflict severe physical or mental pain or suffering in order to fulfil a certain purpose, such as the extortion of information or confessions or the punishment, intimidation or discrimination of a person.[398] In the case of *J. L. Massera v Uruguay*, the HRC found a case of torture, because the applicant was forced to remain standing with his head hooded for many hours, which finally led to his collapse and a broken leg.[399] Without further explanation, the HRC considered this to be

---

Netherlands against Greece after the 1967 military coup in Greece. The applicant states brought a whole list of allegations concerning torture and all kinds of ill-treatment; see also Ch. 6, below.   [393] Ibid., para. 163.

[394] Ibid., para. 167. The alleged violations by British police in Northern Ireland were considered by both the ECommHR and ECourtHR to be easily within this ambit.

[395] UN GA Res 3452 (XXX), adopted 9 December 1975. The ECourtHR's reasons why the alleged violations did not constitute torture on the part of the UK remain obscure.

[396] This is rightly observed by Judge Fitzmaurice in his separate opinion, paras. 34–5. He sees the difference between torture and inhumane and degrading treatment in kind not in degree. The former he understands as being an attack on the physical integrity of the victim, whilst the latter entails all other forms of treatment, psychological and mental distress in particular. An approach like this tends to underestimate the importance of the human psyche for the well-being of individuals.

[397] HRC General Comment 20 (Article 7), para. 4, 5.

[398] See Nowak, Art. 7, No. 6.

[399] HRC *J. L. Massera v Uruguay* Doc. A/34/40, 124. For further references to further HRC cases concerning torturous treatment, see McGoldrick, *Human Rights Committee*, 368–9.

'torture'. Such an interpretation is certainly more excessive than that of the ECourtHR discussed above. In fact, the HRC was prepared to accept two of the five techniques seen by the ECourtHR as inhumane treatment[400] as being tantamount to torture.

A definition of torture similar to that of the HRC is given by Cassese: '[t]orture [is] any form of coercion or violence, whether mental or physical, against a person to extort a confession, information, or to humiliate, punish or intimidate that person'.[401] The definition of torture in Art. 1 (I) of the Convention against Torture (1984) is very similar. Inhumane and degrading treatment consists of a combination of numerous acts and circumstances, whereas torture takes the form of a single act against an individual. It need not be conducted with the intent to humiliate, offend, or debase the victim.[402] According to this definition, the essential element of torture is that it aims at breaking the will-power of the victim, understood here as comprising a person's ethnic, cultural, and historical perception of himself. Sine qua non for torture is the deliberate disregard of the suspect's free will. This approach certainly widens the scope of torture to such an extent that the 'five techniques' before the ECourtHR in *Ireland v United Kingdom* would have amounted to torture. But it is a practicable differentiation and fears of an inflationary use of the term torture must be rejected; if the measures involved are employed to break the will of the victim and treat him like a 'thing', it is torture and must be called by its proper name. This approach rightly sees human beings as having a physical and a spiritual existence.

These findings are backed by the privilege against self-incrimination in criminal procedure. The suspect cannot be compelled to testify against his will. This means that torturous measures, which are, as we have seen, *per definitionem* aimed at coercion, are necessarily excluded. The prohibition of inhumane and degrading treatment has consequences for the surrounding circumstances; this means that interview rooms must be adequately heated, lit, and ventilated, and so forth.[403] The threshold for 'torture' is, of course, fluid.

(b) In national legislation Analysis of national legal systems reveals that domestic law generally seems to prohibit torturous or degrading treatment during interrogation. § 136a StPO rules out mistreatment, fatiguing, physical measures, deception, and the like. The list is not exhaustive.[404]

---

[400] ECourtHR *Ireland v United Kingdom* Judgment 18 January 1976, Series A No. 25. Compare also Nowak, Art. 7, No. 5.

[401] Cassese, *Inhumane States*, 47.

[402] Ibid. 48, giving as an example (pp. 49–50), prison cells without sanitary installations, forcing the prisoner to use 'his' bucket in front of his cellmates.

[403] See e.g. PACE Code C 12.

[404] Kleinknecht and Meyer-Goßner, StPO § 136a No. 6.

Anything that affects the freedom of will of the suspect is ruled out. In the USA, the evidentiary rule that coerced confessions may not be admitted developed as a privilege granted by the Constitution.[405] How far the interrogator may go is by no means clear. Circumstances like the suspect's physical condition as well as the number of police officers present may all cause undue pressure in the individual case.[406] Apart from the presence of third persons like a defence counsel or a custody officer, the best way to safeguard proper conduct of the interrogation is to tape the whole interview. The tape would then prove compliance with the procedure and would lay open the behaviour of the interrogator for the trial court or any other review instance.[407]

(c) Law and practice at the ICTY and the ICC   The prosecutor at the ICTY is strictly bound to tape or video the whole interrogation by virtue of Rule 43. This, as I have suggested, is the most effective safeguard against undue pressure from the interrogator.[408] The procedure of the interrogation is laid down in Rule 43. The suspect must be given the opportunity to speak by himself and if necessary to clarify matters. A transcript must be made and handed over to the suspect, together with a copy of the tape. The original tape must be sealed in the presence of the suspect and signed by both the prosecutor and the suspect. With this procedure the ICTY rule reaffirms and clarifies the rights of Art. 14 ICCPR[409] and enhances the ICTY's ability to determine whether a statement was made voluntarily.[410]

Art. 55 (I) b Rome Statute prohibits coercion and torture during the investigation. Art. 55 (II) d Rome Statute requires the presence of the defence counsel during interrogation of the suspect unless the latter has voluntarily waived this right to counsel. This may serve as a safeguard against undue questioning. The Draft Rules of Procedure take ICTY practice as an example and provide for recorded interrogations (Draft Rules 5.9 and 5.10).

---

[405] Compare US Supreme Court *Brown v Mississippi* 297 US 278 (1936) and *Rogers v Richmond* 365 US 534 (1961).

[406] Lidstone and Palmer, 8.19–8.21.

[407] Nsereko, 5 CLF (1994), 507, at 526, calls the recording of questioning a vital element in the proper administration of justice. It deters the interrogator from coercing the suspect during the interrogation and reduces the frequency of allegations of coerced confessions.

[408] Morris and Scharf, *An Insider's Guide*, 201.

[409] ICTY First Annual Report (1994), para. 59.

[410] Bassiouni, *The Law of the ICTY*, 880. The procedure has so far been challenged once, on a motion by the accused in the *Delalic* case (Case No. IT-96-21-T), alleging an irregularity in the recording procedure prescribed by Rule 43. In its decision of 9 October 1996 on the Motion on the Exclusion and Restitution of Evidence and other Material seized from the Accused Zejnil Delalic, the Trial Chamber II denied the complaint; see Jones, *The Practice of the ICTY*, Rule 43, 258.

(II) Questioning of Witnesses

There are three different types of witnesses. A witness may be in the camp of the victim or even the victim himself. He may be on the opposite side and closely connected with the suspect, for example, a relative, close acquaintance, professional assistant (legal, medical, religious), or he might also be a co-suspect. Lastly, a witness can be a neutral person, who happened to be a witness by chance or is an expert witness because of his specific knowledge. At all events, the witnesses must be treated according to their special position.

1. The victim witness

The victim or victim-related witness is of special interest. In a considerable number of cases, his testimony will be crucial for the prosecution. In cases of rape, the victim is generally the only witness to the crime. The overall maxim is protection of the witness. He has a right to be treated according to his situation and to special protection of his honour and reputation.[411] The witness is further under special protection regarding the integrity of his body and life. It is the court's duty to ensure the witness's safety. It is difficult to decide whether or not the witness has a right to anonymity *vis-à-vis* the suspect. This problem will be discussed later on, at the trial stage. The victim must, however, not be subject to coercion and psychological stress. The presence of an adviser should therefore be permitted during interrogations.[412]

2. The suspect witness

One difficulty we have already touched upon is the distinction between suspect and witness. Special provisions must be guaranteed for the suspect, which is why a suspect cannot simply be questioned as an ordinary witness. The main right of the suspect that is of concern here is the privilege against self-incrimination. We could differentiate between a formal and a material right to silence. The former is the right that protects everybody close to the suspect, either because of their special personal relationship with the suspect, that is, relatives, wives, or husbands, or because of a professional privilege, for example, priests, legal counsel, doctors, and the like. This is foreseen, for example, in §§ 52, 53 StPO. The reason for this privilege rests in the conflicting demands to which the witness is exposed as a result of his oath to tell the truth and his strong bonds with the suspect, whom he does not want to incriminate.[413]

---

[411] Kleinknecht/Meyer-Goßner, Vor § 48 No. 10.

[412] Compare the German rule allowing the presence of third persons if so desired by the victim, § 406 f (III) StPO.   [413] Kleinknecht and Meyer-Goßner, § 52 No. 1.

Criminal procedure should recognize this dilemma and solve the problem via a privilege for the person concerned.

A material right to remain silent exists if the witness would incriminate himself or someone towards whom he has a formal right to silence. The latter right is protected, for example, in § 55 StPO. The rationale is similar to that for the formal right to silence. The main aim is to spare the witness a situation of psychological stress; this right is thus ancillary to the suspect's right to silence.[414] One consequence is the witness's right to counsel; the latter is intended to guarantee that the witness's right to silence is properly applied and misunderstandings avoided.[415] This is of particular importance if the witness is detained because he is accused himself. The counsel should not be able to influence the rest of the procedure.

The ICTY has taken up this issue, amending Rule 45*bis* and its Directive on the Assignment of Defence Counsel[416] on 24 June 1996 in the eleventh plenary session. A detained witness who is transferred to the ICTY under the provisions of Rule 90*bis*[417] can be assigned counsel. This was applied four times: in the case of *Djukic* and *Krsmanovic*, who were both detained by the authorities of Bosnia and Herzegovina, and *Erdemovic* and *Kremenovic*, who both were required by the ICTY as witnesses against *Karadzic* and *Mladic*.[418]

3. Neutral and expert witnesses

Neutral and expert witnesses are usually not personally involved in the trial. They have no personal interest in either the outcome of the trial or the fate of the participants. A neutral witness is thereby generally a person who witnessed a criminal act by accident. He is interviewed by the investigator in order to obtain a neutral picture of the situation and learn about the circumstances of the event. However, such testimony is not necessarily as harmless at it may seem. The prosecutor's case may depend on the testimony of one witness. This person might therefore be particularly endangered, and require special protection at this stage.

The expert witness is considered to be a neutral adviser. His testimony might be necessary to shed light on circumstances which require a special technical knowledge. In actual practice, specialists do not always come to

---

[414] Kleinknecht and Meyer-Goßner, § 55 No. 1.

[415] Ibid., Vor § 48 No. 11.

[416] IT/73/Rev. 2, adopted 11 February 1994, amended on 5 May 1994. The reprinted text of the Directive, together with comments, can be found in Bassiouni, *The Law at the ICTY*, 884–95.

[417] Adopted in the 8th Plenary Session, October 1995.

[418] See ICTY, Third Annual Report (1996), para.106; Jones, *The Practice of the ICTY*, Rule 90*bis*, 422–3.

the same conclusions. This problem materializes during the criminal process in various ways. When the evidence is presented by the parties, the experts will be chosen by the latter and will naturally corroborate the hypothesis of the party by whom they are employed. In inquisitorial systems, experts are called by the court, and serve the purpose of assisting the court in finding the truth. The authorities must take care that the expert is not unduly influenced by the parties.

C. DETENTION OF THE SUSPECT

The suspect might be brought into detention or placed under arrest during the investigation. This is indeed a severe infringement of the right to liberty and security of person as embodied in Art. 9 ICCPR, Art. 5 ECHR.

Art. 9 ICCPR
(I)   Everyone has the right to liberty and security of person. No one shall be subject to arbitrary arrest or detention. No one shall be deprived of his liberty except on such grounds and in accordance with such procedure as are established by law.
(II) Anyone who is arrested shall be informed, at the time of arrest, of the reason for his arrest and shall be promptly informed of any charges against him.
(III) Anyone arrested or detained on a criminal charge shall be brought promptly before a judge or other officer authorised by law to exercise judicial power and shall be entitled to trial within a reasonable time or to release. It shall not be the general rule that persons awaiting trial shall be detained in custody, but release may be subject to guarantees to appear for trial, at any other stage of the judicial proceedings, and, should occasion arise, for execution of the judgement.

Art. 5 ECHR
(I)   Everyone has the right to liberty and security of person. No one shall be deprived of his liberty save in the following cases and in accordance with a procedure prescribed by law:
(II) the lawful arrest or detention of a person effected for the purpose of bringing him before the competent legal authority on reasonable suspicion of having committed an offence or when it is reasonably considered necessary to prevent his committing an offence or fleeing after having done so
(III) Everyone arrested or detained in accordance with the provisions of paragraph 1(c) of this Article shall be brought promptly before a judge or other officer authorised by law to exercise judicial power and shall be entitled to trial within a reasonable time or to release pending trial. Release may be conditioned by guarantees to appear for trial.

Undoubtedly, the right to physical freedom lies within the ambit of these provisions.[419] Detention means that the suspect is deprived of his right to freedom of movement (outside his cell) for the duration of detention. It is not merely a violation of the human right to liberty, but a temporary destruction of this right. As such, it needs special justification. Seen in terms of the presumption of innocence, the legitimacy of pre-trial detention called in question, as it can be defined as the detention of an innocent.[420] For the purposes of pre-trial detention, human rights treaties provide for special exceptions from the liberty-right but these exceptions are made subject to specific conditions in order to prevent excessive use of this measure. It must therefore be assumed that pre-trial detention is generally justifiable. The suspect experiences detention as a particular hardship that he must undergo because of the special interests of the community in solution of the criminal offence.[421] The suspect makes a 'special sacrifice' (*Sonderopfer*).[422]

In order to assess pre-trial detention, the general conditions of detention must therefore be examined first of all, then the legitimacy of the purpose of arrest[423] and, finally, the extent to which the lawfulness of the measure can be challenged.

(I) General Conditions of Detention

Before we look at the material conditions of detention, we must discuss the formal requirements that must be met.[424]

1. Formal requirements

We speak of arrest when the suspect is held in custody and the police can use force to prevent him from leaving. If he is at the police station voluntarily, he is, of course, free to leave whenever he wants to.[425] This means that the term 'detention' can only be used if and when the suspect is formally informed in clear terms that he is not allowed to leave.

The police could misuse this formal requirement and lengthen certain time limits by not informing the suspect and thus not formally arresting

---

[419] See e.g. ECourtHR *Engel v. Netherlands*, Series A 22, § 58 (1976).

[420] Hassemer, StV 1984, 40.

[421] BVerfG Decision 15 December 1965, in BVerfGE 19, 342 at 348.

[422] Kleinknecht and Meyer-Goßner, Vor § 112, No. 4.

[423] This differentiation between general condition and legitimate purpose is internationally accepted, as found in the Havana Conference, 158.

[424] The IAmCourtHR clearly distinguishes between the formal and material aspects of article 7 (II) IAmCHR. See recently IAmCourtHR *Gangaram Panday* case Judgment 21 January 1994, Series C No. 16, para. 47.

[425] In such cases he must be cautioned that he is free to leave at any time when interrogated by the police; PACE Code C para. 10.2; cf. also Leigh, *Police Powers*, 131.

him. In England, for example, a suspect can be arrested without charge for questioning and inquiry purposes. Within thirty-six hours, however, a Magistrates' Court must issue a warrant for further detention. Detention of more than ninety-six hours' duration is completely excluded. The suspect must then be either charged or released (see ss. 40–4 PACE). The police could easily extend this period by several hours, probably up to six or eight hours, simply by not legally arresting the suspect. This would be an obvious abuse of the law and unfair treatment of the suspect. The suspect must therefore be told as soon as practicable that he is under arrest.[426]

German law requires a warrant. The police or public prosecutor may only act on their own responsibility if the conditions for a warrant are met but a judge cannot be approached for reasons of urgency (*Gefahr im Verzuge*).[427] The suspect must be brought before the judge the day after his arrest at the latest; the latter will either issue a warrant or order his release (§ 128 StPO).

The suspect must also be informed at the time of arrest of the reasons for his arrest in a language that he understands, as added in Art. 5 (II) ECHR. Precise technical language is not necessary but the arrestor must make sure that the detainee understands the consequences.[428] Finally, if this has not yet taken place, the suspect must be cautioned and informed of his right to silence.[429]

2. Material conditions of detention

(a) Rule-exception One first condition of any practice of detention is that liberty must always be the general rule, and jail the exception. This is expressly stated in Art. 9 (III) 2 ICCPR and was also emphasized at the Havana Conference.[430] Only under exceptional circumstances may a suspect be detained; otherwise he must remain free.[431] This is the result of logical and consistent adaptation of the principle of presumption of innocence to the pre-trial stage.[432]

Pre-trial detention in Germany is regulated in this way by § 112 StPO. In England, the suspect may be held in police custody for a limited period

---

[426] *Alderson v Booth* [1969] 2 QB 216, and see s. 28 (1) PACE.

[427] § 127 StPO. Any eyewitness to a crime is allowed to arrest the offender, which is to be considered a public duty § 127 (I).

[428] *Abbassy v Metropolitan Police Commissioner* [1990] 1 WLR 385.

[429] See the discussion on whether or not the right to silence is applicable in the pre-trial stage.

[430] See Havana Conference, 157.

[431] See e.g. BVerfGE 53, 152 at 158.

[432] Of course, pre-trial detention differs from imprisonment after conviction, as its aim is not to inflict punishment. If it was meant as punishment, pre-trial detention would obviously be in breach of the presumption of innocence. Geppert, JURA (1993), 160 at 161.

of time before being charged, as we have seen. After the charge, he must either be released on bail or may be further detained in police custody. The charged person should be brought to trial without delay[433] and be at liberty pending trial as far as possible. Bail is relatively liberal in England in both law and practice. Some 80 per cent of those who apply for bail are bailed by the police, and an even higher share by courts. Leigh suspects that this high figure merely balances out the prior excessive use of the power to arrest, even in connection with minor offences.[434] S. 37 PACE states clearly that a person must be released if there is insufficient evidence for a charge, unless the custody officer is convinced that further detention is needed for further questioning.[435] It is up to the latter to decide this matter.[436] After the charge, the custody officer also decides whether specific fears exist that speak against releasing the person charged (s. 38 PACE).[437] Generally speaking, there is a statutory right to bail, as encapsulated in s. 4 Bail Act 1976. It is often referred to as the 'presumption in favour of bail'.[438] Only in exceptional circumstances can a suspect be held on remand after the 'charge'.

According to the practice in the USA, the general rule is that the suspect be released unless overriding public interest can be shown. The Eighth Amendment to the US Constitution provides for non-excessive bail, but does not address a right to bail.[439] Although criticized as a cheque-book system, the law certainly allows detention only in the case of strong, specific dangers.[440] It becomes clear from these three examples that detention should be the exception to the general rule of release.

(b) Strong suspicion   As it has become clear that detention should be the exception, the question arises of what conditions trigger this exception and leave the charged behind bars. In the Anglo-American system, the situation of the suspect alters when the charge is laid. The suspect may only be charged if there is strong suspicion against him. The case will be reviewed by the custody officer, who will issue the charge if he is persuaded by the evidence. German law also requires strong suspicion

---

[433] Leigh, *Police Powers*, 117.

[434] Leigh, *Human Rights*, 55–6.

[435] Murphy, *Blackstone's Criminal Practice*, D 5.2.

[436] The custody officer is supposed to be a senior figure in the police station who is independent in the sense that he is not investigating the case against the arrested person. It is his responsibility to ensure the proper safeguard of the rights of the detained, see s. 36 PACE.

[437] Emmins, 22.3.1.

[438] Compare e.g. N. Corre, *Bail in Criminal Proceedings* (London, 1990), 1.

[439] According to the case-law of the US Supreme Court there is no constitutional rule governing the conditions of bail, either. The Eighth Amendment only states that if bail is granted, it must not be excessive; compare E. Witt, *The Supreme Court and Individual Rights* (2nd edn. Washington, DC, 1988), 217.

[440] Osakwe in Andrews (1982), 271–2.

(*dringender Tatverdacht*) in § 112 (I) StPO, which is the case if it is a highly likely that the suspect is guilty of the crime that has been committed.[441]

Since the Bail Reform Act (1984), which was upheld by the Supreme Court,[442] bail may be denied in the United States if the public prosecutor can demonstrate that the release of the suspect would endanger lives or safety. The Supreme Court has been criticized for departing from the presumption of innocence.[443] In its decision, it upheld the principle that the state may restrain the liberty of individuals in the public interest. This can only take place in cases involving an extremely dangerous offence; it is out of the question for misdemeanours.[444]

(II) Legitimate Grounds for an Arrest

In addition to strong suspicion, there must be specific grounds for detention.

1. Human rights

One possible legitimate aim of detention can be easily derived from the wording of Art. 9 (III) 2 ICCPR. There it says that 'release may be subject to guarantees to appear for trial'. Similarly Art. 5 (III) 2 ECHR says that '[r]elease may be conditioned by guarantees to appear for trial'. Although this does not give a direct justification, it means *e contrario* that the first purpose of detention is to guarantee that the suspect will be present for prosecution; in other words, detention might legitimately be ordered if there are grounds for suspecting that the accused will try to abscond. Apart from that, no other reasons can be directly derived from Art. 9 ICCPR. A number of other purposes could be legitimized by 'implicit justification'. They would include the aim of safeguarding the functioning and effectiveness of the judiciary. Detention would thus be justified if there were grounds to believe that the suspect intended to attempt to suppress evidence, either by destroying evidentiary material or dishonestly influencing witnesses. Another reason for taking an alleged offender into custody is if there is a realistic danger that he is likely to commit further criminal acts. Pre-trial custody could be necessary to end atrocities immediately and prevent further acts. Those grounds could be said to be 'necessary in a democratic society'.

---

[441] Kleinknecht and Meyer-Goßner § 112, No. 5.
[442] See Supreme Court *US v Salerno* 481 US 739 (1987).
[443] Bodenhamer, *Fair Trial*, 136.
[444] Epstein and Walker, *Constitutional Law*, 412.

2. National law

According to German law, there are four possible reasons for arrest: (1) if there is a risk of flight and escape (*Fluchtgefahr* § 112 (II) 1 and 2 StPO); (2) if there is a risk of destruction or falsification of evidence (*Verdunkelungsgefahr* § 112 (II) StPO); (3) if there is a risk or repetition of further offences (*Wiederholunsgefahr* § 112a StPO) and (4) in individual cases involving particularly serious offences (*Tatschwere* § 112 (III) StPO). This last reason must be interpreted restrictively in order to conform to the Constitution: § 112 (III) StPO is not an independent norm, but may only be applied in connection with one of the previous conditions (1) or (2). It thus merely serves the purpose of lowering the threshold in cases of serious crimes where the public authorities have to react swiftly.[445] Should one or several of these conditions exist, the judge must nevertheless also decide whether the principle of proportionality is observed. Detention would be unlawful if it were excessive in relation to the importance and seriousness of the offence and the expected sentence (§ 112 (I) 2 StPO).[446]

In England, the statutory right to bail may be denied in cases involving imprisonable offences according to Schedule I s. 2 Bail Act (1976), under the following circumstances: the offender might (1) abscond, (2) commit a further offence whilst on bail, or (3) interfere with witnesses or otherwise obstruct the course of justice, whether in relation to himself, or any other person.[447] The court must be satisfied that there are substantial grounds for believing that one or several of the conditions are met.[448] As in the United States, the main focus is on the exclusion of dangerous individuals from society; the primary condition for the refusal of bail is the prospect of re-offending. The trustworthiness of the offender is the main guideline for the judge, when determining whether bail should be granted.[449]

(III) Potential Remedies against Detention

1. Remedies with respect to the conditions of detention

Art. 9 (IV) ICCPR says that every detainee has the right to have his case scrutinized by an independent judge. It reads as follows:

---

[445] This is how it is interpreted by the Constitutional Court (BVerfG Decision 15 December 1965. BVerfGE 19, 342 at 350–1). The BVerfG refers explicitly to Art. 6 (II) and Art. 5 ECHR and derives the general right to liberty from the constitutional principles of the rule of law and from the nature of the basic rights (ibid. 348–9).

[446] Compare Peters, *Strafprozeßrecht*, 425.

[447] Other conditions mostly intend to protect the offender or come into play if bail has already been broken. They are not important here; see C. Chatterton, *Bail: Law and Practice* (London, 1986), 3.03. [448] Corre, *Bail in Criminal Proceedings*, 4.

[449] Epstein and Walker, *Constitutional Law*, 412.

Art. 9 ICCPR

IV Anyone who is deprived of his liberty by arrest or detention shall be entitled to take proceedings before a court, in order that that court may decide without delay on the lawfulness of his detention and order his release if the detention is not lawful.

V Anyone who has been the victim of unlawful arrest or detention shall have an enforceable right to compensation.

In other words, the conditions I have just discussed must be subject to judicial review. There must be an institution that makes it possible to challenge the conditions governing custody. This institution must have the power to order release of the person unlawfully deprived of his liberty. This provision is a special example of the general human right to an effective remedy.

Art. 5 (IV) ECHR provides for the same protection as the ICCPR in similar words. Under European case-law the 'court' does not need to be part of the traditional judiciary. The authority called upon to decide 'must be independent both of the executive and of the parties to the case'.[450] The matter at stake is recognized by the ECourtHR as being of great seriousness, namely prolonged deprivation of liberty attended by various shameful consequences. Hence, the requirements of a 'court', in the sense of Art. 5 (IV) ECHR, are high.[451] Although the conditions may vary in each case, the 'court', in this sense, must always have the power to order immediate release of the person, if continued detention is not justified.[452] As to procedural guarantees with respect to such a review proceeding, the ECourtHR does not request the full kaleidoscope of judicial rights as laid down in Art. 6 ECHR. It is not necessary, for example, for the proceeding to be oral.[453] Nevertheless, the detained must be given the benefit of an adversarial procedure in some way or another, as the ECourtHR held in *Sanchez-Reisse v Switzerland*.[454] The principle of 'equity of arms' must be complied with.[455]

According to German law, the conditions governing detention must be reviewed ex officio by both court and prosecutor (*Haftprüfung*).[456] The

---

[450] ECourtHR *Neumeister v Austria* Judgment 27 June 1968, Series A No. 8, para. 24 ('the Law').

[451] ECourtHR *De Wilde, Ooms and Versyp v Belgium* Judgment 18 June 1971, Series A No. 12, paras. 78–9.

[452] Jacobs and White, 114.

[453] ECourtHR *Sanchez-Reisse v Switzerland* Judgment 21 October 1986, Series A No. 107, para. 50. This case was concerned with extradition detention, not with pre-trial detention.

[454] ECourtHR *Sanchez-Reisse v Switzerland* Judgment 21 October 1986, Series A No. 107, para. 51.

[455] Jacobs and White, 114–15, state the opposite, although the ECourtHR, ibid. para. 51, calls compliance with the principle of 'equality of arms' indispensable.

[456] This is so despite the fact that an obligation to do so is not explicitly incorporated in the

two authorities must decide whether the conditions, outlined above, still exist and whether detention is still proportionate to the importance and seriousness of the offence. After six months of pre-trial detention, the *Oberlandesgericht* (higher regional court) will review the conditions of the detention, according to § 121 StPO. The detainee may also apply for review of the detention under either § 115 (IV) StPO or §§ 117 ff StPO (*Haftprüfung* and *Haftbeschwerde*). To this end, the detainee will be assigned counsel, if detention has lasted at least three months (§ 117 (IV) StPO).[457]

Common law recognizes the writ of *habeas corpus ad subjiciendum*. Its use according to its original purpose, that is, to secure the release of a suspect held without charge by the police, has largely been made redundant by the provisions of PACE governing police detention. *Habeas corpus* is still of general importance for challenging the legality of imprisonment. The matter will be heard in court in an oral, adversarial manner.[458] Due to its constitutional importance, that is, its human rights relevance, this writ enjoys absolute priority.[459] The judge may order that the detained person be released. However, the writ of *habeas corpus* is a subsidiary remedy and may not be sought until other remedies have been exhausted. This means that the application for bail must be prior to a *habeas corpus* claim. Generally speaking, the 'charged' has a statutory right to bail, which will not be granted if there are exceptional circumstances justifying detention, as seen above. These circumstances can be reviewed in an application for bail by the detainee or his advocate. However, once a full application for bail has been made, the detainee may only apply again if he can satisfy the court that there has been a change of circumstances or that there are fresh considerations.[460]

2. Treatment during detention

Beyond this, treatment during pre-trial detention must also be subject to legal scrutiny. A look at the prohibition of torture and inhumane and degrading treatment showed that torture is the intentional breaking of the victim's will, while inhumane and degrading treatment means that the way the state deals with the individual must show respect for the inherent value of the human being. These principles can be transferred to treatment during detention. Art. 10 (I) ICCPR contains another provision that

---

text of the StPO; for the court, however, it is derived indirectly from § 120 (I) StPO and for the prosecution from § 120 (III) StPO; see Peters, *Strafprozeßrecht*, 428.

[457] According to § 117 (V) StPO, there will be an ex-officio Haftprüfung after three months in detention, if the detainee still has no defence counsel.

[458] Corre, *Bail in Criminal Procedure*, 96.

[459] Chatterton, *Bail: Law and Practice*, 9.39.

[460] Ibid. 3.14.

governs this stage: all persons deprived of their liberty shall be treated with humanity and with respect for the inherent dignity of the human person.

This norm sounds similar to the prohibition of degrading and inhumane treatment in Art. 7 ICCPR. The HRC therefore does not always differentiate between the two provisions, and seems to read them together as one regime controlling detention.[461] The manner of formulation is, however, certainly different: whilst the prohibition of torture in Art. 7 ICCPR is purely negative in character, Art. 10 (I) ICCPR contains a positive commitment to respect. The HRC therefore refrains from counting this right amongst economic rights deriving from a kind of 'sustainable development' approach, when it states in its General Comment:[462]

The humane treatment and respect for the dignity of all persons deprived of their liberty is a basic standard of universal application which cannot depend entirely on material resources. While the Committee is aware that in other respects the modalities and conditions of detention may vary with available resources, they must always be applied without discrimination, as required by article 2 (I).

Although recognizing the fact that differences in resources may produce different standards in a cross-country assessment, the HRC stresses that the responsible government must not discriminate. We can therefore make out a three-stage floating scale: (1) prohibition of torture, (2) prohibition of degrading and inhumane treatment, (3) respect for human dignity. Respect for human dignity, like the second prohibition above, is concerned with the general conditions and does not necessarily aim at influencing the will of the detained.

The detained person must have the possibility of receiving visits. He may not be detained incommunicado. The HRC states in its General Comment the necessity to grant '[p]ersons such as doctors, lawyers and family members access to the detainees'.[463] The source from which the HRC derives this right is unclear, as it is not mentioned in any of the human rights treaties expressly.[464] If the three-stage floating scale is applied, we find this right stemming from level three; respect for human dignity encompasses respect for human dependence on relatives. Hence, the right to be visited. Incommunicado detention might easily constitute level two, if it is arbitrarily maintained over a long period of time, or even level one treatment, if it aims at breaking down the suspect's resistance.

---

[461] See the discussion of the case-law of the HRC in McGoldrick, *Human Rights Committee*, 378.

[462] HRC General Comment 9 (Article 10), para. 3.

[463] HRC General Comment 7 (Article 7), para. 1.

[464] See McGoldrick, *Human Rights Committee*, 368; cf. also HRC *Simones v Uruguay* Doc. A/37/40, 174.

The detainee must furthermore be held in a place that is publicly known and the place of his detention shall be centrally registered and made available to persons concerned, such as relatives.[465] In particular, the detention shall not be detrimental to his health[466] and his health should be regularly monitored.[467] Restrictions on control measures and censorship of prisoner's correspondence fall more within the ambit of the right to correspondence in Art. 17 ICCPR, Art. 8 ECHR. They are, however, connected with the treatment of prisoners as required by Art. 10 ICCPR. Unnecessary supervision of correspondence must be avoided.[468]

The special provision on pre-trial detention in Art. 10 (II) a ICCPR was invoked in *Pinkey v Canada* before the HRC.[469] The allegations concerned non-segregation from convicted prisoners and worse treatment compared to convicted prisoners. The HRC could find no violation, as it held that separation does not necessarily mean separate buildings. In Germany, § 119 (I) StPO lays down that detained persons must not be accommodated in the same room as convicted prisoners. In its General Comment, the HRC emphasizes the reason for such segregation: the '[s]tatus as unconvicted persons who are at the same time protected by the presumption of innocence stated in article 14, paragraph 2'.[470] The suspect detained on remand must be treated as if he were innocent. The reason why he can be held on remand is the proper administration of justice, under the conditions spelt out above and under these conditions only. He must tolerate imprisonment as a member of a society that is strongly interested in punishing the guilty. Although one may, as an innocent person, have to undergo detention to this end, the treatment must be in accordance with these ends; this means that his liberty may only be restricted to the extent necessary for the special grounds for detention or by the need for order and security in the detention unit.[471]

(IV) Consequences for an ICC

A short summary of the conditions governing pre-trial detention reveals the following requirements: (1) detention must be the exception, (2) the formal conditions of arrest must be observed (arrest and supervision by a judge), (3) the material conditions must be met (strong suspicion and

---

[465] HRC *Simones v Uruguay* Doc. A/37/40, 174
[466] HRC *Ambrosini v Uruguay* Doc. A/34/40, 124.
[467] HRC *Antonaccio v Uruguay* Doc. A/37/40, 114.
[468] HRC *Estrella v Uruguay* Doc. A/38/40, 150. Likewise ECourtHR in *Herczegfalvy v Austria* Judgment 24 August 1992, 15 EHRR (1993), 437, where the applicant was handed back six binders of complaint letters at the time of his release from a psychiatric clinic.
[469] HRC *Pinkey v Canada* Doc. A/37/40, 101.
[470] HRC General Comment 9 (Article 10), para. 9.   [471] Compare § 119 (III) StPO.

legitimate purpose), and (4) a judicial remedy against these conditions and treatment during detention must be available. These are the human rights standards an international court must be measured against. Or should these rules perhaps be modified when we are confronted with heinous crimes like genocide, crimes against humanity, war crimes, and the like?

1. Law and practice at the ICTY

The legal regime at the ICTY appears to pay no heed to human rights concerning pre-trial detention. There is, for example, no verbatim reference to Art. 9 ICCPR compared to the transformation of Art. 14 ICCPR into Art. 21 Statute ICTY. However, Art. 20 (II) Statute ICTY states the following:

Art. 20 (II) Statute ICTY

(II) A person against whom an indictment has been confirmed shall, pursuant to an order or an arrest warrant of the International Tribunal, be taken into custody, immediately informed of the charges against him and transferred to the International Tribunal.

(III) The Trial Chamber shall read the indictment, satisfy itself that the rights of the accused are respected, confirm that the accused understands the indictment, and instruct the accused to enter a plea. . . .

The formal requirement condition (2) is fulfilled here. Arrest must be ordered by the tribunal and the detainee must be informed of the charges against him. As the indictment has already been confirmed by a judge, there will be a prima facie case, that is, strong suspicion against the suspect (Art. 19 (I) Statute ICTY). However, no further reference to the material conditions (3) above can be found, unless the unclear reference to the 'rights of the accused' is interpreted as the human rights standard governing pre-trial detention. The matter is addressed in greater detail in Rules 64[472] and 65.[473] These provisions foresee detention on remand as the general rule, liberty of the suspect as the exception. This constitutes a blatant breach of the letter of Art. 9 (III) 2 ICCPR. In the practice of the ICTY 'exceptional circumstances' for release are seldom accepted.[474]

---

[472] Rule 64, amended at the 13th plenary session on 25 July 1997, now allows detention outside the host country in exceptional circumstances. Prior to the amendment, the Trial Chamber II rejected a motion to transfer an accused person to a Kosovo neuro-psychiatric hospital (Sarajevo), *Delalic et al.* Case No. IT-96-21-T Decision 16 January 1997 on Motion for Provisional Release filed by the Accused Esad Landzo; see Jones, *The Practice of the ICTY*, Rule 64, 321–2.

[473] Rule 65 was amended at the 5th plenary session in January 1995, with the insertion of the duty to consult the host country in cases of provisional release; see ICTY Second Annual Report (1995), para. 22, n. 7.

[474] The three exceptions are discussed below.

Neither Blaskic[475] nor Landzo[476] or Kupreskic[477] were granted release. As held in Delalic, the burden of proof that the criteria of Rule 65 B are met rests on the defence.[478]

The approach might possibly be justified by the exceptional nature of international criminal prosecution. It could be argued that the substantive conditions of pre-trial detention earlier outlined are always met in the international context so that detention of the suspect is always imperative. The possibilities of the suspect absconding are far greater in a worldwide situation; there always seem to be entities or states that protect the suspect from the reach of the international organization. For fear of this occurring, the suspect, once arrested, must be automatically detained. It might also be argued that evidentiary material concerning international crimes is far more sensitive than in the national context. Both physical evidence and witnesses may be far away from the international prosecutor, who is unfamiliar with the circumstances in the area where the crimes were committed. In addition, the time lapse between the offence and the prosecution is usually greater than in any comparable national situation, which makes evidentiary material even more sensitive. The suspect therefore has far more opportunity to influence this material than in the case of national prosecution. Finally, the need to prevent future criminal acts could be said to be enhanced in the international criminal law context, mainly because of the hideous nature of the crimes.[479]

A look at the practice, however, reveals that this latter point turns out to be a complete fallacy. With respect to the last point made, it must be admitted that the aim of prevention is still a distant goal in international criminal law. This body of law is hardly ever enforced at all and, if so, only after circumstances had changed and the committing of similar crimes was highly unlikely. This is so despite the fact that the ICTY was established in May 1993, at a time when the war in the former Yugoslavia was well under way. For more than two years,[480] international criminal norms were breached. It

---

[475] ICTY Trial Chamber I, *Blaskic, Decision Rejecting a Request for Provisional Release*, 25 April 1996.

[476] ICTY Trial Chamber II, *Delalic et al, Decision on Motion for Provisional Release filed by the Accused Esad Landzo*, 16 January 1997.

[477] ICTY Trial Chamber, *Kupreskic, Decision on Defence Motion for Provision Release*, 15 May 1998.

[478] ICTY Trial Chamber II, *Delalic et al, Decision on Motion for Provisional Release filed by the Accused Zejnil Delalic*, 25 September 1996.

[479] The extreme gravity of the offences is mentioned by the Trial Chamber I in *Blaskic* Decision Rejecting a Request for Provisional Release, as justification for the principle of preventive detention encapsulated in the ICTY Rules. Likewise, the Trial Chamber II Decision 16 January 1997 on Motion for Provisional Release filed by the Accused Esad Landzo, para. 26; in the case of *Delalic et al.* Case No. IT-96-21-T, the Chamber took issue with the ICTY system of detention and justified this with the extreme gravity of the offences.

[480] That is to say, if one takes the Dayton Peace Agreement in October 1995 as the formal ending date of the hostilities.

may very well be that a future International Criminal Court will be able to intervene at an earlier stage of a conflict, but even then, detention remains improbable, because in the course of an armed conflict hardly anybody will be surrendered to the international court, as the world discovered during and after the Bosnian war. Peace of some kind or a cease-fire is crucial for enforcement of the law. The first two of the above submissions may encapsulate empirically correct observations, but they do not justify making liberty the exception and detention the rule. In theory at least, there is no reason for treating these suspects differently from their national 'colleagues' in that case-by-case evaluation of whether there is a legitimate reason for detention must take place. This may mean, of course, that the rate of alleged offenders against international criminal norms held in pre-trial detention is higher than the national detention rate.[481]

The case of General Blaskic at the ICTY bears witness to the fact that situations where pre-trial detention is doubtful may easily arise in international law, too. Blaskic's motion to be provisionally released was rejected by the Trial Chamber I.[482] However, he is now detained in house arrest outside the Detention Unit by the President of the ICTY. In his decision on the issue of house arrest, the President discussed various topics in connection with decisions as to whether a suspect should be held in custody, for example, the risk of absconding, the likelihood of tampering with evidence, the risk of influencing witnesses,[483] issues that are well-known from the prescriptions in national law.

General Djukic was provisionally released according to Rule 65, but solely on humanitarian grounds.[484] He was allowed to join his family outside the Netherlands, subject to several stringent conditions which were meant to ensure the appearance of the accused. Djukic died before the trial could commence.[485]

Milan Simic was also granted release for health reasons.[486] The Trial

---

[481] This is also the approach taken by the ECommHR with regard to the extended duration of national prosecutions of war crimes; see ECommHR *Jentzsch v Germany* Report 30 November 1970, Appl.No. 2604/65, 14 YB (1971), 876, concerning prosecution of Second World War crimes. The ECommHR opined that war criminals are no special category of criminals with regard to human rights. They are subject to the same privileges and restraints as any other criminal. However, the special nature of the crimes is likely to influence the interpretation of human rights provisions and allow, as in the case of *Jentzsch*, extended pre-trial detention.

[482] *Blaskic*, Case No. IT-95-14-T, Decision 1 May 1996, Rejecting a Request for Provisional Release.

[483] *Blaskic*, Case No. IT-95-14-T, Decision 3 April 1996 on the Motion of the Defence Filed Pursuant to Rule 64 of the Rule of Procedure and Evidence.

[484] ICTY Trial Chamber I, *Djukic* case, Decision 24 April 1996, Case No. IT-96-20-T.

[485] For a detailed analysis of the fate of this prisoner, see de Waart, 9 LJIL (1996), 453.

[486] ICTY Trial Chamber I, *Decision on Provisional Release of the Accused*, 26 March 1998, *Décision sur la demande de l'accusé Milan Simic de quitter son lieu de residence pur des raisons médicales*, 17 April 1998.

Chamber decided in favour of provisional release because Simic had surrendered voluntarily to the ICTY, his physical status was such that he needed daily medical care, the prosecutor did not object and the Republika Srpska had posted a bail bond of US$ 25,000.[487] The provisional release was granted on several conditions comparable to those of municipal law, like handing over one's passport to the International Police Task Force or the Office of the Prosecutor, daily reporting to the police, notification of change of address, prohibition of any contact to co-accused.[488] He was ordered to appear at least two weeks before the start of the trial to the ICTY.[489] Drago Josipovic was only granted provisional release to attend a funeral of a close relative.[490]

Compared to national practice therefore, the rules of detention at the ICTY could be described as threefold: (1) generally the suspect must be detained; (2) if it can be shown that there is no danger of absconding, or negatively influencing evidence or witnesses, the suspect can be put under house arrest outside the detention unit; and (3) only if the condition of the suspect, notably his state of health, are such that they are not compatible with any sort of detention, may he be provisionally released.[491]

The judges introduced a new Rule 40*bis*, dealing with provisional detention before confirmation of the indictment.[492] A judge may order transfer and provisional detention of the suspect, if he is satisfied that a reliable and consistent body of material shows that the suspect may have committed a crime that lies within the jurisdiction of the ICTY and if he considers detention necessary to prevent escape or the slanting of evidence or if it is otherwise necessary for conduct of the investigation (Rule 49*bis* B). Rule 40*bis* D gives a time limit of ninety days at the most, by which time the indictment must be confirmed, which triggers applicability of Rules 64 and 65, or the

---

[487] However, the ICTY is in general reluctant to accept even very high bail bonds; compare ICTY Trial Chamber I, *Blaskic, Order denying a Motion for Provisional Release*, 20 December 1996, where US$ 500,000 was offered.

[488] In greater detail: Jones, *The Practice of the ICTY*, Rule 65, 324–5.

[489] ICTY Trial Chamber, *Order Requiring Attendance of Accused*, 10 May 1999.

[490] ICTY Trial Chamber, *Kupreskic et al., Decision on the Motion of Defence Counsel for Drago Josipovic (Request for Permission to Attend Funeral)*, 6 May 1999.

[491] Compare, for further elaboration of these conditions in ICTY case-law, Jones, *The Practice of the ICTY*, Rule 65, 322–32.

[492] Adopted during the 10th Plenary Session, 22 and 23 April 1996. This amendment has a story to it: two high-ranking Bosnian soldiers, General Djukic and Colonel Krsmanovic, were brought to the Hague under Rule 90*bis*, which allows for the temporary transfer of otherwise detained persons whose appearance as a witness is required by the ICTY. Both men, who were in custody with the Bosnian authorities, were needed to testify against Karadzic and Mladic. While in 'witness detention' in the Hague, Djukic was indicted by the ICTY prosecutor; in other words, he was arrested by Bosnia as a suspect, and transferred to the ICTY as a witness, only to be indicted and detained as a suspect in the Hague. The aim of the amendment of Rule 40*bis* is to respond to this gap in the Rules.

detainee released. The suspect must be brought before a judge immediately (Rule 40*bis* F). The conditions of detention are subject to judicial scrutiny (Rule 40*bis* G). However, although this rule contains a welcome clarification of the previous broad and unsupervised provisional arrest measure in Rule 40 (iii),[493] it still seems troublesome from a human rights point of view. The threshold of 'may have committed a crime' appears to be lower than anything else that allows detention for up to ninety days without a charge. Furthermore, the possibility of ordering detention whenever the judge considers it otherwise necessary for conduct of the investigation seems to be too wide and to grant carte blanche for any detention that appears appropriate.

Altogether, the law at the ICTY concerning detention is unjustifiable in the extent to which it restricts liberty. As concerns conditions during detention, the ICTY is operating the first detention unit in history that is not governed by national rules of detention but by a unique system of international standards especially created by the ICTY.[494] For this reason, the ICTY adopted the 'rules of detention' on 5 May 1994. These rules take into account the 1977 UN Standard Minimum Rules for the Treatment of Prisoners, the 1988 Body of Principles for the Protection of All Persons under Any Form of Detention or Imprisonment, and the 1990 Basic Principles for the Treatment of Prisoners as well as the 1987 European Prison Rules. There are three underlying principles. First, the presumption of innocence must be respected in every case; secondly, the human dignity of the prisoners must be respected; and thirdly, no discrimination whatsoever will be tolerated.[495] In the Yugoslav war, ethnic conflicts played a major role. The ethnic differences between the detainees can be a delicate problem for the detention unit. The ICTY has paid particular attention to this difficulty. Its purpose-built detention unit provides for individual facilities, which should help to make it easier to ensure prisoners' safety.[496] According to Rule 65*bis*, a status conference must be held every 120 days as of commencement of detention, at which the conditions of detention can be raised between the parties and the Trial Chamber.[497] The International Committee of the Red Cross will act as the inspecting authority. In addition, the Bureau of the ICTY may appoint a judge or a registrar to inspect the detention unit and report to the tribunal.[498]

---

[493] Compare the critical approach in this regard in Bassiouni, *The Law of the ICTY*, 874.

[494] Compare ICTY First Annual Report (1994), para. 98.

[495] Ibid., paras. 99 and 100.

[496] Ibid., para. 103.

[497] Rule 65*bis* was adopted at the 13th Plenary Session on 25 July 1997, confirming a practice adopted at the first trials, and amended at the 19th Plenary Session on 17 December 1998; see Jones, *The Practice at the ICTY*, Rule 65*bis*, 331–2.

[498] See ICTY Second Annual Report (1995), paras. 106–7.

2. The system at the ICC

(a) The grounds for pre-trial detention   According to Art. 28 (I) Statute ILC, the prosecutor may request the Presidency to issue a warrant for provisional arrest of the suspect. In order to obtain such a warrant, the prosecutor must prove probable cause that the person under suspicion may have committed a crime. This procedure is seen as an exceptional one by the ILC. The normal procedure would be for the suspect to be either detained by national authorities under domestic law or arrested only after confirmation of the indictment, unless it is clear that the accused will appear for trial.[499] The ground for provisional arrest is fear that the suspect may not be available for trial (Art. 28 (I) b Statute ILC).

Once the indictment has been confirmed, a prima facie case has been established, which means that there is a sufficiently strong suspicion to hold the suspect in custody (Art. 28 (III) Statute ILC). Although the Report ILC stresses that the Statute ILC adopts the stance that detention should not be the general rule but the exception,[500] the arrest warrant will be issued in all cases, unless there are special reasons for not doing so, for example, if the Presidency is satisfied that the accused will appear for trial (Art. 28 (III) a Statute ILC). In the PrepComm, proposals were made with reference to the ICCPR that the detention of a suspect prior to a trial, that is, irrespective of confirmation of the indictment, should be limited to exceptional cases, such as risk of flight of the suspect, threat to others, or the likelihood of destruction of evidence.[501]

Human rights require, as shown above, that the arrest warrant may not be issued unless there are special circumstances for doing so. In this regard, the ILC Statute diverges from the ICCPR. The Rome Conference saw these flaws and avoided them. Art. 55 (I) d Rome Statute prohibits any arbitrary detention and limits the reasons for deprivation of liberty to those given in Art. 58 (I) Rome Statute, where the requirements for the exceptional issuance of a warrant for arrest are listed, namely reasonable suspicion together with a special reason for detention (necessity). The arguably exhaustive list gives three grounds: first, to ensure the person's appearance at trial; second, to prevent obstruction of the investigation; and third, to prevent further crimes from happening. The requirements for detention are not dependent on confirmation of the indictment.

At the time of arrest, the person needs to be informed of the reasons for the arrest and of any charges against him (Art. 60 (I) Rome Statute, Art. 28 (IV) Statute ILC). Upon arrest, the person must be brought promptly before a judicial officer of the state where the arrest occurred (Art. 59 (II)

---

[499] Report ILC Art. 28, para. 3.   [500] Ibid., Art. 29, para. 3.
[501] Report of the PrepComm I, para. 244.

Rome Statute, Art. 29 (I) Statute ILC).[502] Apart from this, neither the Rome Statute nor the Statute ILC give any guidance as to the conditions of detention. Amnesty International submits that the Rome Statute should refer explicitly to international detention standards.[503]

(b) Time limit Concerns have arisen among lawyers that the provisions in the Draft Statute ILC do not live up to human rights obligations. According to Art. 28 (II) Draft Statute, the suspect is entitled to be released if the indictment is not confirmed within ninety days or such time as the Presidency may allow. It is feared that this indefinite extension of detention is contrary to the provision entitling the accused to be tried without undue delay.[504] It is therefore submitted that an absolute time limit for pre-indictment detention should be enshrined in the statute.[505] From a human rights viewpoint the entire arrest procedure seems questionable with regard to the above finding. Detention for ninety days or more only upon 'probable cause' is more than a person can be asked to tolerate.

The Rome Statute does not differentiate between pre-confirmation and post-confirmation proceedings. Confirmation of the indictment does not influence detention, either. As to the time limit, Art. 61 (I) Rome Statute says that the Pre-Trial Chamber shall hold a confirmation hearing within 'reasonable time' after appearance of the suspect before the ICC. Although there still is no precise time limit, the procedure under the Rome Statute seems preferable from a human rights point of view, because the suspect is detained by way of exception only if there are 'reasonable grounds' to believe that the suspect has committed the alleged crime (Art. 58 (I) a Rome Statute).

There are remedies available for the detainee. He may apply for bail, but does not have an explicit right to bail. He may only be released on bail if the Court is satisfied that he will appear for trial (Art. 29 (II) Statute ILC). Again, this reverses the exception to the rule. The accused should have a right to be released, unless there are reasonable grounds to believe that he will not appear for trial (or any other of the above conditions are applicable). However, should the Presidency declare that detention was unlawful, the detainee may be awarded compensation (Art. 29 (III) Statute ILC).

---

[502] See also Report of the PrepComm II, 136–8.

[503] IOR 40/05/94, 39. Likewise Hall in Trifterer (ed.), *Commentary on the Rome Statute*, Art. 55, No. 16, favours the inclusion of international standards and the body of rules at the ICTY and the ICTR in the law of the ICC.

[504] See the Lawyers' Committee for Human Rights, International Criminal Court Briefing Series, Vol. I, No. 1, 13, Vol. I, No. 2, 6–8; Amnesty International IOR 40/05/94. Doubts on the legality of this time prescription were also raised in the PrepComm; see Report of the PrepComm I, para. 242.

[505] Lawyers' Committee for Human Rights, International Criminal Court Briefing Series, Vol. I, No. 2, 7. The Report of the PrepComm II, 131, finds sixty days and a maximum extension to ninety days appropriate.

Again, the better solution from a human rights point is incorporated into the law of the Rome Statute. The Pre-Trial Chamber will review the grounds for detention on request by the detained person and on its own initiative at specific still undefined periods (Art. 60 (II) to (IV) Rome Statute). The Rule of Procedure should lay down a precise period within which the Pre-Trial Chamber should review detention. It is submitted here that this period should by no means exceed Germany's six-months rule, which is already rather excessive.[506] In Draft Rule 5.16 (b), the period is limited to 120 days. Review may also take place at any time at the request of the detained person or the prosecutor.[507] Draft Rule 5.17 provides a list of possible conditions of provisional release. For unlawful detention or arrest, Art. 85 (I) provides for an enforceable right to compensation.

(c) Position vis-à-vis *national jurisdictions* The International Court has a special problem that stems from its existence as a subsidiary court. The suspect may already have been detained for a long time in a national state before he is transferred to the international judicial organ. It would appear that the suspect detained by national authorities has no remedy against detention under the Statute ILC. Amnesty International criticizes the fact that those persons who are most vulnerable to abuse at the hands of a national authority have no chances of seeking relief.[508] Art. 59 Rome Statute addresses the competence conflict between national authorities and the ICC. The state party that has received an arrest order must take immediate steps to arrest the person in question (Art. 59 (I) Rome Statute). The ICC must be informed of the arrest and will send a copy of the arrest warrant in a language the detained person can fully understand (Draft Rule 5.15 a). According to Art. 59 (III) Rome Statute, the arrested person has the right to apply to the competent national authority for interim release pending surrender. The ICC must be informed of this request (Draft Rule 5.15 d). It lies within the discretion of the national authority to decide whether it will be able to fulfil its duty to surrender the person to the ICC, if interim release is granted. The Pre-Trial Chamber shall be notified of any request for interim release and will make recommendations which the national organ must take into full consideration. However, the lawfulness of the ICC's warrant for arrest cannot be reviewed by the national body (see Art. 59 (IV) and (V) Rome Statute). In the event of interim release, the ICC must be informed periodically of the situation of the suspect (Art. 59 (VI) Rome Statute, Draft Rule 5.15 d).

---

[506] See above Ch. 2 C III 1.

[507] Under these circumstances, the doubts expressed by Hall in Trifterer (ed.), *Commentary on the Rome Statute*, Art. 15, No. 16, namely, that the Rome Statute does not expressly recognize the right to have the lawfulness of detention reviewed, no longer apply, if they were ever justified with regard to Art. 60 Rome Statute.

[508] IOR 40/05/94, 38.

D. OTHER INVESTIGATING MEASURES

Several other measures that could jeopardize human rights must be discussed. The investigating bodies collect evidence not only through witnesses and by questioning of suspects, but also by searching and seizing, ordering specific forensic tests using electronic surveillance devices, and keeping records of the private life of the suspect. These measures threaten the right to privacy. A further topic that should be discussed, although it is not directly rooted in the activities of state authorities, is that of pre-trial publicity.

(I) Searching

In order to track down evidentiary material, investigating personnel may wish to search the suspect's private accommodation and/or office. If this would infringe the 'right to privacy', a special justification is needed. We must thus first define the scope of the right to privacy, and look at possible interference with this and how it could be justified. Lastly, I will discuss the imperatives that follow from this, both for the institutions and for the procedure of pre-trial inquiry.

1. Right to privacy

The right to privacy reads as follows:

Art. 17 ICCPR
I   No one shall be subject to arbitrary interference with his privacy, family, home or correspondence, nor to unlawful attacks on his honour and reputation.
II Everyone has the right to the protection of the law against such interference or attacks.

Art. 8 ECHR
I   Everyone has the right to respect for his private and family life, his home and his correspondence.
II There shall be no interference by a public authority with the exercise of this right except such as is in accordance with the law and is necessary in a democratic society in the interests of national security, public safety or the economic well-being of the country, for the prevention of disorder or crime, for the protection of health or morals, or for the protection of the rights and freedoms of others.

We face four terms that describe the scope of application: private and family life, home and correspondence. Numerous decisions have been handed down by the Strasbourg organs concerning Art. 8 ECHR; nevertheless, these terms are imprecisely defined.[509] This is not surprising, as even at first sight it is obvious that there is a considerable overlap between the terms, each one of them attempting to cover part of the overall aim of protecting some vague idea of privacy and excluding all arbitrary interference by public authorities.[510] Certainly, the terms must be given an 'autonomous', Convention-oriented meaning; that is, definitions from the German Constitution, for example, cannot be applied at the international, Convention level.[511] Jacobs and White therefore propose a different approach to Art. 8 ECHR.[512] The best way to deal with the problem is to establish certain case groups. They propose a number of cases that emerge from the case-law of Strasbourg as a classification of topics that come within the ambit of Art. 8 ECHR. They are: family relationships (right to marry and found a family, names, immigration, custody, access and core proceedings, adoption), homosexuality, transsexuals, respect for the home, prisoners (correspondence, family life), surveillance, and personal records.

Velu summarizes the fields of protection accorded to the individual by Art. 8 ECHR as follows. The individual is protected against:

(1) attacks on his physical or mental integrity or his moral or intellectual freedom,

(2) attacks on his honour and reputation and similar torts,

(3) the use of his name, identity, or likeness,

(4) being spied upon, watched or harassed, and

(5) disclosure of information protected by the duty of professional secrecy.[513]

Searching private premises falls within the ambit of respect for the home. The ECourtHR also treats the problem of searches by investigators as falling within the scope of Art. 8 ECHR, covered by protection of both 'private life' and the 'home'.[514] It can easily be concluded from this that a

---

[509] ECourtHR *Niemietz v Germany* Judgment 16 December 1992, Series A No. 251-B, para. 29, where the Court expressly refused to define 'private life' exhaustively, may serve as an example. However, the Court does not seem to be especially concerned about a wide scope of application.

[510] ECourtHR *Marckx v Belgium* Judgment 13 June 1979, Series A No. 31, para. 31.

[511] Harris, 303.

[512] See Jacobs and White, 175–210. Van Dijk and van Hoof, 282, refer explicitly to this approach. However, Frowein and Peukert (Art. 8, No. 1) stress the importance of distinguishing as far as possible between the individual terms.

[513] Velu, in A. H. Robertson (ed.), *Privacy and Human Rights* (Manchester, 1973), 12 at 92. Cf. also Loucaides, Personality and Privacy under the European Convention of Human Rights, 61 BYIL (1990), 175 at 177.

[514] ECourtHR in three judgments confronted with the 'searching' of premises; *Chappell v UK* Judgment, 30 March 1989, Series A No. 152, para. 51; *Niemietz v Germany*, Judgment 16 December 1992, Series A No. 251-B, para. 29; *Funke v France* Judgment 25 February 1993,

person's private dwelling is entitled to special Convention protection and needs justification under Art. 8 (II) ECHR. Before we look at possible justifications, we must address another issue concerning the scope of application to what extent are business premises subject to human rights protection? Are they protected at all? Can professional offices be included within the scope of 'private life' or of the 'home'?

A narrow, literal application would leave the professional part of life unprotected, whereas in reality difficulties will be encountered if an attempt is made to differentiate between professional and private life. A lawyer who mainly works in his front room would perhaps be protected, while the one who leaves home to work in his downtown office would be unprotected. In General Comment 16 (Art. 17), the HRC held that 'home' is to be understood as 'the place where a person resides or carries out his usual occupation'.[515] In *Niemietz v Germany* the ECourtHR also expressed the opinion that a narrow view cannot be the right approach. It therefore first extended the meaning of 'private life' beyond the 'inner circle';[516] the most protected activity within the ambit of 'private life' involves the creation of relations with the outside world, what generally takes place within the sphere of professional life. The ECourtHR also acknowledges the point already made, that it will often be impossible to draw a clear distinction between the private and professional spheres and this will lead to arbitrary discrimination. The ECourtHR then extended the ambit of the term 'home' to include business premises. It did so by invoking the French term 'domicile', which has a wider connotation than the English word 'home';[517] it also stressed the risk of discrimination, as discussed above with regard to 'private life'.[518] Furthermore, the Court placed the issue within the wider context of Art. 8 ECHR, which is intended to protect the individual from arbitrary interference by public authorities. This aim certainly applies to private and professional premises likewise.[519] Lastly, the ECourtHR held that documents which come under the heading of 'correspondence' are protected whether or not they are

---

Series A No. 256-A, para. 48, where 'correspondence' was also an issue as the argument was mainly about handing over letters to the French customs officers.

[515] HRC General Comment 16 (Article 17), para. 5.

[516] ECourtHR *Niemietz v Germany*, Judgment 16 December 1992, Series A No. 251-B, para. 29.

[517] Unfortunately, the ECourtHR gives no reference for this finding. C.-A. Colliard, *Libertés publiques* (6th edn. Paris, 1982), understands *domicile* as 'le lieu même où habite une personne' (p. 367), where there is no allusion to business premises. It is also interesting to note that the HRC quotes all other official languages to endorse the wide interpretation of 'home' (General Comment 16, para. 5). This is a rather unusual approach for the HRC's General Comments.

[518] ECourtHR *Niemietz v Germany*, Judgment 16 December 1992, Series A No. 251-B, para. 30.

[519] Ibid., para. 31.

private. Although the Convention text put the qualifying word 'private' next to 'life', it refrained from qualifying 'correspondence' in this way. It becomes clear *e contrario* that the notion of 'correspondence' encompasses both private and professional documents.[520]

One can see that the protection of 'privacy' as a human right is not limited to the narrow sense of the private home. It is perhaps better defined positively—as seems to be the inclination of the ECourtHR—as freedom from interference by public authorities in any part of an individual's life and in the development of his personality.[521]

2. Exceptions to the right to privacy

Interference with the right to 'privacy' in this wider sense is not completely prohibited. Art. 8 (II) ECHR states a number of aims that would justify invasion of a person's 'home'. It also states that the measures must be in accordance with the law and proportionate to the pursued aim.

(a) Legitimate aim   Which of the objectives of public interest that are listed would permit the state to search an individual's premises for the sake of criminal investigation? The aim that catches the eye most easily in this context is the 'prevention of disorder and crime'. The other objectives are: the interest of national security, public safety, and the protection of the morals, rights, and freedoms of others. None of these explicitly name criminal investigation. The ECourtHR has so far had to deal with rather specific cases. In *Chappell v UK*,[522] the applicant had to tolerate entry authorized by an *Anton Piller* order.[523] In this case, concerning a video store that sold and rented material which was allegedly produced in breach of copyright, the search was justified as necessary for the protection of rights of others, in this case to protect the copyrights of the video production company against unauthorized infringement.[524]

In *Niemietz v Germany*, a lawyer's office was searched to establish the identity and whereabouts of a person wanted for insulting behaviour towards a judge. The ECourtHR found the (uncontested) aim of the action

---

[520] Ibid., para. 32, with reference to its own case-law.

[521] Loucaides, 61 BYIL (1990), 175 at 189. The scope of protection comes close to that found in Art. 2 (I) Grundgesetz. According to the interpretation of Karlsruhe this norm is the most general of all the Basic Rights within the Grundgesetz, protecting everything through which the individual expresses his personality. In the ground-breaking *Elfes* case the BVerfG rejected a narrow interpretation; it found that the limits stated in Art. 2 (I) would not be necessary if the text did not imply a wide interpretation; BVerfG Judgment 16 January 1957, BVerfGE 6, 32 at 36–42.

[522] *Chappell v UK* Judgment, 30 March 1989, Series A No. 152.

[523] For an explanation of the conditions and consequences of these private-law warrants, see R. Stone, *Entry, Search and Seizure* (3rd edn. London, 1997), 10.02–10.34.

[524] *Chappell v UK* Judgment 30 March 1989, Series A No. 152, para. 51.

to be the prevention of crime and the protection of the rights of others (that is, the judge's honour).[525] In this case, the ECourtHR found a violation, because the measure was not necessary in a democratic society.[526]

In the case of *Funke v France*, the ECourtHR had to deal with customs officers investigating exchange irregularities. As the justifying aim of the action, the responding government gave the economic well-being of the country as well as the prevention of crime. The ECourtHR accepted the former as a legitimate aim.[527] However, a violation was found because the measure was considered to be disproportionate. This conclusion was not reached because less intrusive means could have been used but was based on arguments concerning the rule of law.[528]

The only case that matches our problem in the strict sense is *Niemietz*, because it is concerned with the searching of premises for the purpose of criminal investigation. The search was justified by the ECourtHR in order to prevent crime and to protect the rights of others. Can this aim really be applied to criminal investigation? Certainly, the borderline between prevention of crime and repression is flexible, but it cannot be completely overlooked. In some states party to the Convention, the question of whether the deployed measure is repressive or preventive decides which public body is authorized and accountable for implementation of the measures.[529] Depending on whether they enter someone's premises for crime prevention or for crime repression purposes, the authorities require different legal norms as justification.[530] The problem cannot simply be solved by making a general reference to the aim of enforcing criminal law, either. For this purpose, the aim could be seen in general and individual deterrence. The theory behind this aim is far from being commonly accepted. The legislator usually cites prevention as one of several reasons for executing criminal law but does not fail to quote other grounds that are less vulnerable to empirical scrutiny, that is, the just desert approach.[531] The state can therefore not base the investigator's power of search on such theoretical grounds alone.

---

[525] ECourtHR *Niemietz v Germany*, Judgment 16 December 1992, Series A No. 251-B, para. 36.

[526] Ibid., para. 37.

[527] ECourtHR *Funke v France* Judgment 25 February 1993, Series A No. 256-A, para. 52. A similar case is *Miailke v France* Judgment 25 February 1993, Series A No. 256-C, para. 23.

[528] ECourtHR *Funke v France* Judgment 25 February 1993, Series A No. 256-A, para. 57.

[529] See e.g. the German system, as mentioned above, where the public prosecutor is responsible for the enforcement of criminal law, while it is the responsibility of the police force alone to prevent crimes.

[530] See e.g. the § 100 StPO (Hausdurchsuchung) as the legal basis for investigating entry and Art. 13 BayPAG (Police Powers Act Bavaria) as the basis for preventive search.

[531] Compare Safferling, ARIEL (2000), 123, for a discussion of the different models for justification of punishment.

On another occasion, the ECourtHR held that Art. 8 (II) ECHR had to be interpreted restrictively.[532] The need for entry must be convincingly established. Let us then try the opposite approach and establish the meaning of 'searching' by the investigator first and then fit this into the terms that we find in Art. 8 (II) ECHR.

At this stage of the pre-trial inquiry, the investigator needs to collect evidence for the trial. The main aim of these measures is to find out what really happened and whose guilt can be conclusively established. Conviction of the guilty person is the ultimate goal. To this end, it might be necessary to collect evidence by entering people's dwellings.

'National security' cannot be quoted as justification in this case, as it applies to terrorists and organized crime. It does so in a preventive manner, as was the case in *Klaas v Germany*. To say that the main aim of criminal investigation is to protect the 'rights and freedoms of others' again sounds very utilitarian. Repressive measures surely have this kind of impact: they can protect, at least promote, and ensure the rights and freedoms of others. But this is a remote aim and not the reason why the investigator is now entering the premises. Justifying 'searching' with the 'protection of morals' would mean that public morals are being protected through criminal prosecution. This is probably one of the notions of a theory of positive general prevention in criminal law.[533] According to this theory, prosecution and sentencing ensure people's confidence in the system and its functioning. Lastly, 'public safety' could be cited as a justification. This almost seems like a last resort, as very few cases have provoked such justification.[534] If 'public safety' is understood as the functioning of society, then again one could argue that criminal prosecution is crucial for this purpose. The emphasis could also be on prevention, on measures necessary to secure *l'ordre public*.

None of the justifications explicitly stated in the ECHR text seem to be suited to criminal prosecution. The drafters seem simply to have forgotten to mention 'criminal investigation'. On the other hand, it is arguably unreasonable to exclude these measures. All of the discussed aims rightly refer to some aspects of criminal law enforcement. They all refer to long-range goals, rather than the aims and purposes of the investigator who conducts the search of the premises. In our opinion, the protection of 'public safety' would be the most convincing justifying aim of criminal investigation. Criminal law is certainly part of the social order. Its main,

---

[532] ECourtHR *Klaas v Germany*, Judgment 6 September 1978, Series A No. 28, para. 42.

[533] For a critical discussion of this justification of criminal law, which arguably prevails in Germany, see Hörnle and v. Hirsch, Positive Generalprevention und Tadel, GA (1995), 261.

[534] Jacobs and White, 304.

arguably exclusive, aim is to protect individual and collective goods.[535] To ensure the effectiveness of these rules, they are executed by prosecutors. The efficiency of this protection is no doubt in the interests of 'public safety'. We would therefore call the aim of criminal prosecution a subprinciple of and inherent in the general aim of 'public safety'.

(b) In accordance with the law Invasion of an individual's privacy by public authorities is only legitimate if it is executed in accordance with the law. In Art. 17 ICCPR, we find protection against 'unlawful' attacks. For the HRC, this clearly means that any interference with the right to privacy needs justification in national law.[536] This law must be in accordance with the Covenant as a whole.[537] The requirements pertaining to 'law' in the sense of the ECHR are discussed more precisely. With regard to Art. 8 (II) ECHR, the ECourtHR held that the restrictions and conditions provided for by law should not be 'too lax and full of loopholes'.[538] Any law that justifies interference must therefore conform to the rule of law, that is, it must be sufficiently clear with regard to the foreseeability of state measures and with regard to the separation of powers.[539] Lastly, the specific act of interference must be proportionate to the legitimate aim.

3. Searching procedure

To safeguard these requirements many legal systems have developed a procedure that is dependent on the issue of a judicial warrant prior to execution of the search. The US Constitution, for example, rules out general warrants (Fourth Amendment). A search warrant necessitates an individual authorization. Protection under the German *Grundgesetz* is similar; Art. 13 (II) GG requires an individual judicial authorization for entry into private premises. In general, contemporary English law also requires a warrant. In practice, however, only 12 per cent of searches are based on a magistrate's warrant.[540] Apart from search upon a warrant, there is a variety of possibilities for searching premises without a warrant (ss. 17, 18 PACE). S. 18 PACE (1984) now includes the former common law practice of entry and search after arrest.[541] The usual conditions for a

---

[535] Roxin, *AT I/1*, § 3; protection of legal goods (*Rechtsgüter*) as the main rationale of criminal law. Compare the *Frankfurter Schule*, which emphasizes this notion in particular, cf. Hassemer, in *Alternativkommentar zum StGB*, i (Neuwied), 1990), Vor § 1, No. 274 et sub.

[536] HRC General Comment 16 (Article 17), paras. 2–3. [537] Ibid.

[538] ECourtHR *Funke v France* Judgment 25 February 1993, Series A No. 256-A, para. 57.

[539] For the requirements of 'law', see the quality control of the law in *Malone v UK* Judgment 2 August 1984, Series A No. 82, paras. 67–8; this consists merely in an adaptation of the *Sunday Times* formula; see ECourtHR *Sunday Times v UK* Judgment 26 April 1979, Series A No. 30, para. 29 and 49. Cf. also Jacobs and White, 302–4.

[540] Lidstone and Palmer, 4.07.

[541] This possibility was first ruled out in *McLorie v Oxford* [1982] 3 All ER 480, but then reintroduced two years later by PACE; compare Lidstone and Palmer, 4.21.

search warrant to be issued by the court are to be found in s. 8 PACE (1984): there must be (1) reasonable grounds for a serious arrestable offence, (2) evidentiary, but not excluded material on the premises which is likely to be used at trial, and (3) to obtain this material, the premises must be entered.[542]

German law allows premises to be searched, as seen above, only under authorization by a judge. However, in urgent cases (*Gefahr im Verzuge*), prosecutor or police may act without a warrant (§§ 102, 105 StPO). The search is lawful if there are grounds to assume that the suspect or evidentiary material will be found on the premises.[543]

Recent developments in the USA seem to contrast with these general principles. In *Arizona v Hicks*,[544] the police searched without a warrant and found stolen material. The Court held that no right to seek exclusion of evidence exists unless there is a constitutionally protected interest in keeping criminal activity secret. Obviously, criminals do not have any legitimate interest in maintaining the secrecy of their crimes. The evidence was therefore admitted. One general problem of the *ex post* exclusionary rule becomes obvious here. It follows from the court's finding that criminals do not have a right to keep their crimes secret. Rightly so; the opposite is true, namely, the public has a right to learn about these crimes. However, if a search without warrant is successful, evidence thus obtained will seldom be excluded. The only condition, therefore, that must be fulfilled in order to make a search without warrant legitimate is to find evidence of a crime. This gives the police carte blanche to enter any premises without a warrant and only in the vague hope of finding material evidence.

The ECourtHR finds the necessity for judicial authorization prior to the searching of a premises to derive from the principle of proportionality. A warrant is the only way to ensure that privacy is not arbitrarily invaded.[545] From a human rights point of view, criminal investigation is legitimate grounds for entering and searching premises. However, there must be several safeguards. The normal approach should involve a search warrant and only in exceptional circumstances, basically in emergency, should prior judicial authorization be immaterial. At all events, the search is only legitimate if there are reasonable grounds for believing that relevant evidentiary material can be found on the premises.

---

[542] See F. Hargreaves and H. Levenson, *A Practitioner's Guide to the Police and Criminal Evidence Act 1984* (London, 1985), 34.
[543] Kleinknecht and Meyer-Goßner § 105 No.2.
[544] US Supreme Court *Arizona v Hicks* (1987) 107 S.Ct. 1149.
[545] See Frowein and Peukert, Art. 8, No. 30, referring to *Funke v France* and *Miailke v France*.

4. Law at the ICTY

The power to search is not explicitly mentioned in the law of the ICTY. In Rule 39 (i) and (ii), the prosecutor is entitled to collect evidence and conduct on-site investigations and may undertake such matters as may appear necessary for completing the investigation. Bassiouni finds that these provisions are even broader than the prosecutorial powers of Art. 18 Statute and give no guidance whatsoever on the standards to be applied.[546] According to my interpretation, these norms must be read in conjunction with Rule 39 (iv) and Rule 54. The prosecutor must request such orders as may be necessary from a Trial Chamber or a judge, if the measures he wishes to apply constitute an infringement of human rights. The substantive conditions the judge must find fulfilled are those outlined above, that is, that there must be reasonable grounds for believing that there is relevant evidentiary material on the premises.[547]

Furthermore, the prosecutor may, in urgent cases, request any state to seize physical evidence, as stated in Rule 40 (ii). In the latter case, the legal basis for invasion of a person's privacy must be considered in the light of the domestic law of that state. In the former case, the legal justification for the interference with privacy must be seen in the Rule of Procedure itself. As further elaboration is lacking, the prosecutor has to comply with the necessities that derive directly from human rights law. In particular, it is submitted here that any entry into people's premises needs the authorization of a judge as contemplated in Rule 39 (iv).

5. The ICC

As at the ICTY, the ICC prosecutor has the right to collect documentary and other evidence and conduct on-site investigation. It is submitted here that, whenever this comprises an infringement of human rights, the measure must be authorized by a judge, in this case by the Presidency, in accordance with Art. 26 (III) Statute ILC.[548] In the PrepComm, it was submitted that the right of all persons to be secure in their homes against entries and searches shall not be impaired except upon a warrant.[549] This should be issued only with adequate cause and should specifically describe the place to be searched.

Doubts were also voiced as regards control of the prosecutor's activities

---

[546] Bassiouni, *The Law of the ICTY*, 872–3. A further elaboration on the standards to be applied is probably left to the prosecutor pursuant to Rule 37A.

[547] Compare the test applied by the ICTY President in the Decision 11 November 1996 of the President on the Prosecutor's Motion for the Production of Notes Exchanged between Zejnil Delalic and Zdravko Mucic, rendered in *Delalic et al.* Case No. IT-96-21-T, paras. 38 and 39, as mentioned above.

[548] Report ILC Art. 26, para. 2.

[549] Report of the PrepComm II, 200–1.

by a single judge alone. It was submitted that a special investigation chamber should be instituted that could monitor and authorize investigative activities and give them judicial authority.[550] With regard to national practice, it does not seem compulsory to have an investigatory chamber for this purpose. As the aim of the judicial review is merely to ensure compatibility with the law and the rights of the suspect, it is deemed sufficient to have a single judge authorizing the investigative activity by reviewing the prosecutor's motion.

The Rome Conference took up this proposition and provided for a Pre-Trial Chamber (Art. 56 Rome Statute), which, during the investigation, fulfils the functions previously assigned to the Presidency (see Art. 34 b, and Art. 39 (II) b ii Rome Statute).[551] However, this Pre-Trial Chamber could consist of a panel of three judges or, in some cases, of a single judge only (see Art. 57 (II) a Rome Statute).[552] The prosecutor may request orders and warrants necessary for the investigation (Art. 57 (III) a Rome Statute). He will either cooperate with the states concerned according to Part 9 of the Rome Statute or, if such cooperation fails, he can act with the authorization of the Pre-Trial Chamber (Art. 57 (III) d and Art. 54 (II) b Rome Statute).[553] Draft Rule 5.13 regulates the procedure for the prosecutor's request. Private premises should at all events only be searched after authorization either by a national authority or in the form of a Pre-Trial Chamber warrant.

(II) Seizure

1. Human rights view

Having found evidentiary material, the investigator might want to confiscate it in order to use it as evidence in court. Often the suspect is the owner of material that is about to be seized; we are therefore dealing with a potential threat to the right to property. What is usually referred to in a simplistic manner as 'right to property' encompasses merely something akin to the right to peaceful enjoyment of property, as for example in Art. 1 Prot.1 ECHR.[554] The question is, therefore, whether or not seizure falls

---

[550] Report of the PrepComm I, para. 228.

[551] Behrens, 6 Eur.J.Crime Cr.L.Cr.J. (1998), 431–2.

[552] The number of judges remained quite controversial at the Rome Conference; compare Jarasch, 6 Eur.J.Crime Cr.L.Cr.J. (1998), 335–6.

[553] Before the prosecutor can act, he must, however, prove to the Pre-Trial Chamber that the state party is 'clearly' unable to execute a request for cooperation under Part 9 Rome Statute; Bergsmo *et al.*, in Arbour *et al.*, *The Prosecutor of a Permanent ICC*, 121 at 152.

[554] For a general analysis of the problems arising in connection with the 'right to property' see Schermers, 'The International Protection of the Right to Property', in F. Matscher and H. Petzold (eds.), *Protecting Human Rights: The European Dimension. Essays in Honour of Gérard J. Wiarda* (Cologne, 1988), 565.

within the ambit of this provision. Protection includes ownership and also possession.[555] Generally speaking, in criminal matters, the seized material consists of either stolen or otherwise unlawfully possessed goods, or is material that is lawfully claimed by the person from whom it was seized. In the first two examples, there is no case of violation of any property right whatsoever. The seized material is either lawfully claimed by someone else or possession of the material is unlawful altogether, as is the case with drugs or certain weapons and the like. In both cases, the material seized is not considered to be 'in his possession' in the sense of Art. 1 Prot. 1 ECHR. If the person from whom the material is seized has proper ownership, there is not interference with the right to the property, as seizure is only temporary confiscation of the property. As soon as the reasons for confiscation cease to apply, the property must be given back to the owner.[556] From the perspective of the right to peaceful enjoyment of property, justification is needed only for this temporary removal. This does not affect ownership in itself but consists merely in a restriction in use for a limited period of time.

Traditionally, English law has recognized wider powers of seizure than of search.[557] The only condition for lawful seizure is lawful entry. If a police officer has entered premises lawfully—not necessarily for search purposes[558]—he may confiscate anything that he has reasonable grounds to believe has something to do with any criminal act and needs to be confiscated in order to prevent evidence being concealed, lost, altered, or destroyed.[559] S. 19 PACE corroborates this wide common law approach. In the USA, the law used to be more restrictive. Only material described in a warrant could be lawfully seized by the police.[560]

The justifications for seizure in German law are similar to those for search authority. According to § 98 StPO, either the judge, or, in urgent cases (*Gefahr im Verzuge*), the prosecutor or the police, may order seizure. If no judicial authorization is obtained prior to confiscation this must take place within three days of the measure, if requested by the person in question (§ 98 (II) StPO).

From a human rights perspective, seizure seems to be a minor interference compared with entering premises. Nevertheless, it must meet certain criteria in order to be lawful: (1) seizure should be formally authorized by a judge, (2) the prosecution must have reasonable grounds to believe that the property seized will provide evidence that will assist the investigation,

---

[555] The only precondition the European authorities seem to specify is that 'possessions' in the sense of Art. 1 Prot. 1 ECHR need to have some economic value; compare the excessive case-law quoted in Jacobs and White, 247–50.

[556] Peters, *Strafprozeßrecht*, 446.

[558] Leigh, *Police Powers*, 222.

[560] Osakwe in Andrews (1982), 277.

[557] Leigh, *Human Rights*, 38.

[559] Hargreaves and Levenson, 62.

and (3) must reasonably fear that otherwise the material will not be available for trial.

2. The ICTY

At the ICTY the prosecutor is authorized to seize evidentiary material under Rule 39 (i), (ii), and (iv). It is submitted here that the legal basis for seizure of material is to be seen in this rule. However, prior authorization by a judge or a Trial Chamber is necessary. The conditions are the same as those required by human rights norms and as outlined by President Cassese.[561] If the prosecutor requests a state to seize material, which he is empowered to do under Rule 40 (ii), the national authorities must apply their domestic law. What is not quite clear is the fact that Rule 39 (i) speaks of collecting evidence, whereas Rule 40 (ii) uses the words 'seize physical evidence'.

3. The ICC

The Statute ILC contains no provision as to seizure of material. Possibly the drafters envisaged that national authorities would usually have taken such action before the ICC took over. According to Art. 26 (III) Statute ILC, if the prosecutor seizes material, he can only do so by virtue of a warrant. The statements of the PrepComm as concerns seizure are similar to those concerning the power to search. Seizure must be authorized by a warrant, which must specify reasons and list the items to be seized.[562] Art. 57 (III) a Rome Statute should be read in this way. Orders and warrants issued under this provision are transmitted to states via a request for assistance under Part 9 of the Rome Statute.[563]

(III) Tests

For the purposes of scientific evidence, the offender is often asked to submit to a blood-test or similar medical or biological tests. These modern methods of genetic analysis and the like are used alongside the more 'classical' forms of identification, like the taking of fingerprints, photographs, and so forth. Normally, the aim of these measures is to identify the suspect but this is not the only aim; they may also assist in clarifying factual circumstances of the case, for example, the blood-alcohol concentration or a person's mental state. Virtually no problems arise in this connection as long as the suspect cooperates with the investigator. Things become difficult as soon as the suspect refuses to cooperate. Are there ways and means of forcing him to submit to these measures?

---

[561] See above Ch. 2 D, p. 151.   [562] Report of the PrepComm II, 200–1.
[563] Guariglia and Harris in Trifterer (ed.), *Commentary on the Rome Statute*, Art. 57, No. 10.

1. Applicable human rights norms

According to the definition of 'private life' found before, the measures discussed here fall within the ambit of the 'right to privacy'. These acts intrude upon the physical or moral integrity of the individual. In the case of *Costello-Roberts v UK*, the ECourtHR found, on the other hand, that not every interference with the corporal integrity of the individual constitutes an interference with Art. 8 ECHR.[564] It is not quite clear what the court intended to say with this statement. Frowein and Peukert, however, point out that interference by state organs always falls within the ambit of Art. 8 ECHR, which is especially true of forced identity measures.[565] In *McVeigh, O'Neill and Evans v UK*, the ECommHR accepted this view, in general, concerning identification measures.[566] It also conceded in *X v Netherlands*, that forced blood-tests fall within the scope of Art. 8 ECHR.[567] Medical, especially psychiatric, testing to assess the suspect's state of mind is problematic. In this case, the outcome of the psychiatric test may prejudice the outcome of the trial.

2. Justification for the interference

As an intrusion upon the 'right to privacy', forced identity and other measures require justification. In *McVeigh, O'Neill and Evans v UK*, the ECommHR held that the Convention must allow these measures, if interpreted according to present-day conditions. The special threat that emerges from terrorist activities makes special countermeasures to combat these activities unavoidable. The case was concerned with the gathering and keeping of personal information to fight against terrorism. However, the ECommHR's decision only looked into terrorist activities. Outside the special circumstances of terrorist activities, it could still be argued that the general practice of keeping records would be unjustified.[568] Once more we must distinguish between two issues: preventive measures taken in order to combat crime and terrorism, and the repressive measures taken in order to investigate a crime and collect evidentiary material. The justification for the former, which is not of interest here, is clear, the 'prevention of crime' as found in the text of the Convention. The justification for the second is not so clear. Why must the suspect tolerate a blood-test to ascertain his blood group or analyse his DNA? But again we could say that it is in the public interest that the true offender is found.

---

[564] ECourtHR *Costello-Roberts v UK* Judgment 25 March 1993, Series A No. 247-C, para. 36.
[565] Frowein and Peukert, Art. 8, No. 7.
[566] ECommHR *McVeigh, O'Neill and Evans v UK* Appl. Nos. 8022, 8025, 8027/77, Report 18 March 1981, DR 25, 15 at 49.
[567] ECommHR *X v Netherlands* Appl. No. 8239/78, Decision 4 December 1978, 16 DR, 184.
[568] Loucaides, 61 BYIL (1990), 175 at 187.

A 'genetic fingerprint' provides much stronger evidence to support a suspicion. The innocent person, on the other hand, profits from this measure, because suspicion against him vanishes. The suspect therefore has to tolerate the infringement because of higher public interests.

(IV) Electronic Surveillance

Recent developments in the field of electronic surveillance have led to considerable problems in many Western legal systems. Many judicial decisions have been issued by the highest national and international courts. *Locus materiae* is once again the 'right to privacy', as first held by the ECourtHR in *Klaas v Germany*.[569] Attacks on this right via electronic surveillance devices take many forms. Not only do the investigators extend their ears, but the latest developments also make discussion of the legitimacy of using video surveillance necessary. The question, however, remains the same: to what extent are public authorities justified in invading the private sphere of the suspect? To illustrate the situation, I will look at telephone tapping in greater detail.

1. The national states

States have shown a tendency to increase investigators' powers over the last few decades or so in order to meet the challenges of organized crime and terrorism. This is the case even in Germany, where the limits drawn by the Constitution linger. The right to privacy in Art. 13 GG has suffered major restrictions.

In the United Kingdom, a different course of development can be observed. There has never been and still is no right to privacy, apart from the law that protects a person's proprietary rights.[570] Once more, control over police activity was only gained by rules of evidence established by the courts or through the supervision of senior police officers.[571] After PACE, the law concerning telephone surveillance changed—or rather came into existence in the form of the Interception of Communications Act (1985). Since then, a warrant issued by the Home Minister has been necessary. This warrant will be granted if considered necessary in the

---

[569] ECourtHR *Klaas v Germany* Judgment 6 September 1978, Series A No. 28.

[570] *Malone v Metropolitan Police* Comr (No. 2) [1979] Ch 344, [1979] 2 All ER 620. The discussion about whether or not to introduce a right to privacy is still unresolved in the UK. Whilst implementation of the ECHR into British domestic law makes Art. 8 ECHR applicable in domestic courts, and according to the former Lord Chief Justice, Lord Bingham, has made new legislation superfluous, the press in particular fear the danger of a strict privacy regime established by the judges and are therefore calling for a parliamentary Act, which they hope will lay down more liberal rights. At the time of writing the Freedom of Information Bill has still not been enacted as it is still heavily disputed.

[571] Leigh, *Police Powers*, 255.

interests of national security, to prevent or detect serious crime, or to safe-guard the economic well-being of the state. Interception of telecommunication is somehow the *ultima ratio*, that is, reserved for when other, so to speak ordinary, means have failed. This Act reflects prior practice but introduces a tribunal of five lawyers who review complaints of persons who consider their telecommunications have been intercepted.[572] Save for such interception of telecommunications, no other aural or visual surveillance is regulated by statute. Home Office guidelines govern other such devices.[573] What is certainly questionable in this context is authorization solely by the executive organs. No independent authority, no third person, is involved in the prior review of the planned action. As I have argued before with regard to searching and detaining, *ex ante* control through authorization by an independent judge is desirable from a human rights perspective.

2. Human rights bodies

Several cases have been submitted to the European procedure with little success from the applicant's point of view. In *Klaas*, the ECourtHR declared surveillance compatible with Art. 8 (II) ECHR; for the sake of 'national security', it is necessary, in a democratic society, for police powers to be modernized to keep up with advanced espionage and terrorism in Europe. The pertinent German law has been equipped with safeguarding and reviewing procedures satisfying the ECourtHR. A special review organ outside the main judicial system has been created to deal with complaints; the complaining person can, however, still access the BVerfG in respect of a violation of his basic right to privacy. Although the ECourtHR indicated that normal judicial control would be prefer-able,[574] the procedure under German law fulfilled the Court's arguably rather low threshold test of whether or not possible abuse can be excluded or remedied.[575]

In *Malone v UK*, the ECourtHR found a violation that then led to the change in English tapping law as discussed above. The case was concerned with 'metering', that is, recording the numbers dialed, and the time and duration of each call. As English law did not foresee a legal base for this device at that time, the ECourtHR declared the interception incompatible with Art. 8 (II) ECHR.[576] In two French cases, the ECourtHR further elaborated on this issue. In the cases of *Kruslin*[577] and *Huving*,[578]

---

[572] Interception of Communications Act 1985, s. 7.   [573] Leigh, *Police Powers*, 252.
[574] Loucaides, 61 BYIL (1990), 175 at 187.
[575] ECourtHR *Klaas v Germany* Judgment 6 September 1978, Series A No. 28, para. 50.
[576] ECourtHR *Melone v UK* Judgment 2 August 1984, Series A No. 82, para. 72.
[577] ECourtHR *Kruslin v France* Judgment 24 April 1990, Series A No. 176-A.
[578] ECourtHR *Huving v France* Judgment 24 April 1990, Series A No. 176-B.

the necessity for precise legal provisions was stressed because intrusion into the private sphere is a particularly sensitive issue; '[i]t is essential to have clear, detailed rules on the subject, especially as the technology available for use is continually becoming more and more sophisticated'.[579] A violation was found in both cases; the authorizing legal norm must be in accordance with the rule of law,[580] that is, it must lead to predictability (*Vorhersehbarkeit*) and legal certainty (*Bestimmtheitsgebot*), which means that if the law permits a margin of appreciation, it must indicate the scope of that discretion.[581] The decisions found a violation of Art 8 with regard to the requirement that the interference must be 'in accordance with the law'. The government was condemned not because of what it did but because of how it proceeded. In *Lüdi v Switzerland*, the legal basis for the telephone tapping was indisputable.[582] The ECourtHR, without wasting many words, recognized the whole procedure as necessary in a democratic society for the prevention of crime, thus denying a violation of Art. 8 ECHR.[583]

Possibly the most interesting case is *A v France*, as it deals with a clever investigation method, the 'telephone trap'.[584] Basically, the trick is to find an acquaintance or accomplice of the suspect, induce him to call the suspect and entice the latter into a conversation about the crime, while the police are listening and taping the whole conversation. The French government contested the applicability of Art. 8 ECHR on two grounds; first, the conversation was recorded on the initiative of one of the interlocutors and, secondly, the preparation of a crime is of public interest and therefore does not fall within the private sphere. The ECourtHR rebutted this argument, but relied for its final reasoning on the undisputed respect for 'privacy of correspondence'.[585] Once again, however, intrusion did not have a legal basis in French law and was therefore declared unjustifiable

---

[579] ECourtHR *Kruslin v France* Judgment 24 April 1990, Series A No. 176-A. para. 33.

[580] In *Huving v France* Judgment 24 April 1990, Series A No. 176-B, paras. 28–9, the ECourtHR found, overruling the ECommHR, that well-established case-law must also be taken into consideration in civil-law countries. Law was given a 'substantive' meaning. The differences between common and civil law countries should, in the opinion of the Court, not be overemphasized. This decision is questionable with regard to civil law jurisdiction.

[581] ECourtHR *Kruslin v France* Judgment 24 April 1990, Series A No. 176-A, para. 30; *Malone v UK* Judgment 2 August 1984, Series A No. 82, paras. 67–8; ECourtHR *Sunday Times v UK* Judgment 26 April 1979, Series A No. 30, para. 49 and see n. 477.

[582] Articles 171b and 171c of the Berne Code of Criminal Procedure.

[583] ECourtHR *Lüdi v Switzerland* Judgment 15 June 1992, Series A No. 238, paras. 38–9. The other interesting aspect of the case was the involvement of an undercover agent, who acted as agent provocateur. But neither the use of this agent on its own, nor in conjunction with the tapping, was deemed to be unlawful intrusion of the applicant's privacy. The issue was discussed in greater detail under the auspices of Art. 6 (I) and (III) ECHR. I will look at this later.

[584] ECourtHR *A v France* Judgment 23 November 1993, Series A No. 277-B.

[585] Ibid., paras. 36–7.

with regard to Art. 8 (II) ECHR.[586] The fact that the European authorities rejected the argument that the right to privacy was not concerned remains very important. Although the police are not directly involved, because a private person dials the number and holds the conversation, the latter takes place with the knowledge, and often on the initiative, of investigators using police facilities. It is *de facto* a police interrogation. The crucial question thus emerges of whether the investigator can legitimately circumvent the conditions governing police interrogation, that is, cautioning the suspect and refraining from placing any undue pressure on him. The question was discussed in some detail before the German Bundesgerichtshof. In the end the court held that such a procedure was not tantamount to a police interrogation; the rules governing the interrogation of suspects were thus not applicable.[587] This rather formal approach was heavily criticized in the literature,[588] and rightly so, in particular from a human rights perspective. Never has the ECourtHR been content with a formal interpretation of specific legal terms or procedures. The ECourtHR asks whether or not the applicant is substantially affected. Although this material approach does not always benefit the applicant and is certainly disputable when state conduct is being assessed,[589] it complies with the human rights aim of inhibiting abusive and arbitrary treatment of individuals by state authorities.

To sum up: aural or visual surveillance for the sake of criminal investigation is an invasion of the 'right to privacy'. To safeguard proper administration of the investigation, these devices must be authorized by an independent judge. He may authorize the intrusive measure if he has reasonable grounds to suspect the victim of having committed a serious offence and believes that other less intrusive measures will be ineffective. Situations like the 'telephone trap', which are in effect substantially equivalent to a formal interrogation, must be treated as such, that is, the suspect has to be cautioned.

(V) Retention of Data

One question that has already appeared here and there in the discussion of investigating measures needs further elaboration or clarification. When may data collected during an investigation be retained and when must they be destroyed? It is undisputed that the storing and release of information

---

[586] Ibid., paras. 38–9.
[587] See BGH Großer Senat, in NStZ (1996), 502.
[588] See e.g. Roxin, NStZ (1997), 18.
[589] As seen before in *Huving v France* Judgment 24 April 1990, Series A No. 176-B, paras. 28–9, the ECourtHR allowed case-law to be an adequate legal basis for state interference with a citizen's privacy.

relating to an individual's private life in a secret police register constitutes interference with the person's right to respect for his private life.[590] A justification for storing and release must therefore be found. Three distinct cases can be made out: (1) the suspicion is disproved in the course of the investigation, (2) the suspect is convicted and sentenced, and (3) the suspect is acquitted.

In the first case, that is, when the suspicion vanishes in the course of the inquiry, it would seem that all information that has been collected for investigating purposes must be destroyed. The suspicion was apparently wrong; the invasion of the suspect's private sphere, although justified at the time as a necessary means of investigation, is now illegitimate and no longer necessary in a democratic society. The question has arisen once before the European organs, namely, in *Friedl v Austria*. The dispute was settled amicably and struck off the list, after having been conceded by the ECommHR.[591] In the opinion of the ECommHR, the interference was minor and therefore justified. As a general justification, the Commission referred to the need to prevent crime in modern society. Friedl was photographed and his identity was established and stored by the police in the course of investigations into offences against the Road Traffic Act arising in connection with a demonstration by homeless persons in Vienna. While the complaint concerning the photographs was completely rejected as not within the scope of privacy,[592] the remaining complaints were understood to establish a 'relatively slight interference'. The information was kept separate from the 'proper' criminal files in a general administrative file and not entered into the data-processing system. As such, it was considered necessary in a democratic society for the prevention of disorder and crime.[593] This is certainly an extensive interpretation of what is necessary in a democratic society.

---

[590] ECourtHR *Leander v Sweden* Judgment 26 May 1987, Series A No. 116, para. 48. As this case pertained to national security, the ECourtHR lowered the *Malone* quality control of the law as regards foreseeability and accessibility and found no violation of Art. 8 ECHR.

[591] ECommHR *Friedl v Austria* Report 19 May 1994; ECourtHR Judgment 31 January 1995, Series A No. 305-B.

[592] Ibid., paras. 49–52. The justification cited was the fact that the photographs had been taken in a public place, and therefore did not constitute an invasion of the 'inner circle' of privacy, their purpose being to record the situation and the character of the demonstration. This is rather difficult to follow, as there does not seem to be any necessity for the police to have a photograph of every demonstrator.

[593] Ibid., para. 67. How does this prevent disorder and crime? By deterring potential demonstrators or denying persons who are found in the files the right to participate in further demonstrations? Certainly, it is not as threatening to have one's personal data stored in an administrative file as in a police file. But when a person who is already 'known' to the institutions applies for permission to hold a demonstration, and the application must be filed with the administration, would the record not be found and have consequences for the decision? Would this person not be stigmatized by the mere fact that his name appears in the records?

In the second case, namely, if the suspect has been convicted, the prevention of further crime is certainly an issue. The suspect has been convicted by a competent tribunal of committing a criminal offence. The presumption of innocence has thus been rebutted. As the danger of repetition can never be totally ruled out, the investigating authorities may, for a certain period of time, store and retain information. The test for establishing the length of this period is tripartite: first, the nature and seriousness of the offence plays a major role, especially the question of how dangerous it was and still is for society. For example, a cold-blooded killer who mainly works for organized crime is far more dangerous for the community than a woman who stabbed her husband to death and deeply regretted her action. Secondly, the amount of punishment plays a role. The sentence mirrors the seriousness of the offence. Thirdly, the danger of repetition must be assessed. There is no need to store personal data about the released prisoner, if and when repetition can be excluded.

The last case involves acquittal of the suspect by a competent tribunal. In one European case, this question arose in a slightly different context. The applicant was acquitted of murdering his wife and applied for compensation for one year's detention on remand.[594] The claim was rejected on the grounds that not all suspicion had been banished, that there was still room for arguing in favour of the suspect's guilt and that the acquittal was based on a 7:1 vote, which proved that the jurors only gave the defendant the benefit of the doubt. This reasoning is not convincing. Leaving aside the question of whether the state must grant compensation for this kind of detention anyway, state authorities are prohibited from giving a second verdict on the guilt of the suspect after his acquittal. Either there are grounds for reopening the trial or the presumption of innocence is still applicable. Assumptions that differ from the court's findings on the guilt of the accused are therefore impermissible. If the investigating body stores records of acquitted persons for further inquiries it is presuming that the court's decision was wrong. Furthermore, the danger of a suspect being presumed guilty increases if records of his previous behaviour are kept with the investigating authorities. He is stigmatized for already having had contact with the police and judiciary. For very good reasons this is avoided by criminal proceedings before a jury in English and American law, as the personal circumstances and character evidence of the defendant are irrelevant for the question of guilt or innocence.

---

[594] ECourtHR *Sekanina v Austria* Judgment 25 August 1993, Series A No. 266-A.

(VI) Pre-Trial Publicity

One problem whose primary source is not found in actions by state authorities arises in cases where the independent mass media or public statements of state officials, produce a strong prejudice leading to a situation where conviction of the suspect is almost certain, or, alternatively, to 'social death' despite his acquittal, because the public still sees him as guilty. The danger is even greater in a jury system, as professional judges can be expected to be more skilled at abstracting the truth from biased newspaper reports, etc., than jurors. The state may have a duty to protect the suspect from such a potentially biased environment. This duty could be seen either as part of the general requirement of a fair trial accompanied by the presumption of innocence or as a subprinciple of the right to privacy.

The question of pre-trial publicity has been raised before the European authorities on several occasions. It must be considered in the light of the 'fair hearing' provision (Art. 6 (I) ECHR) and the provision of the 'presumption of innocence' (Art. 6 (II) ECHR). The danger of prejudicial effects stemming from utterances of public figures is perhaps particularly great if a jury decides on the guilt of the defendant.[595] It is, however, not limited to the court room. Any public authority may infringe the protection of Art. 6 (II) ECHR.[596] In the case of *Allenet de Ribemont v France*, the ECourtHR emphasized the dichotomy between freedom of expression (Art. 10 ECHR), which includes the freedom to receive and impart information, and the problem of pre-trial publicity. It is a corollary to Art. 10 ECHR that the state informs the public about criminal investigations in progress. However, this must take place 'with all the discretion and circumspection necessary if the presumption of innocence is to be respected'.[597] In the above case the ECourtHR found a violation, as some of the highest-ranking police officers called the applicant one of the instigators of the murder, without any qualification or reservation. This was clearly meant as a declaration of the applicant's guilt which, 'firstly, encouraged the public to believe him guilty and, secondly, prejudged the assessment of the facts by the competent judicial authority'.[598]

Although the 'fair trial' concept cannot be said to have direct effect on third parties (*unmittelbare Drittwirkung*),[599] the state must protect the indi-

---

[595] ECommHR *X v UK* Decision 16 May 1969, Appl. No. 3086/80, 30 CD, 70.

[596] Jacobs and White, 150.

[597] ECourtHR *Allenet de Ribemont v France*, Judgment 10 February 1995, Series A No. 308, para. 38.

[598] Ibid., para. 41.

[599] See Geppert, JURA (1993), 160 at 162, who submits that the defendant can rely on his *allgemeines Persönlichkeitsrecht* (Art. 2 (I) GG) to complain against reports by the mass media,

vidual against improper reportage by the mass media through effective legislation. The human rights basis for this is to be seen in the 'right to privacy' in connection with the 'presumption of innocence'.[600]

relying on BVerfG *Lebach* Judgment 5 June 1973, BVerfGE 35, 202, where the Court ruled in favour of one of the persons convicted of abetting the robbery of a military arms depot and the killing of four soldiers that his name not be made public in a documentary about this crime that had shocked the conscience of the German people. The equivalent legal basis in the ECHR would be the right to privacy.

[600] This is also the opinion of Peukert, EuGRZ (1980), 247 at 260, who sees the necessity for the state to take positive (legislative) measures in order to protect the suspect against media campaigning, because of the fact that these persons often cannot take civil action to protect themselves against the media. Compare also Markesinis, 'Privacy, Freedom of Expression, and the Horizontal Effect of the Bill of Rights: Lessons from Germany', The Wilberforce Lecture, given on Wednesday, 11 March 1998, in London.

3

Confirming the Indictment

When the investigation is finished somehow a decision has to be made as to whether or not the case is strong enough to be taken to trial. This decision could perhaps be made by the investigating body at an even earlier stage or it may be necessary for the review and the decision to be laid in the hands of an independent judicial institution. It then seems appropriate to take a look at the preparation of the defence, at how much time, information, and facilities are necessary from a human rights point of view. In close connection with this lie potential preliminary motions.

A. THE DECISION TO PROSECUTE

(I) The Different Systems

In a national context the investigating authority starts with an inquiry as soon as it is known that a crime has been committed. This so-called 'principle of legality' (*Legalitätsprinzip*) compels it to investigate when there are facts that give enough grounds for suspicion. In a very clear manner this is embodied in §§ 160 (I), 152 (II) StPO. This principle contests with the opposing 'principle of expediency' or 'opportunity' (*Opportunitäts- prinzip*). According to this persuasion the prosecutor has full discretion whether or not to proceed with the prosecution.[1] The legal systems deriving from the Anglo-American tradition are built around this principle.[2] This conflict must be examined in order to find an answer for an international criminal court.

1. Germany

The objective of the 'principle of legality' is to ensure equality before the law and to prevent arbitrary prosecution.[3] Its roots lie in the belief that the legislator is the proper person to prescribe rules and criminalize certain behaviour. Out of respect for this overall governance the prosecutor, as part of the executive, merely enforces these rules without any discretion on his behalf. He is tightly chained to the legal rules. Any discretion

---

[1] Sessar in W. F. McDonald, *The Prosecutor* (Beverly Hills, Calif., 1979), 255.

[2] But not only these; e.g. the Dutch system leaves similar discretion to the prosecutor, compare Brants and Field in Fennell *et al.*, *Criminal Justice in Europe* (Oxford, 1995), 134.

[3] Kleinknecht and Meyer-Goßner, StPO § 152, No. 2.

would distort the guidance given by parliament and would therefore question the sovereignty of the people. The 'principle of legality' therefore is a 'defender of democracy'. As all executive power, according to the principle of the separation of powers, is strictly bound to the legislature, the 'principle of legality' also expresses the generic *Rechtsstaatsprinzip*, the rule of law. One main component of the rule of law is the principle of security under the law.[4] Security in this regard means that the law must be recognizable and its consequences foreseeable. Therefore all arbitrary decisions must be prevented. There is constant danger of arbitrary decisions in the conduct of executive powers. They must therefore be controlled somehow. The first medium of control is a tight corset of legal rules.

This is in practice a very unattractive principle because it tends to be very costly and time-consuming. Anglo-American lawyers often find it difficult to believe that the prosecution in Germany can comply with this ambitious principle.[5] The legislator, notwithstanding the difficulties, holds onto the 'principle of legality' and he meets the threat of an over-burdensome case-load in three different ways. First, the personnel of the prosecutor's offices is simply increased. This can of course be costly, and at times of budgetary constraint politically unattractive.[6] A second practice is the decriminalization of minor offences. The prosecutor has to investigate whenever a crime occurred, yet what a crime is is for the legislator to determine. In Germany there are, generally speaking, three different types of offences: felonies (*Verbrechen*), misdemeanours (*Vergehen*), and petty misdemeanours (*Ordnungswidrigkeiten*). The last group of offences are not included in the Criminal Code. They are enshrined in the Petty Infractions Code (1969) (*Ordnungswidrigkeitengesetz*). Mostly these comprise road traffic offences and offences in the economic field; they are dealt with by administrative authorities (the police included) with wide discretionary powers. As sanction for an offence a fine (*Bußgeld*) is inflicted upon the perpetrator. This part of the law is governed by the 'principle of opportunity'. The former two groups (felonies and misdemeanours) are defined as criminal acts but of greater seriousness. Here, the principle of legality applies.

A third way of diminishing the size of case-load is to create a number of exceptions to the strict legality principle. The German legislator has done this in several regards relative to the seriousness of the offence. It is therefore generally impossible not to prosecute felonies,[7] but with regard to misdemeanours the StPO gives a number of options.

---

[4] Herzog in T. Maunz *et al.* (eds.), *Kommentar zum Bonner Grundgesetz* (Munich, 1991), Art. 20 S.283 Nos. 61–4.   [5] Sessar in McDonald, *The Prosecutor*, 255.

[6] Still it has been practised in the history of Germany. *Ibid.* 261–2.

[7] The differentiation between misdemeanours and felonies is settled by § 12 (II) StGB. It lies in the amount of punishment that is connected to an offence. It is therefore a purely 'formal' discrimination.

In § 153 StPO certain powers to end proceedings are given to the prosecution. It can end them when the guilt of the perpetrator is considered minor[8] and when there is no 'public interest' in the prosecution. This decision has to be made by the prosecutor, meaning the police themselves cannot terminate proceedings.[9] With the exception of the most unimportant cases, the prosecutor needs the 'blessing' of the judge to discontinue the investigation. Quite controversial was the introduction in 1974 of a second important and now frequently used power to discontinue proceedings, incorporated in § 153a StPO. According to this, the prosecutor's decision is first of all conditional on the consent both of judge and the person charged, and second by certain requirements the charged will have to fulfil in the form of a payment to the state, a charity, or to repair the damage caused by the crime. The discontinuation of the prosecution is temporary; only if the conditions on the offender are met may the proceedings be terminated by virtue of § 153 StPO. This option was created with the aim of reducing the case-load of the prosecution in the field of minor criminality.[10] Its goal is conviction-free peace under the law, not dispensing with sanctions, yet without sentence in the technical sense and without adding to the record of the offender. Some criticize this law as ransom money to reduce the risk of being prosecuted[11] and as unduly favouring wealthy suspects. However, the presumption of innocence is carefully safeguarded and is not compromised by the consent of the charged as this does not amount to a confession.[12] These two are the most interesting and frequently used ways of discontinuing prosecution.[13] The 'principle of legality' is therefore full of holes, giving the investigating authorities some discretion to proceed with the prosecution or not. However, the court judge is also involved, as without his consent the discontinuation would not be lawful.[14]

2. The Anglo-American tradition

In stark contrast to this is the American system. The prosecutor enjoys full discretion over whether to prosecute. Jacoby names four policies that seem to govern the discretionary power of the prosecutors:[15] (1) legal

---

[8] This cautious formulation is necessary because of the presumption of innocence. No state authority may determine the guilt of the offender apart from the court after a trial.

[9] Kleinknecht and Meyer-Goßner § 153 No. 9.

[10] Ibid., No. 2.

[11] Walter, ZStW 95, 32 at 57.

[12] BVerfG Decision 2nd Chamber of the 2nd Senat, 6 December 1995, in NStZ-RR 96, 168.

[13] Other possible reasons are to be found in §§ 153b–154 StPO.

[14] In Dutch law there exist quite similar powers to keep the case out of court; however, these decisions lie solely in the power of the prosecutor; see Brants and Field in Fennell *et al.*, *Criminal Justice in Europe*, 128–9 and 134–8.

[15] Jacoby in McDonald, *The Prosecutor*, 82–6.

sufficiency, which means that there is in general an interest to prosecute offences which constitute a crime; (2) system efficiency, which contributes to the huge overload and backlog of prosecuting agencies (the prosecutor will try to find ways to deal with the case other than prosecution); (3) defendant rehabilitation, which aims at assessing what would be best in the interest of the defendant, opening up possibilities of pre-trial diversion programmes or probation without verdict; (4) trial sufficiency, whereby the possible outcome of a trial is assessed and it is decided accordingly whether or not to continue prosecution. The system is governed by practicability and effectiveness.

These four policies are exercised mainly by three procedural steps. The best known is plea bargaining, which still contributes to the legal sufficiency principle but effectively shortens prosecution and trial. Plea bargaining is most notorious in the US criminal justice systems. It fits into the Anglo-American system which relates the holding of a trial to the accused's plea. If he pleads 'guilty' after he has been confronted with the charges no trial is held, and the defendant is sentenced straight away. In order to achieve either a guilty plea or to discuss a suitable solution outside the court the prosecutor may use what is known as discovery. To this end he exceptionally discloses the entire file to the defence. Finally, he can actually transfer the case to a non-criminal justice agency, which is usually referred to as diversion.

In the English system the main responsibility for the continuation of the prosecution lies with the police. It is for them to decide whether to charge a suspect and refer the case to the CPS.[16] Alternatively they could satisfy themselves by cautioning the suspect, formally or informally, and laying no charge.[17] If they transfer the case to the CPS it is then in its discretion to decide whether or not there is sufficient evidence and whether or not 'public interest' requires a prosecution.[18] The CPS therefore has the power to discontinue proceedings according to s. 23 (III) PACE (1984). It was not always clear whether this meant a presumption against prosecution.[19] Since 1994 and its new Code for Crown Prosecutors the matter has been settled, and a prosecution will usually take place. However, the CPS is formally independent in taking the decision.[20] In practice it is highly dependent on the information presented by the police, which might suggest discontinuing proceedings. If the prosecutors want

---

[16] J. Fionda, *Public Prosecutors and Discretion* (Oxford, 1995), 39.

[17] Brants and Field in Fennell *et al.*, *Criminal Justice in Europe*, 130–1. A formal caution will be added to the criminal record of the cautioned person and will affect future prosecution decisions, which is not unproblematic with regard to the presumption of innocence. It is however widely used in dealing with juveniles.

[18] Fionda, *Public Prosecutors and Discretion*, 24.

[19] Ashworth (1987) CrimLR, 595 at 596–7.

[20] Emmins, 2.2.5.

to discontinue a case and caution the suspect, they have to refer the case back to the police. Similar to § 153a StPO there exists the practice of conditional caution (often referred to as 'caution plus').[21] Conditions might be an agreement to participate in treatment or to pay damages. Thus far, no further legislative action has been taken despite proposals to increase the possibility of 'punitive cautions'. However, discontinued proceedings do not technically amount to an acquittal, which makes later criminal proceedings possible.[22] Similar to the US praxis, pre-trial conferences have become very fashionable and seem to be an accepted means of reducing the case-load of the judiciary by an out-of-court settlement.[23] In these cases the defendant usually pleads guilty so that a second trial is barred by the principle *ne bis in idem*.

3. The practice at the ICTY and the proposals for the ICC

Art. 18 (I) Statute ICTY regulates the beginning of the investigation. The prosecutor will receive information about a crime and has to decide whether or not there is sufficient basis on which to proceed.[24] The letter of this provision supposes that, as soon as the prosecutor learns of a suspicion, either through his own staff or via other sources, he needs to assess whether or not there is sufficient basis on which to proceed.[25] The question of what constitutes a sufficient basis to continue is not elaborated upon, but it seems that the prosecutor is obliged to look into a case and assess the degree of suspicion.[26] He has discretion over whether to discontinue the proceedings. This sounds very close to the 'principle of legality' in the Continental tradition. Nsereko agrees with this[27] and sees two reasons for this: 'the exceptional grave nature of the offences that the prosecutor is mandated to prosecute and the fact that a special tribunal has been established at great cost to try such offences'.[28] This view is supported by the mandatory letter of Art. 18 (IV) Statute ICTY and Rule 47A. Nsereko puts forward a practical argument by saying that public opinion would be outraged, given widespread media coverage, if the prosecutor could discontinue a case on reasons other than lack of evidence.[29]

---

[21] Brants and Field in Fennell *et al.*, *Criminal Justice in Europe*, 132.

[22] Emmins, 2.2.5.

[23] See the empirical study looking at the practice in Nottingham by J. Baldwin, *Pre-Trial Justice* (Oxford, 1985), who seems to try and avoid the term 'plea bargaining' although he admits that this is what the 'settlement conferences' come down to (p. 75).

[24] Morris and Scharf, *An Insider's Guide*, 191.

[25] See also the Report of the Secretary General, para. 93.

[26] Morris and Scharf, An Insider's Guide, 192.

[27] Nsereko, 5 Criminal Law Forum (1994), 507 at 518–19, although he says that the law at the ICTY does not give any indication either way.

[28] Ibid. 519. [29] Ibid. 519.

The ILC proposal for the ICC was different; the prosecutor may only initiate investigations upon receiving a complaint from a state or a request from the UN Security Council.[30] He will then consider whether there is a possible basis for an investigation (Art. 26 (I) Statute ILC). It would be difficult to establish firm criteria that would serve as a screening mechanism and a minimum threshold to filter out complaints that lack sufficient seriousness.[31] What could be clarified in the statute is the degree of suspicion and for what reasons the case could be discontinued. A clear reference to the strength of suspicion in law and in fact should be amended.[32]

The Rome Statute went a step further. The prosecutor shall, when he is of the opinion that the information he received gives a 'reasonable basis' to proceed with an investigation, submit the case to the Pre-Trial Chamber and request authorization of an investigation (Art. 15 (II) Rome Statute). The prosecutor is therefore subject to judicial control at a very early stage of the proceedings indeed.[33] The condition to be met for beginning to investigate is the determination of a 'reasonable basis to proceed with an investigation'.[34] The prosecutor has to take into account the following parameters: (*a*) there must be a reasonable basis to believe that an international crime has been or is being committed, (*b*) there is no conflict with the principle of complementarity, and (*c*) the investigation must not be contrary to the interests of justice (Art. 53 (I) Rome Statute). The Rome Conference was aware of the fact that this last condition is not a purely legal one. In order to prevent any misuse of this condition the prosecutor must in any case inform the Pre-Trial Chamber where he determines that the interests of justice impede an investigation (Art. 53 (I) Rome Statute).[35] The prosecutor has to notify the Pre-Trial Chamber in writing and give the reasons for his decision (Draft Rule 5.4). This pre-investigation control through the Pre-Trial Chamber is not a mere formality. Rather it stems from the efforts to find a widely accepted compromise.[36] Through this early judicial control the political independence of the prosecutor could be increased, a step which must certainly be welcomed.

---

[30] Critical in this regard also Ferencz, 'Von Nürnberg nach Rom', 9–10.

[31] Such a judicial filter has been proposed by members of the PrepComm; see Report of the PrepComm I, para. 226.

[32] Report of the PrepComm II, 112.

[33] In none of the influential systems of criminal prosecution does the Prosecutor have to ask for judicial allowance to initiate the investigation. The control through a separate organ comes on the scene after the investigation has been concluded to decide whether prosecution is appropriate or not; see Ambos, JA (1998), 988 (990).

[34] Bergsmo, 6 Eur.J.Crime Cr.L.Cr.J. (1998), 354–5.

[35] For Cassese this provision is a great tool for the independence of the prosecutor at the ICC, 10 EJIL (1999), 144 at 162.

[36] Compare Bergsmo and Kruger in Trifterer (ed.), *Commentary on the Rome Statute*, Art. 53, No. 3.

4. Summary of the national theory and practice

Having looked at the three systems we find that the differences in principle are greater than in practice. It is quite obvious that in all jurisdictions there exists, first, a sliding-scale according to the seriousness of the offence. With most serious offences the prosecutor will continue the pursuit of prosecution whatever the other circumstances, as it will generally not be in the 'public interest' to leave serious offences unprosecuted.[37] Secondly, the guilt of the suspect plays a major role. This brings the previous criminal record of the suspect into play. As the English system tends to keep 'character evidence' out of the trial, it also finds it difficult to take the criminal record into account at this pre-trial stage.[38] However, if it were not taken into account, a petty persistent offender could constantly slip through the net of public prosecution. When deciding whether or not to prosecute the consideration of the criminal record is part of the 'public interest' test. This contemplation takes place without prejudice as to the guilt of the charged. The decision must be made according to whether or not it is appropriate that this person, concerned with this particular suspicion, be brought to court. This question must be answered in particular with regard to other diverted forms of dealing with criminal offences. If compensation is an appropriate reaction to the crime in question, 'public interest' to prosecute vanishes.[39] On the other hand, taking the wishes of the victim into consideration might alter the outcome of this assessment. Although it is frequently argued that the views of the victim should not dictate the decision of the prosecutor, they are nevertheless to be seen as part of the 'public interest'.[40]

(II) Assessment from an International Human Rights Point of View

After having looked at national and international practice it seems appropriate to look at the human rights issues that arise at this point of the proceedings. One principle that has found its way into human rights treaties as a leading principle crucial to democratic society is of great importance, the principle of non-discrimination. Not only do most human

---

[37] Ashworth (1987) CrimLR, 595 at 597.

[38] Westwood (1991) CrimLR, 591 at 595.

[39] This is the underlying rationale of both § 153a StPO and the 'public interest' requirement in English law; see Kleinknecht and Meyer-Goßner § 153a No. 3 on the one hand and Ashworth (1987) CrimLR, 595 at 602 on the other.

[40] Ashworth (1987) CrimLR, 595 at 603, referring to views that are inclined to give to the victim a right to be consulted before the prosecutor takes his decision, himself submits that the victims should be respected in the way that they are informed about the decision, that it should be explained to them, and that it must be assured that victims are represented in matters of compensation.

rights treaties include a general non-discrimination provision, but it is understood as intrinsic to the 'fair trial' principle that every person is treated equal before the courts.

Art. 14 (I) ICCPR reads: 'All persons shall be equal before the courts and tribunals'. A similar reference is to be found in Art. 8 (II) AmCHR. What does this mean for the stage of the confirmation of the indictment? In the course of investigation, certainly, it might become clear that the first suspicion was without substantial grounds or at least was too weak to base a trial on. Who then decides whether or not to continue with the investigation and to set a date for trial? In other words, can it be the investigator who decides whether or not to call someone to court, even though he is a civil servant dependent on senior ministers who are part of the hierarchy of the executive, or does the human right to an independent and impartial tribunal make it necessary that the decision is taken by a judge even at this early stage of the procedure?

Let us differentiate between two cases; first, it might be that there are just not enough grounds for a suspicion. This is a factual and legal question, not a matter of discretion[41] and can easily be decided by the investigating institution without an independent judicial review because is takes place at a low level. But if, secondly, there is strong suspicion, can it really be left to the investigator to make the decision which is crucial to the suspect? The answer must be in the negative for the following reason: the investigating institution is part of the civil administration. This means that there is a hierarchical dependence on civil servants or ministers of senior rank. It would be fairly easy to put pressure from above on junior officials in order to stop the prosecution of a political or personal friend, while vice versa prosecution could be forced against one's enemies. On the other hand undue pressure, easily crossing the threshold of torture and inhumane treatment, could be put upon the suspect by proposing to him 'easy' ways of how he could be released more quickly. The police might for example demand payment of a certain amount of money to release the suspect. Finally, wealthier suspects could propose a specific payment themselves and bribe their way to freedom. Taking all of this into consideration shows that the idea of non-discrimination and equality before the law is jeopardized if the decision of whether or not to prosecute is left to the investigating agencies. An independent judge is much more unlikely to receive pressure from outside. The investigation can therefore go two different ways. Either it becomes clear at any stage in the course of the inquiry that the suspect is free from suspicion and the investigator, realizing this, stops any further investigation against that person. Or the suspicion remains and the investigation cannot be halted by the prosecution itself; an independent judge must review the case.

---

[41] Kleinknecht and Meyer-Goßner, StPO § 152, No. 4.

The international prosecutor, as we have seen, is supposedly an independent figure compared to his national colleague. The prosecutor at the ICC is not answerable to a hierarchical structure. His position as concerns independence and impartiality equals almost that of a judge. Nevertheless, particularly as the ICC structure follows the common law tradition, the international prosecution has a task that makes it 'naturally biased'. It aims at a conviction. Although it has been argued before that the international prosecuting agency should be objective in the Continental sense, drafting the indictment makes it dependent on a viewpoint of the events that favours a conviction. In this sense the prosecutor is not independent as a judicial person would be. To contemplate discontinuation of the prosecution with this natural slant brings the same dangers of inequality as described above in the national context.

Finally, international criminal law comprises *per definitionem* only the most obnoxious crimes known to humankind. If the prosecution was dependent on the political will of the prosecutor, the seriousness of the matter, as well as the harm done to the victims, would be diminished. Therefore, the only proper reason for discontinuation by the prosecution must be the factual question of whether there is enough evidence to support a trial.

B. REVIEWING THE INDICTMENT

In any case, if the prosecutor considers his case strong enough to be brought to trial, he has to present his case to a judge in order to actually bring it to trial. The judge could then either stop the investigation because he is not persuaded that there is strong enough evidence, that is, he does not share the view of the prosecution, or take the opposite option and set a date for the trial to begin as he is convinced that there is a case for the prosecution.

(I) Insufficient Evidence

The court might decline from opening the main hearing because it is not satisfied by the evidence presented by the prosecution in the indictment. To what degree need the judge be convinced by the evidentiary material? One has to address this question in accordance with the balancing between the 'public interest' to prosecute and the interests of the individual. When is there enough suspicion such that the suspect can be expected to stand trial? What must happen here is a prognosis of the later judgment. Is it likely that the charged person will be sentenced or not?

1. Different jurisdictions

According to German law, the threshold is *hinreichender Tatverdacht* (§ 203 StPO), which means sufficient suspicion that the charged committed the offence. It is therefore necessary to review the entire dossier of the prosecution.[42] This review is done by a professional judge;[43] if he believes that there is sufficient evidence, he will admit the indictment (§ 203 StPO), otherwise his decision will be for a 'non-opening' of the trial (§ 204 StPO).

In English law one could compare committal proceedings or transfer for trial. These proceedings take place before a trial on indictment which will later take place in the Crown Court. During this first or preliminary stage, which takes place in the Magistrates' Court, the examining judges, as they are called here, decide whether there is enough evidence for a reasonable jury to convict.[44] This means that the threshold is not whether the examining judges are convinced by the evidence, but whether a reasonable jury could convict.[45] The evidence is assessed in a similar manner to the actual trial, mainly by presentation and examination of witnesses. After the prosecution has presented its case, the defence has the opportunity to submit that there is 'no case to answer'. If the judges find no prima facie case in respect of an indictable offence, the accused is discharged, that is, he is free to leave.

In the US systems one still finds the institution of a so-called Grand Jury.[46] The prosecutor will present his case to the Grand Jury[47] and may call and examine witnesses. The defendant himself has no right to appear before the Grand Jury, unless upon signing a waiver of the privilege against self-incrimination.[48] The Grand Jury is used by prosecutors as a vehicle for securing sworn testimony, as otherwise witnesses cannot be compelled to appear for testimony.[49] The jurors will endorse the indictment if in their view the state's evidence is strong enough to support the charges.[50] Otherwise the accused is released. In several states alternative

---

[42] Kleinknecht and Meyer-Goßner § 170 No. 1.

[43] How many judges sit on the bench is dependent on the nature of the case, but it can never be lay judges that have a say at this stage of the proceedings; compare § 30 (II) GVG.

[44] The proceeding under s. 6 (2) Magistrates' Courts Act (1980) which leaves out the consideration of evidence is left aside here because it seems to be an irrelevant special procedure, see Emmins, 4.3 and 4.4.

[45] *Practice Direction (Submission of No Case)* (1962) 1 WLR 227.

[46] It was abolished in England by the Administration of Justice Act (1933), which provoked 'rumours of regret but no real opposition'; compare Devlin, *Criminal Prosecution*, 10, see also Ch. 1 above.

[47] Consisting of not less than sixteen and nor more than twenty-three jurors; hence the name Grand Jury.

[48] Paulsen and Kadish, *Criminal Law and its Process* (Boston, Mass., and Toronto, 1962), 942.

[49] D. Karlen, *Anglo-American Criminal Justice System* (Oxford, 1967), 153.

[50] Epstein and Walker, *Constitutional Law*, 333.

review proceedings exist which resemble more of a trial where evidence of both sides is heard and a single judge weighs the prosecutor's case.[51] If in his opinion a trial is justified he will issue an 'information', which is roughly the equivalent to the Grand Jury's indictment.[52] The test is the same in both cases: the reviewing authority has to find 'probable cause' to believe that a crime has been committed, in other words, 'sufficient evidence to warrant a jury's finding the accused guilty'.[53]

In all cases the charged is free to go if the review judges do not find sufficient evidence. However he is not protected by the prohibition of double jeopardy. There was no trial, conviction, or acquittal; the ruling of the court was merely that there was no case to answer. The suspect could therefore face trial at a later stage, but only if there is new evidence or new facts emerge.[54]

2. The law at the ICTY

Art. 19 (I) Statute ICTY relies on a review by a single judge. This judge has to find a prima facie case in order to proceed with the prosecution. Rule 47 regulates the further details of this proceeding. The prosecutor will prepare an indictment in accordance with Rule 47B and C if he is satisfied that there is sufficient evidence for a reasonable suspicion that the suspect has committed the crime (Rule 47B).[55] What follows is a procedure of review before a single judge, during which the prosecutor might be requested to present additional material support for his charges (Rule 47E and F). Rule 47 has undergone several substantial amendments. Therefore, it is no longer necessary to hear the prosecutor on reviewing the indictment.[56] This might have an accelerating effect. The role of the judge has been compared to that of an examining magistrate or that of the Grand Jury, guaranteeing that the prosecutor will not act in a frivolous or wilful manner and that nobody will be prosecuted without strong evidence.[57]

The standard required for a prima facie case (Art. 19 (I) Statute ICTY[58])

---

[51] Karlen, *Anglo-American Criminal Justice*, 149–50, naming the different practices in the US federal states.

[52] Epstein and Walker, *Constitutional Law*, 333.

[53] Goldstein, 69 Yale Law Journal (1960), 1149 at 1166.   [54] See § 211 StPO.

[55] There is a little inconsistency in the wording of Art. 18 (IV) Statute ICTY, which requires a *prima facie* case, on the one hand, and Rule 47A, which requires 'reasonable grounds' for the same process, on the other. This contradictory wording was addressed by Judge McDonald in reviewing the indictment 10 November 1995 *Kordic et al.* Case No. IT-95-14-I, but left open, as Art. 19 (I) Statute ICTY clearly obliges the reviewing judge to find a prima facie case. See Jones, *The Practice of the ICTY*, Art. 19, 173.

[56] 13 Plenary Session on 25 July 1997.

[57] See Ascensio, 9 LJIL (1996), 467 at 470.

[58] Rule 47E, as amended by the 13th Plenary Session on 25 July 1997, now refers explicitly to this standard.

to be established is not clarified in the law of the ICTY.[59] It should be defined restrictively in analogy to the national practice that was outlined above, as a case that provides for a sufficient basis to convict—if not contradicted by the defence:[60] '[A] *prima facie* case for this [Art. 19 (I) Statute ICTY] purpose is understood to be a credible case which would (if not contradicted by the Defence) be a sufficient basis to convict the accused on the charge.'[61] The confirmation decision is unreviewable, except when there is a flagrant violation of the Statutes or the Rules.[62] During the confirmation stage the defence has no say. This has proven difficult in proceedings of confirmation according to Rule 61. The special Rule 61 procedure will be under scrutiny at a later stage when trial *in absentia* is discussed. Also at the ICTY the dismissal of an indictment or of a count does not trigger the principle of *ne bis in idem* (Rule 47I).[63]

In all the jurisdictions considered, the standard test as to the evidence produced is a rather low one. The rationale at this stage is merely to prevent the prosecution from abusing the instrument of the trial. Therefore the test is: does the prosecution develop a logical argument and underpin this with evidence that appears convincing to an extent that would make a conviction look likely?

3. Assessment: fair and speedy trial

There are two main human rights provisions which govern the assessment of this review procedure. First, the procedure may not be prejudicial as to the outcome of the actual trial, that is, may not render the main hearing unfair,[64] and secondly, due respect must be given to the provision of a 'trial within reasonable time' (Art. 14 (III) e ICCPR, Art. 6 (I) ECHR, Art. 8 (I) AmCHR, and Art. 7 (I) d AfCHPR).

It seems to be unclear why there has to be a hearing of the evidence before the actual trial commences as tends to be the case in the English

---

[59] Especially the relation of a prima facie case to 'reasonable grounds' (Rule 47A) or 'probable cause' needs to be determined; see Bassiouni, *The Law of the ICTY*, 898.

[60] See Ambos, 7 EJIL (1996), 519 at 526; this is the wording chosen by Art. 27 (II) Siracusa Draft. This was the definition adopted by Judge McDonald, Review of the Indictment 10 November 1995 *Kordic et al.* Case No. IT-95-14-I.

[61] Judge McDonald, *Kordic et al.*, confirmation of the indictment, 10 November 1995; this dictum was followed in subsequent confirmation decisions, e.g. Judge Hunt, *Milosevic et al.*, 24 May 1999.

[62] ICTY Trial Chamber, *Kovacevic, Defence Motion to strike confirmed amended indictment*, 3 July 1998; similarly the ICTR Trial Chamber I, *Nahimana, Decision on the Preliminary Motion filed by the Defence based on Defects in the form of the Indictment*, 24 November 1997.

[63] As amended at the 14th Plenary Session on 12 November 1997. See Nsereko, 5 CLF (1994), 507, at 528, who calls this the practice according to common law jurisdiction. As we have seen above, this practice is not limited to the common law, but also *usus* in Continental traditions.

[64] Paulsen and Kadish, *Criminal Law*, 918.

system. There are certainly several reasons in favour of such an approach. First, one holds a complete and thorough assessment of the case. If the prosecution's case is weak it will fall apart before the trial even starts, which has undeniable advantages for the suspect; one could say that to bring such a case to trial would be unfair towards the accused. Secondly, the defence gets an early chance to stop the prosecution and present evidence that works in favour of the charged. Interestingly, the defence, out of tactical considerations, seldom presents evidence itself but is normally content with rebutting the prosecution witnesses.[65]

It is true that the hearing of the witnesses, with the opportunity to examine their demeanour and appearance, gives a better chance of scrutinizing the reliability of the evidence against the charged. Yet the hearing is connected with several disadvantages for the witnesses. They are under scrutiny several times, which can be particularly harmful in cases involving child evidence[66] or rape cases.[67] Furthermore it delays the actual trial and thereby may have a negative impact on the witnesses' recollection. This could be to the disadvantage of the defendant. His situation remains uncertain for a longer period of time, which conflicts with the provision of the trial without undue delay, and also because a discharge does not have the same effect as an acquittal.[68]

The balance one has to make is between choosing a procedure that will effectively exclude cases that are not strong enough to support a trial and a procedure that is quick enough not to leave the accused in uncertainty for too long. It therefore seems necessary to review the indictment but in a fairly simple way. Is it then necessary to produce evidence or hold adversarial proceedings? The difficulty the Anglo-American tradition has to solve is the party-type manner of its trial structure. As the prosecution is not called upon to collect evidence which works in favour of the accused[69] the reviewing instance would learn only half the case if it were to rely only on the unfettered evidence of the prosecution. Therefore the further scrutinizing of the allegations is deemed necessary. According to the Continental method, with a more clearly objective and non-party prosecution, it seems sufficient for the purpose of filtering out the weak

---

[65] Emmins, 4.2.5.

[66] In England cases of sexual offences and offences of violence involving child witnesses have been taken out of the committal proceedings by s. 53 Criminal Justice Act (1991). These cases are transferred to trial without evidence being heard in committal proceedings.

[67] The difficulties of balancing the human rights of the witnesses with those of the accused will be discussed at the trial stage.

[68] For these reasons the Royal Commission on Criminal Justice 1993 (p. 90) spoke out in favour of replacing committal proceedings. It recommended, in the case of a submission of no case to answer, an assessment on the paper with the opportunity for both prosecution and defence to advance their views orally but without the possibility of witnesses being heard.

[69] See Ch. 2, p. 74 above.

cases to review the indictment and the files presented by this authority. As I have argued that from a human rights point of view it would be preferable to have the objective and independent Continental-like prosecutor which investigates so as to find evidence that favours the accused, so I am inclined to argue here that a review by a judge of the indictment and the files only is sufficient. It would ensure that a non-case would be discovered and halted. This also contributes to the acceleration of the process and ensures that the accused can be tried within reasonable time.

4. Consequences for an International Criminal Court

Art 27 Statute ILC contemplates the commencement of the prosecution. It is according to this rule a matter of the Presidency to determine whether or not there is a prima facie case with respect to the jurisdiction of the ICC. If so, the indictment will be confirmed and a Trial Chamber be established.[70] Art. 35 Statute ILC provides yet another possibility to halt the prosecution case from going ahead. This provision is intended to give primacy to national jurisdictions. In the words of the ILC it shall 'ensure that the court only deals with cases in the circumstances outlined in the preamble [of the Statute ILC], that is to say where it is really desirable to do so'.[71] This provision means another setback to the prosecutor's independence. The jurisdiction is already relatively narrow, as we have seen before. The additional check of admissibility seems unnecessary for several reasons. First, if the ICC should function only as a subsidiary court to national jurisdictions, that is, not have primacy as the ICTY has, it would seem enough to give the state concerned the possibility of requesting deferral of the case to its national courts in the same way that the ICTY may request of the national state that the case be deferred to its jurisdiction. Secondly, Art. 35 Statute ILC may easily conflict with the provision of *ne bis in idem* (Art. 42 Statute ILC). If the ICC declared a case inadmissible by virtue of Art. 35 Statute ILC, may the ICC then, after the national trial is concluded, prosecute again because it is of the opinion that the national court has been biased or misjudged the international matter of the issue?[72] May the national state request inadmissibility pursuant to Art. 35 Statute ILC once more? A provision should be inserted that protects against this repetition of trial. The ruling on the jurisdiction has to be final and no second trial may be initiated by the international prosecutor.

[70] The *Lawyers' Committee for Human Rights* submitted a profound analysis of how the prosecutor could be politically supervised, which it considers undesirable but probably unavoidable for the time being. The proposals aim at giving the prosecutor more independence in initiating proceedings ex officio which could be consolidated by a stronger and also political supervision upon confirmation. See Lawyers' Committee for Human Rights, Legal Experts Project, 'The Accountability of an *Ex Officio* Prosecutor'.

[71] Report ILC Art. 35, para. 1.

[72] For a discussion of *ne bis in idem* see below, Ch. 5, p. 320.

According to the Rome Statute a confirmation hearing will be held as soon as the suspect is present at Court (Art. 61 (I) Rome Statute). The competent Pre-Trial Chamber will either confirm the indictment and refer the case to a Trial Chamber, reject the confirmation if there is insufficient evidence, or adjourn the hearing and request the prosecutor to conduct further investigation or amend a charge (Art. 61 (VII) Rome Statute).[73] The threshold here is whether or not the Pre-Trial Chamber finds 'substantial grounds' that the charged crimes were committed.

The difficulty described above, as concerns Art. 35 Statute ILC, has not been solved in the Rome Statute entirely. Art. 17 Rome Statute addresses the issue of admissibility. The Pre-Trial Chamber must rule on the admissibility prior to the commencement of the trial by virtue of Art. 18 and 19 Rome Statute. The twofold challenge of the admissibility is likely to protract the proceedings unduly at an early stage of the process.[74] However, Art. 18 (VII) Rome Statute prohibits states from challenging a ruling on the admissibility of a case more than once if there is no significant change of circumstances.[75] Still, it is desirable that the Rules of Procedure address this difficulty in greater depth and prevent repetitive trials and undue delays. The Draft Rules 5.18 and 5.19 encompass an excessive regulatory body concerning preparation and conduct of the confirmation hearing. A considerable number of these rules aim at speeding up the procedure by setting time limits for both the prosecutor and the defence.

(II) Trial is Set

1. The preparation of the trial in national courts

If there is sufficient evidence the court will set a date for the hearings to begin. The review stage has therefore the power to modify the indictment as seems reasonable. This is so in Germany according to § 207 (II) StPO,[76] in England by virtue of r. 7 (6) Magistrates' Court Rules.[77] This power relates only to legal considerations, which means that new suspects or new charges may not be introduced at the review stage; there may only be different opinion as to the legal considerations concerning the charge and its modification accordingly. The court then goes on to prepare for trial. A first obligation in this regard is the setting of a date for the main hearing to begin.

---

[73] See also Ambos, JA (1998), 988 at 990–1.

[74] This danger is also pointed at by Bergsmo *et al.*, in Arbour *et al.*, *The Prosecutor of a Permanent ICC*, 121 at 143.

[75] See Ambos, NJW (1998), 3743 at 3744.

[76] Kleinknecht and Meyer-Goßner § 207 Nos. 3–7.

[77] Compare Emmins, 4.2.5.

On the Continent the preparation warrants a considerable amount of work as the judge needs not only to make himself familiar with the case; it is also for him to inform, that is, to subpoena all witnesses and expert witnesses (§ 214 StPO) to the extent he considers necessary to find the truth.[78] In this matter he is bound neither by the requests of the prosecutor nor by those of the defence.[79] However, both have the right to summon additional witnesses if their request was not granted, § 214 (II) StPO and § 220 StPO respectively.

In the Anglo-American system the burden is on the parties alone to call witnesses and present their arguments and evidence. As the court is still in charge of the proper functioning of the proceedings the parties have to disclose certain points to the judge so that he can act accordingly. In the procedure that is called Plea and Directions Hearing (PDH), introduced in England in 1995, the necessary information has to be produced to allow the judge to fix a date for the trial. This includes mainly information as to the number of witnesses and an outline as to the central arguments concerning law and facts.[80]

2. The law of the ICTY

If the indictment was confirmed by the judge according to Art. 19 (I) Statute ICTY the prosecutor may request such orders as may be required for the conduct of the trial, in particular orders and warrants for an arrest, detention, surrender or transfer of a person (Art. 19 (II) Statute ICTY). The Rules of Procedure give details about the procedure relating to withdrawal or amendment of the indictment (Rules 50 and 51). Generally the indictment has to be publicized (Rule 52). Exceptional circumstances allow the non-disclosure of the indictment (Rule 53).[81]

The warrant of arrest, together with a copy of the indictment and a statement of the rights of the accused, is transferred to the states where the accused was last known to be residing (Rule 55D).[82] Since an order by Judge Jorda under Rule 54 on 24 December 1995, the indictments are also transmitted to the International Implementation Force (IFOR) which was made possible by the Dayton Peace Accord.[83] To ensure the compliance with these precautions a member of the prosecutor's office may be present from the time of arrest (Rule 55G).[84] The local authorities are

---

[78] See Kleinknecht and Meyer-Goßner § 214 No. 3.

[79] Ibid., § 214 No. 7.

[80] For a quick overview see Emmins, 7.1.

[81] See for the cases concerning these provisions that have emerged so far, Jones, *The Practice of the ICTY*, Rules 50–3, pp. 271–81.

[82] As amended at the 9th Plenary Session on 17–18 January 1996.

[83] See Jones, *The Practice of the ICTY*, Rule 55, pp. 294–6.

[84] As amended at the 14th Plenary Session on 12 November 1997; compare Nsereko, 5 CLF (1994), 507, at 529.

obliged to cooperate with the ICTY and execute the warrant as the request by the tribunal overrides both national law and international obligations of the requested state (Art. 29 Statute ICTY and Rule 56).[85] This stage is perhaps the most ineffective and time-consuming one for the ICTY. The unsatisfactory situation that only few indicted persons are actually present in the Hague is due to the fact that crucial states do not cooperate with the ICTY by surrendering alleged offenders to the tribunal's jurisdiction.[86]

3. The human rights issues

Also during this stage time is crucial from a human rights point of view. The human rights norms are clear on the point that the trial has to take place without undue delay. If the court takes too long to prepare the hearing it obviously violates this human rights provision. The danger of this happening is certainly more virulent in Continental systems. In complicated cases it can take a long time before the judge considers himself ready to go ahead with the trial, because he needs to make himself familiar with the case first.

This criticism alone does not justify the quickly drawn conclusion that, in order to avoid this delay, one could turn to the system according to the Anglo-American tradition where the judge is not expected to know the case in detail before it goes to trial. It can be of advantage for the defendant if the person who will judge over him has profound knowledge of the files and of all the circumstances of the case. This is especially true in difficult cases, where otherwise the judging persons may not understand the difficulties in the case during the oral hearing. In cases which involve difficult evidence, documents in foreign languages, or even tricky legal issues, it might be quite impossible to come to a well-reasoned judgment if the judge had no insight into the specifics of the case beforehand.

With a view to the complexity of the matter, as well as to the infancy of the whole area of law, judges at the ICC should have detailed knowledge of the case before it goes to trial. The danger of prejudice is minimized by the fact that the prosecutor is truly objective and that the defence will present its case to the judge in advance.

---

[85] For a detailed analysis of this topic, see Gallant, 5 CLF (1994), 557. Compare also Bassiouni, *The Law of the ICTY*, 909–10.

[86] At the time of writing, 75 persons were indicted but only a mere ten were present at the ICTY, see ICTY Third Annual Report, para. 88 and bulletin No. 19, 4 August 1997, 6.

C. PREPARING THE DEFENCE

There is one main provision that governs the powers of the defence as a whole:

Art. 14 (III) ICCPR
b. to have adequate time and facilities for the preparation of his defence and to communicate with counsel of his own choosing;
c. . . .
d. to be tried in his presence, and to defend himself in person or through legal assistance of his own choosing; to be informed, if he does not have legal assistance, of this right, and to have legal assistance assigned to him, in any case where the interests of justice so require, and without payment by him in any such case if he does not have sufficient means to pay for it;

Art. 6 (III) ECHR
b. to have adequate time and facilities for the preparation if his defence.
c. to defend himself in person or through legal assistance of his own choosing or, if he has not sufficient means to pay for legal assistance, to be given it free when the interests of justice so require.

These provisions of course are not very specific. But one can derive from them three elements that are essential to the preparation of the defence; first, the charged must be given enough time to prepare his case, secondly, documents and texts that he needs for a proper defence must be disclosed to him and, thirdly, he must be given the opportunity to communicate with legal counsel, should he so wish.[87]

First, I must address what legal assistance or counsel means. Then I will reflect upon the adequacy of the preparation time, and finally take a close look at what is actually meant by 'facilities for the preparation of his defence'.

(I) Right to Counsel

1. Right to communicate with counsel

The right to communicate with counsel was inserted into the ICCPR by the Third Committee in its 14th Session (1959).[88] The HRC attributes most of the General Comment 13 (Article 14) para. 9 to this requirement, stressing that the communication with counsel must be conducted according to and in conditions giving full respect for the confidentiality of the lawyer–client relation.[89] This representation must be an efficient one, as the HRC found in a case against Uruguay, especially in the case of a court-appointed

---

[87] G. Seidel, *Handbuch der Grund- und Menschenrechte* (Baden-Baden, 1996), 304.
[88] This was on the initiative of Israel, A/4299 § 39 (A/C.3/L.795).
[89] HRC General Comment 13 (Article 14), para. 9.

lawyer.[90] It cannot be called adequate legal assistance if the counsel neither visits the charged nor informs him of the development of the case against him. Similarly the HRC found a violation in a case where the accused had contact with his counsel only four times in two years.[91] In the context here the right to counsel refers solely to ensuring the preparation of the defence. This becomes clear by a systematic analysis. The right to counsel during trial is separately enshrined in Art. 14 (III) d ICCPR.[92] This is paralleled in Art. 8 (II) d AmCHR, but not in Art. 6 ECHR.

None the less the European system encompasses an implicit right to communicate freely with counsel.[93] Both oral and written communications are protected.[94] This right finds itself in particular jeopardy when the charged is detained on remand. States have often tried to excuse interference into communication with counsel by invoking reasons of order and security inside the prison. These cases are often discussed in relation to Art. 8 ECHR, the right to respect for correspondence.[95] Yet the right to prepare a defence can be seriously hampered if the detained is denied private communication with counsel.[96] In conclusion it can be said that a right to communicate confidentially with counsel, in order to prepare one's defence, is guaranteed as a human right.

2. How to communicate

I turn now to the problem of the extent of communication necessary to ensure the proper preparation of the defence. Can the right to communicate be temporarily interrupted? Can the right be limited to certain times or certain topics?

As said before, this right comes into play in particular when the accused is remanded in custody. Prisons have a strict concept of rules for providing order and security within the unit's walls. In particular it must be ensured that the detained cannot profit from the communication, abscond with the help of the lawyer, or destroy evidence or property. Prison authorities have to employ certain precautions to prevent this from happening. On the other hand, the content of the communication between the lawyer and the client is strictly confidential and so may not be intercepted by guards. A conversation that could be watched and listened to

---

[90] HRC *Scarrone v Uruguay* Doc. A/39/40, 154.
[91] HRC *Estrella v Uruguay* Doc. A/38/40, 150.   [92] Nowak, Art. 14, No. 43.
[93] This is the repeated jurisdiction of both ECommHR and ECourtHR, compare e.g. ECommHR *Can v Austria* Report 12 July 1984, Series A No. 96, 17, para. 52.
[94] Frowein and Peukert, Art. 6, No. 182.   [95] Harris, 255.
[96] ECommHR *Can v Austria* Report 12 July 1984, Series A No. 96, 18, para. 56, where the ECommHR emphasizes the importance of the right to silence which could be interfered with particularly if no free communication is granted.

by a prison or court authority would certainly hinder the charged from freely expressing himself to his counsel.[97]

In Germany § 148 StPO regulates this field; the defence counsel[98] is greatly privileged in communicating with his detained client. In general (offences against § 129 a StGB, that is, terrorist acts are excluded according to § 148 (II) StPO[99]) letters between counsel and the accused are not to be intercepted.[100] Unsupervised visits are to be granted with no limit to time or frequency.[101] To this end the detention unit must provide a room where a counselling talk can be held under normal circumstances without optical or acoustic surveillance. The only restriction to be tolerated is that the ordinary visiting hours have to be respected; but these may not be so limited that counsel's work is severely hampered.[102]

In English law, s. 58 of PACE (1984) provides the right to consult legal counsel. This consultation has to be in private. Although this is not further defined, it is submitted that what is meant is that it should be out of the sight and hearing of a police officer.[103] It is furthermore guaranteed that advice should be accessible at any time. This sounds fairly radical as it does not limit the right by any consideration of practicality or convenience.[104] This norm is however only applicable during police interrogation and not during the time of detention on remand.

From the official point of view the aim is to keep the order of the prison. The defence interest is to keep communication possible and confidential. These two potentially conflicting interests have to be reconciled. It seems that the circumstances are somewhat dictated by the fact that the charged is in detention. So the counsel will always have to come to the detainee and has to respect reasonable visiting times. If those detained on remand are being kept separate from those sentenced, restrictive rules

---

[97] This was rightly stressed by the ECommHR *Can v Austria* Report 12 July 1984 Series A No. 96, 18, para. 56.

[98] It is only the defence counsel in criminal procedure that is privileged in this way; according to cases and literature this law is not applicable to disciplinary proceedings; see Kleinknecht and Meyer-Goßner § 148 No. 3. This fact could be in conflict with the broad understanding of the scope of application of Art. 6 ECHR that the European authorities formed.

[99] The rationale for excluding these activities from the general rule is the prevention of the detained person further exercising leadership of a terrorist organization from within the prison. This exceptional rule is to be regarded as such and to be interpreted restrictively. An application by analogy to similar cases is prohibited; see BGH Decision *Separating Window* 17 February 1981, in BGHSt 30, 38 at 41.

[100] An exception to this general rule is the case where the advocate is under suspicion of having participated in or abetted the crime himself, Kleinknecht and Meyer-Goßner § 148, No. 8.

[101] Ibid., § 148. Nos 9–14.   [102] Ibid., § 148. No. 10.

[103] E. Cape and J. Luqmani, *Defending Suspects at Police Stations* (2nd edn. London, 1995), 53. Here we also find exceptions for terrorist activities s. 58 (14–16) PACE (1984).

[104] Cape and Luqmani, *Defending Suspects*, 53.

concerning order among the sentenced prisoners could be avoided. There certainly has to be control of goods brought into the prison, in particular to prevent break-outs. There is no need for the control of oral or written communication between detained and counsel.

3. Law and practice at the ICTY

Art. 21 IV (b) Statute ICTY enshrines the right to 'communicate with counsel' in strict parallel to the ICCPR. This right can also be found in several provisions among the Rules of Procedure. Rule 62 (i) states that the Trial Chamber has at the initial appearance to satisfy itself that the right of the accused to counsel is respected.[105] Counsel must be present during interrogation (Rule 63), if an accused does not voluntarily and expressly agree to proceed without counsel.[106] Furthermore all communication between lawyer and client is regarded as privileged, with the consequence that it is not subject to disclosure (Rule 97),[107] but must certainly also be free of any influence or control by third persons. In the 'rules of detention' of the ICTY it is laid down that each detainee is entitled to communicate freely and without restraint with his defence counsel. These communications are privileged. Interviews and visits are to be held out of the hearing of the staff of the Detention Unit.[108]

4. Consequences for an International Criminal Court

The Statute ILC incorporates the right to communicate with counsel in Art. 41 (I) b Statute ILC, a provision that has been taken into the Art. 67 (I) b Rome Statute unchanged.[109] The Report of the PrepComm points out that all communication between lawyer and client shall be regarded as privileged, and consequently not subject to disclosure at trial, unless the client consents or has notified a third party of the communication who gives evidence thereof at trial.[110] In accordance with the domestic legal systems in most Western states, further privileges should be taken into account. In particular the confidential words between defendant and a doctor or a priest should be protected and not be considered as third party in this context. The Draft Rules have taken up this issue. Draft Rule 6.4

---

[105] Bassiouni, *The Law of the ICTY*, 913.

[106] In order to comply with Rule 42, Rule 63 was amended at the 12th Plenary Session on 2–3 December 1996.

[107] The ICTY Trial Chamber II, in a decision 27 November 1996 on a Prosecution Motion for Production of Defence Witness Statements, ruled by a majority of two to one that a witness's prior statement, taken by or on behalf of the defence in anticipation of litigation, after the witness has testified, is protected by legal professional privilege and is thus not subject to disclosure to the prosecution, see Jones, *The Practice of the ICTY*, Rule 97, p. 430.

[108] Compare ICTY First Annual Report, para. 109.

[109] Schabas, in Trifterer (ed.), *Commentary on the Rome Statute*, Art. 67, No. 22.

[110] Report of the PrepComm II, 196–7.

widens the privileged status to any communication that is by its nature confidential. It mentions medical doctors, psychiatrists, psychologists, or counsellors, as well as religious clergymen.

(II) Time

The accused must be given adequate time to prepare his defence. Earlier I looked at the right of the charged to be tried within reasonable time. At first sight these two provisions seem to conflict, because the latter aims at accelerating the procedure whilst the former tends to stretch the proceedings.[111] It was in the 8th Session of the Commission of Human Rights in 1952 that the requirement of time and facilities was inserted and the former general invocation of the right of defence abolished.[112] The HRC in its General Comments addresses this requirement with the simple remark that what is 'adequate' has to be considered according to the circumstances of each individual case.[113] A few days will usually be insufficient.[114]

The European context is more enlightening as to the requirement of adequate time for the preparation of the defence simply because there have been more cases. Sometimes the ECourtHR addresses the issue under the scope of Art. 6 (III) c ECHR, which enshrines an overall right to an effective defence.[115] Most crucial is the right in circumstances where a defence lawyer is appointed shortly before the main hearing commences.[116] The complexity of the case,[117] the defence lawyer's workload,[118] and the stage of the proceedings have to be taken into account.[119] A further situation is when the defendant chooses to conduct his defence in person.[120]

---

[111] See above Ch. 2.

[112] This was due to a British motion drafted in obvious analogy to the ECHR, which was adopted unanimously, E/CN.4/SR.323, 15; see also Bossuyt, *Guide*, 296.

[113] HRC General Comment 13 (Article 14), para. 9. ICTY Trial Chamber II, *Delalic et al.*, *Decision on the Applications for Adjournment of the Trial Date*, 3 February 1997, stated that the term 'adequate time' is flexible and begs of a fixed definition outside the particular situation of each case. [114] Nowak, Art. 14, No. 42.

[115] See ECourtHR *Goddi v Italy* Judgment 9 April 1984, Series A No. 76, para. 31.

[116] Frowein and Peukert, Art. 6, No. 180.

[117] ECourtHR *Albert and Le Compte v Belgium* Series A No. 58.

[118] ECommHR *X and Y v Austria* Decision 12 October 1978, Appl. No. 7909/77, 15 DR 160. But the ECommHR held that it is not inappropriate to ask counsel to give priority to important cases. The ECommHR found no violation in this case where the counsel was given notice of his defence obligation seventeen days (including ten working days) before the hearing.

[119] Harris, 253. This requirement is of importance in the context of appeals or other review proceedings. If no further investigation as to the facts and evidence of the case is necessary, it can be expected that counsel needs less time to file a review request than to prepare a trial. Compare ECommHR *Huber v Austria* Decision 4 and 5 October 1974, Appl. No. 5523/72, 46 CD 99 at 107.

[120] ECommHR *X v Austria* Decision 11 February 1967, Appl. No. 2370/64, 22 CD 96 at 100.

(III) Facilities

1. Human rights bodies

In addition to adequate time the charged is also entitled to adequate facilities for the preparation of his defence. The HRC understands this as including 'access to documents and other evidence which the accused requires to prepare his case'.[121] In the case-law of the HRC the question as to the meaning of facilities appeared several times. In *Antonaccio v Uruguay* a violation was found but solely on grounds concerning communication with the appointed lawyer.[122] The HRC did not comment on the accessibility of information. In *OF v Norway* it was held that access to information could be restricted under national law for reasons of public interest, privileges, and confidentiality.[123] In the view of the HRC there is clearly no absolute right to information.[124] As said in the General Comment, the test has to be according to what is necessary to prepare the defence.

The ECommHR explained what the right to adequate facilities means in *Can v Austria*:[125] the charged must have 'the opportunity to organise his defence in an appropriate way and without restriction as to the possibility to put all relevant defence arguments before the trial court'. It becomes obvious that this right is strongly connected to the principle of 'equality of arms'.[126] This right can only be exercised if the charged is given the relevant information concerning the evidence against him. However this right does not go as far as being informed of all the material contained in the defendant's file. Only those documents need be disclosed that are relevant for the preparation of the defence.[127] Amongst those are documents related to the outer circumstances or the subjective elements of the act.[128] In particular the European bodies held, similar to the HRC, that national security,[129] administrative difficulties[130] or secrecy[131] may justify non-disclosure.

---

[121] HRC General Comment 13 (Article 14), para. 9.

[122] HRC *Antoniaccio v Uruguay* Doc.A/37/40, 114.

[123] HRC *OF v Norway* Doc. A/40/40, 204.   [124] Nowak, Art. 14, No. 42.

[125] ECourtHR *Can v Austria* Judgment 30 September 1985, Series A No. 96, Report of the ECommHR, para. 53.

[126] Harris, 255.

[127] Frowein and Peukert, Art. 6, No. 185.

[128] ECommHR *Jespers v Belgium* Report 14 December 1981, Appl. No. 8403/78, 27 DR 61, para. 58; cf. also Frowein and Peukert, Art. 6, No. 185.

[129] Frowein and Peukert, Art. 6, No. 185.

[130] ECommHR *Ofner v Austria* Decision 19 December 1960, Appl. No. 524/59, 3 YB 322 at 350. In this case the ECommHR had to address the question of whether it was justified to discriminate between suspects with and those without legal representation. Only the latter were, according to the practice in Austria, allowed to take notes when consulting their files. The defendant states argued that they did not have the capacity to supervise all the prisoners consulting their files.

[131] ECommHR *Haase v Germany* Report 12 July 1977, Appl. No. 7412/76, 11 DR 78 (91–2).

The opinion of the ECommHR that the prosecution need not reveal all the evidence that it wants to rely on at trial seems doubtful.[132] Whether or not a reliance on the surprise effect by the prosecution is 'fair' towards the defendant is disputable. How can the defence exercise its right to question and challenge prosecution evidence if it learns about it during trial for the first time? It would seem proper to request that adequate time to rebut this evidence be granted. Judging by the reasoning in the above case the ECommHR seems to believe that a defence counsel should always be in a position to rebut prosecution evidence. It might have found otherwise if the applicant had not been represented.

Another practice that is commonly used in many national legal systems was declared compatible with the ECHR by the European authorities. Sometimes disclosure of information is withheld from the charged but granted to his defence lawyer. This is for the simple reason that the lawyer who is compelled to fulfil certain professional standards and has to comply with certain rules is more trusted by the state than the charged, who is under no obligation whatsoever. The leading case in this regard is *Kamasinski v Austria*.[133] This practice stems from the idea that the right to adequate time and facilities is not a right addressing solely the charged, rather it is granted to the defence as a whole.[134] The ECommHR wrote:

whereas, in other words, a defending counsel ... is entitled, *mutatis mutandis*, to the rights mentioned in ... paragraph (III) since these rights are intended to ensure the proper defence of the accused; whereas as a consequence of the foregoing, in order to determine whether the right to have adequate time and facilities for preparation of the defence has been respected, account must be taken of the general situation of the defence and not only of the situation of the accused;[135]

One can justify this as in the interest of an effective criminal justice system, in that not all information should leak through to the defendant, while the defence counsel can be expected to behave properly. This was

---

The case concerned espionage for the German Democratic Republic; the applicant was not allowed to consult the documents, yet his solicitors (according to the facts of the case he had some twenty lawyers working for him) were granted access to the files with some protection for security reasons. The ECommHR found no human rights violation.

[132] ECommHR *X v UK* Decision 12 July 1972, Appl. No. 5282/71, 42 CD 99 at 102; The ECommHR did not substantiate this point further; however, it stressed that the defendant was represented by legal counsel and therefore in a position to challenge evidence against him.

[133] ECourtHR *Kamasinski v Austria* Judgment 19 December 1989, Series A No. 168. See also *Kremzow v Austria* Judgment 21 September 1993, Series A No. 268–B, para. 52.

[134] Ibid. para. 88.

[135] ECommHR *Ofner v Austria* Decision 19 December 1960, Appl. No. 524/59, 3 YB 322 at 352. It is quite interesting in this regard to contemplate an argument against the finding of the ECommHR *X and Y v Austria* Decision 12 October 1978, Appl. No. 7909/77, 15 DR 160, that the defence counsel can claim a violation of Art. 6 (III) b ECHR in his own name; if he is assigned to a client to represent him before the court and he is hindered from performing

the issue in the recent case of *Foucher v France*.[136] This time the defendant wanted to defend himself in person and requested access to his file. The request was denied by the French authorities on the grounds that access would only be granted to legal counsel or insurance companies. The ECourtHR found a violation of Art. 6 (III) read together with Art. 6 (I) ECHR, in as much as these inherit the principle of equality of arms. The Court's previous tenet (*Kamasinski* and *Kremzow*) was declared inapplicable because no lawyer was employed by *Foucher*. In such circumstances his opportunity to file an effective defence must be guaranteed, to which end access to the case file is crucial.[137]

However, it is certainly better for the preparation of the defence if the information is disclosed; it need not necessarily be brought to the knowledge of the charged. There seem to be three levels of state duty to disclose information relevant for the defence: (*a*) ordinary information should be made available to the accused person himself, (*b*) information which contains certain secrets or is of a particular sensitivity should be disclosed to the defence counsel, and (*c*) information that concerns national security need not be disclosed at all.

The European authorities seem to judge the individual case according to the overall test of actual prejudice.[138] In the case of failure to comply with the right to facilities the ECourtHR will only then find a violation of the right to defence, if actual prejudice can be shown.[139] This will not always be easy.

2. National practice

According to § 147 (I) StPO the defence counsel is entitled to have access to the file of his client and to see evidentiary material that has been made available to the court by the prosecution.[140] It is general practice of investigating authorities on the Continent to establish files or dossiers which contain all relevant information obtained during the investigating process. The usual case is that the counsel is allowed to take the files[141] to his office unless important grounds command otherwise (§ 147 (IV) StPO). It is furthermore believed that the right to have access to the files

this task properly by time or facility obstacles, could he not claim victim status in the sense of Art. 27 ECHR?

[136] ECourtHR *Foucher v France* Judgment 18 March 1997, Appl. No. 22209/93, 25 EHRR 234.

[137] Ibid., paras. 34–8.

[138] Jacobs and White, 154, call this a pragmatic approach.

[139] ECourtHR *Bricmont v Belgium* Judgment 7 July 1989, Series A No. 158.

[140] Sometimes it is even pointed out that the defence counsel has a duty to inform himself from the file in order to pursue his obligations properly. This duty exists with regard to his client; see Peters, *Strafprozeßrecht*, § 29 V 2.

[141] Not so the evidentiary material, see § 147 (IV) StPO.

incorporates the right to make notes and to make photocopies.[142] The charged himself, on the other hand, has no right to disclosure of his file.[143] Yet, as the advocate has access and the right to make notes or photocopies, the file may be accessible to the defendant through his counsel. That this is legitimate behaviour seems now to be generally accepted, even more so as it is the duty of the counsel to transmit the material he has to the charged.[144] German law recognizes no restriction on the right to access for the counsel before the trial starts. Only during an ongoing investigation may access be denied if the investigation would be jeopardized (§§ 147 (II), 169a StPO). The right to access relates even to so-called *Spurenakten* of the police. These contain details of different tracks the investigators followed but dropped as unpromising. With this information the defence counsel is enabled to consider and investigate alternative ways in which the crime may have happened.[145]

In English law there seems to be no clear rule giving the defence an unequivocal right to disclosure. Nor does the practice exist of collecting evidence in a file or a dossier. However, if the prosecution does not grant access to its case and introduces evidence during the hearing that was not made known to the defence, the usual procedure is for the judge to grant an adjournment.[146] This handling of the matter has recently been upheld by the Court of Appeal in the case *R v Johnson*.[147] The rules concerning disclosure were recently codified through the Criminal Procedure and Investigations Act (CPIA) (1996).[148] According to this legislation the prosecution must disclose all material in its possession that might 'undermine the case for the prosecution' (s. 3 (1) (a) CPIA 1996). The decision on which material is relevant in this regard lies entirely with the prosecutor. The disclosure will generally be conducted by means of a copy (s. 3 (3) (a) CPIA 1996). However, it goes hand in hand with disclosure by the defence which shall contain 'the nature of the accused's defence, ... the matters on which he takes issue with the prosecution, and ... the reasons why he takes issue with the prosecution' (s. 5 (6) CPIA 1996).

In the United States the rules of disclosure are quite similar, although

---

[142] Peters, *Strafprozeßrecht*, § 29 V 2.

[143] This view is almost uncontested in jurisdiction as well as in literature.

[144] Kleinknecht and Meyer-Goßner § 147, No. 20; BGH Judgment 3 October 1979, in BGHSt 29, 99, at 102.

[145] In principle this is uncontested; the judiciary however tend to be restrictive in the application whereas in literature the prevailing view is in favour of an overall disclosure of these *Spurenakten*. See BVerfG Decision 12 January 1983 in BVerfGE 63, 45, on the one hand, and Peters, *Strafprozeßrecht*, § 29 V 2, on the other.

[146] See Niblett, *Disclosure in Criminal Proceedings*, 32–3.

[147] *R v Johnson* (1996) CrimLR, 504.

[148] The Code applies to a specific type of cases only. I will not discuss this in detail, but take the Code as applicable in the field of the more serious offences before the Crown Court. See for further analysis Niblett, *Disclosure in Criminal Proceedings*, 230.

not codified. The right to disclosure is believed to stem from the Sixth Amendment's right to be informed of the nature and cause of the allegations.[149] The US Supreme Court stated in *Brady v Maryland* that the duty of disclosure lies on the prosecutor as a principle of general fairness and a minimum requirement to conduct the case in an unbiased and unprejudiced manner.[150] The material to be made accessible to the defence contains exculpatory material and material which may be used to impeach prosecution witnesses.

This is an obvious consequence of the adversarial system. The Continental inquisitorial systems may require the defence to disclose evidence and witnesses they want to call in favour of the defendant to the court, but this does not pertain to any tactics or challenges of the prosecution evidence that they intend to employ.[151]

Moreover, in common law countries rules exist that disclosure can be prevented on grounds of public interest. There are several grounds recognized for public interest immunity, like informants, observation points, sensitive investigation and surveillance techniques, national security, and the integrity of the criminal investigation.[152] Where the police want to keep information concealed for reasons of public interest immunity they must at least reveal to the defence that there is such non-disclosed evidence, which will enable the defence to challenge this decision in court. This common law practice remains undisturbed by the CPIA 1996.[153]

3. The system at the ICTY

In general the system at the ICTY follows closely the common law practice of reciprocal disclosure. Rule 66A obliges the prosecutor to disclose to the defence all material that supported the indictment at the time of the confirmation, as well as all prior statements obtained by the prosecutor from the accused, and to disclose statements of witnesses whom the prosecutor intends to call to testify at trial.[154] It seems a bit odd that it is not mentioned what should happen about evidentiary material obtained after this time. In Rule 66B the defence is given the right to inspect any material that is in control of the prosecutor and is important for the defence or intended to be used by the prosecutor as evidence. However, Rule 66B

---

[149] Ibid. 215.

[150] US Supreme Court *Brady v Maryland* 373 US 83 (1963), compare Niblett, *Disclosure in Criminal Proceedings*, 216.

[151] Ibid. 214, who gives a short overview of the main European and other systems, at pp. 198–217.

[152] Recent cases in this regard are *R v Ward* 96 Cr App R (1993), 1, and *R v Keane* 99 Cr App R (1994), 1; see Niblett, *Disclosure in Criminal Proceedings*, 138–53.

[153] Ibid. 153.

[154] This is due to the amendment at the 5th Plenary Session in Jan. 1995.

(not 66A) is subject to Rule 66C, that is, the disclosure must not prejudice further or ongoing investigations, or be contrary to the public interest or affect the security interests of any state. In case of doubt the prosecutor may 'seek the guidance of the Trial Chamber *in camera*' and, indeed, must do so as the Trial Chamber II found in *Furunzija*.[155]

The right to discovery is only triggered after the initial appearance of the accused at the ICTY. Thus counsel to Radovan Karadzic was denied access to material at the Rule 61 procedure against his client.[156] This norm has been interpreted by the Trial Chamber II in the *Celebici* case in adherence to the American case-law. 'Material to the preparation of the Defence' was interpreted as material that was 'significantly helpful to an understanding of important inculpatory or exculpatory evidence' or if it would 'play an important role in uncovering admissible evidence, aiding witness preparation, corroborating testimony, or assisting impeachment or rebuttal'.[157] That the judges are not prepared to follow the Continental approach of full disclosure was made clear by the Trial Chamber II Decision in *Delalic et al.* where the Chamber held that the defence 'must make a *prima facie* showing of materiality and that the requested evidence is in the custody of control of the Prosecutor'.[158] Nevertheless the Trial Chamber I in *Blaskic* paid heed to the rights of the accused referring to US law and French law of disclosure and held that all statements obtained by the prosecutor of the accused and of witnesses must be disclosed immediately.[159]

The request to inspect this material triggers the right of the prosecutor to inspect all the defence material (Rule 67C). Furthermore the prosecutor is obliged to disclose as soon as reasonably practicable prior to the beginning of the trial 'the names of the witnesses that he intends to call in proof of the guilt of the accused' or in rebuttal of any defence (Rule 67A i). The defence on the other hand must notify the prosecutor of any defence alibi or any special defence, such as diminished or lack of mental responsibility (Rule 67A ii). Any evidence that might work in favour of the accused and is known to the prosecutor must be indicated to the defence (Rule 68).

---

[155] Trial Chamber II *Furundzija*, Decision 14 July 1998, to reopen the trial. The ICTY found a misconduct on the part of the prosecutor by which the accused was deprived of his right to a fair trial. Compare ICTY bulletin 27 July 1998, 12.

[156] Trial Chamber I Decision 27 June 1996 Partially Rejecting the Request Submitted by Mr. Igor Pantelic, Counsel for Radovan Karadzic, Case No. IT-95-5-R61/IT-95-18-R61.

[157] See *Delalic et al.* Case No. IT-96-21-T, Decision 26 September 1996 on the Motion by the Accused Zejnil Delalic for the Disclosure of Evidence.

[158] The request was denied in this case as the defence required access to all documents concerning the Celebici Camp, alleging that they were all relevant. Trial Chamber II, *Delalic et al.* Case No. IT-96-21-T Decision 26 September 1996 on Motion by the Accused Zejnil Delalic for the Disclosure of Evidence.

[159] ICTY Trial Chamber I, *Blaskic, Decision on the Production of Discovery Materials*, on 27 January 1997.

The ICTY amended this rule in January 1995 to the extent that now the prosecutor must also disclose evidence which may affect the credibility of prosecution evidence.[160] To trigger the privilege of disclosure the defence must show, according to the ICTY case-law, that the sought material is in the possession of the prosecutor and it must present a prima facie case which would make probable the exculpatory nature of the material.[161] How this scenario could possibly occur without an informant in the office of the prosecutor is not quite clear.

The fact that there is no equivalent obligation on the defence to disclose incriminating evidence can hardly be seen as the reason why the Rules of Procedure 'tilt the scales in favour of the accused', as Nsereko believes.[162] In this regard the accused has a human rights privilege not to incriminate himself. Because of that, incriminating evidence cannot be included in the reciprocal disclosure or be made instrumental for the principle of 'equity of arms' between the parties.

Although the law at the ICTY goes beyond what US courts require, as Bassiouni rightly observes,[163] it is not quite understandable why disclosure is nevertheless limited. Why should the prosecution not just present to the defence all material that is relevant to the case? It would seem intrinsically 'fair' for the prosecution simply to play with a completely open hand and disclose its entire case. This would also erase a matter of complicated rules and a field of potential conflicts producing further delays.

In the *Tadic* case the ICTY Trial Chamber had to deal with a problem of disclosure by the defence. The prosecution requested the publication of a statement a defence witness had made to the defence counsel. The defence argued that this came within legal privilege. The majority[164] held that there was such a privilege referring to the legal practice as it stands in common law (with the exception of US Federal Courts) as well as in civil law.

---

[160] Amended in the 5th Plenary Session, Jan. 1995. See ICTY Second Annual Report (1995), paras. 20, 26.

[161] This finding is in analogy with the interpretation of Rule 66B by the Trial Chamber II, *Delalic et al.* Case No. IT-96-21-T Decision 26 September 1996 on Motion by the Accused Zejnil Delalic for the Disclosure of Evidence; done by Trial Chamber I, *Blaskic* Case No. IT-95-14-T Decision 27 January 1997 on the Production of Discovery Materials, para. 49, followed by the Trial Chamber II, *Delalic et al* Case No. IT-96-21-T Decision 24 June 1997 on the Request of the Accused Pursuant to Rule 68 for Exculpatory Information, para. 18.

[162] Nsereko, 5 CLF (1994), 507 at 536, who seems to contradict himself as he holds the view that reciprocal disclosure was unusual in common law jurisdiction, because the prosecution is considered to be the stronger of the two parties and bears the burden of proof.

[163] Bassiouni, *The Law of the ICTY*, 920–1.

[164] Consisting of Judges Stephen and Vohrah, Judge MacDonald dissenting, Decision on Prosecution Motion for Production of Defence Witness Statements 27 November 1996.

4. Assessment

The ECourtHR dealt with the differences between common law and civil law practice in the case *Edwards v UK*.[165] This case was concerned with a conviction for robbery and burglary which was mainly based on an early confession by the suspect. He later rescinded his confession and alleged it had been fabricated by the police. The prosecution still relied on the confession and kept secret the fact that fingerprints of someone other than the suspect had been found at the scene of the crime and that a prosecution witness failed to identify the accused. The prosecution authority was thereby clearly and undisputedly in breach of domestic English law. The applicant complained that this favouring evidence was not disclosed to him and therefore that it amounted to a violation of Art. 6 (I) and (III) d ECHR. The non-disclosure prevented the applicant's defence counsel from adequately examining the prosecution witnesses. Furthermore, an internal police inquiry report assessing the conduct of the involved police officers was not made available to the defence on the grounds of public interest immunity. The government maintained that the proceedings had to be looked at as a whole when assessing fairness. After the failure of the prosecution to disclose the relevant information the applicant was still given the opportunity to appeal and remedy the failure thereby. The ECourtHR discussed the issue of disclosure within Art 6 (I) ECHR; English law recognizes the obligation on the prosecuting authorities to disclose to the defence all evidence for or against the defendant (*sic!*), the ECourtHR stated rather apodictically.[166] The ECourtHR then came to the same conclusion as the majority of the ECommHR[167] that the failure was remedied by the Court of Appeal, where the applicant was given a fair hearing with regard to the new evidence.[168] Two judges dissented and found that there was a violation of Art. 6 ECHR.[169] Judge Pettiti in particular drew comparisons with Continental systems in his dissenting opinion; in his eyes the concealment of the internal police report amounted to grounds for nullity, which the court had to take into account ex officio. 'On ne saurait en effet laisser à la seule défence, qui peut être inexpérimentée, la charge de faire respecter le droit fondamental procédural qui

---

[165] ECourtHR *Edwards v UK* Judgment 25 November 1992, Series A No. 247-B.
[166] Ibid., para. 36.
[167] Dissenting opinion by Gözübüyük, Weitzel, Martinez, Rozakis, Liddy, and Geus, Series A No. 247-B, 46, holding that there had been a violation of Art. 6 (I), taken together with Art. 6 (III) d ECHR alleging that the Court of Appeal was not in a position to decide whether or not the jury would have decided differently if it had been made aware of the whole evidence.   [168] Ibid., paras. 37–9.
[169] Dissenting opinion of Judge Pettiti and of Judge De Meyer, Series A No. 247-B, 37 and 40. Their criticism is similar to the minority's view of the ECommHR.

prohibe la dissimulation de preuves ou de pièces.'[170] Judge Pettiti thereby approached the Continental practice of inquiry *ex officio*, and left the ideal-type of an adversarial system behind. Yet he thus wanted to protect the adversarial examination of evidence. It was for this reason that he wanted to see all evidence communicated to the defence and showed no under-standing of non-disclosure rules according to 'public interest' or 'defence' and 'state' secrets. Should data like this be involved he would prefer to have a hearing *in camera* rather than conceal relevant information to the defendant.

Judge Pettiti's dissenting opinion seems to be convincing for the following reasons. An issue that is of major importance in this context is the principle of equity of arms, which is, as we have seen before, encom-passed by the general 'fair trial' principle as embodied in Art. 14 (I) ICCPR, Art. 6 (I) ECHR and so forth. Compared to the prosecution the defence team suffers a major structural disadvantage. The investigating authorities are, as part of the state executive, equipped with effective investigative powers and are abetted by the whole state machinery. Their access to information and their methods of obtaining evidence are incom-parably better than those on the defence side. In a purely adversarial system where each side produces its own evidence, the defence counsel would be in a ridiculous situation. Theoretical equality would equal gross practical inequality. The defence, in order to get a fair start, must therefore be given the information that the police collected during the investigation.

Art. 6 (III) d ECHR or Art. 14 (III) d ICCPR seems not to be an issue here. The methodologically better place to discuss the matter of disclosure seems to be Art. 6 (III) b ECHR or Art. 14 (III) b ICCPR. Obviously it is of importance for the cross-examination how much information the defence counsel has about subject and person, yet the right to examine witnesses seems to be a purely procedural prescription; the defence must be given the opportunity to confront the witness with its own assertion of the facts. The right says nothing about the content or the information necessary for this. It is solely concerned with the conduct of the trial. *Sedes materiae* of the right to access to relevant information is prior to the trial. The right to adequate time and facilities seems the appropriate place as it addresses not merely procedural hindrances ('time') but also potential material obstacles ('facilities'), which clearly invokes the right to disclose informa-tion relevant to the defence.

Finally the issue of public interest immunity has to be addressed. Although certain information exists which the state wants to keep secret

---

[170] Dissenting opinion Judge Pettiti, Series A No. 247-B, 39: 'In fact, one cannot leave to a possibly inexperienced defence alone the burden of ensuring respect for the fundamental procedural rule which prohibits the concealment of documents or evidence.'

from the public,[171] there is no logic in withholding it also from the defence. There should be differentiation between the fora in which the topic will be discussed and who will then learn about the secret information. There seem to be three possible addressees: (*a*) the public, (*b*) the defendant, and (*c*) the defence counsel. If some information needs to be kept secret from the public it could be done so by excluding the public from the relevant hearing, as Judge Pettiti proposed. This could easily be done by invoking one of the manifold exceptions human rights norms attach to the principle of a public hearing.[172] Yet one has to keep in mind that, according to the letter of the human rights treaties, the right to adequate time and facility to prepare one's defence has no restriction.

5. Consequences for the International Criminal Court

Art. 27 (V) Statute ILC contains this provision concerning disclosure: the Presidency has the power to order disclosure. Art. 38 gives the power to the Trial Chamber to ensure that Art. 27 has been complied with. A general requirement to disclose material the prosecution intends to use is therefore not embodied in the Draft Statute. Art. 41 (II) Statute ILC enshrines the further requirement that the prosecutor must disclose all exculpatory evidence that becomes available to it prior to the conclusion of the trial. The PrepComm, in discussing this provision, wants it amended in two respects: first, it should be pointed out that inculpatory evidence shall also be made available to the defence prior to the conclusion of the trial and, secondly, it should be clarified that sensitive information supplied by a state should be balanced with the general duty to disclose.[173] The Rome Statute does not alter the proposition substantially, as shown by Art. 67 (II) and Art. 64 (I) c Rome Statute, but completely new is Art. 72 Rome Statute, which addresses the issue of protecting national security information.[174] The Draft Rules 5.28 to 5.34 make the matter even more thorny. Dozens of exceptions and prohibitions give the impression that something needs to be unfairly hidden from the defendant.

From a human rights point of view this seems insufficient. We have seen that, in order to secure a proper preparation of the defence, all material must be disclosed at least to the defence counsel.[175] The extensive

---

[171] However strange it might seem that things of public interest need to be kept secret from the public.

[172] See below Ch. 4, p. 226.

[173] Report of the PrepComm I, para. 274.

[174] The norm constitutes a compromise between the interests of the ICC in having full knowledge of all the relevant circumstances, on the one hand, and the security interests of the national state, on the other. It is not only applicable to documents but includes also the testimony of persons; compare Ambos, NJW (1998), 3743 at 3744.

[175] This is also the view of the Lawyers' Committee for Human Rights, International Criminal Court Briefing Series, Vol. I, No. 2, 9–8.

proposal by Australia and the Netherlands in the PrepComm seems much more satisfying in this regard.[176] It provides for a full reciprocal disclosure of evidence that is material to the defence prior to the trial and foresees exceptions only for the protection of victims and witnesses, which needs special authorization by the Trial Chamber. These rules resemble the situation at the ICTY. It is submitted here nevertheless that these rules could be simplified if a concept of full disclosure were adopted. The prosecutor should be obliged to open his books entirely, with exceptions only allowed in cases where victims and witnesses need protection or in cases of national security.[177] As exceptions these two conditions would have to be interpreted restrictively.

D. PRELIMINARY MOTIONS

The last question I must address is what possibilities there are for the parties to institute preliminary motions. This issue has arisen in almost every case before the ICTY. The frequency of legal disputes on the eve of international criminal trials in the Hague is certainly understandable, taking into account the infancy of the international criminal procedure. Because of this and because of the foggy legal basis on which the ICTY was established, *Tadic* challenged the whole institution of the tribunal.[178] Of course such challenges will most often be a chance for the defence to prevent the actual trial from taking place at all and, if one takes the *Tadic* case as an example, one cannot but call the time between his surrender to the ICTY and his conviction lengthy.[179] Still it seems to be a right of the defendant to challenge the allegations and proceedings as effectively as possible.

The law at the ICTY recognizes several preliminary motions explicitly in Rules 72 and 73.[180] Although this list is not meant to be exhaustive ('shall include'), only those listed motions are under the time limit of sixty days after the accused's initial appearance (Rule 73B). Other motions, which are possible pursuant to Rule 72A, are under no time restriction.[181]

---

[176] Report of the PrepComm II, 177–80.

[177] Pointing in the same direction arguably, Schabas, in Trifterer (ed.), *Commentary on the Rome Statute*, Art. 67, No. 55.

[178] See the two decisions concerning jurisdiction by the Trial Chamber and the Appeals Chamber.

[179] Tadic was arrested in Germany in Feb. 1994, transferred to the Hague on 24 Apr. 1995 and convicted by Trial Chamber II, 7 May 1997, exactly one year after the trial started 7 May 1996.

[180] For a description of the preliminary motions filed so far at the ICTY see Jones, *The Practice at the ICTY*, 355–77.

[181] A summary of the preliminary motions filed and decided upon so far at the ICTY can be found in Jones, *The Practice of the ICTY*, Rule 73, pp. 173–9.

1. Challenges recognized in national jurisdictions

National jurisdictions grant the defendant time and facilities to prepare his defence. In order for the accused to obtain enough of both he may complain to the court if he has the suspicion that the preparation of his defence is jeopardized.

This must be true for both time and facilities. National jurisdictions recognize complaints of insufficient time for the preparation of the defence. The beginning of the hearing can be postponed if some of the participants claim adjournment according to German law. This decision is entirely at the discretion of the judge but it could be complained against if the complaint is based on an error in law.[182] The possibility of granting postponement on request is also known in the English system.[183]

National jurisdictions also allow complaints concerning access to information. German law recognizes an all-embracing right of access to information which is enforceable, if denied by the prosecution by means of disciplinary proceedings,[184] if denied by the court, by means of a complaint (*Beschwerde*) according to § 304 (I) and (IV) Nr.4 StPO. Likewise, English law recognizes the right of the accused to apply to the court for an order requiring the prosecutor to disclose material, s. 8 (2) CPIA 1996. This right exists within the limits of the English law on disclosure, which means that the defence must have reasonable grounds to believe that there exists non-disclosed material that might assist the accused's defence.[185] Finally the defendant is able to complain that the correspondence between himself and his counsel is being interfered with. This is guaranteed in German law by §§ 119 (III) and (VI), 126 StPO.[186]

2. The human rights necessities

As we have seen, the defendant must be given adequate time and facilities to prepare his defence. If he has the impression that the time granted to him does not give him enough time for a proper preparation he must be able to claim an adjournment or postponement of the hearing. This question arose in the European context in *Murphy v UK*.[187] The

---

[182] Otherwise the complaint would generally be excluded according to § 305 StPO; but see Kleinknecht and Meyer-Goßner, § 214 No. 8 with many references to case-law.

[183] See submission of the UK Government in ECommHR *Murphy v UK* Decision 3/4 December 1972 Appl. No. 4681/70, 43 CD, 1 at 7.

[184] This seems to be the prevailing view, see Kleinknecht and Meyer-Goßner § 147 No. 39.

[185] The possibility for a disclosure-order applies only in the case of so-called 'secondary disclosure', that is, after the defence has disclosed its material. The structure has been briefly outlined above; for further detail see Niblett, *Disclosure in Criminal Proceedings*, 228–47.

[186] Kleinknecht and Meyer-Goßner § 148 Nos. 23, 24.

[187] ECommHR *Murphy v UK* Decision 3/4 December 1972 Appl. No. 4681/70, 43 CD 1. In *Goddi v Italy* Judgment 9 April 1984, Series A No. 76, the ECourtHR held that exceptional circumstances might make this claim superfluous.

ECommHR treated this as requiring local remedy. In this case a violation of the ECHR was not found because in the case the applicant had had the opportunity of claiming adjournment in the national court, which would have been granted if requested. Therefore he had not exhausted domestic remedies (Art. 27 (III) ECHR). For our context it tells us that, from a human rights perspective, the right to adequate time and facilities has to be enforceable by means of asking for an adjournment or postponement.

3. The ICC

Art. 19 (II) a Rome Statute provides an opportunity for the suspect for whom a warrant of arrest or a summons to appear has been issued (Art. 58 Rome Statute) to challenge the jurisdiction of the ICC. Apart from this the Draft Statute ILC and the Rome Statute do not explicitly refer to preliminary motions that the defendant can submit in order to protect his situation. At the commencement of the trial the Trial Chamber has however to satisfy itself that the rights of the accused were respected, Art. 38 (I) c Statute ILC, Art. 64 (I) Rome Statute. It is inherent in this provision that complaints of the misconduct of the prosecution must be heard.[188] Albeit that Art. 38 (V) Statute ILC and now Art. 64 (VI) Rome Statute contain several motions that the Trial Chamber may grant, these pertain to the preparation of the trial and not to the protection of the rights of the accused. In the PrepComm it was submitted by Australia and the Netherlands that a rule addressing potential preliminary motions should be inserted.[189] This submission resembles Rule 73 at the ICTY,[190] a norm which has enjoyed quite extensive use since the commencement of prosecutions at the ICTY.[191] For the protection of the accused it seems essential that he has the right to challenge the justification of the proceedings against him before the main hearing begins. Thereby he could effectively avoid a potentially stressful trial to prove his innocence. To prevent extended delays, a time limit as foreseen in Rule 73 at the ICTY could be inserted.

---

[188] Bitti, in Triffterer (ed.), *Commentary on the Rome Statute*, Art. 64, No. 20–4, does not give any guidance in this regard.

[189] Report of the PrepComm II, 184.

[190] The Report of the PrepComm I, para. 260, buttressed this approach.

[191] See for a list of motions brought before the ICTY, Jones, *The Practice of the ICTY*, Rule 73, 370–7.

4

The Trial

The trial is without doubt the place where the differences between the Continental and the Anglo-American legal traditions are most obvious. In the former, the most prominent figure is that of the inquiring judge, whilst the latter is characterized by the accusatorial system in which the two parties present their evidence, perhaps even before a jury. Therefore, the first issue is the role of the various participants during a trial. All basic human rights treaties embody a whole set of principles concerning how a trial should present itself. Having discussed these principles, I will look at the course of the procedure, where the great differences between the systems must again be taken into account. I will examine in special detail the rules of evidence. In doing so, I will enter a relatively untouched field. Practice in the various traditions differs greatly and is changing fast. Nevertheless, an attempt must be made to find a general yardstick. Finally, it is essential to look beyond the conviction in the first instance and discuss the steps that may follow, such as appeal or review.

A. THE ROLE OF THE VARIOUS INSTITUTIONS

The participants in the process are still the same, court, prosecution, and accused, but the role of each has changed, and the two criminal systems differ considerably in this regard. I shall discuss the differences and the reasons for each institution separately, starting with the court, as most human rights treaty provisions exist for this institution. I will then examine the special issue of the jury; some states recognize a right to a jury, whilst others do not use them any more. How should this be approached from a human rights point of view? In Anglo-American systems, prosecutor and defence are supposed to be parties to the process, while the Continental inquisitorial system denies the existence of parties in criminal procedure. How does this affect the role of the prosecutor and the powers of the defence?

(I) The Court

Human rights norms envisage criminal courts as independent and impartial. I looked at this provision in detail when discussing the pre-trial stage. The HRC in its General Comment emphasizes that no tribunal may be so special as not to have to implement the provisions of Art. 14.[1] In this respect it addresses as problematic the military and special courts that exist in many countries to allow exceptional procedures which do not comply with 'normal' standards of justice.[2] The HRC further reminds states that wish to rely on 'public emergency' by virtue of Art. 4 ICCPR, as justification for establishing special courts with 'special' procedures, that the existence of a public emergency must be proved by the procedure as contemplated by Art. 4 ICCPR.[3]

Another consequence for the institution and the organization of the judiciary flows from human rights treaties. The mere existence of an independent and impartial judiciary is not enough. Efficient and effective functions of the judiciary must also be guaranteed. This is due to the fact that human rights guarantee the suspect trial without undue delay (see Art. 9 (III) and 14 (I) ICCPR, Art. 5 (III) and 6 (I) ECHR). This means on the one hand, as we have already seen, that the trial must start within a reasonable time. For the trial stage it means, as we will see, that the trial must be brought to an end speedily. The judiciary needs to be organized and funded in such a way that proper functioning is secured. It is therefore the state's responsibility to provide sufficient personnel and finance for the courts to ensure that the proper administration of justice is possible. States have therefore not succeeded in pleading a backlog of cases as a tenable excuse for unreasonably lengthy procedures. They attempted to do so before the ECourtHR in *Zimmermann and Steiner v Switzerland*, where the heavily overworked court gave priority to urgent or important cases.[4] The state had made no effort whatsoever to end this practice, apparently exercised over several years. It was therefore condemned by the ECourtHR. Similarly, a violation was found in *B v Austria*, where it had taken the court thirty-three months to draft the judgment.[5] As the responsible judge had in the mean time been subject to a disciplinary penalty and the court had reduced his personal workload, the government argued that it could not possibly have initiated more severe

---

[1] HRC General Comment 12 (Article 14), para. 4.

[2] Apparently the HRC presumes compliance with Art. 14 ICCPR as the 'normal' procedure. Reading the reports and communications before the HRC the IAmCHR and even the ECourtHR give more the impression that states only rarely comply with the 'fair trial' provision.

[3] See Higgins, Derogation under Human Rights Treaties, 48 BYIL (1976–7), 281. The proposition by Swaak-Goldman, 10 LJIL (1997), 215 at 218–19, that the ICTY would be entitled to a limited concept of 'fair trial' as it is comparable to a military court during times of emergency, is certainly difficult to uphold in particular with regard to the precise circumstances of Art. 4 ICCPR.

[4] ECourtHR *Zimmermann and Steiner v Switzerland* Judgment 13 July 1983, Series A No. 66. The case dealt with administrative compensation claims and was not concerned with criminal procedure.

[5] ECourtHR *B v Austria* Judgment 28 March 1990, Series A No. 175.

measures without conflicting with the principle of the independence of the judiciary. Still, the ECourtHR 'considers that the measures in question were insufficient and belated to ensure that the proceedings against the applicant were concluded within a reasonable time'.[6] Although the ECourtHR went on to state that it was not obliged to determine which institution was precisely to blame, as the state was responsible in any case, its ruling implies an obvious censure of the state for not ensuring the proper administration of justice.

(II) Jury or Judge

It is a well-known fact in criminal procedure that some jurisdictions rely on a jury for consideration of the guilt of the defendant; others, in contrast, leave the verdict up to professional judges, possibly assisted by a few lay judges. The difficulty from a human rights point of view lies in the question of whether there is a 'right to a jury'. In the context of international criminal procedure, we have to decide whether or not we want an International Criminal Court equipped with a jury. In order to find answers to these questions, a closer look at the origins and nature of the various jury systems and the practical problems they cause will be of assistance.

In common law countries the jury is considered a central feature of criminal trial.[7] In the Constitution of the United States we find a right to an *impartial* jury in all criminal prosecutions in the Sixth Amendment.[8] No further reference to the jury is to be found in the US Constitution. However, the case-law of the US Supreme Court reveals a right to a jury for the defendant in all criminal prosecutions where the possible punishment authorized by statute as well as punishment for contempt in open court is imprisonment for more than six months.[9] The US jury, in federal cases in particular, consists of twelve members.[10] Impartiality[11] is guaranteed as the jurors are under oral scrutiny by counsel: so-called *voir dire*

---

[6] Ibid., para. 54.　　　　　　　　　　　　　　[7] Lidstone in Andrews (1982), 64.

[8] See Osakwe in Andrews (1982), 283.

[9] US Supreme Court *Baldwin v NY* 399 US 66 (1970). Originally, the jury was not applied on all federal states. It was not until 1968 that the Supreme Court agreed that the right to a jury was embedded in the 14th Amendment and therefore compulsory for the states, see US Supreme Court *Duncan v Louisiana* 391 US 145 (1968).

[10] The figure twelve traditionally represents the country; it developed from medieval times where twelve knight-jurors acted as indictors, representing 'their own hundred'; see W. Forsynth, *History of Trial by Jury* (London, 1852), 217. The number twelve also had symbolic religious significance, see also p. 9 *et subs.*

[11] It is interesting to note that, in the early days of the jury, jurors were expected to be partial; they came from the neighbourhood and were expected to know the accused and all the details of the offence. The jury was meant to represent the *fama publica*, compare Forsynth, *History of Trial by Jury*, 201, see also p. 9 *et subs.*

examination. Within this context, the counsel has a limited number of challenges 'without cause' and can challenge jurors 'with reason' in unlimited numbers, at the discretion of the judge. The verdict must be unanimous as far as serious offences and state prosecution are concerned and must be returned in open court. The judge plays the role of instructor to the jury. He is mainly there to clarify questions of law to the jurors, if they wish to receive detailed information about the legal issues at stake. Finally, the right to a jury can be waived by the defendant.[12]

English law relies on the ancient right to be judged by one's 'peers'. Stemming from the Latin word *pares*, peers means 'equals'. The right to jury is called the 'privilege of the Common People of the United Kingdom'.[13] Yet this privilege has suffered more and more cutbacks over recent years. In 1967, after 600 years of unanimous verdicts only,[14] majority verdicts were introduced—perhaps a rather dubious development, as it shakes the fundamental basis of the idea of a criminal jury, in the author's view.[15] The Criminal Law Act (1977) reclassified offences and created a threefold system.[16] Serious crimes are automatically heard at Crown Court by a jury, minor offences in the Magistrates' Court, and 'dual' offences can be tried either at the Magistrates' or before the Crown Court. In these cases, it is up to the offender to choose which court he wants to be judged by, but the approval of the Magistrates' Court is necessary if the suspect wishes to be tried there. In a 'brief' trial, which is exclusively presented by the prosecutor, the magistrates decide whether their upper penalty limit (twelve months) will suffice. If they consider the case more serious than this, they must refer it to the Crown Court, which means that the offender's choice of venue was to no avail. The reasons for reducing the jurisdiction of juries are mainly financial. To hold a trial before a jury is three times more expensive than to do without.[17] Below I will take a closer look at the reasons for abandonment of the jury in Northern Ireland.

One major difference between the US and the English system lies in the role of the judge. The English system gives him a more prominent position. This is mainly seen in what is called the 'summing-up'. After the

[12] C. H. Whitebread, *Criminal Procedure* (New York, 1980), 22.05.

[13] Devlin, *Trial by Jury*, 3.

[14] Maher in M. Findlay and P. Duff, *The Jury under Attack* (London, 1988), 40.

[15] Lidstone in Andrews (1982), n. 4 is also critical. The main problem lies with the concept of 'reasonable doubt', which I will discuss in detail later. If twelve people representing public conscience are selected to apply this level of proof to the facts at issue and if even one of them dissents, then reasonable doubt must exist; compare Freeman, 1981 Current Legal Problems, 65 at 69. Furthermore, majority verdicts imply disapproval of the one or two dissenting; their doubts are considered 'unreasonable'.

[16] Criminal Law Act (1977), Part III ss. 1–4.

[17] Lidstone in Andrews (1982), 66.

pleadings of the parties, the English judge summarizes the facts and the presented evidence for the jurors before they are released for deliberation. Although, *de jure*, this presentation is supposed to be unbiased and objective, *de facto* the judge has a great deal of influence on the outcome of the trial. It is, however, possible that the role of the adversarial parties is diminished as a result of the summing-up. In a common law system, a system that relies heavily upon the ethical behaviour of the professional lawyers involved, there is a certain risk that the parties will pursue their own interests in an irresponsible manner. In the summing-up the judge has an opportunity to rectify what has gone wrong during the examination of the evidence by the parties and clarify the matter for the jurors.[18] However, some people see this as an opportunity for the judge to slant the evidence.

The procedure of ensuring an impartial jury is similar to the one in the USA. What has emerged as a problematic feature is the CPS's practice of allowing the jurors' private lives be checked by the police, although disclosure of the occupation of the jurors is not permitted to the defence.[19]

In *Holm v Sweden*, the ECourtHR found that the principles of impartiality apply to professional judges and likewise to jurors and lay judges.[20] In this case, concerning party membership of jurors, the ECourtHR held that fears as regards their impartiality were objectively justified and found a violation of Art. 6 (I) ECHR.[21] In general the line between ensuring an unbiased jury and producing a biased jury is a fine one.

But what is the underlying rationale behind the use of a jury? Jurors are supposed to ensure that the verdict comes from the people. After all, it is in the name of the people or at least on the people's behalf that the legal system exists and prosecution and conviction take place. Conviction and censure of those who infringe the legal system of the state must be the job of society.[22] It is also felt that matters such as finding 'reasonable doubt'

---

[18] This might also be one of the reasons why the criminal justice system works better in England than in the USA, in addition to the fact that the English Bar is far smaller, more specialized, and therefore better controlled, compare J. McEwans, *Evidence in the Adversarial Process* (Oxford, 1992), 11.

[19] The checking of jurors by the police is called 'jury vetting', see Lidstone in Andrews (1982), 68–9. Gallivan and Warbrick, 5 HRR (1980) 176 at 177, observe that the defence hardly ever challenges jurors with cause, simply because it could not substantiate its plea bereft of information about the candidates; they rightly pose the question whether non-disclosure is 'fair'. Furthermore, they hold the view that in principle the accused's right to a fair trial and the jurors' right to privacy come into conflict here and have to be weighed against each other.

[20] ECourtHR *Holm v Sweden* Judgment 25 November 1993, Series A No. 279-A, para. 30.

[21] Ibid., para. 33.

[22] It is interesting to note that, legally speaking, the judge is not bound by the jury's verdict. The jury assists the judge in finding the right decision, but the jury derives all its power from the judge. Without the judgment being entered upon the verdict, the jury's finding has no legal effect whatsoever, compare Devlin, *Trial by Jury*, 13. That this is not unusual

are better judged by lay people and by several persons.[23] The jury is not told what lawyers understand by terms such as 'reasonable doubt' and jurors cannot rely on long-term experience, as jurors are seldom called upon more than once to perform this service. However, this lack of knowledge and experience is intentional, indeed is the *raison d'être* of the jury; legal judgments are supposed to be tempered by sympathy or compassion where appropriate.[24] Juries thus serve as a buffer in the conflict between the individual and the state that takes place in criminal trials.[25] The high legal standards that state authorities expect of their citizens are applied by members of the governed society. Jurors are expected to judge from the perspective of ordinary people, having perhaps more understanding for offender and victim, and thus, possibly, a greater sense of justice. It is for this reason that the jury system is referred to as 'the grand Bulwark of liberty' by Blackstone,[26] or, in the words of Lord Devlin, 'the lamp of freedom'.[27]

The decision as to whether a jury should be used or not appears to be largely a question of policy. All the reasons cited in favour of juries could also be used, vice versa, to argue against them. On the one hand, lay judgments could be said to be more reasonable; on the other, criticism could be voiced and arguments brought forward in favour of professional knowledge as necessary for judging a defendant's guilt.[28] From a theoretical point of view it is thus impossible to make out a good case for a right to a jury as a human right, nor for the fact that it is intrinsically better for the defendants to be convicted by twelve jurors. The ECommHR has also repeatedly held that Art 6 (I) ECHR does not encapsulate a right to be tried by jury, most recently in the case *Callaghan and others v UK*.[29]

One major difficulty stemming from these theoretical underpinnings is the question of whether decisions by a jury are reviewable and, if so, to

---

in the American experience was recently a matter of worldwide attention, when Judge Hiller Zobel overturned the jury-verdict in the *Woodward* case from second-degree murder to unintentional manslaughter, 10 November 1997, in Cambridge, Massachusetts, see *The Times* (11 November 1997), 1.

[23] People who are professionally biased, i.e. lawyers, are excluded from jury service according to the Juries Act (1974).

[24] Baldwin and McConville, 1979 CrimLR, 230 at 231.

[25] Whitebread, *Criminal Procedure*, 22.01.

[26] Quoted by Lidstone in Andrews (1982), n. 5.

[27] Devlin, *Trial by Jury*, 164.

[28] It seems almost anachronistic that, whereas there is increasing reliance on the judgment of professionals and technical experts in every other field of society to such a degree that some sociologists declare this to be a main feature of modern society (U. Beck, *Risikogesellschaft* (Frankfurt, 1986), Part III), when it comes to convicting individuals—even when the death chamber may be the ultimate outcome—the matter is deliberately entrusted to lay persons.

[29] ECommHR *Callaghan and others v UK* Decision 9 May 1989, Appl. No. 14739/89, 60 DR 296 at 301, with references to the earlier cases.

what extent. Can an offender possibly appeal against the verdict of a jury, if we understand by appeal a reassessment of both fact and law?[30] In both jurisdictions, England and the United States, an appeal against a jury verdict can only be directed against a miscarriage of justice stemming from procedural irregularities, from misunderstanding of a question of law or of the evidence. There is no general review of the facts.[31] The evidence as presented to the jury remains exempt from scrutiny. There is an intrinsic logic to this; if the defendant has a right to be convicted by a jury, this conviction cannot be altered by a panel of judges. Twelve people elected to judge the case cannot be wrong—this is the theoretical idea— the truth is a question of numerical superiority. Historically, the jury inherited this 'divine inscrutability' from the verdict of God expressed through trial by ordeal.[32] For this reason, only the conduct of the trial is open to appeal. Another reason why it is difficult to appeal against a jury verdict is the fact that the jury obviously returns an unreasoned verdict. Appeal judges have no motivation behind the jury decision that they can examine and censure. They therefore cannot argue that the jury's opinion was based on blatant misjudgment of the evidence, or was not supported by adequate evidence at all. Hence the jury verdict must stand for no other reason than that it was arrived at by a jury.[33] This corollary to the very idea of the jury has often been criticized.[34] It seems a bit odd from a human rights point of view that a jury should considerably limit the recti- fiability of a verdict.

Empirical evidence shows first of all that jury trial is a rare event. As, in England, it only takes place at the Crown Court and only comes into play when the defendant pleads not guilty, only about 7 per cent of all criminal cases are judged by a jury.[35] It then becomes evident that a jury is more likely to acquit the defendant than a judge.[36] Allegedly, there is more research on wrongful acquittals than on wrongful convictions.[37] Yet acquittals do not infringe on human rights, as Forsynth says: '[f]eeling of compassion for the prisoner, or of repugnance to the punishment which

---

[30] A detailed analysis of the right to appeal as found in human rights treaties can be found at the end of this chapter.

[31] Osakwe in Andrews (1982), 292.

[32] Field and Young (1994) CrimLR, 264 at 268.

[33] With regard to the Court of Appeals treatment of jury verdicts, the dissenting opinion handed down by Gözübüyük, Weitzel, Martinez, Rozakis, Liddy, and Geus against the majority opinion of the ECommHR in *Edwards v UK* Report 10 July 1991, Series A No. 247-B, 46, is worthy of attention; they express doubts as to whether the Appeals Court can predict the influence of certain facts upon the jury's verdict, as it is never clear what the jury considers important.

[34] Baldwin and McConville (1979) CrimLR, 230 at 237.

[35] A. Ashworth, *The English Criminal Process* (Oxford, 1984), 103.

[36] Lidstone in Andrews (1982), 66, comparing the rates at Magistrates' and Crown Court.

[37] This is observed by Baldwin and McConville (1979) CrimLR, 230.

the law awards, are sometimes allowed to overpower [a jury's] sense of duty'; but this is '[a]n error at which humanity need not blush'.[38] None the less, the unpredictable nature of jury behaviour can be a source of annoyance to the executive. Arguing that the criminal justice system would have collapsed if it had been based on a jury system, the jury was abolished in Northern Ireland in 1978. The system was believed unable to cope with serious terrorist offences. The single judge, in contrast, is thought to be more inclined towards government policy and apply the law without undue compassion.[39] The belief that a jury is less susceptible to irrational tendencies is highly erroneous. Jurors are influenced to an even greater extent (than judges) by fears and anxieties often kindled or fuelled by state agencies. This can make juries much harsher and more malevolent than a single judge.[40] Evidence of this kind of jury behaviour is furnished by the infamous convictions in England in terrorist cases, now considered blatant examples of the miscarriage of justice, like the Birmingham Six, Guildford Four, or Maguire Seven.[41] We therefore cannot say that a jury is a better 'bulwark of liberty' than a judge and preferable from a human rights point of view. Furthermore, there are cases in which the jury convicted, whereas a judge would not have done so, or imposed a more severe sentence than a judge would have done. Although this is true of 3–5 per cent of cases, which many people see as a tolerable outcome,[42] this figure is anything but negligible and could perhaps be avoided if the jury system was abolished. It would seem that a jury contributes neither to a fair trial nor to a mitigated judgment; it only adds to the insecurity of the defendant as the outcome is by no means predictable and above all not reviewable in a higher instance. The fact that jury verdicts can seldom be predicted can hardly be contested. It is usually justified as the consequence of a case-by-case verdict, silently implying that civil law systems do not look at individual cases properly but rather technically applies statutes.[43] The jury therefore might foster

---

[38] Forsynth, *History of Trial by Jury*, 430–1.

[39] If the US Supreme Court has singled out the importance of the jury in death-penalty cases; see U. P. Hans and N. Vidmar, *Judging the Jury* (New York, 1986), 250, it is more an argument to rethink the death penalty than to keep the jury as a welcomed excuse for judges imposing death sentence.

[40] In the recent *Woodward* case Judge Zobel had to overrule the jury's verdict in order to come to a 'compassionate judgment', see the edited version of the judgment in the *Guardian* (11 November 1997), 4.

[41] For a short description of the events around these cases see J. A. G. Griffith, *The Politics of the Judiciary* (5th edn. London, 1997), 204–13.

[42] Baldwin and McConville (1979) CrimLR, 230 at 238.

[43] G. Robertson, *Freedom, the Individual and the Law* (6th edn. London, 1989), 278, draws attention to this very point, when he says: 'Freedom, of course, is alive and well in most European countries, which have long abandoned the jury in favour of trial by professional judges'.

uncertainty, but it brings the verdict nearer to the *aequum et bonum*[44] and is simply a sign of the obvious gap between law and practice. With all due respect, it can be argued this has nothing to do with predictability. If unpredictability is an element of justice, as Devlin seems to imply, how would one define arbitrariness? Certainty and predictability are amongst the main achievements of any legal system.[45] If a law cannot be applied in a just manner to a certain case, then the law is wrong and must give way. But if citizens cannot rely on the enforcement of criminal law, the system runs the risk of being weakened. Furthermore, what seem to be neglected in this context are the consequences for the defendant. If conviction is tantamount to social and ethical censure,[46] this implies that the accused needs to understand the reasons for the conviction in order to be given a fair chance of rehabilitation. But how can he do so in these 3–5 per cent cases in which not even the judge understands the jury's verdict. This kind of treatment tends to run counter to respect for the dignity of human beings.[47]

The jury therefore seems more like a 'bulwark of tradition' rather than one of liberty. As tradition must not be pursued for its own sake but needs a modern justification,[48] the institution of the jury should at least be reconsidered or abolished entirely.[49] The international context brings further difficulties and instituting a jury at an international criminal court proves to be completely impossible. If one applies the principle of being judged by one's peers, who are these peers? Schiller has Maria Stuart exclaim, when confronted with the verdict of the House of Lords:

---

[44] Devlin, *Trial by Jury*, 157.

[45] Radbruch saw the merits of a legal system in three elements: (1) justice (*Gerechtigkeit*), (2) security (*Rechtssicherheit*), and (3) public welfare (*Gemeinnutz*). For Radbruch, a bad law was nevertheless better than no law at all, because it at least provided for certainty under the law. See G. Radbruch, *Rechtsphilosophie* (8th edn. Stuttgart, 1973), 344–6.

[46] Hirsch, *Censure and Sanctions*, 9.

[47] Hörnle and Hirsch, GA (1995), 261, where the authors mainly criticize the fact that, according to a theory of positive general prevention, the state is not honest with the defendant, because it censures him but is only aiming at utilitarian effects on society.

[48] A. Giddens, *Beyond Left and Right* (Cambridge, 1994), 45–50. In Giddens's terminology, tradition that is continued solely for its own sake is tantamount to fundamentalism. In modern society, tradition needs a solid and reasonable justification in order to survive as legitimate practice.

[49] Hans and Vidmar, *Judging the Jury*, 251, arrive at a positive assessment of the jury. Although they concede some flaws, they still claim that the jury, in view of its flexibility and adaptability over the centuries, must survive. After over 700 years of success, time is evidence for the suitability of the jury. The burden of proof, they allege, lies on those who want to curtail or abolish the jury. But the argument of the defenders of the jury can be reduced to the argument that the jury's deflects are bearable and that time speaks for itself. As already argued, this justification of traditionalism is surely inadequate and unacceptable.

Verordnet ist im englischen Gesetz,
Daß jeder Angeklagte durch Geschworene
Von seinesgleichen soll gerichtet werden.
Wer in der Committee ist meinesgleichen?
Nur Könige sind meine Peers.[50]

Similarly, a black teenager from Brixton does not have a lot in common with a white barrister residing in South Kensington and it is doubtful whether they could be judged by the same jury, if the principle were to be strictly applied.[51] But who then should sit on an international jury? Should there be different juries for Somalia and Cambodia? If so, what would be the criteria by which the election of the jurors would work? If we set up a link with the national state we will not have a truly international court; but otherwise we will have no pattern of differentiation, because an international crime is an offence against global society, so that virtually everybody is a potential juror. Another difficulty would lie in coming up with an unbiased jury. If, for example, jurors had to deliver judgment on participants in a civil war charged with crimes against humanity, many people would have followed these events on television and already have a strong opinion about the wrongs and rights of this conflict.[52] Furthermore, the costs of using a jury would be enormous.

These are the reasons why no one seriously considers establishing an international criminal court equipped with a jury. Although a number of legal systems rely on a jury, there is no human right to a jury. In general, the jury is a more than dubious institution and should be reconsidered. For an international criminal court, it is entirely out of the question.

(III) The Role of the Judge

What specific function does the judge perform during the trial in each of the systems? When reference is made to the 'judge' in the singular form, it should be borne in mind that sometimes a bench or a chamber consisting of several judges is the correct institution under the pertinent system. Legal systems attribute functions sometimes to the presiding judge, sometimes to a single judge, and sometimes to an entire bench. These differences in detail

---

[50] Friedrich Schiller, *Maria Stuart*, I. vii, pp. 702–6. 'In England it is ordered by law that each accused is to be condemned by jurors by its-same. Who in the Committee is my-same? Only kings are my Peers' (trans. by author).

[51] It is quite remarkable that it was not until 1972 that almost all those who were entitled to vote were made eligible for jury service. Previously, only those who owned property could serve on juries. Robertson, *Freedom, the Individual and the Law*, 296 and 300.

[52] Hans and Vidmar, *Judging the Jury*, 64–7, report on difficulties in the USA in producing an impartial jury. In the case of the death of a child about which they did empirical studies, almost 70% of the people questioned had detailed knowledge of the case and almost 40% used prejudicial terms in describing the case and the suspect.

scarcely matter for an understanding of the structure and are therefore left aside in the following description. The 'judge', as the word is used here, refers to the judging institution as a whole, that is, a body consisting of several judges or the presiding judge.

1. The Continental judge

The inquisitorial structure has the judge as the head of the procedure; he is the most prominent figure, the inquisitor, so to speak. He presides over the procedure, which means that he is empowered to start, end, or adjourn the proceedings, grant or reject motions, monitor the proper conduct of the participants. In addition to these functional powers, the Continental judge is in charge of presentation of the evidence and the questioning of witnesses (§ 238 StPO). The judge asks for and hears all the evidence he considers crucial for finding out the truth. Although prosecution and defence may request admission of evidence they consider indispensable, the decision as to which evidence will be presented in court is solely in the hands of the judge (see §§ 244–57 StPO). It is also up to the judge to question the witnesses. It is seen as the judge's task to arrive at the truth through inquiry. Finally, the judge comes to a verdict and immediately sentences the accused as seems appropriate according to the law. The judge must base his judgment on the 'Eindruck des Inbegriffs der mündlichen Verhandlung' (§ 261 StPO), that is, on the 'impression the judge gained from the oral hearing as a whole'. We could summarize the role of the judge as consisting of perhaps three elements: (1) the procedural element of presiding over the conduct of the trial, (2) the inquiring element, that is, presenting and examining the evidence, and (3) the judging element, that is, the convicting and sentencing or acquitting the accused.

2. The Anglo-American judge

The role of the judge in an accusatorial system is comparatively limited. The judge only presides over the conduct of the trial and its process. He is obliged to direct the jury as to the law, and to explain and advise them also in matters of evidence. The judge is, however, not directly involved in the presentation of evidence and the questioning of witnesses. This is left entirely up to the prosecution and defence. After the jury has come to a verdict, sentencing is the judge's task.[53]

Often enough, the role of the judge in an adversarial system is

---

[53] It is interesting to note that the public in England seems to be convinced that judges are too lenient in this regard. Public opinion, according to the latest survey, does not support and trust judges' judgments. A closer look reveals, however, that this public opinion is not supported by empirical evidence. On the contrary, judges are far harsher in their sentencing practice than the average person would be, see the *Guardian* (7 January 1998), 1 and 4.

compared with that of the 'umpire' in a sports contest.[54] Although this analogy may seem to do mockery to the seriousness of the matter, it deserves some merit. The judge has the functional powers to safeguard the procedural fairness and supervise the conduct of the parties. However, he is not involved in material questions of the case apart from imposing the penalty on the convicted person. The functions of this judge could be summarized as consisting of perhaps two elements: (1) the procedural element (see above) and (2) the sentencing element, which is part of but not equivalent to the above judging element.

3. The system at the ICTY

The ICTY is mainly patterned on the adversarial structures. The judge's role is thus designed to be more or less that of an independent 'umpire' for the presentation of the case by prosecution and defence. However, there is no jury deciding on the guilt of the offender; instead, there are judges, three in the Trial Chamber, five on appeals (Art. 12 Statute ICTY), called upon to give judgment (Rules 87 and 88). This constitutes a major shift in the role of the judge away from a purely adversarial trial. Rather than functioning solely as an 'umpire' he is involved in the substantive side of the case. The judge at the ICTY is equipped both with the 'procedural element' and the 'judging element'. He seems to lack genuine powers of inquiry, but the 'inquisitorial element' is not entirely missing. Under Rule 85B, the judge has the power to put any question to the witness at any stage. Although Rule 85B relies in its wording on the idea of finding the truth by means of cross-examination[55] and leaves the calling of the witnesses, that is, the presentation of the evidence, up to the parties, it gives the judge the additional power to intervene in the questioning at any stage of the examination and pose questions himself.[56] The Rules of Procedure and Evidence go even further. The Trial Chamber can intervene in the presentation of evidence and order either party to produce additional evidence. Furthermore, it may itself summon witnesses and order their attendance (Rule 98) after the presentation by the parties (Rule 85A v). The Trial Chambers at the ICTY have used these powers and summoned witnesses on their own initiative on several occasions.[57] It was ruled that in such cases witnesses

---

[54] Herrmann, *Reform der deutschen Hauptverhandlung*, 152–3, with further references.

[55] I will discuss this stage of the procedure later.

[56] Nsereko, 5 CLF (1994), 507 at 538, coming from a common law background, is bewildered by this additional power of the judges. He calls for the behaviour of judges to be restricted in this regard.

[57] ICTY Trial Chamber, *Kupreskic*, Order pursuant to Rule 98, 30 September 1998; *Blaskic*, Decisions 25 March, 13 May and 21 May 1999 to order General Philippe Morillon, Colonel Robert Stewart, and others.

would be examined by the judges, then by the prosecution and finally by defence counsel.[58]

This indicates that the judge is not intended to be on the same level as the prosecution or defence. His intervention in the presentation of evidence is not governed by party interests but considered truly independent, aimed solely at seeking of the truth, 'inquisitorial' in this sense.[59] This means that the judge incorporates both the 'procedural' and 'judging' elements and approximately half the 'inquisitorial element'. The only difference to the Continental judge lies in the fact that the latter is exclusively responsible for presentation of the evidence, whereas the judge at the Hague has only an ancillary responsibility in this sense. Does this mean that the role of the judge at the ICTY is closer to that of the Continental judge than that of Anglo-American judges? The ICTY system is at all events a mixture.[60]

4. The ICC

The Rome Statute contains several recommendations concerning the role of the judge at trial, as contemplated by the authors. First of all, Art. 64 (IX) (b) and Art. 64 (VIII) (b) Rome Statute give the judge the power to maintain order in the course of the hearing and give directions for conduct of the proceedings. He is envisaged as presiding over the conduct of the main hearing, therefore fulfilling the 'procedural element'. It is clear that, for the duration of the trial, the Trial Chamber is supposed to be in charge of all procedural questions arising (Art. 64 Rome Statute). Furthermore, as the Rome Statute does not propose the institution of a jury, the judges are also called upon to give the verdict. The ICC judges, three at the Trial Chamber (Art. 39 (II) b (ii) Rome Statute) and four plus President on appeals (Art. 39 (I), (II) b (i) Rome Statute)[61] are thus supposed to incorporate the 'judging element' (Art. 74 Rome Statute). Originally, the rules of procedure and evidence for the trial were intended to be drawn up by the judges themselves (Art. 19 Statute ILC).[62] Art. 51 Rome Statute decided in favour of a

---

[58] Jones, *The Practice of the ICTY*, Rule 98, p. 430.

[59] Bassiouni, *The Law of the ICTY*, 955, sees in this testimony for the approach taken by Statute and Rules, to 'selectively incorporate civil law concepts into a predominately common law framework'.

[60] The ICTY First Annual Report (1994), para. 73, calls this one of the three main deviations from the adversarial system.

[61] As to the difficulties concerning the organization of the chambers, see Jarasch, 6 Eur.J.Crime Cr.L.Cr.J. (1998), 335–6.

[62] There was some discussion about the question of whether the judges should be burdened with this task of drawing up the rules of procedure or whether a group of experts should be established to perform this task with perhaps close cooperation with the states, Report ILC, para. 75. In the PrepComm it was considered that states should participate in the drafting of the rules of procedure and evidence. It was pointed out that the experience of the ICTY, which has amended its Rules several times, shows that a flexible procedure is

decision of the Assembly of States Parties, with some vague power for the judges to establish provisional rules in a case of necessity. The extent to which they will incorporate the 'inquisitorial element' cannot be foreseen. However, the Report of the ILC comments:

[d]etails of the procedure of the court should be laid down in the rules, and will no doubt evolve with experience. It is intended that the court should itself have the right to call witnesses and ask questions, although it may also leave that task to the Prosecutor and defence counsel, and the right of the accused to present a defence must not be impaired.[63]

The PrepComm did not envisage that Art. 38 (II) Statute ILC would encompass anything more than the 'procedural element', that the 'President should play an active role in guiding the trial proceedings by conducting the debate and monitoring the manner in which evidence for or against the accused was reported'.[64] Art. 69 (III) Rome Statute includes the power of the Trial Chamber to request the production of further evidence. This may exceed the passive 'umpire'-like role of the judge in England, and give the judge the task of taking more active steps to prevent abuses during the presentation of evidence, but cannot be equated with the 'inquisitorial element'. It has been said that the role of the judges at the ICC is thus closer to that of Continental systems.[65] The Draft Rules do not further elaborate on this point. Draft Rule 6.20 obliges the Trial Chamber to make necessary orders with regard to further evidence as soon as possible and include strict time limits. An expeditious trial is certainly desirable but should not prevent determination of the truth as the primary aim of the trial (see Art. 69 (III) Rome Statute).

Arguably, the judges should also play an active role in the presentation of evidence and more actively request further evidence and put questions to the witnesses.[66] This submission will be explained and clarified further in the following paragraphs on the various roles of the other participants and in particular those parties that deal with the presentation of evidence and the examination of witnesses.

needed for dealing with the rules of procedure, see Report of the PrepComm, para. 50. The Rome Statute decided in favour of Rules adopted by a two-thirds majority of the members of the Assembly of States. A Committee of Experts was convened for the first time in early 1999 to prepare a draft (Art. 51 Rome Statute).

[63] Report ILC, Art. 38, para. 3.

[64] Report of the PrepComm I, para. 265.

[65] Behrens, 6 Eur.J.Crime Cr.L.Cr.J. (1998), 439. The same author spells out clearly that the court is not allowed to call evidence on its own authority but does have the power to compel the parties to cooperate and produce additional evidence, see Trifterer (ed.), *Commentary on the Rome Statute*, Art. 69, No. 40.

[66] Germany's proposal concerning the determination of proof is similar: the court should extend the taking of evidence to all facts and evidence that are deemed important for the decision; see Report of the PrepComm II, 207.

(IV) Role of the Prosecution

Another major difference between an English (or American) and a Continental trial is the role played by the prosecutor during trial; the two trials can be characterized as a legal battle between two parties on the one hand (adversarial system), in the course of which the truth will hopefully come to light, and an institutionalized search for the truth through the questioning of a judge, on the other (inquisitorial system). Adversarial systems do not seem to have their main focus on finding the truth. What matters at the trial stage is to prove that the defendant is 'guilty as charged'. In each system, the prosecutor has a completely different role.[67]

1. Adversarial system

In an adversarial system, the prosecution is one of the two parties in the legal battle. It is the prosecutor's task to represent the interests of the state, that is, to convict the offender. This does not sound dangerous. It implies a very restricted view of the prosecutor's competence; pleading the case at whatever cost is clearly prohibited. The prosecutor is believed to be a servant of truth and justice.[68] His public mandate does not exceed prosecution of the guilty.

Although the adversarial trial is frequently thought of differently, this is an accurate view. Stemming from the presumption of innocence and the principle of equality of arms, the prosecutor can only be guided by the goal of finding out the truth. The comparison of the adversarial trial with a sports contest, made above when the role of the judge was being discussed, might be misleading with respect to the role of the prosecutor. It most definitely does not mean that the two parties have the same starting conditions. The prosecutor is totally committed to the principles of truth and objectivity, his counterpart not necessarily so, as will be seen later. This was expressed in *R v Banks*: '[the prosecuting counsel] ought not to struggle for the verdict against the prisoner, but they ought to bear themselves rather in the character of ministers of justice assisting in the administration of justice'.[69]

This has several consequences. The prosecutor may never resort to lies, and must not knowingly use perjured testimony.[70] He should even reveal any previous conviction of his witness to the defence, thereby certainly

---

[67] Sigler, in McDonald, *The Prosecutor*, 69, constantly argues in his comparative study of prosecutors against overestimating the difference between the systems, but admits that if there is meaning to the distinction, then it is at the trial stage.

[68] R. M. Honig, *Beweisverbote und Grundrechte im amerikanischen Strafprozeß* (Tübingen, 1967).

[69] *R v Banks* (1916) 2 KB 621.

[70] Osakwe in Andrews (1982), 289.

running the risk of offering the defence a welcome line of cross-examination.[71] He must also refrain from misrepresenting facts in cross-examination. If the prosecution adheres strictly to the truth, it need not fear the defence case; rather, the prosecutor must unfold evidence that is favourable to the accused. It is arguable whether there is a requirement for the prosecution to give to the defence a complete and detailed account of all police investigatory work on the case.[72] However, it is certain that any evidence that is favourable to the accused must be revealed, whether requested by the defence or not.[73]

The organizational structure of the prosecution differs widely. In the USA counselling is done by state attorneys,[74] whereas in England, at least in Crown Court cases, the CPS needs to instruct counsel. The English counsel for the prosecution is therefore not part of a government structure and not under the disciplinary power of the executive.[75]

This understanding of the role of the prosecutor, which is a consistent development from the prosecutor's previous role during the investigation, reveals the maxim 'guilty as charged' to be a myth. The prosecution is committed to finding out the truth throughout the entire trial. Objectivity cannot stop at the 'charge', which then only has to be proven during trial by whatever means. In its procedural activities and moves, the prosecutor has to be objective and truthful until judgment is given.

2. Inquisitorial system

In the Continental system, the role of the prosecution at the trial stage is clearly defined. The prosecutor's task is mainly to collect evidence, indict the offender, and present the evidence to the court. According to the principle of accusation (*Akkusationsprinzip*, § 151 StPO), it is the duty of the prosecutor to initiate proceedings before the court, which cannot try people itself (§ 152 (I) StPO).[76] As the judge takes over the leading role from the prosecutor as soon as the indictment is confirmed, the prosecutor does not have the huge influence on the outcome of the trial that his Anglo-American colleague has. As an institution, the prosecution remains

[71] Emmins, 9.1.1, for this reason referring to *R v Paraskeva* (1983) 76 Crim.App.R. 162. Cross-examination concerning previous convictions of a witness is however an ambiguous avenue for the defence, because it opens up the possibility of the prosecution making the character of the accused an issue.

[72] The US Supreme Court found that there was no such requirement to be found in the US Constitution, see *Moore v Illinois* 408 US 786 (1972).

[73] For the United States, see Osakwe in Andrews (1982), 290; US Supreme Court *Giglio v US* 405 US 150 (1972).

[74] Compare the detailed study by J. Eisenstein, *Counsel for the United States* (Baltimore, 1978).

[75] Unlike the CPS solicitor who is permitted to present the case at the Magistrates' Court. See Emmins, 9.1.1.

[76] Compare Kleinknecht and Meyer-Goßner, § 152 No.1.

the same; it represents the public interest, has to fulfil its duty in an objective manner, and is committed to finding out the truth. During the main hearing the prosecutor reads the indicted charges at the beginning of the process (§ 243 (III) StPO). Yet the interrogation of the witnesses is performed by the judge (§ 238 (I) StPO). Although the prosecutor may question the witnesses after the judge has finished his examination (§ 239 StPO), he will often refrain from doing so in order to avoid confusing the judge.[77] However, this depends very much on the individual character of the prosecutor and the interaction between him and the judge.[78] At the end of the main hearing, the prosecutor will present his view of the case as it derives from what was heard, and will enter a plea as to the guilt of the accused and as to the sentencing (§ 258 (I) StPO).

3. The system at the ICTY

The structure of the procedure is along the lines of the Anglo-American system. Consequently the prosecutor greatly resembles his counterpart in the accusatorial procedural systems. The prosecutor at the ICTY is called upon to present his case at the trial. After the opening statements (Rule 84), the prosecutor presents his evidence and after the defence's presentation produces evidence in rebuttal (Rule 85A). The examination of the witnesses is mainly a matter of the parties. The prosecutor must therefore examine and cross-examine the witnesses, and may then give a closing argument.[79]

4. International system

The precise role of the prosecutor during the trial is not defined in the Rome Statute. However, it can be safely assumed that it will be similar to that of the ICTY prosecutor. Art. 64 (VI) and also Art. 69 (III) Rome Statute presume that presentation of evidence will mainly be the duty of the parties.[80] They may be assisted by the court, only if they cannot take action themselves; such assistance may lie in the issue of an arrest warrant, enforcement of the attendance and testimony of witnesses, or the production of evidentiary material. Such trial procedure is clearly

---

[77] Sigler, in McDonald, *The Prosecutor*, 69.

[78] There have even been reports of prosecutors' reading novels after their opening statements during the conduct of the examination; see Langbein, 41 University of Chicago Law Review (1974), 439 at 448.

[79] Whether there is a general right to re-cross-examine a witness has been denied by the ICTY Trial Chambers. However, re-cross-examination may be allowed under certain circumstances, e.g. if new material is introduced during re-examination. On such new material re-cross-examination may take place. Cases reported by Jones, *The Practice of the ICTY*, Rule 85B, p. 405.

[80] Hermsdörfer, 40 NZWehrr (1998), 197 (199), suggests that this is the way to read the draft; compare also Bitti in Trifterer (ed.), *Commentary on the Rome Statute*, Art. 64, No. 23.

envisaged by the submissions of Australia and Netherlands in the PrepComm. It is again reminiscent of the proceeding at the ICTY.[81]

(V) The Defence

The other party, the defence, is not subject to the same restraints as the prosecution. The counsel for the defendant is not representing the state. He is working merely in the interests of the accused. The counsel is therefore not a servant of justice, and need not be objective and fair towards the prosecution.[82] He need not tell the prosecution about previous convictions of his client,[83] for example, or of one of his witnesses. In general he may use all means at his disposal to secure an acquittal for his client.

There are, however, a number of rules which the defence counsel must respect, rules that stem from the way in which the lawyer's profession is seen. A problem arises, for example, if counsel knows that his client is guilty but the latter refuses to confess to the court or plead guilty. May the defence counsel then behave as if he was unaware of the defendant's guilt, may he really work towards his client's acquittal? By so doing, he would indirectly lie or deliberately mislead the court. The defence counsel has several possibilities in such circumstances; he may either withdraw from the case, which, if the trial has already reached a certain stage, may ruin the defendant's chances of acquittal, or he may continue but is then barred from arguing in favour of his client's innocence. He may work towards a mitigated charge or sentence but not pursue an acquittal.[84] The consequence is that, like the prosecutor and the court, the defence counsel is committed to truth and justice, the only difference being that he must nevertheless act in the interests of his client. This means that, if he is aware of the defendant's guilt, he may not deliberately mislead the court and the prosecution, but may not disclose his knowledge either, if his client officially denies his guilt.[85] It is his duty to address the court 'fearlessly and without regard to his personal interests'.[86] Even in cases of legal aid, where client and counsel have not chosen each other, the counsel is still obliged to argue the case without regard to his personal opinion as to the truth or falsity of the defence, or the character of the accused, or the nature of the charge.[87] The duties of the defence counsel could be described as threefold: the duty to advocacy, commitment to the truth, and silence.[88] He must (*a*) raise all issues that speak in favour of the accused and point to procedural

---

[81] See Report of the PrepComm II, 191–2.   [82] Emmins, 9.1.2.

[83] In civil law countries this will be irrelevant as the court routinely consults the criminal record of the defendant.   [84] See Emmins, 9.1.2.

[85] See Roxin, *Strafverfahrensrecht*, § 19 A II 3 b.

[86] Chairman of the Bar in 62 Crim.App.R., 193 at 194.   [87] Emmins, 9.1.2.

[88] See Roxin, *Strafverfahrensrecht* § 19 A II 3. These duties are found in §§ 258 and 203 StGB.

misgivings; he must (*b*) not lie to the public authorities, and must (*c*) not disclose what the client has told him in secret.

According to the Anglo-American structure of the criminal trial, the role of the defence is without doubt an active one. The defence counsel may present evidence and call witnesses; he tries to dismantle the prosecution case by cross-examining the witnesses called to testify by the prosecutor. The Continental defence lawyer is much more restricted in his powers. He can argue in favour of the defendant and ask the court to call additional witnesses on behalf of the defendant. The questioning of these witnesses as well as of those who give testimony for the prosecution is however left entirely up to the judge. The defence counsel may submit further questions to the judge, who will decide whether or not to admit the point raised.

At the ICTY the defence counsel plays a similar role in the proceedings to that of the defence lawyer in the Anglo-American system. As a party to the procedure, the defence has the power to call witnesses and present evidence (Rule 85) and rebut evidence presented by the prosecution. The defence evidence is presented after the prosecution case. The presentation of evidence may be preceded by an opening statement.[89] The Registrar at the ICTY has issued a Code of Professional Conduct for the Defence Counsel, which can be seen as a compilation of the modus operandi in a number of (Western) states.[90] The principles outlined above are summarized in this body of rules. According to these rules, counsel must act independently and diligently in order to protect the client's best interests (Art. 6 ICTY Code of Conduct for Defence Counsel). The ICTY also sees defence counsel to be obliged to the truth, as he is not allowed to openly lie to the court (Article 13 ICTY Code of Conduct for Defence Counsel). The role of Defence Counsel is perhaps best expressed by the preamble of this ICTY Code of Conduct: '3. Counsel have an overriding duty to defend their client's interests, to the extent that they can do so without acting dishonestly or by improperly prejudicing the administration of justice.' The Statute ILC, in particular in the interpretation and submissions in the PrepComm, assigns a similar role to the defence.[91] The ICTY Code of Conduct for Defence Counsel should be adopted by the ICC, as it represents the practice in national countries and would seem to be a suitable basis for the relationship between court and counsel.[92]

---

[89] Defence counsel have done so, e.g. in *Tadic* (7 May 1996), *Furundzija* (8 June 1998), *Blaskic* (7–8 September 1998); compare Jones, *The Practice of the ICTY*, Rule 84, p. 402.

[90] ICTY Registrar, The Code of Professional Conduct for Defence Counsel Appearing Before the International Tribunal, 12 June 1997, UN Doc. IT/125 (= ICTY Code of Conduct for Defence Counsel).

[91] See Report of the PrepComm II, 191–2.

[92] Draft Rule YY foresees a code of professional conduct to be proposed by the Registrar and adopted by the Assembly of State Parties.

B. PRINCIPLES OF THE TRIAL

Before looking at the actual course of the trial, we must discuss the principles that are commonly associated with a criminal trial in an abstract manner. These principles have a considerable influence on the structure and the process of the procedure. The rights or principles discussed in the following are enshrined in all of the major human rights treaties but unfortunately in a very confusing and unsystematic manner. The wording of the relevant provision is generally simple but interpretation becomes complex. A single word within Art. 6 ECHR, for example, can produce a considerable number of varying decisions. Let us pick out six principles that govern the structure of the trial and discuss their meaning according to human rights treaties.

(I) The Principle of Publicity of Proceedings
(*Öffentlichkeitsgrundsatz*)

The principle of a public trial is embodied in Art. 14 (I) 2 ICCPR and Art. 6 I ECHR in the same words: 'everyone is entitled to a fair and public hearing'. Art. 8 (V) AmCHR formulates, '[c]riminal proceedings shall be public'. However clear this provision is, a fair number of exceptions are cited in the next sentence, which reads as follows:

Art. 14 (I) 3 ICCCPR
(I) The Press and the public may be excluded from all or part of a trial for reasons of morals, public order (*ordre public*) or national security in a democratic society, or when the interests of the private lives of the parties so requires, or to the extent strictly necessary in the opinion of the court in special circumstance where publicity would prejudice the interests of justice; but any judgment rendered in a criminal case or in a suit at law shall be made public except where the interest of juvenile persons otherwise requires or the proceedings concern matrimonial disputes or the guardianship of children.

The principle of a public trial is a genuine democratic principle. Thereby the independence of the judiciary in the sense of a separation of powers should be safeguarded. Justice shall be made transparent and accessible to everyone. The drafters of the ICCPR saw 'publicity' as a bulwark against arbitrary action on the part of the courts.[93] The HRC sees the principle of publicity as 'an important safeguard in the interest of the individual and of society at large'.[94]

---

[93] A/2929, Chapt. VI, § 78, cf. also Bossuyt, *Guide*, 284.
[94] HRC General Comment 12 (Article 14), para. 6.

However, although the public nature of the trial at first seems advantageous for the accused, since it provides for control over procedure and judgment, it might easily prove disadvantageous. The accused might have good grounds for keeping his identity anonymous, whilst it might also be safer for the victim and witnesses too, if they do not have to identify themselves in public, as seen in the recent case of a Tutsi woman in Rwanda, who was murdered the day after she testified in a Rwandan court. For this reason, the principle of publicity cannot possibly be an absolute principle but must be balanced against the interests and rights of the accused, victim, and witness. But, in principle, the right to a public trial is not only a right for the defendant to guarantee the proper conduct of the trial. It is also a right for the public in a democratic society.[95] As the administration of justice is carried out in the name of the people, the public has an interest in overseeing the process.[96] A suitable balance must therefore be sought between the two sides, the participants, who may have conflicting interests, and the public.

The overall principle of publicity may be divided up into three separate questions: public access to the actual hearing, pronouncement of the judgment in public, and the general freedom of information in society.

1. Public hearing

Nowak calls this stage of publicity during the procedure 'dynamic publicity'.[97] By this he means the presence of the public during the time the court comes to a decision, the conduct of the trial. Of particular importance is the presence of the press.[98] The text of the covenant mentions the press explicitly and so does the HRC in its General Comment. Press presence seems to be a special guarantee for the safeguarding of 'fairness'.[99] Attendance of independent press representatives also makes it impossible for states to pack the court room with persons paid by the government, as has apparently been done by a number of states.[100] The requirement of a public trial was called into question by Latin American states in particular. Many of these states conduct trials in written form. For these states, it was considered sufficient if the documents were publicly accessible.[101]

---

[95] Nowak, Art. 14, No. 24.
[96] Compare J. E. S. Fawcett, *The Application of the ECHR* (Oxford, 1987), 161.
[97] Nowak, Art. 14, No. 22.   [98] Harris, 218.
[99] The effect of press presence is described by the former British Bosnia Commander Bob Stewart in the different context of dealing with warlords in Bosnia: 'The Press was often the most powerful weapon available to me. Condemnation of the international or local airwaves was something that even the most hardened warlords would wish to avoid. The mere presence of cameras was often enough to change the situation.' *The Sunday Times* (12 October 1997), section 5, 2.
[100] See McGoldrick, *Human Rights Committee*, 403.
[101] Compare Nowak, Art. 14, No. 23.

This historical fact is the reason for the wording of the AmCHR: 'Art. 8 (V) Criminal procedure shall be public, except in so far as may be necessary to protect the interests of justice.' It is necessary to find the exact scope of application for the right to a public hearing. Sometimes it is stated that the principle of a public hearing only applies to hearings in the narrow sense, that is, 'to the submissions of the opposing parties in a specific matter'.[102] Those parts of the procedure that do not concern determination of the facts, as for example appellate or cassation proceedings that exclusively deal with questions of law, therefore do not need to be held in public.[103] This narrow interpretation conflicts with the wide approach of the Strasbourg organs, which will be looked at below.

The text of Art. 14 (I) ICCPR and Art. 6 (I) ECHR allows several exceptions.[104] So far, on the level of the HRC, no state party has ever invoked any of these exceptions in order to answer allegations against it,[105] although states have been condemned for holding 'secret trials'.[106]

The situation at the European level is different, despite the wording of Art. 6 (I) ECHR regarding the exceptions being exactly the same as in Art. 14 (I) ICCPR, apart from an explicit reference to juvenile offenders in the European document. Some of these exceptions appear as justifying arguments in the second paragraph of a number of other articles enshrined in the ECHR.[107] For these reasons, an assessment of Strasbourg case-law will be of help.

There are five exceptions, each of which deserves to be looked at separately, although Fawcett argues that these terms are so broad that the protection is doubtful as a whole.[108] The public may be excluded only for the following reasons: protection of (a) morals, (b) public order (*ordre public*), (c) national security in a democratic society, to the extent that such protection is (d) in the interests of the private lives of the parties, or (e) strictly necessary in the opinion of the court in special circumstances where publicity would prejudice the interests of justice.

Before I look at each of these terms, here are some general observations. Although it is not stated *expressis verbis*, such exceptions must have a legal basis and be decreed by a judge. The first condition stems from the general requirement that all restrictions on human rights can only be justified if rooted in the law. This is not only obvious from the various human

---

[102] Ibid., Art. 14, No. 24.   [103] Ibid.

[104] Some of these are also to be found in other articles, like Arts. 12(III), 13, 18 (III), 19 (III), and 22 (II).

[105] See McGoldrick, *Human Rights Committee*, 419.

[106] e.g. *Estrella v Uruguay* Doc. A/38/40, 150.

[107] It may suffice as an example to point to Art. 8 (II) ECHR, which was discussed earlier in some detail. There one can find the terms 'national security', 'morals', and 'democratic society' justifying state intrusion into the private lives of individuals. Compare Harris, 219.

[108] Fawcett, *Application of the ECHR*, 161.

rights treaties, it is also a basic principle of the rule of law (*Rechtsstaats-prinzip*). The second condition is a consequence of the fact that the court of decision (*erkennendes Gericht*) presides over the procedure, as seen when the role of the court was discussed in detail.

(a) *Protection of morals*   Without doubt the protection of morals is a broad and indeterminate concept. The problem is enhanced by the jurisprudence of the ECourtHR which attaches to 'morals' a wide margin of appreciation for the state parties.[109] Nevertheless the ECourtHR has repeatedly held that this discretion is not without limits. Whatever restriction the state imposes, it needs to be proportionate to the legitimate aim pursued.[110]

(b) *Protection of* l'ordre public *in a democratic society*[111]   The drafters of the ICCPR discussed whether or not to use the term 'prevention of disorder' in English, rather than 'public order', as the former comes closer to what is meant by the French term *l'ordre public*.[112] The idea was rejected,[113] but this fact may help to make the meaning of 'public order' clearer. The main difficulty lies in the question of whether 'order' refers to the court room or goes beyond this.[114] Nowak gives a somewhat ambiguous answer by saying it relates 'primarily' to the court room.[115]

The ECourtHR has dealt with this problem in two cases in particular. In the first, *Le Compte v Belgium*, it found that public order entails more than just the prevention of disorder.[116] The ECourtHR seems to presume that protection of the private lives of a physician's patients comes within the ambit of protecting *l'ordre public*. In *Campbell and Fell v UK*, the ECourtHR had to deal with the matter of disciplinary proceedings against imprisoned persons held in camera inside the prison. The government justified this procedure as necessary by virtue of 'public order' and 'national security in a democratic society'.[117] The underlying reason for this trial behind bars was security problems. Although the ECourtHR drew attention to the security problems arising in ordinary trials, it

---

[109] See the case ECourtHR *Handyside v UK* Judgment 7 December 1976, Series A No. 24.

[110] Ibid., paras. 48–50.

[111] The notion of a 'democratic society' will be discussed together with national security, although it is clearly related to both elements; see A/4299, § 55, Bossuyt, *Guide*, 288.

[112] Harris, 219 n. 2, presumes that the French *l'ordre public* goes beyond the term 'public disorder'.

[113] A/2929 Chapt. VI, § 79, but it was later decided to clarify the matter by putting the French expression *ordre public* in parentheses in the English and Russian texts, A/4299, § 55, Bossuyt, *Guide*, 289.

[114] This question is stressed by Fawcett, *The Application of the ECHR*, 162.

[115] Nowak, Art. 14, No. 25.

[116] ECourtHR *Le Compte, van Leuven and De Meyere v Belgium* Judgment 23 June 1981, Series A No. 43, para. 59.

[117] ECourtHR *Campbell and Fell v UK* Judgment 28 June 1984, Series A No. 80, para. 86.

accepted the argument that the exigencies of the situation involved particularly great problems with respect to transport and attendance at hearings. The exclusion of the press and public from the proceedings was thus
justified by virtue of 'public order and security'.[118] The Court appears to
be using the term 'public order and security' to describe what is meant by
l'ordre public. It is very unlikely that the allusion to security is meant to
refer to 'national security', because there are no matters of national interest involved.[119] In the above case, the ECourtHR based its argumentation
on considerations of proportionality and found no violation, as a public
hearing conducted under these circumstances would impose a disproportionate burden on state authorities.[120]

(c) Protection of national security in a democratic society   It seems remarkable that the term 'national security' has been supplemented by the words
'in a democratic state'. It seems, at first sight, to be there as a restriction.
And apparently it was indeed intended as such by the drafters, who
speak of a 'salutary safeguard'.[121] National security in the court room
mainly concerns cases where the secrecy of important military facts plays
a role,[122] as might be the case in espionage trials, for example.[123]

(d) The interests of the private lives of the parties   The *travaux préparatoires*
reveal the original aim of this exception: the protection of juvenile offenders.[124] Yet no verbatim reference to juveniles was made in Art. 14 (I)
ICCPR, unlike Art 6 (I) ECHR, where juveniles are mentioned separately
alongside the interests of the parties. The protection of young offenders is
therefore not necessarily the only notion that is included in 'the interests
of the private lives of the parties'.

    The scope of protection entails private lives. But what is meant by the

---

[118] Ibid., para. 88. The UK has abolished the system of the Boards of Visitors in prisons in
the mean time so that prisoners are now transported to the courts, compare Harris, 219 n.
20.

[119] This view is shared by Harris, 219 n. 1.

[120] ECourtHR *Campbell and Fell v UK* Judgment 28 June 1984, Series A No. 80, para. 87.

[121] The restriction was retained in the text despite criticism from the USA (E/CN.4/SR.323,
4) and France (ibid. 10) that this provision was too wide and ambiguous.

[122] Nowak, Art. 14, No. 25.

[123] It is interesting to note, however, that espionage trials with an international background are very rare. As the very concept of espionage is extremely ambiguous in international law, as neither allowed nor prohibited but definitely not protected, spies seem to
operate outside the law, and as every state entertains a legion of secret agents, no state dares
to prosecute a spy from another state; they quite rightly fear that this other state will do the
same to their own agents. After a conflict of some kind or other, spies are usually exchanged
or granted amnesty. On the other hand, rather rigorous treatment is laid down for the
nationals who spy against their own state. For the problem of the punishment of former
GDR spies after the unification of Germany, see Simma and Volk, NJW (1991), 871, who are
in favour of an amnesty for these spies.

[124] Some states felt it safer to refer explicitly to the interests of juveniles; see France
(E/CN.4/SR.318, 11) or the USA (E/CN.4/SR.323, 4).

term 'private life' in this context? Can we draw parallels to the content of 'private life' in Art. 17 ICCPR or Art. 8 ECHR? Nowak believes that special protection must be given to family matters, sexual offences, and other cases concerning private and family life. The Strasbourg organs have found the private lives exception legitimately applied explicitly in divorce proceedings,[125] and implicitly in sexual offences against children.[126] In *Guenoun v France*, once again involving disciplinary proceedings against a doctor, the ECommHR weighed the applicant's right to a fair trial against the rights of the applicant's patients to protection of their private lives.[127] The ECommHR mentioned both the private lives of the parties and the 'interests of justice' as justifying grounds, but based its decision, rather oddly, on the fact that the applicant failed to invoke his right to a public hearing earlier than before the Conseil d'État, where his request was granted. 'The Commission therefore considers that the applicant cannot claim to be the victim of a violation of one of the Convention's provisions, since he did not assert his right to a public hearing before the disciplinary tribunals.'[128]

The other question arising from this exception is, who counts as a party? The Continental trial does not use the term 'party' and indeed commentators point out that 'parties' are foreign to criminal procedure on the Continent.[129] But it would be wrong, here as always, to apply a literal meaning stemming from one or several legal systems to the human rights norm. An 'autonomous' human rights meaning has to be found. To this end, the norm must be interpreted teleologically. Art. 14 ICCPR is intended first of all to protect the defendant, who must be presumed innocent until the verdict. His integrity is more endangered than that of any person involved. He is definitely meant to be within the scope of protection. Further inquiry into the identity of other persons whose privacy could be threatened in the course of a trial will lead to the victim and witnesses. The other participants, judge, prosecutor, and defence counsel, do not seem to be affected, as their lives are not under scrutiny and as they are fulfilling their public duty. Victim and witnesses on the other hand can be severely harmed by publicity. Not only their public reputation but even their lives may be harmed. Both must not only be presumed innocent, but are indeed innocent persons for the course of the trial. Furthermore, the trial is held partly as compensation for the harm done to the victim. Applying a wide grammatical interpretation to the norm one

---

[125] ECommHR *X v UK* Appl. No. 7366/76, 2 Digest 452.

[126] ECommHR *X v Austria* Appl. No. 1913/63, 2 Digest 428.

[127] ECommHR *Guenoun v France* Decision 2 July 1990, Appl. No. 13562/88, 66 DR 181.

[128] Ibid., at 187. The suggestion of Harris, 220, that the justification in this case was the protection of the private lives of the parties, seems doubtful.

[129] Kleinknecht and Meyer-Goßner, Einl. No. 9.

could even argue that the victim is part of the prosecution and therefore a
'party' in the sense of Art. 14 (I) ICCPR. The privacy of the victim is thus
protected.[130]

The situation with respect to the witnesses is less clear. A witness has
no particular interest in the outcome of the trial. The prosecution is not
interested in his 'compensation' or 'satisfaction'. Therefore it is questionable whether a witness should be protected by excluding the public.

Other persons who might deserve protection are those with whom one
of the participants of the trial has a special relationship, for example a
particular duty of secrecy, as doctors have towards their patient or
lawyers towards their clients. In the above-mentioned case *Guenoun v
France* the ECommHR did not specify this problem.[131] In our view, these
persons are too far remote from the trial to be considered as belonging to
one party. Their relationship with one of the participants is too vague to
invoke the 'protection of the private lives of the parties'. Similarly, in
Imberechts v Belgium the ECommHR considered a similar case as legitimate, 'on the grounds that such publicity might be prejudicial to the
public interest'.[132]

(e) Publicity would prejudice the interests of justice   As this exception clause
was discussed in detail, the *travaux* of the ICCPR unveil the underlying
intent of the drafters here, too. In them, they refer to secret industrial
processes and legally incapable persons and first offenders.[133] The provision is flanked by two conditions; it can only be invoked in 'special
circumstances' and only 'to the extent strictly necessary in the opinion of
the court'. The exclusion of the public is therefore only permissible in
highly extraordinary cases. Nowak cites as an example the danger of
emotional reactions on the part of the spectators.[134] This exception had
been invoked by a Belgian court in a case concerning certain narcotic
offences; a public trial would, in the opinion of this court, encourage the
use of habit-forming drugs.[135]

I intend to extend the ambit of this exclusion rule to all cases in which
conflicting rights have to be balanced against the right to a public hearing.
All cases involving the right to privacy of persons who are not party to the

---

[130] Compare Nowak, Art. 14, No. 26. However, Nowak is not willing to go even further
and include 'other innocent persons' in the protection; ibid. n. 77.

[131] ECommHR *Guenoun v France* Decision 2 July 1990, Appl. No. 13562/88, 66 DR 181.

[132] ECommHR *Imberechts v Belgium* Decision 25 February 1991, Appl. No. 15561/89, 69 DR
312. It remains unclear which of the mentioned exceptions the ECommHR wants to refer to.
It could be public order, but the most likely is the exception in the interests of justice.
Unfortunately the ECommHR does not do so explicitly.

[133] E/CN.4/SR.155, §§ 20–2 (United Kingdom), § 24 (Australia), § 29 (United States).

[134] Nowak, Art. 14, No. 26.

[135] Quoted by Fawcett, *The Application of the ECHR*, 162 n. 1, who finds the case uncon-
vincing.

trial will thus be included here. Cases like *Guenoun v France* and *Imberechts v Belgium* should be discussed under this heading. So, too, should cases involving the safety of witnesses. In *X v UK*, where several professional journalists who had witnessed a terrorist murder in Northern Ireland were screened, that is, their faces were made invisible to the public as well as to the defendant, as they feared for their safety, the ECommHR followed the track proposed here. Although evidence must generally be given in open court and publicly,[136] non-disclosure of the identity of the witnesses to the public was justified as it was in the interests of justice.[137] According to this interpretation, Fawcett's argument, that it is 'difficult to imagine in what special circumstances not already covered by other wide exceptions, a court might be of opinion that it was strictly necessary to prevent publicity from prejudging the interests of justice'[138] is unacceptable; indeed, the 'interests of justice' provision should be made one of the main exceptions to the principle of publicity.

(f) Obligation on the part of the state to provide for a public hearing   As I have discussed the exceptions to the principle of publicity, I must now examine what the state needs to do to ensure a public hearing. Again, this provision is not merely a so-called negative right. It places a financial burden on the state. First, if the public does not know about the date and place of trial, it can obviously not attend. The state is therefore obliged to publish the time and venue of the oral hearings.[139] Secondly, it would be a mockery of the publicity principle if only two seats were available in trials of great public interest. The state must therefore ensure that there are adequate facilities. This might involve assessing potential public interest, possible duration of the oral hearing etc. beforehand, in order to select a suitable venue.[140] These obligations must be fulfilled within the limits of reasonable proportionality. The state authorities do not have to grant access to everybody who wishes to attend, nor choose huge rooms or even city halls or football stadiums in which to hold the trial, should public interest be that great.

When these principles are transferred to an international level, difficulties rooted in the dichotomy between national and international interests are encountered. First, 'the public' must be an international one.

---

[136] ECourtHR *Asch v Austria* Judgment 26 April 1991, Series A No. 203, para. 27.

[137] ECommHR *X v UK* Appl. No. 20657/92 15 EHRR (1993) CD 113–15. The ECommHR emphasized that, by means of screening, the interference with the right to a public hearing was kept to a minimum. It furthermore invoked public order and national security as justifications, which is probably due to the special circumstances in Northern Ireland, where almost everything is considered a matter of public order and national security.

[138] Fawcett, *The Application of the ECHR*, 162.

[139] HRC *van Meurs v the Netherlands* No. 215/1986, paras. 6.1, 6.2.

[140] Ibid., Nowak, Art. 14, No. 24.

Conceivably, there will be problems in addressing and inviting a 'world-public'. Secondly, if what I said above is true, that the publicity principle is a necessity in a democratic society, the 'world society' (whatever that may be) would consequently be seen as the international equivalent of the national 'democratic society'. But can the national society in which the crime occurred be dismissed that easily? Is it not this very society, after all, that has a special right to be involved and present when international crimes that occurred on its territory are tried? Is it therefore acceptable for the international community if the venue is set in a distant country, out of reach for most of this state's nationals, maybe even unaffordable for national journalists?

The answer must be found in the aim and purpose of the publicity principle as it stems from human rights. According to what was said above, this principle aims at achieving two rather antagonistic goals, one being control of the procedure through the presence of the public, the other being the pedagogical influence of the trial on the public. In other words, the public, which protects its fundamental goods by the enforcement of criminal law, must ensure that this enforcement is effected in a non-oppressive manner; such enforcement enhances public trust in the protective nature of the criminal system. These interrelated and mutually dependent elements are consolidated in the international society through participation both of the public from the regions in crisis and of the 'neutral public'. The 'neutral public' is called upon in particular to safeguard the upholding of the basic rights of the involved persons. The enforcement of criminal law is, on the other hand, an attempt to overcome the desire for revenge and to establish trust; it is also intended to discourage further violations with immediate effect in the territory where the atrocities occurred, and thus also discourage offences against the international legal order all over the globe.

This brief sketch of the aims and purposes of the public trial indicates that an international public is needed to watch over the conduct of the proceedings and to be positively influenced by them. Of particular importance, however, is the society that has suffered from the violations being prosecuted. Steps must be taken to ensure that this society is given an opportunity to attend the trial through enhanced media coverage and possibly by choosing a venue in a neighbouring state. The 'rest' of the international community must be kept informed about the proceedings by frequent reportage.

2. Public pronouncement of judgment

This stage Nowak calls 'static publicity'.[141] The proceedings having been

---

[141] Nowak, Art. 14, No. 22.

completed, judgment has to be presented to the public as a means of supervising the conduct of the trial *ex post*. *Ex post* control like this may aid and substitute control while the trial is being heard. If, for some reason or other, the trial has been conducted behind closed doors, by way of exception, the decision at least will have to be made public.[142] The exceptions to this principle are different from those discussed above for the conduct of the trial. This is clear from the wording of Art. 14 (I) ICCPR; an additional clause like 'from all or part of the trial (including the judgment)' as proposed by several states in the fifth session of the Commission on human rights (1949) was rejected by the majority.[143] It was further emphasized that some factors which might justify a secret hearing would not justify delivery of a judgment in private.[144] Only in two explicitly stated cases may the judgment be kept secret, that is, if the interests of juvenile persons so require or if the dispute is concerned with the guardianship of children. In criminal cases, therefore, the only cases that can be tried without the decision being made public are those involving protection of juveniles. The ECHR does not incorporate any exceptions. As with the ICCPR, it is not justifiable to apply the grounds that were intended to apply to the 'public hearing' to publicity of the judgment.[145]

There is an interesting difference between the wording of the ICCPR and that of the ECHR. While the ICCPR orders judgments to be made public, the ECHR instructs states that decisions have to be 'pronounced' publicly. It was on an Argentinian motion that the wording was altered from the HRComm draft, which referred to a public pronouncement as in the ECHR.[146] A glance at the original phrasing, in this case Spanish, reveals the precise meaning: the judgment has to be published (*todo sentencia . . . será pública*). At first sight, the ECHR seems to be stricter in the sense that the judge actually has to read the judgment out aloud. In several European countries decisions are often made public by other means, such as depositing the document with a registry, where it can be accessed publicly.

The ECourtHR was confronted with this very question in the case

---

[142] This is the interpretation by the HRC in its General Comment 13 (Article 14), para. 6.

[143] Proposal E/CN.4/286 by Chile, Egypt, France, the Philippines, and the United States.

[144] A/2929, Chapt. IV, § 78. The differentiation was still criticized and discussed in the Third Committee (1959) but finally accepted unaltered, see Bossuyt, *Guide*, 288. Compare also Nowak, Art. 14, No. 28.

[145] This was clearly found by the ECourtHR in *Campbell and Fell v UK* Judgment 28 June 1984, Series A No. 40, para. 90. The government argued that the right to public pronouncement of the decision could not be unlimited; limitations had to be implicit, as the Court had found earlier in the case *Golder v UK* Judgment 21 February 1975, Series A No. 18, para. 38. The ECourtHR admitted that a system of implicit limitations did exist. The entire right to access to a court as found in *Golder* was an implicit right and needed further definition. This right nevertheless carries implicit limitations.

[146] See E/2573, 67.

Pretto v Italy.[147] The Court, comparing the drafting languages, acknowledged that a literal approach would render the depositing of decisions insufficient with regard to the public pronouncement requirement in Art. 6 ECHR. Nevertheless, the Court found that many Member States of the Council of Europe have a long-standing tradition of making decisions public in other ways besides reading them out aloud. The authors cannot therefore have intended to abolish these practices.[148] However, each case has to be assessed separately in the light of the special features of the proceedings in question and by reference to the object and purpose of Art. 6 (I) ECHR with regard to the entirety of the proceedings and the role of the court therein.[149] The case before the Court concerned the fact that the Italian Court of Cassation handed down its decision after holding a public hearing but did not deliver judgment in open court. Instead, it deposited it with the registry of the court. With regard to these facts, the aim of Art. 6 (I) '—namely to ensure scrutiny of the judiciary by the public with a view to safeguarding the right to a fair trial—is, at any rate as regards the cassation proceedings, no less achieved by a deposit in the court registry, making the full text of the judgment available to everyone, than by a reading in open court'.[150] It is important to note that the judgment has to be made accessible to everybody, that is, not only to professional lawyers for their academic work,[151] to the parties only,[152] or to persons who can establish a specific interest in the decision.[153]

As can be seen, the protection granted by the ECHR does not differ from that of the ICCPR.[154] The judgment must be made accessible to the

---

[147] ECourtHR *Pretto v Italy* Judgment 8 December 1983, Series A No. 71.

[148] Ibid., para. 26.   [149] Ibid., para. 27.

[150] Ibid. Similarly, ECourtHR *Axen v FRG* Judgment 8 December 1983, Series A No. 72, para. 29–33, a case again concerning civil procedure before the German Federal Court (BGH), and *Sutter v Switzerland* Judgment 22 February 1984, Series A No. 74, paras. 31–4, a case involving a dispute between the applicant and the military authorities about the length of his hair. Fawcett, *The Application of the ECHR*, 163, agrees with this finding, as for him the overall aim of a fair hearing might overrule the maxim of a public hearing.

[151] This was the case with decisions by the Austrian Supreme Court, in so far as they were not contained in the official publication until the Austrian Constitutional Court declared this practice unconstitutional (decision 28 June 1990, G 315/89, G 67/90; cf. also Nowak and Schwaighofer, EuGRZ (1985), 725 at 730, 732.

[152] This may be intimated by van Dijk, SIM Special No. 1, 1 at 31 (1983).

[153] In this regard, the majority ruling in ECourtHR *Sutter v Switzerland* Judgment 22 February 1984, Series A No. 74 seems questionable. The Court upheld the practice of the Swiss Military Court of Cassation, whose judgments are available by applying to the registry or the military prosecutor, if an interest can be established (ibid., para. 20). This was incompatible with the Convention, according to the dissenting judges, Cremona, Ganshof van der Meersch, Walsh, and MacDonald (ibid., para. 16). The ruling of the ECourtHR is mitigated by (1) the fact that the *Sutter* judgment had been made public and (2) that Swiss law has changed in the mean time and judgments by the Military Court of Cassation now have to be delivered in public.

[154] See Nowak, Art. 14, No. 29.

public, be it via public pronouncement of the verdict or by depositing the written judgment in such a way that it is accessible to everybody.[155] In an international context, the global public has to be taken into account and judgments and decisions made accessible to a worldwide audience.

3. The law at the ICTY

Art. 21 (II) Statute ICTY orders trials at the ICTY to be 'public'. Publicity is also absolutely crucial for the international criminal process. The ICTY recognizes this.[156] Yet the principle of publicity is subject to Art. 22 Statute ICTY, which aims to protect victims and witnesses. Publicity of the trial is further elaborated in Rules 78 and 79. First the general public nature of the proceedings is reiterated (Rule 78). Rule 79 then states several exceptions. It reads as follows:

Rule 79. Closed Sessions
A The Trial Chamber may order that the press and the public be excluded from all or part of the proceedings for reasons of:
i   public order or morality;
ii safety, security or non-disclosure of the identity of a victim or witness as provided in Rule 75; or
iii the protection of the interests of justice.
B The Trial Chamber shall make public the reasons for its order.

This list of exceptions reads differently from that found in human rights treaties as discussed above.[157] The first exception, public order and morality, is phrased even more vaguely than in a human rights treaty, but is surely compatible with them, if interpreted in the restrictive sense outlined above. In contrast to the ICCPR, the ICTY does not refer to protection of the private lives of a party as a justification for excluding the public. On the contrary, it refers to the private lives of victim and witness that need protection.[158] We have submitted above that the protected victim should be understood as a 'party' to the trial and the protection of witnesses as stemming from the 'interests of justice'. From this point of view, it seems hard to ascertain which situations the ICTY envisaged as

---

[155] The ECourtHR noted *obiter* that although that German terminology distinguishes between *Beschluß* (decision) and *Urteil* (judgment) this does not alter the fact that both fall within the meaning of 'judgment' in the sense of Art. 6 (I) ECHR and have to be made public. See *Axen v FRG* Judgment 8 December 1983, Series A No. 72, para. 29.

[156] Compare the Trial Chamber II *Tadic* case (IT-94-1-T) Decision 10 August 1995 on the Prosecutor's Motion Requesting Protective Measures for Victims and Witnesses, para. 32.

[157] Compare Bassiouni, *The Law of the ICTY*, 960–1.

[158] ICTY Trial Chamber II commented on Rule 79 in its decision of 31 July 1996 on the Prosecutor's Motion Requesting Protective Measures for witness 'R'. It called for a restrictive interpretation of the provision and held that closed sessions should only be held when other measures would not provide the degree of protection required (para. 7).

being covered by its third exception. The Rules of Procedure, however, seem to establish a 'vicious circle', as Rule 79A (ii) refers to Rule 75, which itself refers to Rule 79, and none of them gives further clarification of the prerequisites for exclusion of the public. It should be stressed that Rule 75A contains the principle that the measures applied for the protection of victim or witness must be consistent with the rights of the accused. It is unclear why the ICTY leaves out several of the exceptions mentioned in human rights treaties, whilst clearly considering the protection of victims and witnesses to be of particular importance.

The judgment of the ICTY must be delivered in open court and in the presence of the accused (Rule 98*ter*).[159] This rule is in accordance with the ECHR because it speaks of 'public pronouncement'. No exception to this rule is attached. In practice, judgments and decisions are rapidly made available to the interested public and the press via copies at the Registry and, since the *Tadic* verdict, via the internet.

4. Assessment of the Rome Statute

Art. 64 (VII) Rome Statute, like its predecessor, Art. 38 (IV) Statute ILC, envisages several exceptions permitting exclusion of the public from the trial. This article has been criticized as being too vague and in particular for allowing the whole trial to be held in closed session. The members of the Lawyers' Committee stated that they could 'conceive of no circumstances which would justify closing an entire trial to the public, and the Statute should not suggest this possibility'.[160] The text itself seems to limit the possibility of closed sessions to parts of the proceedings and not to the entire trial. Yet the Report ILC clearly wants to include the possibility of excluding publicity from the whole trial.[161] From a human rights point of view, it is obvious that the exclusion can only go as far as necessary to achieve the aim.

Art. 64 (VII) Rome Statute states as an exception a situation where confidential or sensitive information that must be protected is to be produced in evidence. This exception was not entailed in the ILC Working Group Draft.[162] As it was inserted into the Statute ILC, alongside the protection of the accused, victims, and witnesses, it must allude to something other than the parties. Amnesty International calls upon the Court to interpret this exception in a manner that is consistent with the right to

---

[159] Ex-Rule 88 was renumbered as Rule 98*ter* at the 18th Plenary Session on 9–10 July 1998. The presence of the defendant is not compulsory, as was clarified in the amendment of Rule 88 at the 5th plenary session in January 1995; see ICTY Second Annual Report (1995), para. 21, n. 6.

[160] Lawyers' Committee for Human Rights, International Criminal Court Briefing Series, Vol. I, No. 2, 11.

[161] Report ILC, Art. 38, para. 7.

[162] See Art. 40 (II) Statute Working Group.

a fair and public trial.[163] As this provision is enshrined in Art. 67 (I) Rome Statute (previously as Art. 41 (I) Statute ILC), the Court must indeed do so in order to avoid being in breach of its own statute.[164] It is submitted that this means that interpretation must be in accordance with the human rights provisions discussed above. The exception applying to the protection of sensitive information can only be understood as the safeguarding of a state's 'national security' as found in the human rights treaties. It is thus proposed that the text should be amended in this respect.

The other exception serves the aim of protecting the accused, victims, and witnesses (Art. 68 Rome Statute, Art. 43 Statute ILC).[165] As we have seen before, the protection of each of the three groups is a legitimate reason for excluding the public. The discussions of the PrepComm testify to the fact that members of this committee were not quite satisfied with the ILC proposal. They wanted to include as well an explicit statement concerning the protection of minors and cases including sexual violence, whilst there were concerns about the exception made with respect to confidential or sensitive information provided for in the ILC draft.[166] The Rome Conference has taken this into account and inserted a special paragraph allowing a non-public hearing for the protection of victim, witness, or the accused (Art. 68 (II) Rome Statute).[167] Art. 74 (V) Rome Statute (Art. 45 (V) Statute ILC) states that the judgment shall be delivered in open court.[168]

Altogether, the reasons why the Rome Statute (as previously the ILC draft) deviates from the requirements of human rights treaties concerning the principle of a public trial are not clear. It is submitted here that the law at the ICC should preferably be interpreted in strict accordance with human rights law.

(II) The Principle of an Oral Trial *(Mündlichkeitsprinzip)*

Generally speaking, criminal procedure cannot be a written procedure.[169] This principle is not spelt out literally in human rights treaties but is to be read into several sentences of the 'fair trial' norms. First, it follows from

---

[163] Amnesty International IOR 40/05/94, 44.

[164] Schabas, in Trifterer (ed.), *Commentary on the Rome Statute*, Art. 67, Nos. 59–63, contemplates the role of Art. 67 Rome Statute within the statute. He attributes to this provision a hierarchically superior status.

[165] Behrens, 6 Eur.J.Crime Cr.L.Cr.J. (1998), 435.

[166] Report of the PrepComm I, para. 267; Report of the PrepComm II, 182–3, and the proposals therein contained of Australia and Netherlands, which are again drafted in accordance with the ICTY Statute and Rules, and that of France.

[167] Bitti, in Trifterer (ed.), *Commentary on the Rome Statute*, Art. 64, No. 26.

[168] Report of the PrepComm II, 223.

[169] This is not always true of civil litigation, which is not an issue here.

the principle of a public trial that the trial must be oral, otherwise it would not make much sense to invite the public.[170] Secondly, the right to examine or have witnesses examined, specially provided for in Art. 14 (III) e ICCPR, Art. 6 (III) d ECHR, is a right that can only be fulfilled via oral confrontation with the witnesses.[171] Many consequences follow from this principle; it is a way of ensuring that the trial (*Hauptverhandlung*) is the place where all the evidence on which conviction will be based is finally presented. Nothing may be decided in secret, no evidence may be hidden, everything must be spoken out, and presented to both the accused and the public. This is the way to ensure the reliability of witnesses, as they can be subject to proper scrutiny only if they are present. This is the only way the public can properly fulfil its duty as a watchdog preventing arbitrary behaviour on the part of judicial authorities. For these reasons, the fact that the term 'public hearing' required an oral hearing was uncontested in the Third Committee of the GA.[172] In the case *Touron v Uruguay*, the HRC found a violation of the principle of public trial because the proceedings took place in written form only.[173] Similarly, in *Fredin v Sweden (No.2)*, The ECourtHR found a violation of the requirement of a 'public hearing' in the fact that the Swedish court did not hold an oral hearing.[174] The ECourtHR found a violation because (*a*) the Swedish court was the first and only judicial instance in the contested proceedings, (*b*) the jurisdiction of this court was not limited to matters of law but also extended to factual issues, and (*c*) in the particular circumstances of the case, questions of law and fact were addressed. In the opinion of the ECourtHR, not every occurrence of written proceeding is tantamount to a violation of Art. 6 (I) ECHR. However, the situation of the defendant is believed to be particularly sensitive if questions of fact are involved. A first-instance criminal trial can then hardly ever be held in camera.

Although the law of the ICTY does not say so explicitly, it derives from several other components that the trial must be oral in its nature. In particular, the fact that there is an adversarial examination of the evidence (Rule 85), that the trial needs to be public (Rule 78), and that the accused has a right to be present during trial (Art. 21 IV d Statute ICTY) presume that the trial is oral. The same is true of the ICC. If all the human rights requirements, in particular those incorporated in Art. 67 Rome Statute (Art. 41 Statute ILC), are to be respected, the trial has to be 'oral'.

---

[170] Harris, 218.

[171] Stavros, *Guarantees*, 189, states that the principle of an oral trial derives from the letter of Art. 6 ECHR.   [172] See A/4299, § 53; cf. also Nowak, Art. 14, No. 24.

[173] HRC *Touron v Uruguay* Doc. A/36/40, 120.

[174] ECourtHR *Fredin v Sweden (No.2)* Judgment 23 February 1994, Series A No. 283-A, paras. 21–2.

(III) The Right to be Present during Trial

One special feature of the ICCPR is the prohibition of a 'trial in absentia', Art. 14 (III) d ICCPR. It is considered to be a fundamental right of the defendant to be given a fair chance to properly defend himself. The idea behind this right has an obvious Anglo-American origin. Continental criminal systems are not half as anxious about the defendant being absent, and most of them do practise some kind of trial *in absentia*.

1. National jurisdictions

In Italy for example, Art. 497–501 Code of Criminal Procedure foresee a 'trial by default' (*contumacia*). The accused does not appear for trial, although he has been duly summoned, and neither requests nor agrees to be tried in absentia. This occurs if the accused is untraceable (*irreperibile*). The trial follows the ordinary procedure and the accused has the same rights as if he were present; in particular, a defence counsel has to be appointed.

In Germany, the trial in absentia is addressed in §§ 230–9 StPO. The general rule is enshrined in § 230 (I) StPO. There it is said that the main hearing cannot be commenced against an absent defendant. The court has several means of coercing his presence. Usually, the accused must be present throughout the hearing (§ 231 (I) StPO). A trial may be continued against a defendant who is present and subsequently leaves the hearing voluntarily and unexcused.[175] After his examination, the trial may be continued if the court considers his presence unnecessary (§ 231 (II) StPO). There are several other occasions on which the hearing may be held without the accused being present; they are conditioned by the defendant voluntarily putting himself in a situation in which he is unable to follow the trial.[176] § 232 StPO permits trial in absentia if the defendant was lawfully informed of the hearing and of the possibility of being tried in his absence and voluntarily chooses not to appear. This option is, however, only open to the court if the potential penalty is a minor one; it is not permissible if there is the possibility of imprisonment. After his conviction in absentia, the defendant may file an objection within one week (§ 235 StPO). In principle, German law thus requires the attendance of the defendant. The aim is not only to fulfil the constitutional principle of a right to a hearing (Art. 103 (I) GG) and to guarantee a thorough

---

[175] This is what the German term, *eigenmächtig*, means in this context; see Kleinknecht and Meyer-Goßner § 231 No. 10.

[176] § 231a StPO allows a hearing to be continued if the defendant intentionally and culpably puts himself in a situation where he is unable to stand trial; § 231b StPO regulates cases in which the defendant is absent because of prior illegal behaviour.

defence, but also to give the judge a direct impression of the accused's conduct, appearance, and demeanour.[177]

There are many reasons why a trial in absentia may be necessary. First, it is believed that the right to be present is not of an absolute nature. It must be balanced against other rights, mainly against the public interest, and notably the interests of justice. Secondly, if no trial was held there would be a risk of disappearance of evidence. Thirdly, the statutory limitation period might expire for the prosecution, which would lead, fourthly, to a miscarriage of justice.

2. Human rights bodies

The most obvious violation of the right to be present during trial is found in *Mbenge v Zaire*, a case before the HRC, already discussed earlier in a different context.[178] M learnt of his two convictions and sentencing to capital punishment by Zairean tribunals from the media in Belgium. However, the HRC stated in this context that the right to be present is not guaranteed in absolute terms. The reasons for the absence of the defendant have to be taken into account. In the interests of the proper administration of justice, a trial in absentia might be permissible. The HRC cites the obvious example of the waiver. Nevertheless, should trial in absentia be justified in exceptional circumstances, '[s]trict observance of the rights of the defence is all the more necessary'.[179]

In the case *Brozicek v Italy*, before the ECourtHR, the government contested the allegations, as in their view the applicant deliberately refused to answer for his actions in court and to exercise his rights. The ECourtHR made clear that, although the right to be present during trial is not explicitly stated in the ECHR, it is nevertheless inherent in Art. 6 as a whole with regard to the object and purpose of this article.[180] It referred to a former judgment, *Colozza v Italy*, where it had found that

[s]ub-paragraphs (c), (d) and (e) of paragraph 3 [of article 6 ECHR] guarantee to 'everyone charged with a criminal offence' the right 'to defend himself in person', 'to examine or have examined witnesses' and 'to have the free assistance of an interpreter if he cannot understand or speak the language used in court', and it is difficult to see how he could exercise these rights without being present.[181]

The ECourtHR then found a violation of this right, as the defendant was not properly informed of the charges against him. In the opinion of the

---

[177] The BGH emphasized the importance of the presence of the defendant. His absence could only be allowed in these cases that are clearly envisaged in the StPO; see Judgment 2 October 1952, in BGHSt 3, 187 at 190; BGH Decision 21 February 1975, in BGHSt 26, 84 at 90.

[178] HRC *Mbenge v Zaire* Doc. A/38/40, 134.

[179] HRC General Comment 13 (Article 14), para. 11.

[180] ECourtHR *Brozicek v Italy* Judgment 19 December 1989, Series A No. 167, para. 45.

[181] ECourtHR *Colozza v Itlay* Judgment 12 February 1985, Series A No. 89, para. 27.

ECourtHR, it is possible for the defendant to waive his right to be present. A waiver of this right, however, must meet the usual conditions of waiver, that is, the mainly free and unequivocal manner of its establishing.[182] What was left unanswered was the question of whether a suspect who absconds automatically forfeits his right to be tried in his presence.[183]

Although the ECourtHR reiterated in this context that the Member States had a wide margin of appreciation as regards the choice of means through which a 'fair' procedure is to be guaranteed, it found a number of safeguards which have to be respected, if the legal system includes the possibility of trial *in absentia*.[184] (1) The person tried in absentia must not be left with the burden of proof as to the reason for his absence. It is up to the prosecutor to prove that the defendant was seeking to evade justice. (2) The defendant must be able to obtain a new determination of the merits of the charge. This means that the entire trial has to be repeated from the beginning. An appeals procedure is not sufficient in this regard, as its purpose may solely be to review the lawfulness of the original trial and the defendant would be left without any opportunity of reviewing the trial.[185]

3. Law and practice at the ICTY

The UN Secretary General states in clear terms that no trials should be held in the absence of the defendant. He believes that such trials would be against Art. 14 ICCPR.[186] Looking at the law and practice of the ICTY, we do find some allusion to a trial in absentia in the so-called Rule 61 procedure. There has been a fair amount of writing about this procedure and the vast majority of commentators have been in favour of this provision.[187] The tribunal itself has not hesitated to apply Rule 61 and has in fact—in the beginning at least—made quite excessive use of it. Thus far, five Rule 61 proceedings have been held and international arrest warrants subsequently issued.[188] The goal of the procedure is to issue an

---

[182] Ibid., para. 28, with further reference to the established case-law of the ECourtHR.

[183] The ECourtHR did not have to answer the question, as, according to the established facts, the applicant had not been seeking to evade justice. The police were simply unable to find him. Ibid., para. 28.

[184] Ibid., paras. 29–30.

[185] The trial against *Colozza* was declared incompatible with the ECHR on both grounds. See also Peukert, EuGRZ (1980), 241 at 256 and the references there.

[186] Report of the Secretary General, para. 101; as has been shown above, Art. 14 ICCPR does not—at least in the interpretation of the HRC—entirely prohibit trial in the absence of the defendant. The Statute of the ICTY therefore goes beyond the requirements of the ICCPR; see Shraga and Zacklin, 5 EJIL (1994), 360 at 376.

[187] See e.g. Greenwood, The Jurisprudence of the ICTY, in 2 Max Planck YB UN Law (1998), 97.

[188] They are, in chronological order: *Prosecutor v Nikolic* 20 October 1995, Case No. IT-94-2-R61, repr. in 108 ILR 21; *Prosecutor v Martic* Decision 8 March 1996, Case No. IT-95-11-R61, repr. in 108 ILR 39; *Prosecutor v Mrskic, Radic and Sljivancanin (Vukovar Hospital)* Decision 3

international warrant of arrest, if there are sufficient grounds to believe that the person charged is guilty (Rule 61C). Evidence is thus presented by the prosecution, and by the prosecution alone,[189] and thereby conserved and recorded. A complete Trial Chamber sits and reviews the indictment and the evidence furnished. There is no finding of guilt.[190] We can therefore call it 'review in absentia' rather then 'trial in absentia'. The whole procedure seems to be an attempt to address the potential risk of a proper trial never taking place because the suspect might never be surrendered to the tribunal. The least thing the tribunal can do in such circumstances is to collect and record the evidence. As Judge Sidhwa stated, it is 'basically an apology for this Tribunal's helplessness in not being able to effectively carry out its duties, because of the attitude of certain States that do not want to arrest or surrender accused persons, or even to recognize or cooperate with the Tribunal'.[191]

The Rule 61 procedure is sometimes referred to as the 'voice of the victims'.[192] With the help of this procedure, it is hoped that the international community can contribute to international peace and security. One might well argue that the actual goal of issuing an international arrest warrant appears ridiculously insignificant when compared with the huge effort a Rule 61 procedure requires. The goal seems even less important if one bears in mind the fact that the indictment has already been reviewed by a judge. In a domestic context, to issue an international warrant of arrest is a matter of a single judge and is to be considered in a written procedure involving prosecution records only. But of course, as we have seen, this is not so much the underlying rationale but rather the formal reason for this procedure.

However, a few potential risks still exist. A full-scale trial held after a Rule 61 procedure or similar review in absentia will have to respond to the outcome of the previous procedure. If, for example, evidence recorded in a 'review in absentia' procedure can be used without being freshly presented, the review procedure that has taken place may prove to be a dangerous disadvantage for the defendant. It means, in effect, that the defendant is entitled to have witnesses examined that can be cross-examined by the

---

April 1996, Case No. IT-95-13-R61, repr. in 108 ILR 53; *Prosecutor v Raijc* Decision 13 September 1996, Case No. IT-95-12-R61, repr. in 108 ILR 141; *Prosecutor v Karadzic and Mladic* Decision 11 July 1996, Case Nos. IT-95-5-R61 and IT-95-18-R61, repr. in 108 ILR 85.

[189] In *Rajic*, the defence counsel was informed of the hearing by the Registry and invited to observe it from the public gallery; likewise counsel to Karadzic and Mladic were not admitted to the hearing; compare Jones, *The Practice of the ICTY*, Rule 61, p. 308.

[190] This fact was repeatedly stressed by the reviewing Trial Chamber, e.g. in *Rajic* and *Nikolic*.

[191] Separate Opinion in *Prosecutor v Rajic* decision 5 July 1996 and 13 September 1996, Case No. IT-95-12-R61, published in 108 ILR 141 at 171.

[192] ICTY bulletin No. 3, 22 February 1996, 3.

prosecution, whereas the evidence furnished by the witnesses for the prosecution does not have to be reopened, that is, the accusing witnesses cannot be cross-examined. Such an outcome would be a flagrant breach of the right to cross-examine witnesses and of the right of equity of arms among the parties. This danger was addressed by Amnesty International.[193] We suggest that a new trial must be a full-scale trial. Witnesses and evidence must be presented anew. To properly safeguard the presumption of innocence, the new trial must be held before a different bench of judges. Another matter is the question of whether or not the legal findings will be considered as precedents for subsequent trials.[194] The Trial Chambers have made several legal or factual findings as to subject-matter jurisdiction, determination of the nature of the armed conflict in a specific area,[195] or identification of the factual and legal requirements of certain criminal norms (*Tatbestandsvoraussetzungen*).[196] Here, too, the issue is unresolved, but the necessity of a 'fair trial' requires that a full-scale trial must take place with the defendant being present.

4. Proposal for an ICC

Before I look at the Rome Statute, I will summarize the developments that led to the relevant norms, namely Art. 61 (II) and Art. 63 of the Rome Statute. Art. 37 (I) Statute ILC enshrines the general principle that trials in absentia shall be prohibited. However, several exceptions follow in subsequent paragraphs. Several of these were fiercely disputed during drafting[197] and have subsequently been the subject of strong criticism by the PrepComm too.[198] The provision in Art. 37 (II) b Statute ILC which foresees trial in the absence of the defendant if he continuously disrupts the trial appears to be unproblematic. By behaving in this way, the defendant waives his right to be present. In the PrepComm it was submitted[199] that the behaviour of the defendant could not constitute a reason for him being excluded. In such a case, it should be possible to ensure the presence of the defendant via video or by creating a secure area for him. Alternatively, the unseemly behaviour of the recalcitrant defendant could also be reciprocated by holding him in contempt of court. This latter proposal, contempt of court, is as foreign to some jurisdictions as the concept of trial in the absence of the accused is to others. Certainly, solutions should be sought

---

[193] Amnesty International, IOR 40/05/94, 49.

[194] This question is rightly raised by King and La Rosa, 8 EJIL (1997), 123 at 142.

[195] Compare e.g. *Prosecutor v Rajic* Decision 13 September 1996, Case No. IT-95-12-R61.

[196] See e.g. the decision in *Prosecutor v Nikolic* 20 October 1995, Case No. IT-94-2-R61.

[197] Report ILC Art. 37 para. 1. The views varied from being entirely against any trial without the presence of the accused to strongly supportive of such a possibility.

[198] The Report of the PrepComm I, paras. 253–4, however, does not say that the extreme position, which would allow trials in absence on a large scale, has been abandoned.

[199] Report of the PrepComm I, para. 256.

that respect the right to be present and ensure presence in such cases, in the widest possible sense. As a last resort, however, he could be dismissed from the hearing.

The provision that the trial may continue if the accused has escaped from lawful custody or has broken bail is a similar one.[200] Arguably, this is the solution that was contemplated by the Working Group in its draft. Art. 44 (I) h Statute Working Group reads: 'to be present at trial, unless the Court, having heard such submissions and evidence as it deems necessary, concludes that the absence of the accused is deliberate'. Priority must in any case be given to recapturing the fugitive.[201] Art. 63 Rome Statute incorporates these proposals. In general, the accused shall be present during the trial (Art. 63 (I) Rome Statute). Paragraph 2 contains the exception to this principle, namely, constant interruption of the trial by the accused. In such cases, he can be removed from the courtroom, but must be given the possibility of following the trial from outside the court room via communications technology and instructing counsel.[202]

The other provisions are more problematic. Art. 37 (II) a Statute ILC provides for an exception for reasons of security. It is clear from the context that the security risk can only be seen in the defendant, who has to be excluded to prevent this risk. The Lawyers' Committee on Human Rights acknowledges that there may be situations that put witnesses or victims in danger; the authorities must, however, deploy reasonable means to protect these persons without excluding the defendant.[203] Publicity might also be refused if the danger to the accused comes from the presence of the public. If these two principles are compared, the right of the accused to be present probably outweighs the principle of publicity.[204] For the defence it might be of crucial importance for the accused to be present; indeed, nor should the purifying effect of the trial on the offender be underestimated; reformation is one of the main aims of criminal law.[205] Furthermore, there may be more risk of the verdict not being considered reliable if the accused is absent, as doubts may remain as to whether justice has been done.[206] The public, on the other hand, can be

---

[200] These are the only exceptions the Lawyers' Committee for Human Rights, International Criminal Court Briefing Series, Vol. I, No. 3, 4, would accept, if they are applied restrictively. Likewise Amnesty International, which would accept trial in the absence of the accused if he deliberately absented himself after the trial began, IOR 40/05/94, 48 and 50–1.

[201] Report of the PrepComm, para. 256.

[202] Schabas, in Trifterer (ed.), *Commentary on the Rome Statute*, Art. 63, No. 15.

[203] Lawyers' Committee for Human Rights, International Criminal Court Briefing Series, Vol. I, No. 2, 3.

[204] Donat-Cattin, in Trifterer (ed.), *Commentary on the Rome Statute*, Art. 68, No. 20, sees no need to protecting the accused by excluding the public. In my view, he misunderstands the conflict between two human rights provisions.

[205] This is also true of international criminal law; compare Safferling, ARIEL (2000), 123.

[206] Compare the view of Amnesty International, IOR 40/05/94, 48–9.

informed about the trial afterwards and the conduct of the trial can be supervised by the parties and any possible mistake be healed on appeal. Exclusion of the public is only a last resort. Protection of the accused can be managed by controlling the spectators, with bullet-proof glass, etc.[207] Similarly, the discussion of the PrepComm suggests that other alternatives should be sought, like temporary relocation of the court or the use of video conferences.[208] If the defendant constitutes a risk to victim or witness, it might perhaps be better, instead of continuing the proceedings without the presence of the accused, to prevent a confrontation by other measures, like a video link to a separate room, or separating walls between victim and accused.

As a further reason for a trial in the absence of the defendant, the Statute ILC cites the ill-health of the accused. The ILC may have had the case of Erich Honecker in mind when it drafted this article.[209] It is certainly unsatisfactory if the wanted person cannot be prosecuted because he is physically too weak to attend the trial. One could say that the defendant's ill-health might justify postponement of the trial but not a trial *in absentia*.[210] But what about situations where the defendant may die before the end of the trial? In my view, the general rule in the case of illness should be that the trial is postponed until the defendant's health is again such that he can stand trial. In cases in which the accused is not expected to survive the outcome of the trial, the interest in criminal prosecution vanishes. Although the utilitarian effects of deterrence and general prevention are still within reach, and independent of the question of whether or not the accused dies before the end of the trial, the offender's human dignity is denied if he is forced to follow his trial. This is the case because the trial is continued although it is known that the outcome can have no effect whatsoever on the accused, as he will not be alive to hear the verdict. Any special preventive theory, in particular reformation and rehabilitation, must fail. Likewise retributive aims are

---

[207] Amnesty International submits that this is the way in which protection of a defendant against whom threats have been made is usually dealt with in national courts, IOR 40/05/94, 49.

[208] See Report of the PrepComm I, para. 256.

[209] Constitutional Court (VerfGH) Berlin, *Honecker prosecution case*, Judgment 12 January 1993, 100 ILR 393. The Constitutional Court of Berlin held that the Constitution of Berlin contained an unwritten constitutional principle, a commitment to respect the dignity of man and an obligation for all its authorities to respect and protect that dignity. This meant for criminal proceedings that a person could not be made a mere object of criminal proceedings. If there was no reasonable prospect that those proceedings would achieve their lawful purpose of conviction and punishment, detention in custody was unlawful. As Honecker most certainly was not expected to live until the end of proceedings, these conditions were met and he was free to go. The proceedings against Pinochet were similar; compare D. Woodhouse, *The Pinochet Case: A Legal and Constitutional Analysis* (Oxford, 2000).

[210] Lawyers' Committee for Human Rights, International Criminal Court Briefing Series, Vol. I, No. 2, 4. Similar in this regard are the suggestions at the PrepComm, para. 256.

inapplicable. The defendant is truly misused as a carrier for social education. He is not seen as an end in himself; thus his dignity is denied. Therefore, if the ICC comes to the conclusion that the physical condition of the defendant will not allow him to live until the end of the trial, the proceedings must be discontinued, in our view, rather than being held in absentia.

One necessary condition for the legitimacy of a trial *in absentia* is certainly that the court must do everything reasonably possible to ensure the presence of the accused, in particular inform him of the charge. This is provided for in Art. 37 (III) a Statute ILC. What is not clear from the text of the statute ILC is the question of whether or not a new trial has to be held, if, after a trial in absentia, the defendant turns up again, be it voluntarily or under coercion. The Comments to the Statute Working Group reveal that those who argued in favour of a trial in absentia also inclined in general to the opinion that such a judgment should be provisional. If the accused should appear before the court at a later stage, then a new trial should be conducted in the presence of the accused.[211]

This view seems to run counter to yet another provision in the statute: Art. 37 (III) Statute ILC rules that the rights of the accused have to be respected and in particular a defence counsel has to be assigned to represent his interests. Are all these safeguards necessary, if the trial must commence *de novo*, should the defendant appear at court? The only aim of the trial in absentia turns out to be to effectively preserve the evidence.[212] In our opinion, this end can be achieved more efficiently and cost-effectively by doing without a trial and relying on a review procedure similar to that of ICTY Rule 61. Like ICTY Rule 61, Art. 37 (IV) Statute ILC recognizes a 'review in absentia'. The Commentary reveals that the ILC was attracted by the idea of such a review proceeding and adopted it with the same formal aim as the ICTY predecessor: an international warrant of arrest.[213] However, several flaws should be pointed out here. First of all, the relationship between this procedure and a trial in absentia is not clear.[214] It seems that the trial in absentia is applicable, if the accused has already appeared before the court and absconded afterwards. That would mean that a trial cannot, in fact, be commenced in the absence of the defendant, but can be continued in his absence. With regard to the provision in Art. 37 (II) c Statute ILC, this does not appear to be the case in all instances. May the court then choose at its own discretion how to proceed?

---

[211] Report Working Group, Art. 44, para. 4.   [212] Ibid., para. 3.
[213] Report ILC Art. 37, para. 7.
[214] e.g. a trial in absentia can take place if the accused has escaped from lawful custody (Art. 37 (II) c Statute ILC) whereas a review in absentia can go ahead if the defendant is deliberately absent (Art. 37 (IV) Statute ILC). The difference between these two scenarios is by no means clear; compare Report of the PrepComm I, para. 257.

Secondly, Art. 37 (V) a Statute ILC allows a practice that we have already criticized as being in violation of several human rights provisions; namely, recorded evidence from the previous proceeding may be used in court during trial.[215] Comparing this to his situation after a trial in absentia, the defendant may be worse off if his indictment has been reviewed. In a trial in absentia, the defendant must be legally represented (Art. 37 (III) b Statute ILC), not so in the review proceeding; the reason is the nature of this procedure, which is not a trial.[216] But even if the defence counsel were there to cross-examine the witnesses presented by the prosecution, several more conditions would have to be fulfilled for these statements to be admitted at trial.[217] The defence needs sufficient time and facilities to prepare the examination. Art. 37 (V) b Statute ILC rightly excludes any judge who confirmed the indictment from sitting on the bench in the ensuing trial.

The Rome Conference took these discussions into account and arrived at a solution that is more in conformity with human rights. First, there is no provision for a trial in absentia, apart from that described above, Art. 63 (II) Rome Statute. The protection of victims or witnesses is generally to be guaranteed by other means, mainly by exclusion of the public for the time evidence is being given or through electronic or other special means (Art. 68 (II) Rome Statute). In very special cases, where the accused remains a danger for victim or witness and their well-being cannot otherwise be safeguarded, the possibility of excluding the accused from the court room is not entirely ruled out, but the measures taken may not be prejudicial to or inconsistent with the rights of the accused, says Art. 68 (I) and (III) Rome Statute. Secondly, Art. 61 (II) Rome Statute foresees a confirmation in absentia, but only in circumstances where the defendant waived his right to be present or he could not be found although all reasonable steps had been taken to secure his appearance. Even then, the person must be represented by counsel, if the Pre-Trial Chamber so determines in the interests of justice. In principle, this will be the case.[218] The aim of this provision is to avoid the

---

[215] Lawyers' Committee for Human Rights, International Criminal Court Briefing Series, Vol. I, No. 2, pp. 4–5.

[216] See ICTY, *Prosecutor v Karadzic and Mladic* Decision 11 July 1996, Case Nos. IT-95-5-R61 and IT-95-18-R61, and in particular ICTY Trial Chamber I Decision 5 July 1996 *Rejecting the Request Submitted by Mr Medvene and Mr Hanley III, Defence Counsels for Radovan Karadzic.*

[217] Lawyers' Committee for Human Rights, International Criminal Court Briefing Series, Vol. I, No. 2, pp. 5–6. The Lawyers' Committee would, however, not accept the admissibility of evidence. This stems from the fact that the Anglo-American tradition seeks its salvation in the institution of cross-examination. The fact that it is erroneous to rely on cross-examination alone will be shown below.

[218] Shibahara, in Triffterer (ed.), *Commentary on the Rome Statute*, Art. 61, No. 13.

difficulties that have arisen at the ICTY in connection with the Rule 61 procedure in *Karadzic* and *Mladic*.[219]

(IV) The Principle of a Speedy Trial (*Beschleunigungsmaxime*)

1. The human rights issue

All major human rights treaties recognize a right to a 'speedy' trial. The defendant must be tried without 'undue delay', Art. 14 (III) e ICCPR, or 'within a reasonable time', Art. 6 (I) ECHR and Art. 8 (I) AmCHR and Art. 7 (I) d AfCHPR. From the wording it is not clear whether this means only that the procedure has to start 'within a reasonable time'. This is especially true of the German version of this provision, where it says, 'innerhalb einer angemessenen Frist', the word 'Frist' alluding to the period of time until trial starts.

The HRC explicitly addresses this difficulty in its General Comments. It finds that '[t]his guarantee relates not only to the time by which a trial should commence, but also the time by which it should end and judgement be rendered'.[220] This seems to stem from the wording 'to be tried without undue delay', which alludes to the verdict, the end of the trial, which must take place within the time limit. The ECHR is interpreted in a similar way, as the ECommHR affirms that the words in criminal proceedings 'refer to the period that elapses between the charge and the sentence, and not that between the offence and the charge'.[221] Possibly a better drafting can be found in the NATO Status of Forces Agreement (1953). Art. VII-9 reads as: 'Whenever a member of a force or civilian component or a dependent is prosecuted under the jurisdiction of the receiving State he shall be entitled: (a) to a prompt and speedy trial.' It is clear from this wording that two separate topics are at issue, first, commencement of the trial (prompt), second, procedural conduct of the trial (speedy).[222]

From a teleological point of view, a restrictive interpretation cannot be sustained for the reasons outlined below. First, the credibility and effectiveness of the whole judicial system would be jeopardized.[223] The aim of the rule is to protect all parties in court proceedings against excessive

---

[219] See ICTY Trial Chamber I, *Karadzic* and *Mladic* Decision rejecting the Application presented by Mr Medvene and Mr Hanley, seeking leave to file briefs challenging the fairness of the Statute and the Rules of Procedure, 24 July 1996, Case Nos. IT-95-5-R61 and IT-95-18-R61.

[220] HRC General Comment 13 (Article 14), para. 10.

[221] ECommHR *X v Austria* Decision 13 December 1962, Appl. No. 1545/62, 5 YB, 270 at 276.

[222] Compare Fawcett, *The Application of the ECHR*, 169.

[223] See ECourtHR *H v France* Judgment 24 October 1989, Series A No. 162-A, para. 58.

procedural delays.[224] The HRC found this right violated in *Pinkey v Canada*.[225] In this case the applicant had to wait thirty-four months for his appeal to be heard, mainly because the transcript of the original trial was not made available to him. In its General Comment, the HRC stated explicitly that the provision of a trial without undue delay applies to all stages of criminal procedure and encompasses the whole trial, both in first instance and appeal.[226] Secondly, and this is specific to criminal procedure, the person charged is still to be presumed innocent, the exact meaning of which I will discuss in more detail in the next paragraph. Before he is legally convicted, it must always be borne in mind that the only legitimate justification for making a person suffer a criminal prosecution is when his personal interests are outweighed by public interest in the effectiveness of the system. Minimization of the inconvenience for the charged person is thus the logical consequence. Treating him in a fair way means ensuring that he does not remain uncertain of his fate for too long.[227] Bearing in mind further that the reputation of the accused is at stake, the court must ensure that a judgment is delivered without delay. The provision of a trial within a reasonable time or without undue delay therefore goes beyond commencement of the trial. The aim is to ensure a speedy trial from start to finish. In order to clarify the issue with the help of the terminology that has already been used, it is best to speak of the requirement of a 'speedy trial' as analogous with Art. VII-9 NATO Status of Forces Agreements, quoted above.

As a similar provision can be found in Art. 9 (III) ICCPR and Art. 5 (III) ECHR ('shall be entitled to trial within a reasonable time') we must distinguish between the two. Art. 9 ICCPR addresses the defendant in the special circumstance of detention. His right to liberty and security is particularly endangered under these conditions, being dependent upon the outcome of the trial. Art. 14 ICCPR is wider than this; it encompasses all defendants, whether held on remand or not.[228] The ECourtHR had to address this issue in the case of *Wemhoff v FRG* and held that the applicability of Art. 5 (III) ECHR ended with the determination of the charge.[229]

---

[224] ECourtHR *Stögmüller v Austria* Judgment 10 November 1969, Series A No. 9, 40 para. 5; Harris, 223.

[225] HRC *Pinkey v Canada* Doc. A/37/49, 101. The HRC drew a link between the right to be tried without undue delay and the right to appeal in Art. 14 (V). This is not very convincing because an appeal finally took place, so that P was not deprived of his right to appeal, but he had to wait more than two and a half years for it to come; compare McGoldrick, *Human Rights Committee*, 432.

[226] HRC General Comment 13 (Article 14), para. 10.

[227] ECourtHR *Stögmüller v Austria* Judgment 10 November 1969, Series A No. 9, 40, para. 5; similarly *Wemhoff v FRG* Judgment 27 June 1968, Series A No. 7, 26, para. 18.

[228] Compare for the European context Jacobs and White, 143.

[229] ECourtHR *Wemhoff v Germany* Judgment 27 June 1968, Series A No. 7, para. 9. This means that the question of whether this conviction is final or not is irrelevant.

In the earlier invoked case, *B v Austria*, the ECourtHR had to distinguish between the two articles.[230] The case was as follows; the applicant was detained on remand on 1 July 1980. On 16 November 1982, he was convicted and sentenced to eight years' imprisonment. Instead of the prescribed period of fourteen days, it took the court until 28 August 1985 to draw up the judgment. A plea of nullity to the Supreme Court was dismissed on 14 November 1985. However, the sentence was reduced to a term of six years on 19 December 1985. The difficulty with this case lies in the question of when to apply Art. 5 (III) ECHR and when to rely on Art. 6 (I) ECHR. The ECourtHR suggests that Art. 5 (III) ECHR is inextricably linked to Art. 5 (I) c ECHR, indeed, these two 'form a whole'.[231] The applicant was convicted on 19 November 1982; Art. 5 (III) ECHR therefore ceases to apply at that point and Art. 6 (I) ECHR comes into play. A minority view of the ECommHR[232] contested this approach. Normally, criminals follow a route that takes them directly from Art. 5 (I) c to Art. 5 (I) a ECHR. As there is no intermediate step, a time must be pinpointed when detention on remand loses its provisional cocoon and becomes detention 'after' conviction. According to criminal procedure in Austria, a conviction becomes final only after appeal and review proceedings.[233] Art 5 (I) a ECHR is not automatically applicable at any stage 'after' conviction. The detention referred to in Art. 5 (I) c ECHR needs to be caused by the conviction.[234] Applied literally to the ECHR, this would mean that the detention on remand ended on 19 December 1985, with the final decision of the Supreme Court.[235] The ECourtHR,[236] however, relied on an 'autonomous' interpretation of the term 'conviction', without saying so explicitly. It asked the opposite question: what would have happened if there had been no conviction? The answer is obvious: the applicant would have had to have been released. Hence the logical conclusion of the ECourtHR: the detention is 'after' the conviction in the causal sense of Art. 5 (I) a ECHR. The provision that applies specifically to detention on remand, namely,

---

[230] *B v Austria* Judgment 28 March 1990, Series A No. 175.

[231] *B v Austria* Judgment 28 March 1990, Series A No. 175, para. 35. This view seems to be settled case-law of the ECourtHR, as can be seen from the references cited in the ECourtHR's judgment.

[232] This is the view taken in the dissenting opinion of Mr Trechsel, joined by Messrs Soyer, Scermers and Campinos and Mrs Thune, *B v Austria* Judgment 28 March 1990, Series A No. 175, 29–31.

[233] Art. 397 Austrian Code of Criminal Procedure.

[234] ECourtHR *B v Austria* Judgment 28 March 1990, Series A No. 175, para. 38, with references to earlier decisions.

[235] The dissenting commissioners relied on earlier judgments of the ECourtHR: *Monnel and Morris v UK* Judgment 2 March 1987, Series A No. 115, para. 40, and *Van Droogenbroeck v Belgium* Judgment 24 June 1982, Series A No. 50, para. 35, where the ECourtHR expressed the need for a causal connection between detention and conviction.

[236] The ECourtHR ruled unanimously in this matter.

Art. 5 (III) ECHR, can therefore not be applied; after conviction, the applicant can only rely on the general provision in Art. 6 (I) ECHR.[237]

However, an exact time limit cannot possibly be set. The circumstances
of each case play a major role and have to be taken into account when the
meaning of the term 'reasonable' is defined in the specific case.[238] The
jurisprudence of the HRC gives no guidance in defining the time limit.[239]
Nor does it give any help in distinguishing the time limit here from the
time limit in Art. 9 (III) ICCPR, according to which the detained must be
brought before a judge 'within a reasonable time'. The shortest term without trial to be condemned by the HRC was in *Sequeira v Uruguay*, where a
detention of nine months without trial was considered enough to constitute a violation.[240]

One of the factors that must be taken into consideration when the
reasonableness of the length of proceedings is being assessed is the
complexity of the case.[241] The complexity of the case may stem, for example, from the volume of evidence,[242] the number of defendants or
charges,[243] the need to obtain expert witness or testimony from people
abroad,[244] or the complexity of the legal issues involved.[245] The fact that

---

[237] The opposite opinion of the minority of the ECommHR certainly leads to inequalities
between the different systems in Europe. This might explain why the majority recoiled from
applying Art. 5 (III) ECHR here; it would have amounted to censure of most of the civil law
countries, which traditionally have greater difficulties with the requirement of reasonableness of the time limit. Compare the Dissenting Opinion in ECourtHR *B v Austria* Judgment
28 March 1990, Series A No. 175, 31.

[238] See Harris, 223.

[239] Compare McGoldrick, *Human Rights Committee*, 422.

[240] HRC *Sequeira v Uruguay* Doc. A/35/40, 127; one aggravating circumstance is the fact
that the jurisdiction according to the Optional Protocol ICCPR was only in force during the
last three months of the detention.

[241] Jacobs and White, 144; Harris, 223.

[242] ECourtHR *Boddaert v Belgium* Judgment 12 October 1992, Series A No. 235-D, para. 37.
The case involved a prosecution for murder which suffered from lack of witnesses and from
two suspects accusing each other of having committed the crime, whilst it was uncertain
what had motivated the slaughter; furthermore, the crime seemed to be connected with
other offences. Here, violation was denied as the Belgian authorities had proceeded properly
(ibid., para. 39).

[243] ECourtHR *Eckle v FRG* Judgment 15 July 1982, Series A No. 51. According to the finding of the ECourtHR it took seventeen years and three weeks until the criminal case against
the applicant, one of the first big cases involving economic crimes in Germany, was finally
settled (para. 79). In this case, the ECourtHR suggested the prosecuting authorities could
have dropped several counts to accelerate the proceedings (para. 84). Although the case was
a difficult one, and although the behaviour of the applicant hindered speedy conduct of the
trial, the ECourtHR could not find the extraordinary duration of the trial acceptable in the
light of Art. 6 (I) ECHR and blamed it on the conduct of the judicial authorities in Germany
(para. 93).

[244] ECourtHR *Neumeister v Austria* Judgment 27 June 1968, Series A No. 8, para. 21, where
the ECourtHR held that the Austrian authorities could not be blamed for having to wait for
response from abroad.

[245] Compare Harris, 224.

international crimes are involved does not make the procedure any shorter or easier; on the contrary, investigation and presentation of witnesses is a long and stressful process, as can be seen from the work of the ICTY.

What must also be taken into account are the obstacles presented by the defendant himself. He may overburden the court with all kinds of motions and challenges; he cannot then complain that the process is not speedy enough. In the case of *König v Germany*, the ECourtHR held that such actions on the part of the defendant must be taken into account when the court rules on the time limit.[246] Certainly the defendant cannot be compelled to cooperate with the prosecution, but behaviour that could be interpreted as indicative of a policy of deliberate obstruction can surely not be blamed on the judicial authorities.[247]

On the other hand, judges who 'take revenge' for an 'uncomfortable' defence are conceivable. But the defence must not be disadvantaged by legitimate behaviour, even if it is annoying and tiring for the judges. The accused is fully entitled to make full use of the remedies available under domestic law.[248] The court must work as quickly as possible in the interests of justice. Any other behaviour would be deemed improper.

As to the conduct of the court, the significance of the prosecution for the persons involved must be taken into account. In criminal cases, where the liberty of the defendant is at stake, the issue of speedy proceedings is an extremely important one. If the accused is detained pending trial, an even more rigorous standard has to be applied in his case.[249] Furthermore, the court cannot rely on the excuse of a backlog of cases.[250] Apart from that, the ECourtHR will assess the difficulty of the case itself and, if necessary, condemn a national court for having taken too long to determine a straightforward case.[251] In summary, three factors can be found that play a role in assessing the length of the proceeding: the complexity of the case, the behaviour of the defendant, and the conduct of the court.[252]

---

[246] ECourtHR *König v Germany* Judgment 28 June 1978, Series A No. 27, para. 111. Although this case did not concern criminal proceedings; the findings are nevertheless valid for both civil and criminal proceedings. This is an established principle of Strasbourg case-law; compare, e.g. in criminal procedure ECourtHR *Eckle v FRG* Judgment 15 July 1982, Series A No. 51, para. 82.

[247] Explicitly ECourtHR *Eckle v FRG* Judgment 15 July 1982, Series A No. 51, para. 82.

[248] Once again, ECourtHR *Eckle v FRG* Judgment 15 July 1982, Series A No. 51, para. 82.

[249] ECourtHR *Abdoella v Netherlands* Judgment 25 November 1993, Series A No. 248-A, para. 24, with references to other cases.

[250] See the above discussion concerning the organization of the judiciary.

[251] Compare Harris, 229.

[252] See ECourtHR *Deumeland v Germany* Judgment 29 May 1986, Series A No. 100, paras. 78–90. This was not a criminal case but the judgment contains a lengthy discussion of the time limit. It is interesting to note, however, that the ECourtHR, despite its relativist approach, condemned all cases where the proceedings exceeded eight years; compare Harris, 228.

It has been argued that trials against war criminals are of a special nature such that the above criteria cannot be employed.[253] This was made an issue before the ECommHR in *Jentzsch v Germany*.[254] The applicant spent six years in detention on remand before his trial eventually commenced; it ended after fourteen months with a conviction. The extensive time in detention, although regrettable, was nevertheless found to be compatible with the ECHR. This was justified not by a general exception for war crime trials but by applying the principle of balancing the time limit outlined above. The special circumstances usually found in the case of war crimes, namely, that they date back several years, that victimized witnesses have to be found, and so forth, must be taken into account, and in this case excused the long period of inquiry.[255]

2. The ICTY

Art. 21 IV c Statute ICTY repeats the words of Art. 14 III c ICCPR and grants the right to a speedy trial in this sense to the accused before the ICTY. This necessity of a speedy trial gains particular importance through the fact that the accused is generally incarcerated pending trial. However, there are no time limits established by either the Statute or the Rules.[256] As concerns preliminary motions by the accused, some of them were under a time limit by virtue of Rule 73C.[257] The motions mentioned in Rule 73A had to be brought to the knowledge of the court within sixty days after the first appearance of the accused, in any case before the hearing started. If the accused failed to do so, his failure was regarded as equivalent to a waiver of his right. The Trial Chamber could have admitted the claim upon 'good cause' (Rule 73C). Although this approach seemed to be compatible with human rights, it was dropped entirely by the Plenary Session. Instead, Rule 73*bis* and 73*ter* were inserted as tools to expedite trial proceedings.

The practice at the ICTY has generally tended to lead to long trials. *Tadic* was transferred to the ICTY on 24 April 1995, the trial started 7 May 1996, and he was finally convicted one year later, on 7 May 1997, and sentenced on 14 July 1997. After the Appeals proceedings the final sentence was given on 26 January 2000. Blaskic surrendered voluntarily to the ICTY on 1 April 1996, after the indictment had been confirmed on 10

---

[253] See the discussion of this issue by Peukert, EuGRZ (1979), 261 at 272.

[254] ECommHR *Jentzsch v Germany* Report 30 November 1970, Appl. No. 2604/65, 14 YB (1971), 876. The facts of the case are given in the Decision on admissibility, 19 December 1967, 10 YB (1967), 218.

[255] This finding of the ECommHR was backed by the Committee of Ministers; see Res DH (71) 2, 5 May 1971, 14 YB (1971), 898.

[256] Bassiouni, *The Law of the ICTY*, 965.

[257] This provision was comprehensively amended at the 14th Plenary Session on 12 November 1997 and by the 18th Plenary Session on 9–10 July 1998.

November 1995. His trial started on 24 June 1997 and an end is not in sight. Blaskic actually complained about the length of the proceedings, in particular with regard to the detention (for him in the form of house arrest). The Trial Chamber I, when rejecting his motion, based its decision on the case-law of the ECourtHR as outlined above.[258] It stated that the length of the proceeding must be evaluated in the light of the circumstances of the case. This evaluation resulted in findings to the disadvantage of the applicant, due to the complexity of the issue on the one hand, and the already privileged conditions of the detention in this case. Many of the delays are certainly due to the fact that much of the law, procedural law in particular, has yet to be created.

3. The ICC

Art. 67 (I) c Rome Statute (Art. 41 (I) c Statute ILC) recapitulates Art. 14 (III) c ICCPR. In my opinion, this provision should be interpreted in accordance with the human rights treaties, as discussed above.[259] It may have been better to have the provision phrased as a right to a speedy trial, as proposed before and during the conference.[260]

(V) The Presumption of Innocence

The principle that the defendant is to be presumed innocent is expressed in Art. 14 (II) ICCPR and Art. 6 (II) ECHR, Art. 8 (II) AmCHR and Art. 7 (I) b AfCHPR. Certain aspects of this provision, which has often been referred to as the cardinal principle of nearly all systems of criminal procedure,[261] have already been discussed, when looking at the controversial question of whether or not this principle applies to earlier stages of criminal prosecution or whether it is related to the trial stage only. This time we are on solid ground; without doubt, the presumption of innocence is applicable during trial. We must explore the content of this presumption. What is actually meant by saying that the accused has to be presumed innocent? Clearly, the provision has many consequences for the institution of criminal proceedings. I have already discussed this aspect, and also the requirement of judicial impartiality, which has its root in this overall maxim. However, for the stage of the trial three separate meanings can be discerned. It means that the burden of proof is, in general, on the side of the prosecution, but it also has something to say about the require-

---

[258] *Blaskic* Case No. IT-95-14-T, Order 14 December 1996 Denying a Motion for Provisional Release.

[259] Compare, as well, Amnesty International, IOR 40/05/94.

[260] Report of the PrepComm II, 197; Schabas, in Trifterer (ed.), *Commentary on the Rome Statute*, Art. 67, No. 26.

[261] Jacobs and White, 150.

ment of the proof of guilt and about the behaviour of court or other public officials.

1. The burden of proof

'The burden of proof of the charge is on the prosecution', we read in the General Comments of the HRC.[262] This seems to be unquestioned in the context of the ICCPR.[263] Similarly, the ECourtHR has held that Art. 6 (II) ECHR requires, *inter alia*, that the burden of proof is on the prosecution, and any doubt shall benefit the accused.[264] However, Fawcett hesitates to attribute this notion to the presumption of innocence.[265] He argues that in some Member States of the Council of Europe, like Germany, it is the duty of the judge to do everything necessary to discover the truth (§ 244 (II) StPO). He presides over the hearing, conducts the trial, examines the accused, and admits all evidence he considers necessary.[266] This would reduce the implications of the presumption of innocence to the principle of impartial judges. Muhammad also argues that in the Continental system the presumption of innocence does not mean that the burden of proof is on the prosecution. He sees the consequence of this tenet for the inquisitorial system in the obligation of the court to 'do all that is necessary to discover the truth'.[267] But maybe it would be too quick an assumption to dismiss the burden of proof idea altogether because of this, as Fawcett perhaps does. His argument is valid only as far as the prosecution is concerned. In the German system, it is still also the duty of the public authorities to establish guilt. So we could either phrase it positively, saying the burden of proof must lie with the public institution,[268] or we could put it negatively, and say that the burden of proof must not lie on the defendant. Consequently, the defendant cannot be convicted if doubts remain.[269]

---

[262] HRC General Comment 13 (Article 14), para. 7. Although the HRC was concerned with a number of cases claiming a violation of the presumption of innocence, it nevertheless never really commented on this provision. It seemed, however, to presume that any violation of Art. 14 (I) and (III) ICCPR also constituted a violation of Art 14 (II), see McGoldrick, *Human Rights Committee*, 419.

[263] Nowak, Art. 14, No. 35.

[264] ECourtHR *Barberà, Messegué and Jabardo v Spain* Judgment 6 December 1988, Series A No. 146, para. 77.

[265] Fawcett, *The Application of the ECHR*, 180.

[266] This fact is probably the reason why some Anglo-American writers presume that a presumption of guilt rather than of innocence prevails on the Continent. See the reference by Sigler in McDonald, *The Prosecutor*, 69. This assumption is certainly wrong, as Sigler rightly observes.

[267] Muhammad in L. Henkin (ed.), *The International Bill of Rights* (New York, 1981), 138 at 150.

[268] Compare, e.g. Judge Mahrenholz, dissenting vote in BVerfG Decision 29 May 1990, in BVerfGE 82, 106 at 122.

[269] Harris, 243, addresses the dissimilarities between common and civil law. According to

What is a matter of concern with regard to the question of the burden of proof is the practice in many jurisdictions of inferring from certain circumstances that the accused has committed a crime. The English case *X v UK*[270] can be cited here, for example. The applicant was living with a prostitute. He was convicted in accordance with the statutory provisions, which states: 'a man who lives with or is habitually in the company of a prostitute . . . shall be presumed to be knowingly living on the earnings of prostitution unless he proves the contrary'. The ECommHR differentiated between a presumption of fact and a presumption of guilt, and found only the latter prohibited by Art. 6 (II) ECHR. The ECommHR tried to expunge the danger of a wide presumption of facts amounting to a presumption of guilt by an examination of the presumption in its substance and its effect. A violation was denied in this case, mostly because the prosecution would be burdened with an impossible task if asked to prove by direct evidence that someone was living on immoral earnings. The matter probably appears more frequently as a question of evidence. The issue of direct and indirect evidence will be addressed later. The ECourtHR had to discuss similar Continental legislation in the case of *Salabiaku v France*.[271] The applicant was convicted of importing illegal goods into France, although it was shown that he had mistaken the package he brought through customs for his own. The government and the ECommHR argued that there was a crucial difference between guilt and liability.[272] The case of the applicant did not constitute a presumption of guilt. It merely combined a finding of facts with a legal presumption; from the fact of possessing illegal goods it was inferred that the applicant wanted to smuggle them into France. Which acts to criminalize is a matter for the Member States.[273] The ECourtHR struggled to apply a more independent and 'autonomous' approach to this matter. It held that the presumption of facts and law is, in any case, not unlimited. States must 'take into account the importance of what is at stake and maintain the rights of the defence'.[274] However, the ECourtHR upheld the legislative

---

him the appropriate terminology for civil law countries would be that 'the court, in its inquiry into the facts, must find for the accused in a case of doubt'. This does not differ from my definition. Likewise the ECourtHR stated that it follows from Art. 6 (II) ECHR that any doubt shall benefit the defendant; see ECourtHR *Barberà, Messegué and Jabardo v Spain* Judgment 6 December 1988, Series A No. 146, para. 77.

[270] ECommHR *X v UK* Decision 19 July 1972, Appl. No. 5124/71, 42 CD, 135.

[271] ECourtHR *Salabiaku v France* Judgment 7 October 1988, Series A No. 141-A.

[272] Ibid., para. 24. The finding of the ECommHR was, however, not unanimous. Mr Tenekides dissented and stressed the fact that the difference between presumption of guilt and of liability is narrow. An 'inference of guilt from pure fact results in *automaticity* and, accordingly, the shifting of the burden of proof to the person charged' (italics in the text). In consequence of this, the burden of proving the accused's criminal intent is taken away from the prosecution, see *Salabiaku* case, dissenting opinion of Tenekides, Series A No. 141, 26–7.

[273] Ibid., para. 27. cf. also Harris, 244.   [274] Ibid., para. 28.

technique in general, and only challenged the way that national courts might apply strict liability norms; in each individual case, the judge must decide whether the accused can be held subjectively accountable for the offence. Thereby the accused must be given a fair chance to challenge the charge.[275] In the case in question, the ECourtHR could not find a violation in this regard.[276]

2. The proof of guilt

It is for the prosecution to prove the truth of the allegations. But how much does it take to prove that the accused is the wanted offender? What threshold must be passed in order to establish the guilt of the accused?

The HRC finds that the requirement is proof beyond reasonable doubt.[277] The drafting history shows, however, that exactly this threshold was deliberately not included in the text of Art. 14 (II) ICCPR.[278] Commentators believe that this 'reasonable-doubt' principle is nevertheless a generally recognized principle of law.[279] The European authorities refrain from unequivocally stating that there is a requirement of proof of guilt beyond reasonable doubt.[280] In *Austria v Italy*, the ECommHR set the standard of proof as evidence that is sufficiently strong in the eyes of the law to establish the accused's guilt.[281] The ECourtHR thus relies on domestic law and the principles of evidence-weighing therein.[282] However, reliance can still be placed on the ECourtHR's statement that 'any doubt should benefit the accused'.[283] The Court thereby admits that the likeliness of the accused being the offender must be so great that all reasonable doubt is silenced,[284] because if doubts remain as to his guilt, they must work in favour of the accused, and therefore be followed by an acquittal. This could be called 'proof beyond reasonable doubt', as understood by the common law.

---

[275] Compare Frowein and Peukert, Art. 6, No. 158.

[276] Ibid., para. 30. Similarly, in *Pham Hoang v France* Judgment 25 September 1992, Series A No. 243, the ECourtHR found no violation of Art. 6 (II) ECHR, as the French court had duly weighed the evidence before it and had not automatically relied on the presumption established by the law. Therefore, the ECourtHR could find no violation.

[277] HRC General Comment 13 (Article 14), para. 7.

[278] An equivalent Philippine motion was rejected in the HRComm, E/CN.4/365; E/CN.4/SR.156, 6.

[279] Nowak, Art. 14, No. 35.

[280] Compare Harris, 244.

[281] ECommHR *Austria v Italy* Report 30 March 1963, 6 YB 740 at 784.

[282] Nowak also admits that the way in which guilt is to be proved is a question of national law; see Art. 14, No. 35. He believes nevertheless that proof beyond reasonable doubt is a general principle of law. Frowein and Peukert, Art. 6, No. 156, agree that determination of the legal requirements for the proof of guilt should be left to domestic law; none the less, the ECourtHR exercises control against abuse.

[283] ECourtHR *Barberà, Messegué and Jabardo v Spain* Judgment 6 December 1988, Series A No. 146, para. 77.

[284] Kleinknecht and Meyer-Goßner, § 261, Nos. 1 and 2.

National systems, it seems, largely agree on the threshold that is needed to convict an offender. The wording differs but the substance remains the same.

It is often said that the civil law principle of *in dubio pro reo* is also a matter of the proving of guilt.[285] The HRC mentions it in conjunction with the finding that the burden of proof remains with the prosecution: 'the accused has the benefit of doubt'.[286] However, it is not very obvious whether the HRC is alluding to the principle *in dubio pro reo* or intends to make a general statement as to the proof of guilt, like the similar statement of the ECourtHR above.[287] The HRC mentions the standard of proof explicitly, so we assume that it intends to address something different here, which can only be the principle of *in dubio pro reo*. Persistent repetition does not make a false assumption right. If, at the end of the pleadings, the judges cannot abolish all doubts concerning the guilt of the accused, the prosecution has simply failed to cross the threshold, which is to prove guilt beyond reasonable doubt. The ancient principle of *in dubio pro reo* means something else; it concerns establishment of each piece of evidence and belongs to the sphere of material criminal law.[288] If the prosecution cannot establish the factual conduct of the crime, or individual details among the facts with certainty, then the *in dubio pro reo* sentence comes into play; only those facts that have the least impact on the accused may be considered. Let us take a hypothetical example: the prosecutor indicts a person for having committed war crimes and crimes against humanity in a detention camp. The defendant argues that he is not the culprit but his twin brother. If the prosecutor cannot abolish all reasonable doubt as to his identity, the defendant must go free on the grounds that the presumption of innocence has not been disproved. If, on the other hand, the identity of the defendant is unquestioned but it is not clear whether the accused had the intent to destroy an ethnic, religious, or otherwise defined group, when he beat and murdered detained persons, *in dubio pro reo* applies and the charge of crimes against humanity has to be dismissed. In this case, the factual question of whether or not the accused fulfilled the requirement of intent attached to crimes against humanity could not be adequately answered, so that the facts speaking in favour of the defendant have to be assumed. In the example, this means that the defendant can only be convicted of war crimes.

---

[285] Nowak, Art. 14, No. 35. Fawcett, *The Application of the ECHR*, 180, also seems to make this doubtful allusion.

[286] HRC General Comment 13 (Article 14), para. 7.

[287] See above, ECourtHR *Barberà, Messegué and Jabardo v Spain* Judgment 6 December 1988, Series A No. 146, para. 77.

[288] Kleinknecht and Meyer-Goßner § 261, No. 26.

3. Conduct of officials

If the accused must be presumed innocent until the prosecution can prove his guilt beyond reasonable doubt, then all state authorities must treat him in this way, that is, officials may not prejudge the outcome of the trial.[289] In the European system, there are two main cases that address the problem of conduct of judges in this regard. In *Adolf v Austria*, the defendant state was criticized for passages in the verdict which, it was said, could be understood as presuming the guilt of the accused. A violation of the ECHR was then denied, as the fault was remedied by the ruling of the Austrian Supreme Court.[290] In *Minelli v Switzerland*, the ECourtHR held that non-formal findings of a court can also presume guilt.[291] '[I]t suffices that there is some reasoning suggesting that the court regards the accused as guilty'.[292] These cases addressed the behaviour of courts. The ECourtHR's main concern appears to be ensuring that the defendant has a proper opportunity to rebut the allegations. The main rationale of the presumption of innocence would therefore be found in the safeguarding of the accused's right to a defence.[293]

Similarly, other public officials must also abstain in their public statements from prejudging the trial's outcome. ECommHR and ECourtHR have repeatedly criticized infringements of this principle, most recently in the case of *Allenet de Ribemont v France*.[294]

There is no need to go as far as prohibiting all official information about the trial. The mere fact that someone must be arrested or charged certainly implies suspicion, but should not prejudice the guilt of the suspect, as long as the person is treated as a suspect in accordance with the law of the pre-trial stage and not as a convicted offender.[295] This was explicitly stated by the ECourtHR as being in accordance with the ECHR; the state has an obligation to inform 'the public about criminal investigations in progress, but it requires that they do so with all discretion and circumspection necessary if the presumption of innocence is to be respected'.[296] In the case of *Allenet de Ribemont*, the minister for internal affairs and several very high-ranking officers referred to the applicant as one of the instigators and as an accomplice to murder, at a time when

---

[289] HRC General Comment 13 (Article 14), para. 7.
[290] ECourtHR *Adolf v Austria* Judgment from 26 March 1982, Series A No. 49.
[291] ECourtHR *Minelli v. Switzerland* Judgment 25 March 1983, Series A No. 62.
[292] ECourtHR *Minelli v. Switzerland* Judgment 25 March 1983, Series A No. 62, para. 37.
[293] Ibid., para. 37, quite explicitly so.
[294] ECourtHR *Allenet de Ribemont v France* Judgment 10 February 1995, Series A No. 308, para. 36.
[295] See Fawcett, *The Application of the ECHR*, 180, with further reference to decisions of the ECommHR in this connection.
[296] ECourtHR *Allenet de Ribemont v France* Judgment 10 February 1995, Series A No. 308, para. 38.

charges had not even been laid against the person. This was held as a blatant violation of the presumption of innocence.[297]

What are certainly not encompassed by the presumption of innocence are incriminating and guilt-presuming statements of witnesses. Witnesses will surely have prejudicial opinions and are sometimes even obliged to make statements as to the guilt or accountability of the accused. Thus, the ECommHR rejected a claim of this nature as inadmissible.[298]

Judges certainly have to refrain from any behaviour that shows prejudice or their personal conviction before the whole hearing is finished. German courts found a judge who was already drafting the judgment while the accused was making his final statement, that is, when the hearing was not yet over, as in violation of the presumption of innocence.[299]

4. The ICTY

Art. 21 III Statute ICTY contains the presumption of innocence:[300] 'The accused shall be presumed innocent until proven guilty according to the provisions of the present Statute.' Procedure at the ICTY follows mostly the structure of the adversarial trial, as we have already seen. The burden of proof lies with the prosecution. The Statute is silent as to the requirements of proof of guilt. Rule 87A 2 lays down the principle that '[a] finding of guilt may be reached only when a majority of the Trial Chamber is satisfied that guilt has been proved beyond reasonable doubt'.

The threshold I found encapsulated in human rights as a principle of law is spelt out literally here. I gave this principle a more precise content by saying that the likelihood of the accused being guilty must be such that all doubt is silenced. The Rules of Procedure seem to relate this to the individual judges rather than to the Chamber as a whole, as it finds a majority verdict sufficient. Taking the Chamber as a whole, one would probably have to concede that if two find the accused guilty and one not guilty, then there remains reasonable doubt as to the guilt of the offender. Although the tradition of dissenting votes (foreseen by Rule 88C) is familiar to common lawyers, it is unknown to Continental lawyers.[301] But is it

---

[297] Ibid., para. 40–1. In this case the applicant was charged in January 1977, released in March 1977, and eventually discharged in March 1980. Quite understandably, he was angry with the officials.

[298] ECommHR *X v Denmark* Decision 2 September 1959, Appl. No. 343/57, 2 YB, 413, at 446–7.

[299] BGH Judgment 22 November 1957, in BGHSt 11, 74. The BGH argued that the judge may make notes during trial and even draft the verdict before the defence counsel's final pleading or the defendant's last words, as this does not imply that the judge is not willing to change his mind before he passes the actual verdict.

[300] Bassiouni, *The Law of the ICTY*, 961–2.

[301] In Germany only the BVerfG practises dissenting votes (§ 30 (II) Bundesverfassungs-gerichtsgesetz, Constitutional Court Act 1993); all other courts, the Supreme Court included, need to agree on a single verdict and a single reasoning.

really a good idea to transfer this practice to the international law context? The majority verdict and dissenting opinions are traditionally the practice of courts in common law states. However, this is not the case in convictions in criminal matters. The jury assumes responsibility for the conviction, and although majority verdicts have been introduced, there are nevertheless differences from a Trial Chamber consisting of three professional judges. The voice of the people that emanates—as it were—unbiased and irrevocable from the jury is not comparable with the legal reasoning of three professional judges. In higher courts, dissenting opinions are the practice in criminal matters, too, but these courts are restricted to giving judgments on questions of law. Judges have no say in the guilt of the offender. Leaving aside the fact that they can discharge the wrongdoer altogether, they cannot convict criminals. The justification for separate and dissenting opinions is mainly the further development of the law, and certainly international criminal law and procedure desperately needs further developing. But in the case of convictions of criminal offenders, common law countries do not rely on as slim a majority as two to one, nor would it be appropriate. In my opinion, the ICTY Trial Chambers should therefore abstain from dissenting opinions on the question of guilt. Dissenting opinions should be left solely to questions of law and better be avoided altogether at the Trial Chamber stage.

5. The law at the ICC

Art. 40 Statute ILC already enshrined the principle of the presumption of innocence. Art. 66 Rome Statute puts it more clearly. It reads as follows:

Art. 66 Rome Statute
I Everyone shall be presumed innocent until proved guilty before the Court in accordance with the applicable law.
II The onus is on the Prosecutor to prove the guilt of the accused.
III In order to convict the accused, the Court must be convinced of the guilt of the accused beyond reasonable doubt.

This provision clearly encapsulates the above findings. The burden of proof is on the prosecution. Furthermore the quantum of proof is one beyond reasonable doubt. According to the ILC Commentary, this should apply to every element of the crime.[302] However, Amnesty International criticizes the interpretation of the former Art. 40 Statute ILC by the ILC as too narrow. According to the ILC, the provision, 'according to the law', refers only to the Statute itself.[303] It is true that this restriction seems exaggerated, in particular with regard to the incomplete status of procedural

---

[302] Report ILC, Art. 40.
[303] IOR 40/05/94, pp. 44–5.

and material international criminal law. Because of this, it would seem appropriate to extend this concept of 'law' to human rights and general principles of law. 'Law' would then be defined as in Art. 33 a and b Statute ILC (Art. 21 Rome Statute).

The majority quorum that exists at the ICC by virtue of Art. 74 (III) Rome Statute is similar to that of the ICTY. For the presumption of innocence to be rebutted, it suffices if a majority of the three trial judges convict.[304] It was submitted by some delegates in the PrepComm deliberation that the verdict should be unanimous, at least in the case of convictions.[305] Both views were represented, one in favour of dissenting and separate opinions, as is the alleged practice in common law jurisdiction, the other critical of this, pointing out the differences between criminal and civil cases, and emphasizing the potential danger of undermining the credibility and authority of the Court that comes with separate and dissenting opinions.[306] In the author's opinion, the latter view is correct. The greatest caution should be adopted towards proposing dissenting opinions and majority verdicts at the trial stage of criminal proceedings.[307] The presumption of innocence would be discarded too lightly if a potential two to three discrepancy were permitted to carry a guilty verdict in criminal matters. The Rome Conference voted in favour of a compromise: Art. 74 (III) and (V) Rome Statute stress that there is only one decision. From this it follows that dissenting opinions are not feasible. If, however, unanimity cannot be reached by the judges, which they must strive to achieve as their foremost objective, the decision must give the views of both the majority and the minority.

German and French proposals further emphasize the fact that the judges must bear the entire trial in mind when weighing the evidence.[308] The German proposal reads as follows: 'The court will decide on the taking of evidence according to its free conviction obtained from the entire trial.' The French version states that the court shall decide 'in accordance with its innermost conviction'. This means that there are no precise rules of proof. The judges are called upon to decide the case and come to their verdict by looking at the evidence as it presents itself from the entire trial, and then to draw their conclusions as to the guilt of the accused freely and in accordance with their own conscience. These proposals are mirrored in Art. 74 (II) Rome Statute, where it is laid down that the decision shall be based on

---

[304] The fact that the majority will always be a two-thirds majority is a mere coincidence and due to the number of trial judges; no significance whatsoever should be assigned to it, as Trifterer does in Trifterer (ed.), *Commentary on the Rome Statute*, Art. 74, No. 25.

[305] Report of the PrepComm I, para. 291.

[306] Ibid., para. 293.

[307] For reasons, see also the above discussion of the practice at the ICTY.

[308] See Report of the PrepComm II, 207.

evaluation of the evidence and the entire proceedings, limited to the facts and circumstance submitted and discussed before the Trial Chamber at the trial.

(VI) The Principle of Equality of Arms

The principle of the procedural equality of arms is a product of the over-all principle of a 'fair trial'. It is not found explicitly in general human rights treaties, but is believed to be a general principle of law.[309] The reference to 'equality before the courts' in Art. 14 (I) ICCPR establishes the general principle of equality (Art. 26) for special treatment before courts. The drafters did not intend to enshrine the principle of equality of arms therein.[310] This principle stems from the ancient principle of *audi alteram partem*,[311] also referred to as *audiatur et altera pars*.[312] The principle has more significance in an accusatorial system, where opponent parties engage in combat and must be equipped with equal weapons so that the battle can be a fair one. Of course a battle between two equally equipped persons may well end undecided, or with the death of both.

Equality thus does not mean equity of powers and rights but rather the balancing of the powers and rights of each participant according to the specific differences in their procedural roles.[313] Each party must have the opportunity to present its case, both with respect to fact and to law. Each must furthermore have the opportunity to comment on the opponent party's case.[314] The leading Strasbourg cases in this respect are four Austrian cases. In *Ofner*[315] and *Hopfinger*,[316] the reviewing court heard the Attorney-General but not the accused during appeals proceedings before the Austrian Supreme Court. *Pataki*[317] and *Dunshirn*[318] involved similar questions before the court of second instance (Oberlandesgericht), which heard the public prosecutor but not the accused, who were neither present nor represented. Although the facts differed in the two sets of cases, the ECommHR found that the legal problem that had to be addressed was the same. The ECommHR did not think it necessary to specifically consider the 'minimum guarantees' of Art. 6 (III) ECHR and whether or not any

---

[309] Nowak, Art. 14, Nos. 20–1.

[310] See Nowak, Art. 14, Nos. 5–8, as to the drafting history and the specific meaning of the principle of non-discrimination in this respect.

[311] Fawcett, *The Application of the ECHR*, 154.

[312] Nowak, Art. 14, No. 20.

[313] Kleinknecht and Meyer-Goßner, Einl. No. 88.

[314] Fawcett, *The Application of the ECHR*, 154.

[315] ECommHR *Ofner v Austria* Appl. No. 524/59, Report 23 November 1962, 6 YB, 680.

[316] ECommHR *Hopfinger v Austria* Appl. No. 617/59, Report 23 November 1962, 6 YB, 680.

[317] ECommHR *Paraki v Austria* Appl. No. 596/59, Decision 19 December 1960, 6 YB, 714.

[318] ECommHR *Dunshirn v Austria* Appl. No. 789/60, Decision 15 March 1961, 6 YB, 714.

particular norm therein had been unlawfully infringed. It felt that it was a question of the general, wider notion of a 'fair trial' and of the principle of 'equality of arms', as embodied in Art. 6 (I) ECHR.[319] The ECommHR considered three elements in order to assess whether there had been inequality of arms; first, it observed the role of the party that was heard, that is, the role of the Attorney-General in the first two cases and that of the public prosecutor in the second two cases. Secondly, it looked at the precise circumstances of the hearing and, thirdly, it examined the result of the proceedings for the accused, in particular whether there was a *reformatio in peius*.[320] In *Ofner* and *Hopfinger* a violation was not found because the Attorney-General's role had been to secure respect for the law (*Wahrung des Gesetzes*). The Attorney-General is recognized by law as a fair and objective figure *per se*. There was therefore no immediate threat to the rights of the defendant. The situation was different in *Pataki* and *Dunshirn*, where the public prosecutor's interest was mainly in convicting those accused. Therefore, non-admittance of the accused to the appeals hearings constituted a violation of the principle of 'equality of arms'.

The threefold test the ECommHR applies is clearly an *ex post* test. Whether or not the defendant suffered from the conduct of the trial is very important. This becomes particularly clear on the third level of the test. We can nevertheless sum up the situation by saying that 'equality of arms' must be respected in the role of the parties, ensured throughout the proceedings and especially facilitated in cases where the situation of the accused might be aggravated (*reformatio in peius*).[321]

1. The Anglo-American systems

If we apply these findings to both the accusatorial and the inquisitorial systems, we find the former somehow naturally inclined towards granting 'equality'. Because it recognizes the existence of opposing parties, this system is based on the presentation of the pros and cons by these parties. This is so in theory at least. This inherited approach perhaps underestimates the development of technical devices as used by prosecutors, and the swift advance of state surveillance that has engulfed society. The prosecutor is in a far superior position to trace information and produce evidence and it becomes more and more difficult for the defence to rebut such evidence. However, there is nobody else besides the defence counsel to assist the defendant; for example, there is no well-informed judge to challenge the evidence presented by the prosecutor. The problem of expert evidence also proves to be a problem of 'equality of arms'. In the

---

[319] Ibid., 730–2.
[320] Fawcett, *The Application of the ECHR*, 155.
[321] As to *reformatio in peius*, see in the discussion of appeal proceedings below, p. 331.

common law structure, there will almost inevitably be two experts offering conflicting evidence corroborating the respective parties' hypotheses. The court will have to decide which of the experts to believe.

2. The difficulties on the Continent

The inquisitorial system by very nature does not incline to the principle of 'equality' between the parties. The judge finds the truth; truth does not come into existence through the presentations of the two parties. The main problem in this system is the fact that the judge has full knowledge of the prosecutor's files. It often appears as if judge and prosecutor were closely collaborating. From a theoretical point of view this might play no role at all or only a minor one, as the written files have no immediate effect on the verdict. We have seen that the trial must be oral; purely written statements in the prosecutor's file are of no importance. They must be orally introduced into the trial. In this way, they are made known to the defendant and thus open to his scrutiny. Scholars nevertheless frequently complain about the indirect effects of the knowledge the judge has, which are not always positive for the defendant.

The problem of experts is solved in a manner that differs from that of the common law tradition. Experts are appointed by the court (§§ 72 and 75 StPO). Admittedly, it will be difficult for the defence to challenge evidence given by such an official expert, who will enjoy the respect attaching to such a position.[322] This system has the advantage, however, that the court-appointed expert will be more independent than the Anglo-American expert giving evidence on behalf of the prosecution.[323] Critical voices in Germany have alleged that the outcome of the trial is becoming more and more dependent on these experts so that their expertise is often taken as the basis of convictions by judges without further questioning of the facts and circumstances of the case. It seems that the idea of court-appointed official experts is fine, as long as the highest standard is guaranteed as regards their expertise. The defence must nevertheless also have a proper opportunity to challenge the scientific findings of the court appointee.

3. The ICTY

At the adversarial style ICTY, the Rules make a great effort to balance the rights of the two opposing parties. Care is taken to ensure that the defence always gets opportunity to have the 'last word', so that he has a chance to rebut the prosecutor's allegations (compare Rules 84–6). Furthermore, the defence has the right to be present whenever the guilt of the accused is

---

[322] Compare the criticism by Hatchard *et al.*, *Comparative Criminal Procedure*, 235.
[323] This might be a problem in the case of scientific tests that cannot be repeated.

being discussed. Nsereko submits that the fact that the prosecutor may question the accused after deferral to the ICTY constitutes an unfair advantage to the prosecution, as the defence has no right to question the prosecution witnesses.[324] However, this possibility is, in accordance with common law, clearly phrased as an exceptional measure (Rule 63). Furthermore, several safeguards, such as presence of counsel, recording of the interview, and cautioning of the accused, are obligatory. Besides which, the accused need not comment on any question at all.

Difficulties arose within the Rule 61 procedure. No defence representation is foreseen there. In the cases of *Karadzic* and *Mladic*, this was made an issue by the two advocates claiming access to the proceedings on behalf of the accused.[325] The Trial Chamber I rejected the claim because the Rule 61 procedure was not a trial proceeding but a review proceeding to issue an international warrant of arrest.[326]

4. The consequences for an international procedure

Based on the adversarial system, the Rules of Procedure at an ICC must ensure that both parties, defence and prosecution, have the same rights and powers during trial.

C. THE PROCEDURAL STEPS

A comparison of procedure on the Continent with procedure in the Anglo-American tradition reveals another fundamental difference. Trial in the latter system is split into two main stages, conviction and sentencing, whereas on the Continent both questions are considered together. The background and the consequences of this will be addressed first. Then I will look in detail at the procedure of guilty plea and the problems relating to plea bargaining, a phenomenon which, in theory, cannot exist on the Continent but in reality enjoys widespread practice. We will then take issue with the presentation and questioning of witnesses and their protection. After this we will compare the rules of evidence and how human rights could be safeguarded through them. Finally, we will scrutinize the sentence procedure.

---

[324] Nsereko, 5 CLF (1994), 507 at 531.

[325] See Trial Chamber I, *Karadzic* and *Mladic* Decision 24 July 1996, Case Nos. IT-95-5-R61 and IT-95-18-R61.

[326] Compare Jones, *The Practice of the ICTY*, Rule 61, 308.

(I) The Two Acts of the Trial

On the Continent there is only one act: conviction and sentencing are combined, in the sense that from the beginning of the trial the possible sanction is at issue. In the Anglo-American tradition there are two separate stages; in the first half, the case is presented and discussed with the sole intention of proving the guilt of the accused. Only in the second part, after the conviction, are the circumstances that are relevant to the extent of the penalty presented and disputed.

The original reason for this separation was the fact that the question of guilt had to be considered by a jury, while determination of the punishment could easily be left to the judge. The phenomenon of the jury was discussed earlier and it was shown then that a jury is unnecessary from a human rights perspective and that there is no 'right to a jury'. So we are faced with the interesting question of whether or not separation of guilt and punishment is still appropriate or whether it is outdated. It is argued here that separation still makes sense and indeed supports protection of and fairness towards the accused.

If there is a separate second stage for sentencing, the accused's personal details, his background, occupation, and income, his position as regards previous convictions, are of no interest in the first part of the procedure. There, commission of the criminal offence is the only issue that is under scrutiny. In a single-stage trial, on the other hand, all of the above matters will be mentioned before guilt is established.

The European system of human rights protection had to address the question of whether the mentioning of previous sentences is compatible with the presumption of innocence.[327] It did so by taking the practice of the Member States into consideration. The ECommHR was at that time 'not prepared to consider such a procedure as violating any provision of Article 6 of the Convention',[328] even if the information is given to a jury.[329] In another Austrian case, it found that systems that refer to previous convictions before the verdict work on the assumption that persons with a serious crime record may also constitute a danger to society in future. Assessment of a person's dangerousness does not in itself violate the presumption of innocence.[330] This case was concerned more with Art. 5 (I) a ECHR and preventive detention in an institution for recidivists. Special provisions for detaining extraordinarily dangerous persons exist in all states. Certain conditions have to be met to trigger the possibility of the

---

[327] Fawcett, *The Application of the ECHR*, 181; cf. also Frowein and Peukert, Art. 6, No. 170.

[328] ECommHR *X v Austria* Decision 1 April 1966, Appl. No. 2742/66, 9 YB, 550 at 554.

[329] ECommHR *X v Denmark* Decision 14 December 1965, Appl. No. 2518/65, 8 YB, 370.

[330] ECommHR *X v Austria* Decision 15 October 1981, Appl. No. 9167/80, 26 DR, 248 at 250.

domestic court ordering preventive detention. The issue then is one of social policy rather than of criminal procedure.[331]

In another case, the ECommHR argued that the applicant had already admitted his guilt to a certain extent, so that his past record was mainly taken into account to determine the sentence.[332] This decision confirms the fact that the main reason why the ECommHR does not address this question as violating the presumption of innocence is that it is a widespread practice in several Member States of the Council of Europe. Although the ECommHR shows a certain sympathy towards the applicant's complaints, it refuses to decide in his favour.[333] Unlike with other problems, the ECommHR is not prepared to give the notion of 'fair trial' and 'presumption of innocence' an 'autonomous' Convention meaning. Thus, the only argument it finds to endorse the state's position before it is that what has been the practice in several Member States for a long period cannot be incompatible with the ECHR.

According to Strasbourg case-law, it therefore seems compatible with human rights to take previous convictions into consideration, although the ECommHR hardly discussed the matter on its merits. There are three main reasons for taking personal details into consideration: the wish to obtain the complete picture, the belief that the offence cannot possibly be kept separate from the offender, and the argument that the suspect as a person must be taken into consideration as a matter of fairness.

Criticism mainly arises in connection with the presumption of innocence. A judge who is confronted with a person whom he believes to be a criminal because of his 'record' is more likely to convict than if he thinks he is dealing with someone with a 'clean record'. Arguably, this is even more the case with lay judges or jurors. Furthermore, the argument has been put forward that a person who is acquitted is protected because he does not have to undergo what may possibly be an insulting scrutiny of his character. Therefore, separation of the stages is preferable in order to protect the right to privacy (Art. 17 ICCPR, Art. 8 ECHR).

This short survey reveals the interests and rights that must be balanced. On the one hand, the single-stage system, which looks at the person as a whole, with his background and history, seems to be the more humane approach. Certain knowledge about the defendant's person prevents judges from making assumptions from mere outside appearances. The accused may then run the risk of being convicted because of

---

[331] See Fawcett, *The Application of the ECHR*, 182.

[332] ECommHR *X v Austria* Decision 3 April 1967, Appl. No. 2676/65, 23 DR, 31 at 34.

[333] Frowein and Peukert, Art. 6, No. 170, quote this case to underline the practice of the ECommHR of allowing courts to take previous sentences into consideration when ruling on both guilt and sentence. My impression is that this decision can be read in a way that is more critical towards the practice in Continental courts.

his egregious criminal record, but at least he is not sentenced mainly because of his conspicuous criminal looks. Somehow, the first alternative seems fairer because more deserving. Opponents of a separation also point out that two separate stages tend to protract the trial unduly.

On the other hand, the split system stands for greater protection of the right to privacy and for a proper safeguard against negative inferences as to the guilt of the defendant. The above criticism, that it is fairer to look at the criminal record than to rely on appearances only, fails because looks play an equal role in both instances. The judge will always have to endeavour to ignore the defendant's appearance when ruling on his guilt. If he has to take the accused's criminal record into consideration before ruling on his guilt, this simply adds yet another matter that the judge must ignore in order not to be biased. Not mentioning the defendant's personal record during the procedure therefore means excluding something that is apt to make the judge biased. The argument of a prolongation of the proceeding seems groundless. Reasons for delays are manifold, but they do not seem to include separation of the trial. Another advantage of having a separate procedure to discuss the sentence is that if, for whatever reasons, the investigation into the defendant's person is particularly shameful for persons involved, publicity could be excluded for this part of the trial only. Of course the judge can only order exclusion of the public if the conditions outlined earlier are met. Nevertheless, it might be easier to find a compromise between the interests of the public and the protection of affected persons in a two-stage system.

In Germany, where criminal trial is performed in one stage only, the discussion about whether the system should be changed and a *Schuldinterlokut* (separate guilt-finding stage) be introduced is long-standing. Arguments in favour and against such a change have been brought forward, but never reached the stage of the legislator. Altogether, there seems to be an inclination amongst scholars towards the English system.[334] Most interesting is the field study by Schöch and Schreiber, which discusses all the pros and cons of the separation of the trial.[335] In their view, a system that separates guilt-finding and sentence procedures provides greater protection for the defendant.

The systems of both the ICTY and of the ICC anticipate the 'two act' structure of the Anglo-American tradition,[336] although doubts as to the appropriateness of this approach were uttered in the PrepComm, mainly based on the fact that fragmentation is not justified if the trial is held without a jury.[337] Recently, the ICTY has drifted away from the strict twofold

[334] See Roxin, *Strafverfahrensrecht*, § 42 G with further references.

[335] Schöch and Schreiber, ZRP (1978), 63 at pp. 66 ff. and also Schöch, in *FS Bruns* (1978), 457. [336] See e.g. Art. 76 (I) Rome Statute.

[337] See the discussion outlined in Report of the PrepComm I, para. 292.

structure. Rule 87C has been amended in this regard.[338] It reads as follows: 'If the Trial Chamber finds the accused guilty on one or more of the charges contained in the indictment, it shall at the same time determine the penalty to be imposed in respect of each finding of guilt.'

The merging of the judgment and sentencing stages now practised most probably aims at accelerating the process. There is only one deliberation and a single judgment.[339] With regard to what was said above, this development is regrettable, since separation of the hearing into two stages enhances the protection of the accused as well as the impartiality of the judges. It is not only necessitated by the jury system but also a sensible procedure even when a jury is not giving the verdict as to the guilt of the defendant. It seems therefore appropriate to continue the two separate stages. The proceeding according to the Rome Statute adheres to the two-stage system (see Art. 74 and Art. 77–9 Rome Statute).

(II) The Guilty Plea

One special phenomenon of the Anglo-American system is the guilty plea. The accused has the option of pleading guilty before the hearing starts. If he does so, the first stage of the trial obviously becomes superfluous. No more proof is needed to establish the guilt of the defendant. With the guilty plea, the defendant seems to be automatically waiving his rights under the human rights treaties: as far as the establishing of the facts is concerned, no more defence is needed (Art. 14 (III) b and d ICCPR), no more witnesses must be examined (Art. 14 (III) e ICCPR), and the right to appeal is severely limited (Art. 14 (V) ICCPR). The enormous practicality and speedy termination of the proceedings have been put forward as advantages here.[340] The possibility of pleading guilty enables the prosecuting agencies to focus on important issues and liberates them from the tiring work of detailed judicial scrutiny of the charges.

Can the mere 'plea' really have such a major impact? And if so, what conditions must be established for the plea to be valid? The plea is necessarily foreign to the Continental system of criminal procedure because it cannot be reconciled with its maxim of truth-finding. In Continental proceedings a confession does not have the consequence of terminating the procedure; it merely constitutes one strand of evidence among others. The problem of plea bargaining will not be discussed here. It should be noted that, although it is common practice and widely accepted in US courts, it is dismissed by most German academics as being irreconcilable

---

[338] Added at the 18th Plenary Session on 9–10 July 1998.
[339] Compare ICTY bulletin 27 July 1998, 20.
[340] Hatchard *et al.*, *Comparative Criminal Procedure*, 224–5.

with the StPO, although there is evidence of widespread use in German courts as well.[341]

The ICTY once more follows the Anglo-American tradition and foresees two trial stages, despite the fact that no jury is involved. On his initial appearance before the Trial Chamber, the accused must enter a plea of guilty or not guilty (Rule 62). In the case of a guilty plea, the trial proceeds immediately to its second stage and the hearing only concerns the appropriate sentence (Rule 100[342]). A plea of guilty concerning allegations of crimes against humanity (Art. 5 Statute ICTY) was entered by Erdemovic. The Trial Chamber I was satisfied that the plea was made voluntarily, in full cognizance of the nature of the charge and its consequences, and was unequivocal, and sentenced the defendant to ten years' imprisonment.[343] However, Erdemovic appealed against this judgment and in particular against his guilty plea.[344] The Appeals Chamber delivered its decision on 7 October 1997, overruling the Trial Chamber with regard to the plea on the following grounds: Erdemovic pleaded guilty to the counts of crimes against humanity (Art. 5 Statute ICTY) in the belief that this was the lesser charge compared to the alternative indictment of a violation of the laws or customs of war (Art. 3 Statute ICTY). This proved to be erroneous. The Trial Chamber made a considerable effort to define crimes against humanity as the gravest and most serious crime imaginable, deserving the severest punishment.[345] Had Erdemovic been aware of the real situation, he would most probably have entered a different plea. For the Appeals Chamber, the guilty plea was therefore not an informed one and the defendant was given the opportunity to replead with full knowledge of both the nature of the charges against him and the consequences of his plea before another Trial Chamber.[346] For these reasons, Erdemovic then pleaded guilty to the charge of a violation of the laws or customs of war on 14 January 1998, whereupon the prosecutor withdrew the alternative count of a crime against humanity—the same game as before, this time the other way around. The Trial Chamber gave a second Sentencing

[341] Compare in great detail Schünemann, Strafverteidiger 1993, 657.

[342] Rule 100 was amended to clarify this case during the 11th Plenary Meeting of the Judges, 25 June 1996. It now contains an explicit reference to cases involving a guilty plea.

[343] Trial Chamber I, *Prosecutor v Erdemovic* Case No. IT-96-22-T) Sentencing Judgment 29 November 1996, paras. 10–14 (hereinafter referred to as *Erdemovic I*).

[344] Appellant's Brief field by Counsel for the Accused Drazen *Erdemovic* against the Sentencing Judgment, *Erdemovic* Case No. IT-96-22-T, 23 December 1996, which was supplemented on 14 April 1997 by a further document.

[345] See *Erdemovic I*, paras. 26–8, and the comment by Green, 10 *LJIL* (1997), 363 at 374, who is of the opinion that the Trial Chamber was more interested in a jurisprudential exercise than in the person of the defendant.

[346] ICTY Appeals Chamber *Prosecutor v Erdemovic* 7 October 1997, Case No. IT-96-22-A (hereinafter referred to as Appeals Chamber in *Erdemovic*). The reasons for this are given in the Joint Opinion of Judge McDonald and Judge Vohrah.

Judgment on 5 March 1998, reducing the sentence to five years, having found Erdemovic's second plea voluntary, informed and unequivocal.[347] In order to avoid similar inconveniences in the future, the Fourteenth Plenary Session adopted Rule 62*bis*, where it laid down the conditions for a valid guilty plea as follows:[348]

Rule 62*bis*

If an accused pleads guilty in accordance with Rule 62 (vi), or requests to change his or her plea to guilty and the Trial Chamber is satisfied that:

(a) the guilty plea has been made voluntarily;

(b) the guilty plea is informed;

(c) the guilty plea is not equivocal; and

(d) there is a sufficient factual basis for the crime and the accused's participation in it, either on the basis of independent indicia or of lack of any material disagreement between the parties about the facts of the case, the Trial Chamber may enter a finding of guilt and instruct the Registrar to set a date for the sentencing hearing.

This amendment is certainly welcomed as clarification of the Appeals Chamber decision in *Erdemovic*.

As concerns the question of plea bargaining, the ICTY does not intend to introduce such informal talks between the professionals of the trial in its procedure.[349] The First Annual Report in particular rules out the possibility of a plea bargain.[350] Nevertheless, prosecution and defence in the *Erdemovic* case filed a 'Joint Motion for Consideration of Plea Agreement between Drazen Erdemovic and the Office of the Prosecutor' on 8 January 1998. The Trial Chamber II called this a 'plea bargain agreement', not envisaged by the laws at the ICTY.[351] The Chamber considered itself not bound by this document but took it into consideration in determining the appropriate sentence.[352]

Art. 38 (I) d Statute ILC is somewhat more liberal than the Statute ICTY, as it does not require a 'plea'. It allows the defendant to enter a guilty plea. In this case, the Trial Chamber scrutinizes whether it was made freely and voluntarily and assesses its reliability. This can result

---

[347] ICTY Trial Chamber II, *Prosecutor v Erdemovic* 5 March 1998, Case No. IT-96-22-T, para. 23 (hereinafter referred to as *Erdemovic II*).

[348] 14th Plenary Session on 12 Nov. 1997.

[349] Indeed, what happened to *Erdemovic* and his plea was quite the opposite of what is usually understood by 'plea bargaining'. Usually the defendant is called upon to confess to a lesser charge. The unfortunate Erdemovic pleaded guilty to the more serious offence—unknowingly, as the Appeals Chamber held.

[350] ICTY First Annual Report (1994), para. 74.

[351] Trial Chamber II, *Erdemovic II*, paras. 18 and 19.

[352] The Plea Agreement proposed a sentence of seven years as appropriate. The Chamber reduced this recommendation and sentenced the accused to five years.

in the whole prosecution case or at least the key witnesses being heard.[353] If the accused pleads not guilty or does not enter any plea at all, the trial proceeds in the usual way in accordance with the presumption of innocence.[354] In this respect, the Statute ILC seems inclined to treat a 'guilty plea' similarly to the way a confession is treated on the Continent.

The Netherlands Advisory Committee believes that this rule is still inappropriate. It points to the danger of a plea being entered for financial reasons and of a 'plea bargain', which would threaten the whole objective of the ICC. It therefore recommends leaving out the 'plea' altogether.[355] The PrepComm held lengthy and controversial discussions on this topic.[356] Both views were put forward. One side favoured a guilty plea because it would considerably reduce time and costs and give the accused the possibility of waiving the entire trial by admitting his wrongdoing. The other side was of the opinion that the defendant's admission of guilt should be considered as evidence, but no conviction should be based on this admission alone. It was emphasized that the Chamber had a duty to determine the guilt or innocence of the accused notwithstanding any admission. In any case, the Chamber must justify its decision concerning guilt with legal reasoning.

In view of what happened to Erdemovic and his pleas, one is inclined to recommend the above, but for different reasons. Erdemovic must have seen his trial as a mockery.[357] Had there not been such confusion concerning his pleading, the tiring and distressing trial would probably have been over long before 5 March 1998, which was about two years after the original proceedings began. Admittedly, these problems were largely due to the nature of international criminal law, which is judicially far from being a well-developed area of law; nevertheless, had there been no plea at all, the Trial Chamber would have accepted the accused's confession, considered its legal value, and classified the offences. The trial could have taken place on a summary basis, with full cooperation of the defence.[358] His voluntary confession and cooperation with the prosecutor would still have benefited him in court. There would then have been no need to

---

[353] Report ILC, Art. 38 para. 5.

[354] Ibid., para. 4.

[355] Netherlands Advisory Committee, Recommendations, 7.7, in 17 NILR (1995), 225 at 243. In the PrepComm, it had been pointed out that 'plea bargaining' should be excluded as it was in contradiction of the structure of the court, whereas the opinion was also expressed that the 'bargain' was intrinsic in the 'guilt plea' provision; see Report of the PrepComm I, para. 264.

[356] For the discussion, see the summary in Report of the PrepComm I, paras. 261–3.

[357] A critical summary and review of the entire Erdemovic proceedings is given by Linton, 12 LJIL (1999), 251.

[358] This seems to come close to the compromise found in the PrepComm; see Report of the PrepComm I, para. 263.

appeal against the plea and no need for the ludicrous duty of repleading. It is therefore submitted here that the process of 'pleading' should be removed from the system altogether.

Although the Rome Conference did not abolish the 'plea' proceedings entirely, it departed substantially from the Anglo-American structure.[359] It was felt during the conference that the positions of the various states were not so different after all. The Rome Statute therefore incorporates what was found to be the common denominator, based on the proposals of Argentina and Canada.[360] At the beginning of the trial, the defendant will be given the opportunity to make an 'admission of guilt' (Art. 64 (VIII) a Rome Statute), or to plead not guilty.[361] In the former case, the Trial Chamber will first ensure that the defendant was fully aware of the charges and of consequences of his admission of guilt, and that it was made voluntarily after sufficient consultation with defence counsel (Art. 65 (I) Rome Statute). Furthermore, the Trial Chamber will weigh the evidence that has already been brought before it to see whether the guilt of the defendant is supported by it and may request further presentation of evidence or even order the continuation of the proceedings as an ordinary trial (Art. 65 (II) to (IV) Rome Statute). In general, this is the way in which confessions by the defendants are treated on the Continent.

(III) Witnesses

The question of witnesses is addressed by the various human rights treaties. Art. 14 (III) e ICCPR reads as follows: '(III) . . . everyone shall be entitled to . . . (e) to examine, or have examined, the witness against him and to obtain the attendance and examination of witnesses on his behalf under the same conditions as witnesses against him.' The same wording is found in Art. 6 (III) d ECHR. Art. 8 (II) f AmCHR and reads as follows: '(II) . . . every person is entitled to . . . (f) the right of the defence to examine witnesses present in the court and to obtain the appearance, as witnesses, of experts or other persons who may throw light on the facts'. Again, the AfCHPR does not include an explicit reference to this. From the wording, it becomes obvious that at least three separate issues are

---

[359] Art. 65 Rome Statute, which contains the former guilty plea proceedings, is even praised as an example of the constructive approach of the delegates and their willingness to explore new grounds in combining different legal traditions; see Guariglia, in Trifterer (ed.), *Commentary on the Rome Statute*, Art. 65, No. 1.

[360] Behrens, 6 Eur.J.Crime Cr.L.Cr.J. (1998), 439–40.

[361] The fact that the Rome Statute refuses to speak of a 'guilty plea' and speaks of 'admission of guilt' instead is not a mere linguistic modification. In fact, the procedure now in place at the ICC is only an atavistic reminder of the 'plea' practice in the Anglo-American tradition. The consequences on the trial that an admission produces are minimal, as is shown by Art. 65 Rome Statute.

addressed in these articles: first, the precondition already embodied in the principle of an oral trial, that witnesses must appear before the court and give an oral statement; secondly, the right to challenge the witnesses brought forward by the prosecution, and, thirdly, the right to call witnesses on one's own behalf under the same conditions as the prosecution's witnesses.

1. The presence of prosecution witnesses

For a witness to be thoroughly examined, he or she must be present. As the defendant has the right to examine all the witnesses, they must all be present. It is not feasible for the prosecution to have persons interviewed prior to the trial and use the signed record of this examination, for example, as evidence during trial.

(a) Human rights law   Members of the HRC questioned state representatives, within the reporting procedure under Art. 40 ICCPR, as to whether authorities were permitted to rely on written statements alone. Such a practice is presumed to be inconsistent with Art. 14 (III) e ICCPR.[362] The Sixth Amendment to the US Constitution therefore enshrines the accused's right to be confronted with the witnesses against him. Sometimes the prosecution relies on evidence from a witness who is not actually present in court. This is the case with police informers, as in *Kostovski v Netherlands*[363] or with undercover agents as in *Lüdi v Switzerland*.[364] Usually these witnesses are interviewed by either a police officer or a judge; the interviewer then gives evidence in court. The identity of these witnesses is withheld from both the defence and the public. The reason is usually given as protection of these witnesses against potential reprisals. Another obvious reason for such anonymity is that it enables the police to use the agent or informer again in the future.

The admissibility of evidence is seen by the ECourtHR mainly as a matter of national law.[365] What matters from the court's point of view is to ascertain whether or not the proceedings are fair as a whole. In this respect, it seems unfair if a defendant has no opportunity whatsoever of directly addressing and challenging a crucial witness against him, and if the identity of the witness is not disclosed to him, without which it is not possible to challenge the person's reliability properly.[366] Despite the

---

[362] See McGoldrick, *Human Rights Committee*, 409.

[363] ECourtHR *Kostovski v Netherlands* Judgment 20 November 1989, Series A No. 166.

[364] ECourtHR *Lüdi v Switzerland* Judgment 15 June 1992, Series A No. 238.

[365] ECourtHR *Kostovski v Netherlands* Judgment 20 November 1989, Series A No. 166, para. 39, with reference to earlier case-law.

[366] This does not necessarily need to be in open court; it can also take place at a pre-trial stage; see ECourtHR *Kostovski v Netherlands* Judgment 20 November 1989, Series A No. 166, paras. 41–2.

government argument that the measures were necessary to fight serious and organized crime and to protect society, the ECourtHR found that Art. 6 (I) taken together with (III) d had been violated.[367]

The protection of undercover agents is also a highly sensitive area. If the police were to reveal the identity of such an agent, further use would be impossible, as he would then be publicly known as a police officer. In the *Lüdi* case, the ECourtHR drew a fine distinction between police informers, whose identity and background might not even be known to the police, and undercover agents, who are part of the police force and whose actions are supervised by the police or even by a judge.[368] The latter are therefore *per se* more reliable. Nevertheless, even in this case, the ECourtHR found the defendant to be bereft of his right to examine witnesses, an essential fair-trial component.[369]

In view of the general terms used in these and related judgments, the ECourtHR does not seem to be 'wholly consistent' on the problem of witnesses who do not give direct evidence during trial.[370] There is another group of people who need protection in court: witnesses who are victims, or are in danger of becoming victims should their identity be revealed to the defence. This is of major importance in trials concerning sexual offences or cases involving child witnesses in particular. At least the victim-witness's right to privacy is jeopardized by his role as a witness, and often his life or physical safety may also be in danger. Therefore a balance must be found between the accused's right to a fair trial and the rights of the witnesses who are under threat. As M. Leigh teaches us, the term 'balancing fairness' is certainly misleading:[371] the proceeding against the defendant must be fair, always, without exception. So, properly speaking, we cannot speak of balancing trial fairness against anything else, because this would mean that we would accept the trial being a little unfair, which we cannot do. However, if we follow the ECourtHR in this matter, we must look at this by taking all the circumstances of the individual case into account in order to decide this question. If a witness is particularly endangered, for example, because he has

---

[367] Ibid., paras. 44–5.

[368] ECourtHR *Lüdi v Switzerland* Judgment 15 June 1992, Series A No. 238, para.49.

[369] The ECourtHR again argued a violation of a combination of Art. 6 (I) and (III) d ECHR. Interestingly the ECourtHR also mentions that the undercover agent was known to the defendant, physically speaking at least, because he had done the drug deal with him. ECourtHR *Lüdi v Switzerland* Judgment 15 June 1992, Series A No. 238, paras. 49–50. The ECourtHR has upheld a strict opinion against undercover agents who function as agents provocateurs recently in *Teixeira de Castro v Portugal*, Reports 1998-IV. The BGH did not follow the decision but grants a more lenient sentence if the criminal act was provoked by an undercover agent, compare BGH NJW 2000, 1123, or BGH NStZ 2000, 385.

[370] Harris, 212.

[371] M. Leigh, 91 AJIL (1997), 80 at 81.

been threatened, the question that must be asked, taking all the relevant facts of the trial into account, is: can the trial still be a fair one for the defendant, even if the identity of this witness is not disclosed. What must be taken into consideration are the minimum rights listed as essential to a fair trial in Art. 14 (III) ICCPR. Properly phrased, the question is thus: can the trial still be considered fair, if certain provisions of Art. 14 ICCPR are infringed in order to protect other people's rights?

There are certainly several possible solutions to the above problem. First, one could have the witness interviewed outside the trial, for example by a judge, and the record simply read out, or hear the interviewing judge as a witness at the trial stage. The latter method has the great disadvantage of being hearsay evidence, which is inherently problematic in common law.[372] However it does have the great advantage of being quickly available, so that reliance could still be placed on the written statement or the judge even months later and security and anonymity of the witness guaranteed. This applies to child witnesses in particular, and also to rape cases, where the victim-witness may be under pressure or unwilling to give evidence at trial for other reasons. Alternatively, the questioning could be video-recorded and played back as evidence during the trial. To uphold the idea of cross-examination, both parties, prosecution and defence, could be given the opportunity to question the witness separately and have these sessions video-taped. Both recordings could be used as evidence in court.[373]

Secondly, the identity of the witness could be withheld from the public at least, that is, the public could be excluded. As shown above, it is possible to do this without violating the human right to a public trial, either because it is necessary in order to protect a party or because it is necessary in the interests of justice. If excluding the public is not sufficient protection, the witness's identity could also be withheld from the defendant and only revealed to the professional participants in the trial. This was done in *X v UK*; the identity of the witnesses was withheld from the public and the defendant by means of screening.[374] The ECommHR found that this did not infringe the right to examine witnesses, as their identity was disclosed to both prosecution and defence, and they could be questioned without obstacle.

Thirdly, the witness could be protected through a video link, so that he

---

[372] The hearsay problem will be discussed below in greater detail.

[373] A procedure of this type would be possible at the ICTY by virtue of Rule 90A, via a deposition as provided for in Rule 71. This possibility is triggered in cases 'where it is not possible to secure the presence of a witness'. Although this provision is not included among the witness-protection measures, there is no reason why this procedure should not be made available for this purpose via an extensive interpretation of the letter of Rule 90A.

[374] ECommHR *X v UK* Appl. No. 20657/92 15 EHRR (1993) CD, 113–15.

is sheltered from the defendant and the public and can give his testimony in a non-coercive atmosphere, while the judges could still get an impression of the witness's demeanour. This method is used in Germany and England, in particular for child witnesses.[375]

Fourthly, the state could ensure the security of the witnesses by a protection scheme of some kind, guaranteeing his safety through police protection, etc. This would take place outside the court room only and during the trial everything would be as usual. The witness' identity would be made public, and the witness would be under scrutiny by lawyers from both sides. This would certainly interfere less with the right to examine witnesses, but would be less safe for them and often insufficient.[376] National states use this method in order to guarantee immunity to former terrorists who testify against other terrorists.[377] It does not seem suitable for protecting the integrity of witnesses who have been victims of sexual attacks. A great deal of the necessary protection actually concerns the conduct of the questioning in the court room.

The four points can also be ranked in a reverse scale: the more important the witness's right and the more endangered it is, the more readily we can proceed to apply the protection measure. A simple case would make the fourth solution applicable, whilst an exceedingly sensitive case would trigger solution number one. Before I pursue this idea any further, I will take a look at the practice at the ICTY.

(b) Law and practice at the ICTY   The problem of the presence of witnesses has arisen before the ICTY. Even during the drafting stage of the Rules of Procedure and Evidence, the judges took into account the fact that, given the circumstances of the civil war on the territory of the former Yugoslavia, there would be considerable reluctance on the part of witnesses to appear before the ICTY to testify.[378] The Rules of Procedure basically created four measures for the purpose of alleviating this distress

---

[375] Compare Regional Court (Landgericht) Mainz, NJW (1996), 208. In the so-called Mainzer Modell the person is examined by the judge in an ante-room. This examination is transmitted to the court room where the actual trial takes place. Critical with respect to the principle of an oral trial and the principle of the immediacy of evidence is the comment of Dahs, NJW (1996), 178. The so-called English Model is based on a 'two-way closed circuit television'. The German legislator has incorporated witness testimony via video link in § 247a StPO. Under this rule both models are arguably legitimated. Compare the first decision of the BGH in this regard, 15. 9. 1999, JZ 2000, 471, commented by Vassilaki, JZ 2000, 474.

[376] Financial questions should be left aside, but the third alternative would be by far the most expensive one for the state budget.

[377] In Germany, this witness scheme, called *Kronzeugenregelung* (crown witness arrangement), was introduced several years ago (*Kronzeugengesetz*, Crown Witness Act 1989), but has hardly ever been invoked and remains very controversial; compare Kleinknecht and Meyer-Goßner, A3a Vorbemerkung.

[378] See ICTY First Annual Report (1994), paras. 75, 78.

factor:[379] (1) deposition of evidence according to Rule 71; (2) protection of identity from the accused according to Rule 69 or from the public according to Rule 75; (3) the Victim and Witnesses Unit according to Rule 34, and (4) the special provisions for testimony in cases of sexual assault by virtue of Rule 96. These purpose-made provisions will now be examined more clearly.

By virtue of Rule 34, the ICTY operates a Victims and Witnesses Unit under the auspices of the Registry.[380] Its purpose is to provide care, support, and protection to witnesses testifying before the ICTY for both the prosecution and defence.[381] In this way the ICTY contributes to the fourth of the above solutions. The unit has, however, very limited resources and can only operate if and so long as the protected persons are present at the court to give evidence.

On one occasion Trial Chamber II allowed the defence to present a witness by means of a video link from Banja Luka to the Hague.[382] The Trial Chamber stressed that this was an exceptional measure, not even foreseen in the Rules of Procedure. Whether this procedure would also be permitted for the prosecution cannot be anticipated from this decision, which only dealt with a defence witness. However, the Trial Chamber furnished a list of priorities. Accordingly, the general rule is: physical presence of the witness. Video presence does not enjoy the same status, but carries more weight than testimony by deposition (although provided for in Rule 71!). This might lead to the conclusion that, as the testimony of a prosecution witness could also be presented via deposition (Rule 71), presentation via video must be allowed *a minore ad maius*. In 1997, Rule 90A was amended in this regard. Since then, a video-conference link may be held in exceptional circumstances and in the interests of justice.[383]

In the *Tadic* case, the prosecution requested anonymity for several victims and witnesses.[384] The Trial Chamber held that the identities of several victims and witnesses can be indefinitely withheld from the accused and his counsel.[385] The Trial Chamber II discussed the issue of anonymity of witnesses in detail, struggling to find the right balance between the accused's and the witness's rights. In doing so, it laid down

---

[379] Compare ICTY First Annual Report (1994), paras. 79–83.

[380] These provisions are much applauded; see e.g. Bassiouni, *The Law of the ICTY*, 848.

[381] The impressive work of the Victim and Witness Unit is described in more detail in the ICTY Third Annual Report (1996), paras. 118–26.

[382] ICTY Trial Chamber II, *Tadic* case, Decision allowing testimony by video link, 25 June 1996. The witness was heard on 15 Oct. 1996.

[383] 13th Plenary Session on 25 July 1997.

[384] The prosecutor's motion of 18 May 1995 requesting measures for victims and witnesses.

[385] Decision 10 August 1995 on the Prosecutor's Motion Requesting Protective Measures for Victims and Witnesses, Case No. IT-94-1-T.

several guidelines and conditions as to when the identity of the witness may be kept secret from defence and public:[386] (1) There must be real fear for the safety of the witness; the ruthless character of the crime would justify such fears. (2) The prosecutor must establish the importance of the witness for the prosecutor's case. (3) The witness must be absolutely trustworthy and no evidence to the contrary be available. (4) The ICTY's own protection scheme must be insufficient to protect the victim. As to conduct of the trial, the ICTY finds three more criteria. (5) The judge must know the witness' identity and (6) must be able to observe the demeanour of the witness to assess his reliability. (7) The defence must be in a position to question the witness on issues that are unlikely to reveal his identity.

These guidelines, stemming from the ICTY Trial Chamber II majority,[387] were also applied by the Trial Chamber I in the *Blaskic* case.[388] They have nevertheless been heavily criticized as ridiculing the accused's right to a fair trial,[389] although the Trial Chamber has also met with support.[390] Both sides, however, seem to misunderstand the provision concerning the right to examine witnesses. As we have seen before, its meaning in the common law environment differs from its meaning in civil law. In the latter, the judge's familiarity with the facts of the case and the examination of the witnesses by the judge makes non-disclosure of identities less intrusive as regards fair trial. The provision itself states that the right is either to examine or to have examined. From a human rights point of view, both must be accepted as equally 'fair'. We will now scrutinize theory and practice in both systems. Analysis of the shortcomings of both

---

[386] Ibid., para. 77.

[387] The judgment was passed with a majority of 2:1. Judge Ninian Stephen dissented. A summary of both the majority and the dissent is given by King and La Rosa 8 EJIL (1997), 123 at 148–50.

[388] *Blaskic*, Case No. IT-95-14-T Decision 6 November 1996 on the Application of the Prosecutor Dated 17 October 1996 Requesting Protective Measures for Victims and Witnesses. The only difference between the two Chambers is that Trial Chamber I would like to see a very restrictive application of these guidelines. Anonymity can solely be granted if there is proof of 'exceptional circumstances'. The 'armed conflict' which the Trial Chamber II had accepted as 'exceptional circumstances' *par excellence* could no longer be seen as such, because the armed conflict had ceased.

[389] See M. Leigh, 90 AJIL (1996), 216 and 91 AJIL (1997), 80. Leigh agrees with Judge Stephen and criticizes the majority decision mainly on three grounds; first, that Art. 22 Statute ICTY, which addresses witness protection, only relates to non-disclosure towards the public, not towards parties; secondly, that 'fair' cannot be reduced to a 'little bit unfair'; and, thirdly, that the ICTY would lose its credibility if it radically changed due process rules.

[390] Chinkin, 91 AJIL (1997), 75. For Chinkin the protection of the victim or witness must necessarily be in conflict with the fair trial of the accused. This conflict has to be balanced. Art. 14 ICCPR is not an absolute right. Furthermore, the whole establishing of the ICTY aims at contributing to peace and security in the area; witnesses therefore have to be encouraged to come forward and testify. They will not do so if no effective guarantees as to their safety can be given. Compare also Swaak-Goldman, 10 LJIL (1997), 215 at 219.

systems is intended to show that a combination of both systems could provide a remedy. This would result in some modifications to the structure of the trial that would help to solve the problem of protection of witnesses more easily.

2. The right to examine witnesses

Common lawyers will immediately think of cross-examination in criminal cases, which is often spectacular and provides the perfect opportunity for a skilled defence lawyer to pick enormous holes in the testimonies of the prosecution witnesses and so destroy the prosecution's case. Not forgetting that the truth is the aim of the trial, Wigmore called the cross-examination the greatest engine ever invented for the discovery of the truth.[391] This praise of common law practice is contested by most Continental lawyers, as in their view cross-examination does not ensure a free and frank testimony from witnesses.[392] The accusatorial system is based on examination and cross-examination, so that the defendant himself questions the witnesses, or has them questioned by his barrister.[393] It is important to note that the witness is not left to tell his own perception of things. He may only comment on questions asked by the barristers.[394]

The inquisitorial system leaves the examination of the witnesses to the judge. Furthermore, on the Continent witnesses are expected to express themselves 'spontaneously', that is, to tell their story without being asked specific questions.[395] Only then can they be submitted to questioning by the judge. In general, the defence cannot question the witness directly, but only through the judge as an intermediary. Both systems claim to make the truth more accessible. As human rights treaties clearly embrace both approaches and declare them both compatible with human rights, a more detailed examination should reveal which method suits the International Criminal Court better.

The right to examine witnesses is expressed in human rights treaties without restrictions.[396] Yet, it has been held by the ECourtHR that the right to cross-examine is not an absolute right[397] and that we must look at the way in which the examination is conducted. The main concern, as pointed out by the ECourtHR in the *Engel* judgment,[398] lies in the guarantee of

---

[391] Wigmore, quoted by Lidstone in Andrews (1982), 93.
[392] Vouin, 5 ICLQ (1956), 157 at 168.
[393] The US Supreme Court, *Alford v US* 282 US 687 (1931), held that it follows from the Sixth Amendment that the government may not rely on witnesses without submitting them to cross-examination.
[394] McEwans, *Evidence in the Adversarial Process*, 13.
[395] Vouin, 5 ICLQ (1956), 157 at 168.　　　　　　　　　　[396] Nowak, Art. 14, No. 53.
[397] ECourtHR *Engel v Netherlands* Judgment 23 November 1976, Series A No. 22, para. 91.
[398] Ibid.

equal treatment in accordance with the principle of 'equality of arms'. This was assessed by the ECommHR in its report in *Bönisch v Austria*.[399] In this case, the domestic court did not appoint further expert witness, although it knew that the point in question was contested. The ECommHR rejected the government's idea that the expert, as an ancillary organ of the court, is neutral.

We can therefore conclude that equity of arms is a major guideline for this part of the trial. The parties must be treated equally. It might therefore not be sufficient to examine one witness only, if the content of this testimony is contested. The court may have to examine a second witness who contradicts the view of his predecessor in the witness stand. Furthermore it would certainly be wrong to allow one side to ask questions while the other is only permitted to listen to the answers. Defence and prosecution have to be treated equally.

In the adversarial process in particular, it is necessary to assess the problem of whether and to what extent, if any, the judge may control or influence the questions. The European organs in Strasbourg have dealt with several cases that addressed the problem of whether and to what extent questions could be rejected that did not serve to ascertain the truth. The problem undoubtedly goes much further than this. The witness may need to be protected from questioning. The appalling cases of rape victims being cross-examined for hours by their alleged attackers bear witness to this pressing need.[400] The Continental system is quite different; there, prosecution and defence must be silent and are only allowed to play the role of passive protectors permitted to object to questions.[401] The judge formulates the questions even if the point is raised by counsel. This means that on the Continent the judge has full control over every step of the interrogation.[402] As already stated, the adversarial system tends to see the judge more as an impartial 'umpire'. In exercising this role, he can object to questions, and will do so, if the questions seem irrelevant to the case.[403] He must warn the witness that he need not answer a question, if

---

[399] ECourtHR *Bönisch v Austria* Judgment 6 May 1985, Series A No. 92, Report of the ECommHR 12 March 1984, 20.

[400] A recent case in England, in which a subsequently convicted rapist spent days humiliating his two victims by cross-examining them in person, having rejected the services of a lawyer, induced the Home Secretary, Jack Straw, to call for a change in the law. See the *Guardian* (7 November 1997), 7.

[401] McEwans, *Evidence in the Adversarial Process*, 9.

[402] Although the German system includes a clause foreseeing cross-examination in § 239 StPO, it is under the condition that both parties agree to it and it is seldom invoked. It is considered foreign to the German procedural system; see Roxin, *Strafverfahrensrecht*, § 42 D III 2; what is more likely is a so-called informal cross-examination by virtue of § 240 (II) StPO, which implies direct questioning by prosecution and defence but is under the strict control of the judge (§ 241 (II) StPO).

[403] McEwans, *Evidence in the Adversarial Process*, 15.

he is thereby likely to incriminate himself.[404] He can likewise step in to protect a witness against abuse and bullying during cross-examination.[405] This, however, is playing with fire. If the judge goes too far in disallowing certain questions, he will be considered on appeal as having violated the defendant's right to examine the witness. If such a complaint is granted on appeal, the conviction is quashed and the defendant free to go.

To fully understand the differences between the systems, it is necessary to examine the underlying objectives. Both, as should be clear, aim to establish the truth to the fullest, and as quickly and easily as possible. The inquisitorial system relies on the impartiality of the judge, who, in an independent and unbiased manner, interrogates the witnesses and thereby excavates the truth. The adversarial system doubts the judge's ability to do this. Especially with his prior knowledge of the facts and evidence, he will already have a fixed opinion when he starts the interview, and his questions will only aim at having his preconception corroborated.[406] Certainly, the fact that witnesses can give their testimony without interruption enhances the chances of hearing unexpected things. On the other hand, witnesses have been 'prepared' by the police, and the police have most probably helped to refresh their memory. Interrogation by two barristers with opposite intentions, on the contrary, aims at destroying any prefixed opinions. The questions are likely to uncover any uncertainties on the part of the witness. Logical as this might seem, cross-examination is often used to confuse witnesses and get them to contradict themselves in order to establish their unreliability.[407] Furthermore, as counsel has total editorial control over the witnesses, the answers are often reduced to 'yes' or 'no'. This might be very misleading.[408] These two components have the effect that it is fairly easy to make confident and truthful witnesses look uncertain and unreliable. The conclusion has therefore been drawn by some experts that Anglo-American trials are little more than highly stylized dramatizations of reality.[409] It must be kept in mind that the Anglo-American trial is shaped to fit the jury system. It is hard to imagine twelve lay persons inquiring into a case. Therefore, the parties involved present the evidence. They do so in a manner intended to provoke a certain reaction in the jurors. With transferral of the 'judging element' to professional

---

[404] Lidstone in Andrews (1982), 88. Rule 90D at the ICTY provides for the right of a witness not to incriminate himself. As a matter of fairness it seems necessary that he be warned by the judge, should he run the danger of making incriminating statements.

[405] Leigh, *Human Rights*, 75.

[406] Compare Schünemann, Verfahrensgerechtigkeit 1995, 215 at 228; and the same recently in StV 2000, 159.

[407] McEwans, *Evidence in the Adversarial Process*, 16.

[408] Lidstone in Andrews (1982), 92.

[409] W. L. Bennett and M. S. Feldmann, *Reconstructing Reality* (New Brunswick, NJ, 1981), 124.

judges, the situation changes. There is no need to relegate the judges to the role of mere spectators. The philosophy of a system that seeks laymen verdicts is not transferable to a system that is based on the judgments of professional judges. As they are expected to give reasoned verdicts, they must be in a position to influence the proceedings in a way that satisfies their sense of reality and justice.

Again, both systems have their advantages and major shortcomings, too. A more balanced approach may be found in a compromise. As we have already seen, the ICTY provides for an adversarial system with inquisitorial elements both in the presentation and examination of evidence. It is therefore not exclusively based on cross-examination. Judges may ask questions, may even present evidence themselves (Rule 85). Although cross-examination is the main vehicle for finding the truth, it takes place under the supervision of an active judge, which has recently been expressively incorporated in Rule 90G.[410] The judge is not a passive 'umpire' but actively involved in establishing the truth.[411]

This system should be used as a blueprint for an ICC and further developed. The trial at the ICC would adopt a structure based on the adversarial system. Before the hearings start, the trial would be prepared by the judges together with the prosecutor and defence counsel. At the trial, the evidence would be presented to the court by the parties, namely, prosecution and defence. Additional evidence could be requested or presented by the judges as they deem it necessary. Presentation of the evidence and witnesses should, in principle, be left to the interaction between prosecution and defence, that is, cross-examination. This would take place under the active supervision of the judge. He would be permitted to interfere at any time with the questioning by the counsel of either side and address the witness himself.

If one accepts this combined system of judge and counsel working together in establishing the truth during presentation and examination of evidence, the problem of the protection of witnesses appears in a different light. One could imagine a sliding-scale attributing more responsibility to the judge as the need for protection increases.

Generally, a witness and victim unit should counsel and aid those who

---

[410] Rule 90G was added at the 18th Plenary Session on 9–10 July 1998. Although this amendment was inserted mainly for the purpose of accelerating the trial (see Jones, *The Practice of the ICTY*, Rule 90, p. 418), it is nevertheless a confirmation of the inquisitorial element of the role of the judges.

[411] A system based on an inquiring judge 'supervised' by cross-examination can likewise be imagined. The shortcomings of the systems in their pure form could be counterbalanced by implementing a controlling element from the opposite system. As the discussions on the ICC do not contemplate a Continental-based system I shall follow this possibility no further. As to the discussion of modifying the national system in Germany, see Roxin, *Strafverfahrensrecht*, § 42, No. 58, and Schünemann, GA (1978), 161 at 164.

come to the ICC to testify, both for the prosecution and for the defence. This should be available for all persons who request assistance. An unproblematic witness could be examined by the parties with hardly any interference by the judge. The judge would intervene if, for example, the witness was about to incriminate himself, or was put under undue pressure or bullied. In cases where the coercive atmosphere of the court room might harm the witness, for example with a child witness, the examination could be held via video link, where all the participants could see and communicate with each other unhampered. The examination in this case could be left to the parties without interference by the judge. This is a useful method of examination if the presence of the witness in the court room is likely to distort his testimony. The more vulnerable the witnesses, the more they need protection. 'Weak' witnesses are likely to be confused by the questioning of several persons. The examination could then be transferred to the judge, who, as a single examiner with a calming voice, could earn the trust of the testifying person. In a very serious case, he would then examine entirely on his own and act as a mediator for questions raised by counsel. This scale applies *mutatis mutandis* to all the following recommendations regarding the protection of the witness.

In cases where the danger stems from the public or disclosure of the identity of the witness to the public, publicity could be excluded for this part of the trial. We have seen above that the exclusion of the public is possible for the protection of the private life of the victim, just as it is possible for the protection of other witnesses. From the point of view of cross-examination, this exclusion is unproblematic, as examination can go ahead in camera.

If the well-being or the life of a witness is in real jeopardy and cannot otherwise be protected, the identity of a witness may be withheld from the defendant. This could be achieved through technical devices that distort the voice and the face. The effect would be that the witness would be present in the court room, and could be closely watched by the judges, who must know his identity, and questions could be put to him by both parties. In an event of extremely acute danger, his identity could be withheld from the defence counsel, too, who, as a professional lawyer with a public mandate, should otherwise be entrusted with the identity of every witness.

These protection schemes are the exception to the general rule of presence in a public court room and must therefore be interpreted restrictively. The party who applies for enhanced protection of one of its witnesses must show, first of all, that the witness is absolutely reliable and indispensable to the case and, secondly, that he cannot be protected in any other way. These conditions must be assessed by taking into account the seriousness and ruthlessness of the crime involved and the situation with respect to the witness's safety. All other possible means of protection must be considered insufficient. Two issues are extremely important for the examination of witnesses: (1) the judges must always be in a position to observe the witness' demeanour in order to properly assess his reliability, and (2) the defence counsel must always be given the opportunity to scrutinize the testimony. To achieve the latter purpose, the defence need not necessarily be allowed to address the witness personally. It is sufficient if a question raised by the defence counsel is discussed with the witness, albeit through the mediation of the judge.

A system, like the one proposed here, consisting of a combination of an adversarial, cross-examination-based structure on the one hand, and an inquisitorial system with an active judge on the other, would be compatible with the relevant human rights provisions and best suit the aim of an ICC. In particular, the enhanced role of the judge could contribute to the protection of other people involved in the trial without leading to 'unfairness' during the trial stage.

3. The right to call witnesses

According to the General Comments of the HRC, one of the main concerns of Art. 14 (III) e ICCPR is to 'guarantee to the accused the same legal powers of compelling the attendance of witnesses'.[412] Two notions are involved here: first, the power to coerce the attendance of witnesses and, second, the duty of the state to meet the resultant expenses.[413]

It has been held that the wording of Art. 14 (III) e ICCPR, corresponding to Art. 6 (III) d ECHR, restricts the right to obtain the attendance of witnesses considerably by making it subject to 'the same conditions as witnesses against him'. According to the *travaux préparatoires*, the first draft of the HRComm 1949 did not contain the above additional clause.[414] The provision that makes the text correspond to Art. 6 (III) d ECHR was inserted in the final version (1952).[415] This could be broadly interpreted as meaning that the court could choose not to hear any witnesses at all, if the prosecution does not rely on the testimony of witnesses, either. The ECourtHR has certainly restricted the right to call witnesses.[416] It has left it up to the national courts' discretion to decide whether it is appropriate to call witnesses.[417] In accordance with their *quatrième instance* doctrine, the Strasbourg authorities merely supervise the national court's decision

---

[412] HRC General Comment 13 (Article 14), para. 12.

[413] Under German law, the state must pay for the expenses of all witnesses. It is a corollary to the inquisitorial system that the court calls witnesses on behalf of the prosecution and of the defence, see § 71 StPO.

[414] Generally, see Bossuyt, *Guide*, 301.

[415] This originated from a British motion, compare Nowak, Art. 14, No. 52.

[416] ECourtHR *Engel v Netherlands* Judgment 23 November 1976, Series A No. 22, para. 91.

[417] ECourtHR *Vidal v Belgium* Judgment 22 April 1992, Series A No. 235-B, para. 33.

with regard to a fair trial. Although the national courts are thus given relatively broad discretion, they must not violate the principles of fairness
and equality of arms.[418] The minimum guarantee of the right to 'call
witnesses on one's own behalf' is the requirement placed on the judge to
give reason for rejecting the hearing of defence witnesses. This requirement has been established by the ECourtHR in *Vidal v Belgium*.[419]
According to Harris, the judgment of the ECourtHR in this case could also
be read as a substantive criticism; the ECourtHR seemed to have criticized
the decision as such not to hear four witnesses giving evidence for the
defence against a serious allegation, although the defendant was in
danger of being sentenced to long-term imprisonment.[420]

However, the court must ensure the attendance of witnesses whom it
has decided to hear. The ECommHR has repeatedly found that a court
must take appropriate steps to guarantee the presence of the witness.[421]
The consequence of this is that the defence must have some means of
compelling the attendance of the witness. If necessary, the police must
escort the witness to the court room, if he does not appear voluntarily.
Although the Sixth Amendment of the United States Constitution
contains a right of the accused to compel the attendance of witnesses in
his favour, it does not appear to be common practice in the USA for the
government to have to pay the expenses of a defence witness.[422] This
appears to be incompatible with the above human rights standard.

At the ICTY, the defence in *Tadic* requested to be allowed to present
witness testimony via video link from Banja Luka to the court room in the
Hague. The Trial Chamber II granted the request,[423] although it repeated
that the general rule is that the witnesses should be physically present at
the court when giving their testimony. Exceptions arise if the defence can
persuade the court that (1) the witness has been prevented from travelling
to the court (due to the ongoing conflict) and/or (2) the testimony is
important enough to make it unfair to proceed without it. It would then
be in the interests of justice to install the video link, even if this is not foreseen in the Rules of Procedure. The video link must be set up in a manner
that permits as much similarity as possible with the situation in which the
witness is actually present in court; that means that cross-examination
must be allowed (in accordance with the above limits) and each of the
participants (accused, witness, defence, prosecution, and judges) must be

---

[418] Nowak, Art. 52, No. 52.
[419] ECourtHR *Vidal v Belgium* Judgment 22 April 1992, Series A No. 235-B, para. 34.
[420] Harris, 269.
[421] ECommHR *X v FRG* Decision 15 December 1969, Appl. No. 3566/68, 31 CD 31 at 35,
and *X v FRG* Decision 14 July 1970, Appl. No. 4078/69, 35 CD, 121 at 125.
[422] Osakwe in Andrews (1982), 286.
[423] ICTY Trial Chamber II, *Tadic* case, Decision allowing testimony by video link, 25 June
1996.

able to see each other by means of a monitor. A presiding officer will be appointed by the Chamber to ensure that testimony is given freely and voluntarily.[424] The decision concerning whether or not to testify at the ICTY cannot be left to the witness himself. The ICTY Appeals Chamber ruled that, in certain circumstances, in particular if the witness is acting in his private capacity and not as a state official, the ICTY can coerce attendance of the witness.[425] In order to ensure that witnesses are not 'financially penalized' as a result of testifying at the tribunal, the ICTY's Victim and Witnesses Unit has prepared guidelines for their reimbursement.[426]

4. The ICC

The law at the ICC reiterates the relevant provisions of Art. 14 ICCPR, addressing the examination of witnesses in Art. 67 (I) e Rome Statute.[427] For a discussion of these provisions, we can refer to the above discussion concerning Art. 14 ICCPR and take a look at the witness protection scheme at the ICC instead.[428]

Art. 43 Statute ILC addressed the protection of victim and witnesses during trial. Apart from the possibility of excluding the public, it was considered legitimate to present evidence by electronic or other special means. As an example, the Report ILC cites testimony by video camera to allow particularly vulnerable victims or witnesses to speak.[429] It points out that the rights of the accused, in particular his right to cross-examine the witness, must be protected.

The list given in Art. 43 Statute ILC is understood to be non-exhaustive. This situation should be used to achieve a flexible system with many possibilities, in order to react in a suitable way to the needs of the witness. Amnesty International complains that special features for the protection of women and children have not been included in the statute.[430] The Netherlands Advisory Committee calls for more guidelines for the proper conduct of national authorities, as collaboration with them is essential both for the work of the court and the person who is to be protected.[431]

---

[424] The statement, made under solemn declaration, has the same effect as if it were made in the court room, that is, the witness is liable to prosecution for perjury.

[425] ICTY Appeals Chamber *Blaskic* Judgment 29 October 1997, Case No. IT-95-14-AR108 bis. This question is discussed in detail by Hampson, 47 ICLQ (1998), 50.

[426] ICTY Third Annual Report (1996), para. 120.

[427] As to the 'wisdom' of this wording, see Schabas, in Trifterer (ed.), *Commentary on the Rome Statute*, Art. 67, Nos. 37–40.

[428] The importance of witness protection is underlined by the fact that cases have been reported in connection with the ICTR in particular, in which witnesses where killed after they had testified before the tribunal, see V. Morris and M. P. Scharf, *The International Criminal Tribunal for Rwanda* (Irvington-on-Hudson, NY, 1998), 536.

[429] Report ILC, Art. 43, para. 2.   [430] IOR 40/05/94, 57.

[431] Netherlands Advisory Committee, Recommendations, 7.9, in 17 NILR (1995), 225 at 243–4.

The PrepComm likewise complains about the vagueness of the provision.[432] It was suggested that the example of the ICTY should be followed and a Victim and Witness Unit be established. The case-law that has already developed at the ICTY should be taken into account at all events. The most difficult decision to make would be whether and under what circumstances the identity of the witness could be withheld from the defence. The proposals put forward at the PrepComm concerning this possibility are unclear.[433]

Although the wording of the relevant article of the Rome Statute (Art. 68 Rome Statute) is much more excessive than that of Art. 43 Statute ILC, which is rather sparse, it can nevertheless probably not provide a solution for all possible situations. The Trial Chamber at the ICC has the power to hold hearings in camera, and to allow the presentation of evidence by electronic or other special means, and it may permit the views and concerns of the victims and witnesses to be presented by legal representatives. Where the security of the witness or the family is gravely endangered, the prosecutor may withhold evidence or information, but only in proceedings prior to commencement of the trial.

The conclusion can therefore be drawn that the identity of every witness must be disclosed at the trial. More detailed regulations, however, are left up to the Rules of Procedure. As has been argued above, a system could be used where examination is left entirely in the hands of the judges when non-disclosure of the witnesses' identity is necessary for their protection. The Draft Rules give a list of possible tools for reducing the risks of an endangered witness. According to Draft Rule 6.28, the Trial Chamber decides in camera whether the identity of the witness should be withheld from the public, whether a pseudonym should be used, the testimony presented by electronic or other devices, or whether the proceedings should be conducted partly with the public excluded. The list given is not exhaustive and thus provides leeway for special methods best suited to the requirements of the individual case.

To protect and assist victims and witnesses who appear before the court, the Registrar of the ICC will set up a Victims and Witnesses Unit by virtue of Art. 43 (VI) Rome Statute. This unit, as contemplated by Draft Rules 4.1 to 4.3, will provide information, medical and psychological support, and prepare the necessary means for protection of the witness.

(IV) Rules of Evidence

Rules of evidence are part of every procedural structure. Their purpose is

---

[432] Report of the PrepComm I, para. 280.
[433] See Report of the PrepComm II, 204–6.

first of all to promote the discovery of the truth. The second aim is protection of values fundamental to the community, like the dignity and privacy of the individual. This second objective puts a limitation on the first, as the ways in which discovery of the truth may be achieved are restricted to those which also respect the dignity of the offender.[434]

An international court would face a special problem here; as an international body, the court would be confronted to a large extent with evidence that had been collected and investigated by different states. Although the court would have its own prosecutor, there would not be sufficient staff to follow a common codex of rules governing the investigation. The court, and above all the prosecutor, would have to rely heavily on evidence presented by the authorities of national states. However, the different national states each have their own rules for the collection of evidence, that is, mainly police or prosecutor powers. The extent of their compatibility with universal human rights varies—but by no means is there a common standard.

Hearsay evidence can be cited to illustrate the diversity of approaches. When we speak of 'hearsay' we must be aware of the fact that we are using imprecise terminology.[435] What is actually meant by this expression can be seen from the following: '[e]vidence by any witness of what another person stated (whether verbally, in writing or otherwise) on any prior occasion is inadmissible for the purpose of proving that any fact stated by that other person on that prior occasion is true'.[436] Nevertheless, the term 'hearsay evidence' is widely used in connection with the general rule that witnesses must give their testimony orally in court and must testify only as to matters within their own first-hand knowledge.[437] According to Anglo-American persuasion, hearsay witnesses are excluded because their testimony cannot be refuted through cross-examination.[438] The two other reasons given for the exclusion of hearsay evidence are the same in both systems, that is, that the original assertion may be distorted when retold and that the original assertion may not have been made on oath.[439] Although hearsay evidence is therefore certainly not unproblematic in the Continental system, courts there are much more

---

[434] Mann, 'Hearsay Evidence in War Crimes Trials', in Y. Dinstein and M. Tabory (eds.), *War Crimes in International Law* (The Hague, 1996), 351 at 364–5.

[435] See W. M. Best, *The Principles of the Law of Evidence* (12th edn. London, 1922), §§ 492–6. He gives many examples of situations that can be understood as hearsay evidence but are perfectly admissible as part of the *res gestae*, that is, the original proof of what has taken place. For example, the evidence of a witness who has heard the cries of a woman being attacked may, in fact, be the only other evidence available apart from the victim's testimony.

[436] P. Murphy, *A Practical Approach to Evidence* (3rd edn. London, 1988), 6.1.

[437] J. A. Andrews and M. Hirst, *Criminal Evidence* (2nd edn. London, 1992), 17.01, who call the term 'unfortunate' in 17.02.

[438] Herrmann, *Reform der deutschen Hauptverhandlung*, 412. Compare Lord Bridge in *R v Blastland* [1986] A.C. 41 at 54.

[439] Andrews and Hirst, *Criminal Evidence*, 17.05 ff.

generous in admitting hearsay witnesses. How they should be dealt with on an international level will be discussed shortly.

Having discussed the rules that should be obeyed by the ICC prosecutor during his investigation from a human rights perspective, we must also scrutinize not only the consequences of his failure to do so but also—and this may be of even greater practical importance—the consequences of a human rights violation by the national investigating agencies. Using a simple example, is the confession obtained by a national police force, by UN 'peacekeepers', or by a multinational police force using thumbscrews to appeal to the 'reasonableness' of the suspect, admissible as evidence in an international criminal court? This question may be easy to answer in the case of obvious torture but what if the confession obtained in this way is not used itself, but leads the international prosecutor who has taken over the case in the mean time to other evidence, for example, documents that prove the guilt of the accused beyond reasonable doubt, and this evidence is presented during trial—is this admissible or not? The importance of the rules of evidence go beyond the system of the international court. They can easily influence national law and practice. They could emerge not only as a guarantee that human rights are applied by the international prosecutor but also as a means of disciplining national investigating agencies. In the course of time, an international court could develop into a supervising body with more chance of developing a set of rights for the suspect during investigation in all states. This might well be a utopian vision, but, without doubt, the problem of rules of evidence will develop as a major issue at the international court.

Let us now first take a look at the admissibility of evidence in general and what human rights treaties and bodies have to say about this. Then I shall address certain special cases in greater detail.

1. Admissibility of evidence

The HRC did not address this issue explicitly. However, a side-remark in its General Comments could be seen as a hint: '[i]n order to safeguard the rights of the accused under paragraphs 1 and 3 of article 14, judges should have authority to consider any allegations made of violations of the rights of the accused during any stage of the prosecution'.[440] This statement may imply that the court is permitted or even obliged to exclude evidence that was obtained improperly. With regard to confessions obtained by means of torture and improper treatment, the HRC is more explicit: the law must reject the admissibility of statements obtained under any of the above conditions as evidence in trial.[441]

---

[440] HRC General Comment 13 (Article 14), para. 15.
[441] HRC General Comment 20 (Article 7), para. 12.

The European authorities in Strasbourg seem to see the problem of evidence as falling within the scope of Art. 6 (I) ECHR.[442] However, rules of evidence generally lie within the discretion of the Member States.[443] Different standards and approaches therefore seem compatible with international human rights. The ECourtHR stated further that admission of illegally obtained evidence did not, in itself, constitute a violation of Art. 6 (I) ECHR. However, the Court did find several safeguards that had to be complied with to avoid what would otherwise be a violation; first, the defence must have been given the opportunity to challenge the authenticity of the evidence.[444] Although this does not mean that the challenge must be successful, the defence's complaint must be heard. Secondly, there must be other evidence supporting the allegations.[445] The ECourtHR might well have reached a different conclusion in *Schenk v Switzerland*, had there been no other incriminating evidence.[446] Lastly, undue pressure or maltreatment are an issue and may well automatically render the evidence inadmissible.[447]

Rule 95, as amended, of the ICTY Rules of Procedure reads as follows:[448] 'Rule 95. Exclusion of certain evidence. No evidence shall be admissible if obtained by methods which cast substantial doubt on its reliability or if its admission is antithetical to, and would seriously damage, the integrity of the proceedings.' This rule gives a general guideline on the inclusion of evidence. In my view, the amendment does not help to make the rule any clearer. The original wording referred to international human rights norms as yardstick of admissibility. Until 1998, this reference was also contained in the heading of Rule 95, which reads: 'Evidence obtained by Means Contrary to Internationally Protected human rights'. The text, as it is now, originates from proposals made by the United Kingdom and the United States, and was arguably intended to

---

[442] Harris, 210.

[443] ECourtHR *Schenk v Switzerland* Judgment 12 July 1988, Series A No. 140, para. 46. See also Stavros, *Guarantees*, 237.

[444] ECourtHR, *Schenk v Switzerland* Judgment 12 July 1988, Series A No. 140, para. 47. This case involved a non-authorized recording of a telephone conversation by a private person who handed the evidence over to the police. The fact that the police did not breach the law themselves in order to record the conversation was certainly of importance for the ECourtHR's judgment.

[445] Ibid., para. 48. In this case, the tape was considered almost irrelevant, as the testimony of the person who recorded the conversation would have been equally valuable.

[446] See Harris, 210.

[447] The fact that the admission of such evidence is an issue of 'fair trial' was held by the ECommHR in *Austria v Italy* Report 30 March 1963, 6 YB, 740. At p. 784, the ECommHR holds that Art. 6 (II) ECHR is concerned; 'Art. 6 (II) could only be regarded as being violated if the Court subsequently accepted as evidence any admission extorted in this manner'.

[448] It was substantially amended at the 5th Plenary Session in January 1995 and at the 14th Plenary Session on 12 November 1997.

broaden the rights of suspects and accused persons.[449] In my conviction, this aim is not achieved. The new version only covers the internal side of the trial. The reliability of the evidence and integrity of the proceedings constitute the threshold for admissibility. Evidence obtained by methods contrary to human rights does not seem to fall automatically within the ambit of this norm. Even if the admissibility of evidence is left entirely in the discretion of the Trial Chamber, the rule of exclusion is nevertheless a mandatory one.[450] It is submitted here that every human rights violation must likewise hamper the integrity of the proceedings. Evidence obtained in violation of human rights must therefore be declared inadmissible.

The application of national rules is prohibited (Rule 89A), a provision that the judges at the ICTY take very literally,[451] and the Chamber is bound to put forward rules of evidence that best favour a fair trial and are compatible with the spirit of the Statute and the general principles of law (Rule 89B). The Chamber may admit any relevant evidence which it deems to have probative value (Rule 89C) and exclude evidence if its probative value is substantially outweighed by the need to ensure a fair trial (Rule 89D).[452] Although these rules are vague, they nevertheless furnish an approximate idea of what the ICTY appears to consider the correct approach: Evidence that has been obtained by a serious human rights violation must not be admitted by the Trial Chamber as evidence. This must be understood as an absolute principle and *lex specialis* to Rule 89D, and not be restricted by the 'substantially outweighed' test there.

Similarly, Art. 44 (V) Statute ILC declares as inadmissible evidence obtained by means of a serious violation of the Statute or other rules of international law.[453] The fact that the latter comprises human rights law is explained in the Report ILC.[454] However, human rights law is not considered the only possible legal barrier. Other breaches of international law could lead to an exclusion. One possible example would be 'kidnapping' of suspects by one state on the territory of another state. Unfortunately, the Statute ILC does not clearly forbid evidence obtained either directly or indirectly by means of a violation of international law.[455]

[449] Jones, *The Practice of the ICTY*, Rule 95, 427.

[450] Bassiouni, *The Law of the ICTY*, 952.

[451] ICTY Trial Chamber, *Tadic*, Separate and Dissenting Opinion of Judge McDonald on Prosecution Motion for Production of Defence Witness Statements, 27 November 1996; Trial Chamber, *Blaskic*, Hearsay Decision of 21 January 1998, para. 5.

[452] This part of the Rules of Procedure is considered to be another deviation from the adversarial system; compare ICTY First Annual Report (1994), para. 72.

[453] Art. 48 (V) Statute Working Group did not entail breaches of the statute and was limited to violations of internationally protected human rights. This is criticized by Crawford, 88 AJIL (1994), 140 at 149.

[454] Report ILC Art. 44 para. 5. Similar in this respect, the Report of the PrepComm I, para. 289.

[455] This contrasts with Art. 48 (V) Statute Working Group, which stated both types of violation are prohibited.

Art. 69 (VII) Rome Statute rules out evidence obtained by means of a violation of the Statute or of internationally recognized human rights, but only, (*a*) if the violation casts substantial doubt on the reliability of the evidence, or (*b*) if the admission would seriously damage the integrity of the proceedings. These two further requirements remain somewhat doubtful. It is submitted here that any evidence that was obtained by means of a serious violation of human rights will endanger the integrity of the proceedings.[456] Art. 69 (VIII) Rome Statute cautiously states that the Trial Chamber may not defy national law when deciding on the admissibility of evidence collected by a Member State. Arguably, this is meant to exclude debates about national evidentiary standards before the ICC, which will apply its own standard.[457]

2. Special cases

From a human rights point of view, the admissibility of evidence is not automatic. According to Strasbourg case-law, three main criteria aimed at safeguarding the rights of the accused must be fulfilled: (1) a proper defence must be possible, (2) the conviction must not be based on problematic evidence alone, and (3) any evidence stemming from the use of undue pressure on the suspect during investigation must be declared inadmissible.

Below, several 'classical' cases will be closely examined with regard to the three above-mentioned principles, and an attempt will be made to find the best solution for the International Criminal Court.

(a) Direct and indirect evidence   In principle, a distinction can be drawn between direct evidence, such as confessions, the testimony of eyewitnesses of offences, the weapon, and so forth, and indirect evidence (the German term is *Indizien- oder Anzeichenbeweis*),[458] which focuses only on circumstantial matters from which conclusions can be drawn as to what happened, for example the testimony of a witness that the defendant's car was parked outside the house at the time the crime was committed. Circumstantial evidence therefore requires that the tribunal not only accept it as evidence but also draw inferences from it.[459] For example, X is accused of torturing prisoners of war (POW). A witness testifies that he saw him leaving a POW camp on one occasion with a huge knife with obvious signs of blood on it. This testimony is direct evidence for the fact that X left the POW camp with a knife covered with blood but only

---

[456] Likewise Behrens, who opines that 'almost all imaginable cases of violations of human rights' will make evidence inadmissible, 6 Eur.J.Crime Cr.L.Cr.J (1998), 435–6. Similar Piragoff, in Triffterer (ed.), *Commentary on the Rome Statute*, Art. 69, Nos. 76–80.

[457] Behrens, 6 Eur.J.Crime Cr.L.Cr.J (1998), 436.

[458] Kleinknecht and Meyer-Goßner, § 261 No. 25.

[459] Murphy, *Evidence*, 1.2.1.1.

circumstantial as to whether or not X committed murder. The ECommHR found that judges may rely on both types of evidence in their judgment.[460]

(b) Confessions and other self-incriminating statements   With confessions, the main concern revolves, without doubt, around the third principle. In cases where maltreatment or torture led to the confession, the latter cannot be used in court.[461] This is an absolute principle.[462] The main rationale for this maxim is respect for the dignity of human beings which mainly expresses itself in the free will of the individual.

This said, further difficulties emerge with this straightforward-sounding principle. How far should this respect for free will go? When does the investigation cease to be clever and become disrespectful? What does it mean to show respect for free will?

The research of historical development of the right to silence shows that this right is relatively recent. Due to the inquisitorial concept of criminal procedure, the accused was originally forced to incriminate himself through the *ex officio* oath.[463] This practice was adopted in England in the thirteenth century, together with ecclesiastical procedure. As a consequence of the *Lilburne* case, this oath was finally banned in 1641, following struggles between Crown, Parliament, the Church, and dissidents.[464] It is interesting to note that in the colonies there was less opposition; in the United States, the oath was happily relied upon during the 1692 trials in Salem. A century later, the privilege of silence made its way into the various Bills of Rights.[465]

According to common law, it is the duty of the prosecution to prove that the confession was made voluntarily—'in the sense that it was not obtained by fear or prejudice, or hope of advantage excited or held out by a person in authority or . . . by oppression'.[466] The rationale of the exclusion of these kinds of confession is threefold: the confession is unreliable, encourages improper interrogation, and infringes the right to silence.[467] PACE (1984) s. 76 (II) changed this picture slightly; a confession must be excluded, if it was obtained (*a*) by oppression of the person who made it; or (*b*) in consequence of anything said or done which was likely, in the circumstances existing at the time, to render unreliable any confession

---

[460] ECommHR *Austria v Italy* Report 30 March 1963, 6 YB, 740, at 784.

[461] Stavros, *Guarantees*, 225–6.

[462] Compare the unequivocal wording of the ECommHR in this regard in *Austria v Italy*, 6 YB, 784.

[463] See also the historical sketch in Ch. 1, p. 10 *et subs.*

[464] See M. Berger, *Taking the Fifth* (Lexington, 1980), 6–21, for the historical background.

[465] See Ch. 1.

[466] Lord Hailsham L.C. in *D.D. v Ping Lin* (1976) AC, 574, at 600.

[467] Andrews and Hirst, *Criminal Evidence*, 19.21.

which might be made by him in consequence thereof. What we find here can be called the oppression–reliability test.[468] The burden of proving compliance with this test lies with the prosecution.[469]

In English law, in *R v Fulling*, the Court of Appeal narrowed 'oppression' down to the most severe and 'wicked' treatment, clearly excluding bodily or mental uneasiness or distress.[470] In *Mason*, the investigator lied both to the suspect and his counsel that fingerprints had been found at the scene of the crime, although there was no such evidence at all.[471] Advised then by his solicitor to make a statement, the suspect admitted the crime. This time, the Court of Appeal overturned the trial judge and quashed the conviction. The main difference between this and the former case was the involvement of the solicitor. This special relationship between client and his counsel was abused by the police and this was the ultimately the reason why the court overruled the conviction.[472] A confession is unreliable if the judge is convinced that the accused's confession was obtained in consequence of anything said or done which was likely, in the particular circumstances, to elicit an unreliable confession.[473]

The English law may be summarized as follows: A confession must not have been obtained by oppression. If it was, it is excluded, and the question of reliability need not be addressed.[474] Otherwise, the statement must be scrutinized with regard to its reliability. In addition judges have discretion to exclude confessions under the generic exclusionary rule in s. 78 PACE (1984).[475] However, this rule cannot be used as an instrument to discipline the police.[476] Neither breaches of the Codes of Practice nor of PACE itself will provoke automatic exclusion, as shown in *R v Alladice*.[477] In such cases, the burden of proof lies with the defence.[478]

The English approach is therefore very much a normative one that

---

[468] See the admissibility diagram, ibid. 19.49.

[469] So s. 76 (II) PACE (1984) explicitly.

[470] *R v Fulling* (1987) 2 All ER 65. In this case, the detained suspect confessed after the police told her that her husband was having an affair and that his mistress was being held in a neighbouring cell.

[471] *R v Mason* (1987) 3 All ER 481.

[472] A. A. S. Zuckerman, *The Principles of Criminal Evidence* (Oxford, 1989), 333–4.

[473] Cf. *R v Cox* (1991) CrimLR 276. The definition given by the Court of Appeal is not a very good one, as it uses reliability in a circular manner. Be that as it may, this is the definition applied by the court in several cases; see Andrews and Hirst, *Criminal Evidence*, 19.34–19.40, for further references and cases.

[474] Ibid. 19.24.

[475] In *R v Mason* (1987) 3 All ER 481, the Court of Appeal declared s. 78 PACE (1984) applicable to all evidence, including confessions.

[476] Andrews and Hirst, Criminal Evidence, 19.49.

[477] *R v Alladice* (1988) Cr.Ap R. 380, where the appellant was denied access to a lawyer but was otherwise understood to be fully aware of his rights and well able to cope with the situation.

[478] Andrews and Hirst, *Criminal Evidence*, 19.53. Hatchard *et al.*, *Comparative Criminal Procedure*, 240.

focuses on the material content of the confession, that is, its reliability.[479] Respect for individual rights, in the sense of an absolute legal position of the accused, like the privilege against self-incrimination, do not seem to play an important role.[480]

In the United States in contrast, the main reason for excluding confessions is to discipline the police. The right not to be compelled to testify against oneself is enshrined in the Fifth Amendment. Since it remains somewhat nebulous in its wording (when does pressure become compulsion?),[481] we have to consider the Supreme Court's rulings. The original test applied was a 'voluntarily' test. In 1896, the Supreme Court held: 'The true test of admissibility is that the confession is made freely, voluntarily and without compulsion or inducement of any sort.'[482] Stressing the achievements of the accusatorial system, Justice Black held, in *Chambers v Florida*, that the rights and liberties of accused people could not be safely entrusted to a secret inquisitorial process.[483] In *Escorbedo*[484] and *Miranda*,[485] the court started to connect this requirement with the right to a counsel. The Supreme Court thereby presumed that confessions that came about without legal assistance or without the knowledge of the right to counsel were automatically coerced.[486] As Chief Justice Warren expressed it: 'any statement taken after the person invoked his privilege cannot be other than the product of compulsion, subtle or otherwise'.[487] By setting up this link the Court was mainly intent on censuring the conduct of law enforcement agencies. After 1969, the Supreme Court watered down the radical consequences of *Miranda*. Chief Justice Burger held in *Harris v NY*: '[t]he shield of *Miranda* cannot be perverted into a licence to use perjury by way of defence'.[488] In two later decisions, namely, *Oregon v Elstad* where an 18-year-old incriminated himself, without warnings being given, in the totally uncoercive atmosphere of his parents' living-room with his mother present,[489] and *Arizona v Fulminante*, where the criminal confessed to a police agent who had claimed to be

---

[479] Zuckerman, *Principles of Criminal Evidence*, 336–8, who holds that this is the exact intention of the legislator.

[480] Ibid. 333.   [481] Berger, *Taking the Fifth*, 224.

[482] US Supreme Court *Wilson v US* 162 US 613 at 623 (1896).

[483] US Supreme Court *Chambers v Florida* 309 US 227 at 237 (1940).

[484] US Supreme Court *Escobedo v Illinois*, 378 US 478 (1964).

[485] US Supreme Court *Miranda v Arizona*, 384 US 436 (1966).

[486] Years before, the Supreme Court had already found that protracted custodial interrogation amounted to coercion; see US Supreme Court, *Ascraft v Tennessee* 322 US 143 (1944), where the complainant was kept under detention for thirty-six hours for interrogation purposes.

[487] US Supreme Court *Miranda v Arizona*, 384 US 436 (1966), at 474. Four judges dissented and pleaded for an approach that would take into account the 'totality of the circumstances'.

[488] US Supreme Court *Harris v NY*, 401 US 222 (1971), at 226.

[489] US Supreme Court *Oregon v Elstad* 470 US 298 (1985).

protecting him from the violent aggression of other prison inmates without revealing his true identity,[490] the court continued to pay lip-service to *Miranda*, but seemed to have returned in substance to the prior 'voluntarily' test. Although the conviction in *Fulminante* was quashed, this was done mainly on the grounds that there was no other evidence apart from this doubtful confession to prove the allegation. Had there been sufficient evidence to convict him otherwise, the absence of warnings would have been considered as 'harmless errors' by five judges.[491]

We can see from these decisions that the formal *Miranda* approach, although never totally abandoned, has been embedded in a substantive approach similar to that of the English courts. The criteria for the admission of confessions is whether or not they have been made voluntarily. However, the main goal of the US Supreme Court, when rejecting the admittance of evidence, is to discipline the law enforcement agencies.

Looking now at the German approach, § 136 a StPO lays down a number of prohibited methods of interrogation (*verbotene Vernehmungsmethoden*). It sets forth a list of these methods, which is not considered to be exhaustive. It clearly gives the reason for the prohibition as lying in the principle of freedom of will (*Freiheit der Willensentschließung und der Willensbetätigung*). Any statements induced by such methods are inadmissible during trial (§ 136 a (III) 2 StPO). This right cannot even be waived (§ 136 a (III) 1 and 2 StPO). It is commonly seen as an expression of Art. 1 (I) GG, which addresses the inviolability of the dignity of man.[492] As the accused does not forfeit his civil rights because he happens to be under suspicion of a crime, he must be treated as a participant, not a mere object of the proceedings against him.[493] This applies only to interrogations (*Vernehmungen*), a term interpreted by the BGH in a formal and therefore somehow restricted way, as a situation where the interrogator in his official function meets the suspect and asks for information.[494] Because of this interpretation, the BGH could declare evidence coming from telephone conversations tape-recorded with the consent of one of the participants to be admissible. Such a situation, the court has held, does not amount to an interrogation (*Vernehmung*).[495] However, the BGH

---

[490] US Supreme Court *Arizona v Fulminante* US 395 (1991).

[491] Epstein and Walker, *Constitutional Law*, 395.

[492] Kleinknecht and Meyer-Goßner Art. 136 a No. 1.

[493] BGH *Lie Detector* Judgment 16 February 1954 in BGHSt 5, 332 and BGH *Admissibility of Secret Tape Recordings* Judgment 14 June 1960, in BGHSt 14, 358, 364.

[494] BGH GrS NJW 1996, 2940 at 2941.

[495] This was the result of a trial which attracted much attention and discussion even before the decision was handed down, and a lot of criticism after it was publicized; see BGH NStZ 1996, 502. As to the discussion, compare, before the decision, Roxin NStZ 1995, 465, and after, Roxin NStZ 1997, 18, who utterly rejects the approach of the Federal Court, as for him, this practice is a clear circumvention of § 136 a StPO.

found such a technique admissible only during the inquiry into a serious crime and when all other means would be either far less successful or much more difficult to deploy. Apart from inhumane and torturous treatment, the provision also prohibits deception (*Täuschung*). Although this neither infringes human dignity nor interferes with the free will of the accused, it is not decent behaviour in a democratic society.[496] Lying to the accused is clearly outlawed.[497] The inquiring agency is therefore not allowed to pretend to have conclusive evidence,[498] or give incorrect information as to the rights of the defendant.

The German system is closely tied up with basic rights (*Grundrechte*). The exclusion of evidence is necessary for the protection of these rights. Control by the judiciary does not aim at censuring or disciplining law enforcement agencies; it is not even concerned with the reliability of the statement. The court safeguards the rights of the accused because of his inherent human dignity.

In the ICTY Rule 92 addresses the problem of confessions. It states that confessions made in accordance with the procedural guarantees for the accused during the interview by the prosecutor (Rule 63) are presumed to have been free and voluntary, unless the contrary is proved. This is similar to the English approach, namely, that the right to counsel is the guarantor of freedom from self-incrimination and, as long as this is granted, the accused is presumed to have acted voluntarily. The ICTY enhances the guarantee in that the interview must be recorded, as provided for in Rule 43. This would also make it easier to prove improper conduct on the part of the interrogator. Nsereko, however, sees a danger in the sense that the burden of proof is put upon the defendant. He submits that, when the defendant pleads inadmissibility of a confession, the standard of proof should be lowered. The *quantum* of proof should not be 'beyond reasonable doubt', but a confession should be excluded, if coercion is probable or likely according to the evidence presented by the defence.[499] Likewise Sloan, who sees the danger of the presumption of innocence being infringed.[500] However, this presumption is rather narrow in its scope of application. It clearly refers to the prosecutor at the ICTY only and is not to be applied by analogy to a national prosecutor, for example. Furthermore, it literally refers only to the 'accused' and not to the

---

[496] Kleinknecht and Meyer-Goßner Art. 136 a No. 12.

[497] BGH Judgment 31 May 1990, in BGHSt 37, 48. In this case, the police questioned a person who was under suspicion of manslaughter, pretending it was investigating a case of a missing person.

[498] Compare the English case of *Mason*, quoted above n. 475, and BGH Judgment 24 August 1988, in BGHSt 35, 328.

[499] See Nsereko, 5 CLF (1994), 507 at 542–3.

[500] See Sloan, 9 LJIL (1996), 479 at 500, referring to HRC, General Comment 13, para. 7.

'suspect'.[501] In addition, it should be left to the prosecution to prove that the procedure of Rule 63 was complied with during the interview. The accused would otherwise have to bear a double burden: first, to prove non-compliance with the rules and second, to prove the involuntary nature of his confession.[502] If the rule is interpreted in this narrow way, the provision is compatible with human rights.

In conclusion, from a human rights point of view, the rights-based approach appears preferable. Respect for human dignity must be placed at the centre of all state action as an insurmountable barrier against any attempt to subvert it. As we have seen above, the Statute ILC tends towards this approach, as it links inadmissibility with a serious violation of international law and international human rights law in particular. The proposal was made by members of the ILC to exclude from admission only evidence that was obtained in violation of a peremptory norm of human rights law.[503] The majority, however, felt that this was not enough. It is submitted here that the highest human rights standard should be applied. Only if this is the case, will the ICC contribute to the purpose of the UN to 'reaffirm faith in fundamental human rights, in the dignity and worth of the human person'[504] and to promote and encourage respect for human rights among the nations.[505] Similarly, the Preamble of the Rome Statute invokes 'the peace, security and well-being of the world', which is understood as a reference to basic, inherent values of the community of nations.[506] Serious violations of the rights of the individual as outlined in Chapter 3 above should therefore be stigmatized by the ICC by rejecting evidence stemming from such violations. In this way, the Member States will be encouraged to incorporate the necessary human rights standards into their own domestic systems.

(c) Inferences from silence   One problem that follows from the freedom from self-incrimination and is connected with the matter of confessions is the question of what should be done if the defendant refuses to give a statement or refused to do so during police inquiry, and relies on facts during trial that he has not previously mentioned. If the defendant has a right to silence, it seems logical that, if he decides to use this privilege, this cannot be held against him. Otherwise the privilege would be useless, and he would be better advised to get involved and make a statement.

---

[501] See Bassiouni, *The Law of the ICTY*, 946, who is of the opinion that the rule should not be applied to the suspect, because the protection offered by Rules 42 and 43 is not enough.

[502] Pointed out by Bassiouni, ibid.

[503] Report ILC, Art. 44, para. 5.

[504] Preamble Charter UN.

[505] Compare Art. 1 (II) Charter UN.

[506] Trifterer, in Trifterer (ed.), *Commentary on the Rome Statute*, Preamble no. 9.

In English law,[507] this whole matter is closely linked with the right to a solicitor, which is enshrined in s. 58 PACE (1984). The two leading cases in this context are *Samuel*[508] and *Alladice*.[509] In *Samuel*, the conviction was quashed, because the police did not have reasonable grounds for not granting the accused access to legal counsel. The Court found that the real reason for this denial was fears that a solicitor might advise the suspect to invoke his right to silence and, as such, was in breach of the law, although the police claimed the danger of other suspects being warned justified their decision. In *Alladice*, the Court of Appeal narrowed down the previous approach and said that the denial of access to a solicitor must be judged in the light of the circumstances of the case, so that a confession may be admissible if fairness is still guaranteed, in particular if the defendant is fully aware of his rights. The Court further stated that it was 'high time' that the judge be permitted to comment on the silence of the defendant and the caution be adjusted to accommodate this. However, this would not go as far as treating silence as tantamount to an admission.[510] Taking the two decisions together, we can say that (*a*) with a solicitor present, the confession is unlikely to be inadmissible under ss. 76 and 78 PACE (1984), whereas (*b*) if the defendant chooses to remain silent, he runs the risk of suffering disadvantages. In the literature it is also said that inferences should be allowed if a solicitor is present during police interrogations, whilst it is admitted that the right to silence is then entirely abolished.[511] Instead, other rights of suspects should be developed.[512] 'The guilty would then not be able to hide behind the right of silence and the innocent need not be afraid to speak.'[513] In Northern Ireland, the 'right to silence' was abolished in 1988 by the Criminal Evidence (Northern Ireland) Order 1988.[514]

---

[507] See the historical decline of the right to silence between 1972 and 1994, Zander in D. Morgan and G. Stephenson (eds.), *Suspicion and Silence* (London, 1994), 141.

[508] *R v Samuel* (1988) 2 All ER 135.

[509] *R v Alladice* (1988) 87 Crim.App.R. 380.

[510] Compare Zuckerman, *Principles of Criminal Evidence*, 329.

[511] Lidstone in Andrews (1982), 92. See also S. M. Easton, *The Right to Silence* (Aldershot, 1991), 171, who refers to voices that call for abolition of the non-inference rule, especially on the grounds that the right is seldom invoked and is altogether weak. It is interesting that nobody uses such an argument (factual-empirical) in favour of abolishing the right to a jury, which seems to be seldom called for and often waived, as is the right to silence.

[512] Zuckerman, *Principles of Criminal Evidence*, 307; Easton, *Right to Silence*, 171–2, vehemently contests this view. In her eyes the negative image of the 'right to silence' should not result in a fatalistic abdication of this right rather than its further promotion and strengthening.

[513] Lidstone, in Andrews (1982).

[514] There is as yet no official comment on the effectiveness of this Act; this silence—if I may take the liberty to infer from silence—casts a shadow of doubt onto the reasonableness of the abolition. Compare also the quotations from Zander in Morgan and Stephenson, *Suspicion and Silence*, 144.

In the United States a constitutional right is again involved: the Fifth Amendment provides protection against inferences from silence as to guilt.[515] After the Second World War, this right was in the spotlight on two spectacular occasions, during the 1950s McCarthy committee's communist-hunt and during the 1987 Iran–Contra Affair. In *Griffin v California*, Justice Douglas clearly rejects the idea of inferring from silence, calling this a 'remnant of the inquisitorial system . . . which the 5th Amendment outlaws'.[516] This, however, addresses silence during trial only.[517] Silence during interrogation does not necessarily come within the ambit of the Fifth Amendment. The US Supreme Court has brought it under the shield of due process as set forth in the Fourth Amendment.[518] Silence after *Miranda* warnings have been given cannot be taken into account.[519] To properly protect use of the privilege, it is prohibited (*a*) to cross-examine the defendant on the subject of earlier silence, and (*b*) for prosecutors or judges to comment to the jury on inferences which may be drawn from a defendant's failure to testify.[520]

German procedural law outlaws inferences from silence in general.[521] But it discriminates between total silence and partial silence (*teilweise oder beredtes Schweigen*). Total silence does not necessarily mean refraining from any utterance. It is silence in the legal sense if the defendant merely protests his innocence or contests his involvement with the alleged offence,[522] or if he invokes statutory limitations or procedural obstacles. Similarly, statements made by defence counsel concerning factual events cannot be taken into consideration, if the defendant does not explicitly corroborate them.[523] If, however, the defendant testifies in part on the allegations, his silence on other points, on which he refuses to comment or makes incomplete statements, can be taken into account.[524] Nevertheless inferences from silence are conditional on a hypothetical test; only if an innocent man would have defended himself where the defendant resorted to silence may this silence be held against him.[525]

---

[515] Epstein and Walker, *Constitutional Law*, 397.

[516] US Supreme Court *Griffin v California* 380 US 609 (1965) at 614.

[517] Berger, *Taking the Fifth*, 195.

[518] US Supreme Court *Doyle v Ohio* 426 US 610 (1976).

[519] Berger, *Taking the Fifth*, 197.

[520] Osakwe in Andrews (1982), 275.

[521] Kleinknecht and Meyer-Goßner § 261, Nos. 15, 16.

[522] BGH Decision 29 August 1974, in BGHSt 25, 365 at 368; BGH Judgment 26 Mai 1992, in BGHSt 38, 302 at 307.

[523] BGH Judgment 24 August 1993 in BGHSt 39, 305.

[524] BGH Judgment 26 October 1983 in BGHSt 32, 140 at 145.

[525] Kleinknecht and Meyer-Goßner, § 261, No. 17; this view is not uncontested but nevertheless seems to prevail in the literature. Others plead for a wider approach and want to take all the circumstances of the individual case into consideration; see Eser, ZStW 1986, Blei, 160 ff. It is certainly true that the defendant might have other reasons for remaining silent apart from his guilt or innocence.

Furthermore, it cannot work to the disadvantage of the defendant if he chooses to remain silent when questioned by the police but makes a statement at the main hearing before the court.[526] The opposite situation would certainly be a case of partial silence and could be considered by the trial judge.[527] Whether extra-trial statements could be taken into account when the defendant chooses to remain silent before the authorities would be a separate issue. In a situation like this, there is certainly no state compulsion involved. Statements made outside police questioning or court examination may therefore be taken into consideration.

The case of the abolition of the right to silence in Northern Ireland had to be addressed by the ECourtHR in *Murray v UK*.[528] The ECourtHR found that the freedom from self-incrimination and the right to silence were part of a fair procedure required by Art. 6 ECHR, although neither of the rights is explicitly mentioned in the document. It refused to answer the question generally, but stated that these rights are not absolute; an assessment must be made of whether the individual is denied a fair trial by denial of the right to silence.[529] However, a conviction based solely on inferences drawn from the defendant's silence would 'self-evidently' be incompatible with the Convention.[530] 'On the other hand, the Court deems it equally obvious that these immunities cannot and should not prevent that the accused's silence, in situations which clearly call for an explanation from him, be taken into account in assessing the persuasiveness of the evidence adduced by the prosecution.'[531] With these two yardsticks in mind, the ECourtHR tried to decide which of the two was more applicable in the *Murray* case. It found that there was no violation of the ECHR, because the case was 'formidable' for the prosecution.[532]

In conclusion, from a human rights point of view, there seem to be several conditions that must be fulfilled in order to allow inferences from silence to be drawn. First, a conviction cannot be based solely on inferences from silence, that is, if there is no other evidence and the accused refuses to comment, he cannot be convicted. Secondly, it seems that the evidence must be strong enough to carry the conviction on its own. Inferences from silence may only be added as corroboration of the prosecutor's case. It must not be the other way round, so that the main basis for the conviction are inferences. Art. 67 (I) g Rome Statute goes beyond the

---

[526] BGH Judgment 26 October 1965 in BGHSt 20, 281.

[527] BGH Judgment 3 December 1965 in BGHSt 20, 298.

[528] ECourtHR *Murray v UK* Judgment 8 February 1996, 22 EHRR (1996), 29.

[529] Ibid., paras. 45–6.

[530] Ibid., para. 47.

[531] Ibid., para. 47.

[532] Ibid., paras. 52–4, 58. Yet the ECourtHR found a violation of the right to access to counsel in the first forty-eight hours after the arrest as constituting a violation of Art. 6 (I) in conjunction with Art. 6 (III) c ECHR.

text of Art. 14 ICCPR when it says that the silence of the accused cannot be a consideration in the determination of guilt or innocence.[533]

(d) Hearsay The problems with hearsay evidence have already been outlined above. I now intend to take a closer look at the circumstances under which hearsay may be admitted as evidence.

In common law, first of all, the question of what exactly constitutes hearsay must be clarified. I gave a definition above, according to which hearsay evidence includes only what the witness really heard said.[534] This means it concerns only the content and truth of this. For any other relevant purpose, statements made by others may be repeated in court.[535] There are two things that are crucial for finding hearsay: first, the statement which is repeated has to have occurred prior to the giving of the evidence. This will mostly be unproblematic. Secondly, evidence must be furnished to prove the true content of the prior statement. Only if both conditions are met, can one speak of hearsay evidence, which must, in general, be inadmissible.

A glance at the rationale for the hearsay rule now reveals that the categorical exclusion of hearsay is a fairly recent phenomenon. As discussed above, early jurors were expected to represent the *fama publica*. Indeed, hearsay was permitted for hundreds of years, before it was first criticized in 1837 in *Wright v Tatham*.[536] The main reason for the criticism was that jurors were not in a position to properly weigh hearsay evidence. Furthermore, the criticism was voiced that cross-examining was not possible. These two criticisms remain true. Several more reasons have been added, such as the impossibility of taking an oath, distortion of the truth since more persons are involved, and the fact that judges and jury do not have an opportunity to observe the demeanour of the maker of the statement when it is being made.[537]

But the hearsay rule is not an absolute one. Common law and statutory law recognize several exceptions. Those mainly address the availability of witnesses and the admissibility of documentary material.[538] The US Constitution, however, does not contain the common law hearsay rule in the Sixth Amendment, as one might expect; the jurisprudence of the US Supreme Court is clear in this regard.[539] Sometimes it is even said that

---

[533] As to the drafting history see Schabas, in Trifterer (ed.), *Commentary on the Rome Statute*, Art. 67, Nos. 46–8.

[534] Of course, hearsay entails more than just the spoken word. It also applies to written statements and other documents.   [535] Murphy, *Evidence*, 6.3.

[536] See McEwans, *Evidence in the Adversarial Process*, 19.

[537] A. L. J. Choo, *Hearsay and Confrontation in Criminal Trials* (Oxford, 1996), 11.

[538] Choo, *Hearsay and Confrontation*, 102, for the common law exceptions, 142, for the statutory exceptions.

[539] US Supreme Court *California v Green* 399 US 149 (1970). Compare Osakwe in Andrews (1982), 285.

hearsay evidence is necessary. It is needed, for example, for the protection of child witnesses.[540] It also seems a bit odd that a judicial system should entrust the conviction of an accused to a jury and then not trust the jurors to be able to perform their task, that is, weigh the evidence from a common-sense point of view. It may seem rather unjustified to underestimate the ability of the jurors to assign to right amount of importance to hearsay.

German courts have less difficulty in taking hearsay evidence into account. Hearsay, in the strict sense of testimony supporting the truth of the statement, was explicitly admitted by the jurisprudence of the BGH,[541] and this is arguably the prevailing view in the literature.[542] Hearsay could violate the principle that evidence must be direct (*Unmittelbarkeitsgrundsatz*), as enshrined in § 250 StPO. This norm reads as follows: 'If the evidence is based on what a person has seen or heard, this person must be examined during the main hearing. The examination shall not be replaced by the reading of the record of a prior examination or a written statement.' This wording clearly does not encompass hearsay witnesses, as they report on their perceptions directly. Nevertheless, the judge would violate his duty to ensure that all the relevant facts of the case are clearly represented, according to § 244 (II) StPO (*Aufklärungspflicht*), if he did not hear the person who witnessed the event directly, but relied on hearsay evidence only, when it was possible to call a direct witness.[543] In the case of a police informer (*V-Mann*), who, according to German law, needs official permission to testify in court (§ 54 StPO), the trial court can rely on the statements of police officers who questioned the informer, if he does not receive the above permission.[544] Yet, the BGH made it clear that the court must take into account the fact that hearsay evidence is not the best evidence and that the reliability of the informer cannot be properly scrutinized. The court may therefore only rely on the hearsay evidence if it is supported by other important points.[545]

The Rules of Procedure of the ICTY do not contain any concrete mention of hearsay evidence. All cases must be judged according to the general rules in Rule 89, in particular Rule 89C. In the *Tadic* case, the

---

[540] Choo, *Hearsay and Confrontation*, 193. Choo favours the complete abolition of the hearsay rule.

[541] BGH Judgment 30 October 1951 in BGHSt 1, 373 and BGH Judgment 30 October 1968 in BGHSt 22, p. 268 at 270.

[542] Roxin, *Strafverfahrensrecht*, § 44 B IV.

[543] This view is not uncontested; Kleinknecht and Meyer-Goßner § 261, No. 4 are of the opinion that the court could content itself with examining the hearsay witness, even if it would be possible to hear direct evidence.

[544] BGH Judgment 1. August 1962 in BGHSt 17, 382.

[545] Ibid. The BVerfG has confirmed this decision of the BGH, see BVerfG Decision 26 May 1981, in BVerfGE 57, 250 at 292.

admissibility of hearsay evidence (or 'out-of-court statement', as the ICTY phrases it) was made a matter at issue by the defence.[546] The defence sought a ruling that hearsay was generally excluded and only admissible if its probative value 'substantially outweighed' its prejudicial effects.[547] Furthermore the defence wanted the Trial Chamber to rule on the admissibility of evidence without first hearing it. The prosecutor in his response[548] seemed to presume that the hearsay rule is for the sake of the jury and is 'unwarranted in the framework of this Tribunal in which cases are heard by experienced jurists'. The Trial Chamber majority (Judges McDonald and Vohrah)[549] followed this argument in its decision. Professional and experienced lawyers are able to hear the evidence in the context in which it was obtained and determine afterwards whether it had probative value.[550] Furthermore it tried to develop a concept of how to assess hearsay evidence. To that end it defined reliability as a necessary element of 'probative' (Rule 89C, D). It further determined reliable as voluntary, truthful, and trustworthy. In so doing the majority of the Trial Chamber paid tribute to one of the original meanings of hearsay in the adversarial trial only, that is, the difficulty unexperienced jurors have with giving the evidence its proper weight.[551] The other original reason, that hearsay cannot be falsified by cross-examination is not mentioned. The reliability test is an inquisitorial test, giving more importance to the judges than is intrinsic in the adversarial system.[552] Judge Sidhwa issued a separate opinion in the *Rajic* Rule 61 decision, interpreting the Statute ICTY in such a way that it would give preference to direct evidence over hearsay testimony. This kind of evidence needs therefore to be looked at very cautiously.[553] The general admissibility had been confirmed in the final *Tadic* judgment,[554] in *Blaskic*,[555] and in *Aleksovski*.[556]

---

[546] ICTY *Tadic* case, Defence motion on the inadmissibility of hearsay, 26 June 1996.

[547] Nsereko, 5 CLF (1994), 507 at 542, also presumed that in an adversarial system any hearsay evidence must be excluded, mainly because its probity cannot be tested by cross-examination.

[548] ICTY *Tadic* case, Response of the prosecutor to the Defence motion on hearsay, 10 July 1996.

[549] Judge Stephen issued a separate opinion.

[550] ITCY Trial Chamber II, *Tadic* case, Decision rejecting the defence motion on hearsay evidence, 5 August 1996.

[551] This line of reasoning was already alluded to in the ICTY First Annual Report (1994) para. 72.

[552] The ICTY First Annual Report (1994) para. 72, therefore discusses this point as an important deviation from the adversarial system. Bassiouni, *The Law of the ICTY*, 950, also finds that hearsay evidence is admissible in contrast to US practice.

[553] *Rajic* Rule 61 Decision, Separate Opinion Judge Sidhwa, para. 23.

[554] ICTY Trial Chamber *Tadic* Opinion and Judgment 7 May 1997, para. 555.

[555] ICTY Trial Chamber, *Blaskic*, Hearsay Decision, 21 January 1998; Defence motion to admit into evidence the witness statement of deceased witness M. Haskic, 29 April 1998; compare Jones, *The Practice of the ICTY*, Rule 89, 414.

[556] ICTY Appeals Chamber, *Aleksovski*, Decision on Prosecutor's Appeal on Admissibility

In conclusion, the fact that there is no jury at the ICC and that the judges are therefore equipped with the 'judging element' apparently alters the situation of hearsay. Departure from the adversarial system means that the strict exclusionary rule concerning hearsay evidence is not automatically applicable. In this system, it is still crucial that the evidence on which the verdict is based is immediate. Nevertheless, there is no lay jury requiring protection from irrelevant or distorted testimony. The bench of highly experienced and professional judges[557] is capable of distinguishing between reliable and unreliable testimony, after it has been presented. A strict exclusionary rule concerning hearsay evidence is therefore not necessary.

(e) Illegally obtained evidence   I cannot possibly look at all cases of potential misuse of police powers; there are far too many possibilities and, unfortunately, far too many breaches. In general, such misuse occurs when the investigating authorities use methods that are not prescribed in their rules of conduct. Telephones are tapped, surveillance cameras installed, premises searched, and the like. When discussing the conduct of the investigation during pre-trial inquiry, I concluded that it would be best if the use of such methods were ordered and authorized by a judge and that this practice should therefore be applied at an International Criminal Court. Only in a case of urgency could the investigator apply such techniques without warrant. If this code of conduct was not observed, the evidentiary material would have been obtained unlawfully. Two questions now arise: should evidence acquired in such an unlawful way be automatically excluded? What should be done with evidence obtained by national police in strict accordance with their own domestic law but not in accordance with the standard demanded by human rights obligations?

In one respect, these questions have already been addressed. Confessions are a subgroup of illegally obtained evidence. Special rules apply there. I am now mainly concerned with unlawful infringement of the right to privacy through search and seizure, tapping and surveillance.

In English law, the judiciary has always been fairly sympathetic towards the police. In 1870, in *Jones v Owens*, which concerned an offence

of Evidence, 16 February 1999 (Judge Robinson dissenting), admitting as hearsay evidence pursuant to Rule 89 C the record of a witness' testimony in the *Blaskic* trial. The dissenting Judge Robinson sees in this a violation of the right of the accused to cross-examine the witness. Compare ICTY bulletin—Judicial Supplement No. 2, 15 March 1999.

[557] The reader is reminded in this connection that the requirements relating to judicial qualifications in Art. 36 Rome Statute (Art. 9 Statute ILC) propose that the judges at the ICC have long-term experience in criminal trials alongside knowledge of international law. Art. 9 Statute ILC aims at ensuring that the Chambers are equipped with specialists in both fields. Compare Report ILC, Art. 6, paras. 1 and 2, and Art. 9, para. 1.

against the Salmon Fisheries Act (1861–5), the Court of Appeals held that it would be a dangerous obstacle to the administration of justice if evidence obtained by illegal means could not be used against the charged.[558] The trial was understood to be entirely separate from the pre-trial inquiry and was considered the wrong place for trying violations of the law by the investigating authorities.[559] The court is thought to be concerned only with the question of how evidence is used, not with the problem of how evidence was obtained.[560] The exclusion of evidence lies entirely within the discretion of the court and the defendant can do no more than try to persuade the court to use its discretion.[561] The House of Lords upheld this in *R v Sang*, declaring evidence that was gained through an agent provocateur admissible.[562] It conceded more generally that the admissibility of evidence depends on whether, in the opinion of the trial judge, the prejudicial effect of the evidence outweighed its probative value. It quite clearly ruled out the proposition that evidence could be declared inadmissible on the grounds of it being obtained by 'improper or unfair means'.[563] PACE (1984) s. 78 gave this discretionary rule a statutory basis. There, the judge is given full discretion to exclude the evidence if, taking all circumstances into account, including the way in which the evidence was obtained, admitting the material would render the proceedings unfair.[564] In *R v Harwood*, a post-PACE case, the Court of Appeal confirmed *Sang* and made an interesting assessment of the connection between substantive and procedural rules.[565] It held that entrapment was no defence in criminal law. Consequently, s. 78 PACE (1984) cannot apply, as the evidential rule could not abrogate the substantive rule of law.

In summary, the law concerning admissibility of illegal evidence stands as follows: The trial judge has discretion to exclude evidence. He will do so if he is persuaded that admission of the evidence will affect the fairness of the procedure. Furthermore, the judge must balance the interests of the

---

[558] *Jones v Owens* (1870) 34 J. 759. Likewise the Privy Council in *Kuruma v R* (1955) AC 197.

[559] This can be seen e.g. in the writing of Wigmore; see Zuckerman, *Principles of Criminal Evidence*, 343.

[560] Lidstone in Andrews (1982), 99.

[561] Andrews and Hirst, *Criminal Evidence*, 14.03.

[562] *R v Sang* (1979) CrimLR, 655.

[563] Ibid. The exceptions involving drink-driving cases will not be discussed here. For an overview, see Andrews and Hirst, *Criminal Evidence*, 14.05–09.

[564] Whether or not this legislation altered the common law rule is not quite clear. The Court of Appeal denied this in *R v Mason* (1987) 3 All ER 481 at 484, but treated the norm in *R v Fulling* (1987) 85 Cr App R as codifying law that had to be freshly interpreted, whereas Andrews and Hirst, *Criminal Evidence*, 14.17, opine that it has enlarged the judges' discretion. May (1988) CrimLR, 722 at 723 submits that Parliament envisaged a new rule, so that s. 78 has to be interpreted on its own wording. Judges now seem to rely on this rule rather than on the discretionary power under common law. Andrews and Hirst, *Criminal Evidence*, 14.12 admit to have misjudged this development.

[565] *R v Harwood* (1989) CrimLR, 285.

prosecution and the defence. A minor offence against 'fairness' might be outweighed by overall public interest.[566] Evidence will be excluded if its admission would have an adverse effect on the fairness of the proceedings and if the admission would be considered unacceptable.[567]

The US Supreme Court traditionally focuses on violations of the defendant's rights. Constitutional rights would be without value unless protected and enforced through an exclusionary rule. The basis for this ambitious task was laid in *Weeks v US*.[568] Consequently, the 'criminal' goes free because the policeman has blundered.[569] Strong criticism has developed out of this rule. It is believed that the price that must be paid is too high. The rule is inflexible, conceptually sterile, and practically ineffective. This self-inflicted wound is said to encourage criminals and, at the same time, pose an unreasonable impediment to vigorous law enforcement by the police.[570] Alternative proposals have been expressed, the most prominent, arguably, that of Chief Justice Burger in *Bivens v Six Unknown Named Agents*. The exclusionary rule should be abandoned and instead the offender left with the option of instituting civil proceedings concerning the infringement, that is, suing the police for compensation.[571] These rather radical-seeming changes in the treatment of unlawfully obtained evidence have not yet found judicial support. For the time being, the exclusionary rule still exists. Its main rationale can be described as threefold:[572] first, it seeks to exert a deterrent effect on law enforcement agencies; secondly, it enables the judiciary to avoid the taint of complicity in official lawlessness; and, thirdly, it operates to reassure the citizens that the government does not profit from its own lawless behaviour. The exclusionary rule has been narrowed down mainly on two sides. First, evidence is admissible if the police acted in 'good faith'. The reason given is that the price of a technical flaw making the police action illegal would otherwise really be intolerably high.[573] Second, evidence is admissible if the prosecutor can prove that he would have obtained the evidence anyway in a lawful manner. Again, the rationale for this is to combat the consequences of acquittal, which is considered unacceptable from the

---

[566] Andrews and Hirst, *Criminal Evidence*, 14.18.
[567] *R v Walsh* (1989) CrimLR, 822.
[568] US Supreme Court *Weeks v US* 232 US 383 (1914).
[569] Witt, *Supreme Court*, 178.
[570] Compare the summary of the critics by Osakwe in Andrews (1982), 280.
[571] US Supreme Court *Bivens v Six Unknown Named Agents* 403 US 388 (1971). Zuckerman, *Principles of Criminal Evidence*, 349, agrees with this radical shift.
[572] Compare Osakwe in Andrews (1982), 280.
[573] US Supreme Court *US v Leon* 468 US 897 (1984). The 'good faith' argument has also been invoked in English courts; see e.g. *R v Wash* (1989) CrimLR 855, where it was admitted that 'bad faith' might render a police action a substantial and significant breach of their rules of conduct. However, the contrary, that 'good faith' could mitigate a substantial and significant breach, did not follow. The Court of Appeal therefore adhered to an objective approach.

viewpoint of criminal justice.[574] This concept can be called 'inevitable discovery'[575] or the 'hypothetical clean path doctrine'.[576]

In German criminal procedure, there are several grounds for exclusion of evidence. The most straightforward one is a specific provision as laid down in legislation in the law. This applies to interrogations (§ 136a StPO), as we have already seen. This norm is also applicable to the questioning of witnesses (§ 69 (III) StPO). Apart from these cases, the literature and case-law are in conflict when it comes to arriving at a conclusive general rule. The Federal Court of Justice (Bundesgerichtshof) follows a theory of 'circles of rights' (*Rechtskreistheorie*).[577] It looks at the primary rule violated by the law enforcement agencies and then asks whether or not this norm aims exclusively at protection of the individual. If this question is answered in the affirmative, the evidence is excluded. In other cases, the court will balance the interests of the state in resolution of the offence against the interests of the individual in protection of his rights.[578]

Furthermore, exclusion of evidence can be derived directly from the Constitution.[579] This is especially true of the Basic Right laid down in Art. 2 (I) and 1 (I) GG. This guarantees all persons the right to privacy, untouchable by any state authority. Personal diaries, for example, although not automatically excluded if referring only to external factors or to past or future serious criminal offences, are thus generally not admissible as evidence. Privately made audio or video recordings are similarly treated.[580] If evidence was obtained by prosecutors through minor breaches of the StPO, the judiciary will admit the evidence. It will not do so if the evidence was gathered as the result of total circumvention or deliberate breach of legal authorization.[581]

The German system is based on the protection of its Basic Rights. As all prosecuting authority derives from statutory powers, the rules of the StPO must be strictly observed; otherwise there will be a breach of fundamental rights and the evidence obtained must be excluded. Clearly, this does not take place in cases where the law enforcement machinery needs to be disciplined, but when there is a violation of a Basic Right.

---

[574] US Supreme Court *Nix v Williams* 467 US 431 (1984).
[575] Ibid.
[576] Kleinknecht and Meyer-Goßner § 136 a, 31.
[577] BGH Judgment 21 January 1958 in BGHSt 11, 213. This case concerned self-incriminating statements of a witness which led to the conviction of the accused. The cautioning of the witness (§ 55 (II) StPO) was omitted by the judge. The BGH decided that the defendant could not claim this violation of the law as working in his favour, as it was not created for his protection but only pertains to the safety of the witness.
[578] The most recent case is BGH Judgment 9 April 1986 in BGHSt 34, 39 at 53.
[579] BVerfG Decision 31 January 1973, in BVerfGE 34, 238.
[580] Kleinknecht and Meyer-Goßner Einl. 56b.
[581] For telephone surveillance, ibid., § 100a No. 21.

(f) 'Fruit of the poisonous tree' doctrine   Finally, we must address the question of what to do with evidence obtained only with the help of inadmissible evidence. For example, if a weapon is found on the basis of a self-incriminating statement by the defendant that was provoked through maltreatment of some kind, the weapon alone suffices to prove the guilt of the accused.

Most famous in this regard is the decision handed down by the US Supreme Court. It applied a strict exclusionary rule.[582] This exclusionary rule not only applies to direct use of evidence obtained unreasonably; it also excludes indirect and derivative use of such evidence.[583]

The German Federal Court of Justice does not recognize a general exclusionary rule like the 'fruit of the poisonous tree' doctrine (*Fernwirkungsverbot*). None the less, many voices in the literature call for such an extension of the exclusionary rule, mostly relying on the North American practice.[584] The BGH is possibly inclined to apply the 'hypothetical clean-path doctrine'.[585]

(g) Conclusion: an exclusionary rule for the international court   If these last two points are combined, two main bases for the exclusion of evidence can be found: (*a*) vindication of the accused for infringements of his basic rights and (*b*) deterring law enforcement agencies.[586] If the exclusionary rule were centred exclusively on rationale (*b*), these agencies could probably be expected to become more cautious about infringing basic rights. Eventually, their system would be sufficiently protective and cases of breach would become unusual and uncommon. Should an effort therefore really be made to discipline them? A certain deterrent effect is surely useful and necessary. But this function is a helpful side-effect, and should not be made the primary rationale. The underlying reason for the exclusion of evidence should always be a normative one, that is, the protection of the rights of the persons involved. This also seems a workable approach for an international court. If an international body concerned itself with the task of educating and disciplining the police force, it might easily appear to violate state sovereignty. Instead, it should function as a supervising human rights body as well as having the task of criminal prosecution, akin to the ECourtHR or the HRC. If it were to focus on human rights, the main aim would be protection of the individual during the criminal process. The implied censure of the police force of a sovereign state would then be conceived of as a side-effect, not as a declared

---

[582] US Supreme Court *Silverthorne Lumber Co. v US* 251 US 385 (1920).
[583] Osakwe in Andrews (1982), 279.
[584] Compare e.g. Roxin, *Strafverfahrensrecht*, § 24 D IV.
[585] BGH Decision 17 March 1971 in BGHSt 24, 125 at 130.
[586] Zuckerman, *Principles of Criminal Evidence*, 346–7.

purpose. This should make it easier for states to accept the jurisdiction of the international court. This seems to be the policy accepted by the ICTY. In Rule 95, all evidence obtained directly or indirectly by means which constitute a serious violation of internationally protected human rights is excluded. Clearly, the protection of human rights lies at the centre of this exclusion. The ICTY will assess whether a violation is serious enough to warrant exclusion on a case-by-case basis.[587]

Consequently, the clean-path doctrine could be accepted to a certain extent. If the main emphasis is on the rights of the defendant, the outcome of the infringement, the evidence, could arguably have been obtained without the infringement. However, the rules of conduct are there above all to protect the suspect against violations of his rights. Evidence that stems directly from such an interference should generally be excluded. The violation is too serious and too direct to allow hypothetical speculations about what might have been the case, if the rules had been observed. Evidence only indirectly related to the violation could be admitted, if the prosecutor could prove that he did not have to rely on the evidence stemming from the human rights violation, because he obtained it in another way. Yet, one question remains unanswered: if the evidence could have been obtained on a clean path, why was this not done? There are two main possibilities: First, the police knew about an admissible, clean way but considered the unlawful one easier, quicker, and more promising. This excuse cannot be accepted in court. Deliberate unlawful behaviour is no basis for a conviction. Second, the police breached the law accidentally and the outcome would have been the same if they had behaved within the law. What we have then is a combination of a 'good-faith' and a 'clean-path' doctrine. This we would hold as applicable in the 'fruit of the poisonous tree' cases.

(V) The Sentence

What can human rights tell us about the amount of time to which the offender is sentenced? In principle this is not a problem of procedure but of material criminal law. Nevertheless, there are some questions that are worth looking at. The main trouble is the principle of proportionality between offence and sentence. Is this related to a fair trial?

Of importance to a 'fair trial' is the way that facts concerning the amount of sentence are collected. These facts must be either inquired after by the judge (inquisitorial system) or be presented by the parties (adversarial system). The extent of punishment should not be considered an automatic consequence of the verdict concerning guilt. Although statu-

---

[587] Nsereko, 5 CLF (1994), 507 at 545.

tory or mandatory sentences may provide guidelines, every case must be assessed on its own merits. Otherwise, the person of the accused is not taken into account, and the prisoner would be treated as an 'object' of the trial. Like the trial concerning the guilt of the accused, the procedure concerning determination of the appropriate sentence must also be fair.[588]

In Rule 100, the ICTY phrases this by saying that the parties may submit any material relevant in order to assist the Trial Chamber in determining the appropriate sentence. Similarly, Art. 76 Rome Statute foresees further hearings to discover the facts relevant for the sentence as a separate process, distinct from the trial.[589] Art. 24 (I) Statute ICTY refers the judges to the general practice in the former Yugoslavia, when determining the prison term. The reasons for this are not clear from the Report of the Secretary General.[590] The provision is surprising, considering that Western states did not always believe that socialist states could produce respectable law.[591] Furthermore, the Trial Chamber, when called upon to sentence Erdemovic, had difficulties in finding equivalent and applicable law and relied more readily on general principles of criminal law[592] and precedents in international criminal law, like that of the *Eichmann* case of the Supreme Court of Israel.[593]

Guidelines for the determination of penalties are outlined in Rule 101, comprising both the gravity of the offence and the unique circumstances of the individual (Art. 24 (II) Statute ICTY, Art. 46 (II) Statute ILC, Art. 78 (I) Rome Statute). The Trial Chamber accepted orders from superiors and duress, although not excluding individual responsibility, as mitigating factors (Art. 7 (IV) Statute ICTY), while not ruling out entirely the possibility that criminal responsibility might vanish if the offender was under duress, that is, 'extreme necessity'.[594] The Trial Chamber was corrected in

---

[588] This is expressly stated by the Report ILC, Art. 46, para. 1.

[589] Schabas, in Trifterer (ed.), *Commentary on the Rome Statute*, Art. 76, No. 1. As to the previous Art. 46 in the Statute ILC, see Report ILC, Art. 46, para. 1.

[590] Report of the Secretary General, para. 111.

[591] Compare the long discussions by the German Federal Court of Justice (BGH), *First Border Guards case*, Judgment 3 November 1992, 100 ILR 366 and in particular the difficulties finding the right interpretation of the Border Law of the former GDR.

[592] See Trial Chamber I, *Erdemovic* case, Sentencing Judgment, 29 November 1996, para. 40, finding that the reference to the practice in the former Yugoslavia is actually meant as a reflection of the general principle of law. The Trial Chamber is criticized for being more concerned with a jurisprudential exercise than dealing with the convicted person, Green, 10 LJIL (1997), 363 at 376 in particular. The extensive reasoning of the Trial Chamber stands as testimony to the immense difficulties and uncertainties that the ICTY has in applying international criminal law, that is, a poorly developed area of law.

[593] Israel Supreme Court, *Israel v Eichmann* 36 ILR (1968), 257 at 341. See the Trial Chamber I, *Erdemovic* case, Sentencing Judgment, 29 November 1996, para. 64.

[594] Trial Chamber I, *Erdemovic* case, Sentencing Judgment, 29 November 1996, paras. 16–21. The Trial Chamber found that in these cases of 'most extreme duress', in which the defendant had no moral choice, the law at the ICTY provided no guidance. It then held that,

this regard by the Appeals Chamber, which by a majority ruled out the possibility of 'duress' as a complete defence, but held that it must be taken into account as a mitigating factor.[595]

Furthermore, the judges took into account the cooperation of the convicted, who appeared as a witness in the Rule 61 procedures against Karadzic and Mladic (see Rule 100B ii) with the prosecutor.[596] That this 'smallest of the small fry' was nevertheless sentenced to ten years of imprisonment is criticized by Green, who suspects the Trial Chamber of giving in to public pressure.[597] Through the decision of the Trial Chamber II of 5 March 1998, the sentence for the new charge of violation of the laws and customs of war (Art. 3 Statute ICTY) was halved.[598]

When an individual sentence is being determined, factors such as the gravity of the offence, the individual circumstances of the convicted person, and the existence of aggravating or mitigating circumstances must be taken into account.[599] The actual guilt of the convicted person constitutes a limiting principle as to determination of the appropriate and proportionate penalty.[600] As aggravating circumstances, the ICTY accepted the magnitude of the crime and the scale of the accused's role in it.[601] Furthermore, it considered as aggravating the willing involvement in violent 'ethnic cleansing' and the lack of cooperation with the prosecutor.[602]

Does the simple fact that trial and imprisonment take place far away from the offender's home create a mitigating circumstance? The ICTY Trial Chamber supposed that it had to 'take account of the place and conditions of enforcement of the sentence in an effort to ensure due process, the proper administration of justice and equal treatment for convicted persons'.[603] The Trial Chamber considered that the penalty

in these cases of no 'moral choice in the face of imminent danger', a complete defence was possible. However, the facts did not suppose that Erdemovic was in such a position. An earlier study of this issue is available by Y. Dinstein, *The Defence of 'Obedience to Superior Orders' in International Law* (Leyden, 1965). More recently, Paust, in Bassiouni, *International Criminal Law*, iii, 73.

[595] Appeals Chamber *Erdemovic* Decision 7 October 1997, reasons given in the Joint Opinion of Judge McDonald and Judge Vohrah, as well as in the Opinion of Judge Li; President Cassese gave a powerful dissent, arguing in favour of 'duress' as a complete defence, showing that the argument of the majority was too one-sided, and neglected strong precedents proving the opposite. The ruling of the Appeals Chamber was applied by the Trial Chamber II in *Erdemovic II*, para. 17.

[596] Ibid., paras. 55–6.   [597] Green, 10 LJIL (1997), 363 at 378–9.
[598] Trial Chamber II, *Erdemovic II* 5 March 1998, para. 23.
[599] Trial Chamber I, *Erdemovic I* 29 November 1996, para. 42; Trial Chamber II, *Erdemovic II*, paras. 15 and 16.
[600] Trial Chamber I, *Erdemovic I*, para. 53.
[601] Trial Chamber II, *Erdemovic II*.
[602] Trial Chamber, *Tadic* Sentencing Judgment, 14 July 1997, paras. 56–7.
[603] Trial Chamber I, *Erdemovic I*, para. 70.

imposed on persons convicted of international crimes must not be aggravated by the conditions of its enforcement.[604] Furthermore, the fact that the prison term will be served in faraway countries, that cultural and linguistic differences will distinguish these persons from other detainees, will leave the international criminal inevitably in isolation.[605] In the *Delalic et al.* judgment, the Trial Chamber recognized as mitigating circumstances the youth of the offender, his personality problems, his lack of military training or instruction in how to behave towards prisoners, and finally the harsh environment of the armed conflict as a whole.[606]

What also needs to be taken account of here is the time already served in detention prior to the trial. Rule 101D[607] prescribes that credit should be given for the period the convicted person was detained in custody pending his surrender to the tribunal or pending trial or appeal.[608] This provision does not include detention in a national unit until a formal request of surrender to the ICTY has been issued. The reasons for this limitation are somewhat dubious, as the quality of the custody remains the same. Indeed, the convicted suffers a disadvantage if tried at the ICTY, as a domestic court would take the entire time in custody into account. Tadic thus spent almost nine months, from his arrest on 12 February 1994 to the formal request to deferral by the ICTY on 8 November 1994, in German custody, for which he was not given credit.[609] This limitation should be reconsidered. Aleksovski benefited from the credit rule in Rule 101D to the extent that his immediate release was ordered. He had been imprisoned for two years, ten months, and twenty-nine days, when he was sentenced to two years and six months' imprisonment.[610] The proposal of the PrepComm does not include the same limitation as ex-Rule 101E but makes the reduction dependent on the period actually served in detention.[611]

All these circumstances have to be taken into account when a proportionate and appropriate sentence is being determined for the offender at the international court. Several proposals as to aggravating and mitigating factors have been advanced by the PrepComm.[612] The death penalty

---

[604] Ibid., para. 74. [605] Ibid., para. 75.

[606] ICTY Trial Chamber, *Delalic et al.* Judgment, 16 November 1998, paras. 1283–4.

[607] Ex-Rule 101E, as amended at the 5th Plenary Session in Jan. 1995.

[608] ICTY Trial Chamber II *Prosecutor v Erdemovic* 5 March 1998, Case No. IT-96-22-T, para. 23. The Trial Chamber decided further that credit should be given for time already spent in detention since the request for transferral to the ICTY on 29 March 1996, in accordance with then Rule 101E.

[609] ICTY Trial Chamber II, *Tadic*, Sentencing Judgment, 14 July 1997, para. 77.

[610] ICTY Trial Chamber I, *Order for Immediate Release of Zlatko Aleksovski*, 7 May 1999; the written judgment was issued on 25 June 1999; compare ICTY bulletin, Judicial Supplement No. 6, 25 August 1999.

[611] Report of the PrepComm II, 232.

[612] Ibid., 228–34.

was excluded by a majority of the committee members, although it has been pointed out that in some countries the death penalty is exercised for very serious offences.[613] On the other hand, the death penalty is ruled out by major human rights treaties and several national constitutions. For the reasons given in Chapter 1, the death penalty can therefore not be inflicted by an international court.

The Rome Statute took heed of these developments and propositions. Art. 77 Rome Statute contains a prohibition of the death penalty. In determining the sentence, the ICC shall take into account the gravity of the crime and individual circumstances of the convicted person. Prior detention via an order of the ICC will reduce the time of imprisonment; time otherwise spent in detention in connection with the underlying crime may be taken into account when determining the sentence (Art. 78 (II) Rome Statute). Finally, in the case of a conviction for more than one crime, the court will pronounce a sentence for each crime and a joint sentence specifying the total period of imprisonment.[614]

Apart from a vague framework, the Rome Statute does not provide much guidance on the sentencing procedure. It would be desirable from a human rights point of view to try and further clarify the length of the possible prison sentences in particular. Art. 77 Rome Statute only states that imprisonment can be for a number of years up to thirty years. Only in a case of extreme gravity, as is stated in Art. 77 (I) b Rome Statute, can life imprisonment be justified. As such, this distinction does not say much about the appropriate term, since international crimes are generally crimes of extreme gravity *per definitionem*. Further differentiations should be made in the Rules of Procedure, also with a view to Art. 23 Rome Statute (*nulla poena sine lege*). Draft Rule 7.1 (3) links the extreme gravity with the existence of one or more aggravating circumstance. Draft Rule 7.1 (2) furthermore proposes an exemplary list of mitigating and aggravating circumstances. Before this, Draft Rule 7.1 (1) provides guidance on what should play a major role when the crime and the person of the convicted are being weighed up.

---

[613] Report of the PrepComm I, para. 306.
[614] This echoes the German practice according to §§ 53, 54 StGB.

5

After the Conviction

The different traditions hold different views as to what falls within the post-conviction stage. In Anglo-American tradition the trial ends with a conviction or acquittal. Sentence-setting is a problem for the post-conviction stage, as is any appeals or review procedure. For the Continental lawyer the judgment of the court in the first instance (*erstinstanzliches Gericht*) is far from the end of the procedure. Criminal procedure terminates when the final appeal court declares its verdict or when the time limit within which one must appeal (*Rechtsmittelfrist*) has expired. Only then is the judgment legally valid (*rechtskräftig*). The principle *ne bis in idem* only comes into play after the trial has gone through all instances (*Instanzenzug*). The consequences of this will be the first issue. After that we will address the right to appeal as a human rights provision.

A. DOUBLE JEOPARDY (*NE BIS IN IDEM*)

The prohibition of double jeopardy (*ne bis in idem*) guarantees that no one can be tried twice for the same crime. An international court will almost certainly have to deal with a clash; in order to render justice to both victims and offenders national courts may not—to quote another hypothetical case as an illustration—convict a major war criminal of parking in a prohibited zone at the entrance of a concentration camp and inflict upon him a fine of £20. This cannot possibly result in a hindrance to a just and fair trial at an international court where the offender is held responsible for what he really did during his parking in a prohibited area in front of the detention unit: torturing and murdering prisoners of war.[1] In order to prohibit partial and dependent trials designed to shield the accused, a dogmatic proper solution has to be found in accordance with the principle *ne bis in idem*.

This principle is enshrined in the major human rights treaties: 'Art. 14 (VII) ICCPR No one shall be liable to be tried or punished again for an offence for which he has already been finally convicted or acquitted in accordance with the law and penal procedure of each country.' The Council of Europe accepted the right against double jeopardy on 22 November 1984.

---

[1] The danger of 'show-trials' by the successor-states on the territory of the former Yugoslavia is described by Nsereko, Criminal Law Forum 1994, 507 at 516.

Art. 4 Prot.7 ECHR

(I) No one shall be liable to be tried or punished again in criminal proceedings under the jurisdiction of the same state for an offence for which he has already been finally acquitted or convicted in accordance with the law and penal procedure of that state.

This norm had been the subject of major discussion and controversy amongst the drafters. Originally neither the 1954 HRComm draft nor Art. 6 ECHR contained this right. On the initiative of Italy and Japan paragraph (VII) was added to Art. 14 ICCPR. States were concerned that the resumption of a trial which was justified by exceptional circumstances may come within the ambit of this provision. Therefore, many states felt the need to make reservations to the provision. HRC in its General Comment criticizes this false assumption and encourages these states to reconsider their reservations.[2] In two cases the HRC addressed the issue of *ne bis in idem* but found a violation of the principle of a speedy trial instead.[3] In *A.P. v Italy* the HRC expanded upon the meaning of Art. 14 (VII) ICCPR. The applicant was tried in Italy, after already having been finally convicted and punished for the same currency offence by a Swiss court.[4] The HRC took the view that *ne bis in idem* prohibits double jeopardy but only with regard to an offence adjudicated in a given state. A new trial held in a different state is not, therefore, a breach of Art. 14 (VII) ICCPR. McGoldrick believes that this seems to be in accordance with the literal wording of Art. 14 (VII) ICCPR,[5] whereas Nowak finds this interpretation too general and too absolute, but he does not elaborate upon this comment.[6]

The text of the European provision is clearer in this regard as it exempts resumption procedures from falling within the prohibition's ambit. Likewise it is clear that it only pertains to national proceedings and is not applicable across borders.[7] Irrespective of the additional protocol, which has not been signed by all of the Member States of the Council of Europe,[8] a prohibition of double jeopardy could be read into Art. 6 ECHR itself. When the ECommHR first dealt with this problem in *X v Austria* (1963), a case concerning the international application of double jeopardy, it denied that any aspect of *ne bis in idem* would be implied into the ECHR.[9] The

---

[2] HRC General Comment 13 (Article 14), para. 19.

[3] HRC *Schweizer v Uruguay* Doc.A/38/40, 117, and *Nieto v Uruguay* Doc. A/38/40, 201.

[4] HRC *A. v Italy* Doc. A/43/40, 242.

[5] McGoldrick, *Human Rights Committee*, 413.   [6] Nowak, Art. 14, No. 81.

[7] Compare the clear wording and J. Vehn and R. Ergec, *La Convention européene de droits de l'homme* (Brussels, 1990), § 639.

[8] See Harris, 569.

[9] ECommHR *X v Austria* Decision 27 March 1963 Appl. No. 1519/62, 6 YB 346 at 348. The same statement was made in the case *X v Germany* Decision 16 March 1977, Appl. No. 7680/76, 9 DR 190.

matter was left open in *X v Austria* (1970).[10] The case concerned the question of whether disciplinary proceedings could be held alongside a criminal prosecution. The ECommHR held that it was irrelevant whether *ne bis in idem* was included in a fair trial because the two proceedings were of a different nature and imposed different sanctions in different categories.[11] In *S v Germany* the ECommHR ruled out the application of *ne bis in idem* in the international context.[12] The applicant was convicted and sentenced for a narcotics offence in the Netherlands and upon his return to Germany received a much higher sentence from the Regional Court (Landgericht) Frankfurt/M.

In the European context the *ne bis in idem* principle appears yet in another document. Art. 54 of the Implementing Agreement of 19 June 1990[13] of the Schengen Treaty of 14 June 1985[14] prohibits a second trial in any other Member State to the document. It reads:

Art. 54 Implementing Agreement to the Schengen Treaty
Wer durch eine Vertragspartei rechtskräftig abgeurteilt worden ist, darf durch eine andere Vertragspartei wegen derselben Tate nicht verfolgt werden, vorausgesetzt, dass im Falle einer Verurteilung die Sanktion bereits vollstreckt worden ist, gerade vollstreckt wird oder nach dem Recht eines Vertragsstaates nicht mehr vollstreckt werden kann.

A person who has been finally judged by a Contracting Party may not be prosecuted by another Contracting Party for the same offences provided that, where he is sentenced, the sentence has been served or is currently being served or can no longer be carried out under the sentencing laws of the Contracting Party.

This provision is a corollary to the rationale of the original Schengen Treaty, which is the abolition of all border control. Yet not all Member States of the European Union are parties to the Schengen Treaty.[15]

There seems to be some confusion about the actual meaning of the prohibition of double jeopardy. One reason for this is that some states have statutory procedures which allow a retrial if new evidence is found. Other states questioned whether their appeals and review proceedings would fall within the ambit of this prohibition.[16] If the ICCPR itself

---

[10] ECommHR *X* v. *Austria* Decision 13 July 1970 Appl. No. 4212/69, 35 CD 151.

[11] Ibid. 154.

[12] ECommHR *S v Germany* Decision 13 December 1983 Appl. No. 8945/80, 39 DR, 43.

[13] Reprinted in BGBl 1993 II 1013.

[14] Repr. in Gemeinsames Ministerialblatt 1986, 79. Bek. a. BMI, 29 Jan 1986—V II 2—125 760 BEL/6.

[15] The Schengen Treaty was originally constituted by Belgium, the Netherlands and Luxembourg, France and Germany, and has subsequently been ratified by Italy, Spain, Portugal, Greece, Austria, Denmark, Finland, and Sweden.

[16] Harris, 16 ICLQ (1967), 352 at 376 describes these difficulties that can be studied in the drafting history of the ICCPR.

provides for a right to appeal, it is clear that appeals proceedings cannot fall within the prohibition of double jeopardy. Similarly resumption of a trial can remain outside its scope, as the ICCPR justifies domestic proceedings. Nevertheless it remains unclear where the principle *ne bis in idem* is actually applicable. Can the trial be repeated if facts were left undiscussed, or the consequences of the punished act misjudged, and can it be repeated if a lesser or enhanced degree of intent is later discovered? The precise scope of the maxim *ne bis in idem* will be described first. Then I shall take a closer look at the two different meanings one could give to the prohibition of double jeopardy in an international setting, that is *Erledigtenlösung*, and *Anrechnungslösung*, and finally seek a solution for an international court.

(I) What is *Idem*?

We must examine what each national jurisdiction understands by 'the same' (*idem*). In English law the prohibition of double jeopardy is a well accepted principle.[17] The US Constitution enshrines this principle in the Fifth Amendment: no person shall be subject for the same offence to be put twice in jeopardy of life or limb.[18] Likewise German law knows this as a constitutional principle embodied in Art. 103 (III) GG.

All of the jurisdictions apply the principle of *ne bis in idem* from the moment it is believed that the trial is concluded, that is, as soon as the matter is considered *res judicata*. Certainly different systems give different answers to this question: common law jurisdictions generally see the trial terminated when the accused is convicted or acquitted. Civil law tradition understands the matter settled only when the last appeal decision is reached. I will not discuss this here, but operate on the basis that double jeopardy is applicable for *res judicatae* in an abstract sense.[19]

To trigger the applicability of *ne bis in idem* there must be a decision concerning the substantial facts (*Sachentscheidung*). Any other decision, like the non-confirmation of an indictment or decision to discontinue proceedings, leaves the principle untouched.[20] It can furthermore only pertain to the person who was actually indicted. Other persons who abetted or were otherwise involved in the criminal offence cannot claim double jeopardy. A second consideration of what lies within the same course of events is prohibited (*einheitlicher Lebensvorgang*).[21] These are

---

[17] Lidstone in Andrews (1982), 85.
[18] Osakwe in Andrews (1982), 286.
[19] The question will be discussed at the point of the right to appeal.
[20] Compare BVerfG Judgment 17 January 1961, in BVerfGE 12, 62 at p. 331.
[21] Seidel, *Handbuch der Grund- und Menschenrechte*, 323; see also BVerfG Judgment 8 January 1981, in BVerfGE 56, 22 at 27.

delimited in a criminal trial by indictment and confirmation.[22] A false legal classification of the facts at issue is therefore insignificant. Although this may be corrected on appeal, it cannot justify a second trial.

(II) *Erledigtenlösung* (Theory of Final Judgment)

One interpretation of the principle *ne bis in idem* is that after the first decision the state must treat the matter concerning the defendant as at an end (*erledigt*). In this case the consequences are that no other court can initiate further proceedings. A judicial claim would have to be declared inadmissible. In the national context this approach is relatively unproblematic. The case was heard, a judgment produced, justice has been done, the matter is *res judicata* and of no further interest to the prosecuting authorities. In the case of new evidence, as we have seen above, that is, when interest in prosecution is reignited, national states usually have exceptions and have ways of resuming the trial, in accordance with human rights treaties.

In an international setting this approach leads to a direct conflict with state sovereignty. Traditionally states have jurisdiction over offences which occurred in their territory[23] or which involve their nationals.[24] States are obliged to protect their nationals as individuals and as part of society. States usually do this by means of criminal law. If two states have an interest in prosecuting a person, one for example because the offence occurred in its territory, the other because the offender is a national, they will both want to put the suspect on trial. If the rationale for the right of a state to prosecute nationals who committed criminal offences abroad is seen in the fact that the other state did not make use of its right to prosecute by virtue of the principle of territoriality, a prosecution after a conviction or acquittal would be logically excluded.[25] This is only true for the special case of the principle of personality in the passive sense. In other

---

[22] Kleinknecht and Meyer-Goßner, Einl. No. 173.

[23] Principle of territoriality (*Territorialitätsprinzip*). This principle is certainly a main pillar of modern international criminal law, though it has different roots in English and Continental law. The common law tenet 'all crime is local' developed alongside the local juries, the development of which we have already looked at. Compare D. Oehler, *Internationales Strafrecht* (2nd edn. Cologne, 1983), ch. 2.

[24] Principle of personality (*Personalitätsprinzip*). The idea of connecting jurisdiction to the person is of Germanic origin and almost faded in favour of the principle of territoriality because of the practicability of the latter. It is nowadays part of almost every legal system known as *passives Personalitätsprinzip* (principle of personality in its passive sense) to protect its own nationals abroad. By virtue of the principle known as *aktives Personalitätsprinzip* (principle of personality in its active sense) states are justified in punishing their own nationals for committing crimes abroad. Being very closely linked to the principle of sovereignty this has also been introduced into English and related legal systems. Ibid., chs. 2, 9, and 12.

[25] This is the reasoning of Oehler, ibid., No. 747.

cases of conflicting interests the trial is considered to be the medium for establishing peace under the law (*Rechtsfrieden*).[26] If the suspect has been convicted or acquitted in one state and the other arrests him, this state has two possibilities; either it hands the suspect over for new prosecution to its own authorities or it accepts the judgment of the state in which the trial was held. In this case the state would have to utilize the foreign judgment for its own interior peace under the law. Most states are reluctant to do this and do not have the necessary trust in the judiciary of the other state.[27]

This meaning of *ne bis in idem* has been ruled out by the HRC in *A.P. v Italy*, as I have already discussed,[28] despite there being no clear indication in the wording.[29] The German BVerfG had to decide this issue when asked to rule on the question whether or not an extradition into a second state is barred by the fact that the involved person has already been sentenced and imprisoned by a third state, if the former conviction is neither accepted nor taken into account.[30] The Constitutional Court could only have done so by declaring the principle *ne bis in idem* a general principle of public international law by virtue of Art. 25 GG.[31] As to the first possibility that the judgment, conviction, or acquittal has to be accepted, the BVerfG found that, despite it being embodied in many constitutions or legal systems, it is not internationally applicable.[32]

Where Art. 54 of the Implementation Agreement of the Schengen Treaty is applicable, the principle *ne bis in idem* is applicable in the sense of the *Erledigtenlösung*. Any further prosection is prohibited whenever

[26] That a serious crime can cause interior iniquities can be seen from the pressure by families of victims of the 1988 Lockerbie incident on the British government, see the *Guardian* (14 October 1997), 14. They called for a trial that would bring the alleged terrorists to justice. Neither the British nor the US governments were easily prepared to accept a trial in a third state, but have finally agreed to hold a trial in the Netherlands applying Scottish Law. The trial is at present under way, a decision is expected sometime in 2001.

[27] Jung, *FS Schüler-Springorum*, 493, at 501. Compare also Ambos, 7 EJIL (1996), 519 at 533.

[28] HRC *A. v Italy* Doc. A/43/40, 242.

[29] Compare B. Specht, *Die zwischenstaatliche Geltung des Grundsatzes* ne bis in idem (Berlin, 1999), 46.

[30] BVerfG decision concerning the applicability of *ne bis in idem* 31 March 1987, BVerfGE 75, 1. The Constitutional Court denied the existence of such a general principle in public international law.

[31] Art. 25 GG reads: 'The general rules of public international law are an integral part of federal law. They take precedence over statutes and directly create rights and duties for the inhabitants of the federal territory.' Trans. as in D. P. Currie, *The Constitution of the Federal Republic of Germany* (Chicago and London, 1994).

[32] BVerfG decision concerning the applicability of *ne bis in idem* 31 March 1987, BVerfGE 75, 1 at 21–4. Oehler, *Internationales Strafrecht*, No. 906 argues that at least the principle of universality by its very nature excludes a second trial. As this principle gives every state a right to prosecute, this right vanishes as soon as one state has made use of it. It would be a strange thought if all states could prosecute in a cumulative manner.

there has been a decision that terminates the proceedings according to national law of a Member State.[33]

(III) *Anrechnungslösung* (Taking Prior Sentences into Account)

The other way of applying the prohibition of double jeopardy would be to take sentences imposed by other states into account. This could only be done during the stage of enforcement. The state could hold a trial and convict and sentence in the usual way, but the convicted person would only have to suffer imprisonment to the extent that the sentence exceeds what he has already served in the first state.

The HRC as we have seen, categorically denied any application of the principle *ne bis in idem*. But is it not necessary from a human rights point of view to accept this form of the principle as internationally valid? Most European states have implemented this form of *ne bis in idem* in their national legislation: for example, Germany in § 51 (III) StGB and § 153c StPO,[34] Austria in § 66 ÖstStGB, and the United Kingdom in *R v Aughet*.[35] The BVerfG did not find that this development was widespread enough to constitute a general rule of public international law.[36] Even if this is true from a quantitative point of view, it is not persuasive when we look at the theory of criminal law. I will argue below that a failure to give credit for a sentence already served in a foreign state conflicts with the generic justi- fication of punishment. The justifications for punishment are more or less the same in every legal system. In general, the rationale of criminal law is built on three pillars: special and general prevention and just desert. The prevailing view amongst scholars and the view of the legislator is that offenders are punished for a mixture of utilitarian and repressive motives. In the functional sense, the state needs to establish peace under the law, that is, promote a feeling of trust and reliability as well as general deter- rence among its nationals. These reasons may make it necessary to hold a new trial. Through a new trial a state can stigmatize criminal offenders and spread a deterrent effect among its citizens. It may be justifiable to hold a second trial specially to censure the guilty again. From a retribu- tive point of view, just desert demands only as much sentence as deserved. It may well be that two states have diverging ideas of how

---

[33] Specht, *Die zwischenstaatliche Geltung*, 177.

[34] In the case ECommHR *S v Germany* Decision 13 December 1983 Appl. No. 8945/80, 39 DR, 43 the German court consequently credited the time the applicant had spent in deten- tion in the Netherlands towards the sentence.

[35] *R v Aughet* [1918] 118 L.T.658 C.C.A.

[36] BVerfG decision concerning the applicability of *ne bis in idem* 31 March 1987, BVerfGE 75, 1 at 26.

much is justly deserved.[37] Nevertheless there is no reason why what is deserved should be the sum of both ideas. It must necessarily be no more than the higher sentence.

(IV) International Applicability

The International Criminal Court has several problems concerning double jeopardy. It is still doubtful which of the above theories is applicable. I have tried to show that the *Anrechnungslösung* is a human rights maxim in the international context. However, is an International Criminal Court part of the international scene in this sense? Why does it not have to follow the stricter form of *ne bis in idem* which is applicable to national courts?

Secondly, the International Criminal Court is supposed to work against biased and protective national jurisdictions.[38] If, for example, the most heinous criminals on the Serb side of the conflict in the former Yugoslavia were to be tried by a Serb court just for the purpose of shielding them against further prosecution by the international court, the danger of this being a dependent and protective trial rather than an independent and fair trial is real. The International Criminal Court has to find a solution.

1. The solution at the ICTY

Art. 10 Statute ICTY expressly addresses the issue of *ne bis in idem*. According to Art. 10 I Statute ICTY, new prosecution for acts constituting serious violations of international humanitarian law under the statute at a national court is barred if there has already been a trial by the ICTY. According to the letter of this provision it is irrelevant whether the procedure ended with a conviction or an acquittal. A national prosecutor is, however, not prohibited from initiating proceedings if the ICTY merely declared that it had no jurisdiction over the case. The ICTY has therefore primacy over national jurisdictions if it adopts the case to itself. In other words, national states are obliged to accept the decision of the ICTY as that of a national court. It is not enough to merely take the inflicted punishment into account, according to the *Anrechnungslösung*; the national state must consider the case to be finished, as in the *Erledigtenlösung*. Rule 13 contemplates a way of enforcing this obligation. In the case of criminal prosecution being initiated by a national state in breach of Art. 10 (I) Statute ICTY, the ICTY will request the state to discon-

---

[37] In a federalist state like Germany different views on the question what is justly deserved are tolerated in different states.

[38] To counter the failure of the national system is one of the six reasons given for an ICC by the Lawyers' Committee for Human Rights, International Criminal Court Briefing Series, Vol I, No. 1, August 1996, 3–4.

tinue the procedure, and if the national court fails to do so, the President of the ICTY may report the matter to the Security Council.[39] Art. 10 (I) Statute ICTY omits the applicability of the principle *ne bis in idem* to the ICTY itself.[40] However, the same must be valid here: the ICTY may not prosecute a person against whom a decision for the same facts has already been given by the ICTY. In this respect the statute must be interpreted in accordance with human rights—a person must not to be tried twice on the same facts.[41]

It is different if the national court has already given a judgment. Pursuant to Art. 10 (II) Statute ICTY a second trial is possible, if

(*a*) the act for which he or she was tried was characterized as an ordinary crime; or

(*b*) the national court proceedings were not impartial or independent, were designed to shield the accused from international criminal responsibility, or the case was not diligently prosecuted.

By this provision the danger of 'show-trials' in the territory of the successor states of the former Yugoslavia should be excluded. In such a case it is possible for the ICTY to initiate completely new proceedings notwithstanding the result of the national trial.[42] This provision appears to meet the aim of effectively condemning the results of a shielding judiciary. Nevertheless there must be a proper justification for a second trial, in order to satisfy human rights concerns.

In case (*a*) a judicial misinterpretation of the facts occurred.[43] An international crime was falsely interpreted as an ordinary crime. This legal misclassification was deemed to be sufficiently important to be corrected by a new trial at the international level. A possible justification for a new trial could be as follows (procedural justification): the national court was, strictly speaking, not the competent (*zuständig*) body to adjudicate upon international crimes. In such a case, one could argue, the first judgment was not in accordance with the applicable procedural law and a second trial, now according to the law and procedure of international law, can

---

[39] It seems unclear, however, what the Security Council could do with such a recalcitrant state. Would a breach of Art. 10 Statute ICTY, that is, a lack of cooperation with the ICTY, really constitute a threat to international peace and security, so that sanctions could be taken against this state in accordance with Chapter VII UN Charter?

[40] Bassiouni, *The Law of the ICTY*, 334, calls this 'perhaps a drafting oversight'.

[41] Compare Nsereko, 5 CLF (1994), 507 at 515; Reinisch, 47 Austrian JPIL (1995), 173 at 181.

[42] According to Rule 12 the ICTY is not bound by any findings, decision, or judgments of the national court. Yet the national agency has to submit all its materials and files to the ICTY, see Rule 10B.

[43] The Report of the Secretary General, para. 66, paraphrases this point that '[t]he characterization of the act by the national court did not correspond to its characterization under the statute'.

therefore be justified (see Art. 14 VII ICCPR). In the context of the ICTY however, this argumentation must fail. The Statute ICTY, is based on the idea of concurrent jurisdiction at the national and international levels (Art. 9 Statute ICTY). The ICTY enjoys primacy only in those cases where it requests it.[44] If it has done so, and the requested state is recalcitrant and tries the case itself, then one could say, that this procedure was not in accordance with the law applicable in the case. If the ICTY has not requested primacy, the national trial is in accordance with international law. The ICTY even encourages national courts to initiate their own proceedings in such cases.[45]

A second possible justification could be the fact that the misinterpretation itself gives reason for a new trial (material justification). If an offender is tried for ordinary crimes instead of international crimes, he has only been tried for one aspect of the actual offence for which he is accountable. The criminal who committed such heinous offences as international crimes cannot justly rely on a trial that touches merely upon the 'ordinary' half of the atrocities. The ILC draws a distinction on whether the national court lacked in its definition and application of the law the special international concerns of the crime.[46]

This argument also gives rise to serious difficulties. For example, the differentiation between ordinary and international crimes is not always clear-cut and indeed foreign to some legal systems.[47] Ostensibly it was the intention of the Security Council to prevent war criminals from being treated as ordinary criminals and being sentenced to a relatively lenient and mild domestic punishment. Such an intention is not stated anywhere, nor does it derive from stringent logic.[48] For example, a person convicted

---

[44] Although the matter of concurrent jurisdiction (Art. 9 Statute ICTY) and *ne bis in idem* (Art. 10 Statute ICTY) are closely linked, I cannot follow Bassiouni, *The Law of the ICTY*, 312–13, who holds that the conditions of Art. 10 (II) a and b Statute ICTY, should have been placed into Art. 9 Statute ICTY. In my view Art. 9 Statute ICTY grants discretion to the prosecutor of the ICTY to request deferral, whenever it seems appropriate pursuant to Rules 8–10. This norm is applicable until the national court has rendered its judgment. After the domestic judgment (*res judicata*) Art. 10 ICTY comes into play. The prosecutor is empowered to initiate proceedings only under the auspices of the conditions stated there. This seems to be the way the ICTY interprets the law (see below, the discussion of the Tadic motion concerning double jeopardy and ICTY First Annual Report paras. 20, 87–9).

[45] See e.g. the Report of the Secretary General, § 64. This encouragement is not exclusively, nor even primarily aimed at the successor states on the territory of the former Yugoslavia, which the Lawyers' Committee for Human Rights (May 1995) seems to presume (reprinted in Bassiouni, *The Law of the ICTY*, 315). Indeed, several European states have endeavoured to try war criminals that they found residing in their territory. Tadic was indicted in Munich, before being deferred to the ICTY, Djajic was as the first ex-Yugoslav war criminal tried and sentenced by the Bavarian High Court (Bayerisches Oberstes Landgericht) Judgment 23 May 1997, published in 1998 NJW, 392. Compare Safferling, 92 AJIL (1998), 528.

[46] Report ILC, Art. 42, para. 6.

[47] Crawford, The ILC's Draft Statute for an International Criminal Court, 88 AJIL (1994), 140 at 149. [48] Ibid.

of intentional murder will be automatically convicted to life imprison-ment according to § 211 German Penal Code (StGB). A more severe sentence is unknown to German criminal law. Even genocide, penalized by virtue of § 220 StGB, has no higher punishment, indeed, mitigating circumstances may be found to exist (§ 220 (II) StGB). The severity of the punishment can therefore hardly be the reason why the offence needs to be classified as a war crime by means of a breach of the principle *ne bis in idem*. If the facts have been correctly investigated and everything relevant been taken into consideration (in any other case Art. 10 II b Statute ICTY would be applicable), the punishment might well be appropriate whether the conviction was of murder or of war crimes. A second trial, and a reduction of the principle *ne bis in idem* to the *Anrechnungslösung* (Art. 10 (III) Statute ICTY), in such a case does not seem compatible with the human rights principle.

A third justification could be seen in the need to document the crimes (*Aufarbeitung der Vergangenheit*). As international crimes are offences against the international community, one could argue that they also must be treated as such by a global society. For documentary purposes the classification of the crime does not seem to play a crucial role as long as the facts were completely taken into consideration. More than that, had the Security Council wanted documentation of the atrocities for the international community, it would have given the ICTY exclusive jurisdiction over all international crimes which happened on the territory of the former Yugoslavia. It deliberately declined to do so.[49] The rule of Art. 10 II a Statute ICTY does not therefore seem justifiable from a human rights perspective.

The second alternative Art. 10 II b Statute ICTY is far less problematic. It allows a new trial whenever 'conditions of impartiality, independence or effective means of adjudication were not guaranteed in the proceedings before the national courts'.[50] The text of the statute itself is clear about the underlying reason for this provision. The national trial was intended to exploit the human right not to be tried twice for the same offence. A show-trial should bar a 'real' trial by deliberately making use of the prohibition of a second trial. In such a case, no friction with Art. 14 VII ICCPR exists. First, a 'show-trial' is not in accordance with criminal law and procedure, neither national nor international. It is particularly not in accordance with the human rights guarantees that are applicable during criminal prosecu-tion. Secondly, such a situation amounts to collusion. State authorities and defendant work together in a collusive manner aimed at the shielding of the criminal. This behaviour cannot create a legitimate expectation on the side of the accused not to be tried twice.

---

[49] See Bassiouni, *The Law of the ICTY*, 312–13.
[50] Report of the Secretary General, para. 66.

Art. 10 (II) b Statute ICTY is therefore compatible with human rights. However, a practical problem might arise, should this provision be used. By initiating international prosecution the ICTY implicitly questions the legality of the national procedure. The state will automatically understand the proceedings at the ICTY as a blatant censure of its own judiciary. Another question arising is who has the burden of proof on whether the national decision is improper?[51] These problems can only be solved through a state practice of acceptance and cooperation.

The problem of *ne bis in idem* has already been invoked before the ICTY. The defence in *Tadic* claimed that his referral to the ICTY by the German authorities constituted a second trial. Tadic was indicted by the public prosecutor in Munich. The indictment had been confirmed and a date for the main hearing was set when the prosecutor in the Hague requested his referral to the ICTY pursuant to Rule 9 (iii) on 8 November 1994. After the German Parliament had created the necessary legal base for the deferral,[52] it was executed a fortnight thereafter on 24 April 1995. The defence argued that this would constitute a breach of the double-jeopardy principle and that Rule 9 (iii) could not serve as a valid legal basis because it was not compatible with Art. 10 Statute. The responsible Trial Chamber II rejected these arguments. It rightly pointed out that *ne bis in idem* was not applicable to this situation, because the trial against Tadic had not even started. *Sedes materiae* therefore is not Art. 10 Statute ICTY but Art. 9 Statute ICTY. This provision however has not been violated.[53]

2. The law at the ICC

Art. 20 Rome Statute (Art. 42 Statute ILC) contains the provision for *ne bis in idem* similar to that in Art. 10 Statute ICTY. Art. 20 (II) Rome Statute (Art. 42 (I) Statute ILC) is not limited to previous trial before 'national courts' so that any other potential international tribunal would be included.[54] Neither the ICTY Statute nor the Statute ILC expressly refer to

---

[51] Tallgren, in Trifterer (ed.), *Commentary on the Rome Statute*, Art. 20, No. 20.

[52] Gesetz über die Zusmmenarbeit mit dem Internationalen Strafgerichtshof für das ehemalige Jugoslavien (Jugoslavien-Strafgerichtshof-Gesetz [Act about the cooperation with the ICTY (ICTY-Act)], 10 April 1995, BGBl I 1995, 485. Compare, about the request to deferral and the reaction of the federal government, Vierucci, 6 EJIL (1995), 134. This Act (*Lex Tadic*), although drafted especially for the purpose to 'extradite' *Tadic*, is a general-abstract norm and therefore not contrary to the rule of law. Nor is it in conflict with the principle of non-retroactive legislation, as it is purely procedural in nature, see Kleinknecht and Meyer-Goßner Einl. No. 203.

[53] ICTY Trial Chamber II, *Tadic* case, decision 14 November 1995, paras. 10, 11, 24. The Chamber further emphasized that there was no danger that German authorities would continue their efforts to try the defendant after his trial in the Hague as this would be in breach of Art. 10 (I) Statute, ibid., para. 13.

[54] Report ILC Art. 42, para. 2: which other tribunals or courts the ILC had in mind is, however, not quite clear.

a prohibition of a second trial at the international court itself. The Report ILC nevertheless excludes such a second trial.[55] This has been implemented in Art. 20 (I) Rome Statute. As Art. 20 (II) Rome Statute (Art. 42 (I) Statute ILC) refers explicitly to the jurisdiction *ratione materiae* of the ICC the prohibition of a second trial in national courts does not pertain to charges of a different crime. If therefore a person was acquitted of crimes against humanity at the ICC because, for example, the necessary intent could not be proven, he might still have to answer an accusation for murder in a national court.[56] As to the exceptions in Art. 20 (III) Rome Statute (Art. 42 (II) Statute ILC) what was said earlier concerning the Statute ICTY is equally valid here. Art. 20 (III) a Rome Statute should therefore only be applied if the conditions of Art. 20 (III) b Rome Statute are given cumulatively. In the event of a second trial the ICC must take into consideration the penalty already served given by the national court. The Rome Statute unfortunately omitted this norm. However, the penalty already served should be taken into consideration by virtue of Art. 78 (II) Rome Statute.[57]

B. THE RIGHT TO APPEAL

Having discussed the prohibition of double jeopardy the first problem when discussing appeals is to decide whether appeal and review is actually a matter of *ne bis in idem* or whether this principle is applicable only after the whole procedure is over.[58] This is of special importance to the question of whether both the convicted person and the prosecutor have the right to appeal. What the right to appeal means, and how it differs from a review procedure, will be my second point. Finally, I will discuss to what extent the principles discussed earlier are applicable to the appeals stage.

(I) Who can Appeal

A problem lies hidden in the issue of who has the power to approach the court of higher instance for a review. Art. 14 (VII) ICCPR clearly gives the right to appeal to the defendant. From a human rights perspective this seems clear as a 'classical' means to control state authority, but can the prosecutor also approach the higher court or is it prohibited from a human rights perspective to allow the state authority to claim a violation

---

[55] Report ILC Art. 42 para. 3.   [56] Ibid.
[57] Jennings, in Trifterer (ed.), *Commentary on the Rome Statute*, Art. 78, No. 13, is positive that the ICC will consider a prior detention.
[58] Tallgren, ibid., Art. 20, No. 12.

of procedural law, for example, the false weighing of evidence in favour of the accused which led to an acquittal or too weak a sentence? Art. 14 (V) ICCPR leaves this question open. If states want to organize their system on a two-level basis, they may do so. However, these systems have to allow for appeal against a conviction or an aggravated sentence that only came about at the appeals level.[59]

1. Common and civil law

Common law originally did not recognize a right to appeal.[60] Because a jury has convicted the defendant a higher authority cannot easily review the finding. One could not justify several professional judges overruling the verdict of twelve representatives of the public. This is especially true of acquittals. In both the English and United States legal systems, the prosecution may not appeal against an acquittal.[61] In England the prosecutor may ask the Court of Appeal for its opinion. This cannot, however, affect the situation of the acquitted.[62]

A separate problem arises when looking at the effects of a guilty plea. If the defendant pleads guilty, his case will not be discussed by a jury, the judge will only decide on the sentence. Consequently, the common law tradition does not allow for an appeal against a conviction after a guilty plea but only against the sentence.[63] The defendant who pleaded guilty can only appeal if he claims that his plea was wrong and that he did not appreciate the nature of the charge or did not intend to admit that he was guilty of it or that upon the admitted facts he could not in law be convicted of the offences charged.[64] Harris found that the ICCPR goes beyond what the common law admits and allows appeal against conviction by a person who pleaded guilty.[65]

The civil law system sees the process continuing until the time limit for the institution of further proceedings has expired.[66] Only then is the matter regarded as *res judicata* and the defendant can be certain of his conviction and sentence. The process is considered as one trial. It follows that both prosecutor and defendant have the ability to request an appeal. The sentence of the defendant might therefore be increased by an appeals court decision. German law allows for a limited *reformatio in peius*. According to § 331 StPO the situation of the appellant may not be worsened if he himself appealed or the prosecutor appealed in his favour. This

---

[59] Nowak, Art. 14, No. 68.
[60] Osakwe in Andrews (1982), 292.
[61] Lidstone and Osakwe in Andrews (1982), 102 and 286.
[62] Lidstone in Andrews (1982), 102.
[63] Ibid. 102.
[64] *R v Forde* (1923) 2 KB 400.
[65] Harris, 16 ICLQ (1967), 352, at 272, without giving further explanation of this point.
[66] See above at the beginning of Ch. 5, p. 319.

is believed not to be a corollary to the *Rechtsstaatsprinzip* but only a benefit for the appellant, that he need not fear worsening his position by seeking to ease it.[67]

From a human rights perspective it is difficult to argue that the possibility for the prosecutor to appeal, even against an acquittal, constitutes a violation of human rights, because this possibility exists in many countries.

2. The law at the ICTY

In Art. 25 Statute ICTY refers to 'appellate proceedings'. It empowers both the convicted and the prosecutor to appeal against a decision of the Trial Chamber. According to the text the prosecutor's right to appeal is not limited to appeal against convictions, as the accused's right is. To allege that the statute was not intended to grant the prosecutor the possibility of appeal of an acquittal, as Bassiouni does,[68] would need further substantiation. The law at the ICTY is not quite clear in this respect and clarification will only be brought by a decision of the Appeals Chamber, if such an appeal is filed by the prosecutor.[69] Third parties are not allowed to appeal against a decision.[70]

If one looks at the grounds for an appeal in Art. 25 Statute ICTY, alternative (*a*) would not be dangerous for the situation of the accused. This is because, if an error of law is found, this would invalidate the decision. Alternative (*b*) allows for an appeal on the grounds of an error of fact which occasioned a miscarriage of justice. A miscarriage of justice, however, can also occur 'in favour' of the accused, that is, that his acquittal is a major piece of injustice. As we have argued above, this is a fault, at which 'humanity need not blush'.[71] Should the prosecutor nevertheless be given a chance to correct this error of justice by way of an appeal? To achieve the aims of criminal justice, the system should be organized in a way that greatly reduces the likelihood of errors occurring. The innocent must go free and the guilty be convicted. If a system gives both the defence and the prosecution two chances, it does so in order to minimize defects on either side.

---

[67] See Kleinknecht and Meyer-Goßner § 331, Nos. 1, 8. The prevailing view applies this only to the sentence, not to the verdict as to guilt.

[68] Bassiouni, *The Law of the ICTY*, 979.

[69] Morris and Scharf, *An Insider's Guide*, 295–6, who are also inclined not to allow such an appeal.

[70] In the case *Dragan Opacic* Case No. IT-95-7-Misc.1, Decision 3 June 1997 on Application for Leave of Appeal, a detained witness sought appeal against a decision of a Trial Chamber. These proceedings pertain to so-called interlocutory appeal/review as foreseen in Rule 72B and not to actual convictions. These interlocutory appeals are now also allowed for states since the amendment of Rule 108*bis* on 24 July 1997 at the ICTY 13th Plenary Session.

[71] Above, on 'right to jury', Forsynth, *History of Trial by Jury*, 430–1.

3. The law at the ICC

The ICC foresees in Art. 81 Rome Statute a right both for the prosecutor and the convicted to appeal against a conviction or sentence. The prosecutor may also make an appeal on behalf of the convicted person.[72] As this appeals system resembles the Continental practice,[73] it is submitted that the question of *reformatio in peius*, which is not dealt with in the Rome Statute, should also be answered in accordance with the Continental way: the sentence can only be changed for the worse if the prosecutor appealed to the disadvantage of the defendant.

(II) What to Appeal Against

The appeal may be based on a claim that the facts have been incompletely established and the evidence been misjudged or a claim that a procedural mistake took place or that the court has misinterpreted the law. The first claim would lead to a full rehearing, the second would mean reconsidering the legal issues. I will call the first 'appeal' (*Berufung*) and the second 'cassation' (*Revision*).

Human rights probably only protect the right to have the judgment reviewed in the sense of a cassation procedure.[74] The drafting history of Art. 14 (V) ICCPR reveals that it was intended to leave the contents of the right to appeal to the individual legal system.[75]

1. Common and civil law

According to the Anglo-American tradition it is difficult to allow an appeal in this sense. As we have a right to a jury in this jurisdiction it would be a clear infringement of this right if the Court of Appeal could admit further evidence and weigh the material before it again.[76] A complete retrial would be obligatory, otherwise the judges would usurp the function of a jury.[77] On appeal, courts will abstain from reviewing the facts of a case. Matters that are outside the trial record are never considered, even though these might undercut the legality of the conviction.[78]

---

[72] Report ILC, Art. 49, para. 1. In the PrepComm it was discussed whether to reduce the prosecutor's right to appeal to errors of law, Report of the PrepComm I, para. 295.

[73] Compare Behrens, 6 Eur.J.Crime Cr.L.Cr.J (1998), 440, who rightly observes that the rationale for the prohibition of an appeal against acquittal does not apply to a non-jury trial.

[74] See Bassiouni, *The Law of the ICTY*, 979.

[75] Compare Nowak, Art. 14 Nos. 64, 65.

[76] Lidstone in Andrews (1982), 106.

[77] The English Court of Appeal has been criticized for doing precisely this; compare the criticism of Lord Devlin quoted by Lidstone (ibid.).

[78] Osakwe, ibid. 292. Certainly there are special procedures to complain about the injustice of a conviction. If new evidence is found, a retrial may be ordered; if constitutional rights are involved, the way is open to file a complaint to the Supreme Court.

Appeal Courts may quash the decision because it is erroneous on a question of law, or it contains material irregularities. Furthermore, they could set the jury verdict aside even without there being procedural irregularities, on evidential grounds.[79] In all of these cases the Appeal Court will only touch upon the integrity of the conviction if it finds a miscarriage of justice, otherwise misconduct has to be tolerated by the convicted. According to the common law, appeals are therefore only possible against legal misconduct or serious evidentiary misjudgment. Taken altogether we can hardly call this an appeal in the sense given to it above. It merely comprises what I named 'cassation'.

The Continental system is more generous in allowing appeals. In the absence of a jury a new assessment of all relevant facts and legal issues can be easily embarked upon. Thus the Appeal Court can hear all the evidence again and draw its own conclusions as to the value and reliability of statements and witnesses. The appeal will be heard like a first-instance trial before a court consisting of a greater number and more experienced judges.

2. The system at the ICTY and the ICC

Art. 25 (I) Statute ICTY provides for an appeal both on grounds of error of law and error of fact. It thus interprets Art. 14 (V) ICCPR generously, as compliance does not require a review of the facts.[80] Similarly, at the ICC an appeal is possible on grounds of procedural error, error of fact or of law, or lack of proportionality between the crime and the sentence (Art. 81 (I) and (II) Rome Statute). In this case the Appeal Chamber would have to hear the entire case.[81] It has been proposed that appeals proceedings should be possible against the 'review *in absentia*' decision according to Art. 37 (II) Statute ILC.[82] Why this should be so is unclear. Art. 37 (II) Statute ILC (and now Art. 61 (II) Rome Statute) cannot produce a final decision. It is only an interim finding which leads to the issuing of an international arrest warrant. The result of the ordinary arrest warrant is not that different from the international warrant of arrest. It is illogical to discriminate between the two warrants and to only allow an appeal against the latter. The reason for the appeal must therefore lie in the procedure. By allowing an appeal against the review pursuant to Art. 37 (II) Statute ILC, one attributes too much importance to this procedure and enhances the chances that the trial that has to follow, if the defendant is brought before the ICC, will be unfair towards him. The possibility of appealing against such a decision could have the consequence that

---

[79] Lidstone, ibid. 105, who admits that this is not frequent conduct in the English Court of Appeals.
[80] Bassiouni, *The Law of the ICTY*, 979   [81] Report of the PrepComm I, para. 295.
[82] Report of the PrepComm II, 235.

evidence from the review in absentia proceeding is used against the accused at trial without giving him the chance to properly challenge it as he already had the chance to rebut it in the appeals proceeding. The Rome Statute disconnected the confirmation of the indictment in the absence of the suspect from the question of the arrest warrant. The rationale of the confirmation is one of judicial control over the outcome of the investigation and the decision whether or not the case is strong enough to go to trial. The proposal of allowing appeal proceedings against a confirmation has not been inserted into the Rome Statute. The confirmation decision is—so to say—reviewed by the trial that follows.

The Rome Statute differentiates between appeal against the verdict (conviction or acquittal) on the one hand (Art. 81 (I) Rome Statute) and appeal against the sentence on the other. One could draw the conclusion that the statute allows isolated appeals and it is submitted here that Art. 81 Rome Statute should indeed be read in such a way (Art. 81 (II) b and c Rome Statute).[83] It reduces the workload of the Appeals Chamber if it is specified in the complaint which part of the decision should be reviewed. Certainly the Chamber is not bound by an isolated appeal and can review the decision in its entirety (Art. 81 (II) Rome Statute).[84]

(III) How to Proceed on Appeal

1. The applicability of human rights norms

The question of a speedy trial is certainly of major importance. The HRC stated in its General Comment that the time limit is to be applied to appeals proceedings as well.[85] According to the case-law of the European authorities proceedings on appeal fall within the scope of Art. 6 (I) ECHR and its reasonable time limit, as was held in the cases *Wemhoff v Germany*[86] and *Neumeister v Austria*.[87] It is generally accepted by domestic courts and in literature that Art. 6 ECHR applies to review proceedings.[88]

Another problem which has arisen is whether 'appeals' proceedings have to be oral. If one applies the terminology that we gave to 'appeals' it should be obvious that a retrial of facts and law has to follow the same rules as the trial of first instance. Therefore, appeals proceedings have to be oral. Different considerations apply to 'cassation': only legal questions

---

[83] See also Staker, in Trifterer (ed.), *Commentary on the Rome Statute*, Art. 81, No. 16.

[84] Staker (ibid.) argues that this falls within the inherent powers of the Appeals Chamber, as is proven by the ICTY Appeals Chamber's decision in *Erdemovic*, where the convicted appealed only against the sentence. The Appeals Chamber quashed the conviction holding that the accused's plea was not informed. (Case No. IT-96-22-A, 7 October 1997.)

[85] HRC General Comment 13 (Article 14), para. 10.

[86] ECourtHR *Wemhoff v Germany* Judgment 27 June 1968, Series A No. 7, para. 18.

[87] ECourtHR *Neumeister v Austria* Judgment 27 June 1968, Series A No. 8, para. 19.

[88] Lidstone in Andrews (1982), 102.

are addressed, therefore, it is not necessary for the procedure to be oral. Similarly the ECourtHR held in *Monnell and Morris v UK* that proceedings before the English Court of Appeal for leave to appeal do not necessarily have to be oral.[89] However, it must be ascertained whether or not the legal system provides an equal opportunity for both parties to present arguments.[90]

As proceedings on appeal entail a reconsideration of the facts the court must be concerned with the presentation of evidence. Consequently the right to call and cross-examine witnesses in Art. 6 (III) d ECHR has to apply on the appeals stage just as on the first instance trial.[91] The IAmCommHR held that the provisions of due process as embodied in Art. 8 AmCHR must be applied to any appeals or review procedure.[92]

2. The law at the ICTY and the ICC

According to Rule 107 the same rules that govern proceedings at the Trial Chambers shall apply *mutatis mutandis* in the Appeals Chamber. In particular the principle of 'equity of arms' is verified in the Rules of Procedure through written brief and reply, and an eventual oral hearing of the points at issue (Rules 111 to 114). In the case of new evidence (Rule 115) the same rules as for the presentation of evidence at the Trial Chamber apply.[93] New evidence is however only admissible if a reasonable explanation as to why the evidence was not available at trial can be given.[94] In general the rules on appeal are more lenient, in particular those concerning time limits. Rule 108 grants fifteen days to file a notice of appeal,[95] and Rule 111 gives the appellant ninety days to file a brief, Rule 112 gives thirty days to the respondent to reply, and Rule 113 another fifteen for another reply by the appellant.[96] Because of the unique nature of the ICTY and the complex

---

[89] ECourtHR *Monnell and Morris v UK* Judgment 2 March 1987, Series A No. 151, paras. 57–69. In this case the ECourtHR considered Art. 6 (I) and (III) c ECHR together. A further tricky question arises from the ECourtHR's ruling in this case. The applicants' sentences were protracted by the appeals court on grounds of loss of time. This was meant to be a punishment for an obviously unmeritorious application for leave to appeal. In the ECourtHR's case-law it seems to be the case that, whenever there is a danger of *reformatio in peius*, the defendant has a right to be heard (see above as to 'equity of arms'). In the light of this, the English Court of Appeal should perhaps have held an oral hearing.

[90] Fawcett, *The Application of the ECHR*, 132.

[91] Harris, 266.

[92] IAmCommHR, Res 74/90, Case 9850 (Argentina) 4 October 1990, Annual Report of the IAmCommHR 1990–91, OEA/Ser.L/V/II.79 rev.1, doc. 12, 22 February 1991, para. 18.

[93] This derives unproblematically from Rule 107.

[94] See ICTY Appeals Chamber, *Tadic*, Decision on Admissibility of Additional Evidence, 15 October 1998.

[95] The previous time limit of thirty days was halved at the 14th Plenary Session on 12 November 1997. Two weeks do seem to be enough time to decide whether or not to proceed to appeal. Compared to ten days in the US Federal Rules of Appellate Procedure the limit is still modest (Bassiouni, *The Law of the ICTY*, 981).

[96] In the USA the time limits are forty, thirty, and fourteen days (ibid.).

issues at stake these time limits seem appropriate.[97] The judgment (Rule 117) given by the Appeals Chamber is final, which is emphasized by the fact that the sentence pronounced by the Appeals Chamber shall be enforced immediately (Rule 118A).

The appeals proceedings at the ICC are supposed to be governed by the same rules as the Trial Chamber proceedings (Art. 83 (I) Rome Statute). The time limits are not expressly stated in the Statute, but should be implied into the Rules of Procedure.[98] It is submitted that the ICTY law is appropriate in this regard and should be transferred to the ICC. In particular the Rules of Procedure should abstain from imposing different time limits for different grounds for appeal.[99] By doing this the procedure on appeal is complicated considerably without need. The Appeals Chamber may either reverse or amend the decision or sentence or order a new trial before a different Trial Chamber. The Appeals Chamber may also call evidence itself (Art. 83 (II) Rome Statute). The Appeals Chamber's decision shall be taken unanimously. If unanimity cannot be reached, the judgment shall contain the views both of the majority and the minority. Only on a question of law may a judge deliver a separate or dissenting opinion (Art. 83 (IV) Rome Statute).[100]

(IV) Access to Human Rights Bodies

We have seen that human rights foresee a right to appeal and that this procedure must follow the rules of a 'fair trial' to a similar extent to the first trial. The ordinary criminal who is convicted by a national court therefore must be guaranteed the right of access to a court of higher instance to have his case reviewed. The ordinary criminal has then, however, the possibility of accessing a further judicial or quasi-judicial body. In many countries there exists a Constitutional Court[101] which will not look at the whole evidence again, but at least civil liberties issues can be addressed before these bodies.[102] Furthermore, the ordinary criminal in Europe may access the ECourtHR claiming violations of the ECHR. Outside Europe there either exist regional human rights bodies or a communication to the HRC might be possible, if the state concerned accepts its jurisdiction under the First Protocol ICCPR. In the case of the

---

[97] Bassiouni, *The Law of the ICTY*, 981.

[98] Report of the PrepComm I, para. 296.

[99] Draft Rules 8.2 and 8.6 contemplate different and very short time limits.

[100] This recalls Art. 74 (V) Rome Statute: at the Trial Chamber dissenting opinions are disallowed. Compare above, Ch. 4 B V 5, p. 263..

[101] England is the obvious exception.

[102] See the teaching of the BVerfG, according to which the Court is not to be seen as the *Superrevisionsinstanz*, and Stern, *Staatsrecht* III/2, § 91 V 3 b α, similar to the ECourtHR jurisprudence concerning the *quatrième instance* tenet; see Harris, 15.

International Criminal Court there need to be two instances, so as to fulfil the human right to an appeals instance. Nevertheless this Appeals Chamber appears to be the last court. There is no further way for a person convicted by the International Criminal Court to make a complaint about human rights violations to a court of higher instance. This seems to be a case of inequality. This is not only because it is hard to differentiate between an international criminal and an ordinary criminal. Even if this differentiation was easy, it is by no means certain that the former will end up before the International Criminal Court and the latter in national jurisdiction. The international jurisdiction is, to a certain extent, only meant to be a substitute for unwilling or ineffective national jurisdiction; indeed, the war criminal might easily have to defend himself at a national court anywhere in the world.[103]

---

[103] No need to emphasize again the trials of persons involved in the conflict on the territory of the former Yugoslavia in Austria, Germany, or Switzerland.

6

The Post-Trial Stage

It is often forgotten that whatever comes after the final conviction is part of criminal procedure and is certainly still subject to human rights law. Imprisonment is, as we saw above when looking at pre-trial detention, a serious constraint and indeed an infringement of the right to liberty and security of person. From this some conditions follow about the treatment of the prisoner. In addition, I will look at the possible remedies for the prisoner concerning the conditions of his imprisonment or the validity of his conviction.

A. TREATMENT IN PRISON

Fair treatment of criminal offenders must include the stage of imprisonment. This work is not a criminological analysis of the most appropriate treatment during the time behind bars, but is merely concerned with human rights during the stage of execution of sentence and aims to provide a human rights framework for treatment in prison. What essentially need to be addressed are the difficulties emerging from our international approach. The international court would not have its own detention units where the sentenced criminals could serve their time. It has therefore to rely on cooperation with states that signal their willingness to host international criminals. The international body, however, has to choose the right country in which the individual convicted war criminal will serve his time. Whether or not there are some rules that govern this choice, according to human rights, will also be considered.

(I) Adequate Treatment

What are the human rights that govern imprisonment? Are human rights an issue here or do they cease to protect the criminal after the conviction? There are many human rights provisions that govern the conditions of imprisonment. There is, first of all, the right to life which is enshrined in Art. 6 ICCPR: '(1) Every human being has the inherent right to life. This right shall be protected by law. No one shall be arbitrarily deprived of his life.' A further requirement is the prohibition of torture in Art. 7 ICCPR; we also have to look at Art. 8 ICCPR which occasionally speaks directly about imprisonment.

Art. 8 ICCPR

(3)

(a) No one shall be required to perform forced or compulsory labour;

(b) Paragraph (3a) shall not be held to preclude, in countries where imprisonment with hard labour may be imposed as a punishment for a crime, the performance of hard labour in pursuance of a sentence to such punishment by a competent court;

(c) for the purpose of this paragraph the term 'forced or compulsory labour' shall not include:

    i any work or service, not referred to in subparagraph (b), normally required of a person who is under detention in consequence of a lawful order of a court, or of a person during conditional release from such detention;

    ii . . .

Art. 9 ICCPR

(1) Everyone has the right to liberty and security of person. No one shall be subjected to arbitrary arrest or detention. No one shall be deprived of his liberty except on such grounds and in accordance with such procedure as are established by law.

Art. 10 ICCPR

(1) All persons deprived of their liberty shall be treated with humanity and with respect for the inherent dignity of the human person

2

(a) Accused persons shall, save in exceptional circumstances, be segregated from convicted persons and shall be subject to separate treatment appropriate to their status as unconvicted persons;

(b) Accused juvenile persons shall be separated from adults and brought as speedily as possible for adjudication.

(3) The penitentiary system shall comprise treatment of prisoners the essential aim of which shall be their reformation and social rehabilitation. Juvenile offenders shall be segregated from adults and be accorded treatment appropriate to their age and legal status.

1. Human rights bodies

(a) The ICCPR Perhaps the most important provision for treatment during detention is the duty of the state to effectively protect the life of the detainee. The HRC has repeatedly called Art. 6 ICCPR the 'supreme right' that should not be interpreted narrowly.[1] The responsibility for the lives of persons does not stop when they are convicted and imprisoned. The state has to provide adequate and appropriate means to protect their lives when they are in custody.[2] The HRC found that this provision put a positive

---

[1] HRC General Comment 6 (Article 6), para. 1

[2] Two cases before the HRC are of interest in this context: *Bleir v Uruguay* Doc.A/37/40, 130 and *H.Barbato v Uruguay* Doc. A/38/40, 124. Although the applicants could not produce enough evidence of the concrete circumstances of the case, nevertheless the HRC had serious reasons to believe that the state failed to protect the lives of the applicants. Uruguay

obligation on the state party towards those people who are particularly vulnerable due to their detention.[3] Certainly these positive obligations can be interpreted in a progressive way beyond what is sometimes called an 'all-around effect'.[4] The HRC did not go as far as building a bridge between the civil and political and the economic, social, and cultural rights under the right to life in Art. 6 ICCPR. Had it done so, it would have, as McGoldrick states, risked its international acceptance and credibility. Furthermore it would have provoked serious legal questions about interpretation of documents, the relationship between the ICCPR and the ICESCR,[5] and the jurisdiction of the HRC under the First Optional Protocol of the ICCPR.[6] Whatever one's opinion on the 'reunification' of the two concepts of human rights[7] might be, the 'traditional' criticism against state accountability for food, shelter, clothes, medical treatment, and the like cannot possibly apply to this situation. The detained person is entirely in the hands of state authorities and depends on their benevolent and compassionate behaviour.[8] Behind bars he is not able to look after his own conditions. As the state has total control over his life, this must be protected in all its aspects and whatever the prisoner needs to survive must be granted. If one does not want to follow this interpretation, the requirements mentioned here would have to be met by the state under Art. 10 ICCPR in any case.[9]

The prohibition of torture (Art. 7 ICCPR) and the obligation to respect the human dignity of the detained (Art. 10) are often discussed together.[10] In the eyes of the HRC Art. 7 ICCPR is complemented by the positive

once more did not cooperate with the HRC and did not produce any relevant evidence, see McGoldrick, *Human Rights Committee*, 339.

[3] HRC *Herera Rubio v. Columbia* Doc. A/43/40, 190. General Comment 21 (Article 10), para. 3.

[4] For further explanation of this term see Nowak, Art. 6, Nos. 3, 4; in contrast to the maybe more commonly used terms 'horizontal effects' or 'third-party effects' (*Drittwirkung*), the term 'all-around effects' is meant to paraphrase the fact that the right is supposed to be entrenched in all forms of legislation, civil, criminal, and administrative.

[5] Dinstein, in Henkin, *International Bill of Rights*, 114 at 115, unequivocally calls 'the human right to life *per se*' (whatever this is supposed to mean) a civil right that does not protect economic and social rights found in the ICESCR.

[6] McGoldrick, *Human Rights Committee*, 347.

[7] Civil and political rights and economic, social, and cultural rights are to be found alongside each other in the UDHR (1948) and also in the most recent of the regional covenant, the AfCHPR. See, for an introduction into the status of both sets of rights, M. C. R. Craven, *The International Covenant on Economic, Social and Cultural Rights* (Oxford, 1995), 6–16, and above, Ch. 1, p. 27.

[8] The most probable reason why the HRC called detainees particularly vulnerable is that they depend entirely on the state authority.

[9] See below, 343.

[10] Compare in particular the case-law of the HRC concerning the conditions of detention at the 'Libertad' Prison in Montevideo during the military dictatorship, see Nowak, Art. 10, No. 11.

requirements of Art. 10 ICCPR.[11] However, it does not further define torture or elaborate on a further separation between torture and inhumane and degrading treatment.[12] It mainly states that the classification would depend on the nature, purpose, and severity of the applied treatment, but encompasses mental suffering as well as physical harm.[13] Likewise, in most cases the HRC is satisfied with a simple determination of a violation of Art. 7 ICCPR, without further definition of the single elements.[14] The HRC in its General Comments is concerned about incommunicado detentions; to make sure that neither lawyers or doctors nor family members are denied access to the detained, it proposes that states keep general records of names and places of detention in order to prohibit disappearances.[15] Furthermore, the prohibition of torture would include corporal punishment and even solitary confinement, especially if in connection with incommunicado detention.[16] Overcrowded cells, illuminated constantly by artificial light, prisoners being bound and blindfolded, detention in a truck garage, being forced to sleep on the floor, and given little food have been considered as inhumane and cruel treatment.[17]

As for the implementation of Art. 10 ICCPR, the HRC expressed in the General Comments that states did not take the provision seriously enough; their reports were criticized for not giving information about the measures taken to enforce the respect for human dignity[18] of inmates through their national legislation.[19] The state must provide prisoners with a minimum of services to satisfy their basic needs, like food, clothing, medical care, sanitary facilities, communications, light, opportunity to move about, privacy, and so forth. In this respect Art. 10 goes beyond what is prohibited by Art. 7.[20] The HRC in particular addresses the argument that is often raised against economic and social rights: they

[11] HRC General Comment 20 (Article 7), which is replacing, reflecting, and further developing General Comment 7, para. 2.

[12] HRC General Comment 20 (Article 7), para. 4, see also Nowak, Art. 7, Nos. 4, 5.

[13] HRC General Comment 20 (Article 7), paras. 4, 5. These criteria are clearly taken from the definition of torture by Art. 1 (I) UN Convention against torture; see also Nowak, Art. 7, No. 6, and above Ch. 3.

[14] Nowak, Art. 7, No. 16.

[15] HRC General Comment 7 (Article 7) para. 1 and General Comment 20 (Article 7) para. 11; see also General Comment 6 (Article 6) para. 4 where the HRC expresses its concerns about increasing numbers of disappearances against which states must effectively fight.

[16] HRC General Comment 7 (Article 7), para. 2; General Comment 20 (Article 7), para. 6. See also above, Ch. 3.

[17] Nowak, Art. 7, No. 11.

[18] That the text speaks of both humanity and human dignity is not entirely tautological cosmetics; it reflects the aim of the drafters to be as clear as possible. Apparently, the term 'humanity' does not mean the same in different languages, so the drafters decided to attach 'human dignity' to prevent uncertainties. Compare Bossuyt, *Guide*, 224–5.

[19] HRC General Comment 9 (Article 10), para. 1.

[20] Nowak, Art. 10, No. 14.

allegedly depend on material resources. The HRC goes so far as to deny that the respect for human dignity does not depend on financial power;[21] it concedes that resources may vary but at least these must always be applied without discrimination.[22] The Standard Minimum Rules for the Treatment of Prisoners, however, accept in the preliminary observations that there is worldwide a great variety in legal, social, economic, and geographical conditions, which makes it evident that not all of the rules set out in this document (and those are only the 'minimum rules'!) are capable of being applied in all places at all times.[23]

The HRC understands Art. 10 (III) ICCPR as requesting the state to promote the reformation and social rehabilitation[24] of prisoners through education, vocational training, and useful work; likewise visits by family members are understood to contribute to respecting human dignity.[25] The HRC even suggests a right to be visited by family members in *Ambrosini v Uruguay*.[26] McGoldrick criticizes this progressive step. In his view there is nothing in the ICCPR from which one could derive such a right.[27] These patterns are of particular importance when the state is dealing with juvenile offenders. The HRC further refers to other United Nations texts and documents that were drafted in particular to govern conditions of imprisoned persons.[28] Amongst them are the Standard Minimum Rules for the Treatment of Prisoners,[29] the Body of Principles for the Protection of All

---

[21] It is interesting to note that during the three years between the adaptation of the first Comment concerning Article 10 in 1989 and the second that would replace, reflect, and further develop the first in 1992, General Comment 21 (Article 10), the HRC dropped the word 'entirely'. The latest version reads as: '[t]he application of this rule [Article 10], as a minimum, cannot be dependent on the material resources available in the State party'. Ibid., para. 4. Before it said that this right is 'a basic standard of universal application which cannot *entirely* depend on material resources' (emphasis added), General Comment 9 (Article 10), para. 1.

[22] HRC General Comment 9 (Article 10), para. 1. Also the new General Comment 21 (Article 10), para. 4, stresses the importance of applying this provision without distinction of any kind.

[23] Compare Standard Minimum Rules for the Treatment of Prisoners, Preliminary Observations No. 2.

[24] The second Comment in Art. 10 ICCPR was a bit more cautious about the aims of punishment. There the HRC said that the penitentiary system should not solely be retributory; 'it should essentially seek the reformation and rehabilitation of the offender', see HRC General Comment 21 (Article 10), para. 10. It becomes clear from the *travaux* that the drafters envisaged a wording that would be open for other goals of the penitentiary system. It was intended to resist modern ideas or contemporary trends, see the submission of the Soviet Union [A/C.3/SR.882, 3 2]. The 1992 Comment seems therefore closer to the drafting history than its predecessor.

[25] HRC General Comment 9 (Article 10), para. 3.

[26] HRC *Ambrosini v Uruguay* Doc. A/34/40, 124.

[27] McGoldrick, *Human Rights Committee*, 368.

[28] General Comment 21 (Article 10), para. 5.

[29] Adopted by the First United Nations Congress on the Prevention of Crime and the Treatment of Offenders, 30 August 1955; approved by United Nations ECOSOC Res.663 C

Persons under Any Form of Detention or Imprisonment (1988), and the Code of Conduct for Law Enforcement Officials.[30] A provision worth mentioning is found in s. 38 Standard Minimum Rules: foreign nationals shall be allowed contact with diplomatic and consular representatives of their home state. It is submitted here that this should be applied to the context of international criminals.

Art. 8 (III) ICCPR prohibits forced or compulsory labour. The drafters did not entail a definition in the document, although they contemplated one similar to the one of the International Labour Convention[31] submitted by the United States: 'all work or service which is exacted from any person under the menace of any penalty and for which he has not offered himself voluntarily'.[32] In order not to provide for an exception that would serve for some states as a welcomed loophole, a definition that would allow forced labour if in accordance with a court sentence was rejected by the HRComm in the 5th Session (1949);[33] still imprisonment with hard labour was recognized by the Commission as existing in several states. As the exception in Art. 8 (III) b ICCPR shows, this is to be understood as an exceptional sentence in accordance with the law and a court sentence and not prison conditions.[34] It alludes to the existing classical form of 'hard labour' in work colonies or camps.[35] Likewise, work that promotes the rehabilitation of the detained person, that is, ordinary 'routine' prison work, is allowed by Art. 8 (III) c (i) ICCPR.[36] It is notable that this provision refers to all forms of detention, including detention on remand, which does not seem to be compatible with the aim and nature of pre-trial detention, but is consistent with the drafting history.[37]

Perhaps one could summarize the intentions of the ICCPR as perceived by the HRC as to the treatment during imprisonment by a statement found in its Comment on Article 10 ICCPR:

(XXIV) 31 July 1957; amended by ECOSOC Res.2076 (LXII) 12 May 1977. This body of rules was already considered by the drafters as mirroring in greater detail the aim of Art.10 ICCPR; compare Bossuyt, *Guide*, 233.

A detailed analysis of this body of rules is given by Rodley, *Treatment of Prisoners*, 219–41.

[30] Adopted by the UN GA Res.34/169, 17 December 1979.

[31] Art. 2 (I) ILO Convention No. 29 of 28 June 1930.

[32] E/CN.4/W.25. It is interesting to note that while the emphasis with forced labour is on the element of involuntariness, slavery and servitude are also prohibited in the event of voluntariness, see Nowak, Art. 8, No. 15.

[33] E/CN.4/SR.142, § 36 (USA) and E/CN.4/SR.143, § 13 (GB).

[34] See Bossuyt, *Guide*, 172.

[35] As this exception aims only at keeping this, for some states, 'classic' punishment, an *argumentum a majore ad minus* that 'light' labour must then be allowed in any circumstance is not feasible. Furthermore, the punishment may only be imposed for the most severe offences; see Nowak, Art. 8, No. 22.

[36] The annex 'or of a person during conditional release from such detention' was introduced by the Netherlands in the 3rd Committee 13th Session in 1958 (A/C.3/L.682).

[37] Nowak, Art. 8. No. 25.

[persons deprived of their liberty may not] be subjected to any hardship or constraint other than that resulting from the deprivation of liberty; respect for the dignity of such persons must be guaranteed under the same conditions as for that of free persons. Persons deprived of their liberty enjoy all the rights set forth in the Covenant, subject to the restrictions that are unavoidable in a closed environment.[38]

In one sentence: there should be no further hardship than is strictly necessary for life behind bars.

(b) The ECHR   The ECHR does not deal with imprisonment in such an extensive manner as does the ICCPR. In Art. 2 ECHR we find the absolute obligation to protect the life of everyone.[39] Although the European authorities did not even go as far as the HRC in connecting economic and social rights to the right to life,[40] Member States have to ensure that conditions for a life behind bars are fulfilled.

Art. 3 ECHR rules out torture and degrading treatment. This norm is applicable during detention.[41] The case that addressed the conditions inside prison in the most extensive manner so far is *The Greek case* by the ECommHR.[42] As the ECHR does not contain a provision similar to Art. 10 ICCPR, the ECommHR was left to consider the case under the scope of Art. 3 ECHR, and found a violation. Unfortunately, the ECommHR did not differentiate between specific facts and specific violation; it was satisfied with condemning the situation as a whole, that is, solitary confinement, lack of recreation, no access to open air, lack of visits, denial of medical treatment, and so forth.[43] Similar conditions were condemned in the case *Cyprus v Turkey* where food, water, and medical treatment were withheld from the prisoners.[44] The protection afforded to the prisoner seems somewhat lower than that under the ICCPR. In contrast to the universal level, the fact that conditions of detention do not comply with the 1987 European Prison Rules[45] does not automatically mean that the ECHR has been violated as it cannot be presumed that every violation of the prison rules are tantamount to an inhumane or degrading treatment

---

[38]   HRC General Comment 21 (Article 10), para. 3.

[39]   The ECHR took the way that was refused by the ICCPR by giving a list of exceptions where the right to life could be violated.

[40]   Harris, 54.

[41]   See in particular ECourtHR *Ireland v United Kingdom* Judgment 18 January 1976, Series A No. 25, and above, Ch. 3.

[42]   ECommHR *The Greek case* Report adopted 5 November 1969, 12 YB, 1.

[43]   The description of the situation in the four Greek units under scrutiny is found in the Report of the Sub-Commission in 12 YB, 467–97. A short summary of the prison conditions in this case is given by Rodley, *Treatment of Prisoners*, 223–6.

[44]   ECommHR *Cyprus v. Turkey* Report 4 EHRR 482 at 541.

[45]   Adopted by the Committee of Ministers 12 February 1987, Recommendation No. R(87)3, reprinted in 9 EHRR (1987), 513, as a revised European version of the Standard Minimum Rules for the Treatment of Prisoners.

of a prisoner in the sense of Art. 3 ECHR.[46] Yet, a practice that is incompatible with the European Prison Rules might be criticized by the European Committee for the Prevention of Torture.[47] The ECommHR also found that solitary confinement would not in itself constitute a breach of Art. 3 ECHR,[48] but would under additional circumstances; prolonged solitary confinement is generally undesirable and it is, in any case, to be supervised by medical personnel.[49] Most serious was the case *Kröcher and Möller v Switzerland* involving terrorist activities in Central Europe in the 1970s.[50] The applicants were held in separate cells on a floor not occupied by other prisoners, with no opening to the outside world, constant artificial lighting, permanent surveillance by closed circuit television, were denied access to newspaper and radio, and were allowed little physical exercise.[51] The ECommHR stated that complete sensory isolation coupled with total social isolation can destroy the personality and constitute a form of treatment which cannot be justified by security concerns.[52] However, the ECommHR declared the deployed measures as admissible because of the severity of the situation.[53] Furthermore, it conceded that the conditions were relaxed after a month. The minority of four dissenters was not convinced in particular by this last point and wanted the ECommHR to focus on the first month.[54] In summary the ECommHR gives a wide margin of appreciation to the Member States' prison authorities.[55] Under the regime of the ECHR the states have certainly more

---

[46] See ECommHR *Eggs v Switzerland* Decision 11 December 1976, Appl. No. 7341/76, 6 DR, 170 at 181, relating to the 1973 predecessors of the 1987 Minimum Rules.

[47] At least in effect this might be so, as the Torture Committee seems reluctant to refer directly to the Prison Rules and tends to establish its own set of principles; this is criticized as hampering the Committee's effectiveness and credibility by Murdoch, 5 EJIL (1994), 220 at 238. An interesting insight into the work and the findings of the Committee is given by its former president Cassese in his publication, *Inhumane States*.

[48] ECommHR *Ensslin, Baader and Rape v FRG* Decision 8 July 1978, Appl. Nos. 7572/76, 7586/76, 7587/76, 14 DR 64.

[49] See Harris, 69.

[50] ECommHR *Kröcher and Möller v Switzerland* Report 16 December 1982, Appl. No. 8463/78, 34 DR, 24.

[51] Ibid., para. 54.

[52] Ibid., para. 62.

[53] The ECommHR referred to the kidnapping of Schleyer, the hijacking of the *Landshut* as well as to the suicides in the case *Esslin, Baader, Raspe*. Ibid., para. 63.

[54] Ibid. 57, Dissenting Opinion Tenekides, Melchior, Sampaio, Weitzel, who found the case quite unique in its severity and constituting a violation of Art. 3 ECHR according to the case-law of the ECommHR.

[55] See Harris, 70–1; The ECommHR even declared a case inadmissible (*Delazarus v UK*, Appl. No. 17525/90 (1993) unreported, see Harris, 71) where the applicant complained about the use of chamberpots in cells, overcrowding, and confinement of prisoners to their cells for twenty-three hours at Wandsworth Prison in the UK, relying heavily on evidence by the European Prevention of Torture Committee (see Cassese, *Inhumane States*, 49–50), and the Chief Inspector of Prisons in England and Wales. Because the applicant was under solitary confinement he could not complain about overcrowding.

liberty than under the ICCPR and Art. 10 therein, which more or less incorporates the Minimum Prison Rules into the human rights treaty.

(c) The American and African systems   In the AmCHR we find several relevant provisions. The right to life is protected similarly as in the two already discussed regimes. Art. 4 (I) AmCHR reads as: 'Every person has the right to have his life respected. This right shall be protected by law, and, in general, from the moment of conception. No one shall be arbitrarily deprived of his life.' The responsibility of the state for the life of persons under its jurisdiction has been extended by the IAmCourtHR to effective protection. In the *Velásquez Rodríguez* case disappearances were found to be within the ambit of this provision. It said that the state was responsible if it failed to fulfil its duty to respect and guarantee the rights set forth in the Convention.[56] The suicide of a prisoner, however, was not considered to be within the accountability of the state.[57] Art. 5 (II) AmCHR protects against torture and/or cruel and inhumane or degrading punishment or treatment; all detained persons shall be treated with respect for the inherent dignity of the human person. It contains in Art. 5 (IV) and (V) AmCHR the special provisions for those detained on remand and for juveniles. Art. 5 (VI) AmCHR declares reform and social rehabilitation of the prisoners as 'an essential aim' of the imprisonment. Art. 6 AmCHR protects against forced or compulsory labour, emphasizing the same exceptions as Art. 8 ICCPR, in particular labour as punishment (Art. 6 (II) AmCHR) and the 'normally required' work whilst serving a prison sentence (Art. 6 (III) (a) AmCHR).

The African Charter includes the right to life (Art. 4 AfCHPR), which is derived from the right to respect for human dignity, as is the freedom from 'torture, cruel, inhumane or degrading treatment' in Art. 5 AfCHPR.

2. The practice at the ICTY

Art. 27 Statute ICTY addresses the issue of imprisonment. It states that the sentence inflicted upon a criminal by the ICTY shall be served in a state that has indicated to the UN Security Council its willingness to accept convicted persons. The imprisonment shall be in accordance with the applicable law of the state concerned, however subject to the supervision of the ICTY. The fact that Art. 27 Statute ICTY does not contain a legal obligation for states to host convicted persons, but favours voluntary cooperation with the tribunal, might cause difficulties with finding host states.[58] However, the convicted person is surely much better off in a state which accepts his presence in a national prison cell voluntarily.

---

[56] IAmCourtHR *Velásquez Rodríguez case* Judgment 29 July 1988, Series C No. 4, para. 173.
[57] IAmCourtHR *Gangaram Panday v Suriname* Judgment 21 January 1994, Series C No. 16, para. 62.   [58] This is pointed out by Tolbert, 11 LJIL (1998), 655 at 658.

Rule 103 lays down the rule that the transfer to the 'host-prison' shall be effected as soon as possible after the time limit for appeal has elapsed. Rule 104 leaves the supervision of imprisonment to the tribunal or to a special body designated by it. The Trial Chamber I held, in the *Erdemovic* case, that the following instruments should be guaranteed:[59] Standard Minimum Rules for the Treatment of Prisoners; Basic Principles for the Treatment of Prisoners; Body of Principles for the Protection of All Persons under Any Form of Detention or Imprisonment; European Prison Rules and Rules governing the Detention of Persons Awaiting Trial or Appeal before the Tribunal or otherwise Detained on the Authority of the Tribunal.

To find states that were willing to 'host' war criminals from the former Yugoslavia was probably more difficult than envisaged by the drafters of the statute and the judges of the ICTY.[60] So far the ICTY has concluded agreements with Italy,[61] Finland,[62] and Norway.[63] These agreements are generally based on the Model Agreement[64] and do not apply automatically but on a case-by-case basis.

3. Consequences for the ICC

I have found an international human rights standard for treatment of prisoners but I have not taken into account the huge differences between nations in their behaviour towards the criminal. How should the court react to this phenomenon of higher and lower standards of treatment? Which standard should the international community apply?

To raise the question almost implies the answer. Of course the international community when punishing must comply with the set of rules deriving from its own institutions. Although it is not easy to give legal evidence for this tenet, it seems to be prima facie accepted. In any case it would be desirable to mention the relevant international norms, for example the Minimum Rules, explicitly in the statute.[65] The Rome Statute does not entail an explicit mentioning of these rules. However, it states that both the ICC itself and the host state must apply the 'widely accepted international treaty standards governing treatment of prisoners' (Art. 106

---

[59] Trial Chamber I, *Erdemovic* case, Sentencing Judgment, 29 November 1996, para. 74.

[60] Compare the disenchanted paragraphs in the ICTY Second Annual Report, paras. 135–9 and again in the Third Annual Report, paras. 186–91.

[61] Agreement with the United Nations on the Enforcement of Sentences imposed by the tribunal in Italian prisons of 6 February 1997.

[62] Signed 7 May 1997, entered into force on 7 June 1997.

[63] Signed 24 Apr. 1998.

[64] See Yearbook of the ICTY, 1996, 227.

[65] The Report of the PrepComm, para. 357, at least presumes the applicability of these Rules.

(I) and (II) Rome Statute).[66] This reference is to be understood as an obligation to adopt human rights and the Minimum Rules.[67]

It has repeatedly been said that Art. 10 ICCPR should not be contained within a human rights treaty as it contains no legal value. In particular Art. 10 (III) has been criticized as implementing the outdated modernist views of 1960 criminologists.[68] Whilst it may be admitted that the focus of theories of criminology in the 1990s has shifted, the two concepts mentioned in the ICCPR are still understood as the main pillars of modern imprisonment policy.[69] As we have seen the drafters were cautious enough not to pin the text of Art. 10 (III) ICCPR down to one concept alone. Furthermore a comparative analysis unveils that the concept of the ICCPR has been adopted almost verbatim by Art. 5 (IV) and (VI) IAmCHR some years later.[70] Art. 10 ICCPR should thus be applied by the ICC.

In order to find places that comply with the Standard Minimum Rules the court could get assistance from UN institutions that deal with the supervision of the implementation of this body of rules in national legislation, mainly instituted by ECOSOC.[71] These procedures emphasize the important assistance of the NGOs in this respect. They should definitely be taken into account.[72] Likewise, the international court should take notice of the reports of the European Committee for the Prevention of Torture.

The ICTY follows the procedure of concluding treaties with states that indicate their readiness to host war criminals. This treaty should demand that the hosting state accept the obligations according to the Minimum Rules for Prisoners. Using the analogy of the Status of Forces Agreement (SOFA), the UN usually concludes with the states in which UN troops operate, I would call this contract Status of Prisoner Agreement (SOPA).

The ICC would be in a similar situation. The sentence will, according to Art. 103 Rome Statute, be enforced by states which had indicated their willingness to accept the convicted person. In the case that no other state is found, the host state (that is, the Netherlands, see Art. 3 (I) Rome Statute) will make a prison cell available to the ICC, in which case the cost

---

[66] Kreß, 6 Eur.J.Crime Cr.L.Cr.J (1998), 448.

[67] Clark in Trifterer (ed.), *Commentary on the Rome Statute*, Art. 106, No. 2. Strijards in the same commentary, Art. 103, No. 27, takes the norm literally: The Minimum Rules are not treaty law and therefore not strictly binding pursuant to Art. 106 (II) Rome Statute.

[68] Compare the quotations by Nowak, Art. 10, No. 5.

[69] Ibid., Art. 10, No. 22.

[70] Ibid., Art. 10, No. 5.

[71] See 'Procedures for the Effective Implementation of the Standard Minimum Rules for the Treatment of Prisoners', ECOSOC Res 1984/47, 25 May 1984; generally: Bassiouni, *FS Oehler*, 525.

[72] Rodley, *Treatment of Prisoners*, 239.

will be borne by the ICC (Art. 103 (IV) Rome Statute). Otherwise, the ordinary costs for the enforcement of the sentence shall be borne by the host state (Draft Rule 10.11). The PrepComm points out that, strictly speaking, the Member States of the ICC have the duty to execute the sentence of the court if they are so designated by the court.[73] In practice it will not be feasible without the 'willingness' of the host state. Indeed, states would be obliged to execute the sentence of the ICTY, as its decisions and judgments can have binding force on states.[74] Reliance is placed on special agreements between the UN and the state that has declared its willingness. The Draft Rules prepare a procedure that enables the Member States to indicate their willingness to host international criminals to the Registrar. They can withdraw from the list at any time (Draft Rule 10.3). According to Draft Rule 10.3 (e) the ICC may enter bilateral arrangements with a Member State in order to establish a framework for the acceptance of prisoners (SOPA).

It was further submitted by the PrepComm that the ICC should exercise control in order to ensure consistency and compliance with international norms regarding incarceration, and leave the day-to-day supervision of the prisoner to the host state.[75] This proposal has been incorporated in Art. 106 Rome Statute.

(II) Place of Imprisonment

One cannot deny that it would generally matter a great deal to a criminal whether he is to serve his punishment in, for example, an Italian detention unit or if he is to be sent to Iraq to be imprisoned there. The international court must decide where to send the offenders, but how? After having established certain rules, the fact that there are different standards of human rights fulfilment has to be addressed. Finally, the discussion comes to the consequences of an imprisonment abroad.

1. General rules

Despite Art. 27 Statute ICTY on the practice of sending convicted persons to host countries, the law at the ICTY does not give any guidance whatsoever regarding the selection of the place of imprisonment.[76] The first condition upon the determination of the place of imprisonment is that the host state complies with the minimum standard accepted by the international

---

[73] Report of the PrepComm I, para. 356, and Report of the PrepComm II, 289.
[74] This was held by the Appeals Chamber in *Blaskic* Judgment 29 October 1997, Case No. IT-95-14-AR108 bis.
[75] Report of the PrepComm I, para. 357.
[76] Bassiouni, *The Law of the ICTY*, 707, is complaining about this.

community. If it does not, the ICC is barred from sending convicted persons there.[77]

Several further conditions follow from the main aim of the institution of an International Criminal Court. The international court is there to substitute national jurisdiction that is unwilling or unable to hold criminals accountable if international crimes have been committed. As the convicted persons are by definition then international criminals, because they have offended against the international criminal legal system, they can theoretically be asked to serve their sentence in any state of the world but their home state. There are two reasons for this. First the practical point that, if the judiciary is not working, it is likely that prison service is not working either. Secondly, and more theoretically, the criminal was surrendered to the International Criminal Court because the national population and authorities were feared to be not impartial enough to hold a trial; again there are good grounds for believing that they would not be ready to supervise the convicted person serving a sentence inflicted upon him by a foreign (international) court. This is especially true in cases of civil strife and unrest. The former Yugoslavia is a perfect example of this: the difficulties are far too great for the convicted person to be sent back to his home state. Either he ends up in an area which might almost treat him as a war hero, which would destroy any effect of the punishment, or his life expectancy might be severely reduced, if he found himself in an environment mainly governed by his former enemies. A return to his home state is therefore out of the question. The policy of the ICTY follows this. No convicted war criminal will be sent back to any of the states of the former Yugoslavia.[78]

But this is not the only exclusion that needs to be made. For the same reasons why the home of the criminal cannot be the place of imprisonment, one has to avoid host states that have any particular links with the fatherland of the convicted. This is also true for regions and states that entertain any particular enmity. This need not necessarily be a belligerent ally of the enemy during the former conflict. It suffices if there are religious, ethnic, or cultural (embracing both historical and political) grounds for animosity. Take a simple example: if a Serb war criminal has been convicted of war crimes and crimes against humanity, maybe even genocide, especially because of his torturing, raping, and murdering Muslims

---

[77] The ICTY has its Rules of Detention that have already been mentioned earlier. These, however, do not apply to prisoners confined by national authorities pursuant to Art. 27 Statute ICTY; compare Bassiouni, *The Law of the ICTY*, 710, with a comment and analysis of the Rules of Detention on pp. 711–74.

[78] Compare the Report of the Secretary General, para. 121; this is the case although several successor states of the former Yugoslavia have indicated their willingness to 'host' convicted war criminals, see the ICTY Second Annual Report (1995), para. 138, and the ICTY Third Annual Report (1996), para. 189.

in a detention camp, how welcome will such an inmate be in a Pakistani prison? Far from being a shining sign of reconciliation, this would endanger the life of the prisoner dramatically to such an extent that would constitute a violation of Art. 6 ICCPR.

Likewise, the opposite case seems unfair, that is, to send the criminal to a state which applauded and cheered the atrocities that were the reason for his prosecution. In this alternative the life of the inmate is not threatened rather than his circumstances alleviated. Superficially, this is just a matter of fairness. No human right is obviously jeopardized or infringed upon. The reasons lie in the overall aim and purpose of punishment in the international context. In order for the execution of criminal law to achieve what it socially aims at, that is, to deter crime and strengthen the faith of the people in the legal system, the sentence must be seen to be justly deserved. If exaggerated in either way, too weak or too harsh, the goal of reconciliation is put into danger. If the international community sees the convicted war criminal being received as a hero or martyr by the state that is supposed to imprison him, the credibility and seriousness of the international execution of criminal law vanishes. As the danger of being treated in too friendly a manner is not as imminent a problem for the convicted person, one has to include amongst the prohibited states of detention only those states that were direct or indirect war allies of the home state of the criminal. For example, sending a Bosnian Serb to Serbia to serve the sentence would be a possible situation falling under this prohibition.

This tells us that the country in which the convicted war criminal is to serve his sentence needs to be a 'neutral' country; neutrality is not meant here in the narrow sense of the laws of war, rather than in a broader sense with a view to religious, ethnic, and cultural circumstances.

So far I have included all states that were neutral to the conflict and fulfil at least the minimum standard of treatment of prisoners. There is a third criterion that has to be taken into account. This is the closeness to home (*Heimatnähe*). This stems from the general aims of detention, as they are enshrined in Art. 10 (III) ICCPR: reformation and rehabilitation. First, the programmes that are run by states to resocialize the offender will best bear fruit, if they relate to the linguistic, cultural, and social context of the individual.[79] Teaching, education and re-education, vocational guidance, and training, as proposed by the HRC[80] and in the Minimum Rules s. 77, will be more effective if they take place under conditions that are familiar

---

[79] e.g. the inmate has the right to access to information about the outer world according to s. 39 Minimum Rules. This information must necessarily contain news from his nation-state.

[80] HRC General Comment 21 (Article 10), para. 11.

to the detained. Maybe an example will make this submission more plausible: a person who was working as a farmer in Cambodia before the atrocities started will have major problems in adjusting to the Cambodian society if he has served his ten years imprisonment in a detention unit in Frankfurt am Main (Germany).

Secondly, in a foreign country it will be all the more difficult for the prisoner to have contact with other inmates sharing his heritage. In the most difficult circumstances such a situation might amount to solitary confinement, which the HRC is inclined to condemn as inhumane treatment.[81]

Thirdly, visits from family and reputable friends are more unlikely the further the prisoner is away. Contact with these persons at regular intervals, both by correspondence and by visits, is accepted by the HRC[82] as well as by s. 37 of the Minimum Rules. For the HRC this is a requirement of humanity and a means for reformation and social rehabilitation and therefore an element of Art. 10 ICCPR.[83]

If the offender is imprisoned on the other side of the globe, the measures applied to foster the inmate's rehabilitation will not only have to fight practical difficulties, because he would be the reason for many costly extra measures that might provoke the envy of his 'colleagues', but also their effectiveness would have to be questioned in principle. One might argue against this submission that individuals do get imprisoned in foreign countries, for example the German who murdered a woman in Manila will serve his sentence in a prison in the Philippines. True, but this offender chose to be there voluntarily and might have a social background in this Asian state. In the context of the International Criminal Court the offender might have never left his country and is sent to a foreign prison solely on the grounds that he was unfortunate enough to end up before the International Criminal Court. The case of offenders who were convicted by foreign courts by virtue of the principle of universality likewise fall into another category; they also voluntarily submitted themselves to the foreign jurisdiction.[84]

For now I can summarize three principles that must govern the choice of the host state:

(a) the principle of full compliance with the Minimum Rules standard,
(b) the principle of neutrality,
(c) the principle of closeness to home.

---

[81] See above, Ch. 2 C III 2, p. 140.

[82] HRC General Comment 21 (Article 10), para. 12.

[83] HRC General Comment 9 (Article 10), para. 3.

[84] See the first case decided by a German court concerning an alleged war criminal from the former Yugoslavia: Bavarian Supreme Court (Bayerisches Oberstes Landgericht) *Djajic* Judgment 23 May 1997, in NJW (1998), 392; compare Safferling, 92 AJIL (1998), 528.

2. Free choice despite different standards?

If the choice is made according to these principles the problem still remains that different standards exist between the states. A prison in Frankfurt am Main is probably more comfortable than one in Phnom Penh. Even if we presume that both are complying with the Minimum Rules, the prison in Western Europe will be better equipped and offer more possibilities to the inmates than its Asian counterpart can afford.

We can make out two possible arguments against the application of the above principles. The first is based on the principle of non-discrimination, which is to be considered as a human right. The second root is the 'rule of law', which is also of human rights importance, as it is the underlying foundation of the 'democratic society'.

(a) The principle of non-discrimination Obviously, if the international court sends one convicted individual to Germany and the next to Pakistan it discriminates between the two. This discrimination might face human rights problems. Most of the human rights treaties know of a principle of non-discrimination. The ICCPR knows two general provisions against discrimination alongside special norms that are not relevant in this context:[85] Art. 2 and Art. 26 ICCPR. As the former is not an individual right, but addresses the implementation of the rights entailed in the ICCPR through the national states, I will only take the latter as the general governance in this matter not limited to the rights set forth in the Covenant.[86] Art. 26 reads as:

Art. 26 ICCPR
All persons are equal before the law and are entitled without any discrimination to the equal protection of the law. In this respect, the law shall prohibit any discrimination and guarantee to all persons equal and effective protection against discrimination on any ground such as race, colour, sex, language, religion, political or other opinion, national or social origin, property, birth or other status.

The ECHR does not entail a general principle of equality.[87] In Art. 14 ECHR it only sets forth a right to enjoy the Convention's rights without discrimination.[88] In contrast to this is Art. 24 AmCHR, which establishes a general principle of equality and derives the principle of non-discrimination

---

[85] There are several special provisions against discrimination, like Art. 14 (I) ICCPR, Art. 23 (IV), Art. 24, or Art. 25 ICCPR.

[86] This difference between Art. 2 and Art. 26 ICCPR is expressed by the HRC in General Comment 18 (Article 26), para. 12. That Art. 26 ICCPR should not be limited to the rights in the Covenant was clearly intended by the drafters, see Bossuyt, *Guide*, 485.

[87] See Seidel, *Handbuch der Grund- und Menschenrechte*, 370.

[88] The ECourtHR therefore sees Art. 14 ECHR not as an independent right. The 'non-discrimination' principle is exclusively applied in connection with substantive rights of the ECHR; see e.g. ECourtHR *Marckx v Belgium* Judgment 13 June 1979, Series A No. 31.

therefrom. The AfCHPR again contains two separate provisions, establishing a principle of non-discrimination relative to the right of the
Charter (Art. 2 AfCHPR) and constituting an autonomous right to equality before the law (Art. 3 AfCHPR).

The provision of Art. 26 ICCPR, which I will discuss in the following as
the prototype of a 'principle of equality', can be split up into two clauses:
(1) equality before the law, (2) non-discrimination. The first prohibits any
discrimination in the application of the law, the second addresses also the
substance of the law itself. Maybe one can express this generic principle
of equality in the words of the BVerfG: '[d]er Gleichheitssatz [verbietet]
. . ., daß wesentlich Gleiches ungleich . . . behandelt wird. Der Gleichheitssatz ist verletzt, wenn sich ein vernünftiger, sich aus der Natur der Sache
ergebender oder sonstwie sachlich einleuchtender Grund für die gesetz-
liche Differenzierung . . . nicht finden läßt, kurzum, wenn die
Bestimmung als willkürlich bezeichnet werden muß.'[89] The principle of
non-discrimination is violated, if essentially equal matters are arbitrarily
treated unequally. It is universally accepted that equality by all means
would result in injustice. Therefore, as the BVerfG says, not all discrimination can possibly be ruled out, only if it is arbitrary;[90] if there are objective and reasonable grounds for differentiating between certain groups
and cases, the discrimination is justified.[91] The aim of the differentiation
must certainly be legitimate from a human rights point of view.[92] Finally
the principle of proportionality must be respected.[93]

The first task would be to determine what is essentially equal: the
Bosnian Serb, the Bosnian Croat, and the Cambodian Khmer Rouge
warrior. The second topic would than be to ask whether there is a justification for treating them unequally. All the convicted persons with which
our question is concerned are war criminals. They were sentenced by an
International Criminal Court according to international criminal law to a
sentence that they deserve according to their responsibility. The situations
they are in after the trial are essentially equal in the sense of the principle

---

[89] BVerfG *Restructuring Federal States* Judgment 23 October 1951, BVerfGE 1, 14 at 52. This
has become permanent jurisdiction of the BVerfG: 'the principle of equality prohibits that
essentially equal matters are being treated unequally. The principle of equality is violated if
no reasonable cause, emerging from the nature of things or from otherwise objectively
convincing grounds can be found in favour of the differentiation, in short, if the law has to
be called arbitrary.'

[90] Quite similar as to the following requirements the ECourtHR e.g. in the *Belgian
Linguistic case* Judgment 23 July 1968, Series A No. 6, 34 para. 10.

[91] This is already clear in the discussions of the drafters of the ICCPR in the HRComm,
5th (1949), 6th (1950), and 8th Session (1952), see Bossuyt, *Guide*, 482.

[92] If the aim is to achieve a purpose which is illegitimate under the ICCPR, the principle
of non-discrimination has been violated; clear in this regard is the HRC General Comment
18 (Article 26), para. 13.

[93] See Seidel, *Handbuch der Grund- und Menschenrechte*, 365.

of equality. This is so no matter whether they came from Cambodia or from the former Yugoslavia. Sending one of them to Italy and the other to Vietnam would infringe the principle of non-discrimination.

However, a justification could be found. As we have seen, this must operate in three steps: (*a*) there must be reasonable and objective reasons, (*b*) the aim of the discrimination must comply with human rights, and (*c*) the implemented measure must be proportionate to the envisaged aim. To find reasonable and objective grounds one must separate two sets of possible scenarios: the convicted persons coming from the same national state or coming from different parts of the world, for example, two Bosnian criminals or one Bosnian and one Cambodian. In the case where they originate from the same state, one cannot find objective and reasonable criteria for sending one to Italy and one to Pakistan. Indeed, the principles spelt out earlier of how to choose the right country would contradict any discrimination of this kind. In the second case one could justify sending the Bosnian warrior to Italy and the Cambodian to Vietnam.[94] The reasonable and objective grounds lie in the principle of closeness to home. As we have seen above, this principle roots in the general aim of imprisonment, that is, reformation and social rehabilitation. I have shown that closeness to one's home state is essential to the effectiveness of the programmes employed to reintegrate the offender into society. The aim of rehabilitation is explicitly stated in Art. 10 (III) ICCPR and therefore in accordance with human rights. To send the offender to a country that is closer to home but is lower in its human rights standard does not seem out of proportion to this aimed-at goal. This is so in particular because of the fact that only those prisons are electable that fulfil the minimum standard. We therefore have a discrimination that is justified under a human rights perspective.

One further counter-argument could be that this would result in a discrimination on grounds of national or social origin, which is explicitly prohibited by Art. 26 ICCPR. People from underprivileged areas of the world would always end up in a prison with a lower standard of human rights while criminals from a wealthier background will be in a unit with a higher standard. The reason for this could only be seen in the origin of the offender, therefore the discrimination would be unjust. It is true that the different treatment is rooted in the nationality of the convicted person, but discrimination can still be justifiable. The fact that discrimination on grounds of national origin is mentioned explicitly in the text of Art. 26

---

[94] One certainly has to scrutinize thoroughly whether or not Vietnam fulfils the other criteria stated above, also whether or not Vietnam is for a Khmer Rouge an enemy state as the downfall of the heinous regime of the Khmer Rouge was mostly due to the Vietnamese invasion in 1971. See Ratner and Abrams, *Accountability for Human Rights Atrocities*, 227–65.

ICCPR does not mean that no discrimination is allowed at all. Moreover the justification follows the same lines as above.

(b) The rule of law   But there are other reasons for questioning the outcome of our above principles of selection. Taking the 'rule of law' seriously and referring especially to its subprinciples, security of law (*Rechtssicherheit*) and reliability of law (*Vertrauensschutz*), means that it is prohibited to treat the criminal worse than he could possibly have expected. A criminal in Western Europe can legitimately rely on the fact that, if prosecuted and sentenced, he will be in a prison in Western Europe and will not be sent to an Asian country where the prison regime might be much more severe. It is not enough to point to the minimum human rights standard that is met by both the Western European and the Asian state. The sentenced offender could not possibly have foreseen the threat of becoming familiar with the inside of a Pakistani prison. He cannot therefore be sent to a country that has not an equal or higher standard of human rights protection as his country of origin.

If this is the general rule there are certainly several exceptions. I started from the principle of reliability, also referred to as legitimate expectancy (*Vertrauensschutz*), as the main justification for the general rule. Having said this, the obvious exceptions lie in cases where, for whatever reasons, the offender could not legitimately rely upon the prison standard in his own state. When committing crimes in an Asian state, for example, the person is leaving the jurisdiction of his home state and voluntarily undertakes the risk of being punished and having to serve imprisonment there. He then waives the right to the standards of imprisonment in his home state. By this an adequate balance is reached between the conflicting jurisdictions, the principle that criminal jurisdiction is related to the person who committed the crime (*Personalitätsprinzip*) and to the territory where the crime occurred (*Territorialprinzip*).[95] One could object to this on the grounds of the principle of universality (*Weltrechtspflegeprinzip*) in the following manner; in international criminal law the offender runs the risk of being prosecuted and punished by any state of the world according to the principle of universality. Therefore in the context of international criminal law there are no reasons whatsoever to allow the offender to rely on standards like those in his home state. This would lead to the conclusion that in international criminal law there is no place for the principle that the criminal can rely on a certain prison standard other than the minimum human rights standard.

Two problems arise from such a position. The first concerns the functions of the UN; if a body that is institutionally related to the UN has the

---

[95] For further explanation of the principles see above, Ch. 5, p. 323, fn. 23.

choice between a high and a low standard of human rights fulfilment, does it not have to choose the higher and better protection? Secondly, if certain Member States have a high standard of treating prisoners can they really endorse or even agree with a criminal court that could send criminals to prison facilities under conditions which they themselves consider to be inhumane?

A political counter-argument would be that the burden of hosting international criminals would lie upon countries with high standards and only on those. By so doing, the countries of the UN would again be officially split into several groups according to their human rights standards in their detention units. Equally, I submit that the problems could be solved in a similar manner according to the above principles. Always under the condition that the Minimum Rules are observed, the international criminal court needs to choose the prison that best protects human dignity. This is not necessarily done by a higher prison standard. What needs to be taken into account, as I have tried to show, is the whole concept of prison sentences. Because of this human rights might even dictate differentiation and the choice of a prison that better meets the needs and social background of the prisoner. States that have a higher standard in their prisons still can comply with such a system, because their citizens will be treated according to the standard and the background they are used to. The concerns stemming from the 'rule of law' therefore vanish, when this concept is applied when choosing the right place for the convicted war criminal to serve his sentence in.

3. Far distance as a mitigating circumstance

Having spelt out the principles according to which the international court has to decide where to send the convicted person for imprisonment, I now need to discuss whether, generally speaking, the fact that the criminal will be sent somewhere outside his home state constitutes a mitigating circumstance. If so, one could argue that the further away the prison the more the sentence has to be reduced.

The Trial Chamber I of the ICTY in the *Erdemovic* case held in its sentencing judgment[96] that the sentence against the convicted needed to be mitigated because of the fact that he had no chance of returning to his home state before the sentence was accomplished. To reduce the sentence if the place of imprisonment is far away raises practical difficulties. The choice of the place of imprisonment is usually done by the Registry and is a purely administrative decision. The deciding chamber does not necessarily know the options that are available.

---

[96] ICTY Trial Chamber I, *Prosecutor v Erdemovic*, Sentencing Judgment I, 29 November 1996, Case No. IT-96-22-T.

B. POSSIBLE MOTIONS

Although convicted, sentenced, and in detention the offender never ceases to be a human being with certain rights. The right to take legal action against unlawful treatment in particular does not vanish the moment he enters the prison door. If it did, the whole protection by human rights would lose its teeth and would indeed be destroyed. There are possible legal motions with which to challenge either the circumstances of the imprisonment or the verdict as such. Finally, there is always the possibility of pardon, at least in most domestic systems.

(I) Claiming Inhumane Treatment

1. Effective remedy

To claim a human rights violation during the time behind bars is not an unusual procedure in most countries, indeed it is enshrined in all of the human rights treaties we are looking at. Art. 2 ICCPR provides for an effective remedy against any human rights abuse before a national authority. Similar provisions are to be found in Art. 13 ECHR, Art. 25 AmCHR, and Art. 26 AfCHPR. These regulations exist, first in order to reduce the case-load of the equivalent human rights bodies. They need to be read together with the related procedural provisions concerning the exhaustion of domestic remedies as a question of admissibility of the communication to a human rights body.[97]

Secondly, this right to an effective remedy is not entrenched in the 'fair trial' provisions, that is, not all human rights are 'civil rights'.[98] It therefore does not need an impartial and independent tribunal or court to fulfil this obligation. Art. 2 (III) ICCPR expresses that there are different possibilities for the Member States in choosing the authority to deal with complaints. This provision caused lengthy discussions and several votes in the preparation process; one could say that, although no independent national tribunal is strictly speaking required, the Member States nevertheless have a progressive obligation to develop judicial remedies.[99] Nowak therefore speaks of a priority of judicial remedies.[100] The ECourtHR has, for example, accepted the parliamentary G10 Commission in Germany[101] and the executive control by the Home Secretary in *Silver*

---

[97] Nowak, Art. 2, Nos. 56–7, Harris, 443. About the provision on exhausting domestic remedies before being admitted to human rights bodies, see T. Zwart, *The Admissibility of Human Rights Petitions* (Dordrecht, 1994), ch. 8.

[98] Expressly so ECourtHR *Golder v UK* Judgment 21 February 1975, Series A No. 18, para. 33.

[99] Drafting history, see Bossuyt, *Guide*, 64–71.　　　　　　[100] Nowak, Art. 2, No. 58.

[101] ECourtHR *Klaas v Germany* Judgment 6 September 1978, Series A No. 28.

v UK, a case regarding prisoner complaints.[102] Nevertheless, the call is for an effective remedy, which means that the case needs to be addressed to a body that is 'sufficiently independent',[103] that actually applies human rights law,[104] and is in a position to alter the situation of the claimant.[105] Finally, the remedy must be positively available for the 'victim'.[106]

In addition, the claimant could ask for compensation. A violation of human rights is usually redressed by financial reparation. This right is embodied in Art. 50 ECHR and usually considered to be part of the 'effective remedy' provisions. It is especially acceptable in cases where the applicant was the victim of a miscarriage of justice, as mentioned in Art. 9 (V) and Art. 14 (VI) ICCPR, Art. 5 (V) ECHR and Art. 10 AmCHR.

2. Proposition for an International Criminal Court

From this human rights stand point it appears to be clear that the international criminal system has to guarantee that remedies concerning human rights abuses behind prison walls must be available for the international criminal. For an international court there seem to be generally two avenues in dealing with complaints. Either the prisoner who has been convicted by the court and been sent to some host state stays under the responsibility of the UN or he is entirely integrated into the system of the hosting state.

In the first alternative the complaint needs to be addressed to some independent authority within the UN system. To be compatible with the rules established above this must be a body that has the power to grant relief to the application. According to the structure of the UN this could only be the Security Council, with its power to make binding decisions according to Chapter VII UN Charter, or the International Criminal Court, if so equipped, or any other body to be established with the equivalent

---

[102] ECourtHR *Silver and others v UK* Judgment 25 March 1983, Series A No. 61.

[103] Ibid., para. 116.

[104] It is interesting to note in this regard that—maybe not surprisingly—most of the cases concerning Art. 13 ECHR originate from the UK, where the ECHR was not incorporated into domestic law; compare Harris, 461; the ECourtHR did not decide on the Art. 13 ECHR issue with regard to the UK explicitly, see the cases *Malone v UK* Judgment 2 August 1984, Series A No. 82, and *Murray v UK* Judgment 8 February 1996, 22 EHRR (1996), 29. The whole field has been discussed from a practising barrister's point of view in the study by M. Hunt, *Using Human Rights Law in English Courts* (Oxford, 1997). Hunt sees the monist/dualist dichotomy vanishing in particular in the field of customary international law and human rights.

[105] See Art. 2 (III) (c) ICCPR. See also ECourtHR *Soering v UK* Judgment 7 July 1989, Series A No. 161, para. 120.

[106] See the case ECourtHR *Vilvarajah and others v. UK* Judgment 30 October 1991, Series A No. 215. The ECommHR held in its report that this requirement would not be fulfilled if the applicant in an asylum case was asked to return to the country from where he fled for fear of persecution in order to appeal against the refusal to grant him asylum (Report of the ECommHR 8 May 1990, Series A No. 215, 52, para. 153). The ECourtHR did not address this question.

powers. As the Security Council is primarily concerned with other issues of high policy and as its power to issue binding decisions is conditioned by Art. 39 UN Charter, that is, a case concerning international peace and security, it does not seem the organ best suited for this purpose. Another alternative would be to communicate complaints to the HRC, as is already possible under Art. 1 First Optional Protocol ICCPR. Unfortunately the HRC does not have the power to deliver binding decisions.[107] The International Criminal Court would probably be the best institution to communicate a complaint to. It would then need to be equipped with powers that would enable it to change the situation of the applicant. How this should be done is hard to envisage, because the decision of the international court would need to bind directly national states' authorities. Ultimately the court could choose another country for the claimant's imprisonment.

The second alternative would leave the prisoner to the procedures of the host state. He would have the usual possibilities of addressing national courts or other supervising authorities to seek relief for his situation. In addition he could access the HRC after exhaustion of the available local remedies or any regional human rights body like the Inter-American organs or the Strasbourg authorities if by any chance he is imprisoned under their jurisdiction.

The ICTY seems to follow this second alternative.[108] The ICC adopts a mixture. The conditions of the imprisonment shall be governed by the law of the 'host' state. Yet the enforcement of the sentence is subject to the supervision of the ICC. The ICC may ex officio or upon a complaint of the sentenced person at any time decide to transfer the person to another state (Art. 105 and 106 Rome Statute). The prisoner can be removed to another state (Art. 104 Rome Statute).

An unsolved question is the one of compensation. Certainly the host state will have the primary responsibility for human rights violations with regard to the prisoner. Furthermore, the state would be violating its contract concluded with the International Criminal Court if, as submitted earlier, the issue of Minimum Rules was part of the contract (SOPA). Has not the ICC also a responsibility not to deliver a person into a situation where human rights are violated? In other words, could the prisoner not sue the International Criminal Court in order to gain reparation for what happened to him during his imprisonment? This question arises in the context of UN peacekeepers that breach the law and inflict harm on

---

[107] Compare Art. 5 (IV) First Optional Protocol ICCPR; certainly this way would also be limited to states which have accepted the jurisdiction of the HRC concerning individual communications in the first place.

[108] Compare Art. 27 Statute ICTY, which foresees supervision by the ICTY (also Rule 104).

people.[109] To the best of the author's knowledge, so far no case has been brought successfully against the UN, only against the contributing states. Certainly, in the case of imprisonment in a host state, the allusion to an international legal person is less striking than in a peacekeeping operation, which is conducted entirely under command and control of the UN. In the case of the international criminal the ICC is only involved indirectly through the treaty it concluded with the host state. The best solution would be to solve this problem in the agreement (SOPA). Art. 85 Rome Statute addresses the issue of compensation for arrested or convicted persons. It speaks of an enforceable right to compensation in the case of unlawful arrest or detention, and of compensation in case of a 'grave and manifest miscarriage of justice' which might be awarded in the discretion of the ICC (Art. 85 (I) and (III) Rome Statute). The precise conditions for a right to compensation are left uncertain. A wide interpretation would be desirable, encompassing also human rights violations during detention.

(II) Pardon, Remission, and Parole

1. Possibilities in national jurisdictions

Many if not all national jurisdictions recognize some possibility of gaining a 'pardon'. The criminal is pardoned because there has been a blatant miscarriage of justice (pardon) or further punishment seems to be superfluous (remission), when the goals of the sentence appear to have been achieved without insisting on the full punishment.

In jurisdictions where there is no appeal proceeding in the sense of hearing the evidence anew[110] this institution seems to be even more important. In English law this pardon is exercised by the Crown on instruction of the Home Office. A pardon may be granted independently from any potential appeals proceedings if it becomes tolerably plain after conviction and sentencing that the person is innocent.[111] By this procedure the name of the offender is not cleared, He remains in the eye of the law a guilty person;[112] only the punishment is not enforced.[113] In addition to this, the law gives the option of remitting the sentence. This does not necessarily imply that the former conviction was unjustified. It could be

---

[109] See in detail H. Risse, *Der Einsatz militärischer Kräfte durch die VN und das Kriegsvölkerrecht* (Frankfurt, 1988).

[110] See above, Ch. 6, on the right to appeal, for the difference between cassation and appeal.

[111] Emmins, 19.9.

[112] Because of this the pardoned person is still free to appeal against the conviction; *R v Foster* (1985) QB 115.

[113] There are about 200 pardons every year in England and Wales, see Emmins on sentencing, 13.7.

granted if the prisoner has gained particular merits in the eye of the authorities by helping with the investigation of further crimes or apprehension of other criminals. Another case would be where it is discovered the prisoner is terminally ill and the sentence is remitted so that the person need not die in custody.[114]

In the United States, Art. II Section 2 of the US Constitution gives the right to pardon to the President. After a person has been pardoned he is to be seen innocent. The most famous case of pardon was the pardoning of Richard Nixon by President Gerald Ford on 9 September 1974 for the 'Watergate nightmare', before Nixon was even charged. By accepting the pardon it was held that Nixon admitted to the allegations against him.[115]

Apart from pardoning provisions, parole (*Bewährung*) is a frequent practice in the national systems of sentence execution. This has nothing to do with the innocence or guilt of the offender. It is a means by which the rehabilitation of the offender is fostered.[116] The prisoner is released under the condition of reporting regularly to a probation officer; through this he should be helped to become familiar with the outside world again.

2. The International Criminal Court

There are no rules in international criminal law as to pardon. Usually, as we have seen, the right to grant pardon lies with the highest representative figure of a nation, that is, the president or the monarch. In an international context the equivalent could be seen in the UN Secretary General. Whether this institution should be equipped with this right seems doubtful, particularly as the Secretary General's position is not quite comparable to the one of a monarch or a president. The ICTY therefore leaves the question of pardoning, remission, or parole to the discretion of the host state, keeping the right of the final decision to itself (Art. 28 Statute; Rules 123–5). It is in the discretion of the President of the Court whether the prisoner is granted this alleviation of his situation or not. This procedure seems logical from the point of view of leaving every question concerning imprisonment for the hosting state to decide. On the other hand, this method might be criticized for producing new inequalities. To avoid arbitrariness the President of the ICTY has issued a document that governs the practice of pardon and commutation.[117] A feasible way of redressing this difficulty seems to be the supervision of the International Criminal Court. Through this, any arbitrary exercise of pardon, remission,

---

[114] Ibid. There are about 150 cases of sentence remission every year in England and Wales.

[115] Compare C. H. Rolph, *The Queen's Pardon* (London, 1978), 108 ff.

[116] Paulsen and Kadish, *Criminal Law and its Process*, 198–9.

[117] Practice Direction on the Procedure for the Determination of Application for Pardon, Commutation of Sentence and Early Release of Persons Convicted by the International Tribunal (IT/146), issued pursuant to Rule 19B on 7 April 1999.

and parole can be prevented. The International Criminal Court would be advised to also regulate this matter in the SOPA. According to Art. 110 Rome Statute the ICC has the last word as to reducing the sentence. The ICC will review the sentence after the person has served two-thirds of the sentence, or twenty-five years in the case of life imprisonment, and determine whether it could be reduced. A review prior to this date is excluded. Establishing the criteria for an early release has been left to the Rules of Procedure. With a view to the gravity of the crimes involved it is clear that release is possible only where the sentenced person has the best social prognosis, has constantly shown his willingness to cooperate with the prosecution, and has made attempts to repair the injustice he has committed.

A way to effect parole on an international level has yet to be found. The offender is never serving his sentence in his home state, but needs to be reintegrated into this society. Whether parole in a foreign country, the language of which the prisoner perhaps does not speak, can help in this regard needs further exploration. Other possible options, such as letting the prisoner return to his home state and keeping him under supervision of international social workers, must be assessed.

7

Summary: Towards an International Criminal Procedure

This work aimed to show that human rights law is capable of being a vital guideline for the criminal process. The human rights provisions addressing notions of 'fair trial' owe their precise formation to a conjunction of several players. Most prominent in this is the role of international courts and committees, namely the European Commission and Court of Human Rights and the UN Human Rights Committee. Many other institutions play a direct or indirect role in forming human rights, like special committees and commissions, for example, the European Torture Committee, or international conferences, as well as the work of UN bodies. With the help of all these an impressive human rights imperative has emerged that governs criminal procedure.

Schemes for the protection of persons involved in criminal investigation and trial can also be derived from national jurisdictions. Over decades and centuries national states have developed mechanisms for implementing the respect for human dignity in what is their most repressive means of public policy, criminal procedure. In order to reconcile efficiency of the system with protection for the persons involved states have followed different avenues. Two main systems, adversarial and inquisitorial, have developed which are both compatible with human rights since they can, it seems, easily coexist under the same human rights concept, as for example the United Kingdom and Germany under the Council of Europe. Nevertheless, the adherence of each national state to its traditional criminal justice system and the distrust shown towards 'the other system' is blatant. The deep gulf which exists becomes even more obvious as soon as discussions arise that aim at founding an International Criminal Court. Which procedural order should such a body have to adopt? Even where UN *ad hoc* tribunals operate, namely for the former Yugoslavia and for Rwanda, this discrepancy comes to light. The French repudiation of cooperation with the tribunal in the Hague and the disallowing of French soldiers from testifying at the procedures held at the ICTY provide evidence for this.

The way to bridge this gap can only be to find a consensus in a truly international criminal procedure that all states can accept. In order to achieve this, the discussion must begin with what states have already accepted, that is, universal human rights. From this starting-point a procedure can be extracted that takes into account both what has been transmitted by the different national systems and what is necessary for the international implications such an enterprise has. This work has dealt with this problem from two sides, the view of a comparative criminal lawyer and the view of a human rights lawyer. The different stages of the criminal justice system, namely investigation, confirmation, trial, and execution, have been outlined and analysed from these two poles. This analysis then led to a proposal of how the ICC should operate at each of these levels. The results are summarized in the following.

A. INVESTIGATION

The first stage of criminal procedure is the investigation. In any modern system this stage is conducted in a more or less inquisitorial way. A specific authority, police or prosecution, is empowered to investigate criminal acts that have occurred. This institution must necessarily be independent from the authority which gives the final judgment, which convicts or acquits the suspect. Otherwise, independence and impartiality of the court is not guaranteed. The international court will operate on the same basis and needs to be equipped with an investigating agency that is independent from the judicial body of the court. In many states the investigation is dealt with by cooperation between police and prosecutor to a lesser or greater extent. The complexities and difficulties that arise in the international context, as well as the urge for an effective supervision of the police, necessitate that the responsibility for procedural acts rests with a prosecutor. It has been argued that the need for supervision stems also from the presumption of innocence, which is applicable at every stage of the proceedings until a verdict has been given by the competent court.

The international prosecutor is the representative of the international community. He is empowered to fulfil effectively his task to seek to establish the true events of the criminal act. The mandate given to him by the international community does not encompass working towards the conviction of any suspect, rather he must be convinced that every other possible chronology of events can truly be excluded. The prosecutor is obliged to the truth. Therefore he has to perform his duties in an objective manner. This is understood to imply more than just the proper conduct of the inquiry. Objectivity means that the prosecutor must actively seek for incriminating as well as exculpatory evidence.

Another important feature in establishing international prosecution is the interdependence between the prosecutor and the executive. In national jurisdiction it is a common tenet that the prosecuting agency should be as independent from the political will as possible. The international procedural order must likewise take issue with potential improper influence on the prosecutor's work by members of the executive. States as the main players in international law might be most tempted to control the investigation of the international prosecutor. Precautions have to be taken in order to effectively exclude states from intruding into the prosecutor's task. Another way of influencing the prosecution might be via international institutions, namely the UN. It is regarded as highly critical and conflicting with human rights if the prosecutor is dependent on decisions taken by the UN Security Council, which is a purely political organ. To truly tackle international crime, which mostly derives from systemic policy fostered by states, the influence states have on the initiation or conduct of the investigation—be it as individual states or as members of an international institution—must be reduced to a minimum. It is submitted that, in order to arrive at this, instead of giving the UN Security Council or any state supervisory power over international prosecution, one should rather accept a limited scope of operation for the International Criminal Court according to a motto such as 'small but independent'. In this regard one could reduce the international prosecutor's field of operation in two ways. First, the list of crimes for which he has power to prosecute should be reduced to those generally accepted, comprising genocide, crimes against humanity, war crimes, and grave breaches of the Geneva Conventions. Secondly, the court should be operated by strict adherence to the principle of complementary jurisdiction. States, if they could be assured that the international prosecutor would only take action if the national level was insufficient, might be more likely to accept such a subsidiary jurisdiction of the international institution. In so limiting the scope of the international prosecutor, on the one hand, one could enhance the independence of the investigation by giving the prosecutor ex officio powers, on the other.

The institution of the court itself is similarly influenced by human rights. The court needs to be independent as an institution and impartial in its personnel, both organizationally and subjectively. These categories have to be fulfilled from an outside (objective) point of view. To effectively protect human rights of people drawn into the investigation, it is submitted that it should be for the court to give prior authorization for interference with rights of individuals. The court, in the form of an investigating magistrate, would only assess the lawfulness of the investigative means applied for by the prosecutor, and have no control over the functionality of the measure. Certain other criteria have to be fulfilled. First of all, the intrusion must have a base in the law. Democratic society requires that each interference with human rights should have been previously legitimized by the common will of the people, that is, by a general abstract norm. Otherwise rights could be encroached on by the arbitrary will of the prosecutor. Furthermore, there needs to be some degree of suspicion and reasonable grounds to believe that the infringement would substantially aid the investigation and enhance the finding of the truth. The responsibility for the conduct of the investigation would still rest with the prosecutor. Interference with human rights, though, would need prior authorization and thereby control the prosecutor's conduct *ex ante*, cases of urgency excluded.

The last player in the criminal justice system is the defendant and his counsel. The crucial point is where the offender actually becomes a suspect. From this point onwards, it is submitted, he must be granted assistance by counsel. It is not only that representation in court is better done by a third person trained in legal proceedings. Already at the stage of investigation the position of the suspect might be irreparably damaged if he does not get advice from a jurist who is independent from the investigation. The suspect is under particular pressure when questioned by the investigator. Counsel should be present at all times, first, to monitor the moves of the interrogator and, secondly, to assist the questioned person through the legal and procedural maze he is unfamiliar with. In the case where the suspect cannot afford counsel it must be assigned to him. Upon arrest and before questioning the suspect must be duly informed about the allegation against him, of his right to counsel, and his right to remain silent. While questioned and in confinement the interviewing authority must not resort to torture or inhuman and degrading treatment, but must respect the free will of the suspect. To ensure the proper treatment of the suspect by the investigator, it would be best if every questioning was tape-recorded and a close record of his detention was kept. Preferably the incarceration should be monitored by an independent agency. Regular inspections by the International Committee of the Red Cross, for example, should be allowed. Pre-trial detention is only lawful if certain exceptional criteria are fulfilled, which are again to be assessed by a judge. There must first be a strong suspicion that the person held on remand has committed the alleged crime. In addition, one of the three following criteria must be met: there need to be reasonable grounds to believe that there is a danger of the suspect (1) absconding, or (2) negatively influencing evidence, or (3) committing further offences. These criteria are to be read in proportion to the seriousness of the offence. If none of these options are met, the suspect has to be left in liberty, or set free on bail for the time during which the investigation is continued. With the decision of the prosecutor that the case is in his opinion strong enough to be brought to trial, the investigation comes to an end and the procedure enters its second stage.

B. CONFIRMATION

At this second stage of the proceedings a decision has to be made whether or not the prosecution should go ahead and file an indictment with the court. It seems potentially dangerous, because of the seriousness of international crimes, to leave this decision entirely in the hands of a prosecutor. Although I have argued that the prosecutor should be objective in his conduct, and an impartial and independent institution akin to the judges, he is nevertheless called upon to establish a hypothesis as to how the criminal events have happened, and work towards proving the rightness of his version. The prosecutor is therefore 'naturally biased'. It would also do harm to the trustworthiness of the system of international criminal law if its enforcement were left to the discretion of the prosecutor. To execute criminal law from political motives would mean from a human rights point of view to punish some arbitrarily and severely and to leave others free, where both may be responsible for the same criminal offence. The system would then be unduly discriminatory. It seems therefore more suitable that the prosecutor should be strictly bound by the law and that he should have to prosecute unless the evidence does not support the suspicion. The gravity of international crimes as well as the public outrage that is generally provoked by them would make it impossible to discontinue prosecution for reasons other than lack of evidence. If the prosecutor is therefore persuaded that his case is strong enough to carry a trial he has to submit his version to a reviewing judge, that is, file an indictment. The reviewing judge would then decide independently upon the evidence offered by the prosecutor whether or not the case is strong enough to carry a conviction (prima facie case). If this is denied, the case rests until the prosecutor produces more convincing evidence.

In the case of a confirmation of the indictment by the judge the trial is prepared. This means in the first place that the accused is given time to prepare his defence, the exact amount of which obviously depends on the complexity of the case. He must therefore be granted free access to the counsel who will represent him before the court. He must be fully informed of the indictment and of the evidence the prosecutor relies upon in proving the guilt of the accused. In order to give the defendant the full opportunity to challenge the prosecutor's case, and in order to avoid complicated norms and legal disputes about mutual or unilateral disclosure, it is submitted that the files should be made completely accessible to the defendant.

C. THE TRIAL

The trial is the place where the clash between common and civil law is most obvious. An international criminal court does not necessarily strictly need to follow one or the other. It can adopt a structure that is a combination between the two. There are certain principles that are to be respected as they have emerged both from the adversarial as well as from the inquisitorial system. The combined system that I have proposed here has consequences for one of the focal points of the trial, the examination of witnesses, and for the rules of evidence. Finally, the sentencing practice has been assessed.

(I) Structure

The structure of the trial could be orientated either according to the inquisitorial judge that seeks the truth through his questioning or the adversarial presentation of evidence by the prosecution on the one hand and the defence on the other. It has been suggested in the discussion that neither of the possibilities is infallible. The former relies heavily on the integrity of judges who cannot meet the high (but certainly appropriate) expectations. The latter has the cross-examination at the centre of its procedure, which can easily produce injustice to victim and witnesses and slant evidence.

One of the reasons why common law attributes to the judge a very passive and restricted role is the fact that a jury will decide whether the defendant is guilty or not. It has been suggested here that the jury system is questionable in general, and certainly neither affordable nor desirable in the international context. As the verdict is therefore to be given by judges instead of a jury, the international judge gains a typical continental element, the 'judging element'. The role and person of the judge is, however, fundamentally different from that of the juror. The judge needs far less protection from rhetoric and procedural tricks implemented by counsel to impress the jury. As the judge is familiar with facts and the law he need not quietly listen to the presentations of both sides but, in the knowledge that he has to be satisfied with the questioning, may express his disquietude and intervene in the parties' presentation. Furthermore, the judges are expected to give a reasoned decision and must therefore be at least allowed to ask additional questions. In view of all this, it is submitted that the system employed by an international court should be a combination of continental tradition and common law. The system should still be based on confrontational presentation of the case, with the possibility of cross-examining witnesses.[1] The judge, however, should be given a more active role. His duty would be to actively search for the truth himself, request further evidence, and put questions to the witnesses. In this regard he has a particular role to play towards the protection of victims and witnesses. To avoid the shortcomings of the cross-examination techniques he could intervene and bar questions. With increasing need for protection he could then question the witness himself and exclude direct involvement of counsel. Such a combination neither sticks to the wrong allusion that cross-examination is the only 'vehicle for the truth' nor is glued to the belief that a single person can on his own extract the truth. It acknowledges systematic and practical failures in both approaches and tries to combine their positive effects.

This would be a general starting-point: judge and counsel of both sides have to work together in finding out the truth. Both have the right to request evidence and ask questions of witnesses, whereas the judge has a particular call to care for the protection of the witnesses. Consequently, already at the preparation stage, judge and counsel of both sides would have to work closer together. They would have to make up their minds as to what evidence they would regard as essential to be heard.

The two-act system of the common law tradition, with the determination of guilt made first and independently from the determination of the amount of punishment, should be adhered to. For the protection of the accused it is important that the question as to the guilt is kept separate from the one as to the adequate sentence. Yet the practice of the guilty plea should be abolished. Admission and confession should not be more than one of the pieces of evidence and should not have the effect of skipping the question of guilt altogether. A consideration of other accusing evidence should still take place,[2] although this may take a more summary form in such cases.

(II) Principles

I have looked at six principles in detail that would govern the conduct of the whole trial proceedings. The first would be the principle of a public trial. Date and venue of the main hearing must be made public, and in particular the attendance of the media is necessary. Media coverage is

---

[1] I have argued before that the system could also be adopted from the continental viewpoint. This would mean that the important role of the judge would be kept but the shortcomings of the system could be healed by allowing further questioning and examining of counsel, in fact encouraging cross-examinations. The international discussion does not on a whole seem ready to accept the continental system as a blueprint.

[2] This also has the result of allowing proper assessment of the credibility of the confession.

even more important in the context of international criminal law. Publicity in international criminal law pertains both to the worldwide public in general and to the domestic society of the territory where the atrocities occurred in particular. As international execution serves as complementary to national jurisdiction it is crucial that, in terms of public information, the difference it makes that an international court hears the case is minimized. Only thereby can international enforcement have the effects on the national society that national execution would have, in particular reconciliation and education. This latter effect has also to be achieved on a worldwide basis. It can only happen if the international proceedings reach a global society. As the trial may be held in an arbitrarily chosen country, by chance far away from the society which endured the human rights atrocities that are now prosecuted at the international court, almost the only way to address the people of this society as well as the global society as such is through extensive media coverage and through the tools of modern communication, like the internet.

In cases where the security of persons involved, like victim, witness, or accused, is in danger from the public, publicity could be partly excluded in order to guarantee protection for persons in jeopardy. Before the hearing is held in camera it has to be decided that the protection cannot be otherwise secured by means of non-disclosure of the identity to the public and distorting the appearance and voice through technical devices. There can hardly be a reason for the public to be excluded from the entire trial. The expulsion of public and media should be kept as short as possible.

The second principle is that of an oral trial. It needs to be ensured that the defendant is properly confronted with the allegations and they have been made known to the public. Nothing that is of importance for the question of guilt should be kept in secret.

Thirdly, the right to be present during trial has to be assessed. Again some jurisdictions recognize an excessive possibility of conducting a trial in the absence of the defendant, while in other jurisdictions the prosecution rests entirely when the accused is not present. The presence of the defendant appears to be paramount in achieving the aims of the trial. It is not so important whether or not one allows proceedings in absentia to take place in exceptional circumstances. Of more importance is that the defendant is given a full trial in his presence after the reasons for his absence have been overcome. The previous trial that took place without the defendant must have no influence whatsoever on conduct or outcome of the later proceedings. In this context it is necessary to take a brief look at the so-called Rule 61 procedure at the ICTY. In order to contribute to the conservation of evidence the prosecution case is reviewed by a full Trial Chamber, in particular in cases where expectations are low that the accused will ever be surrendered to the tribunal. It must be remembered that this procedure can only be provisional and the case has to be tried from the beginning should the defendant finally be available.

Fourthly, the principle of a speedy trial is vital for the protection of the defendant. The insecurity about his status has to be kept to a minimum. Although no exact time limit can be established, the court has to operate as swiftly as possible.

Fifthly, the presumption of innocence has several important consequences for the trial. It first recalls that public authorities need to establish and prove the allegations. The defendant cannot be burdened with the task of proving his innocence. Furthermore the threshold which has to be overcome in order to justify a conviction is proof beyond reasonable doubt. This means that the judges have to be convinced from the impression they get from the entirety of the trial that all doubts regarding the guilt of the defendant are reasonably silenced. Whether this threshold allows for majority votes and dissenting opinions is doubtful. As concerns the question of guilty or not guilty, the verdict must be unanimous since otherwise, obviously, not all doubts would have been silenced.

Finally, the principle of equality of arms has to be taken into account. The defence has at all stages to be given a fair chance to challenge the charges put against it by the prosecution. In fact the defendant has to be given an opportunity to comment on any claim that is put against him, in particular if it could negatively influence his position.

(III) Witnesses

One of the core points of the trial proceedings is certainly the examination of witnesses. It is suggested here that an international criminal procedure should recognize the modified role of the judge and allow more supervision or influence by the judge of the examination process. The presentation and examination of witnesses is principally left to the parties. Yet the judge can intervene actively, barring questions of counsel, or address the witness himself.

In an unproblematic case this will mean that the judge will not intervene at all. The more vulnerable the witness is, the more the judge will interfere in order to protect him. This can take different forms. It could mean simply that the judge will disallow questions put to the witness by counsel. Enhanced vulnerability of the witness could mean that he is to be removed from the distressing atmosphere of the court room and that the questioning takes place via video-link. Where traumatic experiences cannot otherwise be prevented, as with children or victims of sexual abuse, the judge himself could examine the witness. In cases where the safety of the witness is in serious danger and cannot be otherwise ensured, the identity of the witness could be withheld from the defendant. Only in the most serious cases could it also be kept secret from the defence counsel. It is crucial that the judge knows the identity of the witness, and that when he examines him has the opportunity to observe his demeanour. In any case the defence must be allowed to put questions to the testifying person, albeit through the judge as mediator. If we accept that the system is a combination of adversarial and inquisitorial procedure and if we take into account that the examination of witnesses is not a presentation of the evidence to lay jurors, but rather the stage for the professional judge to apprehend and appreciate existing evidence, we can, in exceptional circumstances, rely on the integrity of the judge in the overall task of bringing to light the truth about the criminal offence.

(IV) Rules of Evidence

As concerns the rules of evidence one also has to keep in mind that the rules' immense importance in Anglo-American culture stems from their main aim of protecting the jury from irrelevant or slanted evidence. At the international court, experienced professional judges will convict or acquit. The focus of the rules of evidence should therefore shift towards the protection of human rights and the respect for the dignity of the accused.

Taking a look at the 'classical' problems of evidentiary rules, this modified understanding of the function and aim of rules of evidence has influence on the results. At first, one could more widely accept hearsay evidence. The reasons for the strict exclusion of such evidence in a jury-court can be overcome by professional judges who can be relied on to attribute to a hearsay witness the appropriate weight, and by a structure which ascribes an inquisitorial element to the judges. Confession and admission by the defendant have to be under particular scrutiny. It must be ensured that no undue pressure or deception was used on the accused, so that his statement was clearly made voluntarily. It must also be determined whether the defendant's self-incrimination was informed, that is, whether he was fully aware of the consequences of his confession, and whether it is unequivocal. Only if these three criteria are met should a statement of the defendant be taken into consideration. In the case of the defendant being silent, it is submitted that this silence should be excluded as evidence. In particular one should abstain from inferring from previous silence that submissions eventually made at the trial stage are made up. In any case silence can only act as a corroboration of evidence that is already compelling by itself. Finally, evidence that has been obtained by violating human rights should not be taken into consideration at the trial. Reasons for this are, first, that the human rights violation committed against the defendant is thereby vindicated and, secondly, that law enforcement agencies are thereby disciplined. That latter point will be of enhanced importance in cases where the international prosecutor has to cooperate with police forces which do not understand human rights duties as their primary responsibility. The core point, however, is the protection of personal dignity. Evidence that has been obtained directly by a violation of human rights should therefore not be admitted for trial. Evidence that stems indirectly from intrusive action could be heard in court if the law enforcement agencies can prove that the infringement happened accidentally. If the violation has taken place knowingly and deliberately, the disciplinary element of the exclusionary rule necessitates non-admissibility.

(V) The Sentence

The decision on the amount of punishment to be inflicted upon the convicted person shall be taken in a procedure distinct from the procedure where the guilt of the person is being discussed. The procedural structure of this sentencing procedure needs to be the same as the process that was applied to the first act of the trial. This structure consists of an adversarial presentation of evidentiary material, with an actively supervising and inquiring judge. As international criminal law does not know of mandatory sentences and, indeed, gives but poor hints as to the lengths of imprisonment, particular importance should be paid to this stage of the proceedings. All relevant factors need to be taken into account. In addition to the 'ordinary' aggravating and mitigating circumstances, the term to be served should take heed of the aim of resocialization and rehabilitation of the prisoner, which is further complicated by the fact that the prisoner will be imprisoned in an environment that is culturally, religiously, and linguistically foreign to him, which might in severe circumstances even be tantamount to solitary confinement. These circumstances should perhaps result in a reduction of the sentence.

D. AFTER THE TRIAL

A finished trial poses two main human rights concerns: the prohibition of a second trial and the right to appeal. The principle *ne bis in idem* comes into play after a conviction or acquittal. What is prohibited is a second decision concerning the substantial facts of the event, as they are presented by the indictment and the confirmation. Appeal or cassation are allowed and not to be seen as a second trial. However, they should not alter the situation to the disadvantage of the defendant.

The principle of double jeopardy can be understood in two ways,

Erledigtenlösung and *Anrechnungslösung.* Whereas usually international law does not follow the former, the fact that the ICC should act as complementary to national jurisdictions calls for the application of the principle of accepting the judgment as final. The exceptions to this principle that have been put forward have to be looked at cautiously. It is submitted here that the only justifiable exception is where the previous national trial was conducted as a 'show-trial' or tried to shield the defendant, that is, abused the prohibition of double jeopardy. Exceptions purely on the grounds that the national court wrongly treated the crime as an ordinary one have been shown to be misleading and unjustifiable from a human rights point of view.

A review of the judgment in regards both to law (cassation) and fact (appeal) has to be provided for. Both sides, defence and prosecution, should be allowed to take the case to a higher instance. However, the defendant should not be put into a position of fearing an exacerbation of his situation (*reformatio in peius*). For the further elaboration of the law, however, it is highly desirable to allow the prosecution to ask for a review of facts or law.

The proceedings that take place at appeal/cassation have to be structured according to human rights. Generally speaking, the review procedure has to be organized in a similar way to the trial procedure. What was said above about the trial procedure applies here *mutatis mutandis.* Of particular importance is the speedy dealing with the matter and that the defendant is at every moment given the chance to refute the allegations of the prosecution.

In order to prevent inequalities between criminals who are tried internationally and those who defend themselves at national courts, it should be discussed whether or not the possibility of communicating human rights violations to a human rights body, for example the HRC, would be feasible.

E. THE POST-TRIAL STAGE

The trial is to be held exclusively at the international body. The responsibility for the conduct and the result rests exclusively with the international court. This is different at the stage of the inquiry, as we have seen. At that stage the prosecutor has to rely on the work of national enforcement agencies. Yet, as was shown, the responsibility for this inquiry rests with the international prosecutor. The post-trial stage shows the same problems. As the international community does not have its own enforcement facilities it is dependent on Member States to implement the judgments and host war criminals.

International rules have emerged that govern the treatment of people who are imprisoned. A standard set of Minimum Rules for prisoners is generally accepted as providing for humane treatment. It should be ensured that these rules are adhered to by the state which hosts the international criminal. The responsibility for the proper treatment of these prisoners rests foremost with the hosting state. This state has direct influence on the well-being of the inmate and has an international duty to guarantee the security of this person just as it has for all other prisoners. Yet the ICC should supervise this duty. It should do so, first, by implementing a tight agreement as to the status of the prisoner (SOPA). Secondly, the Court should pay regular visits and inspections to the place of imprisonment or ask other agencies, like the International Committee of the Red Cross, to do so. In this regard the international court does not lose responsibility for the person it convicted.

Finally, the place of imprisonment has to be decided upon. The ICC is not unlimited in its choice of possible host states. It must first ensure that the state complies fully with the Minimum Standard for prisoners. This as we have seen could be ensured through a SOPA. Secondly, it must choose a country that is neutral to the conflict in the broad sense of religious, ethnic, and cultural concerns. Thirdly, the country should be as close to the home of the prisoner as possible, in order to enable regular visits of family and friends. These principles governing the election of the place of imprisonment are not unjustly discriminating nor is there an infringement of justified expectations the criminal might have. The prisoner should be in a position to challenge the decision on all three grounds. In particular, complaints about the treatment of the prisoner must be heard at the tribunal and if accepted, the prisoner would eventually have to be moved to a different place. Further provisions that might exist in national law for pardon must be supervised by the ICC.

F. CONCLUSION

An international criminal procedure could be developed as a unique legal order that takes into account the history and experience of criminal prosecution over the last centuries in different traditions and cultures. It would emerge as a system that would try to avoid the difficulties one system has by looking at the other in order to find a solution. The prevalent concern in any respect is compatibility with human rights and the focus must be on the protection of human rights from the beginning of the inquiry to release from prison. In the discussion about a criminal procedure comparative law should be placed at the centre of the discussion. False adherence to domestic legal cultures that emerged for certain political and historical reasons helps no one. Instead there must be a profound rethinking of domestic legal systems with a look at the necessities of such a young and sensitive legal order as international criminal law. Certainly a case-to-case development as attempted by the ICTY can be considered inevitable. Nevertheless, in order to avoid embarrassment of states and individuals, this must take place within a solid theoretical consensus. A well-balanced framework for this consensus is to be seen in the Rome Statute for an International Criminal Court. But this is only the dawn of the entire enterprise. One has to bear in mind that punishing individuals on an international level is no academic enterprise but a very serious matter, more serious than conviction within national jurisdiction as the convicted carries the stigma of being a 'world criminal'. On the basis of a consensus, solutions for each case can be found. Only then can the world move towards an international criminal procedure which merits this name.

Bibliography

1 Commentaries

Currie, David P., *The Constitution of the Federal Republic of Germany* (Chicago and London, 1994).

Dijk, P. van, and Hoof, G. J. H. van, *Theory and Practice of the European Convention on Human Rights* (Deventer, 1984).

Fawcett, J. E. S., *The Application of the European Convention on Human Rights* (2nd edn. Oxford, 1987).

Frowein, Jochen, and Peukert, Wolfgang, *EMRK-Kommentar* (2nd edn. Straßbourg and Kehl, 1996).

Harris, D. J., O'Boyle, M., and Warbrick, C., *Law of the European Convention on Human Rights* (London, 1995).

Jacobs, F. G., and White, R. C. A., *The European Convention on Human Rights* (2nd edn. Oxford, 1996).

Kleinknecht, T., and Meyer-Goßner, L., *Strafprozeßordnung mit GVG und Nebengesetzen* (44th edn. Munich, 2000).

Macdonald, R. St J., Matscher, F., and Petzold, H. (eds.), *The European System for the Protection of Human Rights* (Dordrecht, 1993).

Maunz, T., Dürig, G., Herzog, R., and Scholz, R., *Kommentar zum Bonner Grundgesetz* (Munich, 1991).

Nowak, Manfred, *International Covenant on Civil and Political Rights: CCPR Commentary* (Kehl and Strasbourg, 1993).

Simma, Bruno (ed.), *The Charter of the United Nations: A Commentary* (Oxford, 1995).

Trifterer, Otto (ed.), *Commentary on the Rome Statute of the International Criminal Court* (Baden-Baden, 1999).

Tröndle, Herbert, and Fischer, Thomas, *Strafgesetzbuch und Nebengesetze* (50th edn. Munich, 2000).

Vehn, J., and Ergec, R., *La Convention européene de droits de l'homme* (Brussels, 1990).

2 Books

Abernathy, M. Glenn, and Perry, Barbara A., *Civil Liberties under the Constitution* (6th edn. Columbia, SC, 1993).

Allott, Philip, *Eunomia: New Order for a New World* (Oxford, 1990).

Alpert, Geoffrey P., *The American System of Criminal Justice* (Beverly Hills, Calif., 1985).

Andrews, J. A. (ed.), *Human Rights in Criminal Procedure: A Comparative Study* (London, 1982).

—— and Hirst, M., *Criminal Evidence* (2nd edn. London, 1992).

Ankumah, Evelyn A., *The African Commission on Human and Peoples' Rights* (The Hague, 1996).

An-Na'im, Abdullahi Ahmed, *Human Rights in Cross Cultural Perspectives: A Quest for Consensus* (Philadelphia, 1991).

Arbour, Louise, Eser, Albin, Ambos, Kai, and Sanders, Andrew (eds.), *The Prosecutor of a Permanent International Criminal Court* (Freiburg im Breisgau, 2000).

Ashworth, Andrew, *The English Criminal Process: A Review of Empirical Research* (Oxford, 1984).

Baldwin, John, *Pre-Trial Justice* (Oxford, 1985).

Barry, Brian, *Justice as Impartiality* (Oxford, 1995).

Bassiouni, M. Cherif, *International Criminal Law*, i. *Crimes* (New York, 1986). iii. *Enforcement* (New York, 1987).

—— and Manikas, Peter, *The Law of the International Criminal Tribunal for the Former Yugoslavia* (New York, 1996).

Beck, Ulrich, *Risikogesellschaft: Auf dem Weg in eine andere Moderne* (Frankfurt, 1986).

Berger, Mark, *Taking the Fifth: The Supreme Court and the Privilege Against Self-Incrimination* (Lexington, 1980).

Berlin, Isaiah, *Four Essays on Liberty* (Oxford, 1969).

Best, W. M., *The Principles of the Law of Evidence* (12th edn. London, 1922).

Bodenhamer, David J., *Fair Trial: Rights of the Accused in American History* (Oxford, 1992).

Bossuyt, M. J., *Guide to the 'Travaux Préparatoires' of the International Covenant on Civil and Political Rights* (Dordrecht, 1987).

Boutros-Ghali, Boutros, *An Agenda for Peace* (2nd edn. New York, 1995).

Brewer, John D. (ed.), *The Police, Public Order and the State* (2nd edn. London, 1996).

Buergenthal, T., and Shelton, D., *Protecting Human Rights in the Americas* (4th edn. Kehl and Strasbourg, 1995).

Campbell, Tom, Goldberg, David, McLean, Sheila, and Mullen, Tom (eds.), *Human Rights: From Rhetoric to Reality* (Oxford, 1986).

Cape, Ed, and Luqmani, Jawaid, *Defending Suspects at Police Stations* (2nd edn. London, 1995).

Cassese, Antonio, *Human Rights in a Changing World* (Cambridge, 1990).

—— *Inhumane States: Imprisonment, Detention and Torture in Europe Today* (Cambridge, 1996).

Champion, Dean J., *Measuring Offender Risk: A Criminal Justice Sourcebook* (Westport, Conn., 1994).

Chatterton, Clifford, *Bail: Law and Practice* (London, 1986).

Choo, Andrew L.-T., *Hearsay and Confrontation in Criminal Trials* (Oxford, 1996).

Colliard, Claude-Albert, *Libertés publiques* (6th edn. Paris, 1982).

Corre, Neil, *Bail in Criminal Proceedings* (London, 1990).

Craven, Matthew C. R., *The International Covenant on Economic, Social and Cultural Rights: A Perspective on its Development* (Oxford, 1995).

Davidson, Scott, *The Inter-American Court of Human Rights* (Aldershot, 1992).

Deflem, Mathieu (ed.), *Habermas, Modernity and Law* (London, 1996).

De Haas, Elsa, *Antiquities of Bail: Origin and Historical Development in Criminal Cases to the Year 1275* (New York, 1940).

Devlin, Patrick, *The Criminal Prosecution in England* (New Haven, 1958).

Devlin, Patrick, *Trial by Jury* (London, 1966).

Dickson, Brice (ed.), *Human Rights and the European Convention* (London, 1997).

Dinstein, Yoram, *The Defence of 'Obedience to Superior Orders' in International Law* (Leiden, 1965).

—— and Tabory, Mala (eds.), *War Crimes in International Law* (The Hague, 1996).

Duff, R. A., *Trials and Punishment* (Cambridge, 1986).

Dworkin, Ronald, *Taking Rights Seriously* (London, 1977).

Easton, Susan M., *The Rights to Silence* (Aldershot, 1991).

Eisenstein, James, *Counsel for the United States: US Attorneys in the Political and Legal System* (Baltimore, 1978).

Epstein, Lee, and Walker, Thomas G., *Constitutional Law for a Changing America: Rights, Liberties, and Justice* (Washington, DC, 1992).

Fennell, Phil, Harding, Christopher, Jörg, Nico, and Swart, Bert, *Criminal Justice in Europe: A Comparative Study* (Oxford, 1995).

Ferencz, Benjamin B., *An International Criminal Court: A Step toward World Peace— A Documentary History and Analysis*, i. *Half a Century of Hope* (London, 1980).

Findlay, Mark, and Duff, Peter, *The Jury under Attack* (London, 1988).

Fionda, Julia, *Public Prosecutors and Discretion: A Comparative Study* (Oxford, 1995).

Forsynth, F., *History of the Trial by Jury* (London, 1852).

Giddens, Anthony, *The Consequences of Modernity* (London, 1990).

—— *Beyond Left and Right: The Future of Radical Politics* (Cambridge, 1994).

Griffith, J. A. G., *The Politics of the Judiciary* (5th edn. London, 1997).

Habermas, Jürgen, *Faktizität und Geltung* (Frankfurt/Main, 1993).

—— *Die Einbeziehung des Anderen* (Frankfurt/Main, 1996).

Hans, Valerie P., and Vidmar, Neil, *Judging the Jury* (New York, 1986).

Hart, H. L. A., *Punishment and Responsibility* (Oxford, 1968).

Hatchard, John, Huber, Barbara, and Vogler, Richard (eds.), *Comparative Criminal Procedure* (London, 1996).

Helms, Ludger, *Wettbewerb und Kooperation* (Opladen, 1997).

Henkin, Louis (ed.), *The International Bill of Rights: The Covenant on Civil and Political Rights* (New York, 1981).

Herrmann, Joachim, *Reform der deutschen Hauptverhandlung nach dem Vorbild des anglo-amerikanischen Strafverfahrens* (Bonn, 1971).

Hirsch, Andrew von, *Doing Justice* (New York, 1976).

—— *Censure and Sanctions* (Oxford, 1993).

Höffe, Ottfried, *Vernunft und Recht, Bausteine zu einem interkulturellen Rechtsdiskurs* (Frankfurt/Main, 1996).

Holdsworth, William, *A History of English Law in Sixteen Volumes*, xv (London, 1965).

Hunt, Murray, *Using Human Rights Law in English Courts* (Oxford, 1997).

Jones, John R. W. D., *The Practice of the International Criminal for the former Yugoslavia and the International Criminal Tribunal for Rwanda* (3rd edn. Ardsley, NY, 1997).

Kangaspunta, Kristiina (ed.), *Profiles of Criminal Justice Systems in Europe and North America* (Helsinki, 1995).

Karlen, Delmar, *Anglo-American Criminal Justice System* (Oxford, 1967).

Leigh, Leonhard H., *Police Powers in England and Wales* (2nd edn. London, 1985).

—— *Protection of Human Rights in Criminal Procedure: The British Experience* (Kerala, 1993).

Levenson, Howard, Fairweather, Fiona, and Cape, Ed, *Police Powers: A Practitioner's Guide* (3rd edn. London, 1996).

Lidstone, Ken, and Palmer, Clare, *Bevan and Lidstone's The Investigation of Crime: A Guide to Police Powers* (2nd edn. London, 1996).

Luhmann, Niklas, *Legitimation durch Verfahren* (2nd edn. Frankfurt, 1989).

Lutz-Bachmann, Matthias, and Bohmann, James (eds.), *Frieden durch Recht: Kants Friedensidee und das Problem einer neuen Weltordung* (Frankfurt/Main, 1996).

McConville, M., Hodgson, J., Bridges, L., and Pavlovic, A., *Standing Accused* (Oxford, 1994).

McDonald, William F. (ed.), *The Prosecutor* (Beverly Hills, Calif., 1979).

McDougal, M., Lasswell, H., and Chen, L., *Human Rights and World Public Order* (New Haven, 1980).

McEwans, Jenny, *Evidence in the Adversarial Process: The Modern Law* (Oxford, 1992).

McGoldrick, Dominic, *The Human Rights Committee* (2nd edn. Oxford, 1994).

MacIntyre, Alasdair, *After Virtue* (2nd edn. London, 1985).

Matscher, F., and Petzold, H. (eds.), *Protecting Human Rights: The European Dimension. Essays in Honour of Gérard J. Wiarda* (Cologne, 1988).

Meron, Theodor (ed.), *Human Rights in International Law, Legal and Policy Issues* (Oxford, 1984).

—— *Human Rights and Humanitarian Norms as Customary Law* (Oxford, 1989).

Morgan, David, and Stephenson, Geoffrey (eds.), *Suspicion and Silence: The Right to Silence in Criminal Investigations* (London, 1994).

Morris, Virginia, and Scharf, Michael P., *An Insider's Guide to the International Criminal Tribunal for the Former Yugoslavia* (Irvington-on-Hudson, NY, 1995).

—— and —— *The International Criminal Tribunal for Rwanda* (Irvington-on-Hudson, NY, 1998).

Müller, Jörg Paul, *Demokratische Gerechtigkeit* (Munich, 1993).

Mullerson, Rein, *Human Rights Diplomacy* (London, 1997).

Murphy, Peter, *A Practical Approach to Evidence* (3rd edn. London, 1988).

—— (ed.), *Blackstone's Criminal Practice 1995* (London, 1995).

Niblett, John, *Disclosure in Criminal Proceedings* (London, 1997).

Nino, Carlos Santiago, *The Ethics of Human Rights* (Oxford, 1991).

Oehler, Dietrich, *Internationales Strafrecht* (2nd edn. Cologne, 1983).

Paulsen, Monrad G., and Kadish, Sanford H., *Criminal Law and its Process* (Boston, Mass., and Toronto, 1962).

Peters, Karl, *Strafprozeßrecht* (4th edn. Heidelberg, 1985).

Pollock, Frederick, and Maitland, Frederic William, *The History of English Law before the Time of Edward I* (2nd edn.), ii (Cambridge, 1923).

Poncet, D., *La Protection de l'accusé par la Convention Européenne des Droits de l'Homme* (Geneva, 1977).

Radbruch, Gustav, *Rechtsphilosophie* (8th edn. Stuttgart, 1973).

Radzinowicz, Leon, *A History of English Criminal Law and its Administration from 1750*, i. *The Movement for Reform* (London, 1948).

Ratner, Steven R., and Abrams, Jason S., *Accountability for Human Rights Atrocities in International Law: Beyond the Nuremberg Legacy* (Oxford, 1997).

Rawls, John, *A Theory of Justice* (Oxford, 1972).

—— *Political Liberalism* (New York, 1993).

Raz, Joseph, *The Morality of Freedom* (Oxford, 1986).

Richer, Laurent, *Les Droits de l'homme et du citoyen* (Paris, 1982).

Risse, Horst, *Der Einsatz militärischer Kräfte durch die VN und das Kriegsvölkerrecht* (Frankfurt, 1988).

Robertson, A. H. (ed.), *Privacy and Human Rights* (Manchester, 1973).

Robertson, Geoffrey, *Freedom, the Individual and the Law* (6th edn. London, 1989).

Rodley, Nigel, *The Treatment of Prisoners under International Law* (Paris and Oxford, 1987).

Roggemann, Hedwig, *Der International Strafgerichtshof der Vereinten Nationen von 1993 und der Krieg auf dem Balkan* (Berlin, 1994).

Rolph, C. H., *The Queen's Pardon* (London, 1978).

Roxin, Claus, *Strafrecht Allgemeiner Teil I/1* (2nd edn. Munich, 1995).

—— *Strafverfahrensrecht* (24th edn. Munich, 1995).

Rüping, Hinrich, *Staatsanwaltschaft und Provinzialjustizverwaltung im Dritten Reich* (Baden-Baden, 1990).

—— *Grundriß der Strafrechtsgeschichte* (2nd edn. Munich, 1991).

Rupp-Swienty, Annette, *Die Doktrin von der Margin of Appreciation in der Rechtsprechung des Europäischen Gerichtshofs für Menschenrechte* (Munich, 1999).

Seidel, Gerd, *Handbuch der Grund- und Menschenrechte auf staatlicher, europäischer und universeller Ebene* (Baden-Baden, 1996).

Seidl-Hohenveldern, Ignaz, *Völkerrecht* (8th edn. Munich, 1994).

Shihata, Ibrahim F. I., *The Power of the International Court to Determine its own Jurisdiction* (The Hague, 1965).

Specht, Britta, *Die zwischenstaatliche Geltung des Grundsatzes* ne bis in idem (Berlin, 1999).

Sprack, John, *Emmins on Criminal Procedure* (6th edn. London, 1995).

Stavros, Stephanos, *The Guarantees for Accused Persons under Article 6 of the European Convention on Human Rights* (Dordrecht, 1993).

Stern, Klaus, *Das Staatrecht der Bundesrepublik Deutschland*, iii/2, *Allgemeine Lehre der Grundrechte* (Munich, 1994).

Stone, R., *Entry, Search and Seizure: A Guide to Civil and Criminal Powers of Entry* (3rd edn. London, 1997).

Taylor, Telford, *The Anatomy of the Nuremberg Trials: A Personal Memoir* (New York, 1992).

Verdross, Alfred, and Simma, Bruno, *Universelles Völkerrecht: Theorie und Praxis* (3rd edn. Berlin, 1984).

Volk, Klaus, *Prozeßvoraussetzungen im Strafrecht. Zum Verhältnis von materiellem und Prozeßrecht* (Ebelsbach, 1978).

—— *Wahrheit und materielles Recht im Strafprozeß* (Konstanz, 1980).

Walzer, Martin, *Just and Unjust Wars: A Moral Argument with Historic Illustrations* (New York, 1977).

—— *Spheres of Justice: A Defence of Pluralism and Equality* (Oxford, 1983).

Wasik, Martin, *Emmins on Sentencing* (2nd edn. London, 1993).

Weissbrodt, David, and Wolfrum, Rüdiger (eds.), *The Right to a Fair Trial* (Beiträge zum ausländischen öffentlichen Recht und Völkerrecht, 129; Berlin, 1997).

Whitebread, Charles H., *Criminal Procedure: An Analysis of Constitutional Cases and Concepts* (New York, 1980).

Willis, James F., *Prologue to Nuremberg: The Politics and Diplomacy of Punishing War Criminals of the First World War* (Westport, Conn., 1982).

Witt, Elder, *The Supreme Court and Individual Rights* (2nd edn. Washington, DC, 1988).

Wolf, Christian, *Die institutionelle Handelsschiedsgerichtsbarkeit* (Munich, 1992).

Wyngaert, Christine van den (ed.), *Criminal Procedure Systems in the European Community* (London, 1993).

Zuckerman, A. A. S., *The Principles of Criminal Evidence* (Oxford, 1989).

Zwart, Tom, *The Admissibility of Human Rights Petitions: The Case Law of the European Commission of Human Rights and the Human Rights Committee* (Dordrecht, 1994).

3. Articles and Reports

Alston, Philipp, and Quinn, G., The Nature and Scope of States Parties' Obligations under the International Covenant on Economic, Social and Cultural Rights, 9 HRC (1987), 156.

—— and Simma, Bruno, Sources of Human Rights: Custom, *Jus Cogens* and General Principles, 12 Australian Yearbook of International Law (1992), 82.

Alvarez, Jose E., Nuremberg Revisited: The *Tadic* Case, 7 EJIL (1996), 245.

Ambos, Kai, Establishing an International Criminal Court and an International Criminal Code: Observations from an International Criminal Law Viewpoint, 7 EJIL (1996), 519.

—— 14 examensrelevante Fragen zum neuen Internationalen Strafgerichtshof, JA (1998), 988.

—— Der neue Internationale Strafgerichtshof: Ein Überblick, NJW (1998), 3743.

Amnesty International, Establishing a Just, Fair and Effective International Criminal Court, AI Index: IOR 40/05/94.

Arsanjani, Mahnoush H., The Rome Statute of the International Criminal Court, 93 AJIL (1999), 22.

Ashworth, Andrew, The 'Public Interest' Element in Prosecutions, (1987) CrimLR, 595.

Ascensio, Hervé, The Rules of Procedure and Evidence of the ICTY, 9 LJIL (1996), 467.

Baldwin, John, and McConville, Michael, Doubtful Convictions by Jury, (1979) CrimLR, 230.

Bassiouni, M. Cherif, The UN Procedures for the Effective Implementation of the Standard Minimum Rules for the Treatment of Prisoners, in R. Herzberg (ed.), *Festschrift für D. Oehler* (Cologne, 1985), 525.

Behrens, Hans-Jörg, Investigation, Trial and Appeal in the International Criminal Court Statute, 6 Eur.J.Crime Cr.L.Cr.J. (1998), 429.

Bergsmo, Morten, The Jurisdictional Régime of the International Criminal Court, 6 Eur.J.Crime Cr.L.Cr.J. (1998), 345.

Bloom, Evan T., Protecting Peacekeepers: The Convention in the Safety of United Nations and Associated Personnel, 89 AJIL (1995), 621.

Bourloyannis-Vrailas, M.-Christiane, The Convention on the Safety of United Nations and Associated Personnel, 44 ICLQ (1995), 560.

Cassese, Antonio, Reflections on International Criminal Justice, 16 MLR (1998), 1.

—— The Statute of the International Criminal Court: Some Preliminary Reflections, 10 EJIL (1999), 144.

Chinkin, Christine, Due Process and Witness Anonymity, 91 AJIL (1997), 74.

Crawford, James, The ILC's Draft Statute for an International Criminal Court, 88 AJIL (1994), 140.

—— Prospects for an International Criminal Court, 48 *Current Legal Problems* (1995), 303.

—— The ILC adopts a Statute for an International Criminal Court, 89 AJIL (1995), 404.

Dadrian, V. N., Genocide as a Problem of National and International Law. The World War I Amenian Case, 14 Yale Journal of International Law (1989), 221.

Dahs, Hans, Die gespaltene Hauptverhandlung, NJW (1996), 178.

de Waart, Paul J. I. M., From 'Kidnapped' Witness to Released Accused 'for Humanitarian Reasons': The Case of the Late General Djordje Djukic, 9 LJIL (1996), 453.

DeWolfe Howe, Mark, Juries and Judges of Criminal Law, 52 Harvard Law Review (1939), 582.

Dinstein, Yoram, International Criminal Law, 20 Israel Law Review (1985), 206.

Dugard, John, Obstacles in the Way of an International Criminal Court, 56 Cambridge Law Journal (1997), 329.

Eide, Asbjorn, Realisation of Social and Economic Rights and the Minimum Threshold Approach, 10 HRLJ (1989), 35.

Field, Stewart, and Young, James, Disclosure, Appeals and Procedural Traditions: *Edwards v United Kingdom,* (1994) Crim LR, 264.

Frank, Thomas M., The Emerging Right to Democratic Governance, 86 AJIL (1992), 46.

Freeman, Michael, The Jury on Trial, (1981) Current Legal Problems, 65.

Gallant, Kenneth S., Securing the Presence of Defendants before the International Tribunal for the Former Yugoslavia: Breaking with Extradition, 5 CLF (1994), 557.

Gallivan, T., and Warbrick, C., Jury-Vetting and the European Convention on Human Rights, 5 HRR (1980), 176.

Geppert, Klaus, Grundlegendes und Aktuelles zur Unschuldvermutung des Art. 6 Abs. 2 der Europäischen Menschenrechtskonvention, JURA (1993), 160.

Glueck, Sheldon, The Nuremberg Trial and Aggressive War, 59 Harvard Law Review (1946), 396.

Goldstein, A. S., The State and the Accused: Balance of Advantage in Criminal Procedure, 69 Yale Law Journal (1960), 1149.

Green, L. C., Drazen Erdemovic: The International Criminal Tribunal for the Former Yugoslavia in Action, 10 LJIL (1997), 363.

Greenwood, Christopher, International Humanitarian Law and the *Tadic* Case, 7 EJIL (1996), 265.

—— Protection of Peacekeepers: The Legal Regime, 7 Duke J. Comp.&Int'l L (1996), 185.

—— International Humanitarian Law and United Nations Military Operations, 1 Yearbook of International Humanitarian Law (1998), 3.

—— The Jurisprudence of the International Criminal Tribunal for the Former Yugoslavia, 2 Max Planck Yearbook of UN Law (1998), 97.

Grimm, Dieter, Does Europe Need a Constitution? 1 European Law Journal (1995), 303.

Gutmann, Thomas, 'Keeping 'em Down on the Farm after they've Seen Paree': Aporien des kommunitaristischen Rechtsbegriffs, 83 Archiv für Recht- und Sozialphilosophie (ARSP) (1997), 37.

Hafner, Gerhard, Boon, Kristen, Rübesame, Anne, and Huston, Jonathan, A Response to the American View as Presented by Ruth Wedgwood, 10 EJIL (1999), 108.

Hampson, Françoise J., The International Criminal Tribunal for Yugoslavia and the Reluctant Witness, 47 ICLQ (1998), 50.

Harris, David J., The Right to a Fair Trial in Criminal Proceedings as a Human Right, 16 ICLQ (1967), 352.

Hermsdörfer, Willibald, Zum Statut des Internationalen Stragerichtshofs—ein Meilenstein im Völkerstrafrecht, 40 NZWehrr (1998), 193.

Herrmann, Joachim, Neuere Entwicklungen in der amerikanischen Strafrechtspflege, JZ (1985), 602.

Higgins, Rosalyn, Derogation under Human Rights Treaties, 48 BYIL (1976–7), 281.

Hörnle, Tatjana, and Hirsch, Andrew V., Positive Generalprevention und Tadel, GA (1995), 261.

Jarasch, Frank, Establishment, Organisation and Financing of the International Criminal Court, 6 Eur.J.Crime Cr.L.Cr.J. (1998), 325.

Jung, Heike, Internationalisierung des Grundsatzes *ne bis in idem, Festschrift für Schüler-Springorum* (Munich, 1993), 493.

Kaul, Hans-Peter, Special Note: The Struggle for the International Criminal Court's Jurisdiction, 6 Eur.J.Crime Cr.L.Cr.J. (1998), 364.

King, Faiza Patel, and La Rosa, Anne-Marie, Jurisprudence of the Yugoslavia Tribunal: 1994–1996, 8 EJIL (1997), 123.

Kirsch, Philippe, and Holmes, John T., The Rome Conference on an International Criminal Court: The Negotiating Process, 93 AJIL (1999), 2.

Koskenniemi, Martti, National Self-Determination Today: Problems of Legal Theory and Practice, 43 ICLR (1994), 241.

Kreß, Claus, Penalties, Enforcement and Cooperation in the International Criminal Court Statute, 6 Eur.J.Crime Cr.L.Cr.J. (1998), 442.

Kühl, Kristian, Unschuldsvermutung und Einstellung des Strafverfahrens, NJW (1984), 1264.

Langbein, J. H., Controlling Prosecutorial Discretion in Germany, 41 University of Chicago Law Review (1974), 439.

Lawyers' Committee for Human Rights, International Criminal Court Briefing

Series, Vol. I, No. 1: Establishing an International Criminal Court: Major Unresolved Issues in the Draft Statute, August 1996/Updated.

Lawyers' Committee for Human Rights, International Criminal Court Briefing Series, Vol. I, No. 2: Fairness to Defendants at the International Criminal Court: Proposals to Strengthen the Draft Statute and its Protection of Defendants' Rights, August 1996.

—— Vol. I, No. 4: The International Criminal Court Trigger Mechanism and the Need for an Independent Prosecutor, July 1997.

Leigh, Monroe, The Yugoslav Tribunal: Use of Unnamed Witnesses against Accused, 90 AJIL (1996), 216.

—— Witness Anonymity is Inconsistent with Due Process, 91 AJIL (1997), 80.

Linton, Suzannah, Reviewing the Case of Drazen Erdemovic: Unchartered Waters at the International Criminal Tribunal for the Former Yugoslavia, 12 LJIL (1999), 251.

Loucaides, L. G., Personality and Privacy under the European Convention of Human Rights, 61 BYIL (1990), 175.

May, Richard, Fair Play at Trial: An Interim Assessment of Section 78 of the Police and Criminal Evidence Act 1984, (1988) Crim LR, 722.

Meron, Theodor, War Crimes Law Comes of Age, 92 AJIL (1998), 463.

Müller, Jörg Paul, Kants Entwurf globaler Gerechtigkeit und das Problem der republikanischen Repräsentation im Staats- und Völkerrecht, in Zen-Ruffinen and Auer (eds.), *De la constitution: Etudes en l'honneur de Jean-François Aubert* (Basel, 1996), 133.

—— Wandel des Souveränitätsbegriffs im Lichte der Grundrechte, in René Rhinow, Stephan Breitenmoser and Bernhard Ehrenzeller (eds.), *Fragen des internationalen und nationalen Menschenrechtsschutzes FS Luzius Wildhaber* (Basel, 1997), 45.

—— Föderalismus, Subsidiarität, Demokratie, in Max Vollkommer (ed.), *Föderalismus-Prinzip und Wirklichkeit, Atzelsberger Gepräche* (Erlangen, 1997), 41.

Murdoch, Jim, The Work of the Council of Europe's Torture Committee, 5 EJIL (1994), 220.

Nino, Carlos Santiago, Positivism and Communitarianism: Between Human Rights and Democracy, 7 Ratio Juris (1994), 14.

Nowak, Manfred, and Schwaighofer, Christoph, Das Recht auf öffentliche Urteilsverkündung in Österreich, EuGRZ (1985), 725.

Nsereko, Daniel D. Ntanda, Rules of Procedure and Evidence of the International Tribunal for the Former Yugoslavia, Criminal Law Forum (1994), 507.

Oeter, Stefan, Souveränität und Demokratie als Probleme in der Verfassungsentwicklung der Europäischen Union, 55 ZaöRV (1995), 659.

Peukert, Wolfgang, Die überlange Verfahrensdauer (Art. 6 Abs. 1 EMRK) in der Rechtsprechung des Straßburger Instanzen, EuGRZ (1979), 261.

—— Die Garantie des 'fair trial' in der Straßburger Rechtsprechung, EuGRZ (1980), 247.

Radin, Max, International Crimes, 32 Iowa Law Review (1946), 33.

Reinisch, August, Das Jugoslawientribunal der Vereinten Nationen und die Verfahrensgarantien des II. VN-Menschenrechtspaktes: Ein Beitrag zur Frage der Bindung der Vereinten Nationen an nicht ratifiziertes Vertragsrecht, 47 Austrian JPIL (1995), 173.

Robinson, Darryl, Defining 'Crimes against Humanity' at the Rome Conference, 93 AJIL (1999), 43.

Roxin, Claus, Sinn und Grenzen staatlicher Strafe, JuS (1966), 377.

—— *Nemo tenetur* . . . die Rechtsprechung am Scheideweg, NStZ (1995), 466.

—— Zum Hörfallen-Beschluß des Großen Senats für Strafsachen, NStZ (1997), 18.

Safferling, Christoph, Die Atomwaffe unter der Antarktis, 40 Neue Zeitschrift für Wehrrecht (1998), 177.

—— *Prosecutor v. Djajic*, 92 AJIL (1998), 528.

—— Zum aktuellen Stand des Völkerstrafrechts, JA (2000), 164.

—— The Justification of Punishment in International Criminal Law, ARIEL (2000), 123.

Schabas, William A., General Principles of Criminal Law in the International Criminal Court Statute, 6 Eur.J.Crime Cr.L.Cr.J. (1998), 400.

Schachter, Oscar, Human Dignity as a Normative Concept, 77 AJIL (1983), 848.

Scheffer, David J., The United States and the International Criminal Court, 93 AJIL (1999), 12.

Schöch, Heinz, Strafzumessung und Persönlichkeitsschutz in der Haupt-verhandlung, in W. Frisch and W. Schmid (eds.), *Festschrift für Hans-Jürgen Bruns* (Cologne, 1978), 457.

—— and Schreiber, W., Ist die Zweiteilung der Hauptverhandlung praktikabel?, ZRP (1978), 63.

Schünemann, Bernd, Zur Reform der Hauptverhandlung im Strafprozeß, GA (1978), 161.

—— Wetterzeichen einer untergehenden Strafprozeßkultur? Wider die falsche Prophetie des Absprachenelysiums, Strafverteidiger (1993), 657.

—— Der Richter im Strafverfahren als manipulierter Dritter? Zur empirischen Bestätigung von Perseveranz und Schulterschlußeffekt, 1995 Verfahrensgerechtigkeit, 215; an updated version is to be found in StV (2000), 159.

Schweisfurth, Theodor, Vom Einheitsstaat (UdSSR) zum Staatenbund (GUS), 52 ZaöRV (1992), 541.

Sharp, Walter Gary, Protecting the Avatars of International Peace and Security, 7 Duke J. Comp.&Int'l L (1996), 93.

Shraga, Daphna, and Zacklin, Ralph, The International Criminal Tribunal for the Former Yugoslavia, 5 EJIL (1994), 360.

Simma, Bruno, and Paulus, Andreas L., The 'International Community' Facing the Challenge of Globalization, 9 EJIL (1998), 266.

—— and Volk, Klaus, Der Spion, der in die Kälte kam, NJW (1991), 871.

Sjöcrona, Jan M., The International Criminal Tribunal for the Former Yugoslavia: Some Introductory Remarks from a Defence Point of View, 8 LJIL (1995), 463.

Sloan, James, The International Criminal Tribunal for the Former Yugoslavia and Fair Trial Rights: A Closer Look, 9 LJIL (1996), 479.

Stephen, James F., Criminal Procedure from the Thirteenth to the Eighteenth Century, in *Selected Essays in Anglo-American Legal History*, compiled and ed. by a Committee of the Association of American Law Schools in 3 vols. (Boston, Mass., 1908), ii, 443.

Sunga, Lyal S., The Crimes within the Jurisdiction of the International Criminal Court, 6 Eur.J.Crime Cr.L.Cr.J. (1998), 377.

Swaak-Goldman, Olivia Q., The ICTY and the Right to a Fair Trial: A Critique of the Critics, 10 LJIL (1997), 215.

Thornberry, C., Saving the War Crimes Tribunal, 104 Foreign Policy (1996), 72.

Tolbert, David, The ICTY and the Enforcement of Sentences, 11 LJIL (1998), 655.

Vierucci, Luisa, The First Steps of the International Criminal Tribunal for the Former Yugoslavia, 6 EJIL (1995), 134.

von Liszt, Franz, Der Zweckgedanke im Strafrecht ('Marburger Programm'), 3 ZStW (1883), 1.

Vouin, Robert, The Protection of the Accused in France, 5 ICLQ (1956) 1 and 157.

Walter, Michael, Wandlungen in der Reaktion auf Kriminalität, 95 ZStW (1983), 32.

Walzer, Martin, The Moral Standing of States, 9 Philosophy and Public Affairs (1980), 209.

Warbrick, Colin, The United Nations System: A Place for Criminal Courts, 5 Transnational Law and Contemporary Problems (1995), 237.

Wedgwood, Ruth, The International Criminal Court: An American View, 10 EJIL (1999), 93.

Weller, Marcus, The International Response to the Dissolution of the Socialist Federal Republic of Yugoslavia, 86 AJIL (1992), 569.

Westwood, David, The Effects of Home Office Guidelines on the Cautioning of Offenders (1991) Crim LR, 591.

Zimmermann, Andreas, The Creation of a Permanent International Criminal Court, 2 Max Planck YB UN Law (1998), 170.

Zwanenburg, Marten, The Statute for an International Criminal Court and the United States: Peacekeepers under Fire, 10 EJIL (1999), 124.

Index